HARVARD STUDIES IN INTERNATIONAL DEVELOPMENT

REFORMING ECONOMIC SYSTEMS IN DEVELOPING COUNTRIES

REFORMING ECONOMIC SYSTEMS IN DEVELOPING COUNTRIES

Edited by Dwight H. Perkins and
Michael Roemer

HARVARD INSTITUTE FOR INTERNATIONAL DEVELOPMENT
Harvard University

Distributed by Harvard University Press

Published by
Harvard Institute for International Development
May 1991

Distributed by Harvard University Press

The Harvard Institute for International Development is Harvard University's center for interdisciplinary research, teaching, and technical assistance on the problems of modernization in less developed countries.

Library of Congress Cataloging-in-Publication-Data
Main entry under the title:
Reforming economic systems in developing countries, edited by Dwight H Perkins and Michael Roemer.
p. cm. (Harvard studies in international development).
Includes bibliographical references and index.
1. Developing countries—Economic policy—Congresses.
I. Perkins, Dwight Heald. 1934-; II. Roemer, Michael. 1937-.
III. Series
HC59.7. R368 1991   338.'9 009172 '4 — dc 20   91-17785 CIP

ISBN 0-674-75319-4: $29.95

Printed in the United States of America.

Production credits:

Editors
Dwight H. Perkins
Michael Roemer

Copyediting and management
HIID Publications Office
—Thomas N. Gardner, senior editor
—Nancy Hamlin Soukup, assistant

Proofreading and editorial assistance
Christopher Malloy, Nicholas Philipson, Evelyn Rosenthal, Carol Schrader

Index
Fred L. Kepler

Book and cover design and production
Desktop Publishing & Design, Boston, MA

Printing
Book: Maple-Vail Book Manufacturing Group
Cover: Puritan Press

Distribution
Harvard University Press

Contents

Tables and Figures

Introduction

Reforming economic systems has been at the heart of development since the 1950s. The specific content of reform efforts, however, has changed, often dramatically, over the years. In any given period there is typically a dominant point of view on what reforms best promote development. As efforts to implement that view unfold over a decade or more, the limitations of this dominant vision become increasingly apparent until a new, more complex reform model is brought to the fore. The old ideas are seldom totally rejected, but the simple formulas for growth that seemed to hold so much promise at the outset of a new reform period give way to others that appear to promise more in the way of growth and equity.

The dominant vision of the past decade and more has been rooted in powerful propositions of neoclassical economics: the core of reform efforts should be devoted to achieving development through competitive markets.

This neoclassical vision was itself a reaction to an earlier paradigm that stressed the importance of planning. Planning, it was then argued, was needed to overcome various market failures endemic to developing countries. Critics of this emphasis on planning initially argued that planners put too much emphasis on growth and too little on equity. The greater concern for equity that followed became the intellectual foundation for a whole new set of state interventions that were designed to correct for market influences assumed to be inequitable. It was against this background of two decades and more of state intervention in the economy that the neoclassical economists' view came to the fore. Neoclassical economists had little trouble finding numerous horror stories of state interventions that became the main source of market imperfections. If one could remove government intervention, markets would return to something more closely approximating perfection, and growth would accelerate. Even equity considerations might be better served because state interventions to promote equity quite often served the special interests of the wealthy and powerful instead.

There is little doubt that efforts to improve the functioning of markets in developing countries have had a positive impact on growth in recent years and may have had a positive impact on equity as well, although the latter point is hotly debated. But this neoclassical view has also been oversimplified and oversold. It has been oversimplified because its advocates have not recognized the full complexity of measures needed to make markets work well in a developing country after decades of massive state intervention. The neoclassical prescription has been oversold because it has sometimes been presented as the sole requirement to achieve development. Governments are not going to disappear in even the most market-oriented developing countries any more than they are going to wither away in the idealized state of pure communism. It is imperative, therefore, that reformers understand the role of government in promoting development: what it must do, what it can do effectively, what it need not do, and what it cannot do effectively.

The HIID Experience

The Harvard Institute for International Development (HIID) has been an active participant in the development process in more than forty countries over the past thirty years. In its earlier years, the Development Advisory Service (DAS), as the Institute was then called, was involved in strengthening the economic analysis of planning commissions in Pakistan, Colombia, Ethiopia and a half dozen other countries. DAS's involvement acknowledged that governments were inevitably going to be heavily involved in a wide range of development activities and that their personnel ought to be trained to carry out those functions efficiently. Ours was not an effort to promote planning over the market, but to do well whatever degree of planning and government policy intervention in the economy was deemed appropriate. The issue of equity versus growth was raised at an early date and played a particularly prominent role in the later stages of our involvement in Pakistan.

In the 1970s and even more so in the 1980s, HIID has shifted its efforts to help make markets work better. "Getting prices right" was a slogan that many outside of HIID, and some within as well, thought was virtually synonymous with the economics work of the Institute. To some, "getting prices right" meant little more than getting governments out of setting prices and letting markets do so unfettered.

Increasingly, however, the people in HIID working on economic systems reform—a group that includes anthropologists, political scientists, lawyers, management specialists, and economists—have recognized that our own work goes well beyond the neoclassical menu of reform. We have tried to convince governments to depend more on markets to promote development, but this has not meant a retreat for government out of the development business. Most often we have helped governments build their capacity to work through markets to achieve more rapid and equitable growth. The national and international aid agencies, who aggressively endorse the neoclassical prescriptions, also fund— and implicitly endorse—these efforts.

It became increasingly apparent to us that HIID had to have a clearer picture of what we were really doing to help reform economic systems. If we were to provide advice and training to others, we needed to better understand ourselves what the reform process involves. To that end, in 1988 we established a framework for analysis of various reform efforts and invited those in the Institute who were so inclined to write papers based on their research and their own experience with reform. Drafts of these papers were presented and discussed at an HIID conference held in Marrakech, Morocco, in November 1988, and after further revisions an appropriate subset of those papers was compiled for the present volume. These papers are based heavily on case studies of actual reform experience, in many instances reforms in which the paper authors themselves participated. Some papers deal with single instances of reform; others look at a number of cases in a comparative way.

What Does Reform Involve?

Reforming an economic system in the 1980s and 1990s does involve making markets work better. Most reforms are implicitly based on the proposition that high productivity growth is necessary to sustain rapid development. This proposition contrasts with the standard view in the 1950s that higher levels of capital formation are central to successful development. Neoclassical reformers further assume that competition stimulates productivity growth, a relationship that has not been well established empirically. Our introductory essays will explore the empirical foundations for this relationship a bit further, but for the moment we shall take it as a given.

There are three basic propositions about the nature of most reform efforts that will be stated in abbreviated form and then elaborated below.

1) Making markets work efficiently in developing countries is more complicated than textbook economic theory would lead one to believe. It is not that the textbooks are wrong. But they assume certain kinds of behavior and certain types of institutions that cannot be taken for granted in most developing countries. The typical industrial enterprise manager in a developing nation, for example, does not maximize profits in the face of output and input prices over which that manager has no control. More often than not that manager has a great deal of influence over the prices he pays and receives.

2) The state plays an active and essential role in the development process. One cannot treat the state as simply an impediment to the proper functioning of free markets. The real issue is not so much whether the state should be involved, but how state involvement should be handled. What are the rules or principles that should govern different kinds of state intervention in the economy? Put more generally, many economic controls are implemented by bureaucratic commands or rules rather than through market forces, but the development literature has relatively little to say about the principles that should underlie these commands and rules.

3) Technocrats may be inclined to ignore distributional issues, but no one else will. As a result, distributional issues play a pervasive role in economic systems reform. Rural people contend with the urban population over the price of food, and bureaucrats fight with each other over who should command what government resources. The success of any reform effort depends critically on how these diverse political forces are brought to bear. Analysts and practitioners of reform, therefore, must understand political economy and not just economics.

There is nothing surprising about these three propositions taken individually. Together, however, they provide a framework for the analysis of reform that is more complete and systematic than most of the formulas currently extant. Certainly catch words and phrases such as "privatization" or "getting prices right" deal with only one or another corner of the problem. The World Bank's concept of "structural adjustment" is more inclusive, covering a wide variety of specific reforms, but does not provide a systematic framework that indicates why some reforms are included and others are not.

Making Markets Work

Much of neoclassical economics is devoted to spelling out the price-setting rules that will maximize social welfare. When uncertainty or asymmetric information in principal-agent relationships is included, deriving the price rules that maximize welfare can become a sophisticated exercise in mathematical economics. In development economics, however, as Michael Roemer's essay points out, the dominant neoclassical view is that welfare-maximizing prices and free market or world prices are more or less synonymous. Deep down this is almost as much a political judgment as an economic one.

It is not that development economists are ignorant of the various studies that show how state intervention in the setting of prices can sometimes improve the welfare of a nation. But development economists feel that most states are incapable of implementing such rules. Private interests or political forces will always divert prices from the welfare ideal. Only a general rule, such as total abstention from state price fixing, the argument goes, is politically feasible.

Clearly, there is some truth to this point of view. Development specialists have an armory of examples of irrational price distortions. But although governments may be incapable of implementing sophisticated interventions, they are also politically unwilling to let prices be set wholly by the market. Almost all developing countries, including some very successful ones, regularly intervene in the setting of prices. South Korea, as Dwight H. Perkins's paper points out, is one among several examples.

The job of "getting prices right" should thus involve a more realistic analysis of how welfare-maximizing prices can account for distributional and political realities. Food policy analysis, as C. Peter Timmer's essay elaborates, does just that. Few nations can afford to let rice prices fluctuate with short-run world market forces, nor is there any reason why they should do so. It does not follow, however, that the state can interfere according to any criterion that catches its fancy. There are systematic ways of including both economic and distributional considerations, as food policy analysis tries to do.

Shantayanan Devarajan and Jeffrey D. Lewis stick more closely to pure economic analysis but make a similar point. In the real world of developing countries the standard rules of thumb of most development economists are based on economic models bearing little relationship to reality. In the second-best world of development, as a result, these price-setting rules of thumb can involve substantial departures from welfare maximization. Alternative rules, which Devarajan and Lewis spell out, come closer to the mark. It may be that these alternative rules of thumb are not readily implementable, but that is a political judgment, one to be faced explicitly and not buried in economic analysis purporting to be purely technical and politically neutral.

Getting prices right, though not an easy task, does have the virtue of being a goal where the tools of economic analysis, tempered with politics, are well developed and clearly useful. The same cannot be said for the second critical component of successful markets.

The pervasiveness of state involvement in the economy of most developing economies means that profit maximization by enterprises, particularly the larger ones, has little to do with such traditional market-oriented behavior as cutting input costs or increasing sales. Instead, enterprises spend much of their energy gaining subsidies or protected markets from the state. Subsidies and protection can take many forms, ranging from loans at below-market interest rates (loans that often do not have to be repaid) to import quotas that guarantee local firms monopolies.

This problem is apparent in the relationship between enterprises and the government bureaucracy in Bangladesh as described by Richard D. Mallon and Joseph J. Stern. Government officials intervene in enterprise decisions in

Bangladesh at every step from quotas on key inputs to soft loans from the state banking system. Entrepreneurship is as much a matter of manipulating state interventions as it is actually running the business itself. Inefficient enterprises can survive and prosper indefinitely on government largesse. Efficient enterprises that really contribute to Bangladesh's development are stifled or never allowed to get started. The dominant enterprises face what is known in the literature on Eastern Europe as the "soft budget constraint": they do not need to worry about keeping costs down because they can always get bailed out by the state if they run losses.

In Indonesia, as in Bangladesh, the state banks until recently were little more than subordinate units of the central bank and the Ministry of Finance. The main function of the banks, as described in the paper by David C. Cole and Betty F. Slade, was to channel funds from the government budget to other state enterprises. Bank losses, which were large, were made up by subsidies from the government. The banks, in effect, faced a soft budget constraint which in turn allowed them to provide a soft budget constraint to their borrowers, mainly the larger state industrial firms.

When enterprises and banks are maximizing profits through manipulation of their ties to government, even getting prices right will not necessarily increase welfare or promote development. Making markets work means, in these cases, breaking the connection between government and enterprises, creating hard budget constraints, and eliminating discretionary interventions by the state. That, in essence, is one key feature of financial reforms in Indonesia where the government is trying to turn the state banks into publicly owned but genuinely autonomous commercial banks. If the government efforts succeed, not only will the banks behave according to market rules, but enterprises that borrow from the banks will also have to become more autonomous as their managers pay more attention to cutting costs or increasing their sales to repay loans of commercial rates of interest. That is, all enterprises will have to behave in ways required by well-functioning markets.

A third component of effective markets is competition. Lack of competition is an acute problem in developing countries, where markets are often too small to sustain many firms in a single industry and import quotas are regularly used to enforce cartel-like arrangements. Import liberalization is one of the primary measures for promoting competition and, through competition, the more energetic pursuit of growth and efficiency by enterprises. Policies that promote small and medium scale enterprise development, as contrasted to large conglomerates, can also be a means for achieving more vigorous competition, as suggested by Tyler S. Biggs and Brian Levy in their essay comparing the industrial structure of South Korea, Taiwan, and the Philippines.

In industrialized countries, competition is fostered by legislation attacking restrictive business practices as exemplified by antitrust legislation in the United States. As Clive S. Gray's paper points out, however, few developing countries have such legislation and those that do often use it more to restrict foreign investment than to promote competition. A central issue is whether legislation can really limit restrictive business practices in developing countries or whether such rules will become another weapon in the bureaucrat's arsenal to make collusive arrangements with favored enterprises. Gray emphasizes an independent judiciary as one way to deal with this latter problem, but independent judiciaries are not the rule in developing nations. Creating strong legal institutions is one of the lengthy processes of development, not something that can be done as part of a short-term reform.

Finally, there must be some degree of macroeconomic stability if markets are to function properly. This set of essays is mainly about systems reform rather than stabilization, but the two subjects cannot be divorced. High rates of inflation divert investment into unproductive channels. If the price increases reach politically intolerable levels, and cannot be controlled by macroeconomic measures, the inevitable result is a proliferation of price controls leading to rationing, formal or informal, and a declining role for market forces. Balance-of-payments disequilibrium can lead a country down the same path. The Gambia in the late 1970s and early 1980s, for example, experienced both accelerating inflation and disappearing foreign exchange reserves. Borrowing postponed the inevitable, but, as Malcolm F. McPherson and Steven C. Radelet describe, by the mid-1980s the country was in a deep crisis with shortages everywhere and per capita income declining. Escape from macroinstability is seldom easy. For The Gambia a combination of political forces made possible a rapid economic turnaround within two years.

Making markets work efficiently, therefore, is a complex and difficult task in developing countries. Not only must one get prices right where prices have been subject to massive distortions; a reformer must also alter the behavior of enterprise managers often in quite fundamental ways. Autonomous enterprises must also be made or allowed to compete with each other rather than collude to control the local market. And all of this must be done within a stable macro-economic environment. The more a country has departed from the rules of the market as a result of interventions in the past, the more difficult it is to bring market forces into play.

The Role of the State

Complex as it is, market reform is only one of three components of economic systems reform. Although market reforms suggest a lesser role for the state, any well-functioning economic system still requires a well-functioning government. The state performs two distinct functions related to economic development. First, it taxes and regulates economic agents. Second, it actively promotes development. There is an inevitable tension between government and the market because government generally operates through hierarchical systems of control, using bureaucratic commands rather than impersonal market forces.

All governments must tax their citizens and regulate some of their activities. How taxation and regulation are implemented are of central importance to how well markets will work. If government bureaucrats have a high degree of discretion, they will use taxes and regulation to bring enterprises under their control, moving the economy away from market forces. Glenn P. Jenkins's study of tax reforms around the world illustrates these issues. Tax systems have been used by countries to achieve a more equitable income distribution and to pursue any number of other social goals. But even in advanced industrial countries tax systems have often worked out quite differently from the intentions of their designers. In developing nations complex tax systems with highly progressive

6

rates and a multitude of exceptions to general rules have been powerful weapons in the hands of government officials who wish to control the economy or line their own pockets. To avoid discretionary interventions tax systems must be as simple and have as many self-enforcement mechanisms as possible.

If the rules that should govern the state's tax and regulatory functions are relatively straightforward, the same cannot be said of the state's development role. The wide scope of state development activities, from infrastructure investment to public enterprises, is outlined in the paper by Dwight H. Perkins. The complexity of getting state enterprises to behave in a way that promotes development is illustrated by Donald R. Snodgrass and Richard H. Patten in their essay on the reform of one of Indonesia's state banks. It is also well illustrated in Thomas P. Tomich's analysis of why so much of Indonesia's tree crop development has been handled through large-scale block planting schemes that rely more on hierarchical command systems of control than on market forces. In the case of tree crops, there is a smallholder, market-oriented alternative that may be more efficient. But market alternatives may not exist for some state interventions or may not be politically acceptable.

Both state and private enterprise are usually managed through hierarchical systems involving commands rather than market forces. But the principles that should govern the operation of hierarchical systems in a state enterprise are very different from those in a regulatory agency. Maximum flexibility is required in the former and minimum flexibility in the latter. Maximum flexibility, however, requires that incentive systems within the enterprise be closely tied to the firm's objectives. Designing incentive systems that keep employees from going off in unproductive directions is a complex management task, as HIID's experience with reform in the Bank Rakyat Indonesia Project illustrates.

Hierarchical or bureaucratic command systems have been used to control entire economies. China before reform and the Soviet Union are extreme examples, but South Korea's economy in the 1960s and 1970s was run to an extraordinary degree by the commands of Presidents Park and Chun and those who did their bidding in various government bureaus.

The principles that should govern state guidance of the economy as a whole are probably very similar to those that should govern internal management in producing enterprises: clear and simple goals with incentives clearly tied to the achievement of those goals. This whole field of management of hierarchical systems within a developing country context is poorly understood, however, and most development agencies and academic institutions do not deal systematically with the subject at all. Our efforts in this volume point out the void but make only a few tentative steps toward filling it.

The Politics of Economic Reform

Politics enters at all stages and levels of economic systems reform. Even the most technical subjects, the setting of relative prices in a second-best world for example, turn as much on political judgments as on technical analysis. It is not good enough, as economists have typically done, to say that successful reform requires "political will." Such an assertion begs the question of why some leaders carry out clearly needed reforms while others do not. The will to reform is rooted in the values of a society, in the nature of its political and social institutions, and in the nature of the reforms being attempted. It is not simply, or even primarily, a question of individual psychology.

The essay by Merilee S. Grindle and John W. Thomas attempts to build on case studies of reform efforts to generalize about the political underpinnings of successful reforms. Their focus is on policy-making elites, including politicians representing broad class interests, bureaucrats fighting over their piece of government's turf, technical advisers both domestic and foreign, and even the officials of foreign assistance agencies. Which of these groups has the greatest influence on any given reform depends in important ways on the nature of the reform itself and the circumstances pushing a nation toward reform. Politics internal to the bureaucracy, for example, are most likely to determine the outcome of reforms that take a long time to implement, are technically complex to carry out, whose benefits are widely dispersed and not readily apparent to the beneficiaries for some time, and whose initial costs are born mainly by the government budget. Reforms that can be implemented quickly and are more or less self-implementing, as in the case of a devaluation or a change in food prices, are more likely to be fought out in the public arena among political leaders reflecting broad interest groups within the population at large.

It is no accident that much of the political economy literature to date deals with the politics of short-term stabilization efforts rather than with longer-term, more fundamental reforms of the economic system. The political forces surrounding short-term stabilizations are much more visible, making it easier to describe just who won and who lost, and how each of these winners and losers reacted. Most of the reform cases studied by Grindle and Thomas deal with long-term structural changes ranging from land reform in the Philippines to decentralization of decision making in Kenya.

Economists have attempted to approach the politics of reform through an analysis of the proper sequencing of different reforms, as Michael Roemer and Steven C. Radelet point out. Should quantitative restrictions on imports be removed before rationalizing tariffs? Should capital markets be liberalized only after trade liberalization has made substantial headway? Some of these issues are largely economic in nature. Trade liberalization without correcting for an overvalued currency, for example, will lead to a run on foreign exchange reserves and an end to liberalization efforts. But most issues of sequencing turn on the interaction of political and economic forces. Whether quantitative restrictions on imports or high and uneven tariffs on those imports should be reformed first is largely a question of which set of measures will generate the greatest resistance to further reform. Economists who attempt to deal with these sequencing issues without understanding the political forces at work are not likely to produce many useful guidelines for policymakers.

Finally, politics is deeply rooted in the domestic culture and history of a nation and, in some important cases, in the nation's international environment as well. No generalizations can fully capture the diversity of forces at play, and there is no short cut to a more profound understanding of any given nation's politics. The dominance of bureaucratic politics in Bangladesh is not simply the playing out of universal forces found in all countries. Bangladesh's bureaucracy and its army are among the few strong institutions in the nation, products of Bangladesh's relatively recent emergence as a nation from the tutelage of Pakistan and a bloody civil war. Two decades since the civil war have proven too short a time to create alternative political institutions.

The contrast between the political foundations of reform in Chad, as described by Anne-Marie and William Foltz, and those in The Gambia, as described by Malcolm F. McPherson and Steven C. Radelet, is also profound. In Chad political power was based on a system of feudal alliances between military commanders who led troops from one or another ethnic group within the country. In The Gambia the ruling political party based its power on elections dominated by the rural population of the country, largely made up of one ethnic group, the Mandinka. Both Chad and The Gambia, however, faced real external threats to their governments and even to their existence as nations. In Chad the threat was a military one emanating from Libya. In The Gambia the danger was that domestic mismanagement would lead the international community to force an amalgamation with Senegal. In Chad and particularly in The Gambia, this external danger had more than a little to do with the government's attitude toward reform. External threats also help explain why the now famous economic reforms of South Korea and Taiwan were politically feasible.

This third theme, the central role of politics in economic reform, was not incorporated into these essays simply to be comprehensive. Policy and politics are deeply intertwined, as the terms themselves imply. Economic reforms dominated solely by technocratic considerations are doomed to failure except occasionally when the technocratic solution and political requirements coincide. Not everyone involved in economic systems reform needs to understand politics. There is a role for the specialist on the taxation of capital gains or the measurement of effective rates of protection. But the designers of the economic reform itself must understand what is politically possible. Sometimes the designers of reform are elected or self-appointed political leaders of the nation acting alone. More often these political leaders interact with their own and expatriate technicians and with the external aid agencies that help fund many reform efforts.

Outline of this Volume

The three major themes outlined above are woven into most of the essays in this volume. The technical requirements of efficient markets interact with the conditions for effective bureaucratic command systems. And politics is present at every step of the way. Consequently, this collection of essays cannot be divided, with one section for each of the major themes.

Instead we start with three overview papers: Dwight H. Perkins on the rules governing well-functioning market and bureaucratic-command systems, Michael Roemer and Steven C. Radelet on the neoclassical economist's view of economic systems reform in a static and a dynamic world, and Merilee S. Grindle and John W. Thomas on the interaction of economic reform with politics. These three general papers are followed by Malcolm F. McPherson and Steven C. Radelet's essay on the interaction of politics with stabilization efforts in The Gambia, and by Anne-Marie and William Foltz's story of the interaction of politics and reform in providing health services in Chad.

The next five papers all deal in one way or another with international trade-related issues. These begin with Shantayanan Devarajan and Jeffrey D. Lewis's essay on the limitations of standard trade liberalization prescriptions, followed by two case studies of trade liberalization in which HIID was involved: Richard D. Mallon and Joseph J. Stern's analysis of the Bangladesh experience and later Richard Barichello and Frank Flatters's study of the Indonesian trade liberalization since 1986. The other two papers in this section, C. Peter Timmer's on food price policy and Thomas P. Tomich's on smallholder tree crop development, deal with, among other things, the interaction between trade and the agricultural sector.

The remaining chapters of this volume cover fiscal and financial reforms and some nontrade aspects of industrial policy. The paper by Glenn P. Jenkins deals with the conditions necessary for successful tax reform. David C. Cole and Betty F. Slade explore the key elements in financial systems reforms. Donald R. Snodgrass and Richard H. Patten describe the implementation of an innovative reform of rural credit and savings in Indonesia. The final two papers in the volume are by Tyler S. Biggs and Brian Levy on industrial structure in developing countries and by Clive S. Gray on competition and antitrust policies.

It is important to reiterate, however, that this volume is not about trade policy or financial reform per se. It is about the underlying conditions needed to make market systems and hierarchical systems work in a way that promotes development. The particular economic reforms covered in the case studies are often of central importance in their own right, but they are presented here because they illustrate one or more of the three underlying themes of this collection.

Dwight H. Perkins
Michael Roemer
Cambridge, Massachusetts
March 1991

1

Economic Systems Reform in Developing Countries

Dwight H. Perkins

Dwight H. Perkins is the Harold Hitchings Burbank Professor of Political Economy at Harvard University and director of the Harvard Institute for International Development. His research and consulting experience in developing countries has been mainly in East and Southeast Asia. He has written, co-authored, or edited eleven books and more than sixty articles on topics of Asian economic history and development.

Introduction

Our contemporary world is alive with both talk and action about reforming our economic systems. From *perestroika* in the Soviet Union to "structural adjustment" in Africa, there is a sense that current systems are inadequate and badly in need of change. The direction of change is toward a greater role for market forces, but there is considerable confusion over what a greater role for market forces means and how that role is to be accomplished. It is often not even clear why one wants a greater role for the market other than as a reaction to a current economic system in place that is presumed not to be working well. Under the circumstances there is room for more than a little ideology, with "structuralists" of various sorts fighting a rearguard action against the increasingly dominant "neoclassicists."

This essay represents an attempt to bring greater clarity to what is meant or should be meant by economic systems reform in developing countries. A central point of the essay is that increasing the role of the market and making markets work better is a much more complex process than is commonly supposed. Many of our notions of how markets work in developing countries come from studies of the agricultural sector with small household-based producing units, but the lessons gained from agriculture give one an oversimplified picture of what is involved when one tries to introduce market forces into an industrial sector with large-scale units. In China, for example, it was a comparatively simple matter to introduce market forces into the rural economy once the communes had been abolished and replaced with household farming. Reforming large urban state enterprises has proved to be much more difficult.

China is an extreme case of the difficulties involved in introducing market forces, but similar problems can be observed throughout the developing world. Even in mixed market command economies, state-owned enterprises are often not very responsive to market forces. In the private sector as well, enterprise success in many developing countries may have more to do with manipulation of government controls and subsidies than with efforts internal to the enterprise to maximize profits.

A second point of this essay is that markets, even in the most market-oriented economies, determine only a fraction of the economic decisions that are made. Hierarchical or bureaucratic commands play a major role in deciding what is produced and distributed in all economies. The internal management of an enterprise, for example, is usually governed by hierarchical commands rather than market forces. If all firms were small, atomized units, it might make sense to treat internal management as a separate subject presumably of lesser importance for economic systems reform than the external control system.[1] But what happens when a few large conglomerates dominate the economic landscape, as is the case in South Korea? In the latter case, a much larger number of economic decisions take place within the enterprise than is the case when small independent firms dominate the economy, as in Taiwan.

One extreme is the hierarchical command system introduced by the Soviet Union and adopted by China, North Korea, Vietnam, and Eastern Europe, where most economic decisions are made without reference to the market. Economists tend to treat the Soviet style bureaucratic command system as fundamentally different from what goes on in most developing economies. But a closer look at the industrial and banking sectors of many developing countries suggests that there are differences in degree but not in kind.

The economic systems of all countries, in fact, lie within a spectrum that ranges from the pure bureaucratic command system of the Soviet Union in the 1930s through the 1950s to the atomistic market-based competition of Hong Kong today or rural America in the nineteenth century. The first part of this essay is devoted to placing developing countries in the 1980s along this spectrum. Measuring the relative strength of bureaucratic versus market forces for a given economy is a complex task, and it is essential to go into the subject at length. Until one has a clearer picture of the nature of the system to be reformed, it is impossible to talk systematically about what reforms are required.

It is also difficult to analyze and describe reform of an economic system unless or until one has a clear view of the purpose of reform. The primary economic goals of reform are either to increase the quantity of goods and services available to the population or to improve the equity with which those goods and services are distributed. The second part of this essay, therefore, is devoted to a brief discussion of what is known and not known about the relationship between the efficiency of an economy, on the one hand, and the degree of bureaucratic intervention in that economy, on the other. Equity issues will be mentioned only in passing because of space limitations.

The remainder of the essay is devoted to the central theme of what is involved in economic systems reform, given the nature of the economic systems that exist today and the goals of increased efficiency and equity. The task is both to increase the scope of market forces and to improve the operation of the many bureaucratic levers that are inevitably retained. Neither task is as simple as code words such as "privatization" have led some advocates of reform to believe.

The Relative Strength of Bureaucratic versus Market Forces

State Investment and Ownership

The role of the state in most contemporary developing economies is pervasive. To begin with, the public sector in most developing countries plays an often dominant role in capital formation. Selected figures from a number of nations presented in Table 1 illustrate the main point. Whether the country involved is "socialist" interventionist India or resolutely capitalist Taiwan or Japan, the government on average accounts for half or more of all gross domestic capital formation. The government builds roads, railroads, schools, and public buildings. The government also provides most of the infrastructure of research and irrigation systems for agriculture, and the plant capacity to produce military equipment is often provided by government. Even when the firms producing weapons are nominally private, the control over their plant expansion, as well as what is produced, typically rests with the government. The same applies to construction. The contractors putting up the public office buildings and building the highways may be private, but funding and control are in the hands of the government.

Table 1 The Public Share in Capital Formation (selected years)

Country	Period	Gross Domestic Capital Formation Public (% of total)	Gross Domestic Capital Formation Private (% of total)
Japan	1892-1901	55.9	44.1
	1902-1911	57.3	42.7
	1912-1921	47.0	53.0
	1922-1931	54.1	45.9
Taiwan	1960	45.3	54.7
	1980	48.5	51.5
India*	1970-1971	46.0	54.0
	1975-1976	56.9	43.1
Bangladesh*	1980-1981	60.1	39.9
Malaysia*	1965	44.6	55.4
	1970	35.9	64.1
Hong Kong	1975	16.0	84.0
	1980	14.8	85.2
Kenya	1980-1985	41.9	58.1
Ivory Coast[a]	1980-1985	61.0	49.0
Botswana[a]	1980-1985	45.0	55.0
Egypt[a]	1980-1985	65.0	35.0
Turkey[a]	1980-1985	68.0	32.0
Argentina[a]	1980-1985	58.0	42.0
Colombia[a]	1980-1985	40.0	60.0
Mexico[a]	1980-1985	31.0	69.0
Peru[a]	1980-1985	29.0	71.0
Dominican Rep[a]	1980-1985	24.0	76.0
13 Industrial Countries	1980-1985	30.0	70.0

*The figures for India are for Net Domestic Capital Formation and those for Bangladesh and Malaysia are for Gross Investment.

a. These figures are public sector investment (including investment by state-owned enterprises) as a percentage of total investment.

Sources

1. *Bangladesh Bureau of Statistics*, Statistical Pocket Book of Bangladesh, 1982 *(Dhaka: Bangladesh Bureau of Statistics, 1983),* 262-63.
2. *Census and Statistics Department, Hong Kong*, Estimates of Gross Domestic Product, 1966-1983 *(Hong Kong: Government Printer, 1984),* 16-17.
3. *Central Statistical Organization*, Statistical Pocket Book, India, 1977 *(Delhi: Government of India Press, 1977),* 14-15.
4. Council for Economic Planning and Development, Taiwan Statistical Data Book, 1987 *(Taipei: Council for Economic Planning and Development, 1987),* 47.
5. *Republic of Kenya*, Statistical Abstract 1986 *(Nairobi: Central Bureau of Statistics, 1986),* 43.
6. *Henry Rosovsky*, Capital Formation in Japan *(Glencoe: Free Press, 1961),* 2.
7. Second Malaysia Plan, 1971-1975 *(Kuala Lumpur: Government Press, 1971),* 26.
8. *World Bank*, World Development Report, 1988 *(Washington, D.C.: World Bank, 1988),* 47.

As a percentage of GNP, the government's share of capital formation and its control of military production may not be large. If the share of total capital formation in GNP is 25 percent with a government share of half, and military expenditures are another 2 percent, then the government only directly controls 14.5 percent of GNP through these two levers. But in the developing countries, particularly those with per capita incomes below $1,000 (in 1980 prices), the agricultural and services sectors together account for from 60 to 80 percent of GNP.[2]

The industry, construction, and utilities share is only 20 to 40 percent, and most investment and military expenditures relate to these latter sectors, not to agriculture and services.[3] When government controls over half of capital formation, therefore, it controls from a third to over half of all modern sector industry and construction.

Such a large share of the modern sector for government is not absolutely necessary in the sense that governments must do these tasks or the country will go without. Hong Kong illustrates how most infrastructure can be built by the private sector, at least where the private sector is large, capable, and organized to carry out such tasks. But in most developing countries the modern private sector is not large, capable, and organized to carry out these tasks, and the job devolves on government, even governments that would be quite content if they were not involved. The appropriate role for government in the development process used to be a common theme in the literature.[4] The subject is discussed today mainly in the context of how to increase the role of privatization and reduce the role of government,[5] but the reality is that government remains a major direct actor in the economy of most developing countries, not simply an indirect manipulator of broad macro controls.

Government's direct control over modern sector economic activity is not confined to investment and the military. State-owned enterprises dominate many of the key sectors. There is no systematic survey of the share of public ownership around the world despite the current emphasis on privatization. Data for selected countries, however, give an overall view of the role of public ownership.

Public enterprises appear to be most dominant in sub-Saharan Africa. The roughly 3,000 public enterprises in this region account for 15 percent of GDP, 25 percent of investment, and 14 percent of employment, figures that are generally higher than those of Asia and Latin America.[6] If one takes into account that two-thirds of GDP in Africa is in agriculture and services that are largely private, it is clear that the public sector plays a very large role in the urban modern sector. Formal sector employment figures presented in Table 2 tell the main story. The share of the public sector in formal sector employment in the six countries sampled ranged from 39.2 percent in Malawi to 73.9 percent in Ghana.

The experience of Kenya, believed by many to be one of the more market-oriented countries in the region, is illustrative. By 1985, 49 percent of all Kenyan wage employment was in the public sector. Public sector employment in manufacturing was only 22 percent, but electricity and water were 100 percent public, construction was 48 percent public, and the transport and communication sectors were 63 percent public.[7]

Africa may be the continent where public enterprises are most dominant, but their presence is pervasive in parts of Asia and Latin America as well. In Asia, for example, China, Vietnam, and North Korea have manufacturing sectors completely dominated by public enterprises, even if one excludes China's small-scale collective enterprises from the public sector, as one should. In South Korea, the public enterprise share in transport and communications value added was 30.5 percent, and in electricity, water, and sanitation it was 66 percent. In manufacturing, however, the public sector share was only 15 percent.[8] In India's industrial subsectors, public ownership dominates in mining, fertilizers, steel, and telecommunications. It also accounts for half of electronics and petrochemicals,

15

and a quarter of motor vehicles, cement, and even textiles. In Latin America, Brazil is one major nation where public enterprises are pervasive, accounting for three-quarters of mining, fertilizers, steel, and telecommunications, and half of petrochemicals.[9]

Table 2 Public Employment in Africa

Country	Year	Formal Employment as a % of Population	Public Employment as a % of Formal Employment
Ghana	1957	—	51.4
	1972	10.1	73.9
Tanzania	1962	—	27.0
	1974	6.3	66.4
Zambia	1976	14.2	71.5
Kenya	1963	—	29.6
	1977	12.4	41.7
Malawi	1968	—	33.4
	1976	9.6	39.2
Uganda	1962	—	41.8
	1970	5.9	42.2

Source: World Bank, Accelerated Development in Sub-Saharan Africa: An Agenda for Action (Washington, D.C.: World Bank, 1981), 41.

There is, to be sure, some overlap between the value added in state-owned enterprises and the value added in capital formation controlled by the state, but there is no one-to-one relationship. In Korea, for example, the state accounts for over half of all capital formation, but only 5 percent of the value added in construction is contributed by state-owned enterprises.[10] Thus when the issue under consideration is the degree of direct state control over modern sector value added, the contribution of many state-owned enterprises needs to be added to the government's share of capital formation.

In principle, these state-owned enterprises could operate in much the same way as private enterprises, maximizing or at least concentrating on profits by cutting costs or increasing sales. The literature on market socialism, in fact, assumes that such will be the case.[11] In practice, however, state-owned enterprises are rarely pure profit maximizers. Most often the state appoints their managers and expects those managers to be responsive to the goals of the bureaucracy that appoints them. Those goals can and often do include everything from meeting specific employment goals and providing below-cost services to favored groups, to support of the government's political machine. The state may set the prices, guarantee a market by prohibiting private firms from entering that sector, and do much else.

16

State-owned enterprises play a major role in some countries in one sector whose influence on the economy cannot be properly gauged by looking at its share of GNP; that sector is banking and finance. It is not a sector where market failures dictate that the state play a major role, but concerns with questions of economic power have led many governments to take over direct ownership of at least the larger banks.

The experience of Asia illustrates the range of possibilities for state intervention. Hong Kong is at the extreme end of the public-private spectrum. In Hong Kong, even central banking functions are handled by the private sector, notably the Hong Kong and Shanghai Bank. In Singapore, Malaysia, and Thailand most of the large commercial banks are also private, although certain important components of the financial sector, notably the Employee Provident Funds in Malaysia and Singapore, are public and hold huge assets. The financial systems of China, North Korea, and Vietnam are, of course, entirely or largely publicly owned. But so are the banking systems of South Korea, Indonesia, India, and Bangladesh.

In the Republic of Korea and Indonesia the larger banks are not only government owned, they are used as one of the prime vehicles for carrying out the government's industrial policy. In Korea bank interest rates have typically been held well below market rates, and the resulting rationed allocation of bank credit has been controlled in part by government. In Indonesia and Bangladesh there is a symbiotic relationship between government, the banks, and other state-owned enterprises. In Indonesia, major state industrial enterprises have more or less permanent ties to a particular state bank which in turn receives a large portion of the money it lends out from the government. Interest rates are kept low and even the question of repayment of loans can be a subject for negotiation. In Bangladesh, loan repayment by state and other favored enterprises is often the exception rather than the rule.[12]

In Africa there is a comparable range of experience. Historically, the dominant banks were the large private international banks of the colonial power, such as Barclay's. Most of these foreign banks remained after independence, but state-owned banks rose quickly to a prominent position. In Ghana, for example, the government-owned Ghana Commercial Bank as early as 1970 controlled 75 percent of the commercial bank assets in the country, and other government-owned financial institutions included the National Investment Bank and the Agricultural Development Bank.[13] In Kenya the biggest banks were the state-owned Kenya Commercial Bank and three private British banks, although there were also private Kenyan banks. In The Gambia there was also a large (by Gambian standards) state bank and private British banks. In all of these countries the state-owned banks were regularly used as vehicles to channel funds to investments and investors favored by the government.

State Regulation of the Private Sector

Up to this point the discussion has been about those sectors of the economy owned or directly managed by government, such as state-owned enterprises and public investment. But even when the modern sector is privately owned and managed, those private owners and managers often have little autonomy from government control. The list of such controls to be found in most developing economies is a long one. They include:

17

(1) Central bank control over commercial bank interest rates with rates typically set well below market equilibrium levels.

(2) Quotas limiting imports of key inputs and numerous licenses and approvals needed to get access to those quotas.

(3) Controls over the purchase and sale of foreign exchange.

(4) Licensing of new investments by the private sector above a certain size.

(5) Discretionary use of government tax authority over business.

(6) Government-set prices for products deemed to be of particular importance for one reason or another.

What distinguishes developing countries from industrial market economies in the area of regulation is not so much the existence of these various regulatory measures as it is their pervasiveness in the system. In industrial market economies, foreign exchange controls are the exception rather than the rule; import quotas are increasing in number but still apply to a relatively small share of total trade; and government sets prices for key agricultural products and certain public utilities but little else. Licensing and taxes are governed by published rules which allow little discretion on the part of the licensing and tax bureaucracies.

Developing countries, outside of their agriculture and services sectors, fall along a range that varies from states where virtually all modern sector enterprises are heavily regulated to states where laissez-faire policies prevail. But only a handful of countries fall into the laissez-faire category. The great majority of developing nations cluster at the highly regulated end of the spectrum.

The experience of Asia can be used to make the point. In the socialist states of China, North Korea, and Vietnam, enterprises have almost no autonomy from government and are really integral parts of the bureaucracy. The degree of autonomy for larger enterprises, and some smaller ones, is also low in India, Bangladesh, South Korea, the Philippines, Taiwan, and Indonesia. In this latter group of countries, foreign exchange controls are tight (except for Indonesia) and imports of items that compete with domestic products are or were largely prohibited. Imports of essential items not produced domestically required numerous approvals from the foreign trade bureaucracy (seventy approvals on average in the case of Indonesia) before they could be brought in. Licensing is actively used to limit and direct investments of any size in India and Bangladesh. In South Korea in the 1970s, licensing was not used to limit private sector activity, but government instead took a proactive role, virtually ordering private firms to carry out investments deemed desirable by the government or by the president personally.[14]

The comparison of India and Bangladesh with South Korea in the 1970s illustrates the point that import and investment controls could be used for varying purposes. In South Korea, the government relied on such controls to prod and encourage enterprises to take risks that would accelerate growth of the nation. In India and Bangladesh, controls were often exercised to restrict private activity seen as undesirable for one reason or another. The latter approach emphasizing controls as a means of limiting private sector competition often degenerates into what economists refer to as "rent seeking."[15] Whatever the goal of these numerous government control devices, these controls were more often than not the dominant force governing enterprise actions. Success for enterprises in this kind of system depends more on how these controls are administered than on market forces, with one notable exception. No government control system other than outright subsidies could ensure success for manufacturing enterprises producing mainly for export. But even in South Korea where manufactured exports were a large share of GNP, exporting enterprises often generated much of their profits on the highly protected domestic market.

There are nations in Asia where market forces predominate in the sense that enterprise success is primarily determined by how successfully the enterprise responds to such forces. Hong Kong did not calculate national income and other economic aggregates, in part as a way of making even macroeconomic government interventions impossible. Although Singapore did not go to such extremes, the government largely avoided specific interventions as contrasted to generalized policies that affected all enterprises in a nondiscretionary manner. Malaysia's economy, with its rich natural resource base, is less controlled than some others, although state enterprises and Bumiputra promotion regulations are an ever present reality for most enterprises. Thailand lies somewhere between Malaysia and the more control-oriented regimes.

This survey, however, is impressionistic and subjective. Ideally one would like a more objective measure of the relative importance of market and bureaucratic influences on enterprise behavior. There are several measures that would move one a long way toward this goal if they were available for most developing nations. These measures include:

(1) the share of imports that are limited by quotas and the share of domestic modern sector industry that faces no competition from abroad because imports are effectively banned, either formally or by prohibitively high tariffs;

(2) the degree to which domestic prices deviate from international prices for traded goods because of the kinds of import restrictions listed above;

(3) the degree of concentration of domestic industry by sector;

(4) whether interest rates deviate from market rates or at least are positive in real terms;

(5) and the rates of input inventories to inventories of final products. This last ratio, sometimes referred to as the Kornai index, measures the degree to which enterprises are oriented toward meeting market demand on a timely basis, and, hence, have large final product inventories, or are concerned with ensuring their input requirements in a world where inputs, particularly of the imported variety, are available only with long delays in delivery because of government controls and a weak commercial infrastructure.[16]

Measuring the Degree of Bureaucratic Intervention

Given the amount of attention that has been lavished on such issues as the desirability of structural adjustment to ensure greater reliance on market forces, the need for privatization, and the like, it is surprising how little effort has gone into collecting empirical data with which one could assess the current situation in developing countries or measure change. This is not a gap that can be filled by a single analyst in a short essay. Here, we will cite a few examples of the kinds of information desired, not a definitive cross section of the current situation with respect to the role of market forces in the modern sectors of industry in the developing world. We are not concerned with describing the situation in agriculture or in much domestic commerce and services. In these latter sectors, market forces prevail in part because it is impossible to control so many individual units through hierarchical commands. The bureaucracy can distort the price signals reaching these small units, but it cannot effectively intervene directly in their decision making in a discretionary way.[17]

One attempt to measure price distortions for thirty-one countries appeared in the *World Development Report* for 1983 and was based on a study by Ramgopal Agarwala.[18] The summary results of this study are presented in Table 3.

Table 3 Price Distortion Indexes

Country	Distortion Index	Country	Distortion Index
Malawi	1.14	Ivory Coast	2.14
Thailand	1.43	Egypt	2.14
Cameroon	1.57	Turkey	2.14
Korea, Republic of	1.57	Senegal	2.29
Malaysia	1.57	Pakistan	2.29
Philippines	1.57	Jamaica	2.29
Kenya	1.71	Uruguay	2.29
Yugoslavia	1.71	Bolivia	2.29
Colombia	1.71	Peru	2.29
Ethiopia	1.86	Argentina	2.43
Indonesia	1.86	Chile	2.43
India	1.86	Bangladesh	2.57
Sri Lanka	1.86	Tanzania	2.57
Brazil	1.86	Nigeria	2.71
Mexico	1.86	Ghana	2.86

Source: World Bank, World Development Report, 1983 *(New York: Oxford University Press, 1983), 60.*

The Agarwala estimates are a start, but only a start, on a systematic effort to measure price distortions in developing economies, and price distortions in turn are only a part of what one needs to know in attempting to measure the degree to which an economy is governed by market forces versus bureaucratic commands. Two of Agarwala's measures are the average effective rate of protection in manufacturing and in agriculture, and a third is the closely related movement in the real effective exchange rate. For the purpose of reaching some conclusion about the degree of intervention in setting domestic prices, the variation in effective rates of protection between sectors or individual products would be more useful than average rates for such large aggregates as all of manufacturing and agriculture. A high uniform rate of protection, for example, would imply relatively little discretionary bureaucratic intervention in the setting of relative prices. A high average rate of protection would also normally be accompanied by an overvalued exchange rate so that the two measures are really measuring much the same thing.

Agarwala's use of differences in real rates of interest between countries is straightforward, and his data will be reproduced below. His measure of labor market distortion, the relationship between real wage growth and growth of GNP per capita, is based on weak data and subjective judgments. And his final two measures, the rate of return on power utilities and high and accelerating rates of inflation, are only indirectly related to relative price distortions. Furthermore, all seven indicators are reduced to simple indexes of low, medium, and high distortion. Drawing the line between the three categories involves subjective judgment as well.

Some of the problems involved in interpreting this index can be illustrated using the example of Korea. Korea is said to have a low level of distortion in five of the indicators and a high degree of distortion in two, interest rates and the effective rate of protection in agriculture. The inflation index ranks Korea as low because inflation did not accelerate much in the 1970s, even though the average rate of price increase, 19.8 percent per year, was above that of twenty of the thirty other countries. Korea's average rate of effective protection was low (see Table 9 below), but the variation in effective protection was quite high.[19] Some revision in the measures used, therefore, could easily move Korea into at least the medium distortion range for two additional categories, raising the overall index from 1.57 (11/7) to 1.86 (13/7).

Furthermore, all of the countries in the Agarwala calculations are developing countries. How would these developing-country price distortions compare with those of Western Europe and North America? One would have to create more than three categories to allow for the fact that effective rates of protection in manufacturing in the industrialized nations of the West are far lower and show much less variation than in almost all developing countries. Inflation rates are also typically much lower with little long-term acceleration, and interest rates are not just positive, they usually reflect market forces. In short, relative to true market economies, the price distortions in most developing countries are likely to appear large.

There is one set of price data that allows one to get part of the way around the limitations of exercises such as those undertaken by Agarwala, but only part of the way. The data set that eliminates the subjectivity inherent in these kinds of measures is that collected under United Nations and World Bank auspices, guided by Irving Kravis, Alan Heston, and Robert Summers.[20] Most important, these price data are the only ones where one can have some confidence that the prices being compared are for goods with identical specifications. Most price comparisons across countries are subject to a wide margin of potential error, precisely because of the range of variation in product quality and other specifications.

While these data are the best available, they are not ideal for the purposes of the analysis in this essay. They cover only a small number of countries. More important, they include nontraded goods where one would not expect prices to be the same across countries even in the absence of trade distortions. The solution to this problem would be to look only at traded goods, but that is impossible because all goods sold on the domestic market have a nontradable component, namely the cost of wholesale and retail services needed to bring that good to the market. Domestic retail prices are not border prices, and only border prices can be expected to be similar across countries, although even there one must take into account cost, insurance, and freight charges (cif). Finally, these data are grouped into 151 to 153 categories. One does not have access to the individual product-by-product prices. Still, with all these limitations, the comparisons are useful. *(See Appendix A for a further discussion of these limitations.)*

The principal comparisons are presented in Tables 4 and 5. The data are based on product-by-product (or service-by-service) comparisons of purchasing power parity, or the domestic prices of the country listed relative to an "international" price. The international price in most cases is the U.S. price. The data for Germany are included to show that there is more than a little variation in prices even when comparing high-income countries with relatively open trading systems. In effect, a coefficient of variation around 0.3 is probably the minimum achievable in the real world.

Table 4	Deviations from International Prices in 1975		
	(1) All Goods and Services	(2) Tradable Goods Only	(3) World Bank Distortion Index
	(Coefficient of Variation)		
Sri Lanka	1.217	1.028	1.86
Zambia	1.105	1.042	—
Pakistan	.936	.797	2.29
Uruguay	.913	.813	2.29
Philippines	.871	.764	1.57
Colombia	.864	.713	1.71
India	.843	.688	1.86
Syria	.818	.777	—
Korea	.790	.689	1.57
Thailand	.758	.651	1.43
Malawi	.735	.616	1.14
Romania	.733	.642	—
Iran	.686	.635	—
Malaysia	.662	.552	1.57
Kenya	.625	.517	1.71
Mexico	.617	.530	1.86
Brazil	.614	.484	1.86
Jamaica	.511	.430	2.29
Germany	.401	.377	—

Source: Derived from raw data in Irving Kravis, Alan Heston, and Robert Summers, World Product and Income: International Comparisons of Real Gross Product (Baltimore: Johns Hopkins University Press, 1982), 208-15. The statistics were calculated from unweighted purchasing power parity estimates for 151 categories of goods and sources.

If all prices were the same around the world, the figures in columns 1 and 2 of Table 4 would all be zeros. The actual figures in Table 4 indicate that prices vary a great deal around the world. A coefficient of variation of 1.0 implies that over 30 percent of the prices in that country vary by 100 percent or more from the international standard, and over 60 percent vary by 50 percent or more.[21] Only a small part of differences of that magnitude can be explained by variations in commercial services costs due to differences in standards of living. The rest is presumably explained by government trade restrictions, price support policies, transport costs for imported goods, and much else. Even a coefficient of variation of 0.5, a fairly low figure in practice, implies that over 30 percent of all prices in that country fall more than 50 percent above or below the international standard price. Most developing countries have a coefficient of variation above 0.5. Put differently, it would appear from these figures that price distortions in most developing countries are large.

Table 5   **Price Distortions and Overvaluations** *(1975 data)*

| | Per Capita Income in 1975 (as % of U.S.) (1) | Exchange Rate (1975) (2) | Purchasing Power Parities (Tradable Goods) | | |
			Average (3)	Coefficient of Variation (4)	Average/ Exchange Rate (3)/(2) (5)
Malawi	4.90	.866	.962	.616	1.111
Kenya	6.56	7.411	8.53	.517	1.151
India	6.56	8.65	6.85	.688	.792
Pakistan	8.23	9.9	8.83	.797	.892
Sri Lanka	9.30	9.0	9.58	1.028	1.065
Zambia	10.3	.643	.999	1.042	1.553
Thailand	13.0	20.379	18.28	.651	.897
Philippines	13.2	7.248	6.97	.764	.962
Korea	20.7	484.0	428.7	.689	.886
Malaysia	21.5	2.402	2.287	.552	.952
Colombia	22.4	30.93	27.13	.713	.877
Jamaica	24.0	.909	1.145	.430	1.260
Syria	25.0	3.7	3.13	.777	.847
Brazil	25.2	8.127	8.9	.484	1.095
Mexico	34.7	12.5	13.35	.530	1.068
Iran	37.7	68.17	71.10	.635	1.043
Uruguay	39.6	2.299	2.76	.813	1.202
Germany	83.0	2.46	3.46	.377	1.405
United States	100.0	1.00	—	—	—

Source: These figures were taken or derived from data in Irving Kravis, Alan Heston, and Robert Summers, World Product and Income: International Comparisons of Real Gross Product, 15, 208-15; and the World Bank, World Tables (Third Edition) Vol. I, various pages.

Nor do these variations from the international norm differ systematically by level of per capita income. As the data in Table 5 indicate, the coefficient of variation appears to have little relationship to per capita income. There are some elements of price variation across countries that relate systematically to per capita income, but they are overwhelmed by government policies that are anything but systematic. Mexico, for example, which is close to the United States and hence limited in its ability to distort prices from the U.S. level, has a much lower coefficient of variation than Uruguay, which had a slightly higher per capita income but was much further away from the United States. When price structures of developing countries are compared with each other rather than with the United States, the coefficient of variation is often larger than when the same countries' prices are compared to those of the United States.[22]

There also seems to be little relationship between the distortion measures derived here and the World Bank's distortion index (see Table 4). The two measures are built up in quite different ways, of course, but they are both trying to get at the same phenomenon — the degree to which government interventions distort prices. It is unlikely, given the large differences between the two indexes, that both are right. The index derived by Kravis and others has the virtue of being based, not on subjective judgments, but on concrete data derived with a systematic methodology.

Finally, these indexes of price distortion can be used to come up with a crude measure of the relative competitiveness of the manufactured goods of these countries in international trade. The major flaw in these comparisons, as in the data on relative price distortions, derives from the fact that the price data include the costs of getting the goods to the final consumer or investor. If these service costs were stripped from the data, the purchasing power parities of the poorest countries would rise substantially relative to those of the United States. Thus when the average purchasing power parity calculated by Kravis et al. is divided by the official exchange rate, a resulting figure of 1.0 for a poor country implies a substantial degree of overvaluation. To be competitive on the international market the purchasing power parity, including retail services for a given good, would have to be well below 1.0. For textiles and clothing in Korea, where these items are major exports, for example, the average purchasing power parity is 0.48. From the data in Table 5, therefore, Korea, with an average figure of 0.886, is known to be a major exporter of many manufactured products. Zambia, by way of comparison, depends mainly on copper exports whose price, being that of an intermediate good, is not included in the Kravis et al. data set. A systematic attempt to use these data to analyze where a particular nation's comparative advantage may lie, however, is well beyond the scope of this essay. Here all we can suggest is that the figures in Table 5 lend weak support to the widespread view that the currencies of most developing countries are seriously overvalued.[23]

We shall return to some of these issues when we discuss effective rates of protection later in this essay.

Another data set that lends some support to the view that bureaucratic intervention has led to distortions in key prices are the estimates of interest rates and rates of inflation put out by the International Monetary Fund. Of the seventy-two developing countries for which both interest rates and the inflation rate are reported, in thirty-nine nations the inflation rate is higher than the interest rate, and in twenty-seven it is lower (in 1985).[24] In the remainder the two rates are about the same. In only eleven countries was the interest rate 3 percent or more above the inflation rate, as was true in the United States and the United Kingdom at that time. These data are not ideal for these kinds of comparisons, to be sure. For many developing nations the only interest rate reported is the discount rate, which may not reflect the true risk-free rate faced by borrowers on the organized money markets of these countries. A better data set is that collected by Agarwala for twenty-eight countries, which is presented in Table 6. The only nation in the table with a positive real interest rate is Thailand. Together, these two sets of data certainly suggest that most organized capital markets in developing countries are controlled more by direct government rate setting than by market forces.

Table 6 Real Interest Rates in Developing Countries

Country	Nominal Interest Rate	Inflation Rate	Real Interest Rate
Kenya	5.7	10.2	- 4.1
Malawi	6.1	9.8	- 3.4
Tanzania	4.5	13.2	- 7.7
Cameroon	6.9	9.6	- 2.5
Ghana	9.3	34.8	-19.0
Ivory Coast	6.9	12.0	- 5.5
Nigeria	4.4	18.2	-11.7
Senegal	6.9	7.6	- 1.0
Korea	13.7	19.8	- 5.0
Philippines	7.7	13.2	- 4.9
Thailand	10.5	9.9	0.5
Bangladesh	7.3	20.3	-10.9
India	8.2	8.5	- 0.3
Pakistan	8.6	13.5	- 4.3
Sri Lanka	8.1	12.6	- 4.0
Egypt	6.6	11.5	- 4.4
Tunisia	5.3	8.2	- 2.7
Turkey	11.0	29.7	-14.5
Yugoslavia	9.0	19.1	- 8.5
Argentina	58.8	130.8	-31.2
Brazil	25.8	36.7	- 8.0
Chile	99.0	224.1	-38.6
Colombia	19.6	22.0	- 2.0
Jamaica	8.2	17.0	- 7.5
Mexico	4.5	17.0	-10.7
Uruguay	28.3	61.5	-20.6
Bolivia	13.8	22.3	- 7.0
Peru	16.2	30.7	-11.1

Source: Ramgopal Agarwala, "Price Distortions and Growth in Developing Countries," World Bank Staff Working Paper No. 575, 23.

25

Table 7 — International Comparisons of Input to Output Inventories
(Kornai Indexes)

Country	Year	Ration of Input to Output Inventories (excluding semi-finished goods)	Ration of Input to Output Inventories (including semi-finished goods)
S. Korea	1984	1.17	1.74
	1978	1.92	2.74
	1973	1.33	1.83
India	1978-79		
	1984-85	1.78	2.44
Thailand	1984	1.49	1.82
	1979	1.33	2.48
Chile	1980	1.79	2.11
	1977	1.90	2.21
	1971	4.14	4.30
Brazil	1979,1980	1.62	2.15
	1974,1975	1.99	2.47
Mexico	1977,1978,1980	1.65	2.11
	1970-1972	1.23	1.63
Colombia	1983-1986	1.47	1.83
	1967,1968,1970	1.71	2.13
United States	1982	1.03	2.05
	1977	1.15	2.17
Canada	1960-1975	—	1.06
Hungary	1978-1984	—	4.90
	1974-1977	—	5.72

Sources: The Canadian and Hungarian data are from a study by Attila Chikan as reported in Janos Kornai, "The Hungarian Reform Process: Visions, Hopes, and Reality," Journal of Economic Literature *34 (December 1986): 1719.* The author is indebted to Tsur Somerville for help in constructing this table.

Finally, there is the question of the ratio of input inventories to final output inventories. Systematic international comparisons of this variable will have to await further data collection efforts. The variable, however, appears to be sensitive to the nature of the system. For the United States, for example, the ratio varies from 0.9 to 1.2. For China in 1984-85, after some market-oriented reforms, the ratio varied from 3.8 to 4.4 and in the Soviet Union a few years earlier between 9.2 and 12.3.[25] Data for several developing and industrial countries for a few recent years are reported in Table 7. (These figures suggest significantly more bureaucratic interference in many developing countries than in advanced industrial nations, but far less than was found in pre-1990 socialist states such as Hungary.)

Another related and more widely available kind of data that gets at some of the same phenomena are the national accounts figures on changes in inventories. These data are not as useful for our purposes as the ratio of input to output inventories, but a case can certainly be made that there is a positive correlation between the size of inventories of all types and the degree of bureaucratic intervention. Bhagwati, for example, makes the argument that inventories tend to be larger where exchange control regimes exist.[26] Inventories, however, are probably also negatively correlated with the level of development in general and that of commerce in particular.[27] Some relevant figures derived from the national accounts of various Asian countries are presented in Table 8. The ratio of inventories to GDP was derived by averaging the share of annual changes in inventories.[28]

These average levels of inventory changes across countries appear to conform with the hypothesis that bureaucratic intervention and size of inventories are positively correlated. The size of inventories is very low relative to GDP in laissez-faire Hong Kong. In Korea, Taiwan, and China, liberalization efforts in the 1980s have been accompanied by declines in the ratio of inventories, although the Chinese data should be treated with special caution. Some developing countries do not even calculate changes in inventories because the data are too unreliable (Bangladesh, for example), but further research should tell us much more about how well inventory ratios to GDP track the degree of bureaucratic intervention.

Table 8   Change in Inventories as a Share of GNP

Country	Years	(Change in Inventories/GNP) x 100
China	1965-1977	7.38
	1979-1987	6.55
Philippines	1974-1983	5.17
Indonesia	1984-1986	4.66
India	1974-1982	4.06
Singapore	1974-1984	2.98
Hong Kong	1974-1984	2.70
South Korea	1963-1979	2.47
	1980-1987	0.43
Thailand	1974-1984	1.62
Japan	1974-1983	0.73

Sources: Economic and Social Commission for Asia and the Pacific, Statistical Yearbook for Asia and the Pacific (years cited above) (Bangkok: Economic and Social Commission for Asia and the Pacific, United Nations); Economic Planning Board, Major Statistics of Korean Economy, 1988 (Seoul: Economic Planning Board, 1988), 32; State Statistical Bureau, Zhongguo Tongji Nianjian, 1988 (Beijing: China Statistical Press, 1988), 25, 60, 66.

None of the above figures is conclusive. Much more work remains to be done before a reasonably clear picture emerges of the relative importance of bureaucratic and market forces in the economies of developing countries. Nevertheless, the portrait painted in this and the previous section of this essay is one of pervasive controls by government over the economy. Discretionary bureaucratic commands are the norm, not the exception. This conclusion should not come as any surprise to someone who has worked for a developing country's government or tried to do business in such a society. But the implications of this pervasive world of controls for how one reforms a developing-country economic system are often only dimly perceived. Economists in particular think of these controls as an aberration rather than the norm. All reform requires is for government to remove its controls and the system will function the way a market economy should. In reality, reform, even where the objective is to increase the role of the market forces, involves much more than the simple removal of controls. The control system is pervasive and fundamentally shapes the behavior of enterprise managers and other economic decision makers. Reform must be equally far-reaching to have a chance for success.

The Objectives of Economic Systems Reform

We have established that government intervention in the economy is pervasive in developing countries, but why does it matter? The presumed answer is that the degree of government intervention is directly responsible for the good or bad performance of the economy. An increase in the use of bureaucratic commands in the economy leads either to a higher or a lower growth rate or to a more or less equitably distributed income. But which is the correct answer? In the 1950s economists confidently argued that more government planning and intervention were necessary in order to achieve higher growth. By the 1970s and 1980s, development specialists, at least those in the West and in the international aid agencies, pushed for less government and more private market activity. But was the 1980s bias against government intervention anything more than the disappointed reaction to the failures of such interventions in the past? Certainly there was no theory of growth and development that had evolved in the 1960s and 1970s that established a clear relationship between the rate of growth and the nature of the economic system.

What kind of growth theory could be used to establish a connection between growth performance and the nature of the economic system? The aggregate production function provides a useful framework for the analysis of the source of growth, but most growth models based on the aggregate production function stress the role of capital formation. If savings and capital formation are the main driving force behind growth, then economic reform should be directed at raising the rate of savings. People are poor in developing countries; historically, personal savings rates in these countries have been low, so the appropriate reform measure was to have the government take on the task of raising savings. The stronger and more interventionist the government is, the higher the savings rate is likely to be. The Soviet Union in the 1950s was the model for this approach, with its tight restrictions on personal consumption, its relatively high savings rate, and its rapid rate of growth in gross national product.

Most economists of an empirical or historical bent, however, have argued all along that capital formation is at best only a part of the growth story and possibly not the most important part, particularly for developing countries. It is Gerschenkron's view of European development updated and extended to the experience of Asia since the 1960s that provides the theoretical foundations for this alternative view of the sources of growth.[29]

The core idea of this approach is that there are "advantages to backwardness" — that nations late in entering into modern economic growth can take advantage of an enormous backlog of technology and experience from those countries that started earlier. The longer these follower nations wait, the bigger the backlog and, consequently, the greater the potential for an accelerated catch-up period. The potential for accelerated growth did not mean that it would be realized in practice. Developing countries were replete with barriers to development, which is why they lagged behind in the first place. At any given time only a few nations were likely to overcome these barriers completely and achieve the full potential of accelerated growth. Others would either not grow at all or would be constantly battling against internal barriers to growth.

In this view of the growth process, several different patterns of development are possible. They are:

(1) The industrialized nations on the frontiers of the world economy. Growth is likely to be determined by the rate of capital formation and the level of research and development effort. The costs of pioneering new paths of development are high, and per capita growth of GNP is not likely to exceed 2 or 3 percent per year on a sustained basis.

(2) Follower nations that make the necessary changes in policy and in their economic systems to realize the full potential of being a follower. As several countries in East Asia have demonstrated, this potential is very great. Increases in per capita GNP of 6 to 8 percent a year over two decades or longer, as much as a fivefold rise in per capita income, have proved to be possible. What are the changes that make this kind of performance possible? In particular, are the critical changes ones that raise the rate of savings and capital formation, or are they reforms that accelerate productivity growth?

(3) Follower nations that overcome only some of the barriers to growth and hence realize only some of the potential of being a follower. As in (2) above, the critical issue is to identify these barriers to a higher performance. Is the objective to remove barriers to higher rates of savings, or is it to remove elements that inhibit the more efficient use of those savings? In some cases the answer may be both.

(4) Nations that have not yet entered into a period of modern economic growth of any kind. Is it an inability to raise capital formation above a replacement level that leads to stagnation, or is it an inability to use more than ample inputs effectively?

It is the contention here that differences in productivity growth have more to do with the differences between countries in category (2), (3), and even (4) than do differences in the rate of capital formation. The argument turns on rather impressionistic evidence and a very broad definition of what constitutes productivity growth.

Given the limited data available and the small number of studies of the sources of growth in developing nations, one has little choice but to use a very broad definition of productivity growth. Productivity growth, as used here, includes everything other than increases in the quantity of capital and the size of the labor force. Specifically, it includes:

    (a) improvements in the quality of labor and capital;
    (b) economies of scale;
    (c) better management of capital, labor, and other resources; and
    (d) greater or more purposeful effort on the part of labor.

In growth accounting terms, productivity as used here includes everything that would either increase the size of the residual or would raise the elasticity of output response to an increase in capital or labor. Put formally,

$$y = a + b_1 k + b_2 l$$

where y = growth rate of GNP
       k = the growth rate of the capital stock
       l = the growth rate of the labor force
       b_1, b_2 = the elasticity of GNP with respect to capital
         and labor respectively
       a = the residual.

Productivity as used here includes not only "a," the residual, but also changes in "b_1" and "b_2." As we shall see below, the breadth of this definition makes it difficult to establish a causal relationship between higher growth performance and particular economic reforms. The calculations, however, do allow one to reach some tentative conclusions about whether high growth in follower countries is driven more by productivity or by savings and capital formation.

What is the nature of the evidence? Several historical examples shed light on the issue. The most recent cases in point are the Chinese reforms of 1977-79 and after. Prior to 1977, Chinese GNP growth averaged 4 to 5 percent a year, with a gross capital formation rate that rose steadily to a level that in the early 1970s was above 30 percent of GNP. After 1977, China's rate of capital formation actually fell slightly to under 30 percent of GNP before rising again, but the GNP growth rate accelerated to an average of 9 percent a year for a decade.[30]

The nations of Africa provide another example, only in reverse. In the 1960s, thirty-eight nations in sub-Saharan Africa grew at an average rate of 3.8 percent a year. In the 1970-82 period, in contrast, despite a rise in the rate of investment from 16 to 19 percent a year accompanied by an increase in the growth of the labor force from 1.9 to 2.2 percent a year, the GNP growth rate actually fell to 3.0 percent a year.[31] Japan provides a different kind of example of reversal of productivity growth. In the 1950s and 1960s, Japan sustained growth rates of around 10 percent a year as gross capital formation rose by the 1960s to over 35 percent of GNP. After 1973 Japan's growth rate for the next decade fell to just over 4 percent a year, despite the fact that the gross capital formation rate stayed above 30 percent of GNP.[32]

Put differently, these variations in growth and capital formation rates imply widely differentiated capital-to-output ratios. Japan in the 1960s and China in the 1980s had incremental capital output ratios of 3 or 3.5 to 1. Africa in the 1970s, Japan in the 1970s and early 1980s, and China before 1977 had ratios of

6 or 7 to 1. In the Soviet Union in the 1980s the incremental capital:output ratio may have been as high as 10 to 1.[33] Clearly, something is going on in the growth performance of these economies that cannot be explained by the accumulation of greater and greater quantities of capital alone.

By putting these observations in a formal growth accounting framework, the argument can be taken a step further. The growth accounting framework used is,

$$y = a + b_1 \cdot I + b_2 \cdot l$$

where y = the growth rate of GDP
$\quad$ I = the investment rate as a percent of GDP
$\quad$ l = the growth rate of the labor force
$\quad$ b_1 = the marginal product of capital
$\quad$ b_2 = the elasticity of output with respect to labor
$\quad$ a = the residual.

The coefficients "b_1" and "b_2" are assumed to be equal to 0.12 and 0.6 respectively. These are plausible estimates comparable to those obtained in some econometric estimates of these coefficients for specific countries. In reality, "b_1" and "b_2" will vary across countries, but we here are interested in all sources of difference in growth rates other than what can be explained by increases in the quantity of capital and labor. Differences across countries in "b_1" and "b_2" will show up in the residual, "a," along with all other sources of productivity growth.

The data used to investigate this issue come from a sixty-eight country sample compiled by the World Bank. The nations are all developing countries and the sample covers the period 1963 to 1982. The principal results of the calculations using these data are presented as a correlation matrix in Table 9.

The correlations in Table 9 tell a clear and dramatic story. While differences in levels of factor inputs, notably differences in the rate of investment, do "account" for some of the variation in the growth rate of GNP between countries, it is the productivity residual that "accounts" for most of the differences, nearly 83 percent of the total. Crude as these calculations are, they suggest that any effort to explain why some countries grow faster than others should begin with an effort to explain why some nations use their factor inputs so much more efficiently than others. No doubt a nation also must achieve a certain level of capital formation in order to attain sustained increases in per capita GNP, but most nations of the world by the 1960s had investment rates of 15 percent of GNP, a figure some economic historians suggest should be sufficient to begin modern economic growth,[34] as contrasted to the 5 percent rates in many countries or colonies in the pre-World War II era, which were probably barely sufficient to cover depreciation. In the sixty-eight country sample used here, for example, only seven nations had investment rates below 15 percent of GNP in both the 1963-73 and 1974-82 periods.[35] The average rate of GNP growth over the two decades of even these seven low investors was 2.9 percent a year, although the data in the case of several of these countries are of suspect quality. More to the point, for the nations that were able to invest more than 15 percent of GNP, there is only a limited correlation between GNP growth and the level of investment achieved. Nor is there much of any correlation between the level of investment and the rate of productivity growth. Thus, one cannot use these data to tell a story of how productivity growth is embodied in capital.[36]

Table 9 Growth Accounting Correlation Matrix

	Investment	Labor	Total	Productivity	GNP
Investment	1.000	—	—	—	—
Labor	0.010	1.000	—	—	—
Total Factor Inputs	0.653	0.005	1.000	—	—
Productivity	0.004	0.002	0.001	1.000	—
GNP	0.156	0.0002	0.155	0.826	1.000

This table was compiled from World Bank data for sixty-eight developing countries during two time periods, 1963-73 and 1974-82, for a total of 136 observations. The productivity residual and the total factor input contributions to growth were derived using the following equation:

$$y = a + b_1 \cdot I + b_2 \cdot 1$$

where		
	y =	growth rate of GNP
	b_1 =	the marginal product of capital or the shadow interest rate
	I =	investment as a share of GNP
	b_2 =	the elasticity of GNP with respect to labor
	1 =	the growth rate of the labor force.

The coefficients b_1 and b_2 were derived by assumption, namely that b_1, the marginal product of capital, was 0.12 and b_2, the elasticity of GNP with respect to labor, was 0.6. The actual regression derived from these same data gives a figure of 0.15 for b_1 but only 0.0007 for b_2, and b_2 is not statistically significant. It does not follow from this latter result that increases in the labor force contribute nothing to growth. It may be, for example, that countries with a high labor force growth rate have a host of other problems that slow growth while those with a low labor force growth rate do not. The host of other problems, however, may not be caused by the high labor force growth rate, only correlated with it.

If productivity growth, broadly defined, is the main source of growth in developing countries, the logical next step would be to try to relate that increase in productivity to particular policy reforms and other explanatory variables. This step, it turns out, is extremely difficult to accomplish. The research for the essay by Michael Roemer in this volume, for example, tried to relate the degree of openness of an economy and the role of manufactured exports in that openness to productivity and GNP growth, but without success. For the purposes of this essay, it would be desirable to relate the Kornai index to the growth rate of the economy, but we don't yet have an adequate measure of this variable for more than a handful of economies.

For fifteen of the countries in the World Bank sample used here, we do have a measure of the degree of price distortion (see Table 4). Regressions using the Kravis price distortion indexes as the explanatory variable for differences in either productivity or GNP growth rates do have the right sign (negative) but are not statistically significant. These results are heavily influenced by the performance of Jamaica, which had a low distortion index but also had low GNP and productivity growth. Dropping Jamaica does improve the results, but then one can always improve one's results by dropping observations that don't conform with the a priori hypothesis being tested.[37]

Thus, productivity growth is essential for achieving high rates of modern economic growth, but we don't know very much about what drives productivity growth in developing countries. The importance of productivity growth, however, does suggest that how a country manages its economy does matter. It may not be possible with data now available to establish quantitatively which kinds of economic management have the greatest impact on the efficiency with which inputs are used, but there is a presumption that doing the job well will make a large difference. The remainder of this essay will suggest key features of good economic management, beginning with a discussion of what it takes to make a market work in a way that promotes dynamic efficiency. The final section of the essay will examine the rules for achieving comparable results from a bureaucratic command system.

The Nature of Economic Systems Reform

Thus far, this essay has made two simple points. First, developing countries' economies are dominated by a wide variety of bureaucratic controls. Second, there may be reason to believe that the existing degree of bureaucratic control in many developing countries is detrimental to high productivity growth and hence to a rapid increase in per capita national product. It follows that growth could be accelerated either by increasing the role of market forces or by improving management of bureaucratic controls. But how is this to be done in practice? The popular notion that all that needs to be done is to abolish state controls or privatize the economy does not come close to capturing the many changes that are required.

The Steps to Making Markets Work

There are four components to a market system, and all four must be in place before one can speak of a system where market forces predominate. Three of these components are commonly discussed in the economics literature. The fourth component, the profit motive which compels producers to respond to market forces, is usually taken for granted, but should not be. The absence of these four elements is most apparent in countries such as China or the Soviet Union, where in modern industry and much of commerce the market has been historically rejected as a means for determining production and distribution. The contention here is that the full command economy of the Soviet type is really just the extreme end of a continuum that starts from the pure market economy. Most developing countries are quite a long way toward the bureaucratic command end of that spectrum. As a result, the problems of introducing a market system into a nation such as China have much in common with the problems of making markets work well in most developing countries. Put differently, China, as an extreme case of moving from a system dominated by commands to one dominated by market forces, brings into relief the nature of the issues that most developing countries must face in trying to enhance the role of market forces.

The four components of a well-functioning market system are described below.

(1) Goods must be available for purchase and sale on the market. Items allocated through official licensing procedures or government-determined quotas are not distributed through the market.

(2) Prices on these markets must reflect true relative scarcities in the economy. In no economy will this condition hold for all products, but there is some point where prices are so distorted that bureaucratic commands may be a more efficient allocation mechanism than markets. Where that tipping point is will vary from country to country depending in part on the skills possessed by the bureaucrats responsible for making such allocations.

(3) The markets must be competitive. Much of economics is concerned with how price distortions in a static context lead to departures from efficient allocation (Pareto optimality). Most attempts to measure the gains from improving static allocative efficiency, however, come up with quite small numbers. Simulations with computable general equilibrium models of a major across-the-board elimination of trade restrictions, for example, result in static efficiency gains ranging from 1.8 percent of GDP if high elasticities of substitution are assumed, to 2.9 percent of GDP if low elasticities of substitution are assumed. An estimate for Turkey in 1978 suggested that import restrictions resulted in a one-shot GDP loss of 3.1 percent. A dynamic input-output simulation for Korea of the consequences if Korea had abandoned export promotion and followed an inward looking strategy results in estimates of a larger magnitude, a 2 percent decline in the growth rate each year or a 20 percent decline over a ten-year period, but the limited substitution allowed in the input-output framework probably leads to overstatements of the efficiency loss.[38]

Whatever one thinks of the assumptions underlying these simulations, they clearly do not explain more than a small part of why some countries grow rapidly and others do not. National growth rates can vary by as much as 5 to 8 percent a year. Even after eliminating differences in rates of capital formation, the residual or productivity growth between nations can range from negative rates to 4 percent a year and more, as was demonstrated above.

One plausible hypothesis is that it is competition that plays a major role in generating these productivity gains. The gains from competition come not so much from better allocative efficiency, but because of better X-efficiency. Competition forces entrepreneurs to be constantly on the lookout for better ways of doing things rather than relaxing behind a state-guaranteed market monopoly. At this time, however, this possible relationship between competition and high productivity growth remains a hypothesis. There is no theoretical argument that establishes unequivocally such a connection,[39] and empirical studies to date have not done so either.

(4) Those who make decisions on markets, notably producers, must behave according to the rules of the market. Specifically, they must pursue profit maximization or some goal that approximates profit maximization.[40] Furthermore, the pursuit of profits must take place through efforts to cut enterprise production costs or increase sales. Profits generated by manipulating the bureaucracy to grant the enterprise favors violate the rules of market behavior and move one toward the bureaucratic command system. Economists typically take the appropriate kind of profit maximization for granted. The reality of many bureaucracy-dominated developing economies is that decision rules by producers do not come close to approximating those required by well-functioning markets. Changing these rules is one of the greatest challenges to the effective introduction of efficient markets.

34

The four components and how they relate to current efforts in developing countries to increase and improve the functioning of markets will be discussed one by one, but in reality, substantial progress must be made on all four before any one of them will produce the desired results.

(1) For socialist countries such as China, it is possible to speak in concrete terms about the share of inputs and outputs that are distributed through the government allocation bureaucracy versus those distributed through the market. In China, for example, material inputs supplied through the market to state enterprises rose from 16 to 27 percent of total inputs supplied during the early phase of reform in 1984-85.[41]

For most developing countries, however, measuring the share of industrial inputs supplied through market mechanisms is a complex task. A critical area for many developing countries is how imports are handled. Are they imported by trading companies and sold to the highest bidder, or does the state issue import licenses to those it deems to have priority? When a state firm is the sole producer of an important input such as electricity or steel and demand for that input is greater than the supply, does the state firm raise its prices so that the market clears? Or is the firm expected to allocate its output to users on the basis of state-set priorities or some other administrative mechanism?

The issue of bureaucratic control applies mainly to modern sector inputs that are in chronically short supply. Surplus inputs are likely to be freely available to whoever will purchase them. Most developing countries, however, have balance-of-payments problems, which means that most imports face excess demand situations. Imports in turn are often the main source of equipment for plant expansion and for key intermediate inputs. If enterprises regularly bid openly for licenses to import these shortage items, allocation would still be through the market, but how many countries allocate import licenses in this way? Currency devaluation may also alleviate a balance-of-payments disequilibrium that then allows the free import of industrial inputs, but the number of developing countries with overvalued exchange rates is legion.

Among nontraded goods, electric power is often in short supply relative to demand. If shortages of electric power are combined with shortages of imports and both are allocated in accordance with government priorities, enterprise success will depend critically on receiving a high enough priority. Those who do receive priority in allocation will have a substantial cushion against failure. Those who do not are likely to go out of business.

(2) The issue of "getting the prices right" is such a central part of the economics literature that only the most cursory treatment is called for here to put the subject in its proper context with respect to this essay.

Much of the literature on price distortions deals with agriculture and the impact on consumers. These are important subjects, but are not central to the discussion here. Even when agricultural and consumer prices are highly distorted, allocation is still through the market. Given the numbers of farmers and consumers, rationed allocation through bureaucratic channels is very difficult for a developing nation to implement. Even the Chinese in the prereform era relied on the market for the allocation of many, although not all, of these goods.

In other developing countries there are times when key farm inputs such as chemical fertilizer are in short supply and governments are tempted to allocate these supplies through channels they control, but the results are usually disastrous and soon abandoned.

Table 10 Variation in Effective Rates of Protection

	Mean ERP	Standard Deviation of ERP
Singapore 1967	7.6	8.8
Norway 1954*	9.8	20.7
Malaya 1965*	10.4	31.9
Taiwan 1969	18.2	31.2
Mexico 1960*	23.1	36.7
Philippines 1965*	26.5	43.8
Israel 1968	77.5	52.7
Korea 1968	6.1	53.7
Colombia 1969	32.2	60.3
Argentina 1969	75.4	64.6
Pakistan 1963-64*	89.4	108.4
Chile 1961*	64.1	130.8
Brazil 1966*	102.9	134.0

Source: *These figures were derived from data in Bela Balassa,* Development Strategies in Semi-Industrial Economics *(Baltimore: Johns Hopkins University Press, 1982), 28-29; and from Bela Balassa and Associates,* The Structure of Protection *in Developing Countries (Baltimore: Johns Hopkins University Press, 1971), 66-67. The figures in this latter source are for the net effective rate of protection and are starred (*).*
The figures in the second source are not strictly comparable to those in the first source because they are grouped into fifty-seven separate categories whereas those in the first source are grouped into only fifteen categories.

The central issue here has to do with setting prices of investment goods and intermediate inputs for industry and of the output of industry. How large are the distortions typically found in developing countries in these sectors? The discussion of international comparisons of prices above would suggest that these distortions are often substantial. Even in export-oriented Korea the departures from international prices for most domestic outputs appear to be very large.

Among the more careful measures of the degree of distortion of prices found in developing countries, outside of the estimates of Kravis et al., referred to earlier, are those that attempt to calculate the effective rate of protection in particular countries on an item-by-item basis.

Some estimates done with 1960s data by various analysts are presented in Table 10. These data are broadly consistent with the figures derived from Kravis et al. that were presented in Tables 4 and 5. Once again it is the standard deviation of the effective protection rate rather than the average level of protection that is most interesting when analyzing the level of bureaucratic intervention and the degree to which that intervention was ad hoc in character.

A standard deviation of 100.0 in these effective rates of protection data is roughly comparable to a coefficient of variation for the Kravis data of 1.0. The implication in both cases is that over 30 percent of all relative prices deviate from international relative prices by 100 percent or more. In fact, if one compares the data in Table 10 with the figures in Table 4 there is a considerable degree of correlation between the two, although the estimates are for different periods in the two tables and hence not strictly comparable. Brazil, however, is an anomaly with a high level variance in its effective rates of protection, but a purchasing power parity structure closer than most developing countries to that of the United States. Brazil by 1975 was more oriented toward manufactured export than in 1966, but it is doubtful that alone accounts for this seeming inconsistency. The Korean data are consistent with a view of Korean economic policy in the 1960s and 1970s where bureaucratic intervention was substantial and ad hoc — hence a high variance in the effective rates of protection — but did not create a cost structure that inhibited industries' capacity to export, hence a low average effective rate leaving average prices close to world prices.

Given the magnitude of the distortions in domestic industrial input prices caused by trade policies, a case might be made that bureaucratic allocation is necessary in order to overcome these distortions. But bureaucratic intervention, for the most part, caused the distortions in the first place, and further intervention is as likely to reinforce as to offset the original distortions.

(3) Competition, or the lack thereof, is also primarily a problem for the industrial sector, particularly sectors with large enterprises. Farmers cannot form cartels, and most rural trade is competitive despite widespread popular feelings that such is not the case.

In many industries in developing countries, vigorous competition is the exception rather than the norm. Again, import restrictions often stifle competition in two separate ways. First, quotas on imports or outright prohibitions effectively insulate domestic producers from competition from producers abroad. Second, the government administration of key investment and intermediate goods has the effect of creating or reinforcing domestic cartels. When imports are allocated through quotas and licensing arrangements, the simplest procedure is to make allocations on the basis of existing capacity, essentially the same criteria used in most cartel agreements.

Bureaucracies, it should be noted, abhor competition. Competition is by nature disorderly, and bureaucracies are not well constituted to deal with disorder. The better a bureaucracy functions, the more likely it is to impose "order" on the markets it controls, and orderly marketing is another name for suppression of competition.

(4) Economists assume that enterprise managers are rational utility maximizers and that this assumption of rationality ensures that the firm will pursue profits. Risk, uncertainty, and incomplete information will modify how profit maximization is pursued, but the underlying goal remains.

In a world of extensive state ownership and bureaucratic control over both private and public sectors, enterprises may be pursuing success criteria that are not even indirectly related to profit maximization.[43] There are two general reasons why success criteria for enterprise managers often have little to do with profits.

First, enterprise managers in state-owned firms are typically selected by politicians or high government civil servants. The criteria for selection are frequently political. The enterprise controls jobs and funds, and the nation's political leaders want to be sure that those jobs and funds are used to support the party in power. The heads of large parastatals in Africa and Asia are even more powerful politicians than many cabinet ministers. Pertamina in Indonesia or the National Cereals Produce Board in Kenya are two important but not unusual cases in point. Individuals picked as managers because of their political skills and connections will define success in their parastatal management job in terms of how that job can be used to further their political ambitions. Only rarely will profit maximization be the logical route to political success.

Private firms with boards of directors who represent the firms' owners are only partly insulated from these political pressures. If controls by government determine whether an enterprise will succeed or fail, a board of directors will appoint managers who can elicit the desired kinds of government support. In many cases, government regulators will simply leave the government to take high paying jobs in the firms that they previously had regulated. The practice is widespread in advanced industrial market economies such as Japan and even in those sectors of the United States economy where bureaucratic procurement is the main source of demand for a company's goods or services—notably the United States Department of Defense. No systematic surveys exist of the extent of these practices in developing countries, but there is little doubt that they are pervasive in some. Managers put in place because of their connections to a regulatory bureaucracy will make every effort to maintain their ties to that bureaucracy, in part by doing the bidding of their former superiors in exchange for special favors for their new firm.

A second reason why enterprises in a bureaucratic system pay little attention to raising profits through cutting costs or increasing sales has to do with the ease with which some enterprises can escape financial trouble. In the terminology of socialist economics this condition is referred to as the "soft budget constraint."[44] In developing countries the phenomenon occurs with great frequency.

One reason for the prevalence of the "soft budget constraint" is that governments are reluctant to allow large enterprises to fail. In China a bankruptcy law was put forward with great fanfare, but two years later the law was still used on a trial basis and only one major enterprise had actually declared bankruptcy. Bankruptcy of a large firm throws many workers out of a job, and those workers, particularly in state-owned enterprises, may have powerful political allies. Bankruptcy of an enterprise built with government subsidies behind a wall of protectionist legislation, Krakatoa Steel in Indonesia for example, would be politically embarrassing or worse for the politicians and government officials who supported the idea in the first place. From the political perspective of these officials, it is usually easier to perpetuate the mistake by reinforcing the subsidies and the wall of protection than it is to acknowledge failure. For small enterprises and for individual farmers, on the other hand, the consequences of bankruptcy are of little political significance unless small enterprise and farm failures become widespread.

A second reason for the "soft budget constraint" facing many large modern enterprises in developing countries is the way bank loans to these firms are handled. China, again, is an extreme example of a widespread phenomenon. In China, as in most Soviet style economies, the banks make loans at interest rates far below market levels. More important, these banks are virtually required to provide a firm with credit for any activity that is in conformity with the state plan.

Government and banking rules are written to ensure that banks will always have enough money on hand to meet these needs. The fact that an enterprise may be running at a loss and is unable to pay back past loans is not a reason for refusing to tender new credits.

Indonesia is currently in the middle of an effort to reform the nation's banking system, but in the past, and to a significant degree the present as well, there has been a symbiotic relationship between the state banks and the larger state enterprises. Particularly in the days of sizable oil-generated budget surpluses, banks were a prime vehicle for funneling state funds to these enterprises. For enterprises losing money and unable to repay these loans, the solution was to make new loans to cover the shortfall. The enterprise knew this would happen and hence felt little pressure to become profitable so that it could lower its debt burden. The banks, in turn, had little to worry about because the government could always be counted on to bail them out if they made losses.

Banking reform, therefore, is one way of eliminating the soft budget constraint. If the banks are cut loose from government subsidies and forced to survive on their commercial skills, soft loans will gradually disappear or be reduced to manageable proportions. Manufacturing enterprises, unable to cover chronic losses, will be forced to bring their costs under control or fail. Interest rates will tend to rise toward market clearing levels because banks will want the added income. Higher interest rates will reduce or eliminate credit rationing by banks, and government officials will no longer be in a position to provide banks with "advice" on who should receive rationed credit. Thus, a thoroughgoing banking reform accomplishes much more than just allowing banks to approach a static Pareto optimum allocation of credit.[45] A major bureaucratic lever of control over industrial and other enterprises is eliminated, and pressure is felt throughout the modern sector to improve performance and profits in order to ensure survival.

If the budget constraint facing the modern large scale sector is not hardened, then firms will not behave in accordance with the rules of the market. If market rules are not followed, getting the prices right will not help much. Competition between firms will also be reduced or eliminated. In short, markets will not work well, and productivity growth will be slowed.

Privatization

A centerpiece of reform efforts in the 1980s is and was the pressure brought by the international agencies and USAID to privatize many formerly public activities. A look at privatization from the point of view of the above analysis is a useful way of highlighting what is and is not important in the way of reform, if the objective is to make markets work and achieve higher productivity growth. Privatization (and its opposite, socialization), of course, may not be carried out with the goal of higher productivity growth in mind at all. Privatization versus socialization is often an argument over the distribution of power between different ethnic groups or between the bureaucracy and private industrialists. Ideologies of various sorts also play an important role.[46] Here, however, we are only interested in whether privatization leads to changes consistent with what it takes to make competitive markets work and achieve higher productivity.

Is privatization either a necessary or a sufficient condition for achieving the elimination of bureaucratic controls over the proper functioning of markets? It is certainly not a sufficient condition. A public steel mill or oil refinery sold to private sources but allowed to retain a domestic market monopoly and receive highly subsidized bank credit won't necessarily change its behavior. Success still depends primarily on support from the government. It is probably true generally that government is less willing to subsidize the private sector than it is state-owned enterprises directly under government control, but how much less willing will vary depending on the political and personal interests of the government officials involved. On average, private firms face harder budget constraints than public firms, but the difference is in degree, not in kind.

Is privatization a necessary condition? The theory of market socialism makes it clear that there is no logical flaw in the view that state enterprises can behave in accordance with market criteria. The early theorists, however, assumed that enterprise managers would behave as they were supposed to if ordered to maximize profits.[47] Few today are so naive as to believe that this is all that is required. The objective function of state enterprise managers includes many elements other than profits, and getting rid of most of these other elements can be very difficult because political and bureaucratic goals will often be in conflict with the requirements of economic efficiency. The key, as above, is to break the connection between the government bureaucracy and the enterprise, and privatization will often help toward that goal. But there are also examples of efficient state enterprises that have managed to achieve a degree of independence of the government bureaucracy comparable to that of much of the private sector.

Many of the reforms that really matter for making markets work apply whether the enterprises involved are public or private. Creation of an independent commercial banking system that must survive without infusions of government money will tighten the budget constraints for all enterprises, not just the banks or the private sector. Devaluation of an overvalued currency to a level that makes broad-based trade liberalization possible will create competition for domestic enterprises, public as well as private. Trade liberalization will also break an important level of bureaucratic control over these enterprises, again public as well as private. Investment licensing procedures may be one area where bureaucratic control is tighter over the private sector than over public investment. In any case, eliminating or regularizing and speeding up the licensing procedures is likely to improve productivity in both sectors. Promoting small-scale industry may be desirable in part because competition among small firms is likely to be vigorous and the budget constraints they face hard; also, small-scale firms are usually, though not always, private.

There is nothing unusual or surprising in this list of reforms. If there is a departure from the normal shopping list of market-oriented economists, it is in the analysis of what these reforms are designed to accomplish.[48] Markets are excellent vehicles for promoting decentralized decision making and vigorous competition. Closer approximations of static Pareto optimality are also useful, but it is doubtful that the improvements in allocative efficiency involved account for growth rate differentials of 4 or 5 percent *per year*. Put differently, it is possible to conceive of a situation, however unreal in practice, where all traded goods prices were set at world price levels but each private enterprise was given a government guaranteed monopoly of the domestic market, easy access to credit to cover losses, and prohibition on imports of competitive items. Alternatively, a system with distorted prices (because of uneven tariffs), but with vigorous competition both domestically and internationally between private and public firms, and domestic commercial credit available only on hard terms, is also conceivable. The question raised here is which of these systems would be most likely to produce the highest rate of growth in productivity? It is unlikely to be the former of these two extreme choices.

Government's Role in Making Markets Work

Many involved in the discussion of government's role in making markets work have argued that the government bureaucracy should get out of the task of manipulating enterprises through direct and discretionary controls in order to make state-owned enterprises, where they exist, behave in accordance with market rules. There are important areas, however, even in a market economy, where the government's role is essential to making markets work efficiently. Market-oriented reforms require that governments do these tasks well. Much of HIID's work, in fact, has involved efforts to improve the functioning of the government bureaucracy, not just measures designed to circumscribe the role of that bureaucracy.[49]

One area where government must function well if markets are to work is in control of key macroeconomic variables, notably inflation and balance-of-payments disequilibrium. This is an empirically based statement, not a theoretical one. In theory, markets could function well in the presence of rapid increases in prices. In practice there is some level of inflation that each nation finds politically intolerable. That level may be 50 percent a year or more, as in parts of Latin America, or it may be 10 percent or less, as in China. Whatever the level, once it is passed, government will be tempted to impose price controls, and price controls will lead to queues and other forms of informal rationing. Informal rationing will be deemed inconvenient and inefficient, and the government will take steps to introduce formal controls over distribution, in effect undermining what was left of the market system and replacing it with bureaucratic allocation mechanisms.

Balance-of-payments disequilibrium caused by inflation is similar. If the currency is not devalued fast enough to match domestic price increases of traded goods, imports outstrip exports, causing a foreign exchange shortage. The typical response to a foreign exchange crisis in the developing world is to tighten import quotas, and the economy is rapidly on the way back to a world of bureaucratic control. Devaluation might make such controls unnecessary, but devaluation is not always politically feasible even when the economic need is clear.

All governments are responsible for collecting taxes, and all governments perform some regulatory functions. How these tasks are carried out can have a fundamental impact on whether markets function well or not. From the standpoint of making markets work, the important step is to remove as much discretion as possible from the tax and regulatory authorities. Discretionary authority in the hands of tax and regulatory officials is a common means of achieving bureaucratic control over the direction of the economy, taking that control away from the market. Discretionary authority also leads to delays, and delays are often artificially generated in order to elicit bribes. In effect, private bureaucratic agendas in this situation replace both market forces and public command direction of the economy.[50]

Fortunately, the kinds of nondiscretionary tax and regulatory systems that fit well with the needs of the market fit well with a widely held view of how government bureaucracies should behave in any case. The Weberian view of bureaucracy stressed the need for systematic rules to govern official behavior. The contrast was with the societies of the past where good governance depended on good people. If dedicated people controlled the bureaucracy, they could be given wide discretionary authority and the public good would be served.[51] The modern view has stressed how discretion could corrupt even well-intentioned bureaucrats. In a field such as taxation the needs were for a sales tax with only a single rate, an income tax with an inclusive definition of income and few deductions, and so on.[52] The more advanced a society and the more skilled its tax bureaucracy, the more feasible it was to introduce complexities without introducing too much tax collector discretion. In developing countries, complexity inevitably reintroduces discretionary authority that undermines society's goal of a better-functioning market.

Making Bureaucratic Commands Efficient

Unfortunately, the rules that fit well such government activities as taxation and regulation, fit poorly with other essential government functions. A nation cannot fight a war or manufacture products by following rigid, nondiscretionary rules. The issue of how governments fight wars is the subject for another essay. The issue here is how governments directly manage economic production because government either chooses to do so or is forced to do so. As the data earlier in this essay suggest, governments in developing countries either choose or are forced to directly manage a large share of modern-sector economic activity outside of agriculture and commercial services. Even a fanatic privatizer would allow a role for government in deciding military procurement. More to the point for most developing nations, much of a nation's transport, communications, and electric power infrastructure are in public hands. And state-owned enterprises will continue to exist in many other sectors as well, for any number of political and social reasons. How are these activities to be managed?

A few of the principles one finds in books about well-managed private enterprises illustrate the nature of the dilemma.[53] These principles of good management include the following.

(a) Clear, simple goals for managers should be communicated. Profit maximization would be such a goal, but many of the elaborate sets of goals facing many state enterprise managers would clearly not meet this principle. In regulatory bureaucracies it is often quite difficult to reach any general conclusion about appropriate success criteria.

(b) Rewards to individuals should be clearly related to the attainment of these goals, particularly at senior management levels. Most government personnel systems, however, stress seniority and such criteria as an individual's educational level in determining promotions. Rewards cannot be tied to meeting specific goals if appropriate goals are hard to define in the first place, as in regulatory agencies. Seniority is a good system for avoiding promotion based on family or ethnic criteria, as would be the case in Kenya (or Boston) in the absence of a seniority system.[54]

(c) An organizational structure is needed that is fluid and adjusts easily to new circumstances. Private company structures are determined by senior management and can be dismantled and rebuilt at the will of those managers or by lower-level personnel in a decentralized system. Government organizational structures are created by legislation and by presidential or ministerial decrees. Even a highly authoritarian system finds it difficult to change these structures rapidly or easily.

(d) Individuals are allowed and encouraged to take action quickly and on their own initiative without going through elaborate layers of approval.

Other analysts might come up with a somewhat different list. The essential point, however, is that management within a hierarchical command system of a private corporation requires simple goals, few rules beyond those simple, clear goals, and a great deal of flexibility and discretion in meeting those goals. Excessive mistakes within the organization are handled by demotions, reductions in bonuses, or firing. If the organization as a whole is prone to error it can go out of business, or stockholders can vote in a new management.

The requirements of a good tax or regulatory system are virtually the opposite of the above criteria. Fairness and avoidance of corruption demand a minimum of discretionary flexibility at any level, including that of the chief tax collector or regulator. Since most governments were established in an era when these kinds of functions were most of what a government did, it is rigid rules such as these that govern the behavior of most government officials.[55] When such rules are extended to manufacturing enterprises and the like, the results in terms of economic efficiency are disastrous.

It is not the case, however, that all government bureaucracies in charge of economic production activities follow the rigid rules of the Weberian bureaucracy. The more successful ones do not fit the Weberian prescription at all. The experience of the Republic of Korea in the 1960s and 1970s illustrates this point. Half of Korean capital formation was in the public sector, and there were many state-owned enterprises. The entire industrial sector in the 1970s was to an important degree run out of President Park's office in the Blue House. The levers of control were a set of state banks issuing subsidized credit, quotas on imports, a corporate tax system, and much else. With each of these levers there was enormous discretionary authority not only in the hands of the president but in the hands of mid-level bureaucrats as well. The degree of discretion involved fostered corruption, but somehow the level of corruption was never such as to undermine high growth in the economy.[56] In the Philippines, in contrast, a similar level of discretionary authority and presidential involvement led to massive corruption that ultimately undermined the overall performance of the economy.

How does one account for these results? The simple but probably correct answer is that President Park had a few clear goals and everything else was subordinated to the achievement of those goals. The goals were rapid economic growth in general and exports in particular. Everyone, not just President Park, knew what the goals were and that they would do well if they contributed to them and would do poorly if they did not. Discretionary authority, therefore, was used to carry out national goals. There was also private rent seeking by individual bureaucrats, but it was kept within bounds that did not do serious damage to the economy.

The more puzzling question is, how was Korea able to make its bureaucratic command system work in this way? Part of the answer may rest with Park Chung Hee himself and his commitment to the nation rather than to personal indulgence and wealth, as was the case with President Marcos. Another part is that President Park's power base was in the army and the police-security apparatus and, to a lesser degree, the rural as contrasted to the urban population. The army was a modern, disciplined combat army, not a collection of feudal style units with personal loyalties to various individual commanders. Politics did not require that industrial subsidies be carried out for particular political ends. Agricultural price supports in the 1970s did play such a role, but subsidies in industry were directed at economic ends.

China is another "hard" state that has been able to use highly discretionary bureaucratic commands to achieve rapid growth since 1976 and even to a degree before that time. Since 1978 in particular, the goal of rapid economic growth, the "four modernizations," has been clear and unequivocal. While China has elaborate bureaucratic rules governing its economy, implementation of those rules is highly flexible. The carrying out of national goals is less clearly in the interests of lower-level bureaucrats in China than was the case in Korea, but somehow the leadership can cut through the layers of obstructionism when they interfere too much with development.

Again this system, like that in Korea, seems to work reasonably well, for a variety of underlying, mostly political, reasons. Deng Xiaoping's personal dedication to these goals is part of the story. The Chinese Communist Party, for all its splits between "reformers" and "conservatives," was not, at least prior to the upheavals brought about by the student movement, a collection of feudal satrapies, who must be paid off with control over different pieces of the economy. Beyond that, there is the relatively high level of education and organizational experience of the Chinese people, and the even higher level of the Korean people. The Chinese and Korean officials who control these bureaucratic structures have the skills necessary for making such a complex system of control function with adequate efficiency. It may be that as China decentralizes authority and liberalizes its political system, the center will lose its ability to make the bureaucratic system work. Inflationary pressures in 1987 and 1988 were in part a result of such a loss of control, but at least through 1988 that degree of loss of control had not seriously undermined development.

Are there many developing countries in situations similar to those of Korea or China? Few, it would appear, have the combination of political conditions and human resources to run a national bureaucratic command system. Even Cuba in the Latin American context has not been able to make such a system become a vehicle for development. In Africa the few attempts in that direction, Tanzania for example, have been clear disasters.

All nations, however, have some elements of a hierarchical command system. Large enterprises are always run this way internally. Some countries, however, have considerable difficulty making even this level of a hierarchical command system work. For such countries the only choice is to concentrate on family farming and very small-scale industrial and commercial enterprises until the human resources and political preconditions are developed that can make larger bureaucratic structures work efficiently.

Conclusion

Reform in the management and control of an economic system, therefore, is a complex process. The economies of all nations are governed in part by bureaucratic commands rather than market forces, and in developing economies the scope of the command forces is typically wider than in industrial market economies. Reducing the scope of these bureaucratic commands is one kind of reform that may promote higher productivity growth, but making markets work is a much more complex process than slogans such as "getting the prices right," "privatization," or "getting rid of controls" would imply. Making markets work involves fundamental changes in enterprise behavior in most cases and substantial changes in the way government itself carries out its functions. Finally, most developing nations are never going to be willing to turn as much over to the market as, say, Hong Kong. Nonmarket controls or hierarchical commands will continue to play a major role in many sectors of most economies. Reform, therefore, is not just a matter of getting rid of such commands. A high-growth economy must learn to make both the market and the bureaucracy perform efficiently. ✑

A Appendix

Price Distortions and International Purchasing Power Parity Data

The work under U.N.-World Bank auspices on the international comparison of prices and national products by Irving Kravis, Alan Heston, and Robert Summers, (KHS),[1] is one reasonably reliable source of price data that can be used for making international comparisons of price structures. The prices in this study, however, are not ideal for the uses made of them in this analysis because of a number of features of the KHS project. Specifically,

(1) The prices are not border prices with or without cost of insurance and freight (fob or cif), but instead are prices actually paid by consumers and investors, in essence retail prices. As such, these prices include the commercial services involved in getting the goods to market. Commercial services are, for the most part, nontraded, and, as in most developing countries, these services cost much less per unit of goods delivered than comparable services in industrial economies. On average, the developing country purchasing power parities stripped of these services would be significantly higher than is the case when services are included. For purposes of comparing the degree of distortion caused by tariff policy or an overvalued exchange rate, the relevant prices are those stripped of commercial service costs, but no reliable data of this sort are available for a large number of countries.

(2) The KHS data apply to final demand goods and services, not to intermediate products or raw materials. Intermediate products including raw materials, however, are a major part of foreign trade, but the KHS data tell us nothing about price distortions for these goods. The KHS data basically measure distortions in food, manufactures, and services only.

(3) The KHS data are not the raw price data, which are not available to the public, but grouped price data. The purchasing power parity prices are published for thirty-four categories and for 151-153 categories. The way the commodities are grouped and the weights used in adding up prices within and between groups do affect the results. KHS themselves calculate a raw correlation coefficient based on the thirty-four categories data (weighted), and I have calculated a coefficient of variation using the 151 categories data (unweighted). The results, presented in Table A.1, are similar but by no means identical. These differences appear in both the 1970 and 1975 data (see Table A.2), and it is not always readily explainable why the two indexes give different results.

For all of their limitations for our purposes, however, the KHS data are by far the best available. Individual efforts to make price comparisons seldom have the resources and degree of official cooperation that went into producing the KHS estimates. Price comparisons are not an area that rewards casual empiricism.

Quality differences between similar goods are so great that errors of orders of magnitude are commonplace in casual or even conscientious efforts to make individual price comparisons.

Table A.1 **Similarity Index and Coefficient of Variation Compared**
(1975 data)

	Similarity Index (weighted) (34 categories)	Coefficient of Variation (unweighted) (34 categories)
Sri Lanka	711	1.075
Pakistan	728	0.813
India	734	0.740
Malawi	748	0.664
Philippines	756	0.693
Uruguay	766	0.787
Colombia	803	0.878
Romania	805	0.616
Thailand	836	0.691
Kenya	846	0.536
Zambia	853	0.594
Korea (R.O.K.)	853	0.699
Syria	855	0.546
Iran	864	0.671
Brazil	867	0.412
Malaysia	876	0.610
Jamaica	899	0.458
Mexico	915	0.527
Germany (F.R.G.)	980	0.304

Source: All data taken or derived from raw data in Irving Kravis, Alan Heston, and Robert Summers (1982), 176-79, 208-15, 352-53.

Table A.2 Price Structures in 1970 and 1975

	1970		1975	
	Similarity Index	Coefficient of Variation	Similarity Index	Coefficient of Variation
Korea (R.O.K.)	.780	.889	.853	.790
Colombia	.814	.827	.864	.864
Philippines	.729	.787	.756	.871
India	.717	.728	.734	.843
Malaysia	.837	.647	.876	.662
Germany (F.R.G.)	.926	.424	.980	.401

Note: The similarity index is the "raw correlation coefficient" between the prices of the country in question with international (or U.S.) prices. The coefficient of variation is the standard deviation divided by the mean of the purchasing power parities (domestic prices relative to international prices) for 151 or 153 categories of goods and services for the country in question. The similarity indexes are based on only thirty-four categories.

Sources: These figures were taken directly from or derived from data in Irving Kravis, Alan Heston, and Robert Summers (1982), 208-15, 352-53; and Irving Kravis, Alan Heston and Robert Summers, International Comparisons of Real Product and Purchasing Power (Baltimore: Johns Hopkins University Press, 1978), 146-53, 234-35.

Notes

1 From the point of view of the firm, of course, internal management issues would be the primary concern. But hierarchical management issues would not be a major concern of government officials and others involved with the operation of the system as a whole. From the point of view of the system, as contrasted to the individual firm, bad management would be eliminated by competitive forces driving the bad managers out of business.

2 The share of primary production (agriculture plus mining) plus services at $100 per capita (in 1964 prices) as predicted by a cross country regression of 101 countries was 82.2 percent; at $500 per capita this figure fell to 61.7 percent. To convert 1964 into 1980 prices, multiplying by three would give one a close approximation. The 1964 price data are from Hollis Chenery and Moises Syrquin, *Patterns of Development, 1950-1970* (Washington, D.C.: World Bank; distributed by Oxford Univ. Press, London, 1975), 21.

3 There is some government investment in agricultural infrastructure, research, and irrigation systems, for example, but the share of this investment in total state investment is usually quite small.

4 See, for example, Edward S. Mason, *Economic Planning in Underdeveloped Areas: Government and Business* (New York: Fordham Univ. Press, 1958).

5　For a recent discussion of many of the issues surrounding the subject of privatization, see Raymond Vernon, ed., *The Promise of Privatization: A Challenge for American Foreign Policy* (New York: Council on Foreign Relations, 1988).

6　World Bank and the United Nations Development Program, *Africa's Adjustment and Growth in the 1980's* (Washington, D.C.: World Bank, 1989), 25.

7　Republic of Kenya, *Statistical Abstract, 1986* (Nairobi: Central Bureau of Statistics, 1986), 224.

8　Leroy P. Jones and Il Sakong, *Government, Business and Entrepreneurship in Economic Development: The Korean Case* (Cambridge: Council on East Asian Studies, Harvard Univ.; distributed by Harvard Univ. Press, 1980), 50.

9　These Indian and Brazilian estimates are from Mahmood A. Ayub and Sven O. Hegstad, "Management of Public Industrial Enterprises," *World Bank Research Observer* 2 (January 1987): 81.

10 Jones and Sakong, *Government, Business and Entrepreneurship*, 150.

11 The classic works on market socialism both make this assumption. Oscar Lange and Fred M. Taylor, *On the Economic Theory of Socialism*, ed. Benjamin E. Lippincott (New York: McGraw Hill, 1938); and Abba P. Lerner, *The Economics of Control: Principles of Welfare Economics* (New York: Macmillan, 1944).

12 For a survey of the recent literature on financial development and state intervention in the financial systems of Asia, see David C. Cole, "Recent Research on Financial Development in Asia" (HIID Development Discussion Paper No. 270, June 1988).

13 J. Clark Leith, *Foreign Trade Regimes and Economic Development: Ghana* (New York: National Bureau of Economic Research; distributed by Columbia Univ. Press, 1974), 90.

14 This discussion is based on HIID experience in a number of these countries, research visits to others, and other forms of personal exposure to Asian economic systems.

15 Anne O. Krueger, "The Political Economy of Rent-Seeking," *American Economic Review* 64, no. 3 (1974): 291-303.

16 Janos Kornai, *The Economics of Shortage* (Amsterdam: North Holland Publishing, 1980).

17 This may be an overstatement, although it is generally true. The Chinese under the commune system did give direct commands to farmers on what to produce. And in some systems certain services, notably banking, are directly controlled by hierarchical commands.

18 See Ramgopal Agarwala, "Price Distortions and Growth in Developing Countries" (World Bank Staff Working Papers no. 575, July 1983); and World Bank, *World Development Report, 1983* (Washington, D.C.: World Bank, 1983), 60.

19 The question of whether or not Korean prices were subject to a high degree of distortion caused by trade policies has been the subject of considerable controversy. The earlier view, that they were not, was based on the work of Charles R. Frank, Jr., Kwang Suk Kim, and Larry E. Westphal, *Foreign Trade Regimes and Economic Development: South Korea* (New York: National Bureau of Economic Research; distributed by Columbia Univ. Press, 1975). The basic conclusions on this point by Frank, Kim, and Westphal, however, have been called into question by a more recent study by Richard Luedde-Neurath, *Import Controls and Export Oriented Development: A Reassessment of the South Korean Case* (Boulder, Colo.: Westview Press, 1986).

20 Irving Kravis, Alan Heston, and Robert Summers, *International Comparisons of Real Product and Purchasing Power* (Washington, D.C.: World Bank; distributed by Johns Hopkins Univ. Press, Baltimore, 1978).

21 Price distortions of this magnitude may not fit a normal distribution since prices generally are not negative and 100 percent below the average would imply a price of zero. One should use caution, therefore, in deriving percentages of prices above and below a certain norm where those percentages are derived from a normal distribution.

22 The coefficient for Korea and the Philippines in 1970, for example, is 0.95, whereas the Korea/United States and Philippines/United States comparisons are 0.74 and 0.63 respectively.

23 The support is weak because a country can be a major exporter of manufactures even if it is competitive in only a few products. The average purchasing power parity divided by the exchange rate across 100 commodities is not really what matters for foreign trade, but rather the purchasing power parity divided by the exchange rate for these few items. Still, if the average rate is higher than another country's, that could imply that it is competitive in only a few final products. If it is a major exporter of natural resources, however, it would still not be correct to refer to the currency as being overvalued.

24 International Monetary Fund, *International Financial Statistics* (Washington, D.C.: International Monetary Fund, December 1985), 78-521.

25 General Survey Group of the Chinese Institute for Economic Systems Reform, *Gaige: Women Mianlin de Tiaozhan yu Xuanze.* Beijing: 1986, trans. and ed. Bruce Reynolds, under the title *Reform in China: Challenges and Choices* (Armonk, N.Y.: M. E. Sharpe, 1987), 18.

26 Bhagwati, using evidence from Leith, *Foreign Trade Regimes*, suggests that exchange control regimes may "have led to increased holdings of inventories of raw materials and intermediates." Jagdish Bhagwati, *Anatomy and Consequences of Exchange Control Regimes* (National Bureau of Economic Research; distributed by Ballinger, Cambridge, Mass., 1978), 110-12.

27 This statement is based on impressionistic evidence. I am not aware of any studies that have tried to establish the point empirically.

28 For shorter time series and for the early years, the initial stock assumptions will dominate the estimates. One could use incremental changes in stocks and GDP, but the same problem would apply to those figures as well.

29 Alexander Gerschenkron, *Economic Backwardness in Historical Perspective* (Cambridge: Harvard Univ. Press, 1962).

30 State Statistical Bureau, *Zhongguo Tongji Nianjian, 1988* (Beijing: China Statistics Press, 1988), 29, 60-61.

31 World Bank, *Toward Sustained Development in Sub-Saharan Africa: A Joint Program of Action* (Washington, D.C.: World Bank, 1984), 58, 61.

32 Economic and Social Commission for Asia and the Pacific, *Statistical Yearbook for Asia and the Pacific, 1984* (Bangkok: United Nations, 1984), 274-76 (and earlier editions of the same yearbook).

33 In the early 1980s, the U.S.S.R. was investing 33-34 percent of GNP, but the GNP growth rate was under 3 percent per year. Stanley H. Cohn, "Soviet Intensive Economic Development Strategy in Perspective," and Laurie Kurtzweg, "Trends in Soviet Gross National Product," both in Joint Economic Committee of the United States Congress, *Gorbachev's Economic Plans* (Washington, D.C.: United States Government Printing Office, 1987), 16, 133, 135.

34 W. W. Rostow, for example, in discussing the conditions necessary for "takeoff," speaks of a rise in the rate of net investment from 5 percent or less to over 10 percent. The latter figure would be roughly equivalent to a gross capital formation rate of 15 percent.

35 Another seventeen nations had investment rates below 15 percent in one of the two decades for which data were available.

36 It does not follow that productivity growth was not sometimes embodied in capital. It may be, for example, that nations with high productivity growth achieved that growth by importing high quality capital while those with low productivity growth imported low quality capital or relied on low quality domestic sources. The critical question in such a case would be why one country imported high quality capital and the other did not, and not why one county achieved a particular level of investment without regard to quality.

37 The regression equation with Jamaica included, using GNP growth as the dependent variable, is,

$$GNP_{growth} = 6.995 - 1.996 \text{ (Price distortion index)}.$$
$$(2.746)$$

With Jamaica excluded the result is

$$GNP_{growth} = 9.851 - 5.100 \text{ (Price distortion index)}.$$
$$(2.318)$$

The figures in parentheses are the standard error of the coefficient.

38 These various estimates are reported in Kemal Dervis, Jaime de Melo, and Sherman Robinson, *General Equilibrium Models for Development Policy* (Cambridge: Cambridge Univ. Press, 1982), 118, 313, 355.

39 On the theoretical side of this issue, see Dani Rodrik, "Closing the Technology Gap: Does Trade Liberalization Really Help?" (National Bureau of Economic Research Working Paper no. 2654, July 1988).

40 Lesser deviations from profit maximization, "satisficing" rather than "maximizing" behavior, for example, do not fundamentally undermine the proper functioning of markets and are, in fact, prevalent in market systems. Objectives such as maximization of gross value of output or increasing employment of one's political supporters, however, do fundamentally undermine the functioning of the market.

41 General Survey Group, *Gaige: Women Mianlin*, 45.

42 In the early years of chemical fertilizer use in both Korea and Indonesia, for example, fertilizer was allocated through cooperatives that were, in practice, arms of the state or directed by the state. The fertilizer often arrived long after it was needed or in combinations (packages with specific combinations of N, P, and K) that were not suitable for local conditions. The Indonesian experience is discussed in studies by the Center for Policy and Implementation Studies in Jakarta. The Korean experience is described in Sung Hwan Ban, Pal Yong Moon, and Dwight H. Perkins, *Rural Development: The Republic of Korea, 1945-1975* (Cambridge: Council on East Asian Studies, Harvard Univ.; distributed by Harvard Univ. Press, 1980), 108-109.

43 For a discussion of the many different goals that state-owned enterprises are often required to include in their objective function, see Robert H. Floyd and Clive Gray, *Public Enterprise in Mixed Economies: Some Macroeconomic Aspects* (Washington, D.C.: International Monetary Fund, 1984).

44 Kornai, *Economics of Shortage*.

45 There is now an extensive literature on how banking reform can eliminate financial repression and how this will end fragmentation in capital markets and improve the allocative efficiency of capital as well as raise savings. One of the earlier theoretical pieces with this as a theme is Ronald I. McKinnon, *Money and Capital in Economic Development* (Washington, D.C.: Brookings Institution, 1973). For a more recent analysis of how well or badly this view fits the Korean experience, see David C. Cole and Yung Chul Park, *Financial Development in Korea, 1945-1978* (Cambridge: Council on East Asian Studies, Harvard Univ.; distributed by Harvard Univ. Press, 1983).

46 The various motives behind privatization and the establishment of state-owned enterprises are discussed at length in Raymond Vernon, ed., *The Promise of Privatization: A Challenge for American Foreign Policy* (New York: Council on Foreign Relations, 1988).

47 See Lange and Taylor, *Economic Theory*, and Lerner, *Economics of Control*.

48 There is a considerable literature on banking and trade reform, and activities in this area have been a mainstay of HIID for years. Justification of these efforts, however, has been most often stated in the standard neoclassical improvement in allocative efficiency framework, not in relation to the basic issue of whether markets work at all when interventions of this type are pervasive.

49 HIID, for example, has been involved in reform of customs and tax administration in Indonesia, improvement in the budgeting practices of the Ministries of Agriculture and Finance in Kenya, and the development of a

more effective information system for the Ministry of Health in Chad. Developing a project appraisal capacity with government planning agencies has been a mainstay of HIID work since the early days of working with the Pakistan Planning Commission.

50 Under some circumstances, discretionary tax authority can be used to promote broad development goals. It was part of the package, for example, that President Park used to stimulate investment in sectors he favored. But the efficient use of discretionary tax authority for development goals is the exception to the more common use of such authority for private ends.

51 This in essence is the Confucian view of how good government is achieved. See, for example, John K. Fairbank, ed., *The Cambridge History of China* (Cambridge: Cambridge Univ. Press, 1978), 10:1-34.

52 These principles have been a basic part of the tax reform activities to which HIID has provided assistance in such countries as Indonesia, Malawi, Kenya, and The Gambia.

53 There is, of course, a very large literature on how enterprises should be managed. Two sources that influenced how this section was written were Herbert A. Simon, "Management of Productive Enterprises" (Carnegie-Mellon Univ., September 6, 1987); and Thomas J. Peters and Robert H. Waterman, *In Search of Excellence: Lessons from America's Best Companies* (New York: Warner Books, 1984).

54 In the private sector, personal gain (profit) is a powerful incentive to resist favoring reliance on family and ethnic ties except where those ties clearly enhance that gain. In the public sector, however, hiring one's relatives rarely carries with it any financial loss.

55 This situation is particularly true of colonial bureaucracies whose procedures still play such a large role in the newly independent developing countries. Colonial bureaucracies were interested primarily in the maintenance of peace and a stable environment for commerce, not in the development of modern enterprises.

56 This and the discussion of Korea that follows is based on interviews with Korean officials and studies such as Jones and Sakong, *Government, Business and Entrepreneurship*, and Stephan Haggard, Byung-kook Kim, and Chung-In Moon, "The Transition to Export-Led Growth in Korea, 1954-1966," paper presented at "Conference on the Role of the State in Economic Development: Republic of Korea," Univ. of California, Los Angeles, August 14-16, 1987.

2

Macroeconomic Reform in Developing Countries

Michael Roemer and Steven C. Radelet

Michael Roemer is an Institute fellow, senior lecturer on economics at Harvard University, and former executive director of HIID. He has worked on trade and macroeconomic policy issues as a resident adviser to the governments of Ghana, Kenya, Tanzania, and Indonesia, and has published several books and articles on economic development.

Steven C. Radelet, is an Institute associate at HIID and a lecturer on economics at Harvard University. From 1986 to 1988, he was an adviser to the Ministry of Finance and Trade of The Gambia.

The Scope of Economic Reform

D uring the 1980s, developing countries around the world adopted economic reform measures aimed at correcting international payments imbalances, reducing inflation, and reviving growth. The seeds of today's economic problems were sown in the mid- to late 1970s, when oil prices soared and the prices of many primary commodities first rose, then plummeted. Worldwide inflation, high real interest rates, and the slowdown of industrialized economies exacerbated the situation.

In many countries, domestic economic policies made a bad situation worse. To avoid adjustment, some governments adopted expansive monetary policies and overvalued exchange rates, policies they could not sustain in the long run. Several countries borrowed heavily in international capital markets, a strategy which led to the debt crisis of the 1980s. By the mid-1980s, with stagnant economies and no access to capital, many countries had little choice but to adjust their policies and restructure their economies.

This paper reviews the (mostly recent) literature on economic reform, providing a context for the subsequent papers in this volume that deal with specific aspects of economic reform. It is written for economists and non-economists who are interested in, but not closely familiar with, the recent literature on economic policy reform in developing countries. The paper begins by presenting the rationale for reform as provided by the neoclassical paradigm in economics; follows with a review of the development literature as it swung from pessimism to optimism about the role of markets; discusses stabilization as a precondition for reform; examines the components of the structural adjustment package; explores the frontier problem of the sequencing of the various components of stabilization and structural adjustment; addresses related issues of credibility, timing and the magnitude of change; and suggests some distributional consequences of reform. In the last two sections we touch on issues of political economy, but do not cover the topic systematically.[1] Throughout, the paper traces the very different contours of reform in East Asia, Latin America, and Africa.

"Economic reform" is a broad term, encompassing different strategies and policy approaches to economic development. The following definitions help to relate the various concepts to one another:

1. **Economic reform**: Changes in government policy, institutional structure, or administrative procedures designed to alter economic activity and improve performance.

2. **Stabilization**: Correction of imbalances in foreign payments, government budgets, and the money supply, with the aim of controlling inflation and otherwise reducing macroeconomic instability.

3. **Structural adjustment**: Reforms aimed at changing the structure of production (towards tradable goods) and consumption (towards nontradable goods) and increasing the efficiency and flexibility of the economy. Stabilization is generally considered a precondition of longer-term structural adjustment policies.

4. **Outward-looking (-oriented) strategy**: A complex of policies in which export expansion is the engine of economic growth and development.

Policies in this strategy can employ market forces or government interventions, but have in common the establishment of incentives for export growth (and efficient import substitution), with pivotal domestic prices closely related to world prices. Structural adjustment is often designed to achieve an outward-looking economy.

5. **Liberalization or deregulation**: A subset of structural adjustment, dealing with removal of government interventions of all kinds: price controls, quantity restrictions, investment and import licensing, and other barriers to entry.

6. **Privatization**: The sale of government-owned corporations to private investors and the contracting of formerly governmental functions to private agents.

7. **Budget rationalization**: Reforms to bring government's resources more closely into balance and to make them more productive in support of economic growth.

8. **Institutional reform**: Changes in government (and sometimes private) institutions that make it possible for economic reforms to work, predominantly involving shifts away from administered controls towards mechanisms that support private activity.

This paper deals with all of these concepts.

The Neoclassical Case for Reform

The genesis of the case for economic reform, especially the liberalization agenda, is the neoclassical paradigm of competitive markets. In its strong form, the theory of competitive markets requires small firms or economic agents, none of which has any power to control prices; no externalities;[2] and no government intervention. Under these ideal conditions, the value of output is determined jointly and automatically by the buyers (consumers) and sellers (producers) of goods, services, and factors of production (land, labor, capital). Higher prices create higher returns to factors of production, including future workers and investment, which therefore move into activities that create the greatest value. Competition among producers, whether from home or abroad, forces them to use factors as productively as they can, or else fail. Static efficiency is achieved, in the sense that at any time, returns to factors of production (rents, wages, interest, and profits) are maximized, as is consumers' satisfaction.

If time is added to the neoclassical model, the idealized system can also maximize income growth. Investment in both human and physical capital is then treated explicitly and is allocated to the highest productivity uses. New technologies, broadly defined to include new ways of doing old things, raise productivity and attract investable resources. Modern growth theory, which began with Solow's 1956 article, is based on a highly aggregated form of this neoclassical model (Jones 1976).

In real economies, markets deviate from this idealized model in a number of ways. First, some firms gain market power, defined as the ability to influence prices and raise profits within limits by restricting output. These monopolies and oligopolies can arise either through market forces, as economies of scale encourage larger size, or through policies that protect large firms from international or even domestic competition. Second, external costs of production, such as pollution or the overuse of natural resources like forests, are borne by society at large but not by firms. Because firms do not pay the full cost, they produce more than society considers optimal. Third, and conversely, firms underinvest when some benefits, available to society at large, cannot be realized by the firms that create the benefits. Irrigation schemes that combine flood control and recreational facilities provide such external benefits, as do firms that train new workers who later leave to work elsewhere.

Fourth, quantum changes in economic structure that may eventually enhance growth, such as the development of heavy industry, may never be profitable in markets that necessarily reflect current structure and discourage infant industries. Fifth, in developing countries, market institutions are themselves poorly developed and do not function efficiently; indeed, large segments of the population are excluded from some important markets. Sixth, governments may have policy goals, especially concerned with self-sufficiency, income distribution, and poverty alleviation, that are not well served by markets.

Neoclassical economics prescribes corrections for some of these market failures. Monopolies can be regulated or forced to compete with imported goods. Firms can be taxed or subsidized, and in some cases regulated, to correct for external costs or benefits. Infant industries can be protected or subsidized until they mature and become competitive. Governments can promote private institutions to improve market performance. Government itself can invest in infrastructure that supports private activity. Though distributional goals sometimes conflict with productivity and growth, especially in the short term, interventions can often be designed to mute such conflicts in the medium to long term.

When interventions are necessary to correct for market failure, neoclassical economics suggests a set of priorities: (1) try first to improve or enhance the way markets work by providing infrastructure and promoting market institutions; (2) prefer market-based mechanisms, such as taxes, subsidies, and administered prices, over quantity controls, such as import bans or credit allocations; and (3) when regulations are necessary, use them sparingly and target them carefully. Thus, neoclassical economics accepts the need for some intervention, including some regulation, to overcome market failure and achieve optimal outcomes.

However, governments in developing (and many industrial) countries have often intervened to a much greater degree than these neoclassical guidelines suggest. For a variety of reasons, including attempts to correct for market failures, enhance growth, and improve income distribution, governments control and frequently distort foreign exchange rates, interest rates, wages, prices of essential commodities (especially food), the quantity of imports, credit allocations, and many other market variables. Governments also enter directly into production, establishing firms that are insulated from the rigors of market competition. Although such interventions may sometimes succeed, typical interventions are either poorly designed to achieve government's goals or poorly implemented.

Any regulation establishes incentives for rent seeking and corruption, as private agents try to circumvent the rules and civil servants gain the ability to earn income from their administration of regulations (Krueger 1974). When government actions become more important than market forces in determining incomes, economic agents have less incentive to produce efficiently and instead concentrate on seeking governmental favors. Interventions of this magnitude almost always work against productivity and economic growth. For these reasons, interventions often work against the distributional and other policy aims they are meant to achieve.

A common intervention can illustrate these points. Many governments have imposed interest rate ceilings below the levels that would be set by freely operating credit markets. Their goals are to encourage investment (by lowering its cost) and consequently to attain more rapid growth and employment creation. Instead, low interest rates discourage the channeling of savings through the banking system (and may reduce overall savings), which in turn reduces the loan capital available for investment. Below-market rates also cause greater demand for credit, so that bankers have to ration their loans. Some loans then go to projects that are less profitable and therefore less productive than other projects that are denied finance, so that the available credit results in less growth than it might. Also, rationing gives banks, including government banks, the opportunity to channel finance to political and other favorites, rather than to those best able to manage the investments. The consequence is less investment at lower productivity and therefore less economic growth and job creation than might result from market-determined interest rates, exactly the opposite of the intended results.

Market Pessimists and Market Optimists

The development literature has seen a struggle between those skeptical of market-driven strategies and the neoclassical adherents. The latter are now clearly in the ascendancy, but as little as ten years ago economists were more divided.

The roots of market pessimism go back to the postwar period. The depression had destroyed confidence in market capitalism. Keynesianism was a growing force in economics during this period and it, too, suggested government intervention to maintain healthy economies. The Marshall Plan required reconstruction planning by the recipient governments, and Europe's later recovery reflected favorably on government planning. India, after its independence in 1947, followed the Fabian socialist tendencies of its leaders (and, no doubt, the interventionist tendencies of the British colonial regime) to a planned and regulated economy. As other countries gained independence from colonial powers over the following two decades, many of them emulated India. For some, the example of the Soviet Union's industrialization under communism added to the appeal of planned economies.

Three strands of the development literature reinforced this tendency for governments to plan and regulate their economies. First, one of the more influential articles to emerge from the war was Rosenstein-Rodan's (1943) argument for "balanced growth" or a "big push." He reasoned that, in order to create domestic markets for industrial output, all industries would have to grow together, each employing workers who would demand the output of other industries. The market alone would never yield such a big push, so government planning, direct investment, and control would be necessary. The structural transformation of the Soviet Union lent weight to this argument. Even Hirschman's

(1958) counterargument—that unbalanced growth and induced shortages provided a more effective path to industrial development—seemed to invite planning and intervention in the form of import protection and large government investments in infrastructure.

A second, closely related, and much more influential strand ran through the trade literature. In his famous study for the United Nations, Prebisch (1950) concluded that the terms of trade of primary product exporters had been declining since the late nineteenth century. He, along with Singer (1950) and Nurkse (1961), built a case that declining income elasticities of demand for primary products in the industrial countries would condemn developing countries to slow export growth and hence slow income growth, so long as they depended on traditional export products. Prebisch (1959) translated this export pessimism into a case for import substitution as a strategy for development, reinforcing Hirschman's (1958) identification of import substitution as an unbalanced growth strategy.

Protection had been the dominant strategy for industrialization in Europe and North America since the early nineteenth century, so these arguments really only updated the strategy and reinforced existing interventionist tendencies. Governments of newly emerging countries soon introduced a wide variety of interventions in search of industrialization, including overvalued exchange rates; high protective tariffs and import controls; taxes on primary exports; controls over prices of key commodities and interest rates; minimum wage and benefit regulations; investment licensing; state trading; government ownership of key industries; and so on.

The third strand demoted agriculture to a lagging sector. Lewis's (1954) seminal article on the labor surplus economy gave birth to a widely followed strategy of extracting surplus labor and savings from agriculture for use as inputs to growing industry. As development proceeds over decades, employment in and output from agriculture decline while that of industry rises. Development economists used this empirical observation to support the Lewis strategy, even in the short run (Eicher and Staatz 1984). This approach was reinforced by two other observations about agriculture: (1) productivity is substantially lower in agriculture than in industry (Lewis 1954; Fei and Ranis 1964); and (2) agriculture provides fewer linkages to other sectors than does industry (Hirschman 1958). Moreover, there was a widely held belief that small farmers are traditionalists who do not maximize profits nor adopt new technologies, hence are not dynamic contributors to development (Schultz 1964; Eicher and Staatz 1984). This kind of thinking reinforced planners who wanted to quicken the pace at which resources could be moved from agriculture to industry, another apparent justification for intervention.

In the development economics literature, few issues remain settled for very long. The pendulum began to swing against import substitution soon after Prebisch published his defense of the strategy. Power (1966), Bruton (1970), and their colleagues at Williams College completed a group of studies that analyzed the distortions caused by interventions to promote import substitution. They concluded that the strategy led to a structural dead end and advanced several reasons, rooted in economic principles, why this should be so. Little, Scitovsky, and Scott (1970) directed a series of country case studies that further documented the failures of protectionist regimes and laid down perhaps the first version of the reform agenda we discuss below. By the time that Bhagwati (1978) and Krueger (1978) completed their nine-country study of import control regimes, and Balassa (1982) supported the outward-looking strategy on both theoretical and empirical grounds, liberalization had become the new orthodoxy in the economics literature.

Schultz (1964) began to reverse the image of agriculture as a traditional, stagnant industry. He demonstrated that farmers were rational decision makers who, over years of experimentation, weighed economic costs and benefits to evolve an efficient farming system, given resource constraints and the risks of crop failure. If farmers had evolved efficient techniques, then new technology was essential to increase agricultural productivity. Productivity gains would also enable agriculture to give up resources to other sectors while both feeding the urban population and providing export crops. And in Asia and Africa, where farmers were both a large share of the population and among its poorer workers, improved farm productivity was likely to mean a more equal income distribution as well. One implication of this change in attitude is that market-based incentives are the most effective techniques to stimulate numerous small farmers to adopt new technologies and achieve higher productivity. By the 1970s, the green revolution made agriculture into a dynamic sector, at least in Asia, and by the 1980s a productive rural economy had been established in the literature as essential to development (Eicher and Staatz 1984).

The evolution of the literature sometimes followed, but often led, trends in the Third World. At early stages of industrialization, import substitution is capable of giving a spurt to growth, and during the 1960s and early 1970s growth rates in import-substituting countries were satisfactory. Several import-substituting countries, including Mexico, Pakistan, the Philippines, Turkey, Colombia, and Tanzania, achieved GDP growth rates greater than 5 percent per annum between 1960 and 1980 (Gillis et al. 1983). However, despite income growth, it became evident that throughout the developing world urban employment was not keeping pace with population growth (Turnham 1971). Poverty seemed to persist, and in many countries incomes appeared to be more concentrated (Lipton 1977; Ahluwalia 1976). Manufactures were produced at high cost and could not penetrate export markets (Bruton 1970; Little et al. 1970).

In the 1970s and 1980s, as oil prices rose and then fell, and as debt accumulated, most developing countries had great difficulty adjusting to new circumstances, and growth rates fell (Balassa 1982; Killick 1984; Michalopoulos 1987). The new orthodoxy of neoclassical economics now appeared to offer strategies to deal with these structural problems. Perhaps even more influential was the growth experience of the East Asian Four: South Korea, Taiwan, Hong Kong, and Singapore. Their success was seen to coincide with their strong outward-looking strategies (Frank et al. 1975; Kim and Roemer 1979; Kuo 1983; Myers 1986). Indeed, their policies were the inspiration for economists who defined that strategy (Bhagwati 1978; Krueger 1978; Balassa 1971). Brazil's similar, if more limited, success with outward orientation in the decade after 1964 suggested a lesson that could be generalized beyond East Asia (Tyler 1976). Countries in the southern cone of Latin America, led by Chile in the 1970s, instituted sometimes draconian reforms. The International Monetary Fund, through its stabilization programs, and the World Bank, through its structural adjustment programs, converted neoclassical economic principles into practical policy advice, which has been increasingly accepted by recipient countries all over the world.[3]

The Empirical Case for Reform

The debate between market optimists and pessimists also has an empirical dimension. For nearly thirty years, economists have measured the sources of economic growth in industrial and developing countries. They discover that, as incomes rise, the growth of the labor force and the capital stock generally account for a diminishing share of economic growth: over 80 percent for the poorest countries but only about half for countries with incomes over $2100 (Syrquin 1986). The unexplained residual, which is a measure of the growth of total factor productivity (TFP), can be attributed to technological change, better organization of economic activities, improved markets, economies of scale, education, more effective management, and other changes. To enhance growth, then, it is not enough to save and invest more. The productivity at which all resources are engaged plays a major role in determining the rate of growth.

Can we argue that deregulated markets are more likely to promote the kinds of changes that lead to sustained growth of factor productivity and incomes? To some extent the case has already been made in the discussion of the neoclassical paradigm: in principle, market forces promote the most efficient use of resources, both in static equilibrium and over time. Pure competition in the domestic market is not necessary for this argument. If the economy is open to trade, then domestic monopolies and oligopolies can be exposed to competition from foreign firms in their home and export markets, stimulating static efficiency and long-term productivity growth. That is a central reason for the outward-looking strategy of development. Firms protected from competition can survive without exacting the greatest output at the lowest possible cost. And government intervention, even in aid of market forces, has a strong tendency to induce entrepreneurs and managers to expend more effort on the politics of government intervention than on improving the productivity of their firms. Market forces, from home or abroad, are a strong antidote to these unproductive tendencies.

A great deal of research has been conducted on the possible links between market forces, productivity gains, and income growth, centering mainly around trade policy. Much of this work has estimated the benefits from liberalization by measuring the welfare gains in comparative static models. A summary of this type of research is presented in Table 1. Studies that have assumed a perfectly competitive, neoclassical world have found only small gains, typically less than one percent of gross domestic product (column 1). However, when the models incorporate economies of scale, imperfect competition, rent seeking, or X-inefficiency gains, increases in welfare range as high as 8 to 10 percent of gross domestic product (column 2). Because these characteristics are common to many LDCs, the estimates in the second column are probably more relevant. X-inefficiency is the loss of potential output due to the non-income-maximizing behavior of firms, households, and individuals. It is a way to capture in a model potentially the most important gain from reform, the change in behavior due to competitive forces. But we know very little empirically about its impact.

Table 1 Estimated Static Gains from Trade Liberalization
(% of gross domestic product)

Author	Perfect Competition Models	Other Models	Comments
Harberger (1959)	2.5	—	Chile: cost of protection
Scitovsky (1958)	0.05	—	EEC: gain from specialization
Johnson (1958)	1.0	—	Britain: gain from free trade zone
Grais (1986)	—	5 - 10	Turkey: cost of rent seeking with quotas
Bergsman (1974)	0.3 - 1.0	2.5 - 7.1	Brazil, Mexico, Pakistan, Philippines; col. 2: X-inefficiency, monopoly
Harris (1984)	0 - 2.4	4.1 - 8.6	Canada; col. 2: scale economies, free entry, imperfect competition
Rodrick (1988)	—	1.2 - 9.2	Turkey: scale economies, imperfect competition, free entry, rents
Devarajan & Rodrick (1989)	—	2.0	Cameroon: scale economies, imperfect competition

Source: *Lal and Rajapatirana (1987) and original studies.*

Are these gains large? They represent one-time increases in gross domestic product, not continuing gains. However, to take a mid-range estimate, suppose that all of a 5 percent increment in GDP gained from liberalization were reinvested. Under the very simple Harrod-Domar growth model, which might apply in a labor surplus economy, this could result in a sustained increased growth of 2 percent or more per year, a very substantial gain. After ten years, the cumulative gain in GDP would be approximately 28 percent. As a lower bound estimate, if only 10 percent of the 5 percent increment were reinvested, the cumulative gain after ten years would be 7 percent of GDP. Under the alternative neoclassical model, which assumes full employment, additional investment of 5 percent of GDP would yield a large but one-time gain in per capita income, with no effect on the long-term rate of growth.

A second line of research has consistently found a positive correlation between exports and income growth (Michalopoulos and Jay 1973; Michaely 1977; Balassa 1978; Feder 1983). However, Michaely found that the relationship was limited to middle-income countries. Moreover, export growth would be correlated with income growth if both were caused by a third factor (such as training of the labor force). Jung and Marshall (1985) and Darrant (1986) were unable to demonstrate direct causality in either direction between exports and income growth.

A third line of research based on a small number of country studies has explored the relationship between types of trade regimes and income growth. Little et al. (1970), Balassa (1971), Donges (1976), Bhagwati (1978), Krueger (1978), and the World Bank (1987) all concluded that countries experience higher growth rates with incentives that favor exports or are neutral between home and foreign markets. Chenery et al. (1986), using a 1963 computable general equilibrium model of Korea, found higher growth rates and lower capital-output ratios associated with an export-promoting rather than import-substituting strategy. Several studies have indicated that outward-oriented countries were better able to adjust to the external shocks of the 1970s (Balassa 1986; de Melo and Robinson 1982).

However, Helleiner (1986) found no association between trade orientation and GDP growth in a study of low-income countries and concluded that the instability of import volume was more important than trade orientation in explaining slow growth in Africa. Kovoussi (1985) and Singer and Gray (1988) found a positive relationship, but it was weaker during the mid-1970s, a period of unfavorable world trade. They conclude that world demand is generally more important than trade orientation in explaining growth.

The central question for the neoclassical case for reform is the relationship between trade orientation and productivity growth. Bhagwati (1978) found that restrictive regimes were associated with low productivity in Ghana, Israel, and Chile. Krueger and Tuncer (1982) examined eighteen Turkish manufacturing sectors between 1963 and 1976 and found that periods of slower productivity growth coincided with periods of more stringent trade controls.

Feder (1986) extended the basic growth accounting framework to allow for contributions to growth from reallocation between sectors that display different marginal productivities. In a two-sector analysis (export, nonexport) of thirty-four semi-industrial countries between 1964 and 1973, he observed a substantial difference between productivity in the export and nonexport sectors, especially in economies with small export sectors. He found that the higher productivity in the export sector contributed 1.9 percentage points to growth in gross national product, or about 30 percent of overall growth. However, he found no association in other developing countries and during other time periods. Nishimizu and Robinson (1986), in a study of Korea, Yugoslavia, and Turkey, found that "import substitution regimes seem to be negatively correlated with TFP (total factor productivity) change, whereas export expansion regimes seem to be positively correlated with TFP change." Thus, export-oriented economies promote economic growth because of their "ability to maintain productivity in the face of a rapid absorption of factors from lower productivity uses in both agriculture and the urban informal sectors..." (Pack 1989).

Although several authors (Taylor 1988; Helleiner 1986; Singer and Gray 1988) point out the deficiencies in some of these studies and suggest more limited conclusions, there is little empirical evidence indicating the circumstances under which an inward-looking trade strategy is superior to outward orientation. However, the poor performance of import-substituting countries in recent years should not be attributed solely to weaknesses in the strategy itself. In many countries, poor performance is caused more by conflicting policies, the lack of any coherent strategy, and poor implementation, rather than the failure of a well-articulated strategy (Bruton 1989). Indeed, at least part of the success of the East Asian Four lies in the implementation of their strategies, which was decisive and consistent. An inward-looking strategy is demanding, both technically and politically. Much work is needed to determine the appropriate type, magnitude, and duration of protection and incentives. Many governments have found it difficult to make the transition to a more open economy after offering protection for an extended period. In the end, the most compelling argument for the outward-looking strategy may be that most developing countries simply do not have the institutional capacity to manage import substitution effectively from its early protective stage to a more outward-looking posture.

Reform into more outward-looking economies is now the conventional prescription. The consensus rests firmly on a set of economic principles which argue that markets guide economies better than governments can, and on empirical evidence that depends heavily on a few country examples and models which are suggestive rather than totally convincing. The case in favor of reform is enhanced by many negative instances of poor performance using inward-directed strategies. Nevertheless, within this consensus there remains some doubt. Many advocates of reform are looking critically at its implementation and outcomes, giving rise to the lively debates of the 1980s that we now review, beginning with stabilization and going on to structural adjustment.

Stabilization

Stabilization of an economy, either to bring inflation under control or to correct deficits in foreign payments and the government budget, is frequently a precondition to structural adjustment. Reform packages depend on attaining and maintaining relative prices that reflect economic scarcities: what matters for exporters is the price of exportable goods relative to other goods; what matters for employers is the cost of labor relative to output, capital, and land; what matters to savers and investors is the return on deposits and the cost of borrowing relative to the rate of inflation. These relative prices are strongly influenced by the rate of inflation, which changes the prices of goods and services that do not enter into international trade, raises the cost of producing all goods, and reduces both the return to savers and the costs to borrowers.

If inflation is uniform and anticipated, it poses no serious problems. However, in an inflationary environment, groups that are effectively organized and wield political power, such as unionized labor, large businesses, the military, and civil servants, compete intensely to protect their income shares. The result is a distortion of relative prices from their scarcity values towards some manifestation of political power. Partly because of these political forces, inflation is not uniform, so relative prices are volatile, reducing the information they convey to economic agents. For example, with rapid inflation, real interest rates are typically low and negative, so lenders concentrate on short-term finance, reducing the supply of long-term investment. Exchange rates, especially if established by governments, tend to become overvalued, with consequent balance-of-payments problems. Overvalued exchange rates, low real interest rates, and uncertainty about future rates of inflation cause private wealth holders either to flee into foreign currencies or to invest in assets in relatively fixed supply, especially land and gold, the value of which is likely to appreciate with inflation (Khan and Knight 1985). Entrepreneurial energies are bent towards finding ways to beat inflation and away from means to increase productivity. After all, large, sustained productivity gains might reduce costs by 3 to 5 percent a year, not much compared to rates of inflation from tens to hundreds of percent a year.

The International Monetary Fund is the inventor, curator, and chief proponent of what has become the standard orthodox stabilization package. The central idea behind IMF programs is the notion that inflation is a monetary phenomenon, i.e., that prices can rise only as fast as the money supply. To oversimplify just slightly, the core components of a typical IMF stabilization package include:

1. reduction of balance-of-payments deficits, principally through devaluation of the exchange rate, which may also have to compensate for another typical element of the package, import liberalization;

2. reduction of government's budget deficit, through higher taxes, long-term tax reform, and reduced expenditures;

3. debt rescheduling, if necessary;

4. shift of government deficit finance from the banking system to domestic private bondholders, which along with deficit reduction helps to control the money supply;

5. increases in certain prices, such as interest rates (to reduce investment demand and increase saving), food prices (to reduce the costs of subsidies), and charges for government-supplied goods and services (to increase revenues); and

6. wage restraint, to reduce the relative costs of production and contain inflation.

The many problems with this approach to stabilization are assessed in a large and growing literature on IMF-supported programs in developing countries (Williamson 1983; Killick 1984; Taylor 1988) and a great flowering of work on Latin American stabilizations, which have almost always gone hand-in-glove with liberalization (e.g., Diaz-Alejandro 1981; Harberger 1982; Foxley 1983; Corbo, de Melo, and Tybout 1986; Sachs 1986; Edwards 1987). Much of this controversy is best treated in the sections on sequencing and on income distribution, but one current conflict is more singularly a stabilization issue.

A school of "heterodox" economists, represented by Taylor (1988), has challenged the IMF orthodoxy that inflation is a purely monetary phenomenon. Taylor and others argue that important participants in the economy, particularly urban workers and industrial firms, set wages and prices by predetermined rules, such as (1) the indexing of wages to match inflation, and (2) percentage mark-ups to cover the rising cost of manufacturing and thus preserve profit margins. These rules, which prevent changes in relative prices, become the mechanisms by which different economic groups fight to maintain their income shares under changing conditions. Under these circumstances, if the money supply does not grow as rapidly as inflation, reduced liquidity will force manufacturers—who are reluctant to change their mark-up rules—to lower their output instead and so reduce employment. Moreover, two other components of orthodox stabilization programs—exchange rate devaluation and interest rate increases—add to the costs of production and hence, under mark-up pricing, add to inflationary pressures.

In economies with these relative price rigidities,[4] orthodox stabilization packages not only cause substantial losses in jobs and incomes, but may also fail to cure inflation. This was a typical pattern in Latin America in the 1970s (Foxley

1981). The antidote for inflation becomes much more complex and eclectic. It may encompass all the IMF measures, although most heterodox economists reject some elements of the IMF's monetarism, but must also deal directly with the rules that lead to stagflation: indexing and mark-up pricing. The goals are (1) to change expectations that have become accustomed to rapid inflation, and (2) to establish flexibility in setting wages and prices so that real wages can adjust to changed economic conditions (Corden 1989). Among the methods advocated by heterodox economists in Latin America are price and quantity controls, which are generally opposed by neoclassical economists and the IMF, and political compacts with employers, unions, and other strong interest groups. Governments have also used political and military repression, especially of organized labor. Most economies have a mixture of fixed and flexible prices, so elements of both orthodox and heterodox programs may be needed to halt inflation. This adds to the complexity of economic reform programs: policies must be carefully designed for the particular circumstances facing individual countries.

Structural Adjustment

With a stabilization program in place, the next task is to undertake reforms to restructure the economy for economic growth. A complete reform package, derived from the neoclassical paradigm, contains five components:

(1) freeing markets to determine prices ("letting markets work");

(2) adjusting controlled prices to scarcity values ("getting prices right");

(3) shifting resources from government into private hands (privatization);

(4) rationalizing government's remaining role in development (budget rationalization); and

(5) reforming institutions to carry out government's new role.

The crux of neoclassical reform is to free markets as completely as possible to equate supply and demand, thus allowing prices to reflect opportunity costs. Transactions made under these prices would move goods and factors towards maximum output and an optimal rate of growth. Governments would intervene only to improve markets by regulating monopolies, taxing or subsidizing external costs and benefits, protecting infant industries, investing in infrastructure, and developing new market institutions.

Even the staunchest advocates of reform accept that some prices will be controlled by governments, especially exchange rates, possibly interest rates, and the prices of basic foods. But price controls should be kept to a minimum and in no case ought governments control quantities. Controlled prices should be adjusted to reflect real scarcities or opportunity costs of goods, services, factors of production, and time. In this way, controlled prices can approximate free market prices. Oskar Lange (1938) suggested this as a means of managing socialist economies, with managers instructed to maximize profits under government-determined prices.

The rationale for freeing markets, as already discussed, is to introduce a greater degree of competition and flexibility into all aspects of economic activity (Fischer 1986). Government controls over quantities, such as import controls and credit allocations, work against competitive markets because allocations depend on the administrative competence and, often, on the favors of government regulators rather than on the ability of firms to compete. Such controls almost always result in rent seeking and bribery, so that the reward structure favors political skills rather than entrepreneurial and managerial skills.

In small economies, it is unrealistic to expect domestic competition in all fields, especially those involving modern industry, much of which is characterized by economies of scale or scope, rapid technological change, product differentiation on the basis of quality, and large-scale international competition. Thus, the freeing of markets is not a call for a Smithian world of atomistic competition. However, when domestic competition is limited, it is crucial that international competition be present, either through easily available, competitive imports or through export markets. This is where the outward-looking strategy comes in: whatever the degree of competition in the home market, an open economy ensures international competition, providing the stimulus for productivity gains that are necessary for sustained growth. It also requires that at least certain prices be close to opportunity costs as determined by world markets and domestic scarcities: exchange rates, prices of importable and exportable goods, and preferably wages, interest rates, and the prices of nontradables that are important in the cost structure of firms producing for export.

The agenda for the first two components of market reform—letting markets work and getting prices right—dates to at least 1970, with the publication of Little, Scitovsky, and Scott's comparative study, *Industry and Trade in Some Developing Countries.* Several later contributions reaffirm the program (Bhagwati 1978; Krueger 1978; Little 1982; Balassa 1982; Khan 1986; Michalopoulos 1987). Its main elements include:

1. trade reform: eliminating controls over imports, reducing tariff levels, achieving a more uniform tariff structure, and subsidizing nontraditional exports;

2. reducing restrictions on foreign investment;

3. adjusting the exchange rate to establish and then to maintain the profitability of more export industries and to compensate for part of the reduction in protection from competing goods;

4. financial reform: adjusting interest rates to levels above the rate of inflation, in order to eliminate the excess demand for credit, or, preferably, freeing credit markets to determine interest rates, and promoting new credit instruments and institutions;

5. removing minimum wage controls and other regulations that artificially increase labor costs, or at least permitting inflation to erode the real value of these costs;

6. freeing or at least adjusting prices on farm products to encourage investment and increased productivity in agriculture; and

7. generally eliminating controls over prices and otherwise reducing regulations that inhibit market behavior.

Market reforms are expected to raise the productivity of private activities. But price signals alone will not be enough (Chenery et al. 1986; Streeten 1987). To take advantage of a more effective private sector, reform packages include as a third component the shift of resources from government to private hands.

68

"Privatization," which encompasses the sale of government-owned firms to private investors and the contracting of government services to private firms, is one part of this reform. Of possibly greater importance is the reduction of government deficits, advocated for macroeconomic stabilization, but also as a means of reducing government's drain on private saving to finance the deficit.[5] A complementary approach would focus government services and investments increasingly on support of the private sector, emphasizing infrastructure development, agricultural research and extension, credit institutions, health, and education.

The fourth component of reform packages is the rationalization of government's remaining activities. Not only must resources be shifted into private hands, but those left to government need to be used more efficiently, a process sometimes called "budget rationalization." Project appraisal and other techniques are employed to channel more resources into activities with the highest returns. When investment funds are in short supply, those available must be channeled to fewer investments so that projects can be completed and brought into use quickly. Government corporations should be held more accountable by limiting their borrowing or establishing performance contracts with government. The first call on revenues should be to finance the operating and maintenance costs of completed projects and existing government facilities (World Bank 1984). Rationalization also means a reduction in government's own work force, or at least in its rate of hiring. For obvious reasons, this is seldom accomplished.

For governments used to widespread interventions, these reforms suggest fundamental changes in the way government—and sometimes private—agencies operate. The fifth component of structural adjustment is the reform of institutions to carry out government's new economic role. For example, import liberalization requires the licensing authority to be dismantled and the customs authority to be made more efficient and honest; financial market reform includes the creation of new financial instruments and new institutions; and efficient infrastructural investment may be helped by decentralization of government activities and the upgrading of disbursed planning and implementing agencies. Success in economic reform often depends heavily on the completion of complex institutional reforms.

As already suggested, it is difficult to separate economists' advocacy of this structural adjustment program from their admiration of the economic growth performance of the four East Asian exporters. But what exactly was the experience of Korea, Taiwan, Hong Kong, and Singapore? All are certainly outward-looking, in the sense that exports constitute at least 40 percent of gross domestic product and export growth has been the path to success for both the countries and their individual manufacturing firms. However, only one of them, Hong Kong, is an example of a truly liberal economy, and even there the government provides free or heavily subsidized education, health, and housing. Singapore, though providing free trade and capital mobility, subsidizes not only social services but also public enterprises (Balassa and Williamson 1987).

Korea, which has been studied more than the other three, provides the most interesting test for reform advocates. The literature of the 1970s pictured Korea as a country whose government had kept the real exchange rate at levels rewarding to exporters; kept effective protection low and relatively uniform among sectors and industries; subsidized exports in a number of ways, especially through artificially cheap credit; maintained a relatively free labor market in which the market determined wages; and intervened in the market single-mindedly and sometimes heavy-handedly in support of export growth (Frank, Kim, and Westphal 1975; Bhagwati 1978; Krueger 1978; Kim and Roemer 1979; Jones and Sakong 1980; Balassa 1982). These policies were clearly outward-looking. Many observers have suggested that the policies were also market-oriented.

More recent studies have emphasized other aspects of the Korean experience. The revisionists agree with the earlier literature on some of the "right" prices, notably the exchange and wage rates, as well as some of the "wrong" prices, particularly the highly subsidized interest rates. But revisionists find more flaws in the outward-looking story. Although average effective protection rates were low, they note substantial differentiation among industries, contrary to neoclassical prescription. More critically, though import controls were relaxed during the 1960s, complex and often informal arrangements have kept competitive imports very scarce in Korea to this day. Many financial incentives were highly differentiated, by activity and by firm. Moreover, though markets played an important role in resource allocation, Korea's government exerted strong controls over highly subsidized credit, promoted large firms at the expense of small ones, then leaned on these *chaebol* to meet export targets and, in the 1970s, to invest in infant heavy industries. Taiwan stayed closer to the neoclassical norm, promoting smaller firms and relying more on market mechanisms, though government itself owned most heavy industry and allocated subsidized credit. (Haggard and Moon 1983; Scitovsky 1985; Cheng 1986; Balassa and Williamson 1987; Lueder-Neurath 1986; Amsden 1989)

This revisionist picture suggests a couple of hypotheses. First, a determined and effective government can do more than the market alone to make reforms work in favor of rapid development. Though Korea's experience is consistent with this hypothesis, we probably owe it more to the experience of the Soviet Union, China, and other socialist countries whose strong and determined governments successfully pushed development against market forces for years or even, in the case of the Soviet Union, decades. To be effective in this way, a government must have its own comprehensive view or ideology about development; must be able to induce or compel its civil servants to implement this program; and must enjoy substantial autonomy from the efforts of groups in society who would lose from development as conceived by the government.

The second hypothesis is that even effective governments are likely to have greater success if they work with, rather than against, the market. This is the appeal of the outward-looking strategy, which binds both government and private firms to a market test though competition in world markets. Korea's government was able to distort credit markets and exclude competitive imports, but their export performance depended on realistic exchange rates and other market-based incentives. A command economy could not have achieved Korea's success. China's market-based economic reform since 1978 suggests a similar lesson.

However, recent history does not teach that intervention, even in support of the market, is essential for rapid development. In Taiwan, an effective government, though it did intervene, depended much more on impersonal market forces than did Korea and achieved equal success (Scitovsky 1985; Cheng 1986). In Africa, South Asia, and parts of Latin America, where most governments are inherently ineffective in managing their economies to achieve rapid productivity increases, there is little hope of the kind of disciplined and sustained intervention practiced by Korea. For this large majority of developing countries, the market may be the only mechanism with a chance of producing sustained growth (Berg 1981; Roemer 1982).

Sequencing Reforms

Although it is easy to distinguish stabilization from structural adjustment in principle, it is nearly impossible to disentangle them in practice. There are enough common elements to make this division artificial: exchange rate devaluation, interest rate increases, reductions in food subsidies, higher charges for services supplied by government enterprises, and so forth. Although stabilization may be a prerequisite for structural adjustment, there is usually a very short interval, if any, between implementation of these two aspects of reform. When the two are considered together, the interesting questions deal with the sequencing of policies contained in the two packages. It is to this frontier of economic theory that we now turn.

Until recently the literature on economic reform has been conducted in comparative static terms. Neoclassical theory tells us that a liberalized economy is more efficient (and thus productive) than a controlled economy. "However, theory tells us virtually nothing about optimal transition paths from a distorted system to one that is more fully liberalized. Unfortunately, this is the most important problem for any successful reform" (Bruno 1985). The theory of the second best tells us that partial reforms—the adjustment of only some prices or the removal of some controls—does not necessarily lead to overall gains in efficiency and welfare (Khan 1986; Kahkonen 1987). The path to comprehensive reform is likely to pass through phases of lower average incomes as well as shifts in the distribution of income. Experience with liberalization in Latin America suggests that even a feasible, never mind optimal, sequencing of stabilization and reform measures can be elusive (Corbo and de Melo 1985). Virtually all the literature on sequencing derives from Latin America, where severe macroeconomic imbalances, rooted deeply in political and social patterns, have been attacked by comprehensive packages of stabilization and liberalization. Chile is the extreme and most studied case, with considerable literature on Argentina, Uruguay, Brazil, and, to a lesser extent, Bolivia, Mexico, and Peru.

The sequencing issue is a highly technical one. Our intention here is only to impart some of the flavor of the problem and to illustrate two basic points about economic reform. First, even at the general level of technical macroeconomic analysis, stabilization and structural adjustment programs are complex and fragile. The sequencing of measures and their predicted outcomes are difficult to explain to decision makers, indeed are often counterintuitive. On some issues, there is no settled judgment among economists. And much depends on the economic history, structure, and expected response of the particular economy.

Second, the ramifications of sequencing for income distribution and political acceptability, both discussed later, can be substantial. Comprehensive packages of stabilization and reform are not for the timid. Implementation of these packages requires robust but nimble governments, capable of experimenting with the economy under political pressure. It is not surprising that only a handful of governments have tried to implement comprehensive reform programs, and few have been totally successful.

The sequencing problem has been framed as succinctly as possible by Sebastian Edwards (1987), and this account follows his. Begin with the classic unbalanced, distorted economy characterized by high inflation, large budgetary deficits substantially financed by money creation, controlled interest rates, high tariffs, and controls on foreign capital flows. Edwards is describing Latin American countries, especially Chile. If this were Africa, we would start with lower inflation, but add controls over imports and an overvalued exchange rate. With many possible reforms, there are many possible conflicts in sequencing.

If reform is to adjust the structure of the economy, it is essential that land, labor, and capital can be moved from one use to another. This in turn requires the early liberalization of factor markets, especially those for labor and credit (Krueger 1984; Michalopoulos 1987). The dynamic East Asian exporters enjoyed highly flexible labor markets, with market-determined wages. The Korean government did control the credit market, but used credit allocation to shift resources towards export industries (Scitovsky 1985).

If domestic credit markets are liberalized early in the reform and if lenders, not trusting the efficacy of stabilization, anticipate renewed inflation, then interest rates will shoot up, as they did in the Southern Cone[6] reforms of the 1970s and 1980s. Should controls over foreign capital also be relaxed, both foreign and domestic investors will borrow abroad to finance investment in the country, because high domestic interest rates make peso loans much more expensive than dollar loans.[7] The inflow of foreign capital adds to the money supply, exacerbating inflation and the interest rate differential that caused the problem in the first place. This was Chile's particular problem, repeated in other Latin American countries, and it led to increasing concentration of ownership as those with access to foreign capital bought out other firms (Foxley and Whitehead 1980; Edwards 1987).

A real depreciation of the currency—devaluation in excess of the rate of inflation—is central to promoting exports and liberalizing imports. But when controls over foreign capital are reduced, or if a large aid package supports the reform program, the inflow of capital will cause the currency to appreciate in real terms, squeezing the profitability of producers of exports and import substitutes. Attempts by Southern Cone countries to control inflation by limiting the rate of nominal devaluation of the exchange rate also reduced the profitability of exporting and contributed to the failure of several reform programs (Corbo and de Melo 1985; Edwards 1987).

Sequencing problems affect sectoral strategies as well. Import liberalization and tariff reform are mostly aimed at increasing the productivity of manufacturing. If import controls are important, it will be easier to relax them while tariffs are still high enough to protect the affected industries. This sequence has the advantage of moving first to a price-based system of protection. However, the conversion can take a long time (Michaely 1986). Moreover, the rationalization of tariffs then becomes more difficult because quantitative controls no longer mask the reduction of tariff protection. Tariffs on imported inputs are sometimes reduced before duties on competing imports to make industry more competitive, but this increases effective protection and makes future tariff cuts on competing imports more difficult.

Whatever their sequence, trade reforms typically involve major changes in the way institutions such as the customs and import licensing authorities work and can take years to implement. During this period, if foreign capital controls are relaxed before the import regime is thoroughly rationalized, then private investment will be channeled into some inefficient industries whose eventual decline is one of the aims of the reform program (Corbo and de Melo 1985; Edwards 1987).

Agricultural productivity and food security often require that prices of domestically produced foods be raised from controlled levels. But if this is done before the exchange rate has been devalued, resources may move out of export crops into food crops, contrary to comparative advantage and hence contrary to government's goals for macroeconomic productivity and growth (Krueger 1984).

Very few clear rules survives from the literature on sequencing. Stabilization survives intact as a prerequisite for liberalizing reforms, as does the critical importance of a near-equilibrium exchange rate. One implication of the literature—though still subject to debate—is that the deregulation of foreign capital probably ought to be delayed until trade and domestic capital market reforms have been put in place and domestic interest rates have settled down to levels consistent with international rates. Other prescriptions are much more tentative and depend more on particular circumstances.

Credibility, Timing, and Magnitude

All these reforms, in whatever sequence, depend crucially on the credibility of the entire package (Bruno 1985; Edwards 1987; Edwards and Van Wijnbergen 1989). If budget deficits remain high, or if for any other reason money creation is not slowed, the public will anticipate continued or higher inflation. If the real exchange rate is allowed to appreciate because inflation outruns nominal devaluations, as happened in Chile and elsewhere, export industries become unattractive to investors. If import liberalization is undertaken tentatively, or if past attempts have been reversed, investors will put their money into the old protected industries. To establish credibility, governments need to manage their reform program decisively, despite its complexity.

Credibility also depends on perceptions about stabilization and liberalization, which often differ from reality (Krueger 1984; Sheahan 1980; Corden 1989). Nelson (1984) observes that, in judging the effects of policies, the public is most likely to compare situations before and after, when the proper comparison is with and without. A stabilized economy may look worse than the observed pre-crisis economy but could well be an improvement over the unobserved situation without stabilization. The public, government leaders, and officials, not many of whom are well schooled in economics, may also be baffled by counter-intuitive predictions, such as that lower wages may improve the income distribution (by increasing employment). Leaders and officials in many countries have a deep-seated statist bias towards controls and a belief that prices are a policy tool to effect desired outcomes. They maintain an illusion that government controls are effective even in circumstances where they clearly are not. These perceptions by government and the public make it more difficult to plan and implement reforms.

Disappointing results with past stabilization and reform efforts make it more difficult to sell new ones to the public.

The influence of foreign aid institutions on credibility is double-edged. The IMF and World Bank provide additional resources that can ease the transition to an open economy and help to protect incomes during the transition. Nelson (1984) notes that foreign aid can enhance the position of reforming elements within a government and can be used by government to sell stabilization programs to the public. However, additional resources also make the crisis seem less intense. Moreover, IMF presence and the conditions it attaches to its loans have increasingly become focal points for opposition to economic change. Although governments such as Egypt and Zambia have deflected public ire by ceasing to negotiate with the Fund, the result is only to delay necessary stabilization, quite possibly to a more difficult time.

Public debt plays a similarly dual role. To a point, the need to pay off foreign creditors can be used to steel the public to a degree of necessary austerity. But at some point debt becomes a liability, as the public begins to wonder why their standard of living should decline so that foreign bankers' profits can be maintained. In the long run, it probably requires convincing arguments about the population's own well-being to sustain either stabilization or reform efforts.

Implicit in the discussion of sequencing and credibility are the questions of timing and magnitude. Should reforms be pushed through quickly, or phased in gradually? There are times in a country's history when economic and political forces provide a brief opportunity for dramatic reforms. Probably the single most convincing observation on timing is that the beginning of a new regime is the time to act (Nelson 1984). Recently elected regimes have the momentum of popular support, used to good effect by Jayawardana in Sri Lanka, less so by Siaga in Jamaica, and dramatically by Paz in Bolivia (Sachs 1986). New regimes of any kind have a brief initial period when they can blame problems on the previous government. Early success obviously has political benefits for the regime. But as time goes on, growing ties between government and its clients make policy change increasingly dangerous for any regime. Nelson observes that it may be easiest to stabilize and reform totally devastated economies, such as Ghana, Tanzania, and Uganda in the 1980s, because in such circumstances few if any benefits are being channeled to any cohesive group by government.

In these circumstances, credibility is probably enhanced by rapid, decisive, comprehensive action. Such "shock treatment" is also consistent with the economics of reform (Edwards and Van Wijnbergen 1989). The move from an inward-looking, distorted economy to an outward-looking, liberal one requires policy action on many different fronts. We have already seen how changes in only some of these can create sequencing problems. If all can be changed in a very short time, many of these conflicts can be resolved.

However, shock treatment across the board is unrealistic. Few governments have the decision-making or managerial capacity to implement such draconian programs. Fundamental organizational and behavioral changes, both inside and outside of government, are often essential, yet they take months or years to implement. Such reforms may involve not only the operation of government agencies, but also the functioning of labor and capital markets. For example, when capital markets are deregulated, both central and commercial bankers have to learn to operate with new credit instruments in more competitive markets.

These considerations suggest "gradualism" (Michaely 1986). A slower pace for reform, however, means that the benefits of reform take longer to materialize, making it more difficult to mobilize support. Gradualism also gives opposition forces a better chance to mobilize and throws a shadow over government's credibility (Nelson 1984). Asian governments have been more adept at implementing reform over long periods than have governments in Latin America, with the exception of Chile.

How large are the necessary changes? To the extent that some prices will remain controlled—especially the exchange rate, interest rates, and food prices—government must decide both how fast and how much to change them. The technical answer depends on the economy's ability to respond quickly, represented by the relevant supply and demand elasticities. The lower these elasticities, the greater the changes needed to accomplish a given balance or shift of resources. Yet if elasticities are low, then large and rapid changes in prices will cause greater disruptions, more unemployment, and more idle capacity, thus more opposition to reform (Michaely 1986). If stabilization is part of the reform package, then rapid and decisive action can mean severe contraction of the economy, exacerbating the disruptions and encouraging political challenges to reform (Foxley 1983; Michalopoulos 1987). Latin American structuralists have long maintained that economic change is tightly inhibited by economic, social, and political obstacles, so reform is likely to be ineffective or to cause severe disruptions and hardship (Taylor 1988). Neoclassical economists argue that economies are flexible enough over the medium term to base reforms on market rules (Little 1982).

Income Distribution

The distributional impacts of economic reform have been an integral part of the neoclassical literature at least since Stolper and Samuelson (1941) wrote about tariff reform. The recent literature is suffused with attention to the gainers and losers in reforms (e.g., Demery and Addison 1987; Helleiner 1987; Huang and Nicholas 1987; World Bank 1988; Kahkonen 1987).

Measuring the impact of any policy change on income level, income distribution, or poverty is always difficult, but studying the impact of stabilization and structural adjustment is especially laden with problems. First, economic reforms are typically triggered by external shocks to the economy. These can have severe impacts on income levels and distribution that are difficult to separate from the effects of the policy reforms that follow. Second, historical data only permit us to compare situations before and after an event. However, the correct comparison in the face of external shocks (or other disturbances) is with and without the policy change, a comparison that cannot be observed. Third, reform packages are complex, consisting of many policy changes, each with potentially different impacts on particular economic groups. Even predicting, let alone measuring, the net impact of all policies on all groups is a Herculean task (Dethier 1986; Demery and Addison 1987; Huang and Nicholas 1986).

The most promising method for analyzing these impacts is to use computable general equilibrium models to run counterfactual experiments for the with-without comparisons, dealing with single policy changes and with small groups of policy changes. An early attempt, Adelman and Robinson's (1978) study of Korea, and a number of later studies based on large macroeconomic models show that the more neoclassical the world is, in the sense of easy substitution among goods and factors, the less will be the impact of government intervention on income distribution, in any direction.[8] Put another way, economic reform is more likely to have a significant distributional impact in economies marked by structural disequilibrium and large distortions, precisely where reform is needed most. De Melo and Robinson (1982), in examining trade reform in three archetypal developing economies, note that outcomes are complex and depend heavily on the choice of adjustment policy. However, there is little to say beyond this, as the literature on macroeconomic simulations of reform packages is in its infancy.

Thus, we are left with predictions of outcomes based largely on reasoning from first principles and some rough economic indicators. Not surprisingly, there is a general concern that stabilization programs reduce incomes, especially of the poor (Diaz-Alejandro 1981; Crockett 1981; Taylor 1983). The main impact of stabilization is to reduce expenditures of both government and the private sector, so incomes fall and unemployment rises. Food subsidies are a particular target for IMF programs, for example, and the constituencies for health, education, and other social services are often not as effective in protecting their programs as are the military, civil servants, and other groups.

However, Killick (1984) and Pastor (1987) found that the overall impact of IMF programs on income was negligible. Demery and Addison (1987) show, on both theoretical and empirical grounds, that the distributional impact of stabilization programs is complex, even in the short run. They find no clear presumption from the literature that stabilization should or does in fact worsen income distribution. The impact depends heavily on where the government chooses to cut expenditure. Heller (1988) and the World Bank (1988) cite stabilization efforts in Chile, Ghana, Kenya, and Korea in which governments protected outlays on poverty groups and in some cases increased them.

Structural adjustment programs do not so much reduce expenditure as switch expenditure from foreign to domestic goods and move resources from public to private hands. The impact on poverty and income distribution is complex, but potentially beneficial, particularly in the long run. Much depends on the structure of the economy and the particular mix of policies chosen.[9]

Reform of the trade and foreign exchange regimes will boost the incomes of exporters and reduce those of import substituters. This could improve the income distribution if exporters include small farmers, as in Africa; even if exporters are large farmers, but their demand for workers and expenditures in the rural areas add to rural incomes, as might be true in parts of South Asia and Latin America; and if export industries are smaller in scale or more labor-intensive than others, as in East Asia during the 1960s. Decontrol of import licensing and other restrictions opens access to a wider group of importers, including small-scale manufacturers, and reduces the rents of entrenched businessmen and their political and bureaucratic patrons. The presumption that trade liberalization improves income distribution may not hold, however, in economies marked by mineral exports; capital-intensive, large-scale, export farming; and concentrations in industry that extend to exporting firms.

Liberalization of labor markets is likely to improve income distribution. In a typical prereform situation, organized labor lobbies for high wages and other benefits for employed workers, and government acquiesces as a political expedient or from ideological conviction. Latin American "populist" regimes have favored organized workers this way (Foxley and Whitehead 1980; Diaz-Alejandro 1981). If reform challenges these arrangements and the real wages of organized labor fall, the demand for urban labor will rise. The beneficiaries are employers in organized industries, workers in unprotected sectors with lower wages, and those unemployed urban workers and migrants from rural areas who subsequently gain jobs. The losers are higher-income organized workers, small-scale employers in the unorganized sector, and farmers who employ labor. Depending on the nature and size of the latter two groups, on balance, poorer groups probably gain and richer groups lose from these shifts, especially in Africa and Asia. But in Latin America, where organized workers have been a particular target of stabilization-liberalization programs, it appears in many cases that unemployment rose as real wages fell, so that employers as a whole gained and workers lost (Sheahan 1980; Foxley and Whitehead 1981).

The distributional impacts of financial market reform are more problematic. Higher interest rates that balance supply and demand for funds will make savers better off, raise the costs of investment while screening out low-productivity uses for funds, reduce credit rationing and open access to more borrowers, and attract funds from informal credit markets into the modern financial system. The latter is likely to hurt smaller, poorer borrowers until major structural changes are implemented to unify credit markets (Foxley 1983; Roemer 1986). On other counts there is no presumption about income distribution. However, higher interest rates are likely over time to encourage more labor-intensive activities, increasing employment creation and equalizing distribution.

Rising food prices help farmers who produce food surpluses, but not those who are net consumers of food. Among farmers, larger and better-off ones are more likely to benefit; within society, these may be high- or low-income earners, depending on the country. Rising food prices hurt low-income consumers more than the rich, because food is a larger proportion of their expenditure. Thus, higher food prices are likely to concentrate incomes unless, as in some African and Asian countries, food surpluses come from small farmers (Timmer 1986). However, the existence of parallel markets in the face of price controls can change these outcomes, especially if low-income consumers have been purchasing a large share of their food at high black market prices (Devarajan, Jones, and Roemer 1989).

Evidence from East Asia suggests that over the long run an outward-looking strategy can be associated with egalitarian outcomes. Korea and especially Taiwan, paragons of the export-driven economy, enjoy two of the most egalitarian income distributions in the developing world. However, both countries had undergone war, decolonization, military occupation, and land reform before their export-led episodes began. Thus, asset and income distribution were relatively equal before economic reform. In Taiwan's case, it appears that liberalization favored small-scale and rural producers, maintaining income equality through more than two decades of rapid growth (Fei et al. 1979). In Korea, a more urban-based strategy nevertheless maintained equality for a time, until the 1970s when wages of skilled workers began to rise more rapidly than others and government began to emphasize heavy industries and to pursue a more concentrated industrial structure (Mason et al. 1980; Scitovsky 1985).

Income distribution is a major point of departure for understanding the political economy of reform. It is not only a question of knowing who gains and who loses, and who may therefore support or oppose the reforms. Even if, on balance, the distributional impacts of reform are egalitarian over the long term, there remain the crucial issues of timing and especially of the short-run perceptions of distributional change. The potential losers from reforms include well-defined, politically articulate groups whose losses are likely to be large and who are quick to recognize the threat to their well-being: organized workers, owners and managers of highly protected firms, civil servants, and other urban consumers. Mancur Olson (1982) has observed that the concentration of losses on relatively small groups is likely to make these interests work more intensively than others to preserve their positions.

The gainers, though often more numerous, tend to be less powerful: smaller farmers, informal sector workers, and the unemployed. Because the gains are spread over larger numbers of people, gainers are likely to be less effective in lobbying for change (Olson 1982). Even in flexible economies, but especially in structurally rigid ones, the benefits are likely to be delayed for many months, in some cases for years. Potential beneficiaries who have spent years or decades under inflationary, controlled economic conditions have difficulty imagining the kinds of changes that can be wrought by stabilization and liberalization (Krueger 1984). With foreseeable near-term losses concentrated among the powerful and less predictable long-term gains spread widely among the politically weak, it is far easier to mobilize popular opposition to reform than to gather support for it (Roemer 1982; Krueger 1984).

One particularly influential set of losers from reform are the "clients" of a regime: individuals and narrowly defined groups who support and are rewarded by those who control government. The clearest examples of "clientelism" are in Africa, where local and tribal affinities frequently breed governments whose power depends heavily on the support of local leaders and successful business-men (Hyden 1983; Haggard 1985; Lancaster 1986). Robert Bates (1981) suggests that African governments, while keeping agricultural prices low for the usual urban-based reasons, have created clients among small numbers of farmers and rural workers through targeted schemes such as infrastructure development, state farms, subsidized agricultural credit, and subsidized fertilizer. The economically better alternative, raising prices of farm products, confers some benefits on the large mass of farmers, whose resulting incentive to support the regime, if we follow Olson's reasoning, is positive but small. In contrast, low farm prices combined with targeted subsidies confer greater benefits on a few, who thus develop a more active interest in preserving the regime.

The notion of clientelism has very broad application. It fits particularly well with the concept of rent seeking (Krueger 1974). To take one of many possible examples, an import control system is an ideal instrument to reward clients. Access to import licenses is extremely profitable, because shortages create high prices and thus excess profits or rents. Politicians and officials who control licensing can reward their friends and supporters, while making money themselves through bribes and other forms of rent sharing, at the expense of large numbers of mostly unsuspecting consumers, farmers, and others. Once a regime has developed clients through the creation of rents, the system becomes very hard to reform. Import liberalization means an end to the profits from obtaining scarce licenses, which hits directly and immediately at those who most visibly support the regime. And in general, incentives that work through the price system reduce government's ability to maintain its clients compared to incentives based on controls and rents. In countries with well-developed clientelistic governments, economic reform can be politically irrational (Haggard 1985).

Conclusion

From this review of the literature on economic reform in developing countries, a few points emerge as crucial to understanding why economic reform is desirable, how it can be made to work, and why it often fails.

First, reform is desirable because freer markets introduce more competition, which is believed to spur growth in productivity and hence in incomes. Economists believe that competition enhances productivity because first principles of neoclassical economics strongly suggest it and because there is empirical evidence to support it, although this evidence is based on a few cases rather than comprehensive cross-country data.

Second, the agenda for reform, though extensive, has attracted a wide consensus among development economists and practitioners. Because competition is the crucial ingredient of reform and the strongest dose of competition is likely to come from outside the economy, the reform agenda is closely associated with the outward-looking or export-oriented strategy of development.

Third, the major doubts about the reform agenda are those of implementation: with such a large agenda, how much can be done, in what order, and how soon? Reform programs are technically complex, with many opportunities to make fatal mistakes. Experience offers few convincing general lessons about the sequencing, timing, and magnitude of reform measures. Differing country circumstances demand tailor-made programs, which increases the chances for error.

Fourth, over several years a well-implemented reform should raise average income. Despite popular belief to the contrary, evidence is mixed that stabilization and structural adjustment necessarily lower incomes in the short run, especially if the correct (though difficult) comparison is made with the situation as it would have been without reform.

Fifth, reform ought to improve the income distribution in many circumstances, especially in Africa and Asia where economies are characterized by small farmers and a labor surplus. But in the most successful reforming countries in East Asia, reform has probably had a marginal impact on income equality, compared to the impact of war and land reform. And in Latin America it appears that stabilization may concentrate incomes.

Sixth, even if reform does raise income and equalize it, losses are likely to be concentrated among the most powerful groups in the society, who have both motive and means to thwart structural adjustment. This is especially true in clientelistic regimes, whose main support comes from favorites of the regime who benefit enormously from the controls that are a principal target of structural adjustment.

Finally, technical complexity and political fragility make it much easier to explain why reforms fail than why they succeed. Yet reforms do succeed, not only in East Asia, but in some unexpected places such as Indonesia, Bangladesh, Bolivia, and, increasingly, in some African countries. Research on reform can make its greatest contribution by explaining how these programs have worked. This volume attempts several steps in that direction. ღ

Notes

1 For a recent review of the literature on the political economy of reform, see Grindle (1989).

2 Externalities are defined below.

3 A significant fraction of the proreform literature has been produced or inspired by the World Bank. A notable example of its wholesale application to a large group of countries is in *Accelerated Development in Sub-Saharan Africa* (World Bank 1981).

4 The IMF model assumes, unrealistically, that production and hence employment are fixed in the short term; only prices vary.

5 Expenditure cuts reduce the government's drain on private saving to the full extent of the cut; tax increases take a fraction of this back in the form of reduced saving to pay taxes.

6 Argentina, Chile, and Uruguay.

7 The reverse order, to liberalize first the cross-border flow of capital and then domestic financial markets, could result in immediate and massive capital flight.

8 We are grateful to Dwight Perkins for this point.

9 For another, though consistent, treatment of the ensuing issues see Streeten (1987). Demery and Addison's (1987) discussion of stabilization programs is also relevant for structural adjustment.

3

Policymakers, Policy Choices, and Policy Outcomes:

Political Economy of Reform in Developing Countries

Merilee S. Grindle and John W. Thomas

Merilee S. Grindle is a specialist on the comparative analysis of policy making, implementation, and public management in developing countries and has written extensively on the political economy of economic policy change. She is a research associate at HIID and lecturer on public policy at the John F. Kennedy School of Government, Harvard University.

John W. Thomas is an Institute fellow at HIID and a lecturer on public policy at the John F. Kennedy School of Government, Harvard University. His research has focused on agriculture and land policy, and he has served as an adviser in the design and implementation of development programs in several Asian and African countries.

This article was originally published in *Policy Sciences* Vol. 22:213-48, 1989; copyright 1989 Kluwer Academic Publishers, printed in the Netherlands. It is reprinted here by permission of Kluwer Academic Publishers. Themes in this article are expanded upon in the authors' book, *Public Choices and Policy Change: the Political Economy of Reform in Developing Countries* (Johns Hopkins University Press, Baltimore, Md., April 1991).

The Political Economy of Reform in Developing Countries[1]

T he development message of the 1980s is clear: for a large number of countries, little can be accomplished to enhance growth and welfare unless major policy and institutional reforms are undertaken and sustained by developing country governments. The bearers of this message—many development specialists, international aid and lending agencies, development advisers, academic specialists, and industrial country governments—have become increasingly convinced of: 1) the importance of establishing a macro-policy climate to improve economic performance; 2) the need for adjusting sectoral policies to encourage efficiency and responsiveness to market forces; and 3) the imperative to lessen bureaucratic constraints on economic interactions. The debt crisis in Latin America and the food crisis and apparent failure of two decades of development in many African countries, contrasted with the apparent success of a number of Asian countries in achieving and sustaining high rates of growth, have helped focus extensive attention on the issue of appropriate macroeconomic, sectoral, and institutional contexts for development.[2]

Nevertheless, in the 1980s, the ranks of opposition to reform were full: economic elites supported by existing policies; ethnic, regional, and religious groups favored in allocative decision making; bureaucrats and bureaucratic agencies wielding regulatory power; policy elites sustained through patronage and clientele networks; military organizations accustomed to spending generous budgets with few questions asked. Moreover, decision makers, even those convinced of the economic need for the reforms, could not escape considering the political wisdom of adopting and pursuing them. In the name of efficiency and development, most changes implied a significant decentralization of decision making, a shrinking of the size of the public sector, and an important shift in the strongly interventionist role of the state in the economy. For policymakers schooled in the importance of state building, practiced in the methods of centralizing power in order to survive politically, familiar with the use of the public sector for patronage and regulation, and imbued with development doctrines emphasizing planning and control, the logic of the new orthodoxy was not always politically or philosophically obvious.

Despite substantial barriers to introducing reform, changes in macroeconomic and sectoral policies were made, and organizational reforms were adopted in many countries, and similar changes were contemplated in many more.[3] How can these changes be explained? Although techniques of policy analysis to generate recommendations for economic and organizational reforms are well developed, the process by which policy and institutional changes are adopted and sustained is much less well understood. There is little theory to explain how issues of reform come to the attention of government decision makers or how reform of policies and institutional arrangements becomes part of their agenda. Even less is known about how policy elites weigh the often urgent and well-articulated advice they receive about policy and institutional changes, their own intellectual and political commitment to such changes, and economic and political pressure to alter policies, against equally pressing concerns about the impact of their decisions on existing political and bureaucratic relationships. The factors that affect whether policies will be pursued, altered, reversed, or sustained after they have been decided upon are also generally left unexplained because implementation and sustainability are often considered to be mechanical, not political, processes.

This chapter addresses how changes in public policies and public institutions come about. Our interest in the process of policy and institutional change has led us to investigate policy making within government and to focus on the factors that appear to influence decision makers. We take instances of reform as our unit of analysis, policy elites as our focus of attention, and the processes of agenda setting, policy making, and implementation as critical arenas for understanding the factors that account for how, why, and when policy and institutional changes occur.[4] Our analysis builds on case histories prepared by individuals who were intimately involved in reform initiatives as part of their professional experience, either as officials responsible for particular policy areas or as advisers to government.[5] Those who prepared the cases were asked to consider three central questions: 1) How did the issue of reform get on the agenda of government decision making? 2) What political, bureaucratic, and technical criteria were important in promoting or inhibiting the process of change? and 3) What factors led to the sustainability or abandonment of reformist initiatives? The twelve reform experiences we consider here span the range of macroeconomic change, sectoral initiatives, and organizational innovation, as indicated in Table 1.

In this chapter, we advance three principal arguments:

(1) First, we are convinced that the outcomes of policy reform initiatives are not adequately explained by dominant theories in political science and political economy because such approaches do not systematically address the role of decision makers and managers in the policy process. The autonomy of these officials to shape policy and its implementation is neither as constrained nor as independent as current theoretical approaches suggest. Our cases indicate that policy elites play important roles in shaping policy and institutional outcomes but also demonstrate concrete ways in which options available to them are constrained by contextual factors. We will explore the degree of autonomy with which they operate and the factors that influence their action within the space available to them.

(2) Second, we believe circumstances unique to a particular policy initiative affect the dynamics and process of decision making, although they do not necessarily determine the outcome of that process. Accordingly, we give particular attention to the circumstances that surround how a reform measure gets on the policy agenda and is deliberated within government. In particular, whether a reform initiative is considered under conditions of perceived crisis or under conditions that can be termed "politics-as-usual" is critical in understanding the stakes involved in reform, the type of public official involved in decision making, the degree of change introduced, and the timing of decision making. We will consider differences in agenda setting and decision making that occur under conditions of crisis and those corresponding to politics-as-usual.

(3) Third, we argue that the characteristics of particular reforms determine the type of conflict and opposition that surround their implementation. In fact, our cases show that the characteristics of a policy have a powerful influence

on whether it will be implemented as intended or whether the outcome will be significantly different. The distribution of the costs and benefits of a policy or institutional change, its technical complexity, its administrative intensity and its short- or long-term impact determine reaction to the initiative, how that reaction is likely to be manifested, and the resources policy implementors require if the change is to be pursued successfully. Thus, implementation is a filter that often alters intended policy. We will use the cases to analyze the characteristics of policies and their implications for implementation.

In the following pages, we develop each of these arguments because we believe they can explain the outcome of many reform initiatives. First, we review current theoretical approaches to explaining policy outcomes and compare them to what our cases suggest about the role of policy elites and the factors that influence their decisions. Then, we consider the role of circumstance in shaping the process through which issues get on reform agendas, are deliberated within government, and are pursued and sustained. The third major section of the chapter considers the role of policy characteristics in shaping the task of implementation and in determining reform outcomes. We believe that our approach, which builds on state-centered theories about policy choice, is able to go beyond current theory because it also builds on the unique experiences and insights of participants in reform efforts. The resulting arguments and hypotheses advanced here are intended to encourage further research into the analysis of policy and institutional change.

Explaining Policy and Institutional Change: The Role of Policy Elites

In current theory, there are several alternative responses to the question, "How can we account for policy (or organizational) change?" Society-centered responses to the question argue that the causes of decisions made to adopt, pursue, and change public policies lie in understanding relationships of power and competition among individuals, groups, or classes in society or in international extensions of class-based or interest-based societies. In contrast, state-centered approaches argue that the perceptions and interactions of policy elites and the broad orientations of the state more generally account for policy choices and their subsequent pursuit.[6] Our cases indicate that state-centered approaches provide a useful beginning point for explaining the role of policy elites, but do not deal adequately with the evidence that decision makers are also systematically constrained by societal interests, past policies, and historical and cultural legacies. Following a review of the models most widely adopted to explain policy outcomes, we use our cases to outline several critical elements of decision making and the criteria adopted by policymakers in assessing options available to them. These factors provide insight into the concerns of decision makers, the constraints within which they operate, and the utility of current theories about how, why, and when reform occurs.

Society-Centered Explanations of Policy Choice

Explanations that emphasize the centrality of social class and interest group formations to policy choice dominate current research in political science and political economy. In class analytic and pluralist/public choice formulations, the activities of states and policy elites are understood to be dependent variables. Thus, choices of policy and the behavior of policy elites can be predicted on the basis of an analysis of class and group formations in society or in the international arena. As discussed below, the values, perceptions, behavior, and institutional contexts of public officials are much less important than the values, perceptions, behavior, and historical and/or international contexts of social classes and interest groups.

Class Analytic Approaches

Marxist analyses locate the source of policy—and of policy change—in relationships of power and domination among social classes. Dependency analyses, which have been widely adopted to explain the political economy of development, begin with relationships of domination and subordination that emerge through an international context of capitalist development and subsequently incorporate class relationships within a society (see, for examples, Amin 1976; Dos Santos 1970; Cardoso and Faletto 1979). In both cases, political interaction is derivative of economic conflict and politics is a significant manifestation of class conflict. Within this context, the primary function of the state is to ensure the legal, institutional, and ideological hegemony of the dominant class or class alliance over subordinate classes. Under normal conditions, the state is therefore an instrument of domination that reflects the structure of class relationships, and policy change is explained by changes in the composition of the dominant class or dominant class alliance.[7] Neo-Marxist perspectives introduce somewhat greater possibilities for autonomous action by the state. In one view, the state acts periodically to ensure the persistence of the capitalist system, even if the interests of specific fractions of the capitalist class or the class as a whole are constrained by such actions (see especially Poulantzas 1973; see also Carnoy 1984). Autonomy of policy elites is possible when dominant classes are profoundly at odds with each other and unable to establish a ruling coalition or when the interests of the capitalist economy as a whole are threatened (see Skocpol 1985). Reformist initiatives are adopted in order to resolve these infrequent crises of political legitimacy or economic disorder. For Marxists, neo-Marxists, and dependency theorists, then, the process through which decisions are made is not a useful focus of inquiry; what is important are the social class formations that give rise to policy initiatives and the differential impact of policy on particular classes in society (see, for example, Stallings 1978).

Pluralist and Public Choice Approaches

In pluralist approaches to political analysis, public policy results from conflict, bargaining, and coalition formation among a potentially large number of societal groups, organized to protect or advance particular interests common to their members.[8] These interests are usually economic, but groups also form around shared concerns for neighborhood, ethnicity, religion, values, region, or other issues. For pluralists, political society is composed of large numbers of such groups that compete and coalesce around the promotion of common policy goals. Like the economic efficiency derived through an open and competitive market, the public interest is thought to be best served when policy emerges out of competition among large numbers of organized interests. The state acts as an arbitrator among competing interests; public officials may register preferences, and at times seek to negotiate compromises among divergent interests, but their principal role is to respond to the pressures placed upon them by organized groups in society. Not only is the initiative for policy linked to the mobilization of interests in society, but the source of policy change must also be sought in changes in the coalitions of interest groups or in their relative power in bargaining, negotiating, marshalling votes, and otherwise influencing the policymakers.

Like pluralist perspectives, public choice theory assumes that political society is composed of organized interests. Interest groups, which form around relatively narrow issues of special importance to their members, are created by individuals seeking to acquire access to public resources (see especially Olson 1965). They use money, expertise, political connections, votes, and other resources to extract benefits, or rents, from government through lobbying activities, through elections and other direct forms of political involvement, or through the imposition of rewards and sanctions on public officials (Colander 1984; Srinivasan 1985, 43). Complementing the interest of groups in capturing favored status in the distribution of resources in society are elected public officials who are overwhelmingly concerned with remaining in power (see Ames 1987; Anderson and Hayami 1986; Alt and Chrystal 1983). In order to do so, they consciously seek to provide benefits to a range of interests, systematically favor certain groups over others, and maximize their returns from the allocations of public expenditures, goods, services, and state regulation as a way of attracting and rewarding supporters (Bennett and DiLorenzo 1984; Anderson and Hayami 1986; Bates 1981). Nonelected officials respond also to the pushing and hauling of interest groups because they can derive rents from providing favored access to public goods, services, and regulations (Colander 1984; Brock and Magee 1984; Krueger 1974; Wellisz and Findlay 1984). Politics, then, is a sum total of individuals seeking special advantage through public policy and individual officials seeking to benefit from public office through reelection and rents. This "political marketplace" generates negative outcomes for social and economic interaction—a state that is captured by narrow interests, policies that are distorted in economically and socially irrational ways by self-seeking groups, and public officials whose actions are inherently corrupt (see especially Bates 1981; Brock and Magee 1984; Colander 1984, 6; Olson 1982; Srinivasan 1985; Krueger 1974).[9] Thus, while the public choice approach shares basic assumptions with pluralist theory, its assessment of politics stands in considerable opposition to the pluralist perspective that wise policy results from fragmented interest articulation in the political arena.[10]

State-Centered Models of Policy Change

While political science and political economy have emphasized society-centered approaches in explaining policy choices, the policy sciences literature has been more explicitly focused on the analysis of decision making within the organizational context of the state. As such, it takes as a principal unit of analysis the decision maker or the organization responsible for decisional outcomes. Not surprisingly, much of this literature credits the decision maker with considerably more capacity for choice and substantially more complex motives for making those choices than is the case with the society-centered approaches. Similarly, constraints emanating from societal contexts are considerably less powerful in explaining what policymakers can and cannot do.

Rational Actor Models

Much discussion of policy decision making has revolved around the question of the extent to which policymakers can be considered rational actors who accumulate information, assess alternative courses of action, and choose among them on the basis of the potential to achieve the decision makers' preferences (see, for discussions, Allison 1971; Frohock 1979; Killick 1976; March 1978; Robinson and Majak 1967).[11] Much decision-making theory has involved modification of the perfectly rational actor model by introducing concepts such as "bounded rationality," "satisficing," and "incrementalism" (see Kinder and Weiss 1978; March 1978). These revisionist perspectives generally argue that because of the complexity of perfectly rational choice, and its costs in terms of time and attention, decision makers (whether individuals or organizations) do not usually attempt to achieve optimal solutions to problems, but only to find ones that satisfy their basic criteria for an acceptable alternative or ones that meet satisfactory standards (see March and Simon 1958, 140-41). Moreover, individuals and organizations operate on the basis of "bounded rationality," a concept suggesting that organizations develop means of dealing with recurrent problems in ways that obviate the need to assess separately each issue that requires a decision (March and Simon 1958, 169-71). In subsequent formulations, the concept of "incrementalism" was introduced, asserting that decision makers, when confronted with the need to change policy, attempt to reduce uncertainty, conflict, and complexity by making incremental or marginal changes over time (see Braybrooke and Lindblom 1963). Thus, rational actor models establish a set of assumptions about the conditions under which decisions are made, focus on the options and strategies available to the policymakers, and make it possible to view discrete decisions as part of an overall decision-making system with characteristics that can be described and that shape outcomes (see Frohock 1979; Killick 1976).

Bureaucratic Politics Approach

Decision makers are also the focus of analysis in the bureaucratic politics approach to explaining policy outcomes. In this model, state policy is the result of competing activities among bureaucratic entities and actors constrained by their organizational roles and capacities (see Allison 1971; Halperin 1971). Executive and bureaucratic "players" compete over preferred solutions to particular policy problems and use the resources available to them through their positions—hierarchy, control over information, access to key decision makers, for example—to achieve their goals. The issue position of each player is defined by the bureaucratic position he or she occupies, such that "where you stand depends on where you sit" (Allison 1971, 176). The autonomy of decision makers to shape and pursue policy is very great in this approach, for it is constrained only by the power and bargaining skills of other bureaucratic actors and by their own hierarchical position of power, their political skill, and the bureaucratic and personal resources available to them. Change in policy results from the potential for variable outcomes in bargaining, negotiation, and conflict among the actors involved.

State Interests Approach

In a state interests approach, a broader perspective on the role and influence of government decision makers is adopted as a way of accounting for instances in which the state appears to have some autonomy in defining the nature of public problems and developing solutions to them. In contrast to class and interest group models, states are analytically separable from society and considered to have "interests" that they pursue or attempt to pursue (see Bennett and Sharpe 1985; Grindle 1986a; Bardhan 1984; Haggard and Moon 1983). Among the interests of the state, for example, are the achievement and maintenance of its own hegemony vis-à-vis societal actors, the maintenance of social peace, the pursuit of national development as defined by policy elites representing particular regimes, and the particular interests of regime incumbents in retaining power (Krasner 1978; Nordlinger 1987, 36; Stepan 1981; Skocpol 1985, 15; Trimberger 1978). The state, and by extension, policy elites, strive for autonomy to make and pursue policy choices, but do not necessarily achieve it because of the variable power of societal classes or groups that constrain the state. In the state interests approach, policy or institutional reform comes about because of the interaction of policymakers attempting to generate responses to public problems and the constraints placed upon them by political, economic, and social conditions and by the legacy of past policy.

Reflecting on Current Theory: What the Cases Suggest about Policy Elites

Policy elites were central actors in our twelve cases of reform, but their activities are not fully explained in the models of policy choice described above. In society-centered approaches, policy elites do not assume much initiative in making policy choices. Instead, they reflect societal preferences mechanistically, collude with societal groups to circumvent or exploit the public interest, or, at best, broker agreements among groups. In contrast, our cases suggest that policy elites often initiate reforms by placing issues on the agenda of government decision making. In so doing, they may shape the debate over such issues and use technical expertise to influence discussions within and outside government. Moreover, policy elites often shape reform strategies by influencing the timing and content of proposals so they are made more politically or bureaucratically acceptable. A good example of the leadership role assumed by policy elites comes from our analysis of the case of planning reform in Colombia:

> The intention of the president, the foreign adviser, and his chief counterpart was to make planning the serious heart of development in the country. Their strategy involved: 1) carving out an important and useful role for the national planning agency as a source of information; 2) gaining access to policymakers and encouraging them to rely on the information and analysis provided by the agency; 3) building support among prominent technocrats and important officials within the bureaucracy in order to have wide access to decision makers of different political persuasions; and 4) strengthening the competence, image, and staff spirit of the agency. Overall, their strategy was one of building a coalition of support within the government and within the society at large. (See note no. 4.)

More generally, the cases suggest that policy elites can provide initiative, orientation, leadership, ideology, expertise, and political sensitivity to major issues of reform. None of these contributions is easily predicted from society-centered approaches to understanding public policy.

If society-centered approaches give insufficient recognition to those who work within government, some state-centered approaches reduce policy decision making to a set of interactions among policy elites who are little encumbered by societal pressures, historical context, or the legacies of prior policies. Their activities correspond to rational choices or to bureaucratic games in which the stakes are personal, organizational, and positional. In contrast, our cases indicate that policy elites are always at least partially constrained by political, economic, and historical contexts. Moreover, while the stakes in decision-making situations frequently involve the individual power of policy elites, bureaucratic organizations, and the state more generally, decision makers are also influenced by ideological predispositions, their professional expertise and training, and their memories of similar prior policy situations. The constraints that face policy elites, as well as their role in shaping policies, is evident in the development strategy shift that occurred in Costa Rica in the 1980s.

> The past years have been witness to an active search for an alternative development strategy. There has also been the effort to construct a new hegemonic alliance among the state elite, the private sector, and the popular sectors. There is a preliminary consensus with respect to an export-led development strategy, yet the speed of adjustment and the decision as to which sectors will carry the burden of the transition remained only partially resolved issues. After a push-and-pull struggle with domestic and international actors, the state elite had settled on an equilibrated, balanced path towards an export-led strategy where adjustment costs would be rotated among different sectors, where the key word would be gradualism, and where the country's social stability would be a major concern.

The cases uniformly indicate the importance of policy elites to the initiation and outcome of reform experiences. Thus, they present policy elites as potentially active, but systematically constrained strategists in efforts to bring about change. They often articulated goals for their societies and for the activities of the state. Goals frequently reflected the predispositions of decision makers which were in turn often influenced by bureaucratic positions, professional training, and experiential learning. The cases also indicate that policy elites represented the concerns of a particular regime and shared a sense of the importance of regime survival and their own responsibility for it. Societal pressures and interests, historical contexts, and bureaucratic capacity and compliance were among the factors that limited the options available to these policy elites. Aware of these constraints, they often sought to maneuver within them and to craft policy solutions that would be politically and bureaucratically acceptable.

If, as our cases suggest, policy elites are key actors in determining policy initiatives and choices, it is important to try to identify more specifically the criteria they use to make decisions about major policy and institutional reforms. In contrast to the other discussions of the decision-making concerns of policy elites, which generally focus on case-specific explanations, we have used our cases to generalize about these criteria and to provide insight into the kinds of factors that influence the choices made by policy elites. In the specific decision-making contexts we investigated, they were frequently influenced by or concerned about at least four criteria: the technical advice they received; the impact of their choices on bureaucratic interactions; the meaning of change for political stability and political support; and their relationships with international actors.

The Influence of Technical Analysis

In the case histories, decision makers frequently appear to have been strongly influenced by technical analyses of the problem area and advice about how best the particular problem could be solved. Important to the explanation of reform outcomes, therefore, was the insistence that technical tools and advice based on sound problem analysis were persuasive to decision makers and central to the issues they considered. In explaining a reform initiative from this perspective, the reliance of decision makers on their technical advisory teams or on foreign technocrats and the quality of information available to them were stressed.[12]

Technical analyses and technical advisers were particularly prominent in shaping decisional outcomes in Korea and Indonesia; decision makers in these cases responded to the technical input and applied it to the problems they sought to solve.

> On the decisions to pursue export-led growth in South Korea—"[as] early as 1961, American-trained Koreans understood the importance of macro-economic and market-oriented policy reforms but were not in positions of power.... Later, a foresighted deputy prime minister brought these young technocrats up through the ranks, often skipping them past more senior people."

> On rice price policy in Indonesia—"With solid evidence of the correspondence between consumption and price for wheat flour, the Indonesians adopted a pricing policy that helped finance the development budget....This relatively simple work legitimized price analysis to the minister of trade, the director of trade research, [and the food logistics agency], and enhanced the role of the technical analysts."[13]

In terms of the conventional models of policy change reviewed earlier, only the rational actor and state-interest models explicitly recognize that policymakers may have goals and perceptions about national development that are not reducible to self-interest (pluralist/public choice approach), class interest (class analytic approaches), or positional games (bureaucratic politics approach). But even these models do not tell us how goals for national development are identified nor how technical advice is factored into choices and options. The case histories emphasize the importance of this process and suggest that reformers need to know under what conditions information or analytic output would be taken seriously by decision makers. The case of Ghana reflects well the complex way in which technical information combines with other factors—such as bureaucratic rivalries and concerns about political support—in actual decision-making contexts.

> At the end of 1971, the governor of the central bank called an emergency meeting to discuss ways of meeting the economic crisis. No one from the Ministry of Finance attended, underlining the antagonism between the minister and the rest of the economic decision makers. Without his assessment of the economic consequences of the decision, the prime minister and cabinet decided to undertake a major devaluation in opposition

to the position of the minister of finance. The decision makers believed that a major devaluation would bring more revenues from export taxes to buy off urban elites and cocoa farmers. It later became clear that the cabinet was not well equipped to evaluate the complex economic information given them in reports that were intended for an audience of trained economists at the central bank. Simpler memos with fewer recommendations should have been prepared to offer clear alternatives to the cabinet.

The Power of Bureaucratic Interactions

A second perspective that emerged in the cases signalled the way policy elites are influenced by the bureaucratic politics that surround the selection of policy and institutional changes. With regularity, decision makers within government were concerned with making decisions or supporting positions that would enhance their own career opportunities and/or the fortunes—in terms of budgetary resources, influence over programs, prestige, or clienteles—of the bureaucratic entities they led or were part of.[14] Statements such as the following were used to account for the fortunes of reform initiatives:

Building a planning agency in Colombia "evoked antagonism from other ministries because such a new agency might challenge their influence."

On planning reform generally—"To become a premier technical agency, someone in power needs to turn to the planning agency and enhance its prestige, because of the weaker position it usually occupies in relation to the ministry of finance."

On decentralization in Kenya—"A minister or other senior official builds up his group of followers within the organization and these people don't want to disappoint him, so they don't send bad news up the ladder. Hence, information useful for change does not reach decision makers."

On ministry reorganization in Kenya—"As he observed the functioning of his staff, the Permanent Secretary began to notice that there was an informal power network that ran vertically within the ministry but often across formal lines of authority. This network was based on tribal affiliations: each officer was tied into an informal tribal-based network that often conflicted with formal lines of authority and responsibility in the ministry."

On health policy in Mali—"The Mali Health Project was part of a weak ministry.... If changes in laws or regulations were needed, cabinet approval was required. With such a weak ministry, this process took too long and was oftentimes unsuccessful."

In fact, in the case of Mali, the health project faltered and then died in large part because bureaucratic concerns came to dominate decision making.[15] But these cases also provide us with evidence that to understand the way decisions are made, we need to look outside the bureaucracy for additional political and situational inputs and inside it to assess such factors as the technical information and advice that is available. In the Kenya decentralization case, for example, bureaucratic politics influenced the acceptance of reform, but so did a major political change that altered the support group most important to the regime. Moreover, nonbureaucratic factors were frequently introduced into decision-making contexts that corresponded closely to the bureaucratic politics model.

For example, in India, the refusal of a number of bureaucratic entities to assume responsibility for water management reform was endemic because public officials were well aware that the reforms pressed upon them by the World Bank could easily incite political instability if they were pursued. In this case, bureaucratic buck-passing was engendered by extrabureaucratic concerns.

The Significance of Political Stability and Political Support

A third concern of policy elites that emerged in the case histories stressed the importance of political stability, political opposition and support, and the political use of policy resources. Thus, policy reform options were assessed by decision makers in terms of how reaction to them would affect the longevity of the regime in power or the particular leadership group wielding authority. Explicitly political criteria were applied to decision making and they indicated the importance of building or maintaining coalitions of support for incumbent political elites.[16]

> On health policy in Mali—"The project sites were selected on the basis of political criteria. The Malians had recently fought a 'soccer war' with Burkina Faso (then Upper Volta), and wanted to have a presence in the border area. [In another area], the government wanted to ... forestall any shifts in political loyalty."

> On agrarian reform in the Philippines—"Adoption of an agrarian reform was considered by some leaders of the government to be central to weakening the appeal of the insurgent National People's Army, but the fact that top leadership saw it as potentially disruptive of its support coalition meant that it was consistently given low priority in the government's policy agenda."

> On decentralization in Kenya—"President Jomo Kenyatta had pursued a successful policy of centralization since independence in 1962. His strategy was to increase the central government's capacity to provide benefits to his fellow tribesmen and therefore help sustain the political regime. As a result, by the 1970s, 95 percent of the development budget was controlled from Nairobi. A policy of decentralization conflicted with political and bureaucratic interests in maintaining control of economic resources."

Central to decision makers in Ghana was concern about how devaluation would affect the groups thought to be important to the sustainability of the regime—cocoa farmers and urban elites. In Korea, decision makers believed that rapidly improving economic performance was a critical ingredient in building legitimacy for a new regime that had taken over power extraconstitutionally. Water management reform in India, involving fee increases for users, was resisted because of concern about adverse political reaction. To a considerable extent, then, the cases affirm the theoretical assertions that underlie the state interest and public choice models. But the cases, by focusing on the process of decision making, demonstrate—in a way that neither of the models can—how political stability goals actually influence the policy process and how judgments are shaped and altered by such concerns.

The Persuasiveness of International Pressure

A fourth factor that was regularly considered important by policy elites in the case histories emphasized the role of international actors and international economic and political dependency relations in determining the outcome of decision making about reform.[17] In our case studies, explanations for reform included reference to the strong influence of international actors or international dependency relations:

On structural adjustment in South Korea—"In early 1963...the U.S. Ambassador was withholding PL480 food aid to put pressure on Park to quit politics and to get the Koreans to commit to a stabilization program. This pressure was decisive."

On rice pricing policy in Indonesia—"Indonesia experienced considerable problems with inflation in the late 1960s and early 1970s. The IMF put pressure on the ministry of finance to tighten up on credit. In turn, the ministry used the leverage provided by IMF to put pressure on other agencies in the government."

On health policy reform in Mali—"The Mali Health Project...originated at the request of the Mali government, which was seeking funds for medical inputs. USAID wanted to look at the entire health care system.... After more than two years of study, a plan was drawn up that reflected USAID's interests more than those of the government of Mali."

On export promotion in Jamaica—"The government, on the advice of the World Bank...decided that Jamaica had comparative advantage in [several industrial subsectors].... These were then designated the seven priority subsectors which would be the focus of the government's program of assistance.... External funding agencies such as USAID and the World Bank supported this choice."

The cases also indicate how international actors become engaged in bureaucratic interactions in developing countries, suggesting the appropriateness of including them within a bureaucratic politics analysis. In the Latin American cases of planning reform, for example, resources made available through the Alliance for Progress were used effectively within bureaucratic agencies to enhance the prestige and bargaining power of the agencies. In India,

The Finance Ministry's general approach towards foreign aid is to maximize its volume on the most concessional terms available while minimizing external interference with established national policies....[In the case of water management reform] the point repeatedly made by the Indian authorities was that...the [World] Bank was welcome to present its point of view for discussion...but that India could not accept wholesale policy change leveraged on particular projects....Detailed discussions between the Bank, the Finance Ministry, and the Ministry of Works resulted in a compromise.

Technical analysis, bureaucratic interactions, concerns about political stability and support, and international leverage were factors that emerged repeatedly in the explanations offered by "insiders" in reform experiences to explain a variety of outcomes. As we have suggested, presenters of the cases often utilized more than one factor to explain the choices that were made by decision makers. In the next section of the paper, we suggest that the salience of specific concerns influencing decision makers tended to vary depending on the circumstances surrounding considerations of reform. More specifically, we believe that policy elites are differentially influenced by specific criteria depending on whether a particular policy issue is being considered under conditions of perceived crisis or under conditions that approximate politics-as-usual in any particular regime (see Hampsen 1986).[18] Important to our perspective is the evidence that a shift in circumstance (from crisis to politics-as-usual or vice versa) can alter the decision criteria adopted by policy elites by altering the nature of the stakes for change. Importantly, a shift in circumstance can introduce or destroy windows of opportunity for reform.

Agenda Setting and Decision making: The Role of Circumstance

Circumstance—the particular conditions surrounding the emergence, consideration, and pursuit of particular reformist initiatives—is an important intervening variable in explaining policy choices. In the cases of policy reform reviewed here, the process of policy making was significantly different when policy elites perceived they were dealing with a crisis situation from when they believed that reform initiatives were worthwhile but not critical to the political or economic health or survival of the regime they represented. In cases in which the perception of crisis surrounded the consideration of policy changes, considerable pressure developed to "do something" about a problem if dire economic and social consequences were to be avoided. Devaluation in Ghana, structural adjustment in Korea, agrarian reform in the Philippines, development strategy change in Costa Rica, and rice pricing policy in Indonesia would fall into this category of crisis-ridden reforms. In many other reforms, however, less pressured circumstances of "politics-as-usual" prevailed. Decentralization and ministry reorganization in Kenya, planning reform in Argentina and Colombia, water management in India, trade reform in Jamaica, and health policy reform in Mali correspond to this pattern.

Crisis and Politics-as-Usual

We believe the distinction between crisis-ridden and politics-as-usual reforms is useful for explaining how issues got on the agenda for decision makers in our cases, and also for predicting how those issues would be treated in the decision process. The cases demonstrated systematic differences in terms of the pressures for reform, the stakes involved in change, the level of decision makers involved, the degree of change considered, and the timing of reforms, depending on whether the reform initiative was thought necessary to resolve a crisis or whether it was treated as a useful but not necessarily critical change.

Pressing and Chosen Problems

Circumstances of crisis or politics-as-usual tend to distinguish between whether problems are "pressing" or "chosen." Albert Hirschman (1981, 146) has suggested that pressing problems are those "that are forced on the policymakers through pressure from injured or interested outside parties"; chosen problems are those that decision makers "have picked out of thin air" as a result of their own preferences and perceptions. In several cases, actors outside of government played significant roles in placing issues for debate within government. In Ghana, for instance, the IMF and the British government were particularly important in pressing the need for reform on the policymakers, and in the

Philippines, insurgent forces and international donors were among those pressuring a frequently reluctant government to consider agrarian reform. Pressing problems tended to predominate when policy elites perceived that a crisis existed, and the pressures added to their sense of urgency about the problem. Those pressing for reform did not necessarily determine how the policy elites would respond, but only that they would feel the need to respond in some way to it. In the cases of chosen reforms, however, conditions of politics-as-usual predominated and policy elites had much greater autonomy to decide whether and how to push for policy or institutional change. The case of water management reform is particularly apt here, for it demonstrates that in the absence of sustained public demand for improved service, the initiative for reform had to emerge from within the government's bureaucratic system.

Stakes

Circumstances of crisis or noncrisis surrounding the emergence and consideration of a particular policy issue also systematically raised or lowered the stakes for policy elites. A situation of perceived crisis appeared to raise the concerns policy elites had about macropolitical conditions such as political stability, legitimacy, and regime vulnerability, and cautioned them to assess carefully the political and economic consequences of the options available to them. This was evident in all the cases of crisis-induced agenda setting—Korea, Ghana, the Philippines, Costa Rica, and Indonesia. In noncrisis situations, these anxieties were largely absent and were replaced by more mundane concerns about short-term political and bureaucratic support and opposition. For example, in Mali:

> Malians had a vital interest in the project inputs, especially medical supplies and vehicles. Malian staff were particularly interested in project perquisites; at the local level, this meant the steady paychecks that came from the project, and at the regional and national level, it meant access to vehicles and medical supplies.

Status of Decision Makers

Conditions of crisis or noncrisis alter the identity and often the hierarchical position of decision makers and the kinds of societal interests they are most concerned about. Crisis situations tend strongly to move the level of concerned officials upward in the decision-making hierarchy of government while situations in which the crisis threat is low tend to remain at lower hierarchical levels. This distinction is clearly related to the level of threat to macropolitical conditions of political stability and legitimacy; the higher the perceived stakes, the more likely that high-level officials will take a personal interest in the decision— Ghana is a good case of this, as is the revision of development strategy in Costa Rica, where critical decisions were made by small groups at the highest level in government.[19] When politics-as-usual prevails in the decision-making process, policy changes are more likely to be considered as routine matters and policy elites are more concerned with micropolitical interactions with societal groups and the bureaucracy. The example from India is instructive:

> No domestic actor considered this [water management reform] to be something which required urgent and forceful action. Because of its low problem status, it was considered unnecessary to raise the matter to the political level at either the center or the state. Bureaucracies within the

central and state agencies had, over the years, developed sufficient under-standing of what were politically possible alternatives and of the time-frame in which they would become implementable. This was not considered an issue that required forcing onto the higher political level, or likely to be accepted within the kind of short period the World Bank had in mind.

Innovation or Incrementalism

Distinct circumstances also alter the perceptions of decision makers about the causes, consequences, and remedies of a particular policy issue. Crisis-ridden reforms tend to emphasize major changes from preexisting policies. That is, prior policies are often considered to be fully implicated in the causes of the crisis and must be rejected if the crisis is to be overcome. Moreover, policy elites may feel under considerable pressure to appear to be taking decisive action in response to a dire situation. In Costa Rica, a development strategy that had been in effect since the early 1960s was reversed in the 1980s; in Ghana, after avoiding devaluation as a no-win policy for four years, the government decided on a major change in 1971; Indonesia systematically altered its strategic approach to rice pricing policy in response to crisis situations—in one instance as a result of a domestic and international shortage of rice and in another instance as a result of an economic crisis. Thus, although the stakes are high for the decision makers in crisis-induced reforms, they are also pushed in the direction of major reform initiatives when a perception of crisis exists. Innovation rather than incrementalism is likely to result.

In contrast, under noncrisis conditions, change is often incremental, with considerable scope for trial and error or scaling up if initial efforts provide positive results. Implementation capacity was a concern of decision makers in these cases, and improving this capacity tended to prolong the duration of the reform. This became a major component of reforming trade relations in Jamaica, as the list of things that "had to be done" before the policy would be effective grew longer and more complex. In general, in these reforms there was greater potential for the initiative to become sidetracked by other issues or pushed to the bottom of the policy agenda by more pressing issues. As in the cases of water management in India, health in Mali, and the planning reforms in Latin America, more bureaucratic maneuvering and concern with possible sabotage or resistance was characteristic of reforms undertaken under circumstances of politics-as-usual.

Timing

Finally, the timing of policy response can be altered by circumstance. Under conditions of perceived crisis, decision makers often believe they have little alternative but to act, however much they might wish to avoid making difficult and risky decisions. They will not be without power or room to maneuver in cases of crisis-ridden reforms, but their control over timing may be significantly reduced. The case of rice price reforms in Indonesia is a good example of how the timing of change is affected by crisis conditions.

> The specific policy options adopted indicated the government's confidence in the technical advice it received from a team of food policy analysts. The timing of the changes, however, reflected broader political concerns about food prices during periods of perceived economic crisis.

While the perception of crisis affects the timing of reform initiatives, it does not necessarily result in either predictable or recommended policy changes. For example, in the Philippines, policy elites, at least until mid-1989, rejected a major land reform as too destabilizing politically and sought instead to address a political and economic crisis through negotiations with insurgent groups.

When noncrisis circumstances surrounded a reform initiative, more time was available to decision makers for studying the implications of change, and policy elites were able to determine the extent to which it would be actively pursued. When moments appeared to be propitious for reform, they encouraged its pursuit but then placed the issue on a back burner when conditions seemed to be adverse to success. Institutional reforms in Colombia, Argentina, and Kenya were shelved for long periods of time when little political support was available for pursuing them. While such conditions provide policy elites with greater control over the timing of reform, they may also be without the pressured political environment that can act as a stimulus to change. Thus, under conditions of perceived crisis, the likelihood of change occurring may be greater than when the policy reform is considered a matter of routine.

Given these characteristics of the agenda-setting and decision-making process under different circumstances, our cases provide an opportunity for considering when and why policy elites will be particularly likely to apply particular criteria to the choices they make. The hypotheses presented below are based on the experiences considered in the cases and attempt to specify the relationship between circumstance (perceived crisis or politics-as-usual) and the decision-making criteria most salient to policy elites (technical advice, bureaucratic interactions, political stability and support, and response to international pressure). We believe that, overall, the cases suggest that crisis-ridden reforms are adopted or rejected most frequently in conformance to the criteria of political stability and that politics-as-usual reforms most frequently reveal the priorities of bureaucratic interactions. Technical advice and international pressures often figured as important factors that decision makers considered, but they were generally subordinated to the political and bureaucratic concerns of decision makers.

The following three hypotheses indicate our effort to generalize from a limited number of cases of policy and institutional change in order to stimulate further research into the process of reform. The relationships that we identify between agenda-setting circumstances and decision-making criteria have not been specified in this form in prior scholarship. We believe they provide a basis for understanding the content of reform decisions by understanding the conditions under which issues emerge and are acted upon.

Hypothesis 1:
In crisis-ridden reforms, decision making tends to be dominated by concern about major issues of political stability and control. Technical analysis, bureaucratic interactions, and international pressures often assume importance in these decisions, but usually remain subordinate to concerns about the stability or survival of the regime in power or the longevity of its incumbents.

Example: In Ghana, a decision to devalue was taken by political elites in the expectation that the resulting economic changes would benefit groups whose support was critical to the incumbents. In the event, however, their decision contributed significantly to the overthrow of the regime, a fact explained in large part by the policymakers' failure to understand the economic dynamics they were putting in motion.

Example: The agrarian reform issue in the Philippines was a controversial one. Many members of the Aquino cabinet as well as other politically and economically powerful Filipinos were adamantly opposed to agrarian reform. Moreover, President Aquino's family had large land holdings that would be affected by any agrarian reform measure. Her family holdings were well run and productive. So in addition to family and class interests, which could affect her thinking, she was familiar with the model of an efficient large land owning system. On the other side there was also powerful support for action. International donors, peasants, leading educators, and business people advocated agrarian reform. But, after the coup attempt of August 1987, the Aquino government's political base seemed too insecure to undertake serious land reform.

Hypothesis 2:

When noncrisis reforms concern policy issues, decision-making outcomes tend to be dominated by bureaucratic and micropolitical concerns. Technical input and international pressure are important, but not decisive, in explaining policy choice under these conditions. Major issues of political survival and support building are usually not salient to decision makers.

Example: In the Mali project to develop low cost health care through the training of village health workers and the establishment of village dispensaries, decisions made in the process of project design and implementation were strongly influenced by bureaucratic politics. The inability of the project to achieve greater impact on the health sector in Mali largely reflected the intragovernmental concerns of the decision makers.

Example: In the case of decentralization in Kenya, resistance to the idea of reform was primarily based on the desire of political elites to maintain control over the allocation of resources in society so that traditional tribal clienteles could be maintained. In this period, when there was no political support and little bureaucratic interest, the approach taken by project personnel was to build up a constituency for reform. This meant finding important groups in national and local administration and interesting them in activities that could advance the goals of the project.

Hypothesis 3:

When noncrisis reforms concern issues of organizational change, decision making tends to be dominated by bureaucratic concerns. International pressures often emerge as part of bureaucratic interactions in these reforms. Technical input and concern for political survival are usually not salient to reform decision makers.

Example: Planning reform in Argentina was introduced over a considerable period of time and was based on efforts to establish the bureaucratic prestige and importance of a technical agency in government. Although international and domestic nongovernmental actors were involved in urging the development of planning in Argentina, reformers did not perceive that dire consequences would result if they were not successful in introducing change. Instead, they perceived that they had considerable time to engineer institutional change; they gave considerable attention to the strategies available for strengthening the planning apparatus within the organizational structure of the government. The planning agency attempted to acquire information and use its technical expertise to enhance its influence in government decision making.

Example: In the case of the ministry reorganization in Kenya, opposition to change came from high-level civil servants who believed that the new system shifted power to the permanent secretary....They raised questions within the ministry about the appropriateness of the new system, including attacks on the permanent secretary for not being familiar with how things were done in Kenya and being too interested in foreign management ideas. There was also resistance from those who did not like what appeared to be a heavier work load, less free time, and being held accountable for continuing performance.

Table 3 summarizes the hypothesized linkages between agenda-setting circumstances and decision-making criteria. The possible relationships among the variables suggested in the hypotheses require considerably more research if they are to be posed as useful reflections of a wide variety of reform experiences in developing countries. Nevertheless, we believe they are interesting enough to stimulate further study; if they have some validity, they can provide guidance to reformers about how they can most fruitfully encourage the adoption of significant changes in policies and institutions that affect the potential for economic development in a large number of countries.

Implementation and Sustainability: The Role of Policy Characteristics

The task of policy and organizational reform is only begun when issues are placed on a problem agenda for decision makers and choices are made among a variety of responses to these problems—including decisions not to address the issues at all. At times, the process of policy choice may even be relatively easy compared with a much longer and more conflict-ridden process of reform implementation. For most reforms, sustainability is determined during their implementation. It is during this phase of the policy process that conflict, resistance, "slippage," and the rejection of change will become most apparent to advocates of reform and when the often contradictory goals of development policies will become most evident. Our cases suggest that the distribution of implementation outcomes is not bi-modal, with the policy being successfully or unsuccessfully implemented, as is usually assumed. Instead, they make clear that there is frequently a third outcome: the policy is significantly changed during implementation and the final outcome is very different from that intended by the decision makers.

After a decision to change policy is made, the variety of potential outcomes is great, largely due to conflict and resistance engendered by efforts to alter established practice. The decision to introduce change upsets the equilibrium surrounding an existing policy mix and, depending on the characteristics of the reform, will set in motion responses, some of which will occur largely in the public arena, others of which are played out largely within a bureaucratic context. These responses vary from those that have only a minor impact on effective implementation, to those that bring the pursuit of the new policy into question, to those that can even threaten the existence of a regime. Thus, policy characteristics condition the type and degree of conflict that emerges during the implementation of reforms and in large part determine the kinds of problems that will be encountered in efforts to sustain them. The extent to which the costs and benefits of a reform are dispersed or concentrated, the technical and administrative content of a reform, and the length of time it takes for results to become apparent are significant characteristics of policy and organizational changes that shape the conflicts that will surround implementation. They also signal the kind of resources needed by reform advocates to sustain the policy or organizational initiative.

More specifically, some implementation outcomes are primarily determined by conflict that emerges in the public arena, among the societal groups and interests that are most affected by the reforms. For example, in Ghana, the implementation of a major devaluation fed public discontent with the government's management of the economy and probably acted as a trigger event to encourage a military coup that had been brewing for some time. Soon after the coup, the new political regime revalued the domestic currency. In other cases, the outcome of implementation efforts is significantly altered in the bureaucratic arena, through the activities of implementors within government. A good example of this is the case of Jamaica, where the government developed a policy of export-led growth and selected the medium-scale apparel industry as the leader for that strategy.

> In the process of implementation, those responsible...created conditions that brought multinational garment manufacturers to Jamaica and in the process virtually destroyed domestic producers who were the intended beneficiaries of the policy. They also encountered conditions very different from those expected. The most serious was that the labor force was not well prepared for working in a large factory environment. The result was an outcome that was a serious departure from the original understanding of the policy statement. It was a case of the implementors actually determining the policy.

In another case, that of water management reform in India, an outcome was determined by the implementors who opposed the reform and effectively stymied a proposed change before it was ever officially decided upon. The demands of the World Bank for placing charges on water were rejected, even at the risk of losing Bank funding, because the implementors recognized that they did not have the political or administrative capacity to collect fees from millions of water consumers. Again, the implementors played a key role in determining the outcome of a reform initiative. In each of these examples, policy characteristics strongly influenced the arena of resistance and response.

Characteristics of the Reform

Identifying the inherent characteristics of a reform enables analysts and policymakers to predict responses to the decision, understand the stakes involved, and assess the resources available to deal with that response. In the following pages we indicate important characteristics of reform content that strongly influence whether response to implementation will occur in the public or the bureaucratic arena. In this, we go beyond most analyses that either ignore implementation or assume that implementation problems are a result of insufficient "political will" or weak institutions of government.

Scenario One: Reaction in the Public Arena

The outcome of some reforms is largely determined by societal response to efforts to change existing conditions. An assessment of our cases suggests a series of hypotheses about the characteristics of reforms that are sustained, shaped, altered, or rejected in the public arena. In large part, the characteristics of these reforms result in changes that 1) have a direct impact on broad sectors of the society or on politically important interests in society, and 2) are readily visible to the affected publics. In such cases public response is likely to be strong, as it was in Ghana after the devaluation. Moreover, the stakes in pursuing such reforms can be very high and even threaten the existence of a political regime. In such cases, reformers must be able to count on considerable political "capital" if the reform is to be sustained. Where this is not the case, considerable thought needs to be given to accumulating support and managing public opposition as part of a strategy of implementation devised by policymakers.

Based on evidence in our cases, we propose that reforms with the following characteristics will create a response that is public, will involve stakes in managing that response that are high, and will require skills in political management, solid political support, and considerable regime stability and legitimacy if the reform is to be sustained.

Dispersion of Costs

If the costs or burden of the reform have a direct impact on the public or on politically important groups in society, opposition will emerge during implementation. The best example of such a policy is increasing the price on an important commodity such as water or food, especially as such a decision often represents the reversal of a previous policy to subsidize such prices. The costs of such a decision are borne by a large segment of the population and are generally met with considerable protest. Economists are frequently concerned with the issue of who bears the burden of short-term costs of policy change. Dispersion of costs is a characteristic that captures much of this issue but without making a set of inferences, common among economists, about the primacy of short-term utility maximization over the distribution of longer-term benefits (see Olson 1965). Instead, in this analysis the dispersion of cost is used as an indication that reactions to policy change will be in a public and political arena.

Concentration of Benefits in Government

Frequently, reforms that impose broadly dispersed costs directly on a population also generate direct benefits that are not widely understood or valued by the same population. Thus, when the benefits of a reform are concentrated within government, such as those that accrue to the public budget or the efficiency of the public sector, their impact is not likely to be directly felt by the public. Using the same example of price increases, the benefits of such increases accrue to the public budget, a situation that is unlikely to create significant popular support. A similar case would be one in which a public enterprise is to be privatized. Opposition to such a change could be anticipated from managers and staff of the enterprise and a variety of groups who might have benefited from the public enterprise. In contrast, the anticipated benefits of a stronger budget or more efficient and profitable management of the enterprise would be unlikely to generate support other than among decision makers. Concentrated benefits generally do not create a countervailing force to offset the public opposition that widely dispersed and felt costs have generated.

Low Administrative and/or Technical Content

If the implementation of a policy change does not require depth and continuity of administrative resources or highly technical skills to sustain it, it is more likely to be introduced as planned. In some cases, such reforms—such as a price increase—are almost "self-implementing." Nevertheless, sustainability will be determined by public reaction, which is often strong because of the same reform's broad and relatively undifferentiated impact. Policies such as devaluation or changes in mandated prices that are relatively self-implementing, in the sense that they require little in the way of technical or administrative infrastructure to carry them out, will have a broadly felt and immediate impact and any negative reaction that is generated will be forthcoming quickly.[20]

Short Duration

The length of time needed to implement a reform also has an important influence on the response it generates. If the full impact of the change is immediately visible—again, the example of a price increase is relevant—the response is likely to be stronger and more public. Thus, the effect of the Ghana devaluation was easily apparent to most Ghanaians. Within days, the results were very clear in the market in terms of much higher prices and many fewer foreign goods. The reaction among those adversely affected was also not long in coming.

Reforms with some or all of these four characteristics create strong reactions that are likely to be played out in the public arena. Politically, they frequently bring about the mobilization of existing pressure groups or encourage the formation of new ones to oppose the reform. These groups exert pressure on political leadership and public officials to reverse or alter the decision in a variety of ways. Some of the more dramatic make international headlines, such as the protests that followed the partial removal of the subsidy on bread in Egypt or the coup that followed devaluation in Ghana. Moreover, reforms with these characteristics can give impetus to longer-term organized opposition to the government. Policy reforms that generate response primarily in the public arena therefore often carry very high stakes for the regime and for incumbent political elites. The legitimacy of the regime itself can be called into question, as was the case in Ghana. Less dramatically, the stability of a government and its capacity to take other needed measures may be affected by such reactions. Certainly the sustainability of the reform is called into question if strong public reactions emerge during its implementation.

The political calculus of reformers, confronted with a decision that will precipitate reaction to implementation in the public arena, must be grounded in an evaluation of the resources available to deal with such reactions. A series of questions illuminate the political resources that can be important in introducing and sustaining this kind of visible reform. First, how legitimate is the regime? If the government has strong, broad-based public support, it is not likely to be threatened by public opposition on a single issue. A tradition of political stability that makes changes of government unusual on the basis of a single issue is thus an asset. A related question is whether the reform stands alone or is one of a series of unpopular actions so that it might become the "straw that breaks the camel's back." If so, the question of timing becomes important, to allow the government the opportunity to assess and replenish its political bases of support. Third, how autonomous is the government? If it depends on one or two extremely powerful interests, then the issue of how the reform will affect those interests becomes exceedingly important. Finally, is there an elite consensus in support of the reform? What is the likely response of the press, the financial community, the private sector, the military, or religious leaders? If the government can rely on these groups for overt support or obtain some assurance that they will not be mobilized in the opposition, then prospects for sustaining the policy, the administration, or the regime improve. An example of this type of elite consensus comes from the case of Costa Rica, where a new export-led growth strategy was carefully negotiated and tailored to achieve a broad elite consensus and to rotate the costs of adjustment among affected groups.

In some cases, policymakers appeared to have decided that such political resources were not sufficient to overcome the strong reaction in the public arena that they anticipated. In the Philippines, agrarian reform was supported by some officials, some members of the elite such as the church and leaders of nongovernmental organizations, and the international community as a way of countering the insurgent New People's Army and creating greater equity in the countryside. However, decision makers anticipated serious opposition to land reform from some powerful elites and believed that to move ahead could bring the regime into serious jeopardy. Therefore, they delayed action by referring the issue to the new Congress, then to various committees, and finally, almost two years later, they enacted a much modified agrarian reform act. The case of water management reform in India is a case of implementors resisting a proposed policy reform because they believed that they could not count on sufficient political resources to impose an unpopular change. In Ghana, policy elites would have benefited from such a realistic assessment of their political resources prior to moving ahead with a major devaluation.

Scenario Two: Reaction in the Bureaucratic Arena

The outcome of some reforms is largely determined by how bureaucratic agencies, public officials, and administrative routines respond to the changes. In some of our cases, characteristics of the reforms meant that such agencies, officials, and routines sustained, shaped, altered, or rejected the changes. In these cases, the results 1) did not have a direct impact on large sectors of the population, and 2) were not as readily apparent to the public as they were to insiders in government. In Kenya, decisions to decentralize and to reorganize a ministry were actively supported or resisted by public officials, but went largely unnoticed by the general public. In Mali, the implementation of a new health program was stymied within the bureaucracy. During its unraveling, little protest or reaction was heard from low-income rural Malians who were to have been the beneficiaries of a more available and appropriate health system.

Based on cases such as these, we propose that the implementation of reforms with the following characteristics will be played out primarily in the bureaucratic arena, the stakes for the government will be much lower than if response is generated in the public arena, and the emphasis in implementing and sustaining the reform will be on competence and compliance of the bureaucracy.

Concentration of Costs in Government

When the costs of a reform are narrowly focused to affect primarily the government budget or government institutions, they are not likely to be felt directly or immediately by the public. Resistance or opposition to such change will tend to arise in the bureaucracy. The reorganization of the Ministry of Agriculture in Kenya and the resuscitation of the planning agencies in Colombia and Argentina meant shifts in power in the bureaucracy, but had little apparent impact elsewhere. The outcome in each case thus rested on the response of the administrative system.

Dispersion of Benefits

Reforms that concentrate costs in the government often have broadly dispersed benefits that become visible only in the longer term. Thus, the public may benefit over the long term from the reorganization of a ministry or the creation of a primary health care system, but the direct impact is initially borne by officials and institutions that are required to alter accustomed forms of behavior and relinquish accustomed forms of security. The public support such reforms generate may eventually be a countervailing force to opposition to change that may arise in the bureaucracy but the administrators are likely to become aware of the costs long before the public appreciates the benefits. This situation is illustrated in the case of a new rural health system in Mali.

High Administrative and/or Technical Content

If the administrative content of implementing a policy is high or if it is technically complex, it requires the coordinated efforts of public officials and institutions to see that it is correctly carried out. In this case of nonself-implementing reforms the public is unlikely to be immediately affected by its implementation or to be fully aware of the costs and benefits it may impose. In this situation, implementation depends on competence and support in the bureaucracy. This was the case with trade reform and the apparel industry in Jamaica, where the policy was significantly altered by technicians in the government long before the targeted beneficiaries became aware that these changes were harmful to their interests.

Long Duration

The longer the time needed to implement a reform, the more likely that conflict, resistance, and capacity within the administrative system will determine the implementability and sustainability of the reform. In Indonesia, the rice marketing agency, BULOG, responded to the government's price and supply stabilization program over a twenty-year period. Time allowed BULOG to solidify its bureaucratic power so it could do things in the mid-1980s that it could not have accomplished in the early 1970s.

If a reform has some or all of these four characteristics, reaction will take place largely within the bureaucratic arena and the success of implementation will depend on the capacity and support of the bureaucracy. Opposition in the bureaucracy often comes from resistance to change or loss of power and may range from overt opposition to quiet sabotage or inaction. In some cases, alliances between factions in the bureaucracy and external interests or clienteles can result in piecemeal sabotage of the intent of the policymakers. In addition, lack of capacity within the administrative apparatus can lead to implementation failure, however inadvert.

When the response to a policy reform takes place in the bureaucratic arena, the political stakes for a government are relatively low. The real issues are whether the capacity exists to implement the reform and whether there is support for the reform that will cause the bureaucracy to comply with the intention of the decision. Whatever happens, the issue is the viability of the reform and not the survival of the regime. Stakes tend to focus on individual or agency goals. The government and the decision makers have a stake in the implementation of the reform or they probably would not have undergone the risks of change. Individual and collective credibility can be enhanced by effective government action and weakened in its absence. Individual officials in government may have very high personal stakes in being perceived as effective leaders, moving upward in their careers, acquiring greater resources for their agencies, or achieving greater efficiency in their work. Nevertheless, compared to the high stakes of reforms played out in the public arena, these are not ones that are likely to imply major political or economic upheaval.

From organization theory and experience we know that bureaucracies fight intensely for territory and power. We also know that change is hard to achieve and that hierarchical directives do not necessarily bring action. In Kenya, for instance, the directive of the permanent secretary of agriculture was not enough to bring about the reorganization of the top administrative staff of the ministry. Thus, the task of implementing a policy change cannot be taken for granted and those with a stake in a policy change need to consider what resources they have available to encourage the implementation and sustainability of reform.

The resources for bringing about change in a bureaucracy are relatively well-known: high-level political support; organizational or hierarchical authority; capacity for consensus building; behavioral incentives; and administrative capacity. The support of political leaders is often critical in such reforms. For example, in Kenya, decentralization of development planning and implementation stagnated for three years before anything of substance happened. It was only after a new president assumed office in 1978 and gave his full support to the policy because of his need to broaden the base of participation in the political system that real change took place. Organizational power may come from a public reputation or from alliances with organizations or interests outside the bureaucracy. Control of budget, personnel appointment and promotion, and control of support services ranging from transportation to purchasing are important elements of bureaucratic power, as we saw in the case of Mali. Moreover, decision makers need to think clearly about the administrative capacity of the organization to implement change. In Indonesia, BULOG's mission was important enough that, over time, it was given the authority and financial and human resources needed to carry out its policy mission. In Colombia, the combination of high-level political support and authority, the building of an elite consensus for planning over time, and the enhancement of technical capacity enabled the planning agency to strengthen its position in government.

It is clear that decision making is only one step in the policy reform process. Policymakers who focus on the decision and neglect the implementation process do so at their own peril. In Jamaica, decision makers left the implementation of trade policy reform entirely to the bureaucracy. The result was not at all what the policymakers intended. More generally, our cases suggest that an assessment of the characteristics of a policy is critical because it enables policy reformers to determine where response to policy change will occur, what the stakes will be, and what resources will be needed to implement and sustain the policy reform. The review of the hazards of introducing change should not discourage policy elites from making such difficult decisions, but rather should help them develop a strategy for dealing with the public and bureaucratic responses to their actions. Table 4 summarizes the hypotheses about policy characteristics, response to change, and stakes. It also suggests the kinds of resources that reformers should try to mobilize within implementation strategies.

Conclusion

Policy reform will continue to be an important issue facing the governments of many developing countries as they seek to enhance opportunities for economic growth and social welfare. It will also continue to be a process that varies from one country to another in important ways and that will require intimate knowledge of a particular country's environment and immediate situation if its potential is to be fully analyzed for that country. Indeed, current practice in defining the conditions necessary for the introduction and pursuit of reform has relied, in significant measure, on the often well-developed political instincts of policymakers in particular contexts. In contrast, this chapter has presented an initial discussion of more generalized dynamics of policy and institutional changes as they are understood by participants in such initiatives. In this undertaking, we have attempted to illuminate aspects of agenda setting, decision making, and implementation that are conventionally treated as if they occurred within a "black box," especially by dominant theories in political science and political economy.

Going beyond most political economy frameworks, we have tried to link theory and practice and to make some of the concerns of policymakers more explicit. The chapter has suggested that decision makers have considerable scope to shape and influence the space available for reformist initiatives. We have focused on the role of the circumstances that surround a decision because they appear to be an important determinant of the who, how, and why of decision making. Finally, we have attempted to close the gap between decision and implementation, too often ignored in both theory and practice. Unlike much current thinking, we suggest that outcomes of policy change are not just successful or unsuccessful implementation, but a range of possible outcomes. Thus, a strategic plan of implementation must accompany any decision to change policy.

A global look at the political economy of policy reform runs the risk of generalizing so broadly that it is meaningless; alternatively, discussions of particular situations in specific countries often focus on the idiosyncratic. This chapter has attempted to avoid those two extremes and provide some new insights, based on a range of country experiences, that can serve as the basis for further research into the political economy of policy reform. Ultimately, such work should assist policy reformers to pursue change more effectively. ∾

Table 1   Cases In Policy and Institutional Reform

Policy Type	Country	Year(s)	Source(s)
Macroeconomic policy			
Devaluation	Ghana	1971	Policy advisers Published and unpublished papers
Structural adjustment	Korea	1960-66	Policy adviser Published and unpublished papers
Development strategy	Costa Rica	1948-81 1982-88	Senior policymaker Supporting documentation in Ph.D. thesis
Sectoral policy			
Agrarian reform	Philippines	1986-88	Policy adviser Supporting documentation Published and unpublished papers
Primary health care	Mali	1975-79	Policy adviser Published papers
Rice pricing	Indonesia	1972-73; 1986	Policy adviser Published and unpublished papers
Public water supply	India	1980-88	Senior policy implementor
Export manufacturing	Jamaica	1982-88	Senior policy implementor
Organizational change			
Decentralization	Kenya	1976-78	Policy adviser
Planning	Colombia	1966	Policy adviser
Planning agency	Argentina	1962	Policy adviser
Reorganization of ministry	Kenya	1978-79	Policy adviser

Table 2 Factors Influencing Policy and Institutional Reform Choice

Factors Influencing Decision making	Criteria of Choice	Influential Actors
Technical analysis	Information, analyses, and options presented by technical advisers, experts	Technocrats, ministers, and other high-level bureaucrats; Foreign advisers
Bureaucratic motivation	Career objectives of individuals; Competitive position of units; Budgets	Ministers and other high level bureaucrats; Middle-level bureaucrats; International bureaucrats and advisers
Political stability and support	Stability of political system; Calculus of costs and benefits to groups, classes, interests; Military support or opposition	Political leadership; Dominant economic elites; Leaders of class, ethnic, interest associations; Military
International leverage	Access to aid; Loans; Trading relations	IMF, USAID, World Bank; Governments of former colonial powers; USA, international banks

Table 3	Agenda Setting and Decision making	
Agenda	Characteristics of Decision Process	Policy Elites Most Concerned About ...
Perceived crisis	Frequently, problems pressed upon decision makers by interests outside of government; High political and economic stakes; Small groups of high-level decision makers closely involved; Major changes from prior policy (innovation); Sense of urgency to act, "do something."	Macropolitical issues such as legitimacy, social stability, costs and benefits to major national interests, duration of regime in power.
Politics-as-usual	Frequently, problems "chosen" by decision makers for action; Low political and economic stakes; Middle- and lower-level officials involved, dependent on high-level support for action; Incremental changes in existing policy or institution; Little sense of urgency, with promoters of reform able to control extent of emphasis on change.	Bureaucratic issues such as careers, budgets, compliance and responsiveness of implementors, incentives to modify bureaucratic behavior and procedures, agency power within government; Micropolitical issues such as clientelism and narrow coalition building.

Table 4   Characteristics of Policies and Their Implications for Implementation and Sustainability

Characteristics of Policy	Arena of Response	Stakes	Resources for Sustainability
Scenario I			
Impact			
Dispersed cost			
Concentrated benefits		High:	Government
benefits		At risk is	legitimacy, stability,
	Public	the government's	support of elites,
		viability	or relative auton-
			omy from elites;
			Skills in political
Visibility			management
Low administrative/			
technical content			
Short duration			
Scenario II			
Impact			
Concentrated costs			
Dispersed benefits		Low:	Bureaucratic
		At issue is	capacity, high-level
	Bureaucratic	the substance	support, hierarchi-
Visibility		of the reform	cal discipline,
High administrative/			consensus, behavioral
technical content			incentives
Long duration			

Notes

1 This is a revised version of a paper written in October 1987 under the auspices of the Employment and Enterprise Policy Analysis Project at the Harvard Institute for International Development and funded by the Agency for International Development. Tony Killick, Richard Hook, Richard Mallon, Joseph Stern, Michael Roemer, David Cole, Stephan Haggard, Richard Cash, and Peter Timmer contributed insightful cases through an HIID workshop. Gregory Gottlieb served as rapporteur for the workshop. We have also benefited from the useful suggestions of Dwight Perkins, Michael Roemer, Richard Hook, Donald Snodgrass, Richard Mallon, Marguerite Robinson, Brian Levy, John Sheahan, Judith Tendler, Ravi Gulhati, and others. We are particularly grateful to numerous public officials from developing countries who have helped shape our perspectives about the political economy of reform. Those who have been mid-career students at the Kennedy School of Government have been generous in sharing their experiences with us. Among others, we would like to thank Shyam Bajpai, Raymond Broize, Ncedo Mlamla, Evelyne Rodriguez-Ortega, Valerie Veira, and Yiwei Wang for their participation in a seminar on policy reform. Eduardo Doryan-Garrón also contributed substantively to our research effort.

A slightly revised version of this chapter also appeared in *Policy Sciences* 22:213-248, 1989.

2 We define macroeconomic issues as those which have a wide impact on a national economy, regardless of sector. Exchange rates, interest rates, and inflation rates are examples of macroeconomic issues. Sectoral issues refer to those which primarily affect the economic conditions or performance of a particular sector of the economy, such as agriculture or industry. Organizational issues refer to those that affect the performance and responsiveness of public institutions such as ministries and state-owned enterprises. The advocacy of reforms in macroeconomic and sectoral policies and institutions is reflected in publications such as World Bank (1984; 1986); Balassa et al. (1986); and USAID (1982). For a discussion, see Cohen, Grindle, and Walker (1985).

3 The term reform is used advisedly throughout this paper. Those promoting particular policy and organizational changes consider that they are attempting to bring about reform, a change that will lead to a more desirable outcome than current practice permits. However, policies do not always achieve the goals intended by their proponents. Moreover, what is a more desirable outcome for one may be a less desirable outcome for another. We do not consider reform necessarily to constitute improvement. We personally do not consider all the proposed reforms advocated either in our own cases or in the broader literature of policy liberalization and reform to be necessarily better. We believe that we can analyze the process and why it worked, or didn't, without making any judgment on whether the reform proposition should have been adopted.

4 The term *policy elites* is used throughout the paper to refer to political and bureaucratic officials who have decision-making responsibilities in government and whose decisions become authoritative for society. It is a term used

interchangeably with "decision makers," "policymakers," and "policy planners."

5 During the academic year 1986-87, the Harvard Institute for International Development sponsored a workshop series on "Promoting Policy Reform in Developing Countries" through the Employment and Enterprise Policy Analysis Project. At each session, individuals who were involved in reform initiatives as advisers to government described processes of change in which they participated. During the academic year 1987-88, the Kennedy School of Government at Harvard University offered a six-week seminar course in which officials from developing countries prepared cases about reform initiatives in which they had been involved. The quotations in the paper all come from oral or written presentations of these cases.

6 The differences between society-centered and state-centered theories are not trivial. Promoters of reform who adopt a society-centered explanation of policy, for example, would be well advised to concentrate efforts on mobilizing interest group activities or attempting to create coalitions and alliances of classes and interests to influence authoritative decision making by government. If, on the other hand, a state-centered explanation of policy is adopted, reformers might better concentrate effort on directly influencing the perceptions of decision makers about the goals and content of policy. Useful discussions of society-centered and state-centered theories of political economy are found in Skocpol (1985) and Nordlinger (1987).

7 Early in the Marxist literature, Engels (1968, 290) argued that at particular historical moments, no class may be dominant, allowing an enduring apparatus of the state to acquire some independence and ability to establish and pursue policies, even those that have a detrimental impact on the possessing classes.

8 Pluralist approaches to explaining policy choice are found in many texts on American politics. A classic statement of "interest group politics" is Truman (1951). See also Dahl (1961; 1971) and Lane (1959). Early political science discussions of political development implicitly adopted pluralist models that focused on "inputs" and "outputs" but not on how one was transformed into the other. See, for example, Almond and Coleman (1960) and Apter (1965). More recently, Tony Killick (1976) has used a pluralist approach in explaining development policy making as a "balancing act" among competing interests, "a process of conflict-resolution in which social tranquility and the maintenance of power is a basic concern ..." (176).

9 Olson (1982) argues that the search for rents constricts a country's economic growth rate and eventually brings it to a stop. Only a major crisis—a war, for example—will break the stronghold of rent-seeking groups on economic development. The solution to the problem of the state and the capacity of policy to distort resource allocation is to limit closely the activities permitted to fall under the regulatory power of the state (Buchanan 1980; Colander 1984, 5). According to Bennett and DiLorenzo (1984, 217), "the problem of reforming the rent-seeking society is widely perceived to be the adoption of an appropriate set of rules to limit the burdens of government. The power of the state and its burden on the private sector have been associated with public

service expenditure and employment, both of which have increased dramatically over the past decades in both the United States and the rest of the industrialized world. Thus, reform has centered on efforts, particularly in the United States, to restrict by constitutional amendment the ability of the government to borrow, tax, and spend. Revenue is regarded as the lifeblood of the public sector, so that, if public sector income is limited, the intrusiveness and burden of government can be controlled and the negative-sum game of rent-seeking contained."

10 Public choice theory promotes a view of politics that is both negative and cynical, perhaps in reaction to earlier assumptions among many economists that the purpose of the state was to facilitate the workings of the market and to safeguard "the public interest" (Srinivasan 1985, 45). There is little room in this perspective for public officials who adhere to particular ideologies, whose professional training provides them with independent judgement in the analysis of policy issues, or who may adopt goals that transcend the interests of any particular group. See Adler (1987); Orren (1988, 15).

11 In the sense used here, rational actors are those who accumulate all available information in order to understand and assess a particular problem. They consider all possible options for responding to the problem and select the alternative that most efficiently enables them to achieve their stated goals.

12 The important role ascribed to technical analysis in policy choice may reflect the fact that technocratic elites are central figures in policy making circles in many developing countries and the process of decision making itself is relatively closed and even secret. A supporting factor may be the complexity of the issues that political leaders are expected to address in shaping development policies in their countries, and the need to explain their decision in terms of the promotion of the national goal of development.

13 See chapter 8, "Food Price Stabilization: Rationale, Design, and Implementation," in this volume for a discussion by Peter Timmer of the role of technical analysis in decision making in Indonesia.

14 For cases in the literature, see Grindle (1977) and Thomas (1975).

15 In addition, the principal funder, USAID, terminated the funding for the reform initiative.

16 In a considerable amount of scholarly work, regime maintenance goals have been adopted as a way of explaining why certain policy options are "off-limits" because they impose heavy costs on important groups in the society. They are also used to explain how government actions are employed as "pay-offs" to maintain the loyalty of important groups or interests. See Bates (1981); Haggard (1985). This element of decision making is frequently salient in many developing countries because of the fragility of the coalitions that support incumbent regimes and because of the limited legitimacy that makes them vulnerable to the performance expectations of supporters (see Ames 1987). At the broadest level, Bates (1981, 4) has argued that regime maintenance becomes the single most important factor in explaining the perpetuation of economically irrational development policies. "Governments want to stay in power. They must appease powerful interests. And people turn

to political action to secure special advantages—rewards they are unable to secure by competing in the marketplace."

17 The international leverage element is of considerable importance in a period of international economic crisis when foreign donors, governments, and international agencies can put extensive pressure on developing country governments to make recommended choices and can command extensive technical expertise to influence decision makers. It is also encountered in efforts to explain such issues as technology choice and institutional reform that become conditional on "rewards" from international actors.

18 As we have defined it, a situation of crisis exists when 1) decision makers believe a crisis exists; 2) there is general consensus among them that the situation of crisis is real and of a threatening nature; and 3) they believe that failure to act will lead to even more serious economic and political realities.

19 In addition to a situation of crisis, however, it should be recognized that some policy decisions—such as a devaluation—must be decided secretly and announced as fait accompli to minimize opportunities for speculation.

20 It should be noted that policies that are relatively self-implementing may have a high technical content during the decision-making process.

4

Economic Reform in The Gambia:

Policies, Politics, Foreign Aid, and Luck

Malcolm F. McPherson and Steven C. Radelet[1]

Malcolm F. McPherson is a research associate at HIID. From 1985 to 1989, he was director of the Economic and Financial Policy Analyses Project and senior adviser to the Ministry of Finance and Trade of The Gambia.

Steven C. Radelet is an Institute associate at HIID and a lecturer on economics at Harvard University. From 1986 to 1988, he was an adviser to the Ministry of Finance and Trade of The Gambia.

Introduction

In 1985, the government of The Gambia introduced the Economic Recovery Program (ERP) in response to an economic crisis which had been deepening since the early 1980s. Within eighteen months, the economy had stabilized and was growing. The Gambia's reform effort has been unusual because of the quick economic turnaround and because the government implemented the program with remarkably little overt public opposition. President Sir Dawda Jawara and his People's Progressive Party (PPP) were reelected with 60 percent of the vote just nineteen months after introducing the ERP.

This paper gives a brief summary of The Gambia's economic crisis and subsequent recovery. The factors that contributed to the recovery—the ERP reforms, foreign aid, lucky breaks in rainfall and world prices, and The Gambia's political environment—are examined. The paper concludes with some observations on the government's experiences in implementing its reform program.

The Emergence of Disequilibria

The Gambia is the smallest and one of the most densely populated countries in Africa. It stretches along the banks of the Gambia River in the western-most part of Africa, completely surrounded by Senegal, except for its narrow Atlantic coast. Agriculture and trade are the mainstays of the economy, and groundnuts are the leading domestically produced export. Other important exports include fish and shrimp. The Gambia's location, open borders, and low tariff structure make it an active entrepot for reexports to the rest of the subregion.

Many factors, both external and internal, were associated with the economic deterioration which preceded the introduction of the ERP. Rapidly rising prices for imports (including petroleum products), the long Sahelian drought, low world prices for groundnuts, declining foreign aid flows, high international interest rates, poor planning, mismanagement, and inappropriate fiscal and monetary policies all contributed to the growing imbalances. The adverse effects of some factors, such as the overvalued exchange rate and the government budget deficit, were evident in the late 1970s (McPherson 1979). However, it was not until early 1982, when foreign payment arrears began to accumulate rapidly, that the full extent of The Gambia's difficulties emerged. From that point on, the economy rapidly deteriorated.

One way of placing the change in The Gambia's economic circumstances in perspective is to compare the country's economic performance during the first and second decades after independence, 1965/66 to 1975/76 and 1975/76 to 1985/86. The year 1975/76 is a useful dividing point as it marks the time when several important structural changes occurred. Externally, the first oil shock began to have a major impact on world prices, the international donors sharply increased their aid, and the pattern of rainfall became increasingly erratic. Internally, the introduction of the First National Development Plan dramatically changed the government's role in the economy. The comparison ends with 1985/86 because by then some of the measures introduced under the ERP, particularly the exchange rate reform, the liberalization of rice marketing, and improved budget discipline, were beginning to take effect. It was also the time when The Gambia's international financial standing began to improve once the country's arrears to the International Monetary Fund (IMF) were paid. Table 1 gives selected data from the two decades. (The data in column 4 will be examined later in the chapter.)

A comparison of the second and third columns reveals a marked divergence in economic performance over the two decades. During the first decade, aggregate real income increased substantially, average per capita income rose, inflation was moderate, and the foreign exchange rate was stable (indeed, the dalasi was revalued 20 percent in 1973[2]). Foreign exchange reserves accumulated, foreign debt was small, the government's recurrent budget was in balance, average groundnut production was high and increasing, and imports were broadly in line with exports. However, during the second decade, aggregate real income grew slowly (after 1981/82, real income declined), average per capita income fell, inflation accelerated, the foreign exchange rate depreciated, foreign debt increased sharply, and foreign payment arrears reached $114 million—equivalent to 58.5 percent of Gross Domestic Product (GDP)—by mid-1986. The government budget became unbalanced, development expenditure expanded rapidly with no major positive impact on aggregate output, foreign exchange reserves were depleted, average groundnut production declined, and imports increased well beyond the country's export capacity.

Whereas the decade 1965/66 to 1975/76 had left The Gambia in basic balance, both internally and externally, the decade 1975/76 to 1985/86 left the economy with unsustainable imbalances in both the domestic budget and the balance of payments. Real income was declining, the currency was unstable, the marketing board was insolvent, inflation was accelerating, and the country's foreign debt could not be serviced.

The economic deterioration had several causes.[3] Externally, the petroleum price increases of 1973 and 1979 sharply raised the foreign exchange cost of fuel; the prolonged Sahelian drought reduced agricultural production, simultaneously lowering agricultural exports and raising staple food imports; international inflation increased the costs of manufactured imports; and foreign aid and soft loans, which had increased dramatically in the second half of the 1970s, declined in the early 1980s as developed countries reoriented their aid programs. The international prices of agricultural products (specifically groundnuts) fell as the agricultural surpluses generated by subsidies in the EEC, United States, and Japan depressed world market prices; and international interest rates rose as the major industrial countries tightened their monetary policies in order to control inflation and the United States increased its borrowing to cover its budget deficit.

The impact of these external events on the Gambian economy was aggravated by inappropriate economic policies and administrative weaknesses. In retrospect, the planned development expenditure was too large and too poorly managed to have produced a long-term positive effect on economic growth and development. The high levels of subsidies on rice, fertilizer, electricity, and transport services increased parastatal losses, and diverted resources from productive investment. Price controls on staples, such as rice, cooking oil, and meat, undermined farmers' incomes. The overvalued exchange rate and export tax on groundnuts depressed revenues from, and investment in, agriculture. The result was that the contribution of agriculture to GDP declined by 7.5 percentage points during the decade 1975/76 to 1985/86 (Table 1). Government budgetary

Table 1 The Gambia: Selected Data, 1965/66 to 1987/88

Item	1965/66-1975/76	1975/76-1985/86	1985/86-1987/88
Real GDP	+69.6%	+34.2%	+11.2%
Real GDP per capita	+36.7%	-4.5%	+3.9%
Consumer prices	+70.6%	+251.8%	+64.2%
Value of dalasi (rel. to U.S. $)	-24.0%	-98.6%	-56.2%
External debt (U.S. $)	+$10.1m	+$488.8m	+$168.3m
External arrears (U.S. $)	0	+$101.0m	-$67.0m
Gov. exp.(% of GDP)	17.5%	33.5%	37.1%
Development exp.(% of GDP)	3.9%	12.8%	13.4%
Gov. def.(excl. grants) (% of GDP)	2.6%	13.2%	19.5%
Gov. def.(incl. grants) (% of GDP)	1.6%	8.3%	7.7%
Net foreign assets	+D51.3m	-D652.5m	+D408.7m
Net domestic credit	+D41.0m	+D469.3m	-D245.1m
Commercial bank loans/advances	+D30.3m	+D367.6m	-D107.3m
Net bank credit to government	+D10.6m	+D101.7m	-D137.8m
Money supply	+421.6%	+338.6%	+73.4%
Avg. annual g/nut purchases (thousand tons)	122.9	88.5	59.8
Avg. g/nut price (1976/77 U.S. $)	$556.6/t	$490.8/t	$298.3/t
GPMB's reserves	+D78m	-D108m	—
Agricultural output (share in GDP)	37.5%	30%	29.4%
Average annual rainfall Yundum	1049mm	870mm	841mm
Georgetown	843mm	708mm	853mm
Basse	607mm	822mm	867mm
Domestic exports annual average	D42.1m	D68.6m	D78.1m
Exports (incl. reexports)	D43.2m	D139.8m	D431.3m
Imports (annual average)	D56.8m	D272.5m	D741.0m
Current account deficit	D15.9m	D187.7m	D344.2m
Official transfers and net loans (annual average)	D2.7m	D92.6m	D292.0m

D = Dalasi, currency of The Gambia

Source: Statistics and Special Studies Unit, Ministry of Finance and Trade

118

discipline eroded as public employment expanded sharply,[4] supplementary appropriations became a regular feature of government budgeting, and revenue collection procedures broke down. In addition to its impact on agriculture, the overvalued exchange rate switched demand to imports and reduced the profitability of nonagricultural exports and import substitutes. Further pressure on the balance of payments resulted from the drought-induced decline in groundnut production and food crops.

Despite the massive increase in foreign borrowing and investment relative to GDP, productive capacity per worker declined. The government's increased involvement in the economy through the creation of parastatals and investment incentives such as tax abatements, guaranteed loans, and subsidized credit did not provide the anticipated impetus to development. Due to administered prices, unproductive investment, mismanagement, and poor cost recovery, the parastatals made no net positive financial contribution to the economy. Indeed, during the period 1979 to 1982, parastatal losses were D121.6 million (World Bank 1985, Table 7.1). Together with the government budget deficit, the whole public sector became a serious drain on the economy.

Many developing countries have sustained internal imbalances for long periods with policies which insulate them from the rest of the world. Because The Gambia is a small, open economy, with a liberal pattern of trade and exchange, insulation did not (and could not) occur. However, there was some delay in the onset of the economy's difficulties. Many of the adverse trends, such as the decline in exports relative to imports, higher rates of inflation, mounting pressure on the budget, and the erosion of foreign exchange reserves, were evident as early as 1977/78. Nevertheless, the economy was cushioned from these difficulties for several years by the availability of foreign exchange reserves (which had reached the equivalent of ten months' imports in 1974/75), the country's ability to borrow abroad, and the low levels of debt service (because most of the loans contracted in the 1970s had grace periods of six to ten years).

Pressure on the economy increased in phases. Net foreign assets became negative in 1979, payment arrears began to accumulate in mid-1980, and the parallel foreign exchange market emerged in 1982. The government's attempt to raise groundnut producer prices in 1982/83 (in response to IMF pressure to increase farmer incentives) technically bankrupted the Gambia Produce Marketing Board (GPMB) when world prices fell sharply. The 25 percent devaluation of the dalasi in February 1984 merely postponed more decisive action. The foreign exchange position was further aggravated by the large food imports needed to cover the shortfalls in the 1983/84 harvest. By late 1984, the cumulative effects of these factors had seriously affected business confidence. Private investment activity virtually ceased, and capital flight increased significantly.

Though the situation had been serious, it became untenable when The Gambia fell into arrears with the IMF and the standby program which had been negotiated in mid-1984 was cancelled. The foreign exchange situation continued to deteriorate. Gross foreign exchange reserves fell to the equivalent of two weeks of imports, and arrears to the IMF and other international creditors mounted rapidly. By mid-1985 they were approximately SDR (Special Drawing Rights) 58.5 million (U.S. $75 million). Disbursements on many development projects were suspended, normal short-term credit facilities were withdrawn, and rice and petrol shortages became common. The premium for foreign exchange in the parallel market reached 50 percent. A general sense of malaise was evident. The pressure intensified when the managing director of the IMF began formal proceedings to have The Gambia declared ineligible to borrow. Other donors added to this pressure when they made it clear that, unless the government changed its economic policies, there was little that they would, or could, do to assist.[5] Time had run out for The Gambia in international financial circles.

The Economic Recovery Program

When it became evident that the international community had no intention of rescuing The Gambia financially, the government had to act. Accordingly, Minister of Finance and Trade Sheriff Sisay assembled a task force of senior officials in June 1985 to develop a reform program. Sisay assigned staff from the Ministry of Finance and Trade,[6] the Ministry of Economic Planning and Industrial Development, and the Central Bank of The Gambia (Central Bank) to the task force. He also asked two expatriates to participate—an economic adviser in the Ministry of Finance and a World Bank economist. Sisay told the members of the task force to design as comprehensive a program as was needed to reverse The Gambia's economic decline and return it to a sustainable growth path. He instructed them not to be concerned with the political consequences of reform measures. Sisay wanted the task force to design an economically sound program—others would deal with political acceptability.

After meeting continuously for a week, the task force produced a report which formed the basis of the Economic Recovery Program. The major elements of this program—exchange rate reform, the promotion of agriculture, the promotion of other productive sectors, civil service and parastatal reform, monetary and fiscal policy measures, and the reorientation of the Public Investment Program (PIP)—were announced in the 1985/86 Budget Speech. Implementation began immediately. The Ministry of Finance liberalized rice importation and marketing, sharply increased the producer price of groundnuts, and eliminated the fish export tax. The government affirmed the previously adopted ban on the creation of new civil service posts and the freeze on civil service wages. In September the Central Bank raised interest rates. In December the Gambia Public Transportation Corporation increased public transportation fares, the Ministry of Finance raised the prices of petroleum products, and the government adopted a moratorium on contracting or guaranteeing new nonconcessional, medium-term debt. In January the Gambia Utilities Corporation raised both water and electricity charges, and the government liberalized the fertilizer market. Also in January, the Ministry of Finance floated the dalasi by establishing an interbank market for foreign exchange and lifted all restrictions on capital flows. The government initiated a crackdown on customs fraud in February; and in May, it laid off 1,644 temporary employees and abolished 280 vacant civil service posts, reducing the number of government employees by nearly 10 percent.

During the second year of the ERP, the government sharply increased the producer price of groundnuts for the second year in a row, this time to well above world market levels, on the insistence of the IMF (see *The Nature of the Reforms* section for more details). It raised taxes on petroleum and rice and lowered import duties on many other items.[7] The Central Bank established a Treasury Bill tender system to determine market interest rates; the Ministry of Finance and Central Bank rescheduled debts with the Paris Club; the government laid off an additional 291 temporary employees and 922 established staff and abolished 816 vacant civil service posts, reducing the number of government employees by an additional 8 percent; and the Ministry of Economic Planning and Industrial Development revised the Public Investment Program to include stronger investment criteria. The government divested its shares in a local bank and a trading company and took over D72.6 million of government-guaranteed (and mostly nonperforming) debts from the Gambia Commercial and Development Bank (GCDB). The Gambia Utilities Corporation (GUC) and the Gambia Public Transportation Corporation raised their rates for the second year in a row, in order to better cover costs.

New initiatives continued in 1987/88: the Ministry of Finance introduced a national sales tax and restructured the income tax system; the Central Bank refinanced its debts with the London Club; and the government paid off D80 million of the GPMB's accumulated debts with the Central Bank. The president signed performance contracts with three parastatals; the government reorganized the Ministry of Agriculture and the Gambia Commercial and Development Bank; and Parliament ratified a revised Development Act. The government is planning more reforms, including performance contracts with other parastatals, divestiture of additional government holdings and activities, and further reorganization of parastatals.

Progress of the Recovery Effort

As the foreign exchange market stabilized in mid-1986, and the government further tightened its control over the budget and monetary policy, the Gambian economy began to recover on a broad front. The extent of the recovery since 1985/86 is shown in column 4 of Table 1.

Aggregate real income has increased significantly, providing a welcome increase in per capita real income. The annual rate of inflation has fallen to below 10 percent, the government budget deficit (net of extraordinary transfers[8]) has been reduced to more sustainable levels, net credit to the government from the banking system has contracted sharply, and exports have increased relative to imports. The current account of the balance of payments, after initially increasing, is now steadily declining. The overall balance of payments was positive in 1987/88 for the first time in fourteen years, allowing the government to reduce its debt service arrears (from SDR 75 million to SDR 25 million) and increase gross foreign exchange reserves (to the equivalent of eleven weeks of imports). Groundnut and livestock production have increased, tourism has expanded, construction activity has surged, the range of financial services has broadened, the transport and communications sector has expanded, and wholesale and retail activity has been buoyant.

Of all the changes which have occurred, perhaps the most welcome has been the increase in per capita incomes. Real GDP increased approximately 5 percent in both 1986/87 and 1987/88. Particularly noteworthy is that the sharpest increases occurred in the rural areas, where the poorest Gambians live. GDP in agriculture grew by nearly 20 percent during the first three years of the ERP. After years of poor harvests, low producer prices, and the relative neglect of agriculture in the national development effort, this improvement has been a major vindication of the measures taken under the ERP. More importantly, because the ERP has redirected income to the poorest members of Gambian society, it has been one of the most potent forces for economic development in The Gambia since independence.

Though it is important to highlight these improvements, the hardships created by the ERP should not be overlooked and ought not be minimized. The devaluation of the dalasi eroded the incomes of civil servants and those on fixed incomes; high interest rates have raised the cost of institutional finance for individuals and enterprises; the reduction in government employment and redirection of government expenditure has required some painful adjustments, particularly among the urban population; the reorganization of the parastatal sector has increased the costs of basic services such as transport, ferries, electricity, and water; the customs clean-up made competition in the business community keener (and fairer); and higher user charges and commodity prices, particularly for petrol, have raised costs for businesses and individuals.

Nevertheless, these difficulties must be seen against the hardships which would have occurred in the absence of an adjustment program. Shortages of basic commodities would have increased in severity and duration; parallel market commodity prices, foreign exchange rates, and interest rates would have risen; more development projects would have been canceled as debt service arrears mounted; both inflation and unemployment would have increased; and the quality of basic services would have continued to deteriorate.

Viewed broadly, the government has achieved the first goal of the ERP—stabilizing the economy—and has made some progress toward the second—sustained economic growth. The economic gains of the last two years stand in stark contrast to the declines of the early 1980s. Several factors contributed to the turnaround, including:

   (i) the reform measures introduced under the ERP;
   (ii) foreign aid;
   (iii) luck; and
   (iv) the nature of the political environment.

The next four sections of this paper briefly examine the impact of each of these factors on The Gambia's economic turnaround. The section on *Sustainability* analyzes the prospects for sustained growth, and the section on *Lessons from the Economic Recovery Program* contains some observations on The Gambia's experiences in implementing reform.

The Nature of the Reforms

In general, the ERP was designed to expand the role of market forces in determining prices throughout the economy and to improve the government's efficiency. In four key markets—foreign exchange, credit, rice, and fertilizer—the government abandoned controlled prices altogether in favor of competitively determined prices. The GPMB equalized the margins paid to groundnut marketing agents, removing the bias which favored the Gambia Cooperatives Union (GCU). The Ministry of Finance eliminated export taxes on fish products, lowered import duties on major reexport items, introduced a uniform sales tax, and restructured the income tax system. These changes lowered overall tax rates, broadened the tax base, and enhanced incentives for private business. In markets where competition is limited (such as electricity, water, and port services), the government raised prices to reflect scarcity values more closely. The government also introduced more stringent economic criteria for the Public Investment Program, its plan for capital expenditure and development projects.

However, market mechanisms were not the basis of all the reforms. In what is perhaps the most intriguing reform of the ERP, the government increased the producer price of groundnuts in 1986/87 to more than double the world price, on the insistence of the IMF. To support this high price, the government transferred D83 million (8 percent of GDP) to the GPMB. The Fund wanted a domestic price high enough to stop farmers from selling their groundnuts across the border in Senegal—which offered an even higher price—in order to maximize the GPMB's purchases and its foreign exchange earnings. The IMF was not willing to rely on the market mechanism of the new interbank market for foreign exchange to encourage Gambian farmers to repatriate the fully convertible CFA francs they would receive for groundnuts in Senegal.

Ironically, one year later, the IMF reversed the strategy, both because the government could not sustain such a large subsidy and the interbank market had functioned smoothly for 16 months. The Gambia lowered its producer price from 85 percent to 70 percent of Senegal's price, reducing the subsidy to D50 million (4 percent of GDP). Gambian farmers sold about 30 percent of their marketed crop across the border in 1987/88, repatriating most of the foreign exchange to the Gambian banking system. Both Senegal and The Gambia lowered their prices in 1988/89, with The Gambia's price approximately 65 percent of Senegal's price. The subsidy was reduced to D13 million (1 percent of GDP). The government has announced that it intends to eliminate the subsidy in 1989/90, which may require a further reduction in the producer price.

Although the IMF recommended too high a subsidy, offering some subsidy to groundnut farmers was in many ways a sensible policy. The subsidy has been one of the most effective and equitable policies of the ERP—effective because the subsidy directly reached the intended recipients, and equitable because virtually all Gambian households produce some groundnuts, and the pattern of production across households is relatively uniform. An additional advantage is that the costs of administering the subsidy were low because the funds were distributed by the groundnut buying agents when they purchased the crop.

The subsidy, together with other changes introduced under the ERP (particularly the exchange rate reform), had a major impact on rural incomes. This has shown up in a number of ways. For example, in the two years after the ERP was introduced, the contribution of agriculture to GDP was 32.2 percent; in the two years immediately prior to the ERP, it was 28.8 percent. The corresponding increase in average real per capita income for rural workers was approximately 15 percent.

Another important reform was the reduction in the size of the civil service to a level more appropriate for the productive capacity of the economy. Between 1974/75 and 1984/85, the government wage bill increased 57 percent in real terms and increased from 38 to 48 percent of recurrent expenditure (excluding debt service). In 1974/75, the government wage bill was approximately 27 percent of farmer earnings from groundnuts; by 1984/85 it had grown to 202 percent.[9] In 1986, the government laid off almost 3,000 workers (approximately 20 percent of the civil service), saving almost D10 million on an annual basis. The wage bill fell to 27 percent of recurrent expenditure (excluding debt service and extraordinary transfers) and 70 percent of farmer earnings from groundnuts in 1987/88. While no formal survey has been made, officials at the Ministries of Economic Planning, Finance, and Agriculture believe that most of those who lost government jobs were reemployed in agriculture (responding to the high groundnut price), small manufacturing, trade, and construction activities. Although the Indigenous Business Advisory Service offered assistance for retrenched workers, few people applied.

In addition to changes in economic policy, the government introduced several organizational reforms. These included performance contracts between the government and the major parastatals, restructuring of the Ministry of Agriculture, and reorganization of the Gambia Commercial and Development Bank (GCDB). In general, the government's aim has been to improve administrative efficiency.

The performance contracts spell out the parastatal's objectives, its strategies to fulfill them, and the responsibilities of both the government and the parastatal. The parastatals involved can no longer rely on unlimited bank borrowing or government subsidies, and the government will no longer require them to set uneconomical prices or pursue noncommercial objectives.

Streamlining the Ministry of Agriculture will reduce costs and strengthen its capacity to carry out its primary functions of research and extension in support of private agricultural activities. Several services the ministry has been performing—such as machinery repair and tractor plowing—will be taken over by private businesses and aid agencies when the reform is completed. The ministry will continue other activities, but with fewer staff.

The government is in the process of completely reorganizing the GCDB, which incurred major losses during the 1980s. A reconstituted board of directors has hired new management personnel, separated commercial and development activities, and instituted new lending and collection policies. The government has recapitalized the bank and is pursuing debtors that have defaulted on their loans.

Other administrative and organizational reforms include the establishment of the Personnel Management Office, the restructuring of the Central Bank, the crackdown on customs fraud, and civil service reform. These reforms generally complement the changes in economic policy, reinforcing the increased reliance on market mechanisms and enhanced incentives for private production.

The Interbank Market for Foreign Exchange

Among the many changes made under the ERP, perhaps the most economically beneficial was the introduction of the interbank market for foreign exchange. This policy change, which floated the dalasi, had a major impact on both domestic and foreign perceptions of The Gambia's adjustment effort. More than any other measure, it demonstrated the government's resolve to make the changes necessary to deal with the country's problems.

Prior to the float, serious distortions had existed in the foreign exchange system for several years. As noted earlier, net foreign assets became negative in mid-1979, the profitability of export activities had declined, imports became increasingly attractive to local consumers, foreign payment arrears emerged in 1980, and the parallel foreign exchange market progressively undermined the official market. The situation had deteriorated to such an extent that the 25 percent devaluation of the dalasi in February 1984 had no perceptible impact.

More radical measures were needed. Options included a series of programmed devaluations; a foreign exchange auction; or a float. For administrative simplicity and its effectiveness in eliminating market distortions, the government decided to float the currency by introducing an interbank market for foreign exchange. This was done on January 20, 1986. During the first weeks after the float, the commercial banks were cut out of the foreign exchange market because they would not actively compete for foreign exchange. As a result, the rates offered in the parallel market moved well beyond the rates the commercial banks were offering. This situation changed in late February when, under pressure from the Ministry of Finance, the banks started to compete aggressively. As they began to attract foreign exchange, the discount in the parallel market declined.

Other factors also helped. The customs clean-up, which began in mid-February 1986, reduced the supply of dalasis being converted to foreign exchange as traders who had been undervaluing their imports had to pay the correct duties. The clean-up also sharply increased government revenue, reducing the level of bank credit in the economy. The dramatic fall in the international price of rice in early 1986 reduced the demand for foreign exchange. Fuel grants from the Netherlands and the United Kingdom enabled the government to further insulate the foreign exchange market. By late April, the foreign exchange market had stabilized, the commercial banks began to dominate the market, and confidence in the reform effort increased.

Because the ERP was formulated and has been implemented as a comprehensive package of measures, the effect of any particular reform should not be over-emphasized. Nevertheless, without the float of the dalasi, none of the other measures would have been as effective. Moreover, once the government floated the dalasi and the economy began to stabilize, the donor community had the proof it needed that the government was serious about economic reform. The response was generous.

Donor Support for the ERP

Soon after the Cabinet approved the ERP, the government outlined the program and the country's resource requirements to a Special Donors' Conference in London (GOTG 1985). Initial reaction was favorable. The donors generally agreed that the program was comprehensive and bold. Nevertheless, they were not willing to pledge support based only on the government's intention to initiate reform. In this respect, the float of the dalasi was vital, for it left no doubt about the government's commitment to economic adjustment.

One reason why the donors were reluctant to support the ERP was that The Gambia did not have a standby agreement with the IMF. The major obstacle to such an agreement was the government's arrears to the fund. These arrears were finally cleared in July 1986 through a bridging loan with Standard Chartered Bank (London). Soon thereafter, the government signed an agreement with the

IMF, just one day before the Fund's board was scheduled to meet to declare The Gambia ineligible to borrow.

The IMF lent The Gambia SDR 13 million, contingent on the government adhering to quarterly limits on the level of government and GPMB credit from the Central Bank, net domestic assets, foreign payment arrears, reserves, and short-term debt. It did not insist on many new policy initiatives because the government had already adopted stringent fiscal and monetary policies as part of the ERP. After concluding the standby agreement, the government obtained a Structural Adjustment Credit (SAC) worth U.S. $35 million from the World Bank, co-financed by the African Development Bank, the United Kingdom, and Saudi Arabia.

Donor assistance played a vital role in The Gambia's economic recovery. The IMF, the World Bank, the European Community, the United Kingdom, the African Development Bank, the Netherlands, the United States, Japan, and Saudi Arabia provided over SDR 75 million in balance of payments support between 1985/86 and 1987/88. Over 80 percent was in cash, with the rest as commodity aid. In addition, the government rescheduled SDR 31.8 million of debt with the Paris Club, the London Club, and the Islamic Development Bank.[10] Furthermore, bilateral and international agencies and private organizations provided technical assistance valued at over SDR 55 million. This, too, was vital for the ERP. Without it, the government would not have been able to meet all of the donors' conditions.

Taken together, the donors and commercial banks provided The Gambia with resources equivalent to SDR 31 million in 1985/86 (20 percent of GDP), SDR 74.4 million in 1986/87 (63 percent of GDP), and SDR 41.5 million in 1987/88 (30 percent of GDP). Further assistance of SDR 59.4 million (39 percent of GDP) was expected in 1988/89. Two-thirds of the aid has been grants and the remainder concessional loans.[11]

This support gave the ERP a major boost. It helped The Gambia replenish its foreign reserves, reduce its arrears, meet its current foreign exchange obligations, stabilize the exchange rate, increase its food security, and reduce its bank borrowing. Perhaps most importantly, it allowed investment and consumption to be higher than they otherwise would have been during the adjustment period. The higher level of investment is critical for The Gambia to achieve sustained economic growth; the higher level of consumption helped to reduce public resistance to the ERP.

Given the difficulties The Gambia faced in 1985 (especially the threat of IMF sanctions), this external aid would not have materialized without the ERP. Moreover, without donor support, the effects of the ERP would have been entirely different. Indeed, the ERP would have probably collapsed without external support. The Gambia's experience clearly illustrates the importance of adequate levels of financing to ease the burden of adjustment, promote stability, and stimulate growth.

Luck: Favorable Exogenous Conditions

To some extent, The Gambia benefited from plain luck: fortuitous exogenous circumstances strengthened the recovery. First, after several years of poor rains (annual rainfall between 1980/81 and 1984/85 was 30 percent lower than it had been in the late 1970s), rainfall returned to more normal levels between 1985/86 and 1988/89. As a result, agricultural production increased over the period, raising incomes and reducing the deficit on the current account of the balance of payments (by increasing agricultural exports and decreasing food imports).

Second, the world price of rice fell sharply just after the government floated the dalasi, and higher rainfall increased domestic grain production. As a result, the dalasi price of rice was actually lower in mid-1986 than it had been before the float. This was a key factor in minimizing public opposition to the ERP. The world price of oil fell as well. Although the retail price in Banjul (which is controlled) actually rose during the period, the duty portion of the retail price grew markedly, increasing government revenue and reducing the budget deficit. The lower world price also increased the amount of fuel made available under the United Kingdom and Dutch fuel grants, which were awarded in terms of value rather than volume. In general, international rates of inflation were low,[12] easing the pressure on the balance of payments.

In short, many of the exogenous variables which had adversely affected the economy in the late 1970s and early 1980s reversed and helped the economic recovery. One significant exception was the world price of groundnut products, which continued to decline in real terms between 1984/85 and 1987/88, falling to 36 percent of 1976/77 levels. On balance, however, external circumstances as they affected the Gambian economy greatly improved. Without this fortuitous change, The Gambia's economic performance would not have been as strong.

The Politics of Reform

Both regional and domestic politics have been important in The Gambia's reform effort. Regionally, The Gambia's relationship with Senegal influenced both the government's decision to undertake an adjustment program and public reaction to the reforms once they were introduced. Domestically, the rural constituency of the ruling People's Progressive Party (PPP), the lack of any strong opposition groups, and the relatively quick economic turnaround all mitigated negative public reaction to the ERP.

Relations with Senegal

The existence of The Gambia has long created economic and political problems for Senegal. The Gambia effectively divides Senegal into two regions, making it costly and inconvenient to transport goods from the northern region (where Dakar, the capital, is located) to the southern region, the Casamance. Trucks moving from northern Senegal to the Casamance must cross two borders and take a congested ferry across the Gambia River. The Gambia has contemplated building a bridge/dam across the river, but for both economic and political reasons, it has not been built. A demographic split follows from Senegal's geographic split: Wolofs dominate the northern section and Jolas populate the Casamance. In 1960, the president of Senegal, Leopold Senghor, agreed that there would be a plebiscite on the issue of independence for the Casamance before 1980. The plebiscite was never held. Secessionist sentiment is high in the Casamance.

Relations between The Gambia and Senegal changed after an attempted coup d'état in The Gambia in July 1981. Lasting eight days and claiming over 1,000 lives, the attempted coup was finally put down by 1,500 Senegalese troops called in by Gambian President Jawara under a 1965 mutual defense treaty. Most of the troops left shortly after the uprising was quelled; however, some troops remained until 1989 to guard the State House and the residence of the president.

In December 1981, with The Gambia's security clearly dependent on Senegal, the two countries agreed to form the Senegambia Confederation. Since that time, a Confederal Parliament has met regularly, and the two governments have signed protocols on defense, transportation, arbitration, communications, and cultural exchange. Negotiations continue on a free trade zone, a monetary union, and other issues. The Gambia, fearing complete domination by its larger neighbor, has moved slowly and cautiously in negotiating the Confederal agreements. Senegal, on the other hand, is interested in integrating as quickly as possible. (The confederation was dissolved in September 1989.)

With this history in mind, many people both inside and outside The Gambia believe that in the event of another uprising in The Gambia, Senegal would use the opportunity as a pretext to take power. This situation effectively limits both the potential excesses of the government and the willingness of opposition groups to promote public discontent.

These circumstances influenced the government's decision to undertake a reform program. As the economic crisis deepened in the spring of 1985, The Gambia asked its foreign bankers for loans and several donors for emergency support. Each refused. The bankers were not willing to lend because The Gambia had ceased to be creditworthy. The donors, although recognizing that The Gambia's economic crisis was partly due to external circumstances, felt that the government had been given ample opportunity to adjust to these circumstances and to take steps to redress the domestic causes of the disequilibria. They were no longer willing to finance The Gambia's deficits in the absence of a significant adjustment effort—particularly in light of The Gambia's large debt service arrears. They were aware that in the absence of emergency aid, shortages and disruptions might lead to the downfall of the government. However, the strong possibility that it would be Senegal (and not some unknown group) that would ultimately take power made any potential collapse of the government less problematical. The Senegalese (and the French) would have welcomed such a result; for many of the donors the "problem" of The Gambia would have been solved; and the outcome would serve as a warning to other countries reluctant to undertake adjustment measures that the donors would not necessarily always bail them out.[13]

Thus, continuing economic decline without donor support posed a potential threat to The Gambia as a nation. Minister of Finance Sisay recognized that some kind of adjustment program had to be undertaken to reduce this potential threat. Two years later, in reviewing the progress made during the first phase of the ERP, he observed that "in assessing the impact of the ERP it is also relevant to consider whether The Gambia's integrity as a nation would have long withstood an IMF's declaration of ineligibility and the regional pressures this would have generated."[14]

In chapter 3 of this volume, Merilee Grindle and John Thomas observe that decision making in crisis-ridden situations tends to be dominated by concern for political stability and the survival of the regime in power. In many countries, this concern constrains the pace and scope of reform, as leaders become apprehensive about public reaction to reforms. In The Gambia, these concerns were also important. However, policymakers perceived that the greatest political threat was further deterioration through inaction, and thus they embraced the ERP.

Government Deliberations

Sisay responded to the deepening crisis by establishing the task force described earlier. Once he submitted the ERP for Cabinet consideration in August 1985, only one vote mattered: the president's. President Jawara had been the country's only leader since independence in 1965, and little could be accomplished without his support. By this time the president, who was well aware of the mounting domestic and international pressure, was ready to accept some type of reform program. In considering the content of the reform package, he had to ensure that the reforms were strong enough to attract support from the donors, sound enough to redress the economic crisis, and palatable enough to keep public opposition from derailing the program and his administration.

In addition to the threat of public disturbances and concerns about the donors, the president had to consider that general elections were scheduled for March 1987, just nineteen months away. His concerns over the election were mitigated to some extent by the fact that his power base was in the rural areas (discussed in more detail below) and the task force had recommended promoting agriculture and increasing producer prices. Nevertheless, the prospect existed that the reform program might attract donor support and be received with little public opposition, yet still lead to his electoral defeat.

With his background as a veterinarian, the president had always relied on his advisers to determine economic policy. Most of those whom he could have called on for advice in 1985 were poorly trained in economics, and their earlier economic advice had proven ineffective and even detrimental. None of his advisers—nor anyone else inside or outside of government—presented any credible alternative to the ERP.

Sisay, on the other hand, had been minister of finance in the early 1960s during a period of relative economic prosperity, had been the first governor of the Central Bank, and held a graduate degree in economics. He was also one of the few remaining active original members of the PPP besides the president. Given this background and the fact that he was the only one presenting any kind of coherent adjustment program, the president had little choice but to rely heavily on his recommendations. In fact, he relied on them completely. This proved to be shrewd both economically and politically: economically, it gave coherence and consistency to the program; politically, it gave the president the opportunity to distance himself from the program if it failed. In the end, Cabinet and Parliament adopted the ERP almost exactly as Sisay had presented it to them.

Public Reaction

Perhaps the most striking aspect of The Gambia's adjustment effort was the lack of overt public opposition to the reforms. There were no public demonstrations, no rallies or marches, no strikes, and no hint of an attempted overthrow. The government did not have to ban public gatherings, use force to dissuade opponents, or declare a state of emergency. The public generally reacted to the reforms with skepticism but without much outright opposition. Moreover, in March 1987, nineteen months after the ERP was approved by Cabinet and fourteen months after the dalasi was floated, the president was reelected to a fifth term with 60 percent of the vote and his party won thirty-two of thirty-six seats in Parliament—increasing its majority by two seats.

The types of reforms introduced in The Gambia fit the criteria that Grindle and Thomas suggest will elicit strong public reaction—they affected broad sectors of the economy, were immediate in their impact, and the benefits were not immediately clear. Why was there so little opposition?

The reasons are many and varied. One important factor is the nature of the political system and the political power base in The Gambia. The Gambia is a democracy—a rarity in Africa. There is universal adult suffrage, and voting in the five parliamentary and presidential elections since independence has been widely acknowledged to have been free and fair. Freedoms of speech, religion, and the press are guaranteed by the constitution. Political parties need not register and are free to campaign actively.

These political freedoms notwithstanding, the PPP has totally dominated politics in The Gambia since independence. As mentioned previously, President Jawara, as the head of the PPP, has been the country's only leader (first as prime minister, then after 1971 as president). The party has always held a strong majority in Parliament. The PPP is unusual among African ruling parties in that its main constituency is rural dwellers. Mandinka and Fula farmers dominate the party, whereas urban-dwelling Wolofs tend to support the minority opposition parties.[15]

The rural power base stems partly from simple arithmetic: 75 percent of the population lives in rural areas. The country's small size and the accessibility of rural villages contribute to the rural power base as well. All villages are linked by roads, and even the most distant village is only an eight-hour bus ride from Banjul. Consequently, rural dwellers are not geographically (and thus politically) isolated. The rural constituency of the PPP is important in explaining its easy electoral victory so soon after the implementation of the ERP. The policy reforms of the ERP which tended to hurt mainly urban dwellers—the float of the dalasi, higher bank interest rates, increased utility rates and transport fares, and the retrenchment of civil servants—did little to erode the party's support. Other reforms—the suspension of export taxes, the liberalization of the rice trade, and, most importantly, the increase in the producer price of groundnuts—directly benefited the party's constituents.

Although the nature of the political system helps account for the 1987 electoral victory, it only partially explains why there was so little overt urban resistance to the reforms. One reason is the lack of any group which might have served as a focal point for active protest. Opposition parties tried to seize the opportunity created by the economic crisis to discredit the PPP and increase their own influence. However, as noted above, they are weak, disjointed, and unorganized. Two are led by former vice presidents who split with the president, so political opposition is seen partially in terms of personal animosity and not fundamental issues. In campaigning for the March 1987 elections, the opposition did not attack the ERP or promise an alternative—they simply promised that, if elected, they would implement the ERP better than the ruling party could. They were unable to spark public dissent and actually lost seats in the election.

130

Labor unions, representing urban dwellers on fixed incomes who lost purchasing power because of steadily rising prices, were another possible source of dissent. However, the few existing unions are small and politically powerless. University students are often a source of political opposition, but there are no universities in The Gambia. The military, which might have considered action out of concern for national security, is small, apolitical, and conscious of the larger army in Senegal and how it might react to trouble in The Gambia. Civil servants, also on fixed incomes and facing the possibility of losing their jobs, could have actively opposed the ERP. But they are not organized, and the possibility that troublemakers might be the first to lose their jobs during the retrenchment exercise contributed to the lack of protest. Other factors influencing civil servants are described below.

Urban dwellers bore the bulk of the costs of the reforms. The devaluation of the dalasi and higher user charges, utility rates, interest rates, and commodity prices reduced purchasing power. Civil servants who lost their jobs were particularly hard hit. Nevertheless, the impact on urban dwellers was not as great as it might have been. As noted earlier, the liberalization of interest rates, the customs crackdown, and foreign aid all reduced the extent to which the dalasi depreciated. Many of the civil servants who lost their jobs were either absorbed into small manufacturing or construction activities (both of which experienced rapid growth in 1986/87) or joined relatives on farms to take advantage of the high returns offered to groundnut producers.

Moreover, as noted earlier, the price of rice (the urban staple food) was actually lower in mid-1986 than it had been before the float because of lower world prices and increased domestic production. The large amount of foreign inflows which supported the ERP allowed both consumption and investment to be higher than they otherwise would have been during the adjustment period. All of these factors helped reduce public opposition to the reforms.

By contrast, some groups benefited quickly from the reforms. Besides the obvious example of the farmers, importers who had not been falsifying their customs invoices gained immediately when competitors were forced to pay full duties. Reexporters, who make up a large part of the urban business community, benefited from the easing of restrictions on capital flows and the lowering of import duties on reexport items.

Another reason for the lack of overt urban opposition was the timing of the implementation of the reforms. The government announced most of the reforms well ahead of implementation, giving people time to get used to the idea and prepare for the changes. Moreover, the government introduced the reforms over a long period of time. The opposition to any single reform was not great enough to spark active dissent. Had the government introduced all of the reforms at once, there might have been a stronger popular reaction. The danger with a slow pace of reforms is that it can give the opposition time to mobilize, preventing the government from introducing all of its desired reforms.[16] This did not occur in The Gambia. A long "window of opportunity" for implementing the reforms was made possible by the combination of consistent, strong support for the program from the president and the minister of finance and the lack of any real political opposition to the ERP. To the extent that the particular policies chosen and the foreign aid received contributed to quick positive results, they contributed to diffusing opposition and lengthening the "window of opportunity."

Without diminishing the importance of the above factors, the legacy of the 1981 attempted coup d'état and The Gambia's relationship with Senegal were the major reasons for the lack of opposition. As much as the people of Banjul did not like the ERP and were not happy with their economic situation, they did not want a repeat of the violence and bloodshed of 1981. Moreover, people realized that a large disturbance could threaten the very existence of The Gambia as a nation. Urban dwellers who saw Senegalese troops put down the 1981 attempted coup understood the potential consequences of another incident of civil unrest in The Gambia.[17]

Sustainability

Now that the economy has started to grow, the main issue is whether the growth can be sustained. The Gambia remains highly vulnerable to adverse shifts in external conditions and back-sliding with respect to some of the adjustments undertaken. The budget deficit and external current account deficit are projected to remain high at 6 percent and 21 percent of GDP, respectively, in 1989/90. Foreign payment arrears will not be eliminated until 1990 (and then only if The Gambia meets all the donor's conditions for continued financing). The debt burden will not begin to decline until the amounts rescheduled with the Paris and London Clubs are fully repaid in 1995. Foreign exchange earnings continue to depend heavily on rainfall, either directly through groundnut production or indirectly through trade. Business and consumer confidence could evaporate quickly if the government were to abandon key elements of the ERP, such as maintaining realistic exchange rates and interest rates. Thus, the government must continue its commitment to the basic policies of the ERP if growth is to be sustained.

Two other factors will be important for continued growth. First, sufficient resources must be made available to expand the productive base. Because of the large government budget deficit and low level of private savings, The Gambia has been almost completely dependent on external resources to finance public and private investment. Donors will not continue to supply The Gambia with such extraordinary amounts of aid indefinitely. The government will have to free up more domestic resources if it wishes to continue the current level of investment. Because the potential for mobilizing significant private savings is limited, the bulk of the additional resources will have to come from further reductions in the budget deficit.

Second, productivity must increase. From 1982/83 through 1985/86, investment averaged nearly 18 percent of GDP, yet real GDP fell 2 percent. There was some improvement during the first two years of the ERP, when investment averaged 21.5 percent of GDP and income grew 5 percent annually. Higher interest rates (which discourage unproductive investment), stricter criteria in government investment projects, and the performance contracts with parastatals have all contributed to this improvement. The government can achieve additional productivity growth by improving the analysis and monitoring of its investments, continuing financial reform through the restructuring of the Gambia Commercial and Development Bank and the Gambia Cooperatives Union, and further parastatal reform. Without continued government commitment supported by increased availability of domestic resources for investment and improved productivity, sustained economic growth is unlikely.

Lessons from the Economic Recovery Program

Numerous lessons emerge from The Gambia's experience. First, and perhaps most important, the government's failure to undertake comprehensive reforms in the early 1980s allowed the economy to deteriorate further, making the subsequent recovery effort more difficult. The Gambia's economic difficulties were obvious in early 1983, and fundamental changes were needed then. The delay until mid-1985 simply allowed a difficult problem to become a crisis.

Second, The Gambia benefited from the design of its adjustment program. Two points are relevant. The individual reforms derived from basic economic principles. When an economy is fundamentally out of balance, as was the case in The Gambia, the factors responsible for the distortions are not hard to determine. To illustrate, it was clear that the foreign exchange rate was seriously distorted—the parallel market was progressively undercutting the official market. Similarly, it was obvious that the government could not maintain its rice subsidies—the GPMB ran out of foreign exchange and could no longer import rice. This is not meant to detract from, or minimize, the role of detailed technical analyses in the reform process. It simply makes the point that in formulating a reform program, the principal focus has to be on the fundamental economic reasons for the economy's dilemma.

Moreover, the package of reforms was comprehensive.[18] By 1985, most aspects of the economy had deteriorated seriously. No single policy change or reform measure could have reversed the damage. For this reason, the government had to implement a broad range of changes. This approach spread the costs of adjustment more widely and reduced resistance to individual reforms. Many of the reforms reinforced others, enhancing the overall efficacy of the program.

Third, donor support was important in several ways. The level of financial assistance was large enough to make a major difference to the economy. It eased the process of adjustment and enabled government officials to devote more time and effort to implementing the reforms. Furthermore, donors attached conditions to their assistance that generally conformed with the overall thrust of the ERP. This consistency also allowed officials to concentrate on the essential elements of the program. Although the sheer volume of conditions created some difficulties, the problem was eased somewhat by donors piggybacking their conditions and providing technical support to help monitor the reforms.[19]

Fourth, economic policy reforms have been easier to implement than organizational reforms. For example, the liberalization of the rice trade, interest rate reform, and the float of the dalasi, although difficult politically, required few new administrative procedures and were fairly simple to implement. On the other hand, organizational reforms such as the parastatal performance contracts, reorganization of the Ministry of Agriculture, and reform of the Gambia Commercial and Development Bank, were more difficult. Organizational reforms have often been delayed or modified significantly before implementation, and many require continuous administrative effort to sustain. In general, the more new administrative procedures and changes in bureaucratic roles which a reform required, the more difficult it was to implement. Reforms involving only a change of price were the easiest. This observation is supported by Grindle and Thomas in the cases they analyze in chapter 3.

Because of weak administrative capacity in The Gambia, it was crucial for officials not to have to keep coming back to the same problem repeatedly. Administrative ease was a major reason that The Gambia floated the dalasi. A series of devaluations or an auction would have been too demanding, irrespective of their other benefits. It was also an important consideration in the decisions to liberalize the rice market, adopt market-determined interest rates, and suspend price controls (except on groundnuts and petroleum). Though the disadvantages of market prices were not overlooked, their dominant advantage, as Galbraith (1979) has noted, is that they economize on scarce and honest administrative talent.[20]

Economic policy reforms were also implemented much earlier than organizational reforms. This sequencing was partly because policy reforms were easier, but also because they were more important to the government's immediate objective of economic stabilization. There are good reasons why the government has waited to implement some organizational reforms. The danger is that, because of the improvements achieved so far, its commitment might wane before it introduces all of the intended reforms.

Fifth, The Gambia benefited from designing and implementing its own reform program. The process of designing the ERP focused attention on the nonsustainability of the situation in 1985. Moreover, although donors influenced the program, the government maintained control over its content and timing. This helped minimize resistance and mobilize support for the reforms, easing their implementation.

Sixth, the nature of the political environment also helped. The rural power base of the ruling People's Progressive Party, the weak political opposition, and the relatively quick economic improvement for many people all reduced public opposition and helped the PPP achieve its electoral victory nineteen months after introducing the ERP. The relationship with Senegal helps explain both the government's decision to introduce reforms and the lack of public opposition once the reforms were introduced.

Finally, individual personalities were decisive. Minister Sisay was probably the only one in the government capable of successfully introducing and implementing such a reform program. His background, record, training, and relationship with the donors equipped him to head the effort and enabled him to gain the trust of the president, the public, and the donors all at once. President Jawara's long tenure in office gave him authority and influence. His support was crucial not only for the initial acceptance of the ERP, but for the continued implementation of individual reforms as well. This has been true particularly for organizational reforms, where bureaucratic actors have had more scope to inhibit implementation. The implication is that personalities—as much as content, timing, and process—can be critical to successful reform.

Summary and Conclusion

The economic problems confronting The Gambia in mid-1985 were serious and deep-rooted. Inappropriate domestic policies, reductions in foreign aid, and deteriorating external circumstances caused the economic crisis. In turn, reversals in these factors led to the recovery. The first objective of the ERP has been achieved—the economy has stabilized. However, until the economy grows and the burden of external debt diminishes, it will remain vulnerable. Consequently, the ERP will have to be continued and appropriately reinforced if the second objective—sustained economic growth—is to be achieved. Specific areas which require attention are the mobilization of domestic resources and improvements in productivity throughout the economy.

The ERP has yielded some useful insights into the process of economic adjustment. More are likely to emerge as The Gambia pushes forward. For a small country, this is a considerable legacy. The Gambia's experience provides an example for other countries faced with similar difficulties. Economic reforms can succeed if they are well designed, conscientiously implemented, and receive sufficient domestic and international support. ✌

Notes

1 We are indebted to Dwight H. Perkins, Mike Roemer, and Parker M. Shipton for comments on earlier drafts.

2 Prior to March, 1973, the dalasi was fixed at D5 = 1 pound sterling (PST). It was then revalued to D4 = PST 1, and devalued back to D5 = PST 1 in February 1984. The dalasi was floated in January 1986, and the exchange rate in February 1989 was D12.10 = PST 1.

3 The factors associated with the decline of the Gambian economy have been examined in several places (McPherson 1983; USAID 1985, Annex K; World Bank 1985; and GOTG 1987).

4 Established posts increased by 4,130 or 69.6 percent in 1977/78 alone. The increase in the civil service for the decade 1975/76 to 1985/86 was 96.7 percent.

5 Donors made this point at a UNDP-sponsored conference in November 1984, which, far from generating support for the government's proposed one billion dalasi four-year public investment program, ended with calls for major cuts in it.

6 Throughout the remainder of this paper, the Ministry of Finance and Trade will be referred to simply as the Ministry of Finance.

7 The lower import duties led to increased revenue because of larger volumes of reexports.

8 During 1987/88, the government transferred D80 million and D25 million (a total of 8 percent of GDP) to the Central Bank to retire the accumulated debts of the GPMB and the GUC, respectively.

9 For an estimate of farmers' earnings from groundnuts, see Radelet (1987).

10 For details on The Gambia's Debt Reschedulings, see Radelet (1988).

11 For example, World Bank Structural Adjustment Loans have a grant element of some 90 percent.

12 Based on data reported in *International Financial Statistics*, the world whole-sale price index increased at an annual rate of 1.7 percent between 1984/85 and 1987/88.

13 Members of the donor community made these points in interviews with the authors.

14 GOTG, Ministry of Finance and Trade (1987, 20).

15 Mandinkas are the largest ethnic group in The Gambia (37 percent of the population), followed by Fulas (17 percent) and Wolofs (13 percent).

16 For a fuller discussion of this point, see Joan M. Nelson (1984).

17 Urban dwellers made these points repeatedly in interviews with the authors.

18 See IMF (1989) for a recent observation on the importance of comprehensive reform programs.

19 For example, the condition for continued UK support is that The Gambia maintain an IMF program. In addition, the United Kingdom, United States, UN, FAO, IMF, and World Bank (among others) have provided a large number of technical assistants to help Gambian officials work on various aspects of the ERP. Without this assistance, and some of its spin-offs (such as computerization), The Gambia's progress under the ERP would have been considerably slower than it has been.

20 For a recent comment on the effects of governments overreaching administratively, see Lewis (1989, 73).

5

The Politics of Health Reform in Chad

Anne-Marie Foltz and William J. Foltz

Anne-Marie Foltz has taught at Yale University and New York University and writes on health policy and epidemiology in Africa and the United States. She was HIID resident adviser in Chad from 1985 to 1988.

William J. Foltz is professor of political science at Yale University. He specializes in the study of African politics and international relations.

Introduction

This paper examines an attempt at reform of the health system in Chad, a particularly poor and troubled country. The thesis of this paper is that both the choice of reform and the probability of implementation depend in greatest part on the participants' (policymakers') concerns for their own and the regime's political survival and only marginally for the survival of their particular sectors of the bureaucracy. Thus, some variant of a pure politics model that takes into account a multiplicity of loyalties, obligations, and antipathies seems more appropriate than a standard bureaucratic politics model for describing the outcome of this sectoral/organizational reform in Chad.[1]

The analysis is in four parts. In the first part, we examine Chad's economic and political situation in 1985 as the context in which the question of reform of the health sector arose. Second, we examine Chad's choices for reforming the health sector and why it chose as it did. Third, we turn to the implementation of the reform, and finally, we discuss how Chad's experience can contribute to understanding problems of reform in poor and troubled Third World countries.

Context for Reform in Chad

Chad, a landlocked country, varies in topography from desert to heavily wooded savannah, from the middle of the Sahara to the outskirts of the Congo basin. Historically, Chad had been the center of trade, pilgrim, and slaving routes going north and south, east and west. As a result, the country boasts an extraordinary variety of ethnic groups, 110 by one conservative estimate.[2] In the north, the primary occupation has been herding livestock. In the south, agriculture predominates with a very few industries based on agricultural production (cotton processing, sugar refining, cigarettes).

Chad was the "Cinderella colony" of French Africa, a Cinderella who has yet to meet her Prince Charming. What little investment has gone into the country has been concentrated in the south, known to the colonizer as *le Tchad utile,* useful Chad. The country has been particularly handicapped by its poor road system, which imposes high internal transportation costs (when transport is even possible). Since Chad is 1500 kilometers from the nearest port, imports are expensive and exports must be priced to include high transport costs.

Following independence in 1960, Chad was ruled by an increasingly arbitrary regime dominated by southerners. The first revolts broke out in 1965, beginning a period of bloody civil strife and foreign intervention that ravaged the country for the next two decades and that has not completely ended. This violent period laid bare in dramatic form some of the underlying structure of Chadian political life. It demonstrated the fragility of large, formal structures of rule and social organization, which were undercut by a multiplicity of shifting factional alliances and feuds. Although region, religion, mode of livelihood, or ethnicity might at one moment describe a particular factional lineup, it would not likely explain the participants' motivations. Virtually none of the 110 or so ethnic groups is itself homogeneous or solidaristic. Parochial loyalties and antagonisms divide tiny villages among the animist/Christian Sara, while the Saharan Toubou must come close to world records for harsh individualism.

Fixed political ideology has been virtually absent from politics. When proclaimed, it would be used to provide a facade for factional rearrangement or for brokering an alliance of convenience with a group of foreigners who might take that sort of thing seriously.

Factionalism and short-run calculations dominated and exacerbated the civil wars, which were fought with unstable coalitions, often more jealous of their partners than of the opposition.[3] The so-called Transitional Government of National Unity (GUNT), which was cobbled together by various outside interests in 1979, proved unable to devise a central process for governing the country. Everything had to be divided according to the shifting weight of factional interests. The GUNT lost the capital to Hissène Habré's forces in 1982 in good part because each of the armed factions making up the GUNT waited for the others to commit their troops to battle in the expectation that it could preserve its forces intact and emerge the ultimate winner over its coalition partners. The social scientist will find Chad a challenging laboratory for the study of collective choice, free riders, and prisoner's dilemmas.

Factionalism is a common enough feature of politics in African and other states. In some cases—Senegal is a good instance—factions are based on well-established patron-client relationships, with their own, well-understood rules of distribution, deference, loyalty, and defection. Although factional competition is intense, it follows predictable forms anchored in social structures common to most of the population. For all the swirl of political wheeling and dealing and the rise and fall of political *clan* leaders, the system itself is metastable and provides a high degree of predictability for those who participate in it.[4] No such certainty is available to those who must play Chadian politics. The Chadian political system provides no such common social base or set of stable expectations on which trust can be established. The violent reversals of Chad's recent past inspire the adventuresome few to redefine the rules to fit their advantage, and persuade the prudent many to confide fully only in the smallest circle of friends, while keeping open multiple links to possible patrons who might provide a secure lifeline should things turn nasty.

Instability and factionalism have been increased by outside powers backing "their own" Chadian clients, and sometimes playing one against another. At one time or other, France, the United States, Egypt, Libya, Nigeria, Zaire, Congo-Brazzaville, Gabon, Sudan, Iraq, and Saudi Arabia have provided significant support for one or more Chadian factions. This has left a legacy for entrepreneurial Chadians of looking outside the country's borders for economic and other resources to profit themselves and their clients and close allies. Multiple backers are to be preferred, of course, so that one can be played off against another. Such a legacy inevitably affects the way foreign aid is understood by members of the current Chadian government.

Hissène Habré, who had built an effective fighting force largely on the basis of personal loyalty to himself and a core group of skilled commanders (and with quiet help from France and the United States), proved at first to be a surprisingly effective political leader. By the end of 1985, his government had reestablished civil order over most of the country. He combined military pressure on opposition factions with a policy of "national reconciliation," which distributed political plums to those who submitted to his leadership. Habré seized the high ground of national unity by leading a national effort to chase the Libyans and their remaining Chadian clients out of their last positions in northern Chad. Although he was overthrown in December 1990 by ethnically based factions of his original military coalition dissatisfied with their share of power, Habré left behind a recognizable and functioning state apparatus.[5]

Chad is an exceptionally poor country, even when the rains come and the locusts stay away. Chadian government finances are in a perpetually parlous state of deficit (see Table 1). Well over half of all public expenses, on and off budget, goes for the war and other security purposes. The collapse of Chad's cotton economy, thanks to maladministration and a catastrophic fall in world prices, has deprived the government of 25 percent of its domestic income and sharply cut export earnings. (In 1986-87, Chad lost nearly $1 on every kilo of cotton it sold.)

Since the mid-1980s, Chad has got by with more than a little help from its friends. As the World Bank has noted, "foreign aid is the most important "sector" of the Chadian economy, since it represents more than two and a half times the quantity of receipts from exports."[6] In addition to substantial military aid, both France and the United States have provided direct budgetary aid to prevent total collapse. The World Bank and various European donors have put together a rescue package for the cotton industry, and the International Monetary Fund has negotiated a standby arrangement to reestablish some sort of budgetary order.

The net effect of all of this, however, is that the Chadian people and the Chadian civilian administration are faced with the prospect of a long period of even greater financial stringency than that which has obtained in the past. Pressure is on to reduce public employment, since civil service wages make up over 50 percent of nonmilitary expenditure, despite the fact that by most measures the country is seriously underadministered. Most civil servants are poorly paid; the average Chadian civil servant is paid 30,000 CFA a month (approximately U.S. $100)—except for the month when the salary is "donated" to the war effort, and the one or two months when it just is not paid.[7] Any new governmental enterprises must be made to pay for themselves in hard cash, first by generating new resources either internally or from outside donors, and second by making certain that recurrent operational costs do not become another drag on the regular budget.

The health system was in shambles in 1982 when Hissène Habré began to restore central government rule. More than half the country's hospitals, clinics, medical supplies and equipment had been destroyed. Doctors and nurses, most of whom belonged to southern ethnic groups, had fled into exile or been killed.

The rehabilitation of this health system was slow and depended on massive infusions of aid from outside donors, governments, international organizations, and private voluntary organizations. For example, the European Economic Community contributed U.S. $9 million over three years to permit the Belgian-based Médecins sans Frontières (MSF) to rebuild facilities and train health personnel in the nine northern prefectures. In 1985, this outside aid for the health sector amounted to more than U.S. $12 million, approximately seven times the amount appropriated by the government itself for its health activities.

In addition, religious and voluntary groups support a large share of the health activities, particularly in the southern part of the country. The financing of these

Protestant and Catholic facilities, which account for one-quarter of the country's facilities, is not computed in national aid figures (see Table 2).

Although most facilities had been rehabilitated by 1985, they were scarcely in adequate condition to provide basic health services and were chronically short of trained staff. Some public hospitals lacked basic equipment such as beds and x-ray machines, while facilities at all levels were without routine essentials such as soap.

The number of health personnel was woefully inadequate. In 1985, there were only seventy-five Chadian physicians backed up by an equal number of expatriates to serve nearly five million people. Lacking trained administrative personnel, the Ministry of Public Health assigned nearly one-third of its Chadian physicians to administrative duties, leaving the actual delivery of health care in the hands of expatriate doctors, Chadian nurses, and lesser-trained personnel. As a result, the health system was administered by physicians who were not, as a rule, experienced as administrators, while health facilities were shorthanded.

How well the ministry was meeting health needs could only be estimated because reliable data and a reliable information system were lacking. Nevertheless, the estimates produced alarming statistics: an infant mortality rate over 200 per 1,000 births (compared to 93 in Egypt and 72 in Kenya[8]); a maternal mortality rate of 786 per 100,000 births; high numbers of cases of tetanus, measles, and polio—diseases all preventable by immunization.

The economic and political situation in Chad in 1985, thus, seemed to orient the government less toward reform than toward simply rebuilding an economy and a state apparatus devastated by twenty years of civil war. Neither the government as a whole, nor the individuals who were employed by it, enjoyed the margin of security or of resources which are often thought to be necessary to bring about planned change.

Opportunities for Reform in the Health Sector and Chad's Response

The disappearance of central government and the destruction of facilities and personnel during the civil war had created a vacuum in the health sector, a vacuum which the rehabilitation of buildings and the reassignment of personnel only partially filled. Needed still were the means of organizing and monitoring the system.

To organize, or reorganize, or reform a health system, theoretically an infinite number of choices exist, but those most relevant to Third World countries can be grouped by four types of action, none of them necessarily exclusive:

1. **No reform:** Restore the system that existed before the war.
2. **Economic reform:** Institute a system of financing which would require patients to pay for use of the system and thereby provide the financial support which the central government was unable to provide.
3. **Health services organization reform:** Reorganize the health services system by giving primacy to primary health care at the expense of hospital (secondary) care. To carry out such a program would require training

village health care workers, organizing their supervision by nurses, and emphasizing public education.

4. **Administrative reform:** Reorganize the administrative structure of the health system to assert central control consonant with the assertion of central control by the government as a whole. Conversely or simultaneously, decentralize control in the provinces by giving more resources and responsibility to district doctors.

The first option, to restore, meant rehabilitating a system inherited from the French, a system geared toward infectious disease control (the *Grandes Endémies* approach standard throughout France's colonies) through top-down organization and geared toward high technology. Even in the 1970s, Chad continued to be dependent on technical assistance through expatriate personnel and funding of programs, projects, and administration. After 1983, as calm returned to Chad, restoration became the key word in the Ministry of Public Health.

To restore the health system to where it was before the breakdown of central government rule presented two dilemmas. The first raised the question, restore the health system to what period? To 1965, when civil unrest first began? To 1975, when the Southern-dominated Tombalbaye government was overthrown? To 1978, when the government of unity broke down completely? Or to 1979, when major battles between government factions raged in the streets of the capital? The second dilemma was to know what to restore, since most records had been lost and most personnel dispersed. Thus, any policy of restoration could be ambiguously interpreted; this left a broad scope for policy innovation and conflict.

A policy of restoration was politically advantageous to ministry leaders. They could make extensive demands for resources, whether to the Council of Ministers or to the president or to outside donors, with the straightforward plea for the equivalent of emergency aid to rebuild a war-torn infrastructure. It would be a hardhearted Chadian or outsider who could argue that Chad should do without the minimal health services which had existed before the "events" (as the war was euphemistically called).

Restoration rhetoric underlay most of the ministry's activities during the mid-eighties: the MSF's task was to "rebuild" the health facilities destroyed in the war and to retrain doctors and nurses to run the facilities. Appeals went out to the World Health Organization (WHO) and Swiss Cooperation for assistance to "rebuild" the nursing school.

Not all of the restoration rhetoric actually meant restoration; innovation could be built into the new structure. The ministry by 1984 had already approved a project for the "restoration of health planning." When the HIID/USAID-funded team arrived on site in 1985, it was evident that this phrase was a euphemism for "creation of a statistics and planning unit in the ministry." Thus, the option of restoration was attractive to policymakers throughout the ministry. It could bring in new resources to be used for purposes which went beyond narrow meanings of restoration, thanks to the ambiguity of the term.

Economic reform was a second direction to take. The financing of health facilities and health care in Chad was handled through the ministry except for those facilities supported by religious groups. Health personnel were employed

142

by the ministry. Physicians and nurses were not allowed to engage in private practice, at least not formally, and they were not supposed to charge fees for services rendered as state employees, nor for the drugs distributed free to the facilities. However, traditional healers who practiced outside public or private health facilities did charge fees, and some supervisory doctors did a lucrative abortion business, strictly against the law.

The financing available from Chadian and outside resources was clearly insufficient to support such a public system. The expenditure per capita was U.S. $0.30.[9] To obtain funds for facilities, the government asked them to charge 100 CFA (U.S. $0.30) per visit. These fees, when they were collected, were sent to the treasury where they were never again seen by the Health Ministry. Thus, incentives were slim for this type of financing. Little was collected and none of whatever was passed on to the treasury returned to finance health services.

Reform of health financing is simply a facet of the increasing vogue for economic reform of Third World countries.[10] These proposals usually take the form of proposals for user fees which may be acceptable in some countries.[11] USAID, during this period, supported a project in self-financing of medications in one town in Chad, putting pressure on Chadian officials to think about alternative means of financing.

The prevailing philosophy of leading ministry officials was that health care in Chad should be free and available to all. In fact, the private practice of medicine was forbidden. All Chadian physicians (who comprised the leadership in the ministry apart from the minister and the deputy minister) had been trained abroad, often in Eastern Europe, an experience which impressed them with the ability of government to furnish health care with little or no self-financing. There was even a slight sense that for government *not* to provide health care would make Chad a second-rate country.

Another reason for rejecting self-financing schemes was their impracticality in Chadian social structure. A health worker may be a civil servant in the eyes of the government, but in the eyes of his family he is a financial resource in case of need. Thus, any health worker would be hard pressed to collect fees from members of his family and friends. Even in the ostensibly nonpaying system, such family demands were a constant source of difficulty for health workers. One visitor to the national public pharmacy spent a morning observing drugs dispensed in exchange for favors previously rendered or to meet family obligations. A fee system would not be politically popular and would be extremely difficult to administer in the Chadian social context. Given these constraints, it is not surprising that ministry officials never seriously considered economic reform except for the single project of pharmaceutical self-financing, which USAID insisted on funding in one town and which ended two years later with no sign that it would be tried in other regions. It was clear that if any economic reform were undertaken, it would be only as a result of strong external pressure and strong external funding.

The third option for reform was to recast the health services system itself by emphasizing primary care over secondary and tertiary care. In public health parlance, primary care meant preventive, diagnostic, and treatment care delivered at the site of first contact in a situation where the care-givers were integral members of the community with which they worked. In the international sphere,

143

primary care began to take on a broader meaning particularly after the WHO Conference at Alma-Ata in 1978 which declared:

> Primary Health Care is essential health care made universally accessible to individuals and families in the community by means acceptable to them, through their full participation and at a cost that the community and country can afford.[12]

Putting this definition into operation has proved difficult. The conference specified eight elements necessary for primary care including nutrition, sanitation, maternal and child health care, and disease control, with communities expected to plan their own primary care activities.

In fact, what primary care began to mean through the work of WHO was the delivery of health services by indigenous village health workers (as opposed to doctors and nurses). This development was influenced by the experience of China during the Cultural Revolution when it had trained one million "barefoot doctors" to serve as community workers and sanitation experts, and to provide a minimum of medical care.[13] Unfortunately, this experience has not been successfully replicated elsewhere (and subsequent inquiry suggests that its success in China was limited). The Chinese tried with little success to export their methods to Tanzania. India has been no more successful, despite attempts to place community health volunteers in 600,000 villages.[14] A USAID-funded project to place village health workers in Niger fell far short of its goals, while a USAID-funded project in Mali incurred recurrent costs which went far beyond what local communities were willing to support.[15]

Nevertheless, the goal of training village health workers is still espoused by WHO. Thus, WHO provided Chad with funds for training village health workers and encouraged the ministry to set up a separate administrative division called "Primary Health Care."

Most ministry officials agreed, in principle, with the notion of promoting primary health care, but reacted with skepticism to giving prominence to a new type of health worker with no clear relationship to other health workers. However, as long as WHO provided the funds and clearly was not going to provide those same funds for other purposes, the Chadians were willing to accommodate a small program. At no time did they envision a massive community program. This was a reform which was acceptable so long as outsiders paid for it. The only officials who openly espoused the reform were those whose administrative positions gave them responsibility for the program. This was a reform with the potential to change entirely the face of health services delivery in Chad, but ministry officials, in treating it as just another incremental program, were able to limit its effects.

The fourth option was to reform the administrative structure itself. This became the ministry's major reform activity in two sequential parts: first, to restructure the ministry itself, and second, as a result, to develop a statistics and planning unit.

The Chadian administrative system is based on the Napoleonic model of a centralized bureaucracy, hierarchical in nature, with the central government represented outside the capital by a prefect responsible for all aspects of the administration in his region. The system is a direct descendant of the colonial civil bureaucracy. Before the "events," the Health Ministry had followed a military model developed by the French technical advisers who, like their colonial predecessors, were themselves mainly military physicians.[16] The bureaucracy they dominated and endowed was called the Grandes Endémies. It was organized with mobile teams which spread across the countryside striking down infectious disease wherever it arose. Permanent officers were posted in the "Secteurs" which did not correspond with the geographic lines of the prefectures. The agency was heavily staffed by French physicians and at one time was considered to have an effective disease prevention program. Divisions of the ministry other than the Grandes Endémies, such as sanitation, health facilities, and training, lacked enthusiastic French support and thus garnered relatively few resources in personnel and financing.

With the restoration of ministry activities after 1982, officials had at least five objectives for administrative reform. The first and most important was to strengthen the central ministry to make the power of the central government felt in the regions. Ideally, this would include control over personnel and resources. This objective was part of the whole government's need to reassert central control after years of anarchy. Just how to accomplish this administratively was not clear, but it would involve, among other things, creating regional representatives, a better trained (more competent) central bureaucracy, and the means to gather and process information so the ministry could plan, monitor, and supervise what was going on in the country.

A second objective was to coordinate relations between staff and line agencies, in this case between programs which were created at the ministry and the facilities in which the programs were supposed to operate. Another way of describing this is the problem of coordinating the activities of nationwide vertical programs, such as maternal and child health, with the activities of individual clinics and medical centers. This is a problem which has bedeviled public health officials in all places at all times. In essence, the question boils down to whether you organize by geographic area or by function. New York City, the world's first major public health department, struggled with this issue for more than forty years.[17]

Lest this objective seem an elevated philosophical one, it should be noted that the way an issue such as this tends to get resolved has less to do with the philosophy of administration than with a necessity of self-preservation, which we propose as a third objective. For any individual actor in the Chadian Health Ministry, the objective was to enhance his personal survival and secondarily to enhance any agency in which he had a major role. Since the assignment of roles could easily change under the reorganization, and since it was not necessarily clear who, if anyone, would reassign roles (whether the director general, the highest ranking professional, or the deputy minister, or the minister), negotiations became highly complex. The director general had a particular interest in consolidating the power of his office, but in this objective he could not absolutely count on the support of his political superiors in the ministry, nor necessarily on his inferiors, the directors of divisions/agencies who wanted to retain their autonomy.

The fourth objective was, paradoxically, to strengthen regional administration, to make the regions more capable of solving their own health problems. This was not as much in conflict with centralization as it seemed. The regions had developed a good deal of autonomy thanks to the civil war. For many years, they had been operating without benefit of central government. For example, when a ministry delegation traveled to health facilities outside the capital in 1986, health workers commented that it was the first time they had received a government delegation. However, the autonomy afforded by the lack of central government had also created independently operating personnel, often oblivious to what was going on in the next village or health facility. Hence the need for central government to establish a regional medical officer, called at first "medical prefect," whose task was to coordinate health activities in his prefecture.

The fifth and final objective for some ministry personnel was to decrease the influence of foreign, particularly French, personnel. Residuals of Chad's colonial past, of Chad's impoverished status, and of its intermittent wars, French advisers had a place of honor at the minister's side and all the way down through the hierarchy. Sentiment at this state of affairs ranged from outraged anticolonialism to simple pecuniary interest in controlling the funds the French provided. No one was ready to bite the hand that feeds, but certain Chadians, galled by their semicolonial status, did think it time to limit the amount of poking the fingers of that hand could do.

If those were the five primary objectives of reform, one should not lose sight of an objective frequently cited, the need to "rationalize" the administration. When closely scrutinized, "rationalize" itself turned out to be a rationalization for any of the five other objectives which were not as easily enunciated in polite discourse.

Administrative Reform: Decisions and Implementation: Two Cases

Organizational Reform

The first action was to restructure the ministry. The discussion on administrative reorganization dragged on from 1984 until April 1986 when changes were finally approved by the Council of Ministers. The Chadian description of this process was "créer un nouvel organigramme," that is, to create a new organization chart. The intensity of the debates suggested that much more than a drawing was at stake. The major controversial issue became the number and character of each of the ministry's major agencies, and what the responsibilities of each would be.

The director general preferred as few such agencies as possible, since that would simplify the task of coordination and, fortuitously, consolidate his power. He wanted also to break up or at least submerge the Grandes Endémies in a larger agency, particularly if the director of that agency were one who were closely tied to him. Arrayed against this viewpoint were certain directors who already controlled agencies and wanted to maintain the status quo, if not increase their holdings. Two other important actors were the French advisers, whose extensive investment in the ministry made changes in the administrative structure no trivial matter, and the WHO, which had published recommendations for how Third World health agencies should be organized, including suggestions for assuring the visibility of primary care by giving it its own agency.

The second issue was the creation of the "medical prefects" who were to coordinate health activities in their localities. The Ministry of the Interior had objected to their denomination as "prefects" since there could be only one prefect in each region and he was the representative of the Ministry of the Interior. This objection was easily met by rebaptizing the physicians "Médecins Chefs de Préfecture" (MCPs). However, there remained much ambiguity about their roles. The director general wanted them directly under his authority, a kind of local health czar. The directors of agencies wanted them to be subordinate to their agencies and the programs they directed. Most donors favored the creation of the MCPs but were inclined to take no position on administrative relations, except for the French advisers who wanted to be sure the MCPs did not usurp the authority of the Grandes Endémies' regional agents, the Médecins Chefs de Secteur.

The third issue was whether to move the statistics and planning unit, which had been buried in the agency for training and education, up to become part of the director general's office. The director general favored this proposal because this unit, funded and promoted by USAID, would give him the means to monitor and survey activities of the whole ministry, as well as give him the tools to do some orderly planning. Few other ministry staff saw the potential of such an agency. In fact, no one else seemed to care except for the director of the training and education agency, who was known to be unhappy about the dismemberment of his agency. (His discomfort was resolved when he was rewarded with a major post with the political party and relieved of having to deal with the health bureaucracy.)

The resolution of these questions was worked out in the back rooms, in ministry staff meetings, and ultimately in the Council of Ministers, but not until they had been remanded to lower levels several times. As in all such political compromises, there was something for everybody. Every director got an agency. Primary care had its own agency. The "preventive medicine" agency included all the former Grandes Endémies activities. In addition, it was given management of the special programs such as maternal and child health, nutrition, and vaccination. To give the agency line authority, rural clinics were placed under its supervision while urban clinics, infirmaries, and hospitals were placed under another agency, Hospitals and Urban Medicine. With this splintering of the health facilities, attempts to coordinate line and staff agencies appeared frustrated.

The law gave the MCPs authority over local health services, but since facilities and programs were administered through agencies, and since the relationship between the MCPs and the agencies was not spelled out (in the new organization chart both MCPs and agencies depended on the director general but no lines connected them), the extent of their authority remained murky. The one concession to the director general's interests was the transfer of statistics and planning to his office.

These compromises maintained the independent position of certain agency directors (and even added one), maintained intact the elements of the French-sponsored activities, gave visibility to the WHO-sponsored programs of primary care, and gave the director general his own statistics unit. This result can be seen as typical of bureaucratic infighting, with the agency heads and foreign donors succeeding in protecting their pet projects. The French preserved their Grandes

Endémies structure, yet henceforth their influence in the ministry as a whole could be balanced by the American-supported statistics unit.

Creation of the Statistics and Planning Unit

Although the creation of a statistics and planning unit was originally proposed by a donor, USAID, its implementation became possible because some ministry officials, at least, could benefit from espousing it. The very establishment of this unit gave the director general some of the means to assert central control over the regions, to put in place a regional representative of central authority, to increase the resources available to his office, and finally, to assess resources and plan for their deployment.

The notion of a strong Bureau de Statistiques, Planification, et Etudes (BSPE) had been around since the mid-1970s when it had been particularly promoted by USAID representatives in Chad as in other African countries. By 1983, USAID had revived the idea which met with favor from the director general, and they had funded a two-year project for the restoration of health planning.

When the three-person, USAID-funded HIID team assembled in N'Djamena in October 1985, it found that the ministry lacked the means to gather data on even the simplest activities. It could not report accurately the number of public health facilities in the country, much less the number of private ones. The five agencies trying to gather some data did so with duplicative and less than optimal results.

With the HIID team helpfully pointing out these lacunae, the ministry moved to establish the Commission on the Health Information System (CSIS). Commission members included all agency and program directors as well as donor representatives. Thus, the debate on administrative reform could also be played out in the debate on the information system. The director general asked the BSPE to serve as secretary to the commission, but since the BSPE had no bureau chief and only a modestly trained staff of three, the secretarial work as well as the more directive work of option papers fell in the hands of the HIID team. This additional bureaucratic capacity was essential to the planning process.

The option paper for restructuring the health information system, which the HIID team prepared in May 1986 after much consultation with ministry officials, was circulated to the director general and members of the commission in June 1986. It took account of the needs for data voiced by agency and program directors, the need to minimize administrative burdens of regional and local personnel, and the limited resources available at the ministerial level.

During the next few weeks, a member of the HIID team met individually with the director general and members of the commission to evaluate what options were likely to be chosen, and to see where compromises could be made. As positions were clarified, they were communicated to others to see if agreement could be reached. By the day of the commission meeting on June 30, it was obvious that there was a consensus to scrap the old system and to build a greatly simplified new one.

Three decisions had to be made that morning as the commission assembled in the ministry meeting room with its droning fans and creaking chairs. The first was to select the sources of data to be used in the information system. Many of the directors had earlier insisted that much of the information they needed could be acquired only through surveys of particular populations for particular health problems—for example, malnutrition. Others who recognized the ministry's limited resources felt that it would not be possible to build a capacity for surveys simultaneously with building a routine reporting system. Since a routine reporting system was needed to monitor the activities of the health facilities as well as to assess health needs, the commission decided that the ministry's major source of data for the next few years would be routine reports provided by all health facilities, both public and voluntary/private.

The second decision was to choose the types of reports required. The directors of Administration and of Hospitals and Urban Medicine wanted an annual inventory of all health facilities with information about their personnel, facilities, and equipment. The primary care aficionados wanted this inventory to include information about village health workers, village health committees, and population size. When an inventory was eventually agreed to all these indicators were included, although much doubt was expressed about the reliability of population data and the probability of succeeding in getting facilities to fill out such a form annually.

The old system had required each facility to report monthly on its activities and on the health problems it had treated. Everyone agreed that one of the major reasons this system had not worked before was that the reports were too long, too complicated, and no one did anything with them anyway. As a result, the commission decided that all health facilities would still be required to fill out monthly reports but that less information would be required; that the reporting of health problems would be limited to those problems that nurses even in the simplest clinics were capable of recognizing correctly; and finally, that clinics would receive feedback from their reports.

This agreement to simplify reporting requirements did not sit well with the preventive medicine agency epidemiologists, who feared losing information about (and control over) various diseases running loose in the country. Therefore, the commission decided that health facilities which had greater diagnostic ability (and which were equipped with laboratories) would serve as "sentinel sites" to report on supplementary diagnoses and activities.

Finally, the commission decided to ask a limited number of facilities with good diagnostic capability and access to a radio, telephone, or telegraph to report weekly on a few important infectious diseases against which the preventive medicine division might have to take immediate action. Thus, in all, four routine reports were chosen, with the stipulation that they be the *only* reports used by *all* ministry agencies and programs.

The third and most important decision in terms of administrative reform was how and through whom the data were to be transmitted, and who was to receive and process them. Knowledge is power, as everyone knows. Those in the ministry who until now had been collecting their own data, however badly, were still reluctant to see them going to anyone else. The director general, who had been dissatisfied with previous information efforts, particularly those run by the French, saw an opportunity to revamp information flow and to centralize it within the BSPE, now under his direction. Before the commission meeting, he had conveyed his preference to the directors with the rationale that since the

HIID project would provide two personal computers for the BSPE, the data should be centralized where the computers were. The agency and program directors agreed to this plan only after the director general had reassured them that the BSPE thereby undertook an obligation to provide feedback to the directors and to generate special reports when requested. But they remained skeptical and later, on several occasions, tried to circumvent the new system.

The Preventive Medicine Agency held out that it should receive the weekly telegram simultaneously with the BSPE so that it could immediately take whatever action was needed. Thus, the weekly telegram was the one exception to the pattern of transmission. All the other reports were transmitted by the health facility to the MCP who, in turn, transmitted them to the BSPE for processing and analysis. Agency directors would become dependent on the BSPE for information about activities in the regions.

During the next year, the ministry increased the BSPE staff to eight members and appointed a bureau chief. The HIID team installed computers, trained staff, designed new forms for the monthly reports and annual inventory, and trained the BSPE staff to organize seminars throughout the country for MCPs and local personnel on how to use the new system. By the end of 1988, 88 percent of all health facilities were participating in the monthly reporting system and had managed to send to the BSPE 86 percent of the reports expected during the previous year. This was a remarkable achievement considering the difficult local work conditions and the previous history of poor communications.

Let us now turn to how actors and administrative relations were affected by the burgeoning information system. The major change was in the flow of information and in the consequential change of administrative relationships, much as had been intended by the reform. The MCPs found themselves with the authority to train and supervise nurses and to tell them how to manage information in their clinics. They could stop in the BSPE offices when they were in the capital to review the activities in their region and to assess needs. This information gave them an advantage in negotiating with the Administration and Finance agency for personnel or with the Preventive Medicine Agency for preventive programs. In fact, only one or two of the more energetic and dedicated MCPs took advantage of the new situation. For the others, using this tool to improve their professional performance was less important than other considerations.

The director general benefited from having information about health facilities, personnel, and activities available at any time. When donors presented proposals to develop new facilities, he could marshal lists of current facilities and more easily turn donors toward projects he favored. He could keep an eye on the activities of programs, agencies, and the MCPs.

The high point of the BSPE's early career was reached when a meningitis epidemic swept N'Djamena in March 1988 (in public health, administrative triumphs tend to accompany epidemiologic disasters). The BSPE became the nerve center for directing the successful fight against the epidemic, maintaining daily counts of cases (something which the Preventive Medicine Agency would have done previously), and coordinating the distribution of vaccines.

The new information system did not necessarily clarify administrative relationships. For example, the minister and deputy minister, when they pleased, would go directly to BSPE staff for information and special reports (which took priority over other activities) instead of passing through the director general. The new system also heightened tensions between donors, each in defense of his client agency as well as between the BSPE and other agencies and programs. To illustrate the first case there was the time the HIID team asked if the BSPE could use some empty ministry offices the French had just renovated to set up computers and train BSPE staff during the two months when their own offices were being renovated. The French adviser took this issue to the minister with the statement, "No American is going to use our offices." BSPE tensions with the vaccination program became evident during a vaccination campaign in late 1987, when the latter program set up its own data collection and analysis system. Meanwhile, preventive medicine eyed nervously the BSPE's activities during the meningitis epidemic, while some of the BSPE nervously eyed the HIID team. None of these tensions was serious enough to threaten the information system, but one could see the possibility that the agencies which had lost their data-gathering and controlling capacity when the system was formed were working to erode BSPE's control, or better yet, to contrive to establish their own parallel system, if possible with the help of outside donors.

The implementation of these administrative reforms sounds like the stuff of bureaucratic politics, with bureaucrats defending their turf or expanding it. In fact, the only ones playing a traditional bureaucratic politics game were those who were not part of the Chadian bureaucracy: the donors. They were playing it on behalf of their own bureaucracies back home. Within the Chadian bureaucracy there were other events which did not happen, which you would have expected to happen if everyone were happily being a classic bureaucrat. In the next section, we will examine these events or nonevents.

Bureaucratic Reform in Chad-Like Systems

The most telling nonevents were in the BSPE itself where staff stability and indigenous leadership remained in short supply despite the bureau's enlarged resources and responsibilities. It would be tempting to attribute this either to slow development or to incompetence, but that would be missing the effects of the factional system which creates incentives for actions that are often at variance with the bureaucratic interests that one expects to prevail in a bureaucratic politics model.

From an analytic point of view, bureaucratic politics is a subset of factional politics. In bureaucratic politics it is assumed that the faction is congruent with the bureau and that when a person leaves the bureau, his prime factional loyalties change. Such an arrangement can prevail when a person's objective interests—income, advancement—and psychic well-being—power, status—are tightly bound to the workplace and its success. Chadian factional life is more unbounded than this; where one stands depends only coincidentally on where one sits, because vital personal alliances extend outside bureaucratic structures. They persist when a civil servant changes his bureaucratic position or, as has too frequently been the case, when the bureaucratic and governmental structure collapses around him. Given Chad's recent history of uncertainty, betrayal, and distrust, holding on to as many bureaucratically unbounded alliances as one can find is perfectly rational.

The low level of financial rewards from bureaucratic work further militates against strong identification with the workplace. Thus, making money on the side by tutoring, double-dipping, fiddling the expense account, or cadging a plum like a personal vehicle or a trip abroad has more survival value than intense devotion to a bureaucratic mission.

The chief of the BSPE had been appointed when he returned from study in France, nearly a year after the bureau's creation. Although he and the director general were from the same small central ethnic group, which some said accounted for his receiving his post, the BSPE's chief's strategy seemed to be to increase his own margin of maneuver by building ties to as many sources as possible including the minister and the deputy-minister. The BSPE chief managed his staff with a very light touch because the staff also had patrons among higher officials. If affronted, even on minor disciplinary issues (such as regularly not showing up for work), they took their complaints to their patrons, who then leaned on the BSPE chief. Under such circumstances, the costs of hewing to bureaucratic norms of administration became high.

BSPE staff also found means to opt out of the BSPE completely by obtaining fellowships abroad using their own patron-client networks. Even a much needed secretary, by using his patron-client network, secured a transfer back to his hometown. For an administrator in these circumstances, personal survival may have to take precedence over administrative reform, even reform that, in theory, should increase the power and rewards accruing to his bureaucratic unit.

Although the director general had lost most of the major points in the administrative reform, and although rumors abounded that he would lose his post, he survived. The secret of his survival lay not in his ability to manipulate the forces within the ministry but in his ties outside the ministry. These ties included having been part of the core group of loyalists that fought its way back to N'Djamena in 1982 with Hissène Habré and friendships with politically powerful individuals, not from his ethnic group, but with whom he had gone to school. The director general's survival, like his subordinates' advancement, depended little on bureaucratic performance.

Ministry business was often conducted on the basis of factional alliances, not bureaucratic position. Higher officials frequently blocked proposals or projects put forward by civil servants belonging to other factions, and called in extra-ministry allies to make their point stick. When carried to extremes, this behavior could cause all government business to come to a grinding halt, as when a very senior official insisted on running ministry funds through his personal account where they could be used to bankroll his political faction. An official in the ministry, explaining in late 1987 how factionalism dominated decisions, called the situation "GUNT II."

In the classic model of the civil service, loyalty is owed to the state. In the Chadian version of the civil service, loyalty to political allies must take precedence. Insofar as allies represent the formal state command hierarchy, business can be accomplished. But when the political allies and the state are no longer synonymous, government activity follows patterns bewildering to the outsider (and even occasionally to the insider). Contributing to the bewilderment is the presumption on the part of Chadian participants that others *must* be acting in accordance with personal factional interests, even on those occasions when bureaucratic policy interests may be the motivation.

What conclusions are we to draw about the reform discussed in this paper? The bureaucratic lines were successfully rearranged; MCPs began to monitor their regions; the BSPE was established and has been more than trivially successful in producing reports and information useful to interested policymakers. At the same time, coordination remains a sometime thing; erratic decision making is a frequent occurrence, as are misallocations of resources and bureaucratic undiscipline. The reform may be justifiably seen as a triumph over the chaos of Chad's recent history. Even then, serious questions must be raised about the reform's sustainability after the HIID team leaves.

Grindle and Thomas usefully employ Hirschman's distinction between pressing and chosen reforms to analyze the problems these reforms encounter later.[18] The reform leading to the creation of the BSPE would clearly fall within the category of chosen reform. As such, it does not benefit from the overwhelming pressures of circumstance that might continue to guarantee its survival against the disruptive effects of factional politics. The fact that reform occurred at all owes something to the pressures, at least in the form of resource enticements, provided by USAID, and the pressures exerted by the presence of the HIID team.

This would suggest that proposals for chosen reforms in countries with Chad-like characteristics must include plans to build in continuing pressures that may sustain the reform over time. These pressures could include plans for projects to last five to ten years rather than the two to three years of this project or to require that disbursements for further projects be made conditional upon maintenance of the earlier reform. Ultimately, of course, a reform will be sustained against lower-level factional pressures only if officials at the ministerial level or higher take a direct interest in these reforms.

To understand the effects of bureau and ministerial level factionalism should be the first assignment for those proposing reforms. In effect, something of a "political risk" and "political resource" analysis should be done at these subsystemic levels as part of the preparatory work. While no outside group is likely to penetrate the deepest mysteries of factional alignment, it should at least be possible to arrive at a realistic assessment of the internal factors affecting success and sustainability. Such work is touchy, but reformers should have some idea of what they are getting into. For administrative reforms such an analysis means understanding political factionalism in the bureaus where the reforms will take place.

Outsiders who would be reform-mongers in Chad-like bureaucratic systems might well pay attention to three additional lessons from the experience described above. First, since reform consumes both time and bureaucratic resources, a supplemental team, like the HIID team in Chad, may be required. However, it will prove useful only if it serves instrumental purposes of important officials. Second, adjustment policies that hold down civil-service salaries to present levels make the task of improving bureaucratic performance even harder, however imperative such policies may appear from a macroeconomic perspective. Such trade-offs should be debated and not decided on ideological grounds. Finally, major improvement in bureaucratic performance, and a fair prospect that reforms will be self-sustaining, will in the longer run depend on assuring stability of the governmental system as a whole. Predictability and supervisory attention of senior officials who themselves have a stake in the performance and survival of the regime are essential. In the production of such a felicitous macrolevel environment, outsiders can provide modest help and encouragement, but they cannot hope to direct the process nor to control the prime variables that determine success or failure. ✍

Table 1 **Chad Facts** (estimates)	
Population (est.1987)[1]	5.3 million
Gross Domestic Product (GDP), 1987[2]	U.S. $729 million
GDP/capita, 1987[2]	U.S. $138
External aid for all public activities (gifts and loans), 1987[2]	U.S. $240 million
External aid as percent of GDP[2]	32.9%
External aid for health activities, 1986[3]	U.S. $16 million
Ministry of Public Health	
Average annual expenditures, 1983-85[3]	U.S. $1.2–1.6 million
Personnel costs, 1986[4]	
Budgeted	U.S. $3.2 million
Estimated allocation	U.S. $1–2 million
Operating costs, 1986[5]	
Budgeted	U.S. $1 million
Actual expenditures	U.S. $250,000

[1] Government of Chad, Ministry of Planning and Cooperation, *Statistiques Démographiques du Tchad, 1985-86-87-88*.

[2] Government of Chad, Ministry of Planning and Cooperation, *Comptes Economiques: 1983-1988 -Document Provisoire- (Données recueillies au 31-12-87)*.

[3] World Bank, *Tchad: Situation Economique et Priorités*, 18 June 1987.

[4] Republique du Tchad, *Dotation de Fonctionnement des Pouvoirs Publiques*, 1986.

[5] Government of Chad, Ministry of Public Health, *Rapport d'Activités, 1986*.

Table 2 **Chad Health Data**

A. Health resources per 100,000 inhabitants, 1988

Physicians	2.13
Dentists	0.11
Qualified nurses	17.74
Pharmacists	0.34
Hospitals/med. centers	0.58
Dispensaries/clinics	5.90
Hospital beds and places for beds	74.00

B. Health facilities

	Public	Religious/ Voluntary/ Private	TOTAL
Hospital/med. center	24	7	31
Infirmary/maternity	22	7	29
Dispensary/clinic	193	93	286
Health posts	3	32	35
Other	33	4	37
TOTAL	275	143	418

C. Death rates

Infant mortality estimate, 1987	210/1,000
Maternal mortality rate for births at N'Djamena hospital, 1986	786/100,000

D. New cases of selected health problems per 1,000 inhabitants as reported by 294 health facilities, July 1987-June 1988

	AGE			
HEALTH PROBLEM	0-11 Months	1-4 Years	5 Years and Up	All Ages
Fever	112	65	21	30
Cough of <2 weeks	168	61	15	27
Trauma	35	33	22	24
Diarrhea	179	69	9	23
Dysentery	21	22	7	10
Conjunctivitis	63	26	9	13
Skin infection	47	29	9	13
Otitis media/tonsil	43	25	8	11
Neonatal tetanus	5	—	—	—

Source: Government of Chad, Ministry of Health, Bureau of Statistics, Planning, and Studies

Notes

1 For the "bureaucratic politics" model see Graham Allison, *Essence of Decision: Explaining the Cuban Missile Crisis* (Boston: Little Brown, 1971). Merilee S. Grindle and John W.Thomas use this concept in explaining the outcome of reforms in their paper, "The Political Economy of Policy Change in Developing Countries," Harvard Institute for International Development, Employment and Enterprise Analysis (E.E.P.A.) Discussion Paper No. 10, October 1987.

2 Jean Chapelle, *Le Peuple Tchadien: Ses Racines, Sa Vie Quotidienne et Ses Combats* (Paris: Editions l'Harmattan, 1980), 39.

3 Robert Buijtenhuijs, *Le Frolinat et Les Guerres Civiles du Tchad (1977-1984)* (Paris: Karthala, 1987).

4 William J. Foltz, "Social Structure and Political Behavior of Senegalese Elites," in *Friends, Followers and Factions: A Reader in Political Clientelism*, eds. Steffan W. Schmidt, James C. Scott, Carl Lande, and Laura Guasti (Berkeley: University of California Press, 1977), 242-49.

5 William J. Foltz, "Chad's Third Republic: Strengths, Problems, and Prospects," *CSIS Africa Notes* 77 (October 30, 1987).

6 World Bank, *Tchad: Situation Economique et Priorités (Projet)* (18 June 1987): 127.

7 It is commonly estimated that an African family of four requires 50,000 CFA a month to live with modest comfort in N'Djamena.

8 The source of the infant mortality rate for Chad is from estimates by Chadian and expatriate physicians of infant deaths in N'Djamena. No studies permitting a more accurate estimate have been undertaken in Chad in the 1980s. The source of the Egyptian and Kenyan rates is James P. Grant/UNICEF, *The State of the World's Children, 1987* (New York: Oxford University Press, 1987), 90. This source gives an infant mortality rate of 138 per 1,000 live births in Chad in 1985. No one in Chad could identify the source of this statistic, nor was anyone willing to attest to its reliability.

9 World Bank, *Tchad: Situation Economique et Priorités* Report No. 6785-ch (Washington, D.C., January 1988): 123.

10 See, for example, the volume of nine papers edited by D. Donaldson and D. Dunlop, "Financing Health Services in Developing Countries," *Soc. Sci. Med.* 22, no. 3 (April 1986): 313-85. Each paper develops and illustrates some of the issues in financing health services in particular countries.

11 Donald S. Shepard and Elisabeth R. Benjamin, "Mobilizing Resources for Health: The Role of User Fees in Developing Countries," Harvard Institute for International Development, Development Discussion Paper No. 234, September 1986.

12 World Health Organization, *Primary Health Care*, a joint report by the Director-General of the World Health Organization and the Executive Director of the United Nations Children's Fund (Geneva and New York, 1978), 2.

13 Victor W. Sidel, "The Role and Training of Medical Personnel," in *Public Health and the People's Republic of China*, eds. Myron E. Wegman, Tsung-Yi Lin, and Elizabeth Purcell (New York: Josiah Macy Foundation, 1973), 162.

14 Lincoln C. Chen, "Primary Health Care in Developing Countries: Overcoming Operational, Technical, and Social Barriers," *Lancet* (29 November 1986): 1264.

15 Clive S. Gray, "State-sponsored Primary Health Care in Africa: The Recurrent Cost of Performing Miracles," *Soc. Sci. Med.* 22, no. 3 (1986): 361-68.

16 The military model was the origin for the Public Health Service Corps in the United States, and it is not quite dead yet. During the 1980s, United States Surgeon General C. Everett Koop reinstituted the policy of requiring Public Health Service Corps personnel to wear uniforms when on duty.

17 Herbert Kaufman, *The New York City Health Centers,* Inter-University Case Program (Indianapolis: Bobbs-Merrill, 1959).

18 Grindle and Thomas, "The Political Economy of Policy Change," 31.

Structural Adjustment and Economic Reform in Indonesia:

Model-Based Policies vs. Rules of Thumb[1]

Shantayanan Devarajan and Jeffrey D. Lewis

Shantayanan Devarajan is associate professor in public policy at the John F. Kennedy School of Government, Harvard University. He has been writing, teaching, and advising governments about macroeconomic policy in developing countries for eleven years. His current research focuses on the environmental dimensions of development policy.

Jeffrey D. Lewis is an Institute associate at HIID and has been an adviser in the Ministry of Finance, Indonesia, for five years. He has also consulted in Bangladesh, Turkey, and Colombia, and has taught courses at Harvard University in development economics and planning.

Introduction

Since the early 1970s, a number of developing countries have faced balance-of-payments crises. The causes have been many: adverse external shocks, like oil price increases, commodity price declines, a rise in international interest rates, or cutoffs in international lending; or profligate spending by either the government or the private sector that led to unsustainable current account deficits. Despite their varied causes, the policy responses to these crises have been surprisingly similar, in general aiming at the twin goals of shifting resources towards tradable goods and improving the efficiency of the economy. The specific policies include one or more from the following "package": (1) devalue the exchange rate; (2) set other tradable prices equal to world prices; (3) liberalize trade; (4) unify tariff rates or effective rates of protection; (5) reduce the growth of the money supply; (6) cut government spending; (7) privatize state-owned enterprises; and (8) open up capital markets.

While these policies are familiar, and widely promoted, the mechanism by which they help achieve the twin goals mentioned above are not always well understood. Typically, policymakers (and more commonly their advisers) appeal to intuition derived from the standard model of Walrasian economics. In a "first-best" world (that is, one with no other distortions), reducing or eliminating an existing distortion will unambiguously improve economic welfare. Thus, setting the domestic price of a tradable good equal to its world price eliminates the distortion created by an existing trade tax. Unfortunately, in the real world, no country has but one distortion. However, once this assumption is relaxed, it is not clear whether the standard policy prescription will always improve welfare. Advocates of the policy package respond by saying that, even in actual economies, these measures serve as useful rules of thumb. They associate the problems facing the economy with some of the key distortions (an overvalued exchange rate, say), and claim that eliminating this distortion will steer the economy in the right direction. Besides, the argument continues, to understand the "true" implications of a given policy, a complete model of the economy is needed, which (it is argued) is hard to come by in most developing countries.

The rules of thumb under consideration relate to policies in nearly all sectors of the economy. In the macroeconomic arena, governments are advised to "get the exchange rate right" by maintaining an appropriate real exchange rate. Conventional wisdom identifies "appropriate" adjustments in the exchange rate as those required to offset the difference between domestic and world inflation. In the area of trade reform, the focus is on the *level* and *pattern* of import tariffs (or alternatively, effective protection). According to the standard prescription, the average level should be lowered and the dispersion of rates across different commodities reduced or eliminated.

In fiscal policy, attention is focused on the superiority of certain types of fiscal instruments (value-added taxes are preferable to indirect taxes, for example) and on the need to "get prices right" by setting domestic prices as close to world prices as possible.

These rules of thumb are not completely wrong; rather, they are correct only under restrictive conditions that are rarely met in developing countries. In the absence of such "first-best" simplicity, the magnitude or even direction of reform efforts critically depends on the nature and size of other distortions in the

160

economy—in other words, on the structure of the economy in question. In a second-best environment, the policy package needs to be amended.

In this paper, we consider several common rules of thumb from two perspectives. First, we use an analytic model with just enough detail to analyze each rule and its required assumptions, and assess the circumstances under which these assumptions are valid. Second, we consider the empirical implications of these standard policy measures in a multisector model of the Indonesian economy that embodies many distortions characteristic of developing countries.

Indonesia provides an ideal subject for such analysis. In the last few years, adverse external conditions (especially oil price declines and dollar depreciation) have placed severe strains on the economy, requiring broad-based economic reform in order to bring about the necessary structural adjustment. The Indonesian government's response has been impressive, beginning with systemwide tax reform and sweeping financial liberalization, and continuing with trade liberalization and deregulation packages from May 1986 onwards, including a major devaluation in September 1986. With debates now under way over the nature and extent of further reform, examination of the relevance of rules of thumb to Indonesia's situation is timely.

In the next section, we first present the two models used subsequently in the analysis. Then we proceed with the analysis of several rules of thumb that frequently appear in the adjustment prescriptions. In the final section, we consider the implications of our findings for policymakers and policy advisers.

Models for Examining Policy Reform

A. A Two-Sector Analytic Model

Much criticism of common rules of thumb centers on the simplicity of the underlying model and the implausibility of the assumptions necessary to produce simple rules. However, it is not necessary to rely on much more complex models to demonstrate the fallacy of these rules. Instead, in this section we describe a simple two-sector model,[2] which will be used in subsequent sections to highlight the critical assumptions for different rules of thumb, and to demonstrate what happens to the standard prescriptions when these assumptions do not hold.

Consider a simple economy in which only two goods are produced: an export good (X), whose output is fully exported, and a domestic good (Q), corresponding to the rest of the economy's output that is consumed domestically. Production of each good occurs according to a production function [equations (1) and (2)] that includes fixed sector-specific capital stocks (K), mobile labor (L), and in the case of the domestic good, an imported intermediate input (M_2) demanded in fixed proportions [equation (3)].

(1) $X = g(K_X, L_X)$

(2) $Q = f(K_Q, L_Q, M_2)$

(3) $M_2 = aQ$

Assuming all labor in the economy is fully employed,

(4) $L = L_X + L_Q$

we equate the value of the marginal product of labor between the two sectors:

(5) $f_L [P_Q(1 - t_Q) - a\pi_2 E(1 + t_2)] = g_L [\pi_X E]$

161

where f_L and g_L are the marginal products of labor, P_Q is the price of Q (and is fixed at unity as the numeraire), π_X and π_2 are the exogenous world prices of X and M_2, t_Q is an indirect tax on Q, t_2 a tariff on M_2, and E the exchange rate.

Final good imports (M_1) are subject to a tariff (t_1) and compete with consumer demand for the domestic good (C), albeit as imperfect substitutes. The elasticity of substitution is given by s:

(6) $\quad C/M_1 \quad = \quad k \, [\, \pi_1 E(1 + t_1) \, / \, P_Q \,]^6$

The private sector balances its budget:

(7) $\quad \pi_X XE + P_Q(1 - t_Q)Q - \pi_2(1 + t_2)M_2 E \quad = \quad P_Q C$

The government consumes a fixed amount of domestic output (G), and balances its budget with foreign borrowing (F):

(8) $\quad t_1 \pi_1 M_1 E + t_2 \pi_2 M_2 E + t_Q P_Q Q + F^* E \quad = \quad P_Q G$

Balance-of-payments equilibrium is assured through movements in the exchange rate (E):

(9) $\quad \pi_X X + F \quad = \quad \pi_1 M_1 + \pi_2 M_2$

Finally, Walras' Law guarantees that supply and demand for Q are equal:

(10) $\quad Q \quad = \quad C + G$

Several features of the model that will affect the results deserve mention before proceeding. First, choosing P_Q as the numeraire means that changes in demand for Q will be apparent in the movements of other variables *relative* to P_Q. For example, since the government consumes only the domestic good Q, any reduction in government consumption must translate into lower output of the domestic good, which is brought about by a depreciation of the exchange rate, making exports more profitable and domestic output less profitable.[3] Second, the assumption that the private sector balances its budget while the government borrows abroad to balance is a crucial one (and quite reasonable within the Indonesian context). As a consequence, changes in the government's deficit are reflected one-for-one in the trade deficit. Finally, the imperfect substitutability in consumption between imported and domestic goods is an important feature which influences the magnitude or even the sign of the economy's response to certain policies.

B. A CGE Model of Indonesia

The model of Indonesia that we use to examine empirically the propositions advanced in this paper derives from the class of economywide computable general equilibrium (CGE) models that in recent years have been developed to analyze the complicated interactions between policy reform and structural change in developing economies.[4] In the remainder of this section, we present a brief overview of the characteristics of the CGE model. For more detail, the reader is referred to the two Appendices, which contain a full equation listing for the model and a description of the sectoral structure and data sources used in the model.

Today's CGE models trace their lineage back through two distinct strands of economic literature: first, to the empirical tradition of input-output and linear programming planning models that were widely applied in developing countries in the 1960s, and second, to the theoretical basis provided by Walrasian general equilibrium theory. The contribution of CGE models has been to move beyond the linear, fixed coefficient representation characteristic of the input-output economy towards a simulated market economy, highly nonlinear and embodying a full range of substitution possibilities in production, demand, and trade.

The CGE model simulates the workings of a market economy. A model solution is a set of wages, output prices, and an exchange rate that represent an economywide equilibrium in labor, product, and foreign exchange markets. Note, however, that the model solution represents a market equilibrium *subject to* behavioral and institutional constraints believed to represent a realistic picture of Indonesia. The base year, in fact, incorporates "disequilibrium" elements: fixed sectoral capital stocks, intersectoral wage and profit differentials, external imbalances, and divergence between international and domestic prices.

There are thirteen sectors or product markets. Domestic prices affect supply-and-demand decisions in all sectors. Supply decisions are constrained by sectoral production functions which permit substitution between labor and (fixed) capital inputs; intermediate input use is determined by fixed input-output coefficients. Four labor types are identified: two types (paid workers and unpaid proprietors) work only in the two agricultural sectors, and two types (blue-collar and white-collar) work in all sectors. Firms maximize profits given exogenous (to the firm) prices and wages. The firm's decision to hire a new worker depends on a comparison between the market wage (which includes a sector-specific differential) and the marginal value product of that worker. Aggregate supply for each labor type is exogenous, and wages adjust to clear the labor markets. The Walrasian character of the model (in which only *relative* prices matter) is evident by fixing exogenously a price index (the *numeraire*).

We have argued that the tradable-nontradable distinction is crucial in analyzing the common rules of thumb. Most of the commodities in the model are tradable, although to varying degrees. As in the two-sector model, domestically produced goods and imports are assumed to be imperfect substitutes. Demand for a sector's "composite" good is defined as a constant elasticity of substitution (CES) function of the domestic good and the imported substitute. Elasticities of substitution vary across sectors, with smaller elasticities reflecting greater differences between the domestic and imported good, and hence greater difficulty in substituting one for the other in response to changes in their relative prices. This formulation implies that the sectoral ratio of imports to domestic goods is a function of the ratio of their prices. Following the small-country assumption, Indonesia is assumed to have no influence over the world price of imports (or exports).

Sectoral exports also are assumed to be different from output sold domestically, reflecting explicit differences (such as quality) as well as a range of barriers preventing the costless reallocation of output between domestic and foreign markets (such as market penetration costs). Because of such barriers, domestic and export prices need not be equal. Producers maximize revenue from selling their total output (expressed as a constant elasticity of transformation [CET] function of exports and domestic sales) by dividing sales between export and domestic markets based on the ratio of prices in each market.

Total foreign exchange available for imports depends not only on export earnings, but also on foreign capital inflows: foreign borrowing, amortization and interest payments, direct foreign investment, and so on. Some of these flows may be either exogenous or endogenous, depending on the simulation undertaken. In some cases, a flexible exchange rate will equate supply and demand for foreign exchange.

Accounting and behavioral rules determine how value-added or factor income is distributed among three different classes of income recipients: firms, households, and the government. The distribution of value added in each sector depends on: (1) the size of the wage bill in total value added; (2) the corporate savings rate; and (3) taxes that affect the division of value added between the private sector and the government. Saving and expenditure behavior are specified for each type of income recipient. The income remaining with firms after they have distributed wages to labor households is distributed to capitalist households, who are the owners of capital (including land). The income flowing into the government from various taxes and from its share of foreign borrowing is used for government consumption (fixed exogenously in real terms), for financing investment, and for debt service. Households save a fixed fraction of their disposable income and spend the rest on goods. Private and government consumption is allocated with fixed expenditure shares. Savings-investment balance is assured by setting total investment equal to available savings, although in certain simulations, real investment is fixed and some component of savings must adjust.

Rules of Thumb: An Assessment of Standard Policy Packages

We now examine the implications of widely prescribed rules of thumb in two different areas: exchange rate policy and tariff policy. Using the analytic model presented above, we consider the conditions under which the standard prescription applies, and assess the applicability of these conditions to developing countries. Finally, using the model of the Indonesian economy, we examine the empirical importance of these issues.

A. Exchange Rate Policy

Exchange rate reform is a nearly universal element in the standard adjustment package prescribed for developing economies, reflecting popular recognition of the sweeping influence that this single price has on incentives to produce for export or import-substitution. Exchange rate policy focuses on two distinct issues: first, *changing the level of the exchange rate* (usually through a devaluation) in order to reduce pressure on the balance of payments and to remove distortions in the relative price of tradables and nontradables; and second, *managing movements in the exchange rate* in order to minimize the impact of adverse external developments.

Regarding the first issue, there is no question that major exchange rate adjustment to reduce tradable-nontradable distortions is a necessary step towards successful liberalization in many developing economies. Rules of thumb are, however, of little use in providing a guide in such cases; in most instances policymakers proceed by trial-and-error in choosing how large an adjustment should be made, with political feasibility often constraining the choice. The target policymakers aim for is the equilibrium real exchange rate (ERER), which will lead to a current account of zero (or some other "sustainable" number).

Once this equilibrium level is reached, concern over *preserving* the gains achieved from the devaluation focuses attention on maintaining the real exchange rate. It is argued that adjusting the nominal exchange rate so that the real exchange rate stays constant will be sufficient to preserve the benefits. In the absence of a general equilibrium model, the standard method of performing this real exchange rate calculation is to pick a base year in which the current account was in balance, and then calculate the nominal exchange rate changes that are necessary to keep the real exchange rate constant, given domestic and world inflation rates.[5]

In this section, we show that this simplistic approach is inappropriate if one adopts a more complex representation of the economy. Specifically, we show that: (1) the simple exchange rate adjustment rule is inadequate except under very restrictive assumptions; (2) terms-of-trade movements (that change the *relative* world prices of traded goods) can change the equilibrium exchange rate, making the simple rule inappropriate; and (3) the appropriate response to terms-of-trade shocks depends on the structure of the economy and the sectoral origins of the shocks.

1. A Constant Real Exchange Rate Maintains a Balanced Current Account

Consider the impact of external price shocks on the stylized economy in the model of the section *Models for Examining Policy Reform*(pp. 161-64). For simplicity, assume that all tariffs and taxes are zero. If all world prices (π_x, π_1, and π_2) change by the same percentage (say, increase by 10 percent), then "world inflation" is equal to this percentage change (10 percent). The rule of thumb suggests the exchange rate should be devalued to offset the differential between domestic inflation (zero in this instance, since P_Q is fixed as the numeraire) and world inflation (10 percent). This implies a 10 percent *revaluation* of the nominal exchange rate, E. Examining the equations of the model, it is apparent that wherever a foreign price appears together with the exchange rate ($\pi * E$), the two movements (π up, E down) will cancel each other, leaving each equation unaffected. The uncertainty stems from the presence of foreign borrowing in the government budget constraint and in the balance-of-payments equation. *As long as foreign borrowing is zero, the rule of thumb is correct.* With F=0, the impacts of the higher world prices and revalued exchange rate cancel out. However, if F is not zero, the exchange rate revaluation lowers the domestic currency value of resources received by the government. In the model as specified, the government would respond by increasing borrowing by 10 percent, which would leave the foreign exchange market equation balanced (since each element would rise by 10 percent). However, if foreign borrowing were constrained (that is, F is not permitted to increase), *then this neutrality would be lost.* A series of further adjustments (real exchange rate depreciation, a cutback in government consumption, or tax increases) would be necessary to restore equilibrium.

Table 1	Exchange Rate Adjustments with Across-the-Board Price Changes	
World price change	Real depreciation	
-50 percent	8.2 percent	
-25 percent	2.8 percent	
+25 percent	-1.7 percent	
+50 percent	-2.8 percent	

Turning to our general equilibrium model of Indonesia, we find that this effect can be quite large, as the data in Table 1 illustrate. By imposing uniform changes in sectoral world prices on the model, we find that the prescription for exchange rate management is *insufficient* to generate the necessary adjustment. The additional adjustment required to restore the economy to equilibrium varies with the magnitude of the shock, and is not symmetric for positive and negative price shocks. A 50 percent decline in world prices requires an 8.2 percent real devaluation (in addition to the 100 percent nominal devaluation demanded by the equilibrium exchange rate rule), while a 50 percent increase in world prices requires only a 2.8 percent revaluation relative to the rule of thumb. One might conclude from the results in Table 1 that while the *magnitude* of the rule is wrong, the *direction* is at least right. However, the direction of the error in fact depends primarily on the *sign* of the trade balance. Since Indonesia had a balance of trade surplus in 1985, an across-the-board decline in world prices lowers nominal exports more than imports, and the balance-of-trade surplus declines. With foreign capital inflows fixed, the exchange rate must adjust to increase the surplus to its original value, requiring further depreciation. However, if the economy initially shows a balance-of-trade deficit (as is true in many developing countries), this story reverses, and the smaller deficit resulting from the lower world prices evokes a slight revaluation to return the balance of payments to its starting point.[6]

2. Terms-of-Trade Changes and Real Exchange Rates

Real economies are not subject to the uniform price changes discussed in the previous section, but rather to sectorally differentiated shocks that further complicate the picture. Reference back to the two-sector model reveals the source of this complication: once the various world prices (π) no longer change proportionately, then the rule of thumb is no longer viable even if foreign borrowing is zero. Even if one adjusts the exchange rate by the *average* level of world inflation (as the rule suggests), the domestic price of each traded good will change unless its world price change equals the average price change. Once these relative prices change, intersectoral reallocation of production and demand is required in order to restore equilibrium. Furthermore, for a given terms-of-trade shock, the *direction* in which the exchange rate should move depends on whether s is greater or less than one (see de Melo and Robinson [1988]). A rule of thumb that is based on price changes alone could be seriously misleading.

Using the CGE model of Indonesia, we can investigate the impact of terms-of-trade shocks on macroeconomic adjustment in the economy. In separate experiments, we apply different size price shocks (-50, -25, +25, and +50 percent) to the world prices of three sectors: petroleum and mining; traded agricultural products; and processed wood and wood products. For each shock, we calculate the new equilibrium exchange rate and compare it to the exchange rate implied by the constant real exchange rate rule of thumb.

Table 2 **Rule of Thumb vs. Model-Based Exchange Rate Changes with Terms-of-Trade Shocks**

World Price Change	Traded Agri.		Wood and Prods.		Oil and Mining	
	R-O-T	Model	R-O-T	Model	R-O-T	Model
-50 percent	2.9	9.5	1.4	4.4	22.7	9.9
-25 percent	1.7	4.9	0.8	2.8	11.0	6.5
+25 percent	-1.9	-4.9	-1.2	-3.7	-10.4	-8.5
+50 percent	-4.0	-9.5	-2.8	-8.1	-20.0	-17.7

Note: A positive change indicates a devaluation.

Table 2 shows the results for the three sets of experiments. For each sector we show two columns: the first contains the exchange rate change resulting from application of the real exchange rate rule of thumb, while the second shows the change generated by the model.[7] The pattern of adjustment is quite different across sectors and price changes. For the traded agriculture and wood sectors, the rule of thumb significantly understates the adjustment required. However, for the oil and mining sector, the reverse is true, as the actual adjustment is lower than that predicted by the simple rule. Moreover, the adjustment is asymmetric between positive and negative shocks, with world price increases generally evoking a larger exchange rate response than decreases. Of course, the exchange rate adjustment is only one component of the economywide adjustment that occurs following each shock. Differences among sectors further influence how the adjustment is distributed through the economy. For example, the sectoral origin of government revenues affects the exchange rate response. The dominance of oil sector revenues in the government budget implies that the oil price declines translate directly into falling government revenues, while for the other two sectors, the direct effect of falling prices on government revenue is tiny, and more than offset by the positive impact that the exchange rate depreciation has on the rupiah value of oil earnings, so that in fact, total revenue grows. The sectoral effects will have obvious implications for other results as well, such as rural-urban income differentials (traded agriculture shocks affect rural incomes more), and so on.[8]

One final complication in the constant real exchange rate approach is the assumption that the net inflow into the economy remains unchanged following a shock. In our CGE model, this implies that a whole range of foreign capital inflows and outflows are not allowed to respond. While convenient, such an assumption flies in the face of prudent macroeconomic management in response to external shocks. When Indonesia's oil export earnings fell by more than 50 percent in 1986, the government responded by drawing on existing lines of credit and supplemental foreign assistance, thereby cushioning the negative impact. The real exchange rate rule of thumb provides no guidance in this regard, nor does it suggest that the preferred response to an external shock should depend on whether it is perceived as temporary or permanent. In the next section, we will consider a case where foreign capital inflows adjust in the context of tariff reform. The qualitative results will be similar for a terms-of-trade shock.

B. Tariff Policy

A common ingredient of economic reform programs has been the reform of the country's tariff regime. This is so for at least two reasons. First, any import tariff—or quantitative restriction, for that matter—acts as an implicit tax on exports. If increasing exports is a goal of the reform, the level of import protection must be reduced. Second, it is often argued that the prevailing pattern of tariffs harms the efficiency of the economy. Highly varying tariff rates, for example, mean that relative domestic prices deviate from world prices. This in turn distorts the signals received by domestic producers and consumers, causing production and consumption to be inefficient. Finally, a crucial aspect of the reform of tariff policy is the distinction between nominal and effective protection. Nominal protection is the degree to which the output price of an industry is increased by a tariff on its competing import. Effective protection measures the impact of the entire tariff structure on value added in an industry, taking into account not just the tariff on competing imports, but also tariffs on the industry's intermediate inputs. Much of the discussion of tariff reform centers around reducing both the level and variation in effective protection.

In this section, we demonstrate that all of these widely held tenets of tariff reform are open to question. Specifically, we show that: (1) reducing tariff levels does not always help exports; (2) reducing the dispersion in tariff rates does not necessarily improve efficiency; and, finally, (3) the standard method of calculating effective rates of protection (ERP) does not measure effective protection.

These standard notions of tariff reform fail to hold because they depend on an unrealistic portrayal of the real world. Typically, tariff reform has been guided by rules of thumb which are both intuitively appealing and easy to implement. However, as in the case of exchange rate policy, these rules are appropriate only for highly simplified model economies. With slightly more sophisticated models, the rules break down. In particular, we show that the standard rules of tariff reform neglect at least four facts about the underlying economy: first, that tariffs may be an important source of revenue to the government; second, that there may be other domestic taxes in the system; third, that not all goods are traded goods; and fourth, that imports and domestically produced goods in the same sector may not be perfect substitutes.

In this section, we show how incorporating these features of developing economies leads to different conclusions about the direction of tariff reform. We do so first in terms of the two-sector model so that these features and the key mechanisms can be seen in sharp relief. Next, we demonstrate the empirical significance of our results by simulating the policies on the thirteen-sector model of Indonesia.

1. Lowering Tariffs Increases Exports

To assess this claim, we simplify the model in the section *Models for Examining Policy Reform* (see pp. 161-64). by neglecting all intermediate inputs ($a = 0$) and domestic taxes ($t_x = 0$). These simplifications are for clarity only; they do not affect the qualitative nature of the results. Assume further that s, the elasticity of substitution between imports and domestic goods, is less than one.

Now consider a reduction in the tariff rate, t_1. In the first round, the effect will be a drop in government revenues. Since government expenditure, G, is fixed, the fiscal deficit widens. By assumption, so does the current account deficit. Associated with the larger current account deficit is an appreciation of the real exchange rate (with P_Q fixed, this means a fall in the nominal exchange rate, E). This real appreciation causes exports to fall. Hence, in this case, the tariff reduction has decreased, rather than increased, exports.[9]

This somewhat surprising result is driven by two features of our model. The first is the assumption that the government's deficit is financed by foreign borrowing. If the government were constrained in international credit markets, so that the revenue shortfall had to be made up by higher domestic taxation, the outcome would be different. The second is the assumption that the elasticity of substitution between imports and domestic goods is less than one. Any change in the tariff rate has both an income and a substitution effect. The income effect would cause a reduction in the tariff rate to increase demand for the domestic good (Q), whereas the substitution effect would cause this demand to decrease (because imports are cheaper). When s < 1, the income effect dominates. The increased demand for Q in turn causes the real exchange rate to appreciate.[10]

That this is more than a simple, theoretical point is demonstrated by a similar result obtained when a 75 percent across-the-board reduction in tariffs is simulated on our model of Indonesia. We require that real government spending (both consumption and investment) remain fixed. The lost tariff revenue is made up through foreign borrowing, while other elements of foreign capital inflow remain unchanged. When tariffs are cut by 75 percent, a real *appreciation* of 3.2 percent occurs, borrowing rises by an amount *greater* than the fall in tariff revenues, and aggregate exports *decline* by 1.6 percent, or in value terms by around two-thirds of the fall in tariff revenues. The export drop varies substantially across sectors, with wood and wood product exports dropping by nearly 7 percent.

The lesson from all this is not that those who advocate tariff reduction as a means of export promotion are wrong. Nor is it simply that the revenue implications of a tariff reduction cannot be ignored. Rather, what our model points out is that the drop in government revenues associated with trade liberalization can also have the effect of *reversing* the original intent of the program, namely, expanding exports. This is especially true for developing economies in which tariff revenues are a more important revenue source than in Indonesia, where they represent only 3.5 percent of total government revenue. Too many structural adjustment programs have proposed tariff reductions without paying enough attention to the fact that the government's revenue base is being undermined.[11] When the effect of the program is to widen the fiscal and current account deficits, political support diminishes. Often, then, tariffs are reimposed as a means of shoring up government revenues.

2. Reducing the Dispersion in Tariffs Increases Efficiency

Given that lower tariffs may have harmful effects on revenue, an alternative reform proposal is to leave unchanged the average level of tariffs, but reduce their variance. The argument here is that this brings relative domestic prices of traded goods closer to relative world prices, reducing distortions and improving efficiency. To evaluate this rule with our two-sector model, we need to reintroduce intermediate inputs (a > 0), so that there will be two imported goods, and hence two tariff rates. We must also bring back domestic indirect taxes, as these play a crucial role in our discussion. Finally, we set government expenditure to zero and assume all tariff revenues are rebated to consumers in a lump-sum fashion.

Armed with these changes, we can assess the efficiency implications of a particular set of tariffs. By "efficiency" we mean the utility of the single consumer in this economy. Note that the consumer buys two goods, the domestic good and imports, and his utility is given by the CES function underlying the demand functions for these two goods. As we set the current account deficit exogenously in this version of the model, and there is neither savings nor investment, the efficiency-measuring welfare function is well defined.

If reducing tariff rate dispersion improves efficiency, then a uniform tariff rate must maximize efficiency. We first test this proposition. We compute the tariff rates that maximize consumer welfare and raise a particular level of government revenue. It turns out that uniform tariffs are optimal only in the special (and unrealistic) case when the domestic indirect taxes are also set optimally. For it is only in this case that a uniform tariff rate will leave domestic price signals undistorted. If the domestic tax rate is not optimal, then a uniform tariff rate will distort the relative price between exports and domestic production, say. In Table 3, we present the optimal tariffs from numerical simulations of the two-sector model for various levels of indirect taxes. The model has been calibrated so that tariffs represent about 20 percent of government revenues, with indirect taxes making up the rest.

Table 3 **Optimal Tariffs with Indirect Tax Distortions**

Indirect tax	.102*	.097	.092	.087
Tariff on consumer good	.083	.099	.116	.132
Tariff on interm. good	.083	.048	.013	

*Optimal indirect tax

Note that for suboptimal levels of indirect taxes, the tariff on the consumer good is significantly higher than that on the intermediate import. Although the optimal tariff rates vary greatly with the indirect tax rate (not surprising given the small share of tariff revenues in total government revenues), it should be noted that total welfare does not vary by more than 1 percent across all four scenarios.

In most countries, domestic indirect taxes are not set optimally. Furthermore, it is reasonable to assume that the rate is below the optimal level to raise a given amount of revenue. In this case, the analysis above shows that unifying tariff rates will not improve welfare. In addition, the typical pattern of tariffs in developing countries is a higher rate for consumer goods than for producer goods. This appears to be closer to the optimum than a unified rate.

Once again, we use our model of Indonesia to investigate the pattern of optimal tariffs in a more complex economy. Table 4 shows the optimal tariff pattern that will generate the same tariff revenue as was raised in the base data. Note that the pattern of tariffs observed in the small model is reproduced. The optimal tariffs are zero for petroleum and mining, wood products, and metals, minerals and machinery, and quite high for food agriculture and traded agriculture. In other words, they are low or near zero for the intermediate goods and high (to make up the necessary revenue) for the consumer goods sectors. The model pattern is complicated by another factor: our base data for Indonesia embodies labor market distortions, so that factors earn different rates of return in different sectors. In trying to improve the efficiency of the economy, the model picks an optimal tariff structure that will cause factors to flow to where their returns are higher. This is why there is a tariff on the chemicals and refining sector, even though this sector produces intermediate goods. The influence of this labor market distortion on the economy is confirmed by column B in Table 4, which shows the optimal pattern of tariffs when all factors are assumed to earn the same rate of return across sectors. In this case, the optimal tariff on chemicals and refining is zero. Another factor that will cause our optimal tariff structure to deviate from a simple rule of thumb is the presence of other indirect taxes; for the optimal tariff is one which compensates for the distortions created by other taxes. Hence, in column C, we examine the optimal tariffs when all other indirect taxes are removed from the system. Notice that the pattern evident in column B is accentuated. The tariffs on consumer goods are even higher, and those on intermediate goods lower. Here, the differentiated tariff is due to the application of optimal tax principles (see Newbery and Stern [1987] or Dahl, Devarajan, and van Wijnbergen [1986]).

Table 4 **Optimal Tariffs with Labor Market and Tax Distortions** (%)

	Tariffs in Base	Optimal Tariffs (A)	(A) + No Labor Dist. (B)	(B) + No Tax Dist. (C)
Food agriculture	1.4	20.7	54.3	71.2
Traded agriculture	1.3	46.0	49.5	69.0
Mining and petroleum	0.7	-	-	-
Food industries	6.7	26.1	49.8	36.3
Textiles	8.1	3.2	17.5	14.8
Wood products	6.9	-	6.0	1.5
Chemicals and refining	4.1	13.0	-	-
Metals, minerals, and machinery	4.0	-	-	-
Utilities	-	-	-	-
Construction	-	-	-	-
Trade and transport	-	-	10.5	4.8
Services	0.2	-	-	-
Public administration	-	-	-	-

What are the policy implications of these results? We are not saying that unifying tariff rates always harms welfare, nor that existing tariff patterns in developing countries are optimal. Indeed, we believe that reducing the variation in tariff rates in many countries (including Indonesia) would be beneficial. However, the benefits stem from increased administrative simplicity and reduced rent-seeking behavior, rather than from any improvements in the efficiency of the economy.[12] In addition, our results indicate that the old rule of thumb could be replaced by a new one: maintain no more than two or three tariff rates, with the higher rates on consumer good imports and lower ones on intermediate and capital goods. This will achieve most of the administrative benefits mentioned above while keeping with the spirit of the optimal tax results obtained in this paper.

There has been no mention so far of the role of tariffs as instruments of protection. In our models, tariffs are simply tax instruments. The picture is only slightly changed if we add the protective function. If certain industries are singled out for protection, then clearly the tariff rate on their competing imports should be higher. If the government is uncertain as to which industries to protect, and therefore wishes to protect all industries, then the preferred relative pattern of tariffs will still be that shown by our model, with the absolute magnitude increased by the amount of blanket protection desired.

3. Effective Rates of Protection Measure Effective Protection

Recognizing that protection of value added in an industry depends on tariffs on outputs as well as inputs, economists have proposed the concept of effective protection. They measure it using the following formula, in which the effective protection rate in sector j is given by:

$$ERP_j = \frac{P_j(1 + t_j) - \Sigma P_i(1 + t_i)a_{ij}}{P_j - \Sigma P_i a_{ij}}$$

where P_j is the world price of commodity j, t_j its tariff rate, and a_{ij} the input-output coefficient.

As it is written, the above formula leaves out nontraded inputs. Several methods have been proposed for including these in the calculation of effective rates of protection. In general, they involve subtracting nontraded inputs at market prices from the numerator and the cost of these same inputs in the absence of tariffs from the denominator. While this is correct in principle, in practice it is difficult to determine what the price of nontraded goods in the absence of tariffs will be. Nevertheless, this is crucial if we wish to examine the following question: do uniform nominal tariff rates lead to uniform effective rates of protection? Clearly, the answer depends on what happens to the price of nontraded goods in the absence of tariffs. If the price declines by the amount of the tariff rate, then the answer to the question is "yes." If, however, the prices of nontraded goods do not fall by exactly the amount of the price of traded goods (the latter being equal to the amount of the tariff), then uniform nominal and effective rates of protection are not synchronous.[13] This is more than just a theoretical point: with our model of Indonesia, we show that a uniform tariff rate can lead to quite divergent effective rates of protection. Table 5 contains different measures of effective protection calculated under an assumed 10 percent uniform tariff across all sectors.

The appropriate analogue to the ERP formula in a general equilibrium model is somewhat ambiguous, as the presentation of four different model-based calculations in Table 5 suggests. The standard formula (here called Balassa-Corden, or BC) measures the percentage change in a price—the price of value added—in the absence and presence of tariffs. However, what we are most interested in is quantities: the impact of the tariff structure on the output of various sectors. The point is that with the extremely strong assumptions of the model underlying the usual ERP formula, the price of value added is a perfect signal for the effect of the tariff structure on output.[14]

Table 5	Effective Rate of Protection with Uniform 10 Percent Tariffs (%)			
		CGE Model Results		
	BC	PV	XD	VA
Food agriculture	25.1	-1.9	-1.2	-3.1
Traded agriculture	26.5	3.9	3.5	7.5
Mining and petroleum	25.5	14.2	1.1	15.5
Food industries	26.1	-8.7	-1.2	-9.7
Textiles	26.9	-4.8	2.8	-2.0
Wood products	26.4	-3.3	11.0	7.4
Chemicals and refining	27.2	-10.4	-0.9	-11.3
Metals, minerals, and machinery	26.5	-8.0	-0.3	-8.3
Utilities	-19.5	-10.3	-1.2	-11.4
Construction	-38.9	-15.0	-5.3	-19.5
Trade and transport	27.4	-5.4	0.3	-5.2
Services	28.4	-6.8	-0.4	-7.1
Public administration	0.0	-5.7	0.0	-5.7

Notes on calculations: The four ERP measures are defined as follows:

$$BC_I = 100. * [\frac{ER(PWM_I(1+tm_I) - \Sigma_J AA_{JI} PWM_J(1+tm_J))}{ER_{TM=0}(PWM_I - \Sigma_J AA_{JI} PWM_J)} - 1]$$

$$PV_I = 100. * [(PV_I / PV_{I,TM=0}) - 1]$$

$$XD_I = 100. * [(XD_I / XD_{I,TM=0}) - 1]$$

$$VA_I = 100. * [(PV_I XD_I / PV_{I,TM=0} XD_{I,TM=0}) - 1]$$

However, with the weaker assumptions of our CGE model, this is no longer the case—deviations in the price of value added with and without tariffs capture only part of the effect. Since the CGE model also calculates the changes in output that result from tariff elimination, we also have the desired measure of effective protection. For completeness, we also report the percentage change in value added.[15]

Even the Balassa-Corden ERPs are not uniform, despite the 10 percent across-the-board tariff. This is because of our treatment of nontradables. In calculating unit value added in the presence and absence of tariffs, we subtract the unit costs of nontradable inputs as well. Our hypothesis is that these costs are the same with and without tariffs. Hence, the same number is subtracted from both the numerator and denominator of the formula, whereas the rest of the numerator is scaled by 1.1 (for the tariff rates) times the rest of the denominator. For tradable sectors, the Balassa-Corden measure is nearly uniform; the reason the rate is greater than the 10 percent tariff is because the exchange rate depreciates from the tariff increase, which in turn raises all prices in the numerator by a constant percentage.

The sector with the highest XD ERP is wood and wood products. Meanwhile, construction has a large negative BC ERP and a negative XD ERP from the model because it uses a sizable input of wood in its production. Food agriculture and traded agriculture have similar BC ERPs, but have XD ERPs that differ in sign. This stems from the general equilibrium nature of our calculation. When we perform the hypothetical experiment of eliminating tariffs, there is an appreciation of the real exchange rate due to the increased foreign borrowing to make up for the shortfall in government revenues. This appreciation has a greater impact on traded agriculture than on food agriculture because the price of traded agriculture is more closely linked to the (now lower) import and export prices. The lower price lowers output, and the XD ERP is higher than for food agriculture because the percentage loss in output (in the absence of tariffs) is bigger.

The presence of pure nontraded goods is but one problem with the formula for effective protection rates. Another is the (implicit) assumption that domestic and imported goods in sector j are perfect substitutes. This is what permits us to write the domestic price of good j as $P_j(1+t_j)$. If this assumption is relaxed, then the domestic price will be below $P_j(1+t_j)$. In fact, it can be shown that as the elasticity of substitution between the domestic and foreign good approaches infinity, the domestic price approaches $P_j(1+t_j)$ from below (see Devarajan and Sussangkarn [1987]). This does not mean, however, that effective protection rates are overstated by the formula above. For, although the effect of the tariff structure on the output price is overstated, so is the effect on the input prices. The outcome depends on the net effect of the two.

To assess the importance of this effect, we investigate the effective rates of protection in Indonesia as generated by the model and compare them with those that we would have obtained from applying the formula using the same data as the model. Table 6 shows the Balassa-Corden ERP measure (first column) and the output (XD) measure from the model for the original elasticities (second column) and for five different sets of uniform trade substitution elasticities (0.5 is quite inelastic, while 15.0 is quite close to completely elastic).

Clearly the estimates differ in their ranking of the relative protection afforded each sector. The XD calculations show the importance of imperfect substitution in determining the economy's response. Comparing the BC ERP figures to the XD ERP estimates with the base elasticities, we observe that while some sectors (wood) are high in both rankings, others (chemicals and refining, food processing) are not. Chemicals and refining is a largely imported sector with a low elasticity in the base (0.4). This low substitutability means that the "true" protection it gets is quite low (zero), although the Balassa-Corden measure (assuming it is a perfect substitute) will give it a high ERP. Moreover, as our (uniform) elasticity gets large, chemicals and refining moves up until it is near the top. Textiles starts out as the lowest XD ERP in the model, but as the elasticities increase, so does the ERP, and it ends up ranked number 2, same as with Balassa-Corden. The pattern with high elasticities more closely matches the Balassa-Corden measure; the top five BC ERP sectors are also the top five XD ERP sectors at the highest set of elasticities. The lesson seems clear: to the extent that imports and domestic goods are imperfect substitutes at the level of aggregation at which the ERPs are being calculated, application of the standard formula can be misleading.

Table 6 Changes in Ranking for the XD ERP Calculation from the CGE Model (%)

Balassa-Corden	Orig. Elasticities	Elasticity = 0.5	Elasticity = 0.8	Elasticity = 2.0	Elasticity = 5.0	Elasticity = 15.0
Foodproc 25.8	Woodprod 1.2	Woodprod 0.7	Woodprod 0.9	Woodprod 1.8	Woodprod 4.4	Woodprod 12.7
Textiles 17.6	Metalprod 0.3	Metalprod` 0.5	Metalprod 0.5	Chemical 0.8	Chemical 1.5	Textiles 6.1
Woodprod 15.1	Tradeag 0.2	Construc 0.3	Chemical 0.3	Metalprod 0.7	Textiles 1.3	Chemical 2.3
Chemical 13.5	Construc 0.1	Tradeag 0.2	Tradeag 0.2	Tradeag 0.3	Metalprod 0.9	Metalprod 1.1
Metalprod 5.9	Oil&mine 0.1	Chemical 0.1	Oil&mine 0.1	Oil&mine 0.1	Tradeag 0.3	Foodproc 1.1
Tradeag 1.2	Chemical 0.0	Oil&mine 0.1	Pubadm 0.0	Pubadm 0.0	Services 0.2	Services 0.7
Foodag 1.1	Pubadm 0.0	Pubadm 0.0	Tradtrans -0.0	Tradtrans 0.0	Oil&mine 0.1	Tradeag 0.4
Oil&mine 0.6	Tradtrans -0.0	Tradtrans -0.0	Construc -0.0	Textiles 0.0	Foodproc 0.0	Oil&mine 0.2
Pubadm 0.0	Foodag -0.1	Foodag -0.1	Foodag -0.1	Services -0.1	Pubadm 0.0	Tradtrans 0.1
Services -0.5	Services -0.1	Services -0.2	Services -0.1	Foodag -0.1	Tradtrans 0.0	Utility 0.0
Tradtrans -0.7	Foodproc -0.2	Utility -0.2	Utility -0.2	Foodag -0.1	Foodag -0.1	Pubadm 0.0
Utility -2.8	Utility -0.2	Foodproc -0.2	Foodproc -0.2	Foodproc -0.2	Utility -0.2	Foodag -0.1
Construc -5.3	Textiles -0.3	Textiles -0.6	Textiles -0.5	Utility -0.2	Construc -3.3	Construc -8.8
				Construc -1.1		

175

Conclusion

It appears to be widely accepted that the economics of policy reform is well understood, but that the politics and implementation are not. The purpose of this paper has been to show that even the economics is an open question. Much of what passes for economics is a set of rules of thumb that guide policy. These rules in turn are based on models that bear virtually no resemblance to the economy in question. For example, a rule of thumb used for real exchange rate policy makes sense only when the balance of trade is zero; unifying tariff rates improves efficiency only when all other taxes are set optimally.

Of course, the notion that eliminating one of many distortions in an economy is not necessarily welfare-enhancing is an old one in economics. The practice is justified on the grounds that these second-best considerations are minor compared to the gains to be achieved by addressing the one important distortion in the country. We have shown that not only are these second-best considerations not minor, but they may subvert the intended outcome of the policy. For instance, under some conditions (not mentioned in the rule of thumb) it is necessary to appreciate the real exchange rate in the face of an adverse terms-of-trade shock. Similarly, liberalizing tariffs without protecting government revenues could lead to a decline in export performance.

Why, then, have these rules of thumb enjoyed such widespread use and acceptance? Two reasons suggest themselves. First, in order to question the rule of thumb and replace it with an alternative, one needs a model of the economy. In the past these models have been hard to come by, owing to data and computational constraints, as well as the modelling capacity of the policy adviser. The two-sector model developed in this paper shows that, at least in order to question the rules of thumb, one does not need a sophisticated model. Moreover, multisector models of developing countries are no longer difficult to build and, as demonstrated by our exercises with the Indonesia CGE model, they can provide empirically relevant policy alternatives to the traditional rules of thumb.

A second reason for the tenacity of these rules of thumb is their simplicity. Not only is the intuition on which they are based appealing, but they are easy to implement. For example, a uniform tariff is much easier to administer than a system of highly variegated, albeit "optimal," tariffs. Furthermore, a uniform tariff rate may avoid the welfare losses due to rent-seeking behavior. We find this argument compelling. Our point is that, in these cases, the rule of thumb should be justified on grounds of administrative simplicity and reduced rent-seeking, rather than on the (fallacious) argument that it improves economic welfare.

Even when the rule cannot be justified on administrative grounds, we do not wish to suggest that the only alternative is to build a large, multisector model. The models developed in this paper give us insights we could not have gotten otherwise. These insights could lead to slightly more complicated rules of thumb that capture both the simplicity of the old rules as well as the richness of the characteristics of the developing country where the reform is being undertaken.

❧

Appendix A: Equations of the Model

A.1 Introduction

In this appendix, we present a mathematical description of our Indonesian CGE model. Endogenous variables are denoted by names in capital letters. Lower case names are exogenous variables or parameters. Certain variables that can be endogenous, but which in the current version are exogenous, are capitalized. Subscript conventions used throughout the appendix include:

i,j = sectors
vat = sectors included in the value-added tax
oil = petroleum and other mining sectors
ag = food and trade agriculture sectors
nonag = nonagricultural sectors
k = labor categories
g = household groups
br = borrowing institutions (government = gov; public enterprise = pub; private sector = priv)

A.2 Prices

(1) $PM_i = pwm_i(1 + tm_i)(1 + tv_i)\, ER$

(2) $PE_i = pwe_i(1 + te_i)\, ER$

(3) $P_i = (PD_i * XXD_i + PM_i * M_i) / X_i$

(4) $PX_i = (PD_i * XXD_i + PE_i * E_i) / XD_i$

(5) $PV_i = [(XXD_i * PD_i)(1 - tx_i - tv_i) + (E_i * PE_i)]/XD_i - \sum_j aa_{ji} P_j + \sum_j aa_{j,vat} P_j tv_j$
$\quad (XXD_{vat} / XD_{vat}) + (DK_i/XD_i)tv_i PK$

(6) $PK = \sum_i bb_i P_i$

(7) $PINDEX = \sum_i pwts_i P_i$

(8) $PINDOM = \sum_i pwtd_i PD_i$

Endogenous variables:

ER : exchange rate
PM_i : domestic price of imports
PE_i : domestic price of exports
P_i : composite good price
PX_i : average sales price of domestic output
PV_i : value added (or net) price
PK : price of composite capital good
PD_i : domestic price of domestic output
PINDEX: general (composite) price level
X_i : sectoral composite demand
XD_i : sectoral domestic output
XXD_i : domestic demand for production
M_i : imports
E_i : exports
DK_i : investment by sector of destination

Exogenous variables:

PINDOM : domestic price level

pwm_i : world price of imports
pwe_i : world price of exports
tm_i : tariff rate
te_i : export subsidy rate
tx_i : indirect tax rate
tv_i : value-added tax rate
aa_{ij} : input-output coefficients
bb_i : composite capital good coefficients
$pwts_i$: composite price index weights
$pwtd_i$: domestic price index weights

A.3 Production, Employment, and Final Demand

(9) $XD_i = \alpha x_i * \pi_k(L_{ik}{}^{\mathcal{T}_{ik}}) * K_i{}^{(1-\Sigma_k \mathcal{T}_{ik})}$

(10) $L_{ik} = (XD_i * PV_i * \mathcal{T}_{ik}) / (W_k * gam_{ik})$

(11) $LS_k = \Sigma_i L_{ik}$

(12) $XD_i = \alpha t_i [\text{ß}t_i * E_i{}^{\delta t_i} + (1-\text{ß}t_i) * XXD_i{}^{\delta t_i}]^{(1/\delta t_i)}$

(13) $X_i = \alpha c_i [\text{ß}c_i * M_i{}^{-\delta c_i} + (1-\text{ß}c_i) * XXD_i{}^{-\delta c_i}]^{(-1/\delta c_i)}$

(14) $X_i = INT_i + C_i + G_i + Z_i + STK_i$

(15) $INT_i = \Sigma_j aa_{ij} XD_j$

(16) $C_i = [\Sigma_g YH_g * (1-taxh_g) * (1-savh_g) * cc_{ig}] / P_i$

(17) $G_i = gg_i * GOVCON$

(18) $Z_i = bb_i(INVEST - INVSTK)/PK$

(19) $STK_i = inv_i * XD_i$

(20) $DK_i = [zz_i(INVEST - INVSTK)] / PK$

Endogenous variables:
L_{ik} : demand for labor type k in sector i
W_k : average wage of labor type k
INT_i : intermediate demand by sector of origin
C_i : private consumption demand by sector
G_i : government consumption demand by sector
Z_i : investment by sector of origin
STK_i : inventory investment
INVEST : total investment
INVSTK : total inventory investment

Exogenous variables:
K_i : exogenous sectoral capital stock
LS_k : exogenous labor supply of category k
GOVCON : total real government consumption
gam_{ik} : proportionality ratio of sectoral wage rate to average wage rate for
         labor category k
zz_i : total sectoral investment allocation shares ($\Sigma_i zz_i = 1$)
gg_i : government expenditure shares ($\Sigma_i gg_i = 1$)
cc_{ig} : private expenditure shares ($\Sigma_i cc_{ig} = 1$)
inv_i : inventory coefficients

taxh$_g$: household income tax rates
savh$_g$: household savings rates
α : shift parameters for production (αx), CES composite goods (αc), and CET export supply (αt) functions
τ_ik : exponents in Cobb-Douglas production functions
ß : share parameters in CES (ßc) and CET (ßt) trade functions
δ : elasticities in CES (δc) and CET (δt) trade functions

The production functions are Cobb-Douglas functions of labor and capital, with intermediate input requirements given by fixed input-output coefficients. Equation (10) represents the condition that factor returns equal marginal value products for all labor inputs. With capital stocks fixed by sectors, sectoral rates of return to capital differ. For labor, the wage is assumed to adjust so that the demand for labor equals the supply, and the excess demand equation (11) is satisfied for each category of labor.

Imports and domestic goods are assumed to be imperfect substitutes. Consumers demand a composite good which is a CES aggregation of imports and domestic goods (equation [13]), with a different trade aggregation function for each sector. This specification implies that the price of imports need not equal the price of domestic goods (PM$_i$ does not equal PD$_i$) and that the domestic price system acquires some autonomy not present in standard trade models in which world prices determine domestic prices. Exports and domestic goods sold on domestic markets are imperfect substitutes, paralleling the treatment of imports. Export and domestic prices need not be equal, and producers maximize their revenue from dividing their sales between domestic and export markets (equation [12]).

A.4 Foreign Trade

$$(21) \quad E_i = XXD_i \left[\frac{(1-\text{ß}t_i)\, PE_i}{\text{ß}t_i\, PD_i} \right]^{[1/(\delta t_i-1)]}$$

$$(22) \quad M_i = XXD_i \left[\frac{\text{ß}c_i\, PD_i}{(1-\text{ß}c_i)\, PM_i} \right]^{[1/(1+\delta c_i)]}$$

$$(23) \quad \Sigma pwe_i E_i - \Sigma pwm_i M_i - \text{repat} + \Sigma_{br}(\text{borrow}_{br} - \text{amort}_{br} - \text{inter}_{br}) - \text{forinv} - DFR = 0$$

Exogenous variables:
DFR : net change in foreign reserves
repat : repatriated profits and other nonfactor services
forinv : direct foreign investment
borrow$_{br}$: public and private foreign borrowing
amort$_{br}$: public and private amortization payments
inter$_{br}$: public and private interest payments

A.5 Income and Flow of Funds

(24) $YH_1 = \sum_i L_{i1} * gam_{i1} * W_1$

(25) $YH_2 = \sum_i L_{i2} * gam_{i2} * W_2 + \sum_{ag}(PV_{ag} * XD_{ag} - \sum_k L_{ag,k} * gam_{ag,k} W_k)$

(26) $YH_3 = \sum_i L_{i3} * gam_{i3} * W_3$

(27) $YH_4 = \sum_i L_{i4} * gam_{i4} * W_4 + CORPY(1-ctax)(1-csave) - DEPREC$

(28) $HHSAV = \sum_g YH_g(1-taxh_g)savh_g$

(29) $HHTAX = \sum_g YH_g * taxh_g$

(30) $CORPY = \sum_{nonag}(PV_{nonag} * XD_{nonag} - \sum_k L_{nonag,k} * gam_{nonag,k} * W_k) - OILREV$
$- ER * repat - ER(inter_{pub} + inter_{priv})$

(31) $GR = TARIFF + INDTAX + HHTAX + OILREV + VATREV$
$+ CORPY * ctax - EXPSUB$

(32) $TARIFF = \sum_i tm_i(1+tv_i)pwm_i M_i ER$

(33) $INDTAX = \sum_i tx_i PD_i XXD_i$

(34) $EXPSUB = \sum_i te_i pwe_i E_i ER$

(35) $VATREV = \sum_{vat} [PD_{vat} XXD_{vat} tv_{vat} + pwm_{vat} M_{vat} tv_{vat} ER$
$- \sum_j aa_{j,vat} P_j tv_j * XXD_{vat} - DK_{vat} tv_{vat} PK]$

(36) $OILREV = oiltax * (PV_{oil} * XD_{oil} - \sum_k L_{oil,k} * gam_{oil,k} * W_k)$

(37) $GSAV = GR - \sum_i P_i G_i - inter_{gov}$

(38) $DEPREC = \sum_i depr_i K_i PK$

(39) $INVSTK = \sum_i STK_i P_i$

(40) $SAVING = HHSAV + GOVSAV + (forinv + DFR) * ER + CORPY(1-$
$ctax)csave + \sum_{br}(borrow_{br} - amort_{br}) * ER$

(41) $SAVING = INVEST$ (Walras' Law)

Endogenous variables:

YH_1	:	income to agricultural worker households
YH_2	:	income to agricultural owner households
YH_3	:	income to urban worker households
YH_4	:	income to urban owner/capitalist households
HHSAV	:	household savings
HHTAX	:	household income tax revenue
CORPY	:	nonagricultural corporate income
GR	:	government revenue
TARIFF	:	import tariff revenue
INDTAX	:	indirect (excise) taxes less subsidies
EXPSUB	:	export subsidies
VATREV	:	government revenue from the value-added tax
OILREV	:	government revenue from oil sector
GSAV	:	government savings
DEPREC	:	financial depreciation
SAVING	:	total savings

Exogenous variables:

ctax	:	tax rate on nonagricultural corporate income
csave	:	savings rate out of nonagricultural corporate income
oiltax	:	tax rate on oil sector earnings
$depr_i$	:	financial depreciation rates

A.6 The Operation of Markets

There are three types of markets in the model: those for labor, output, and foreign exchange. The model assumes that these three sets of markets all "clear," which means that the excess-demand equations for labor (11), output (14), and foreign exchange (23) must all equal zero at equilibrium. Indeed, the solution problem is to find a set of wages (W_k), product prices (PD_i), and an exchange rate (ER) such that the three sets of excess-demand equations are simultaneously satisfied.

The full equation system contains one more equation than the number of endogenous variables. As the system is a Walrasian general equilibrium system, the excess-demand equations must satisfy Walras' Law; in our specification, the savings-investment identity (equation [41]) is satisfied automatically. The system can determine only relative prices; rather than choosing a single price as numeraire, we fix the domestic price level (equation [8]), thereby normalizing all other prices.

Appendix B: Data for Our Indonesian CGE Model

B.1 Base Data for 1985[16]

The primary source of data for a CGE model is an input-output table. Work on the 1985 input-output table for Indonesia is not yet completed, so we have started from a preliminary version and made our own adjustments.[17] Several additional data sources were used to provide data for the base year, which will be referred to by abbreviation below.[18]

Data on government finance and expenditure come from the Ministry of Finance and are presented in (WB) and (IMF). Additional data on direct and indirect taxes, including the value-added tax and tariffs, come from the Ministry of Finance and Bank of Indonesia.

Given that one analytic focus of the model's application is on macroeconomic projections associated with the government budget cycle and the preparation of Repelita V (the Fifth Five-Year Plan), we chose to use fiscal year data (the fiscal year starts in April). Data on government accounts and international trade are usually presented on a fiscal year basis. The first step in data preparation and reconciliation was the decision to tie all data to the national income and product accounts for FY85/86. The accounts for the fiscal year were estimated by interpolation from the national accounts, which are given on a calendar year basis (NIPA). Control totals for the various macro aggregates (aggregate value added, private consumption, government consumption, investment, exports, and imports) were all imposed on the available input-output accounts for 1985. The sectoral input-output accounts were then adjusted so as to be internally consistent and to match the aggregate control totals. Preliminary data from the 1985 social accounting matrix were used to provide various parameters to map from sectoral value added to institutional and household income. Where necessary, the 1980 social accounting matrix (SAM) was used to provide parameters. Finally, sectoral commodity demands by institutions and households were adjusted so that they matched the corresponding sectoral totals from the input-output table.

The various adjustments to the data required to create a balanced social accounting matrix were achieved using a computer program called the "SAM Generator."[19] This program runs on a personal computer and provides a powerful tool for achieving reconciliation among disparate data sources. The underlying data were balanced at a twenty-six-sector aggregation. The SAM Generator program can generate any desired aggregation of the data, and we are currently using a thirteen-sector aggregation for the CGE model.[20]

The data on international trade presented a number of problems. In general, the various sources agree in their definition of the current account balance and the balance of trade in goods and nonfactor services (goods & nfs).[21] The difference between these two balances represents "net factor income from abroad," which, in Indonesia, includes transfers and all net interest payments.[22] This item represents the difference between gross domestic product (GDP) and gross national product (GNP).[23]

There are a number of problems, however, in the definition of the balance of commodity trade. In the input-output accounts, exports and imports are valued in producer prices, excluding trade and transportation margins. In the national product accounts, and in trade statistics, imports are valued CIF and exports are valued FOB, and so include various ancillary services. Exports and imports in other services are also treated differently. The input-output table and the national income and product accounts show gross exports and imports of goods and services, while the trade data from Bank Indonesia present only a net trade figure for services. Thus, it is difficult to reconcile data on commodity and service sector trade from the different sources, even though the current account balances are the same.[24]

We decided to reconcile the input-output accounts to match the export and import data given in the national product accounts. Thus, our model incorporates sectoral exports and imports for the service sectors. However, we follow the input-output convention of valuing all flows in producer prices, so that commodity trade data exclude trade and transportation margins. It is feasible to reconcile the different treatments, and we plan to generate estimates for trade and transportation margins so that we will be able to produce tables that follow the definitions in standard trade statistics.

B.2 Aggregating the Sixty-Six-Sector Input-Output Table to Twenty-Six Sectors

Table B.1 shows the mapping scheme that was used for the aggregation. The input-output table in producers' prices was used, so that all trade and transport margins show up as intermediate demands (that is, *only* in the trade and transport rows in the input-output table), rather than as part of the purchase of each input or final good. The twenty-six-sector aggregation was chosen to permit comparability with the sectoral classification in the 1980 SAM, although some limited reconciliation at the full 170-sector level was required for full compatibility with the production sectors included in the detailed SAM.

26-Sector Classification		66-Sector Classification
1.	Farm food crops	1-6
2.	Farm nonfood crops	7-17
3.	Livestock	18-20
4.	Forestry	21,22
5.	Fishery	23
6.	Coal and petroleum	24,25
7.	Other mining	26
8.	Food, beverages, and tobacco	27-34
9.	Textiles and leather	35,36
10.	Wood and furniture	37
11.	Paper and printing	38
12.	Chemicals and refining	39-42
13.	Nonmetallic minerals	43,44
14.	Basic metals	45,46
15.	Machinery	47-50*
16.	Other industry	50**
17.	Electricity, gas, and water	51
18.	Construction	52
19.	Trade and storage	53,59
20.	Restaurants and hotels	54
21.	Rail and road transportation	55,56
22.	Sea and air transport, and communications	57,58,60
23.	Financial services	61
24.	Real estate	62
25.	Public administration	63
26.	Social and other services	64-66

*   Includes sectors 132 to 134 from 160-sector aggregation
**   Includes sectors 135 to 138 from 160-sector aggregation

B.3. *Labor Information from the SAM*

The fully disaggregated (261x261) SAM contains thirty-eight productive sectors and seventy-two labor categories. These seventy-two labor categories derive from nine different types of labor, each split according to urban-rural, paid-unpaid, and male-female divisions (9x2x2x2). We have used only the nine labor types, with the exception of agricultural workers, for which the paid/unpaid distinction was maintained in order to distinguish workers (paid) from proprietors (unpaid). Employment, wage structure, and imputed income information is compiled from the SAM and matched with the twenty-six-sector input-output table.

B.4. *The CGE Model Aggregation Scheme*

The data used in the CGE model are obtained by aggregating the twenty-six-sector, nine labor category data version down to thirteen sectors and four labor categories. The labor and sectoral aggregations are shown in Table B.2 and Table B.3.

The four labor types form the basis for the four household categories used in the model. Capital income from the agricultural sectors (1 and 2) accrues to the agricultural proprietors, while capital income from the nonagricultural sectors (3 to 13) is received by white collar workers.

Table B.2   Aggregation Scheme for 1985 CGE Employment Data

4 Labor Types	Labor Types from SAM
1. Agricultural workers	Paid agricultural workers
2. Agricultural proprietors	Unpaid agricultural workers
3. Low-wage workers	Service workers Manual workers Other workers and armed forces
4. High-wage workers	Professional workers Managers Clerical workers Sales workers

Table B.3   Aggregation Scheme for 1985 CGE Sectoral Data

13-Sector Classification	26-Sector Classification
1. Food agriculture	1. Farm food crops 2. Livestock
2. Traded agriculture	3. Farm nonfood crops 4. Forestry 5. Fishery
3. Mining and petroleum	6. Coal and petroleum 7. Other mining
4. Food industries	8. Food, beverages, and tobacco
5. Textiles	9. Textiles and leather
6. Wood products	10. Wood and furniture 11. Paper and printing
7. Chemicals and refining	12. Chemicals and refining
8. Metal industries	13. Nonmetallic mineral 14. Basic metals 15. Machinery 16. Other industry
9. Utilities	17. Electricity, gas, and water
10. Construction	18. Construction
11. Trade and transport	19. Trade and storage 20. Rail and road transportation 21. Sea and air transport, and communications
12. Services	22. Restaurants and hotels 23. Financial services 24. Real estate 25. Social and other services
13. Public administration	26. Public administration

Notes

1 The authors wish to acknowledge the contributions of Jaime de Melo and Sherman Robinson in developing the ideas presented in this chapter. The Indonesia CGE model was developed in collaboration with Robinson and Sherif Lotfi, with the latter providing invaluable research assistance in the preparation of this chapter. The authors are also grateful to Dwight Perkins and Michael Roemer for comments on an earlier draft. They dutifully retain responsibility for all interpretations and errors in the chapter.

2 The model presented here draws on earlier work presented in Devarajan and de Melo (1987) and Devarajan and Sussangkarn (1987). Discussion of the foreign trade issues appears in de Melo and Robinson (1988).

3 In this two-sector model, with the nontradable price P_Q fixed as numeraire, any movement in E represents a real exchange rate change (simply defined as E/P_Q), since the price of tradables (E) is changing while the price of nontradables is fixed. One can just as easily reverse the story, making E the numeraire, in which case adjustments to a government consumption decline will occur through a decline in P_Q.

4 A current survey of the application of CGE models to development issues can be found in Robinson (1988). An application of the earlier version of the Indonesia model presented here can be found in Behrman, Lewis, and Lotfi (1989).

5 The usual procedure in practice is to calculate changes in the "price-level-deflated" exchange rate. With this measure, the nominal exchange rate must change by the difference between domestic and foreign inflation in order to maintain the real rate unchanged. For examples of the calculation and application of this rule, see Harberger (1988).

6 This point is similar to that made in the literature on the Marshall-Lerner conditions with unbalanced trade.

7 The rule of thumb value is equal to the differential in the domestic and world inflation rates. The world inflation rate is calculated as the weighted sum of import and export price inflation, using the shares of sectoral imports and exports in total trade as the weights.

8 For a more complete analysis of these sectoral effects, see Behrman, Lewis, and Lotfi (1989).

9 This argument is akin to the elasticity side of the transfer debate on German reparations (where Keynes was on the elasticity side and Ohlin on the income side).

10 It may be thought that this outcome is not, in fact, "surprising" if the revenue implications of trade reform are taken into account. Nevertheless, much of the discussion on trade policy reform neglects the government's budget constraint. See, for example, Harberger (1988).

11 The World Bank's first structural adjustment loan to Morocco is a case in point. See World Bank (1989).

12 This is probably the rationale for the preference for tariff uniformity expressed by Mallon and Stern in chapter 7 (1991) and Barichello and Flatters in chapter 10 (1991) in their analyses of trade policy in Bangladesh and Indonesia, respectively.

13 This point was recognized by Corden (1971), among others, but seems to have been overlooked by Harberger (1988).

14 The assumptions are those of the nonsubstitution theorem: constant returns to scale, no joint production, and only one nonproduced factor. In an economy satisfying these assumptions, prices can be solved for independently of quantities. These prices indicate the mix of production (across sectors), while the quantities indicate the scale.

15 For further discussion of the measures used here, see Devarajan and Sussangkarn (1987).

16 This section draws on notes prepared by Sherman Robinson.

17 The cooperation of Biro Pusat Statistik (BPS) in providing us with a working version of the 1985 input-output table and some preliminary social accounting matrix (SAM) numbers is gratefully acknowledged. Our own adjustments to this data have changed them from what they provided, and we therefore bear responsibility for their use in this paper.

18 The sources and abbreviations used are: (WB) = World Bank (1988); (IMF) = International Monetary Fund (1988); (NIPA) = Biro Pusat Statistik (1988); and (SAM) = Biro Pusat Statistik (1986).

19 The basic design of the SAM Generator is described in an appendix to Dervis, de Melo, and Robinson (1982). The program uses a matrix-balancing technique called the RAS method to achieve consistency in the input-output and household expenditure tables.

20 The sectoral aggregation used in the model is discussed in the following section.

21 The World Bank calls the balance of trade in goods and nonfactor services the "resource balance." See WB (1988) Table 1.4, 8; and Annex 1, Table 3, 134.

22 In other countries, only private net interest payments are included. In Indonesia, government interest payments are also included.

23 The definition in the national income accounts, following standard practice, includes only capital income and net interest. See the description in (NIPA) p. 34, where it is also stated that export and import data for the national product accounts "... are obtained from several sources, namely export and import statistics from [Central Bureau of Statistics] CBS, Balance of Payments from Bank Indonesia and International Monetary Fund." The definition of the current account balance used by the IMF and the World Bank includes remittances and transfers. The differences are small—workers' remittances were only U.S. $64 million in 1985-86. See IMF (1988), Table 18, p. 51 and Table 56, p. 100, and WB (1989) Table 1.4, p. 8 and Table 11.4, p. 207. In WB, Table 11.4, Line F.1 is defined as "Current acct bal (excl of trans)" but the reported numbers are inclusive of transfers.

24 The relevant tables are: (1) WB (1989): Table 1.4, p. 8; Table 2.10, p. 32; Table 2.11, p. 33; Table 3.1, p. 36; Annex 1, Table 3, p. 134; Statistical Annex, Table 3.1, p. 162; Statistical Annex, Table 11.4, p. 207; and (2) IMF (1988): Table 18, p. 54; Table 56, p. 100.

7

The Political Economy of Trade and Industrial Policy Reform in Bangladesh

Richard D. Mallon and Joseph J. Stern

Richard D. Mallon was chief resident adviser of HIID's Trade and Industrial Policy Reform Project in Bangladesh from 1983 to 1987. He is currently an Institute fellow, lecturer in the Harvard Economics Department, director of HIID's Public Enterprise Workshop, and consultant to various overseas projects.

Joseph J. Stern is an Institute fellow at HIID and coordinator of HIID projects in Indonesia. He first went to Bangladesh (East Pakistan) in 1962 and has continued to work there in various capacities, serving, until 1987, as a consultant to the Trade and Industrial Policy Project.

Introduction[1]

This paper analyzes the political economy of reforming the highly centralized command economy of the People's Republic of Bangladesh. The focus is on three main areas of reform: investment, credit, and import controls; the market for foreign exchange and export incentive policies; and protection policies for the steel, engineering, and cotton textile industries.

The main hypothesis of the paper is that even in a poor economy, highly dependent on foreign assistance, reforms triggered by a crisis and promoted by foreign donors can succeed in producing tangible results, but the speed and direction of reform will depend on the extent to which local pressure groups, new and traditional, consider the process of reform a positive sum game. Taking advantage of "windows of opportunity" and co-opting the main actors are the critical variables in the political economy of a successful reform.

Bangladesh inherited a tradition of state paternalism and a distrust of free markets. Initial conditions at the time of independence, combined with the beliefs of the ruling party, further encouraged reliance on a centralized, highly controlled, economy. The pervasive control system was run by bureaucrats with a diverse range of motives. Some were altruists motivated by *noblesse oblige* to protect the poor and prevent abuses by the wealthy. Some were personal profit maximizers earning extra incomes from the economic rents engendered by the multitude of permits required to undertake any economic activity in Bangladesh. And some officials simply relished the power to control. A significant portion of the military officers, who have run the government with only minor interruptions since 1975, have recognized the opportunities provided by the control system and have made common cause with the bureaucrats. Although an increasing number of technocrats, many foreign trained, had begun to work in government and the local research institutions, their initial concerns were more with theoretical and ideological questions than with effective policy formulation. Those private interest groups that had been given access to licenses or operated in highly protected markets were, of course, content to keep the system in place.

Three sets of actors emerged in the 1980s to help accelerate the pace of policy reform. First, the aid donors who had initially been concerned only with the provision of increasing flows of aid, in the process becoming virtual hostages of the bureaucrats, moved to tighten aid conditionality. In the 1970s, they began to impose certain microconditions, insisting, for example, on the installation of water meters as a condition for a potable water project. The donors then moved on to sector-specific conditions, such as requiring the decentralization of the fertilizer distribution system as a precondition for an agriculture sector loan, eventually insisting on broader macroeconomic reforms for further commodity aid. Specifically, the donors insisted on trade and industrial policy reforms to strengthen industrial investment and export incentives and improve the overall efficiency of the manufacturing sector.

The government of Bangladesh responded to this pressure by establishing in 1982 the Trade and Industrial Policy (TIP) Reform program which was to analyze policy reform alternatives. The analysis was carried out by a team of Bangladesh technocrats and foreign advisers provided by the Harvard Institute for International Development. Over time, the work carried out by the TIP staff created a realization among some bureaucrats and technocrats that policy reform was necessary.[2] Finally, a growing new entrepreneurial class which had taken advantage of a secondary foreign exchange market to establish new domestic and export-oriented industries, created additional pressure for change.

The emergence of these three groups—foreign donors, local and foreign technocrats, and more enterprising businessmen—succeeded in convincing local interest groups that changing the economic rules was not a zero sum game. In practice, the reforms have been negotiated piecemeal, suffer from inconsistencies and contradictions, and are far from complete. It is thus not surprising that progress in export and industrial development has been limited. But considering the initial conditions from which the reform saga began it remains a remarkable voyage.

Background: 1969-80

As in many developing countries, the early economic history of Bangladesh was characterized by an increasing centralization of economic power and the extension of a system of direct controls that eventually affected nearly all aspects of economic decision making. Although parts of the control system were in place at the time of independence, the system was extended and buttressed by a number of events and ideas that marked Bangladesh's early history. Subsequent efforts to reform the control system had to recognize its historical antecedents in order to formulate acceptable alternative policies.

Bangladesh, which became independent in 1971 after breaking off from Pakistan, has a total area of some 55,000 square miles, a population (mid-1988) of 108.9 million, and a per capita income of U.S. $170, making it one of the most densely populated and poorest countries in the world. Union with West Pakistan proved politically and economically unfruitful, resulting in relatively slow growth for East Pakistan and a widening of the regional income differences.[3] These economic failures, combined with a long-standing feeling by the Bangladeshis that they had been denied their basic political and social rights within the Pakistan nation, fueled a period of increasing political turmoil.[4] On March 26, 1971, Bangladesh declared its independence. There followed six months of bloody guerrilla warfare which was effectively ended when Pakistan troops in Bangladesh surrendered.

Under the leadership of Sheikh Mujibur Rahman (Sheik Mujib), who had inspired the country's independence movement and was recognized as the "father of the nation," Bangladesh began a major economic, political, and social adjustment. Products previously produced or manufactured in East Pakistan, such as matches, newsprint, and tea, and destined for the protected West Pakistan market, now had to find new markets, while, at the same time, many industries had to find new international suppliers of raw materials. This adjustment process had to be carried out in the face of a staggering loss of managerial resources and the destruction of an already poor infrastructure, partly through damage inflicted by the war of liberation, but compounded by a major cyclone and tidal bore which had hit the offshore islands and the coastal areas of Bangladesh on November 12, 1970, a scant six months before the war of liberation erupted.[5]

These events had a devastating effect on the economy. Over a two-year period, 1969/70 to 1971/72, agricultural output fell by some 15 percent, while the manufacturing sector showed an even more dramatic decline, falling by 54 percent. As a result, GDP fell by nearly 6 percent in 1970/71 and by a further 14 percent the following year, cutting per capita income by nearly one-quarter. The already high levels of unemployment rose and the need to create new jobs was further compounded by the demands of the "freedom fighters," who not only expected an improvement in economic conditions following independence, but insisted on special considerations for their role in achieving the nation's freedom.

At the same time, Bangladesh's foreign exchange situation, precarious in the best of times, deteriorated. The major donors had not yet recognized the new government or established aid programs for Bangladesh, so that aid disbursements, especially of nonfood aid, were low. Moreover, Bangladesh's traditional export market in Pakistan had been lost. It was hoped that exports to India, especially of jute, would rise rapidly following the conclusion of a long-term trade agreement signed just after independence, but India never fulfilled its commitments under the agreement, further reducing foreign exchange earnings.[6] The resulting import shortages exacerbated the already difficult economic situation.

In an effort to deal with the unprecedented economic turmoil, the Awami League Government of Sheikh Mujib imposed a complex system of direct controls covering prices and most economic activities, and sharply limiting access to foreign exchange and investment resources. A number of factors persuaded the Awami League to adopt these policies. First, Bangladesh inherited a plethora of controls that had been installed by Pakistan during the 1950s and 1960s. These now seemed validated by circumstances. Second, faced with factories left untended by fleeing Pakistan owners, the government felt it had no choice but to nationalize most of them. As a result, by 1974 some 62 percent of manufacturing output was in the hands of the public sector, a share that rose to 71 percent by 1978, the highest share for any Asian country, except China (Floyd 1984). Eventually, the government extended its control to transportation and the distributive trades. Third, many in the Awami League were committed socialists who believed that direct government control was necessary in a poor country if it was to achieve growth, especially growth with equity.

As a reflection of its economic philosophy, the government, in 1973, set a limit of Tk. 2.5 million ($315,000) on private sector investment, effectively relegating such investments to the small-scale and cottage industries. Public corporations were set up to run the nationalized industries and the *First Five-Year Plan* allocated over 85 percent of industrial investment to the public sector. By the end of the 1970s, public investment constituted over half of total investment while the role of the private sector continued to shrink. Many of the public corporations operated at a loss while their capital intensity raised the cost of each new job created. By 1975, per capita income had not yet recovered pre-independence levels and there was growing popular awareness that the economy was being mismanaged.

Recognizing its policy failures, the Awami League government began to roll back some of the control measures it had implemented, even going so far as to devalue the currency in 1975 in an effort to stimulate the economy. But these measures were too few to reverse the deepening economic malaise. The growing popular disenchantment with the government's economic policies was one of the factors that fueled a bloody coup on August 15, 1975, in which Sheikh Mujib and most of his family were assassinated. A series of coups and counter-coups followed during the next three months, ending when the military installed General Zia Rahman, who remained in power for five years, establishing a political party and eventually ruling as a civilian president. In 1981 President Zia was assassinated, and Justice Sattar, a member of Zia's party, was elected president. But in March 1982 this civilian government was overthrown, bringing to power General Ershad, who continued as president until growing disenchantment against his regime forced his resignation in December 1990.

Under General Zia, the industrial policies put in place by the Awami League government were modified and partly dismantled. In part, this shift in policy reflected a growing recognition by the government that labor absorption had to occur primarily in the industrial sector. This would be feasible only if industrial investment and growth could be increased and made as labor intensive as possible. In an effort to stimulate private sector investment, the government increased the private investment limit in steps to Tk. 100 million, moved to disinvest some of the smaller firms taken over after independence, created the Investment Corporation of Bangladesh to assist private investors, and agreed to pay compensation for units nationalized. By the end of 1978, seventy-seven firms worth Tk. 330 million had been sold back to private entrepreneurs. However, these tended to be mainly smaller, older firms, so that public corporations continued to dominate the manufacturing sector. In a further effort to accelerate industrial development, government instituted a series of export promotion measures, took steps to strengthen investment incentives, and continued to deemphasize the role of the public sector manufacturing enterprises.

While these measures reduced the role of government in the allocation of resources and production, direct allocation and centralized controls remained pervasive. Not surprisingly, the economy responded poorly. Over the period 1974/75 to 1980/81, GDP grew at an annual average rate of 4.0 percent while per capita incomes increased by only 1.1 percent per annum. Although the manufacturing sector grew somewhat more rapidly, at 5.3 percent per annum, the response by private investors to the government's policy initiatives was poor. It was not until the process of policy reform was accelerated, especially after 1982, that the economy evidenced a more robust response.

The Political Economy of Reform

While trade and industrial policy reforms were initiated before the end of the Sheik Mujib regime and continued under President Zia's administration, they accelerated after 1982, when General Ershad came to power and the TIP project was initiated. Policy reform might therefore appear to have been a cumulative process that built up momentum as it went along, feeding on its own success. But this impression is contradicted by the severe crisis experienced by the country at the beginning of the 1980s, a crisis that could have interrupted the reform process. Why did the crisis lead instead to an acceleration of reform, and equally important, why did policymakers turn increasingly to technocrats for guidance?

A partial answer may be found in the literature on the political economy of reform. Grindle and Thomas (see chapter 3) argue that in reform initiatives which emerge under conditions of perceived crisis, decision makers are likely to be concerned with such major issues as political stability, regime maintenance, and support building. They may, under such conditions, seek new supportive coalitions among domestic elites and interest groups. In less crisis-ridden reform initiatives, on the other hand, decision makers tend to be more concerned with how change will affect bureaucratic behavior and gain the support of narrow clientele groups.

To whom policymakers reach out for new support depends in part on the nature of the crisis. Bangladesh's external terms of trade deteriorated by nearly 20 percent in both 1980/81 and 1981/82. In the latter year, the value of petroleum imports alone absorbed 87 percent of reduced export earnings, and foreign exchange reserves fell precipitously. At the same time, foreign aid disbursements declined while the International Monetary Fund's (IMF) Extended Fund Facility, arranged in December 1980, was suspended because of the violation of the domestic credit ceiling, caused in part by a 47 percent increase in bank credit in 1980/81 needed to finance the large deficits of the central government and public enterprises.

The economic crisis was further complicated by the assassination of President Zia in May 1981, creating a leadership vacuum that impeded agreement on solutions to the crisis. The 1981/82 government budget, for example, was quite unrealistic, requiring continued large-scale bank credit financing. Only in early 1982 when "it had become clear that no major increase in aid was forthcoming did government embark on domestic policy adjustments to mitigate the adverse effects of external events" (World Bank 1983, 1). This shift in policy coincided with President Ershad's assumption of power in March 1982 and his appointment of Muhith as Minister of Finance, who accepted the position under the condition that he be given a free hand.

The austerity budget for 1982/83 submitted by Muhith was supported by the president over strong opposition in the cabinet. To overcome this opposition, the finance minister was obliged to organize an energetic lobbying campaign on television and to use all of his persuasive powers with senior civil servants and private interest groups. The support he could count on from international donor agencies was important for implementing his policies, but he would be politically vulnerable if it appeared that he was following their dictates. He therefore pushed through the TIP project to help strengthen the capacity of Bangladesh technocrats to formulate policy reforms and to promote dialogue with international donor agencies.

Consolidation and maintenance of the new regime was undoubtedly a high priority for President Ershad and his ministers when they came to power. Their reform agenda of relaxing government controls and relying more on private initiative was epitomized in the *New Industrial Policy* issued in May 1982, and the decision to return about twenty-five jute and thirty-five cotton textile mills to private ownership. These reforms were certainly designed to please important domestic interest groups as well as the international donors. But they could not have been received very enthusiastically by much of the bureaucracy and by those private business groups that had learned to manipulate government controls for their own benefit, and they were strongly opposed by most existing political parties and labor unions.

Despite the policy reforms introduced by previous governments, the regulatory and control systems for trade and industry differed relatively little in 1982 from those that were originally set up after establishment of the People's Republic of Bangladesh. Close to 70 percent of fixed assets in the modern manufacturing sector was still state owned and operated. The government directly controlled all private industrial investment as well as the allocation of domestic credit and foreign exchange, except for the nascent Wage Earner's Scheme (WES) exchange market.[7] For private manufacturing units the system worked as follows. First, investments had to be sanctioned in accordance with an "Investment Schedule" based on directives from the Planning Commission. Credit was allocated directly for sanctioned investments and for operating capital through state-owned development finance institutions and commercial banks. Only then was foreign exchange made available in the official exchange market through a system of import licenses and passbooks for each individual firm that spelled out precisely how much of each input could be imported as a percent of sanctioned capacity.

These interlocking control systems not only ignored market price signals and incentives, but together with other government policies, actually fostered distortions. Subsidized credit was made available to firms regardless of their credit-worthiness or of the commercial viability of the projects financed; and the credit continued to flow even if loans were not repaid, since the liquidity of development finance institutions was assured by generous rediscounts from the central bank. Effective rates of protection for domestic industries and individual firms ranged arbitrarily from negative to infinite, the result of a vast panoply of import duties which encompassed some twenty-four different rates ranging as high as 400 percent. The rates were also affected by a variety of sales tax rates on imports, numerous quantitative import and export restrictions, including outright bans, and by sundry special regulations and exemptions. Foreign exchange policies were somewhat more market-oriented than they had been in the early 1970s because of the introduction of the WES market and some export incentives for nontraditional exports. But until the crisis of the early 1980s, no more than 8 percent of total imports entered the country through the WES market. Available export incentives were modest and rigidly administered, and the nominal value of the taka had remained virtually constant in relation to the U.S. dollar for close to five years despite the more than 50 percent increase in the domestic price level.

Grossly distorted market price signals and incentives were perhaps less important when most nonagricultural production and resource allocation were under direct government control, but beneficial results from increased reliance on private initiative depended on improved market efficiency. The relationship between private initiative and efficient markets was probably not appreciated by more than a handful of government policymakers and private businessmen in 1982, and most of the bureaucracy had a stake in the preservation of government controls. Policy reforms after 1982 were thus far from assured: the outcome depended on how the five main protagonists—policymakers, government bureaucrats, influential businessmen, international donor agencies, and technocrats—used their persuasive abilities and bargaining powers.

The influence of international donor agencies derived from Bangladesh's heavy dependence on foreign aid. The current account deficit in the balance of payments averaged over 10 percent of GDP during the period 1972 to 1982; export earnings financed less than one-third of imports. About 63 percent of foreign aid disbursements in fiscal 1979 and 1980 was for food and commodity aid, which could be disbursed more rapidly than project aid and generated counterpart funds to bolster the seriously unbalanced fiscal budget. It was thus cause for alarm when the share of food and commodity aid fell abruptly to slightly over 50 percent in 1980/81. Close to 80 percent of the public sector development program was financed by foreign aid inflows, and foreign exchange reserves could not be further drawn down while external commercial borrowing was restricted by the country's limited capacity to pay. The only feasible way to quickly ease the balance of payments and fiscal crises was to increase the flow of commodity aid. International donor agencies were in a strong position to enhance their leverage by attaching policy reform conditions to additional commodity assistance.

Far from pressing the government to relax controls, most influential private businessmen seemed more concerned with preserving the privileges they enjoyed under the existing system. They had become adept at obtaining government sanctions, credit, and import licenses, and they were represented on the committees that recommended changes in tax and duty rates and exemptions. Many of them made a lucrative business out of recycling scarce imported goods to the highest bidder, going so far as to set up "industrial fronts" for the purpose of obtaining import licenses. "Real" entrepreneurs, such as those located in the thriving clandestine industrial town of Jinjira, across the river from Dhaka, probably supported decontrol, but without legal status their voices were not heard as loudly. This cozy situation between government and business was changing as the number of private industrialists increased and the structure of manufacturing diversified and deepened. One indication was the increase in complaints about tax anomalies (chiefly about higher duties and taxes on inputs than on outputs), reflecting demands by domestic producers of industrial inputs for higher protection. Indiscriminate lending by government development finance institutions also began to dry up when "soft budget constraints" hardened and the central bank had to cut back on rediscounts. For the first time in the short history of Bangladesh, entrepreneurs were obliged to risk a significant amount of their own capital to finance new investments. The free ride for "members of the club" was becoming much more bumpy.

Government bureaucrats, of course, had a stake in the existing control system, not only because controls were an important source of power and side payments, but because many controllers were convinced that markets in Bangladesh were fatally flawed and facilitated exploitation of the poor by the rich. Civil servants constituted an especially formidable barrier to decontrol because they traditionally enjoyed high prestige in the Indian subcontinent; no new policy could become effective without their help in implementing it.

Yet most of the proposed trade and industry policy reforms required the bureaucracy to step aside or at least to reduce its direct intervention. This dilemma was resolved in most reform decisions by retaining considerable scope for administrative discretion. The technocrats would have preferred the adoption of a set of general "rules of the game" that would work automatically. For example, they would have favored the elimination of credit allocation controls entirely, rather than raising the ceiling on the size of loans commercial banks could make; permitting private investors to invest freely in unrestricted industries instead of requiring Investment Board approval for projects importing more than 20 percent of their inputs (later raised to 50 percent); auctioning off of garment export quotas and barter foreign exchange instead of distributing them on a firm-by-firm basis.

The technocrats associated with the TIP project were therefore obliged to consider very carefully the roles of other protagonists in designing their own strategy. With respect to the private business community, the most important consideration was the phasing of reforms in a way that would win maximum support. Priority was given to revising the structure of protection for the steel and engineering sector and to promoting the backward integration of nontraditional export industries. It was expected that the rapidly growing number of private ship breakers and steel rerollers would support efforts to reform a protection policy designed mainly to shelter the government-owned Chittagong Steel Mill (CSM), while private engineering firms would welcome a change in import duty exemption and government procurement policies that discriminated against domestic capital goods producers. Likewise, local suppliers of inputs to the export garment industry would appreciate receiving the same incentives that direct exporters enjoyed.

To help break down bureaucratic barriers to reform, an effort was made to channel reform recommendations of TIP through high-level interministerial and interagency committees. It was hoped this strategy would reduce the risk that recommended measures could become bottled up in individual ministries or agencies by middle-level officials who felt personally threatened by the reforms. Wherever possible, policy options were also suggested with the purpose of providing intended beneficiaries with alternatives so that they did not have to depend on the discretion of a single bureaucrat. It was recommended, for example, that nontraditional exporters be allowed to choose among different duty-drawback, bonded-warehouse, and incentive schemes so that they could bargain with various agencies and officials for the most attractive package. Second, third, or even nth best policy options were suggested when it was anticipated that first best policies would not be politically acceptable. For example, instead of insisting that the Chittagong Steel Mill be closed down because it generated negative value added at border prices, a detailed proposal was also worked out for paying explicit operating subsidies to the mill.

With respect to international donor agencies, the TIP advisers tried to keep their distance so as to strengthen their identification with the interests of the government of Bangladesh. This was considered vital in winning the confidence of local officials whose support was needed to reach a consensus on the policy reform measures the advisers would propose in negotiations for additional commodity aid. This strategy worked reasonably well with regard to reforms of investment regulations and the structure of protection, as will be seen below, but it also contributed to a direct confrontation between TIP and international agencies over export incentives. The effectiveness of existing XPB (Export Promotion Bonus) subsidies that TIP proposed to strengthen depended on the size of the exchange rate premium in the secondary exchange market and on ignoring, or at least bending, GATT rules against export subsidies, as many countries do in practice. But the IMF and the World Bank were committed to the unification of foreign exchange markets in Bangladesh and would not countenance explicit export subsidies.[8] The result was that the World Bank brought in a separate team of experts to design a new export promotion and incentive system based on the model used in South Korea.

Little will be said in this paper about the fifth main protagonist in the political economy of reform in Bangladesh—the policymaker—because the authors have no independent information on how policies are ultimately made in Bangladesh. The following sections focus on interactions among the four protagonists mentioned above, the identification of episodes that appear to have triggered reform breakthroughs, and factors that accelerated the reform momentum.

Reform of Controls

The continued direct controls over investment, credit, and foreign exchange, after official policy began to rely more on private initiative, were justified on grounds that the new entrepreneurs were inexperienced and needed guidance, that powerful private interests would exploit imperfect markets if left to their own devices, that the country could not afford to waste scarce financial and foreign exchange resources, and that government controls were needed in pursuit of other objectives, such as the promotion of the regional growth poles and the protection of local "indentors" or import agents against foreign commercial intermediaries. Few civil servants recognized any contradiction between pervasive direct government intervention and the healthy growth of the private sector. And some observers commented that government controls, far from discouraging private initiative, actually stimulated it, arguing in fact that no entrepreneur was worth his salt if he could not find a way around the controls. If transaction costs had to cover the cost of side payments, then the price mechanism was working just fine, a point to which we will return.

In view of these obstacles to decontrol, the relaxation of investment, credit, and import regulations, probably had to be triggered by exceptional circumstances. The first such circumstance was the interest shown by some foreign entrepreneurs at the end of the 1970s in the export garment industry (see *Reform of Prices*). To avoid delays, they were permitted to import capital goods through the WES market, a privilege that, once granted to some, became increasingly difficult to deny others. The second exceptional circumstance was the breakdown of government credit controls. Because existing control systems were highly interdependent, the failure of one link was bound to weaken the whole chain. In this case the link was the government-owned development finance institutions (DFIs), primarily the Bangladesh Shilpa Bank (BSB) and the Bangladesh Shilpa Rin Sangstha (BSRS). In 1982 these institutions were responsible for sanctioning most industrial investments, and they were the major source of long-term industrial credit. In earlier years most BSB and BSRS loans were made to state-owned corporations. But between 1977/78 and 1980/81, credit disbursements to private sector firms increased almost five-fold to Tk. 1.1 billion. They remained approximately at this level for three years and then collapsed as suddenly as they had grown to only Tk. 210 million (about U.S. $7 million) in 1985/86 (World Bank 1988).

The decline in the lending capacity of the DFIs was caused by the sharp fall in the loan recovery rates, the inability of the Bangladesh Bank to maintain its generous rediscount policy while complying with monetary expansion targets under harder budget constraints, and the reluctance of international donor agencies to continue funding the DFIs.[9] Under these circumstances, the government was obliged to encourage waiting clients to finance their investments through foreign suppliers' credits or with their own resources and to import required capital goods through the WES market without the usual restrictions. The response was so strong that, by the second half of 1982, nongovernment WES imports of machinery and equipment exceeded imports through the official market.

This breach in the control system did not lead at once to its complete collapse. But it starkly revealed the policy weaknesses and contradictions that thoughtful policymakers and officials could hardly overlook. One such official became secretary of the Ministry of Industries in 1984 and was asked to revise the New Industrial Policy (NIP) of 1982 in preparation for launching Bangladesh's *Third Five-Year Development Plan*. He turned to the TIP for advice and eventually developed a close professional relationship with the TIP staff. Both the changes he did introduce in the NIP and those he did not (well recorded in TIP memoranda and early drafts of the NIP) reveal political and interest group alignments at the time.

The 1982 NIP had reserved six industries exclusively for public sector development and included thirteen in a concurrent list for both the public and private sectors, subject to their inclusion in the Investment Schedule. The list of "free" industries, that is those which did not require investment sanctioning, was increased. In the 1985 draft of the revised NIP, some marginal changes were made in the reserved and concurrent lists (e.g., electricity distribution and air transport were moved from the first list to the second), the Investment Schedule was made "indicative" instead of obligatory, and the list of free industries was further expanded. After discussion with TIP personnel and others, the final version of the revised 1986 NIP dropped the concurrent list altogether (but moved electricity distribution and air passenger traffic back to the reserved list), eliminated the Investment Schedule, and replaced the free list with an indicative list of industries in which private investment should be given priority or discouraged.

Of even greater significance were the changes made in investment sanctioning and import licensing regulations. The 1982 NIP, decentralized sanctioning powers and significantly liberalized import licensing and passbook procedures. The 1985 draft of the revised NIP made few changes except for requiring industrial projects with more than 20 percent imported inputs to be cleared by the Investment Board. At the urging of TIP staff the import content ratio was raised to 50 percent in the final version of the revised NIP, and it was explicitly stated that no sanction was necessary for investments, unless they were included in the reserved list or financed by official credit. Import licensing regulations were also very similar in the 1982 and preliminary 1985 NIPs, but the 1986 version specifically called for simplification of procedures and did not detail methods for determining import entitlements of individual firms. Most of these changes recognized what was already happening on an increasing scale. Policy making was being overtaken by events. By officially removing some bureaucratic hurdles and simplifying procedures, the 1986 NIP effectively chipped away at the scope for administrative discretion.

Perhaps the most substantive policy changes announced in the 1986 NIP were those affecting regional development incentives. The concessional rate of duty on capital goods imported for use in "developed" areas was raised to the 20 percent minimum level recommended by TIP, while the rate for "less-developed" areas was raised to 7.5 percent, although the TIP staff had recommended 10 percent. However, an additional category, "least-developed" areas, was added and given the previous low rate of 2.5 percent. In a similar vein, interest rate subsidies and the earmarking of certain industries for exclusive location in less- and least-developed areas was dropped in the final version of the document, and despite TIP objections, a provision for fuel subsidies to industries in these areas was retained. In other policy areas, the wording "on a selective basis in phases" was dropped from the section on export incentives, and, at TIP's urging, incentives were adopted to encourage backward integration of export industries. But instead of eliminating a reference to concessional loans to basic chemicals, such loans were granted to "capital machinery."

These and other changes, made and not made, during the drafting of the 1986 NIP give insight into the logrolling that occurred. Regional interest groups apparently were a force to be reckoned with. Consequently, TIP submitted a proposal for charging all imports of capital goods a minimum 20 percent duty, earmarking the additional revenue earned for infrastructure improvements in less- and least-developed areas. This proposal was rejected. TIP then suggested that all imports of capital goods be taxed at 20 percent upon importation and that the difference between this rate and the concessionary rate be reimbursed to importers, but only after they had obtained official certification that the machinery had actually been installed in a less- or least-developed area. While not the optimal solution to removing discrimination against domestic capital goods producers, it was believed that this procedure would substantially reduce the effective rate of subsidy to imports of capital goods because bureaucratic inertia would erode the real value of duty rebates. Regional interests could hardly argue against the proposal and the bureaucracy would support it. This assessment of political and interest group pressures proved correct, and the suggested policy was adopted.

Another example of "successful" technocratic reform-mongering was the replacement of the list of permissible imports by lists of imports that were prohibited or restricted, making import restrictions the exception rather than the rule. But the new lists were so general that substantial administrative discretion was preserved. Manufacturing firms were relieved of the obligation to obtain prior permission from "sponsoring authorities" to import many products, but discretionary bans were continued for a number of imports (e.g., machinery and spare parts for jute and cotton textile mills and the tea industry, raw tobacco for cigarettes, and wool for carpets); and while passbook regulations were significantly relaxed, passbooks were still used to try to ensure that firms imported inputs only for their own use.

What conclusions can be drawn from this experience with investment and import-control reforms? First, the establishment of general rules of the game instead of piecemeal reform does not yet seem possible in Bangladesh. We will return to this theme in *Reform of Industrial Protection*. Second, until general across-the-board reforms become possible, substantial scope for administrative discretion in policy implementation will remain. Third, piecemeal policy making lends itself to extensive logrolling, which can become a serious obstacle to reform.

Another conclusion from this experience is more open to dispute. Did the breakdown of DFI lending that helped foster decontrol entail an excessively high cost in terms of slower future growth of the manufacturing sector? Dynamic development of the ready-made garment industry, discussed in the next section, was not impeded by the drying up of DFI lending. But this industry had been given permission to import through the WES market and is not capital-intensive. The garment industry's most important financial requirement is working capital, which it was able to obtain in the form of rollover credits from the commercial banks. Other Bangladesh industries identified by TIP as having strong comparative advantage (e.g., leather products and electronic goods assembly) are on average more capital-intensive and have longer gestation periods. It has been argued that in these cases pressure on the DFIs to improve loan recovery rates could, if successful, drive many borrowers into bankruptcy, reduce private savings, and impede new investment.

This argument, however, suffers from two major flaws. The first is that DFI lending practices have not contributed to the development of industries with comparative advantage. For example, the most important BSB loans in 1982 were for cinema halls! Moreover "the median delays [in obtaining loans] were 12 months of waiting for a decision from the bank, 23 additional months until machinery is imported, and 15 additional months until production begins" (TIP 1986). DFI equity requirements from borrowers were very low, so that investments tended to be highly leveraged and borrower risks minimal. This was hardly a formula for promoting industrial entrepreneurship, especially in view of the fact that rent-seeking borrowers with good connections were favored in granting loans.

A successful crackdown on delinquent DFI debtors would increase the availability of long-term credit to the extent that more funds become available for relending. On the other hand since little private equity had been committed to projects financed by the DFIs, a crackdown on loan repayments could, if combined with a prudent rescheduling of debt service payments by otherwise healthy borrowers, lead to the liquidation of financially nonviable firms. Such liquidation could promote the redeployment of capital to more profitable activities, assisted by a host of recently established private or joint venture development banks, such as the Islamic Bank of Bangladesh Ltd., the Saudi-Bangladesh Industrial and Agricultural Company, and the Industrial Promotion and Development Company of Bangladesh. Strengthening of a more competitive, market-oriented development finance system could also be expected to reduce transaction cost for new investors. Under the old system low equity exposure and high real resource costs of negotiating side payments must have distorted incentives and contributed to the serious misallocation of investment observed in Bangladesh.

Reform of Prices

The system of import controls and export incentives inherited by Bangladesh left only a minor role for the official exchange rate. Direct licensing of foreign exchange was the rule. Much the same situation had prevailed in Pakistan, but there a system of export bonus vouchers had been introduced which provided at least a partial free market for foreign exchange and allowed exporters of non-traditional commodities to capture some of the rents import license holders normally captured (Bruton and Bose 1963). Initially restricted to manufactured exports, this export bonus voucher system eventually was expanded so that it also covered raw jute and jute goods, the major exports from then East Pakistan. By the end of the 1960s, approximately 60 percent of all exports were covered under the scheme and about 15 percent of imports were purchased using bonus vouchers (Stern and Falcon 1970).

Once independent, Bangladesh fixed its exchange rate at Tk. 7.78/$ compared to the preliberation rate of taka (or, more precisely, rupees) 4.76/$, the rate that had prevailed in Pakistan.[10] This suggests that the exchange rate was substantially devalued. In fact the opposite is the case. Toward the end of 1971, the export bonus rate for raw jute, jute goods, and other exports were 15, 35, and 45 percent, and as the premium on such vouchers averaged almost 200 percent, the effective exchange rate for raw jute was Tk. 6.16/$; for jute goods Tk. 8.09/$; and Tk. 9.04/$ for other export items.[11] The postindependence exchange rate thus represented a marginal revaluation of the currency!

Over the next few years, the government did little to improve the situation. With exports dominated by primary products, with a weak industrial base, and with a small export sector, the idea of seeking an improvement in export performance by raising the price to exporters was dismissed.[12] Given this policy bias, it is not surprising that real export growth was slightly negative over the period from 1972 to 1979, with export earnings financing less than half of imports, the rest financed through various forms of development assistance.[13] Moreover, the Awami League government viewed exchange controls as an important adjunct to its industrial licensing system.

Despite the prevailing pessimistic view about the efficacy of exchange rate movements, the taka was devalued by about 50 percent in 1975, although it was then held constant relative to the dollar for about the next five years. A more important policy reform was the acceptance by the Awami League government of a scheme, the Wage Earner's Scheme, which allowed for the development of a legal secondary exchange market. Established in June 1974, the Wage Earner's Scheme (WES) grew from very modest beginnings to a system that eventually provided a strong incentive to exporters and gave importers greater access to imported raw materials and other goods. In the final analysis, the WES proved to be one of the more dramatic policy changes introduced, sharply reducing the impact of direct controls on imports, production, and investment.

As early as 1964, remittances from East Pakistan workers overseas had become an important source of foreign exchange. However, after the war of liberation, the level of remittances fell sharply. Bangladeshis working in the United Kingdom were reluctant to the use legal remittance channels because of their well-known inefficiency and poor exchange rate offered, but they were also reluctant to use illegal channels, which carried the risk that the investment financed by repatriated funds could be confiscated.

In an effort to attract more wage remittances, it was suggested that a secondary exchange market be established. The government, unwilling to admit that changes in the exchange rate would attract large remittance flows, instituted an administrative fix: the establishment of a telex facility in London to speed up the transfer of funds. This addressed only part of the problem and with little consequence. The proposal for a secondary exchange market for remittances was resubmitted a number of times and repeatedly dismissed for a variety of political and supposed economic reasons.[14] Eventually, those pressing for a secondary exchange market managed to reach the president and, just before the import policy for the first half of 1974/75 was announced, he approved the scheme. Whether he did so because he was persuaded the scheme would begin to alleviate the severe shortage of foreign exchange or because, as has been suggested, he owed a political favor to those pressing for the reform, may never be known. Whatever the reason the scheme was announced as part of the import policy for 1974/75.

Victory was only partial. The scheme had been accepted only on a "trial" basis, only four items could be imported, and those making remittances had to be certified as "legal wage earners"—conditions that severely limited the impact of the scheme. But the rapid increase in the migration of workers to the Middle East, especially after 1973, made it increasingly difficult to administer some of the provisions of the scheme and built up tremendous pressure for reform. Over time the scheme was simplified and the number of commodities that could be imported increased, resulting in a dramatic rise in the flow of wage earner remittances. They rose from less than $30 million in 1975/76, to about $400 million in 1980/81, and to over $700 million in 1986/87, equal to almost three-fourths of the total value of merchandise exports. The proportion of total imports financed under the WES market increased from 15 percent in 1980/81, to 24 percent in 1983/84, and to 42 percent in 1986/87. In 1987 the government extended the scheme to cover all non-government imports, except those financed by foreign aid or through barter arrangements. The only major items still imported under the official exchange rate are food grains, fertilizer, and certain capital goods for officially sponsored projects. Although the WES began as a means of encouraging workers to finance the purchase of four needed commodities, it became a critical instrument in freeing up the foreign exchange market. Investors could import capital goods which were critical in the creation of new industries, such as shipbreaking and ready-made garments for exports, and in revitalizing existing ones, such as steel rerolling.

The WES played an equally dramatic role in stimulating nontraditional exports. Under the Export Performance Licensing (XPL) system, eligible exporters obtained Import Entitlement Certificates (IECs) equal in value to a certain percentage of their gross f.o.b. export earnings. The IECs could be freely traded, and entitled the holder to obtain import licenses for commodities which could be imported through the Wage Earner's Scheme. Exporters were free to use the IECs to satisfy their own import requirements, but, in fact, most were sold in the WES auctions where exporters obtained additional revenue to the extent of any exchange rate premium. Today all commodities except jute, wet blue leather, and tea are included under the scheme. The result has been a dramatic increase in nontraditional exports, which now represent nearly half the total value of commodity exports. As shown in Table 1, nontraditional exports in real terms have grown at an annual rate exceeding 22 percent since 1980/81.[15]

Table 1 Growth of Exports: 1973/74 to 1986/87

| | Annual Rate of Growth [a] | | | Percent Share of Non-traditional Exports in Total Exports(b) |
Year	Total Exports	Non-Traditional	Traditional	
1973/74	-0.1	-0.9	10.7	7.4
1974/75	-18.3	-21.5	16.6	10.3
1975/76	24.5	24.8	19.0	9.5
1976/77	3.3	2.7	1.5	10.0
1977/78	4.2	0.6	37.6	9.5
1978/79	-2.1	-3.6	9.4	12.3
1979/80	-4.1	-4.3	-1.4	12.3
1980/81	11.4	4.5	59.1	13.8
1981/82	4.0	5.1	-0.3	18.2
1982/83	4.8	1.6	20.0	26.9
1983/84	4.7	-1.4	30.7	22.6
1984/85	-3.4	-17.5	39.9	29.7
1985/86	11.0	11.5	10.2	37.4
1986/87	21.4	10.0	42.2	46.8
Annual Averages				
1973/74 to 1980/81	1.9	0.3	12.4	11.1
1980/81 to 1986/87	6.8	1.0	22.4	32.6

Notes: [a] Calculated at constant prices. [b] Calculated at current prices.

Source: Bangladesh Bureau of Statistics and Bangladesh Bank data.

Despite these policy improvements the trade regime remained biased against export development. In 1985/86 the XPL was replaced by an Export Promotion Bonus (XPB) scheme, which, in effect, replaced the IECs with cash subsidies based on the differential between the official exchange rate and the WES rate. As this differential narrowed, the effectiveness of the export subsidy given under the XPB scheme eroded. The growth of nontraditional exports was also heavily concentrated in ready-made garments which were made almost entirely from imported materials. Export activities continued to be handicapped by the impact of the tariff protection afforded to domestic suppliers which acted as a tax on exporting. Rab estimated that "the average level of effective assistance (to exports) seems to lie somewhere around 10 percent, while the lowest appear to be near zero or even negative." (Rab 1984).[16] To help exporters gain access to needed imported inputs, the government had set up a "bonded warehouse system," in effect creating a series of mini-duty-free export processing zones. But exporters who had access to such duty-free imports had no incentive to seek out potential domestic suppliers. Thus, not only was the export sector relatively discriminated against, but exports tended to be highly import-intensive.[17]

The TIP analysts launched a campaign to persuade the government to provide incentives to encourage the backward integration of export industries and to strengthen the effective rate of assistance given to exporters. The analysts recommended that the XPB level should be based on the *net* value of exports, defined as the gross value of export receipts less the value of duty-free imports used with the XPB rate set at 30 percent.[18] This would allow an exporter who used domestic inputs and reduced his access to imported inputs, to raise the *net* export value and hence the subsidy earned under XPB. The additional revenue earned would offset the higher cost incurred by using local producers, or, alternatively, might be used to encourage local producers to upgrade the quality of their products and stimulate production. In fact, differential XPB entitlement rates, providing for higher rates for exporters using domestic manufactured inputs, were introduced in the 1985/86 Export Policy Order. And in 1987, after further analysis by the TIP staff, the Committee on the Textile Sector recommended that the very modest existing differentials be increased sharply.

On the whole, however, the idea of an XPB system based on domestic value added was resisted. In part, this reflected a belief by the bureaucrats that the market would not work: the additional revenues earned by exporters who switched to local inputs would not be used as an incentive to encourage local production but would merely increase their (already presumed high) profits. And demonstrably less efficient alternative measures, such as the use of bonded warehouses, tax holidays, and access to subsidized credit, allowed the bureaucrats to retain a considerable degree of administrative control.

Perhaps more surprising, the efforts to encourage backward integration were not supported by the World Bank, which felt that in doing so it was giving official sanction to export subsidies. The Bank proposed instead the establishment of a new Duty Exemption-Drawback Office (DEDO) to facilitate duty-free imports for both direct and indirect exporters. Under this scheme, which was made a condition of the Industrial Sector Credit, no incentive is provided for promoting the integration of exporting and import-substituting industries. The failure to provide a strong encouragement for backward integration helps perpetuate import-intensive export development with weak industrial linkages.

Despite this notable failure, more progress has been made in other areas of trade and exchange rate policies. The tariff structure is being rationalized, and the most acute anomalies in the tariff system, applicable to textiles and steel and engineering, with over half of manufacturing value added, have been eliminated. Import bans have decreased in number, albeit slowly, and the number of tariff rates has been reduced and simplified.

While controls continue, either explicitly or implicitly, to hamper foreign trade, progress has been made in reforming trade policy. This has been achieved despite a strong belief in the efficacy of controls. And indeed controls continue to hamper the economy and protect inefficient producers. At the same time, however, liberalization has allowed the emergence of a new, dynamic, export-oriented industrial sector, whose overall contribution to national income and employment, while still small, is growing.

Reform of Industrial Protection

Reforming industrial protection constituted the single most important objective of TIP. Dozens of studies were carried out by TIP units in the Tariff Commission and the Planning Commission on the effective rate of protection (ERP) for individual industries. Using these studies, detailed recommendations were formulated to replace quantitative import restrictions with tariffs, to rationalize and simplify the chaotic tariff structure, and to bring most ERPs within a band of 30 to 50 percent.[19] The objective of this reform was to make it possible to use industrial protection as a rational tool of public policy, not to provide uniform protection.[20] Furthermore, a strong effort was made to reduce the great dependence of government revenue on trade taxes by broadening the domestic tax base.

Although TIP's recommendations for reform of industrial protection were not based on a formal model of the Bangladesh economy, neither were they guided by the "rules of thumb" criticized by Shantayanan Devarajan and Jeffrey D. Lewis in chapter 6 of this volume. Careful attention was given by TIP to the impact of tariff reform on government revenue, which was usually estimated to be positive when quantitative import restrictions were replaced by tariffs or prohibitive duty rates were lowered. As most goods could not in fact be legally traded in Bangladesh, TIP undertook a substantial research effort to estimate empirically the difference between domestic and border prices of goods that were imperfect substitutes. Formal models were used to measure the macroeconomic impact of recommended reforms, but, contrary to the model posited by Devarajan and Lewis, the TIP model did not assume that revenues lost through tariff reform would be offset by increased foreign borrowing, an assumption that would not reflect the reality facing Bangladesh.

These technical questions had little to do, however, with the implementation of recommended reforms, which depended primarily on the attitudes and bargaining power of the other main protagonists mentioned earlier. International donor agencies, most importantly the World Bank, supported the majority of TIP's recommendations. But local interest groups, including not only private businessmen and government bureaucrats, but also powerful state-owned enterprises, could be expected to oppose reforms that they feared might adversely affect them.

TIP's substantive reports and policy recommendations began flowing in 1984 to the TIP Governing Council, key ministries, and officials. They were initially received with what can most charitably be described as benign neglect.[21] But reforms in protection policy recommended by TIP began to appear in the 1985/86 Budget Message and became more frequent thereafter. A critical breakthough occurred in 1986 when the secretary of industries, with whom TIP collaborated on revision of the NIP was appointed chairman of the Tariff Commission. He proceeded to set up interagency committees to review TIP's work and make policy reform recommendations to the government. These recommendations were then used in negotiating ISC conditions with the World Bank.

Committees were set up to review TIP work in three industrial subsectors in which TIP had grouped its protection policy recommendations: steel and engineering, cotton textiles, and chemical and allied industries (no committee has yet been established to review protection policies for the agro-industrial subsector). We focus attention on the first two subsectors—steel and engineering and cotton textiles—as these were given priority in the World Bank's Industrial Sector Credits (ISC) and subsequent reforms adopted by the government.

Before turning to the analysis of industrial protection reform, it should be noted that during this period Bangladesh faced a generally favorable macro-economic situation. Real GDP was growing on average by more than 4 percent per year, the annual rate of inflation remained at about 10 percent, the value of exports doubled between 1981/82 and 1987/88 with the current account deficit declining from 12 percent of GDP in 1981/82 to 5.5 percent in 1986/87, while foreign exchange reserves rose. Although the parliamentary and presidential election campaigns created considerable political turmoil, this was not serious enough to destabilize the economy and generate pressure for reimposing controls or abandoning the reform program.

A. **The Steel Industry**. The Bangladesh steel industry had been created as an import-substituting activity and the effective protection received by almost all producers has been determined mainly by quantitative import restrictions. These restrictions took the form of outright bans on imports of competitive products and of complicated regulations on the few permissible imports.[22] The ostensible purpose of these controls was to protect the government-owned Chittagong Steel Mill (CSM), which uses an antiquated technology to produce steel while generating negative real value added in most of its product lines. The only competitive segment of this industry is composed of private rerolling mills using scrap from ship breaking. The incremental domestic resource cost of saving a dollar of foreign exchange from rerolling scrap in these mills was estimated in 1985 at Tk. 14/$, about 40 percent less than the official exchange rate.[23]

The high level of effective protection that steel products other than ship scrap received (from 150 percent to infinite) made steel rerolling extremely profitable. As a result, rerolling capacity expanded very rapidly after the ship-breaking industry emerged and provided a vastly cheaper source of raw material than billets produced by the CSM. By 1987 more than 100 mills had been "registered," and many more unregistered ones were alleged to be in operation. The supply of rerolled products began to exceed demand, putting a downward pressure on prices, further reducing the competitiveness of the CSM. In 1985/86 the government slashed taxes on imported inputs for the CSM and tried to restrict expansion of the rerolling industry, but by then the monster had grown too large to hold down. The rerollers constituted a powerful lobby, and the Shipbreakers Association could claim that their industry provided employment directly or indirectly to 200,000 workers, mainly in the same Chittagong district where CSM employed only a few thousand.

The only viable solution to excess capacity in the industry was clearly to increase demand by cutting prices further. The TIP recommendation that the nominal protection on steel outputs be reduced to about 30 percent and on steel inputs to 20 percent was in general accepted by the committee and was included among the conditions attached to the ISC. In the 1987/88 and 1988/89 budget messages, numerous tariff reductions were announced, lowering duties on some inputs even below the recommended 20 percent minimum level. Duties on outputs, including billets, still remain mostly above 40 percent. Moreover, the committee recommended that restrictions be continued on imports of billets and rods (the latter being the main output of rerollers). No reduction in effective rates of protection is therefore likely to have taken place yet in the basic steel sector.

For a number of other steel products, on the other hand—bolts, nuts, rivets, screws, washers, springs, etc.—the cut in customs duties from 150 to 50 percent must have reduced the effective rate of protection to some extent, even allowing for the fact that there was considerable "water" in the old tariff. These tariff reductions were strongly recommended by TIP to assist users of these products in the engineering sector.

Finally, with regard to the CSM, the committee accepted TIP's second best recommendation: if, for social and political reasons, it was not possible to close down the mill, then an explicit subsidy should be paid to make the fiscal cost of the alleged social benefits more transparent. The committee further recommended that the subsidy be temporary and that the situation of the CSM be reviewed in depth before making any further investment in the mill. Consequently, an "initial step" was announced in the 1987/88 budget message of paying CSM a 10 percent subsidy on billets and a 15 percent subsidy on plates. These subsidies are less than those recommended by TIP and the committee, most probably because the Finance Ministry would like to test whether TIP's estimate of the net fiscal cost of the subsidies (which are expected to be largely offset by savings in government purchases of steel) is correct. It is also interesting to note that most private sector buyers of the products selected for subsidization—billets and plates—belong to two very influential interest groups—rerollers and ship builders.

B. **The Engineering Sector.** There is no other industrial sector in Bangladesh that is affected by so wide a variety of protection policies. On one hand, many major engineering products are protected by selective import bans or special restrictions. On the other hand, protection is eroded by high import duties and restrictions on imported inputs, by concessionary rates of duty on capital goods imports, by policies that discriminate against local sales to foreign-aided projects under international tender, and other measures. Furthermore, preferential treatment of imports of completely or semi-knocked-down (CKD or SKD) parts favors low value-added assembly activities. Estimates of the effective rates of protection for engineering products ranged from over 400 percent to less than -50 percent.

Despite these erratic protection policies, a thriving private engineering sector has developed in Bangladesh, composed mainly of medium- and small-scale firms such as machine workshops scattered throughout the country. The quality of their products usually falls short of international standards, partly because many firms are "unregistered" and do not have easy access to modern technology and imported inputs as do more sophisticated public enterprises and registered assemblers of imported components. Protective measures are tailor-made to serve the special interests of privileged engineering firms, while influential user industries are placated by receiving access to low-duty imports of machinery, equipment, and components not produced by these firms.

As the engineering sector has grown and diversified, it has become more difficult to reconcile conflicting demands for special treatment and to ignore widespread abuses. In meetings of the Committee on Steel and Engineering with local trade and industry associations, engineering firm representatives strongly criticized existing policies, claiming they were responsible for the observed decline in domestic demand for their products.[24] One outcome of these meetings was a decision to prepare a complete list of capital goods produced in the country, and in 1987/88 concessionary rates of import duty on these goods were suspended.

At the same time, import duties were reduced on a wide variety of material inputs and components used by engineering firms. Especially noteworthy was the drastic reduction of duties on imports of electronic components and parts, a measure strongly recommended by TIP to foster development of an internationally competitive electronics industry. Another important TIP recommendation supported by the committee was also partially adopted in the 1988/89 budget message, which announced increases in import duties on imports of CKD and SKD kits for the assembly of auto-rickshaws, buses, trucks, and jeeps.

These reforms almost certainly improved the effective rate of protection received by the engineering sector. Furthermore, the opportunity was wisely seized to increase excise taxes on a wide variety of consumer durable goods, ranging from motor vehicles, refrigerators, and air coolers to stainless steel cutlery and cookware. Much remains to be done to rationalize and simplify protection of the engineering sector, but important first steps have been taken. Perhaps more important, they were taken without much prodding from the World Bank, which had largely ignored the engineering sector in the conditions it attached to the ISC.

C. **Cotton Textiles.** Traditionally the textile industry in Bangladesh consisted mainly of a group of medium- and large-scale spinning mills that supplied yarn to tens of thousands of small handloom weavers, who, in turn, supplied three-fourths of the cloth consumed in the country. Both yarn and cloth have been rather heavily protected by taxes and quantitative import restrictions, but illegal competition from India has undermined much of the protection provided. The Committee on the Textile Sector estimated that about one-third of total yarn supplies was smuggled into the country, as well as a significant amount of cloth. Since it is virtually impossible to close the long border with India to illicit trade, the domestic textile industry cannot be effectively sheltered from import competition.

In recent years import competition for cloth has become even sharper. Little domestic cloth has traditionally been used in the factory production of ready-made garments, which were supplied mainly from imports of second-hand clothing. So when the ready-made garment export industry developed, almost all of its cloth and other inputs had to be imported, mostly into duty-free bonded warehouses. Leakages of cloth from these warehouses or from ports of entry have subsequently undermined the very high protection (ERPs from 150 percent to over 300 percent) given to the fledgling, modern fabric and clothing manufacturing sector. Pressure to tighten controls on duty-free cloth imports has not been effective because of the fear that greater restrictions could injure the nascent export garment industry, which has become one of the country's most important foreign exchange earners.

Faced with widespread, *de facto* import competition, textile producers focused their attention on removing obstacles to increased efficiency rather than oppose reductions in statutory tariff rates for competitive imports. Singled out among the main obstacles to improved efficiency are government interference in the procurement of raw cotton (mainly through the assignment of quotas for cotton imported under barter or from domestic production); restrictions or high taxes on imports of machinery, equipment and such inputs as dyes; and frequent power failures. The Bangladesh Textile Mill Corporation (BTMC), the state-owned enterprise that still owns about 60 percent of cotton spindle capacity in the country, is also saddled with bureaucratic regulations of procurement, marketing, pricing, and personnel that seriously impair its ability to compete in the market. These obstacles were carefully documented by TIP and became more obvious when a number of BTMC mills that were privatized and released from most of these regulations began to operate efficiently.

The policy reforms recommended in the committee's report were therefore aimed primarily at improving the competitiveness of the BTMC and private mills: BTMC mills should be allowed to sell yarn freely and to exercise more autonomy in fixing prices; private mills should be freed from all raw cotton procurement obligations; and the BTMC should be paid an explicit subsidy to cover the difference between the market price and the official price of raw cotton imported under barter or produced locally. Further, BTMC mills should be given "a free hand in handling their labor recruitment, dismissal and other related policies;" mills should be permitted to purchase stand-by electric generators; and programs for the balancing, modernization, and replacement of the cotton mill plant and equipment should be promoted vigorously. The committee also recommended elimination of a number of import controls and the reduction of import duties on most categories of textile inputs and outputs.

The reforms advocated by the committee largely reflected TIP recommendations, except that tariff rates advocated for fabrics and clothing were considerably higher than those suggested by TIP. But duty reductions were announced only for yarn and textile inputs in the budget messages of 1987/88 and 1988/89; no action has yet been taken on the protection of fabrics and clothing. It is therefore likely that the high statutory rates of effective protection these products receive have been increased. This may have been the political price that had to be paid to win support for reducing protection of domestic yarn production, but the price may not be very high in reality because of the water in the tariff created by stiff competition from illegal cloth imports.

Summary and Conclusion

Trade and industrial policy reform in Bangladesh has consisted of the gradual, piecemeal dismemberment of the highly centralized economic planning and control regime established when the country became independent. Unlike the reforms undertaken in Sri Lanka, Jamaica, and Chile, the Bangladesh reforms were not motivated by a strong ideological commitment to a freer market economy. With few exceptions each major policy change had to be negotiated between proponents and opponents, so that logrolling and compromise were often necessary to win support for individual reform items; hence, the reform agenda has followed no clear blueprint or schedule. The *New Industrial Policy* of 1982 and 1986 were statements of general principles concerned mainly with government controls and dealing only peripherally with specific export promotion and protection policies.

Given this environment policy changes tended to be tentative and partial and sometimes contradictory. This may be inevitable when both policy decisions and policy implementation must be negotiated between the bureaucracy and affected interest groups. It also meant that fulfillment of the conditions attached to the Industrial Sector Credit agreed to with the World Bank in 1987/88, which included a three-year timetable for adopting specific trade and industrial policy measures, will require substantial changes in the way policy reforms are agreed upon and implemented in Bangladesh. It is still too early to judge the likelihood of such changes actually taking place, although, as might be expected, initial reductions in quantitative import restrictions have affected redundant controls rather than those that are really binding.

In the absence of a basic reform of the reform process itself, policy advisers are faced with an extraordinary challenge. To be effective in promoting negotiated, piecemeal policy changes in such broad areas as trade and industrial policy, they must come to grips with especially difficult issues of political economy. In order to draw some lesson from the experiences described in the previous sections, we group these under three headings: (i) episodes or situations that trigger reform decisions; (ii) inconsistencies or contradictions in piecemeal policy reform; and (iii) reform momentum and sustainability.

(i) **Reform triggering mechanisms**. It was argued in the *Political Economy of Reform* section that economic and political problems at the beginning of the 1980s helped trigger an acceleration in the pace of reform. The assassination of President Zia created a political power vacuum, and the ensuing economic disarray set the stage for General Ershad who, soon after taking power, proclaimed a number of reforms and a strict monetary and fiscal policy. In view of the country's heavy dependence on foreign assistance, there can be little doubt that international donor agencies, notably the World Bank, exercised considerable leverage in persuading the government to adopt reforms. On the other hand, acceptance of the TIP advisory project was allegedly not due to donor agency pressure but to the interest generated among Bangladesh officials by an earlier study of effective protection.[25] These elements supporting reform were not sufficient, however, to assure a thorough overhaul of the trade and industry policy regime. It was also necessary to overcome strong opposition from influential members of the business elite and the bureaucracy.

The next major step was triggered by a chain of events only indirectly related to the measures first taken by the new government. A boom in migrant worker remittances through the WES market allowed that market to blossom from tentative beginnings into an authentic parallel exchange market in the late 1970s, providing an important new source of foreign exchange for industrial investment. This source of foreign exchange quickly exceeded demand by such a wide margin that the Bangladesh Bank found it necessary to start buying remittances to prevent the WES rate from falling below the official exchange rate!

At about the same time, development finance institutions (DFIs) suffered a liquidity crisis when the Bangladesh Bank was unable to continue providing them with generous rediscounts while staying within the new monetary restraints. Since foreign exchange purchases in the WES market also threatened compliance with monetary restraints, it became possible to solve simultaneously both problems—the sudden accumulation of foreign exchange reserves and the shortage of DFI resources for industrial projects—by encouraging entrepreneurs to use their own resources to import what they needed through the WES market with fewer restrictions.

This greater freedom from investment and import controls allowed the ready-made export garment industry to develop rapidly. In turn, the development of this industry led to the introduction of back-to-back letters of credit and bonded warehouse arrangements providing easy access to duty-free imported inputs. These arrangements proved to be much more effective than the existing duty drawback system, so pressure mounted to make the duty drawbacks more automatic. The success of the ready-made garment industry also spawned greater interest in strengthening nontraditional export incentives, especially for indirect exporters, the suppliers of domestic inputs to export firms. This success generated interest in the "backward integration" policies strongly advocated by TIP as a means of increasing the domestic value added to nontraditional exports.

Decontrol of industrial investment and imports also facilitated rapid development of private ship breaking and steel rerolling production, which increased domestic competition for the Chittagong Steel Mill and made it possible to modify policies designed to protect the state-owned monopoly. Reform of the system of concessionary rates of duty for capital goods imports was made possible by the strong growth and diversification of the private engineering industry that decontrol fostered. And increased smuggling of imports from India persuaded domestic cotton yarn producers to accept lower duties on competitive imports and to focus attention on reducing duties on imported inputs and on measures to improve operating efficiency.

With respect to the lessons that might be learned from these experiences, there is nothing new in saying that reformers must be constantly on the lookout for "windows of opportunity." At times, these windows can be created. This was done, for example, in 1982/83, when strict monetary and fiscal restraints hardened soft budgets. Once a window is identified, new opportunities should be exploited in a way that creates a positive sum game and one that is perceived to yield considerable returns in the short run. Ideally, winners should receive their rewards up front while the losers may not even be certain how much it is going to cost them. Such opportunities often appear when it is possible to offer options, such as permitting industrialists to use their own resources to import more freely through the WES market while retaining controls on imports financed by DFI credit through the official market, or by offering nontraditional exporters a choice between using a bonded warehouse or receiving duty drawbacks. In other cases, it is possible to buy off opponents of reform at a relatively small cost, such as by paying an explicit subsidy to the CSM or offering the BTMC greater operating autonomy.

Policy reformers who follow window-of-opportunity strategies avoid frontal attacks. In Bangladesh, for example, they relied on the withering away of excessive import controls in the official market as more and more transactions were shifted to the WES market; on competition from bonded warehouses to improve administration of duty drawbacks; and on the transparency of explicit subsidies to dramatize the high fiscal cost of maintaining the CSM in operation. Such reformers may actually condone excess capacity in steel rerolling to increase interest-group pressure for a reduction in protective duties, or they might rely on bureaucratic delays to reduce the value of concessionary rates of duty on capital goods imports. These strategies purposefully promote unbalanced policy reform, for the same reason that Hirschman (1958) advocated a planning strategy of unbalanced growth: imbalances generate contradictions and tensions that foster further reform.

(ii) **Inconsistencies in piecemeal policy reforms.** All strategies have their downside. Negotiated, piecemeal reform may generate imbalances that are not purposefully promoted simply because some reforms generate stronger opposition than others. The most obvious examples are the reductions made in taxes on imported inputs without concomitant adjustments in taxes on imports of competitive outputs in the steel and cotton textile industries. Another example is the great resistance encountered in trying to reform procedures for domestic sales to government under international tender, transactions which often involved substantial illegal payments. A third example is the resistance of regional interests to eliminating concessionary rates of duty on capital goods imports, which was overcome only after a list was prepared of locally manufactured capital goods. These partial reforms often produce undesirable changes in effective rates of protection and discourage production of goods not already domestically manufactured.[26]

An even more serious obstacle to the reform of protection policy is the prevalence of selective quantitative restrictions (QRs). Such restrictions increase the scope for administrative discretion and the opportunity for earning side payments. It is therefore not surprising that progress in the reduction of binding QRs has been relatively slow. For example, TIP suggested that the domestic prices of banned articles be monitored and that bans be lifted if price-gouging was detected. Such measures, it was hoped, would at least create a bit more competition for side payments and reduce "rents," although, admittedly, it might also raise real transactions costs. In contrast, the World Bank preferred a frontal attack. In the ISC it called for the phasing out of sixty-nine QRs on industrial inputs over a three-year period. The extent to which this condition is actually fulfilled will provide an interesting test of the frontal attack strategy.

The fiscal constraint on reform of protection policy was not anticipated in designing TIP's terms of reference, although it has proved to be a major stumbling block and a source of policy inconsistency. For example, changes in the rates of protection incorporated in the 1987/88 and 1988/89 budgets, were estimated to substantially reduce government revenue. Since 55 percent of total government tax revenue is derived from import taxes, this was cause for concern. TIP argued that reduction of prohibitive import duty rates and the replacement of bans by taxes could be expected to increase tax revenue, but not much has been done on this score. On the other hand, a number of TIP's recommendations for increasing excise taxes and fuel prices have been implemented. However, to raise necessary revenues and calm complaints about dumping, tariff values (that is, the duty base) and import-development surcharges have been sharply increased. In principle, these measures may well offset the changes made in import tax rates and arbitrarily alter the structure of protection.

Fiscal considerations have also played a role in holding down the level of export incentives, especially after the shift from XPL to XPB, since the latter appears as an expenditure in fiscal accounts, whereas the former did not.[27] TIP recommended raising the level of nontraditional export subsidies to 30 percent of the net value of exports, that is, the export value less the value of duty-free imported inputs. Export incentives would then be placed on par with the minimum ERP suggested for import-substituting industries. An extremely serious policy inconsistency is that it appears politically impossible to place export- and import-substituting industries on a more equal footing. Most firms will not find it profitable to export, or become suppliers of domestically produced inputs to exporters, unless they have access to duty-free imported inputs. This failure drastically reduces the potential domestic value added in export activities.[28] The manufacturing sector is, thus, likely to remain divided in internationally competitive and noncompetitive segments, thus narrowing the constituency of interest groups that support outward-looking policy reform.

(iii) **Policy momentum and sustainability.** It is also possible that the inconsistencies in piecemeal policy reform can undermine the momentum and sustainability of the process by contributing to a new economic crisis. However, it was hypothesized in *The Political Economy of Reform* section (see pp. 193-98) that policy changes made under the pressure of crisis are likely to increase the leverage of international donor agencies, enhance the influence of technocrats, and motivate decision makers to seek broader supportive coalitions. This seems like such a favorable climate for reform that reformers should hope that the crisis does not abate until the reforms are all in place. Yet if easier policy changes tend to be made first, how can one expect harder policy changes to take place after the pressure of crisis disappears? There are, of course, many examples of liberalization programs that were aborted when economic conditions deteriorated. A crisis might help trigger reforms, but if reforms are subsequently suspected of helping to trigger another crisis, controls will almost certainly be reintroduced unless the government is ideologically committed to reform.

Since the government of Bangladesh does not appear to have a strong ideological commitment to reform, what would prevent the retightening of controls if, say, a serious balance-of-payments crisis emerged? It would be relatively easy to tighten controls because the most important control mechanism, administrative discretion, still flourishes. This mechanism is, moreover, controlled by a bureaucracy that often feels threatened by decontrol. Consider the following example. The Investment Board Ordinance of 1988 was ostensibly created at the ministerial level to overcome administrative hurdles that inhibit private investment. But the ordinance also empowers the board to impose "such conditions and limitations as it deems fit" on new investments, decide on the terms and conditions of foreign loans and suppliers' credits, and determine import entitlements. Even the operation of the WES market is still subject to administrative discretion: importers must obtain bank letters of credit and other documentation that has to be officially approved, and old passbooks still circulate.[29]

Nothing in our opinion would contribute more to the sustainability of reform in Bangladesh than reducing the scope for administrative discretion. Among desirable improvements would be greater automaticity in the granting of those approvals that are still needed, the announcement of explicit criteria for granting approvals, and the standardization of tax rates by commodity groups rather than on a product-by-product basis. In short, exceptions should become the exception, rather than the rule.

One would expect that the growing number of beneficiaries of reform would increase reform momentum sufficiently to make it increasingly difficult to retighten controls. But private interest groups have not yet organized themselves to press for the adoption of general rules of the game. Many members of the traditional elite still rely on special favors to make a profit. And the babel of new interest group voices lobbying for contradictory policies reinforces the mediating role of the bureaucracy. The ineffectiveness of private manufacturing and trade associations has been attributed to their loose and unprofessional structure, which often makes it impossible to reconcile differences among members who do not trust each other. The cure for this debility or rent-seeking disease probably requires additional shock therapy.

Tightening enforcement of loan repayments to the DFIs should contribute to curing rent-seeking disease, as would suspension of automatic *ex post* subsidization of public enterprise deficits. And by making the ERP measure a generally accepted criterion for the evaluation of industrial protection, TIP has made a modest contribution to curing this disease. The experience with the BTMC suggests that further privatization of public enterprise units might also help shift energies from operating in political markets to competing in economic markets. But it is unlikely that the disease can be totally cured until the transaction costs of pervasive rent seeking exceed the benefits.

If ideological commitment to the merits of markets is lacking, some window-of-opportunity strategy of piecemeal reform will have to be relied on to alter the cost-benefit ratio of rent seeking. This suggests that it might be a good idea to select reforms that generate the widest possible distribution of benefits in the hope that the possibility of granting special favors or making exceptions is eventually overwhelmed by the sheer number of claimants. Development of the export garment industry contributed mightily to this cause in the past; perhaps there are other industries that can perform the same service in the future. &

Notes

1   The authors would like to thank Dr. Muhith and Dr. Momen for contributing to their discussion of the early economic history of Bangladesh and for providing insights into the reform process. Numerous readers, including Junaid Kamal Ahmad, Ataman Aksoy, Tom Hutcheson, and Robert Warner, as well as the authors' colleagues at the Harvard Institute for International Development, have provided comments and suggested changes. The authors have tried to take this advice into account and hope that in so doing they have improved the paper. As usual, responsibility for errors and conclusions rests with them.

2   The emphasis in this paper on TIP's role in encouraging reform should not be misinterpreted. The authors fully recognize the vital roles played by other actors, but they can speak with greater confidence on the contribution of TIP. The technical assistance to the TIP project was financed under a World Bank International Development Association loan to the government of Bangladesh.

3　It has been estimated that per capita incomes in West Pakistan were 17 percent higher than in East Pakistan in 1950. The gap widened to 27 percent by 1965 and continued to increase until Bangladesh declared its independence. See Stern and Falcon (1970) and Stern (1971).

4　This is not the place to review the history of Bangladesh-Pakistan relations. An impassioned description of the difficult relationship between the two provinces of Pakistan, and the events leading up to the declaration of independence, is given in Muhith (1978). The economic causes of the breakup of Pakistan are detailed in Griffin and Khan (1972).

5　Bangladesh, an extremely flat country, is subject to annual monsoon flooding, which normally enriches the soil and allows double, and in some regions, even triple cropping. But in years of severe flooding, as much as 40 percent of the total land area goes under water, often with disastrous losses in agricultural output and lives. The death toll from the 1970 cyclone was estimated at nearly half a million, while the flooding directly affected some five million people. Many Bangladeshis took the failure to mount an effective relief program as further evidence that union with Pakistan left them at the mercy of an uncaring and remote bureaucracy.

6　It was reported that India had an exceptionally good jute harvest in 1973/74 which was adequate to meet its domestic needs. It is quite likely, however, that "unofficial" (smuggled) jute imports from Bangladesh played a significant role in meeting India's jute needs without resort to legal trade. See Faaland and Parkinson (1976, 178-79).

7　The Wage Earner's Scheme (WES) was a parallel foreign exchange market. For a fuller discussion, see p. 188ff.

8　The value of the export bonus (XPB) originally proposed by TIP depended on the spread between the official and WES exchange rates, which narrowed when Bangladesh began moving toward a unified exchange system. The XPB could at this time have been replaced by an outright subsidy, but the Bank "did not want to put exporters at risk over the longer term."

9　A major investigation of the lending operations of these institutions was undertaken jointly by IDA and the Asian Development Bank during 1982/83.

10　Pakistan took the opportunity to devalue its currency after the war from Rp. 4.76/$ to Rp. 9.90/$. Bangladesh decided to equate its currency with the Indian rupee, aligned with the pound sterling at that time. For convenience, we convert all exchange rates to local currency units/U.S.$.

11　Data on the effective exchange rate is given in Faaland and Parkinson (1976). Since the official exchange rate was initially denominated in terms of pounds sterling, the data have been converted to U.S. dollars using the cross rates reported in the *International Financial Yearbook*.

12　Exports constituted about 7 percent of GDP, well below the average for low-income economies.

13 The following result is obtained by regressing exports, in 1980 prices and dollars, against time, with data taken from the World Bank World Tables:

(Eq. 1) ln Exports = 6.278 - 0.003(T) for 1972 to 1979.

By contrast after some of the antiexport biases had been removed, we obtain:

(Eq. 2) ln Exports = 6.090 + 0.051(T) for 1979 to 1986.

14 Much of the information on the establishment of the WES comes from Abdul Momen, an officer in the Ministry of Commerce during the early 1970s, who worked on the establishment of the scheme. He notes that among the reasons given for opposing the establishment of the WES was the argument that it would help only Sylhet, the area the majority of migrants came from, and that the funds would be used to buy properties abandoned by their previous Pakistani owners so that the flow of funds would help Pakistan, not Bangladesh.

15 The development of the garment industry involved technical assistance from Korean manufacturers who initially had come to Bangladesh to seek a production base not subject to quotas. So successful were the technology transfer and training efforts that in 1985 the United States imposed quotas on garment exports from Bangladesh. The fascinating story of the development and rapid growth of the garment industry is described in Rhee (1988).

16 These estimates do not allow for any correction for the overvaluation of the currency.

17 For example, the gross effective rate of protection for export industries was 11.2 percent while for import substituting activities it was 134.9 percent; the "net" ERPs were -9.1 percent for export compared to 91.9 percent for import substituting activities. Hutcheson and Stern (1986).

18 It may seem that it would be difficult for the government to calculate the net export value. Since the government had good records of commodities moving into and out of the bonded warehouses, it would be, in fact, a relatively simple calculation.

19 Choice of this band was based on TIP's estimate that the taka in the official exchange market was overvalued by a little more than 20 percent and that the average ERP for the economy as a whole was between 35 percent and 40 percent. The band chosen would thus provide a positive real ERP for manufacturing without burdening the economy with a relatively inefficient industrial sector.

20 In fact, the lower tariff rates recommended by TIP generally applied to intermediate and capital goods and the higher rates to final consumer goods.

21 Even the attitude of the chair of the TIP Governing Council was extremely skeptical. In his first meeting with TIP advisers he expressed the opinion that the project's objective of eliminating industrial protection was not politically feasible. Correcting this widely held misconception about what industrial policy reform meant required considerable explanation and time. Two years passed before TIP blue-covered reports became a familiar sight on the desks of responsible officials.

22 One regulation, for example, stated that C.I. sheet of up to 26 BWG containing zinc coating of 1.25 oz. per square foot could be imported up to a value of Tk. 100,000 per registered WES importer based on district-wise quotas allocated according to population.

23 See TIP (1985). In the estimation of this DRC, rerolling and ship breaking are treated as an integrated operation.

24 Representatives of user firms were equally vociferous in insisting on the continued need to have access to cheap imports.

25 This study, financed by the World Bank, was carried out at Boston University and involved a number of Bangladesh students studying there at that time.

26 Arbitrary scheduling of tariff reforms can also lead to undesirable changes in effective rates of protection. See Ahmad (1986).

27 As mentioned in the section on *Reform of Prices*, World Bank opposition to export subsidies also played a critical role. This is both unfortunate and ironic, because new industrializing countries such as South Korea, which relied heavily on export subsidies, especially during their earlier stages of development, are now touted by the Bank as models of dynamic non-traditional export promotion.

28 A Duty Exemption and Drawback Office (DEDO) was set up in the National Board of Revenue (NBR) in 1988, and an inland back-to-back letter of credit system was created to provide incentives to indirect exporters. It remains to be seen how much these measures will actually increase the domestic value added of direct exports.

29 It was suggested to the governor of the Bangladesh Bank that he need not worry about liberalizing import controls because import surcharges or pre-import deposits could be introduced to reduce temporarily the demand for foreign exchange. He replied that he was not worried because he still controlled the speed at which foreign exchange was released to importers.

Food Price Stabilization:

Rationale, Design, and Implementation[1]

C. Peter Timmer

C. Peter Timmer, a faculty fellow at HIID, was a resident adviser with the Harvard group at BAPPENAS, the Indonesian National Planning Agency, in 1970 and 1971 and has continued active involvement with Indonesian food policy issues since then. As Harvard's Thomas D. Cabot Professor of Development Studies, he teaches on food policy, economic history, and development, while conducting research on food policy.

pervasive element of economic reforms in developing countries has been efforts to reduce distortions by eliminating government interventions into price formation in domestic markets. In the arena of pricing policy for basic foods, however, "getting prices right" is not the same thing as free trade. Although border prices are an important ingredient in determining what prices are "right," at least four additional considerations—instability of world prices, market failures in fertilizer demand, concerns for income distribution and nutrient intake, and linkages to the macroeconomy—argue for a more sophisticated approach to domestic food price policy than simply opening the borders to competition from world markets.

The political desire to stabilize prices and the economic benefits from doing so are the major reasons why few countries permit free trade in their basic food grain. World markets are unstable, especially for rice, and unpredictable. No country can set its price policy on the basis of *future* prices in world markets. Any desire to stabilize domestic prices must inherently be backward looking and will thus cause domestic prices to deviate from border prices.

Because of risk aversion, imperfect credit markets, lack of information, and the role of learning by doing in finding optimal fertilizer levels, most developing countries use suboptimal quantities of fertilizer relative to social opportunity costs for the input and the resulting social value of the output. Because fertilizer is usually the most important commercial input into crop production, policy decisions about fertilizer prices and crop prices should be made simultaneously. For rice in Asia, for wheat in northern China and the Indian subcontinent, and for corn in Latin America and parts of Africa, interdependencies between the failure of farmers to use optimal quantities of fertilizer on food grains and the resulting exposure to world markets for these grains mean that domestic food grain prices may need to be adjusted relative to their border equivalents.

Concerns for the distribution of incomes and nutrient intake among the poor are a legitimate element in the determination of optimal economic policy. Where nondistorting instruments to redistribute incomes or assets are not available to satisfy society's desires for more equal food consumption, interventions to alter food prices may be the only feasible instrument available to the government to meet these objectives. The short-run and long-run efficiency costs of such interventions, and their impact on economic growth, are equally legitimate elements in the analysis of appropriate pricing policy, but prices designed to improve poor people's access to food cannot be ruled out on theoretical grounds alone.

Linkages between the level and stability of food prices and growth in the rest of the economy may not be fully reflected by the market value of the commodity at the border. The impact of prices on expectations, budget revenues, export competitiveness, and macroeconomic stability are all outside the static, partial-equilibrium models used to demonstrate the equivalence of border prices and the "right" domestic prices. Price policy for a society's basic food grain must consider the impact of these macroeconomic and dynamic linkages as well as any efficiency losses from short-run deviations of domestic prices from border prices. Consideration of such factors is extremely difficult given present data and methodologies, but that is no excuse for measuring only what is easily measurable.

In isolation, none of these arguments is new. The goal of this paper is to integrate them into an economically coherent rationale for the type of food price policy so often seen for rice in Asia and to use that rationale to understand the evolution of rice price policy in Indonesia. The paper is divided into three parts. The first briefly reviews the two major schools of thought on agricultural pricing—neoclassical as opposed to structural approaches—and concludes that neither is fully relevant in the Asian context, where a single food commodity, rice, dominates both production and consumption patterns. A new approach based on the macroeconomic and dynamic consequences of price stabilization is proposed as the basis for evaluating the benefits of pricing interventions.

The second part addresses important operational issues facing policymakers who wish to stabilize the price of their basic foodstuff. Analytical as well as financial aspects are discussed as a means of identifying the relevant costs that must be matched with the benefits from price stabilization. The political economy of intervention is addressed explicitly in the context of constraints on the implementation of policies that appear desirable on narrower analytical grounds. This section in particular raises questions about the politics of economic reform (never more difficult than when changing food prices) and the role of bureaucracies, especially food logistics agencies and ministries of finance, in designing and implementing major new pricing interventions.

Part three presents an Indonesian case study. It reviews the history of efforts by the government of President Suharto to stabilize rice prices in Indonesia, the main analytical issues that arose during the two decades of that experience, and the debate on agricultural deregulation that took place as the fifth five-year plan was prepared for implementation in April 1989. This debate continues and is a fast-moving target. Rice surpluses in Indonesia in 1985 and 1986 stimulated great interest in diversification away from rice production, but deficits in 1987 and 1988 renewed concern over Indonesia's capacity to maintain self-sufficiency in rice. Price stabilization remains an important policy objective in either setting, but the financial costs, feasible levels of prices, and general policy thrust with respect to the agricultural sector are quite different.

Part 1: The Analytical Case for Price Stabilization

Within the economics profession, a debate is under way on the appropriate role of price policy in agricultural development strategies. The free-market school argues that all agricultural prices should reflect their opportunity costs at the border, no matter what the international market processes are that determine the prices, and no matter what the price levels happen to be. The result of such a pricing strategy is supposed to be optimal efficiency of resource allocation, as well as minimal rent-seeking activity with its associated losses in X-efficiency.[2]

The structuralist school argues that the entire border price paradigm for domestic price determination is misdirected, at least for a select list of commodities, such as basic foodstuffs, that have important roles in the macroeconomy and welfare of consumers. Supply and demand elasticities are quite small for these commodities, so the triangles of allocative losses from not equating domestic prices with border prices are trivial. The border prices themselves are mostly the result of gross distortions in agricultural policies in the developed world; they are highly unstable, and thus carry minimal information on how resources should be allocated in the long run. Accordingly, prices should be set to favor income distribution objectives in conjunction with macroeconomic stability.[3]

The debate over agricultural pricing is just one of several that have been conducted between these two schools of thought in development economics since the 1950s.[4] The free-market approach has clearly won the ear of most large donor agencies in the 1980s, although the structuralist paradigm remains dominant in Latin America. Other developing countries, even the most successful ones in East and Southeast Asia, have openly rejected the free-market approach for primary foodstuffs, especially rice and wheat, in favor of interventions to stabilize and support agricultural prices. At the same time, the structuralist approach has also been rejected because the allocative and budgetary costs of wide, long-run deviations from border prices (including those deviations due to overvalued domestic currencies) have turned out to be substantial. The result has been a mélange of ad hoc pricing interventions intended to satisfy the needs of farmers for price incentives, the needs of consumers for low-cost foods, the constraints imposed by budget-minded finance ministers, and the powerful sociopolitical desire for price stability as the proximate indicator of a society's degree of food security. Figure 1 shows one example of the outcome of such a pricing strategy. Indonesia has sharply reduced the instability of domestic rice prices relative to that in the world market but has tried not to deviate from the long-run trend in world prices.

The analytical underpinnings for this pragmatic approach to agricultural pricing so dominant in Asia are just beginning to coalesce into a third school of thought, tentatively labeled here the "stabilization" school. The main contention of this school is that by *following* short-run price movements in international markets, an economy incurs significant efficiency losses. At the same time, the economy can incur large efficiency losses by *not following* longer-run trends in international opportunity costs (whatever the market processes that determine them). In the stabilization approach, maximizing *efficiency*, the standard goal of economic reforms, thus calls for some degree of market intervention to stabilize short-run prices. At the same time, there must be sufficient flexibility to allow domestic prices to reflect international price trends. Rent-seeking behavior is reduced by using competitive market agents to carry out most marketing activities but within government-established price bands.

While rejecting the call of free-market advocates for no pricing interventions, the stabilization approach also rejects the structuralist's desire to use agricultural prices primarily as an instrument for redistributing incomes. Further, by encouraging the development of a competitive private marketing sector over time, the role of government price interventions can decline as the role of price stability for the basic foodstuff becomes progressively less important to the macroeconomy during the course of economic development. When the opportunity (or budgetary need) comes for such a transition, structuralist- or socialist-inspired stabilization policies that actively seek to displace the private marketing sector have proved unworkable.

Neither the underlying analytical foundations nor workable operational procedures have been satisfactorily developed for domestic price-stabilization schemes to be implemented and evaluated with any degree of coherence.[5] The fact that nearly all countries in Asia attempt to implement such schemes suggests

Figure 1
Indonesia: Comparison of Domestic and International Rice Prices
1969-87 *1987 Constant Prices*

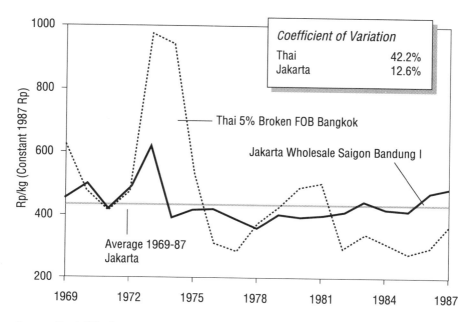

Coefficient of Variation
Thai   42.2%
Jakarta   12.6%

Thai 5% Broken FOB Bangkok

Jakarta Wholesale Saigon Bandung I

Average 1969-87
Jakarta

Source: Frank Ellis, Integrated Planning Unit, Food Logistics Agency (BULOG), Jakarta, Indonesia, 1988.

that the rewards to progress on both fronts—analytical and operational—would be very substantial. This paper is primarily concerned with operational issues of analyzing, designing, and implementing price-stabilization schemes; the underlying theoretical rationale has been addressed by a number of authors.[6] It is important, however, to lay out the basic logic of the analytical approaches in order to focus the discussion of operational issues on pricing strategies that are consistent with the theoretical rationale for their design and implementation.

Potential versus Actual Benefits of Government Intervention

With the early contributions of Smith, Marshall, and Pigou to the economics literature, economists have understood for over a century the basic analytical rationale for government interventions into market price formation. Economies of scale and monopolies, externalities in production and consumption, public goods, and imperfect information in the absence of complete contingency markets have long offered theoretical justification for interventions designed to correct such market failures. The resurgence of the free-market paradigm builds on a crucial lesson from postwar development experience: policies that attempted to strengthen the competitiveness of markets as a way to improve their efficiency outperformed policies that attempted to correct for market failures by suppressing market activities. This success of market-oriented policies came about primarily because government failures in market interventions were often

223

far more serious in terms of wasted economic resources and forgone growth than were the market failures they were designed to correct.

An additional factor grew out of the theory of the second best. Many imperfections in markets, especially in rural factor and product markets, could be explained as second-best adaptations to inherent constraints on first-best arrangements because of imperfect and asymmetric information, moral hazards and high transactions costs, and a significant degree of risk aversion by the very poor in the context of incomplete credit and contingency markets. In such circumstances, government interventions into one market run a substantial risk of lowering the welfare of the poor because of its connections with other markets that provide some degree of welfare insurance. Under the twin banners of "government failures" and models of interlinked markets in a second-best world, neo-neoclassical and social-choice theorists provided a new intellectual foundation to the free-market paradigm.[7]

The basis of this foundation is not theoretical, however, but inherently empirical. Given the reality of widespread market failures in developing countries, modern welfare economics is very clear on the *potential* scope for government interventions to achieve a Pareto-superior position for the economy. Whether a government can improve welfare through an actual intervention in a specific case depends on two factors: whether the market failure itself is "real" within the context of the theory of the second best, and whether the government can actually improve social welfare by intervening. The latter question must be addressed in a dynamic context that explicitly includes the potential for vested interests to capture both the economic gains from the policy intervention and the policy-making process itself, thus leading to further interventions that carry the economy away from the Pareto optimum achieved by the initial, but limited, government intervention.

The stabilization approach builds on these analytical foundations to develop the empirical case for price-stabilization policies. In doing so, however, it rejects the emerging consensus that the welfare gains from price stabilization, although usually positive in theory, are empirically not very important relative to the costs governments must incur in order to stabilize prices.[8] Two key innovations in the analysis, one microeconomic and one macroeconomic, lead to such different empirical conclusions. The first is to consider the farmer as an investor rather than as the manager of a static stock of assets and a flow of variable inputs. The model of farmer as manager is the basis of nearly all theoretical and empirical assessments of risks from price and yield instability, but it clearly excludes important elements in farmer decision making that are strongly influenced by these risks, especially expectations and patterns of investment in physical and human capital. Transforming the problem into one of dynamic portfolio investment decision making enormously complicates the analysis of risk, even when restricted to farm-level issues.

Tracing the macroeconomic ramifications of price instability is even more complicated because general-equilibrium analysis is needed with dynamic investment functions that are conditioned by stability-sensitive expectations.[9] But incorporating these dynamic factors into both the micro- and macroanalyses offers the opportunity to examine the impact of price-stabilization policies on agricultural development and economic growth. The static, microbased models simply do not address these issues; they are incapable of assessing the consequences for the economy of the price-stabilization polices that are widely implemented—consequences that policymakers actually worry about.

The Quantitative Significance of Price Stabilization

The important analytical question is not to demonstrate that the pervasive market failures in developing countries lead to non-Pareto-optimal outcomes, but that they are quantitatively significant relative to the costs governments would incur in order to alleviate them. Large costs from price instability will not be found in the static, microbased models that follow the Newbery and Stiglitz tradition. As noted above, impact on investment behavior and on the macroeconomy are the obvious places to look for more significant benefits from price stabilization, as well as at consumer preferences for price stability in the presence of adjustment costs. No formal model is offered here, but the likely ingredients of a model that would capture these effects include the following: displaced investments in physical capital at the farm level, the marketing sector, and the industrial sector; substitution of consumption and leisure for savings and work; biases in investments in human capital for the farm agent and intergenerationally in children; the transactions costs consumers face in reallocating budgets when prices change; the welfare gains from a psychic sense of food security (and voters in rich countries and poor alike place a substantial economic price on this factor); and the feedback from this sense of security to a stable political economy, which reinforces investors' willingness to undertake long-term (and hence risky) commitments.[10]

These benefits from stabilizing the prices of basic foodstuffs, or other agricultural commodities with significant macroeconomic linkages, are considerably larger than those reflected in the models that have been used so far to analyze relative costs and benefits of price-stabilization programs. While little is known empirically about the size of the dynamic and macroeconomic benefits of stability, it is difficult to agree that they should be ignored in the evaluation of such programs. The pervasive, indeed universal, tendency of Asian governments to stabilize their domestic rice prices relative to unstable prices for rice in the world market suggests that the benefits may be very large. The relatively rapid economic growth in many of these countries argues that the impact of efficiency losses and budgetary costs on growth cannot be too large, at least if the price-stabilization program is well designed and implemented. A focus on these operational issues of design and implementation, which are better understood than the resulting dynamic and macroeconomic benefits, offers some practical guidelines in judging the efficacy of price-stabilization policies. The guidelines are drawn from countries that have been more successful than others in managing the complex tasks of intervening in agricultural price formation without incurring unacceptably large budgetary costs or sacrificing long-run efficiency in resource allocation.

Part 2: Operational Issues in Analyzing Price-Stabilization Policies

All countries in Asia intervene in their rice markets. The primary analytical methodology used by economists to understand the impact of intervention, the border-price paradigm, says they should not. This must be one of the widest gaps between theory and reality in all of economics. No single attempt is going to close that gap, but even a beginning might be useful. The essential starting point is to recognize that the gap exists because of failures at both ends. The analytical methodology has serious problems in purely theoretical terms. Relaxing the assumptions that make the framework simple and elegant, and therefore useful as a conceptual device, comes at a high cost in practical applicability. If analysts insist on realistic assumptions that reflect the pervasive market failures, non-equilibrium outcomes, and lack of information in the economies of developing countries, their methodologies are made progressively more complex, situation-specific, and dependent on the very knowledge that is lacking. On the other hand, most governments do intervene too much, at significant cost to the budget and the efficiency of the economy. One goal of this paper is to find an analytical process that copes with both of these realities, in the hope that out of this process analysts can emerge with better methodologies and price policies.

For this analytical process to work, both the objectives for and problems with market interventions must be recognized.[11] In rice-based Asian economies, rice price policy can affect economic growth, income distribution, and political stability—three important factors in any policymaker's objective function. Economic growth is affected by the level and stability of price incentives to farmers, which stimulate growth in output and rural incomes. Low and stable consumer prices keep real wages low, thus stimulating investment, industrial output, and exports. With purchases of rice still a large share of household budgets in many Asian countries and rice production the single most important farm activity, the impact of rice prices on real incomes by sector and income class is enormous. Most countries have no other policy instrument with a fraction of the potential of rice prices to alter the society's income distribution. Because of the economic significance of rice, maintaining reasonable stability in rice prices contributes directly to political stability. Nothing is more unsettling politically than rapid shifts in real income and wealth among large sectors of the population. Governments can eliminate at least one important cause of such instability by stabilizing rice prices.

Unfortunately, there are serious problems with the price policies used to reach these three objectives. The most visible, and therefore the most important to government policymakers, is the cost to the budget of defending stable prices and of maintaining domestic price levels above or below prices in world markets. But there are important hidden costs as well. The budgetary costs are not painful just because taxes must be collected to pay for them if fiscal policy is to remain in balance. Expenditures for subsidies to producers or consumers have alternative opportunities in investments or other programs that might offer higher payoffs. Static efficiency losses due to misallocation of resources are seldom large when compared with income transfers or GDP, but if distortions are sufficiently large and persist long enough to be built into investment patterns, the losses become truly significant.

This is especially true when prices for a single commodity are the object of intervention and all other commodities are produced and consumed according to market signals, which is the approach suggested by the analytical arguments developed here. The spillover effects of price policy to other markets can be immediately troublesome when close substitutes in production and consumption exist, but the longer-run impact on the structure of the economy is also worrisome. Government policies that keep resources in agriculture that should be encouraged to move to the industrial or service sector can make the entire agricultural sector uncompetitive and, therefore, a high-cost burden to the rest of the economy. Diversification out of rice into commodities and livestock products with greater value added is a natural evolutionary process, which can be slowed or stopped altogether with price support and stabilization policies.[12] Structural change is impeded, rice farmers develop powerful political lobbying groups, and the potential for policy reform then rests with highly polarized sectoral interests. It is not clear whether the larger costs are to the economy or to the political process.

Finally, continuous market interventions and price controls have an impact on the development of a private marketing sector. Investments in physical and human capacity in this sector are not forthcoming if margins are squeezed, policy implementation is erratic, or the middleman is held responsible for policy failures. The loss is the absence of competitive traders in search of marketing opportunities for new commodities or greater volumes. Farmers need this dynamic search process; it provides them with information about what to produce and how profitable it will be. Government traders seldom reach farmers at all, much less with this type of information. Growth and diversification in agriculture is stimulated by transmitting information about changing demand patterns to farmers willing to experiment. Only a competitive, dynamic private trading sector has demonstrated much capacity to establish this link.

The operational dimensions of this issue are crucial. How can government interventions into the level and stability of prices in domestic rice markets be designed to stimulate the development of a competitive private marketing sector rather than retard it? The issue is particularly difficult for policy analysts because the factors that stimulate the private sector are often subtle and hard to measure. Generating positive expectations about the potential role and rate of return on investment is obviously essential, but there is little academic knowledge about the ingredients in such expectations, and few policy analysts have personal knowledge of what makes private traders tick. We do know that positive expectations are fragile; they take a long time to build and can be destroyed overnight with one foolish intervention. Trading is risky enough without having to figure out what the government will do. Perhaps the best that price policy analysts can do to encourage an efficient private sector is to create a stable policy environment, set price margins wide enough for significant participation by the private sector, and eliminate legal and bureaucratic barriers to entry by private traders. Simple as these tasks seem, they often conflict directly with the short-run or long-run interests of policymakers in food price stabilization and of food logistics agencies in implementing it.

Budgetary Costs

Governments enact programs to stabilize commodity prices because free-market prices do not provide a satisfactory degree of price stability. These programs are subject to two basic principles: they are activities of the public sector that require the expenditure of public resources; and price stabilization is inherently destabilizing to some other part of the economy, usually the budget or credit system.

Stabilizing grain prices has two distinct but related components: seasonal price stabilization between postharvest lows and preharvest highs, and year-to-year stability relative to world prices. Stabilizing domestic prices in relation to world prices is most easily accomplished through a national buffer stock operated in conjunction with trade policy. Coordination is achieved by placing monopoly control over imports and exports in the hands of the same agency that manages the logistical operations involved in running the buffer stock. In principle, this role for the agency permits international trade to be the balance wheel that maintains a stable equilibrium between domestic demand and supplies available to the market from domestic production and net trade (and stock changes). Such direct quantitative controls often conflict with GATT rules or desires of trading partners, but they are standard in rice trade in Asia. Of the major countries in Asia, only Thailand does not restrict international trade in rice to a state-controlled monopoly, and even Thailand has often used extensive intervention into its export trade to stabilize (and lower) domestic rice prices.

Unlike seasonal price stabilization, which always costs the government money, monopoly of international trade can sometimes yield revenue for the budget or the state trading company. The key is the level of the domestic price relative to the international price and the direction of trade. Economic forces limit the options, however, and push the results toward subsidies rather than revenues. Countries that keep their prices below border prices tend to discourage production at efficient levels and hence end up importing the needed supplies, at a cost to the budget, to keep domestic prices low (again, the exception is Thailand). In reverse fashion, countries that maintain prices to farmers well above border prices frequently produce surpluses that must be stored or exported at a loss. Consequently, schemes for both seasonal and annual price stabilization require public resources to be effective.

Two distinct forms of financial resources must be committed on behalf of the public food logistics agency. Assuming the agency is implementing a floor and ceiling price policy through a combination of domestic procurement, market injections from short-run buffer stocks, and international trade, it needs a line of credit to purchase domestic grain during the harvest and to store it until needed for market injection, as well as a continuing budget allocation to cover operational losses incurred because of the squeeze on the price margin. The subsidy required to cover losses on international trading (or profits) depends on prices in world markets relative to domestic prices, and this relationship can change dramatically from year to year. South Korea nearly always profits when it imports rice from world markets; Indonesia did in 1983, but its imports required subsidies in 1980 and 1981. In 1985 and 1986, Indonesia had to subsidize rice exports.

With proper financial controls and accounting procedures, central banks and ministers of finance should expect their food logistics agencies to repay, with full interest, the credit used for domestic procurement and seasonal stockholding when the stocks are sold in the market. Continuing losses incurred on behalf of policy-dictated objectives for price stabilization should be visible in the Routine Budget. Such an open financing mechanism for food-price stabilization has the twin advantage of clearly identifying the regular subsidies incurred by society in order to stabilize its staple food prices and highlighting the fact that the instability is transferred to the outstanding debts owed by the food logistics agency. When crops are good and purchases are high, credit needs rise sharply. This credit is not repaid until the stocks are needed to contain domestic price rises. Repayment can take quite awhile if the private sector (including farmers) also holds stocks from the good harvest and provides supplies to domestic markets for longer than normal. The added interest costs on the "excessive" public stocks must then be added to the agency's routine subsidy, or the stocks must be exported (probably at a loss). The main point, however, is that demand for credit becomes unstable as grain prices become stable. Since the outstanding credit held by a food logistics agency is often a substantial share of total credits outstanding from the formal banking system—20 to 30 percent is common—the macroeconomic consequences of this financial instability can be quite dramatic (especially if the country is operating under strict credit ceilings imposed by an IMF standby agreement, as in Bangladesh in the early 1980s).

The transmittal of instability in credit and budget requirements to the rest of the economy can impose significant adjustment costs, no matter whether the food logistics agency is increasing or decreasing its use of credit and budgetary resources. When credit demand rises, interest rates rise or government loans are rationed, budgets of other agencies are cut, investment projects are delayed, or the deficit is financed by increasing the money supply, with attendant potential for inflation (although the large grain crop that generated the requirements for additional credit has a negative impact on inflation). When loans are unexpectedly repaid as stocks are drawn down, money and purchasing power are withdrawn from the economy, with potential recessionary impact. Changes in the real scarcity of food require that adjustments be made somewhere in the economy. The important question for the analysis of stabilization schemes for food prices is which adjustments do the least damage to the growth prospects for the economy and to the desired distribution of income. This requires a general-equilibrium analysis with dynamic investment functions linked to the impact on expectations of instability in food prices, in credit markets, and in budgetary behavior of the government.

The operational significance of the two basic principles—grain price stabilization both costs public resources and destabilizes either the government budget or the credit market—is quite profound. Failure to face them directly is the most common reason for failure of stabilization programs. Planning of stabilization activities can be based on expected values under normal circumstances, and budgets can be drawn up under these assumptions. But actual operations must be conducted as reality unfolds, and reality is likely to hold surprises with respect to the size of the harvest, level of consumer demand, expectations of the private sector and its participation in storage and transportation, world market prices (in

U. S. dollars), and the country's exchange rate.[13] For the logistics agency to cope with these surprises, it must be able to arrange for substantial credit lines on very short notice, often no more than a week or two. Many government agencies have difficulty allocating resources so quickly, unless they understand the need in advance and can trust the logistics agency to spend the money, with adequate financial controls, for the intended purposes. It is no wonder that so few countries have been able to carry out this task successfully over a long period of time.

From Analysis to Implementation of Market Interventions

Making government agencies understand the financial and operational mechanisms that permit a food logistics agency to implement successfully a stabilization program for food prices requires a capacity to analyze and explain the complicated issues involved. If governments are willing to let world markets determine domestic prices, no complicated analysis of price interventions is needed. It is also possible to intervene heavily into market outcomes without any analysis of the likely outcome, but such an idiosyncratic and unsystematic approach to agricultural pricing has proven ineffective in helping societies reach their food policy objectives. The alternative is food policy analysis, a coherent effort to understand the impact of existing and proposed policies on these objectives. The principles and basic methodological frameworks for this analysis are presented elsewhere.[14] The experience of Asian countries in applying these principles and frameworks to price-stabilization policies demonstrates several common issues that all analyses of food price policy must address. Four issues are important, but only one is analytical in the narrow sense.

Analysis—How does an analyst know which policies are best? This is the narrowly analytical issue, but even at this level, a simple determination of optimal answers is not possible. A broad set of objectives must be incorporated into the analysis, as well as a clear recognition of the actual starting point for the food system. The dynamic and macroeconomic benefits from stabilization of food prices are not revealed in the standard analytical models used to evaluate price interventions; this problem alone argues that intuition based on extensive experience in a country is likely to be at least as valuable as formal economic models based on optimization techniques in analyzing the costs and benefits of price interventions.

Communication—How can the results of policy analysis be communicated effectively to policymakers, so that appropriate policy decisions are made? This effort to communicate involves the analyst in a negotiating role in which pedagogy can be crucial to the outcome. Although the negotiating role involves a subtle change in the analyst's task from that of understanding to advising, it does not necessarily require advocacy of specific policy recommendations. Rather, the advocacy is for the analysis itself and for an understanding by policymakers of the trade-offs identified in the analysis.

Communication across agencies is especially important in building the understanding of the resource requirements for successful implementation of food-price stabilization schemes for extended periods of time. Clearly, a full understanding of these requirements might lead to a decision that stabilization is too expensive. A common mistake, however, is to decide that stabilization is worthwhile on the basis of gross underestimates of the costs, with subsequent underfinancing of the logistics agency. Speculative attacks on the agency cause it to fail in its announced mission, thus exacerbating price instability and significantly jeopardizing credibility in all government activities because price-stabilization schemes are usually among the most visible of government interventions.[15] Such government failures are a major justification for the free-market approach to agricultural pricing, but they are not inevitable. Relevant policy analysis that is effectively communicated to policymakers can be an important contribution to more successful policies.

Analysts in donor agencies such as the IMF, the World Bank, or USAID now play an important role in communicating the results of policy analysis. To improve the effectiveness of the aid process, development agencies increasingly conduct independent assessments of policy environments in various countries. These assessments can simply be offered to policymakers as input to their own process of policy analysis and design, in which case little controversy arises. Indeed, the added analytical resources available to governments in this manner are often warmly welcomed.

Increasingly, however, donor assessments of policy form the basis for a policy dialogue with countries, the object of which is to induce policy changes in directions that the donors think advisable. If the analysis has been conducted in a way that genuinely illuminates the problems facing the country, this dialogue can be extremely productive. But such is not always the case. Often there are sharp disagreements over the directions of appropriate changes in policy. In many cases, the donor analysts have the economics right within the context of their models, which claim to represent the policy issues being discussed. But they fail to understand the shortcomings of the models, which do not incorporate the broader dimensions of the economic analysis discussed in this paper, as well as the other ingredients in effective policy analysis. When donor analysts fail to communicate their analytical results in a convincing fashion because the results depend critically on basic assumptions in the underlying models used, challenges to the models can unravel the entire foundations of the policy advice and the usefulness of the policy dialogue.

The importance of basic models to drive policy advice is linked to the very short time horizons in which donor analysts must often work. Three-week trips to unfamiliar environments mean that analysts must rely on readily accessible data, basic models with wide applicability in many countries, and fairly restrictive assumptions to determine results. This approach may be workable for project analysis, with its relatively limited scope to question assumptions about the external policy environment. When that environment itself is the subject of review, however, the "sortie" approach to policy analysis requires reliance on an underlying ideology about appropriate policy interventions rather than an understanding of the complexity of any given country's policy environment. A particular problem with development economics has been its vulnerability to wide swings in the prevailing political ideology and the resulting enthusiasm for particular approaches to the development process.[16] A special advantage to watching this process in one country over a long period is the realization that intellectual fads come and go, but the basic structural problems that must be addressed by policy remain. The only way to improve the effectiveness of the policy dialogue between donor and country is for both sides to recognize the long-run nature of the development process and the necessity for policymakers to live with the complex outcomes of policy changes in the short run.

Implementation—The third issue to be treated in the analysis of price-stabilization schemes is whether a new or revised policy can be implemented. A frequent criticism, especially of economists, is that they are excellent at designing policies, but ones that governments are not capable of implementing. Such criticism misses the main point: policy analysis that ignores problems of policy implementation is simply bad analysis. The problems may be economic, political, social, or cultural, but they must be incorporated into the policy analysis itself if implementation is to be successful.

Many observers feel that implementation of a policy is the most difficult aspect of government intervention into the development process. Frequent failures in this regard cause a wide gap between objectives and outcomes, between rhetoric and results, and they have led to widespread disenchantment about the actual potential of interventions to improve on simple market-determined outcomes. Part of the reason is simply the unpredictable nature of the world and the slower response of government policies to changed environments than the responses observed in markets. But much of the problem stems from efforts to implement policies that are unrealistic, that is, not based on careful analysis of the likely constraints that face policy managers and implementers. For a policy to be adopted, effective policy analysis must be communicated to policymakers in a clear and convincing fashion; likewise, the analysis must incorporate the problems that will be faced after the policy has been approved for implementation. Although incorporating constraints on implementation vastly complicates the analytical tasks, it simplifies the task of communicating with policymakers because it is immediately clear that the analyst understands the problems the policymaker faces in the day-to-day tasks of policy management.

A very wide array of constraints impinges on the potential success of a policy. A major reason why successful policy analysis requires extended time in and knowledge of the country concerned is because constraints on policy change are unique and idiosyncratic. Politics are frequently invoked as the main reason why good economic policies cannot be adopted. Sometimes this means there would be such broad, popular opposition to the new policies that even elected governments would be in jeopardy. Rice riots have brought down more than one government, and promises of cheap rice have elected others. Sometimes it means narrower vested interests will be negatively affected by the policies and can influence policymakers to prevent the change. Trade unions or the military often oppose increases in food prices or devaluations of the country's currency. And sometimes it just means that the minister does not think the change in policy is a good idea. A vague distrust of the market is easily translated into perceptions of political opposition to price incentives and wider margins for traders.

What is often forgotten when officials are criticized for lack of political will to implement needed policy reforms is that virtually all changes in agricultural price policy hurt someone's interests, vested or not. If those interests are the food consumption of the poor, political opposition to changes in pricing is desirable, even if the new price policy is intended to generate more output and employment in the long run. Unless compensating programs for those most negatively affected can be implemented simultaneously with the price reforms, political opposition on behalf of the poor is both understandable and important. This argument obviously does not hold in those environments in which current price policy is so badly distorted or poorly implemented that the interests of the poor are being sacrificed, possibly even to the benefit of the better-off segments of the society. Whatever the political arguments, it is important that the policy analyst determine the actual distributional impact of current policy and the effect of the proposed changes on the distribution of benefits.

For good reasons or bad, political constraint is always important. The task of the policy analyst, however, is not just to incorporate constraints into the policy analysis. Rather, analysts need to determine which dimension of a policy is objectionable, to whom, and to what degree of impact. Is it possible to design compensating programs or an information campaign to clarify exactly who gains and loses under the new policy? This approach can be risky, especially when the vested interests are close to power, or are simply powerful. Sometimes policy analysis is a feeble instrument for inducing change; at other times courage and simple facts bring surprising results. Only individual analysts wrestling with their own consciences and the realities as they perceive them can decide which time has come.

Evaluation—The last issue for the policy analyst is whether the new policy is actually working. After the analysis, communication, and implementation, the policy must be evaluated. Much is to be learned from the evaluation process because unexpected problems always arise. Trying to distinguish systematic elements in these problems from purely idiosyncratic ones provides valuable lessons for the next cycle of policy analysis.

Evaluation is the poor relation of the policy analysis family. Once the analytical design, policy negotiations, and implementation have taken place, few individuals or institutions have much energy or budget left for evaluation. If the policy works, it will be obvious; if it fails, it is better not to stir up a hornet's nest. Unfortunately, this caricature of attitudes about policy evaluation contains too much truth to be dismissed. Opportunities should not be missed to understand the reasons a policy went awry and to channel this information back into the process of policy analysis and design. Policy evaluation not only completes the linear process of design, communication, implementation, and evaluation, but it also provides an important input into the design process itself, thus making the policy process an evolving circle rather than an arrow.

To provide the necessary links in this circle, it is desirable for the original policy analysts to be involved personally in the implementation of the policy and the monitoring of its outcome. They thus develop a heightened sense of responsibility because they must live with the problems created by their own design, and, for individual analysts, it also creates continuity of insight. Such continuity is important for building the intuitive sense of the economy's likely response to various shocks and policy interventions, a skill that is essential to making policy analysis relevant to policymakers. In further support of this "intuition building," analysts can participate in the trouble-shooting that is an integral part of making a new policy work. When this role in ongoing implementation and short-run evaluation is built into the original terms of reference of the policy analyst, analysis and design of policy are likely to be more pragmatic and capable of successful implementation.

Part 3: Indonesia's Experience with Rice Market Interventions

Indonesia's food logistics agency, Badan Urusan Logistik (BULOG), is widely regarded as a successful example of institution building in an area of the economy where government intervention in other countries has generally been counter-productive. BULOG's terms of reference at its founding in 1967 were twofold: stabilization of rice prices and provision of monthly rice rations to the military and civil service. Its success in carrying out this mandate led to other tasks. By the late 1980s, BULOG was still charged with its original role in rice markets but also was responsible for handling or monitoring sugar, wheat, corn, soybeans and soymeal, and several lesser commodities. The chairman of BULOG was also the minister of cooperatives, and BULOG's enormous influence in rural markets was used to foster the development of Indonesia's village cooperatives. From a ragtag staff assembled hastily from the Quartermaster Corps of the army shortly after the New Order government of President Suharto was established in 1966, BULOG has grown in size, stature, and influence in the Indonesian economy to such an extent that it now rivals the former Pertamina petroleum empire.

Inevitably, such growth and influence raise questions about BULOG's perfor-mance, the costs and benefits of the services it carries out, and its appropriate role in the future, as the rest of the Indonesian economy is progressively deregulated under pressures to expand nonoil exports and shift the source of economic growth more to the private sector. BULOG has largely escaped these "winds of deregulation" so far, although not the notice of the World Bank, IMF, USAID, and others who see substantial distortions introduced into the Indonesian economy by agricultural regulations, including BULOG's interventions. Most attention has focused on nonrice commodities, especially wheat, sugar, and soybeans, where the distortions are quite visible. But BULOG's interventions in the rice economy are also under scrutiny, along with crop-specific acreage controls implemented by the Ministry of Agriculture, the fertilizer subsidy which is such a large share of the agricultural development budget, and irrigation subsidies. A combination of new budget realities, a shift in development thinking about the efficacy of free markets, and major structural change in the Indonesian economy since the mid-1960s has focused attention on BULOG's role and mission in rice markets.

Evaluating that role requires a perspective that is inherently historical.

Naturally, in an ideal world analysts would be able to pull fully functioning agencies off the shelf whenever needed and throw them in the trash bin when their usefulness is gone. This is impossible, despite the assumptions of much price policy analysis that somehow implementing agencies will appear and disappear gracefully when it is time for domestic prices to equal border prices. The dynamics of building and dismantling institutions is poorly understood, especially when the policies to be implemented by the agency being built significantly influence how hard it will be to reduce its role and size. (Timmer [1988a], 355)

The history of BULOG offers a unique opportunity to build some of this understanding, starting with how the mission of the agency was formulated in the first place.[17] This dimension of institution building is little acknowledged in the wider applause for BULOG's success in the next phase, establishment of an implementing agency that was able to respond to its radically new mission, and a rapidly changing rice economy. Agency leadership and staff-training efforts have received most of the attention, but the extent of BULOG's integration into macro policy making and access to financial resources also played key roles. In the 1980s, BULOG has been used to "fine-tune" agricultural price policy with respect to goals for production, consumption, and overall food security. The analytical and operational capacities needed for such sophisticated interventions into agricultural policy would have been unthinkable even a decade before.

Parallel to the organizational and institutional efforts to strengthen BULOG's implementation capacity was a series of analytical debates over the appropriate policies to be implemented. Although the basic mission laid out by Mears and Afiff in 1968 was not challenged, reflecting the importance of rice price stabilization to Indonesia's political economy, all of the key parameters were subject to continuous review.[18] The size of the marketing margin to be permitted between BULOG's floor price and ceiling price, the size of buffer stocks needed to supply monthly distributions and market operations, the price of fertilizer relative to the floor price and relative to world prices (and consequently, the size of the fertilizer subsidy) are issues that have received extensive analytical treatment by economists inside and outside the government. As world rice prices fell in the mid-1980s and Indonesia developed rice surpluses, analytical attention turned to the impact of rice prices on production, on the health of the rural economy, and ultimately, to consideration of the dynamic dimensions of rice price stability on the Indonesian economy and society.

Institution Building, 1968-88

The economic and political chaos of the mid-1960s took its toll on Indonesia's rice economy; yields and per capita consumption were lower in 1966 than in 1958. The chaotic conditions also generated widespread support for measures to stabilize the economy, and this meant rice. As an editorial in an influential newspaper put it in late 1967 during another surge in rice prices, "Rice is the barometer of the economic situation in Indonesia." (*Harian KAMI*, September 14, 1967.) To most Indonesians, no return to normalcy was possible without stability in rice prices. BULOG was created in 1967 to fulfill this mission.[19]

The institution was not created *de novo*, however. The Dutch had intervened massively into domestic rice marketing and price formation during the depression in the 1930s and had created a logistics agency to do so. After independence, the new Indonesian government renamed the agency BAMA (the Foundation for Food) and again in 1952 as JUBM (the Foundation for Food Affairs). Whatever the name, the task was the same—to stabilize rice prices. As inflation became a major factor in the early 1950s, a new task was added—the provision of rice rations to the civil service and military (the "Budget Groups") in lieu of cash payments, which were of progressively lower value. When inflation escalated to more than 100 percent per year in the early 1960s, the rice rations were the only real income provided by the government to its employees.

From this historical perspective, it is not so surprising that BULOG would be charged with the double tasks of stabilizing rice prices and provisioning the

Budget Groups. But the dual functions vastly complicated the creation of an agency capable of implementing both dimensions of its mission. Especially in the early days of BULOG, when financial, logistical, and organizational resources were scarce, one mission inevitably took precedence over the other. Since rice rations were the basis of the government's claims on its civil service and military, BULOG always had to be certain that adequate quantities of rice were available for distribution. Since budget resources were limited and uncertain, the rice had to be obtained as cheaply as possible. The price-stabilization policy was designed to support farm prices in rural markets through procurement of unlimited quantities at the floor price, but none at all if the market price was above the floor. Nervous local BULOG purchasing agents (operating from regional offices called DOLOGs), however, tended to buy with quantity targets in mind. In surplus areas they often conspired with rice millers and traders to drive down the market price in order to buy as cheaply as possible. When sufficient quantities had been bought to meet regional distribution needs, procurement stopped, even if prices then plunged. BULOG's procurement activities in 1967 and 1968, rather than stabilizing prices, may well have destabilized Indonesia's rice markets.

In addition, the price-stabilization policy was intended to defend ceiling prices for rice in urban retail markets—a task parallel to provisioning the Budget Groups. Officials in BULOG (and the DOLOGs) quickly learned the logistical routines as well as the political importance of controlling urban rice prices. Imported rice was normally used because it was easier to ship to urban ports, of higher quality than domestically procured rice, and often (until unification of all exchange rates in 1970) cheaper at the official exchange rate used for government imports. When BULOG's mission is disaggregated in this way, four separate tasks are revealed, and a clear hierarchy of priorities for the nascent agency emerges. Rice for distribution to the Budget Groups was of top priority; as a result, regional procurement officers often operated according to quantitative rather than price targets. Defending urban ceiling prices was at the next level of importance, and supplies of rice to inject into retail markets were easier to obtain from imports than from domestic procurement. Consequently, financial and logistical resources for procurement went to imports, which left defense of the floor price for farmers at the bottom of the list of priorities.

By 1969 it was apparent that two key constraints kept BULOG from carrying out its full mission successfully: inadequate and inflexible financial resources for domestic procurement; and a field staff operating with only limited understanding of how to implement a floor price. Much of BULOG's planning during the first five-year plan, from April 1969 to March 1974, was devoted to easing these constraints on its operations. The task was not made easier by the world food crisis in 1973 and 1974; rice disappeared from world markets just as Indonesia needed substantial imports to stabilize urban prices. By 1975, however, the agency had survived the domestic crisis and found its priorities and constraints altered.

A new chairman of BULOG had been appointed during the crisis, General Bustanil Arifin, the former deputy for logistics who was recalled from his position as consul general in New York. Financial constraints were nearly eliminated as petroleum dollars flowed into the Ministry of Finance after OPEC succeeded in raising oil prices. The disappearance of rice supplies from world markets in 1973 clearly established the political vulnerability of relying on large imports of rice.

Farmer welfare received substantially more attention in the late 1970s as the political goal of rice self-sufficiency was translated into operational terms. Because the civil service and military were no longer so dependent on rice rations to maintain their real incomes, the pressure was off BULOG always to keep monthly distributions as the top priority. It had the resources to meet these requirements without difficulty.

From 1975 to 1985, BULOG implemented the government's floor and ceiling price policy and delivered monthly rations to the Budget Groups without a hitch. The changed external constraints noted above account for part of this success, but internal developments also played a major role. With the enthusiastic support of the chairman, massive and expensive efforts at staff recruiting and training were designed and carried out by Sidik Moeljono, the head of the expert staff. Supporting the floor price received top priority as a way of stimulating domestic rice production—a crucial task because of the perceived unreliability of the world rice market. From 1974 to 1978, persistent problems with disease and pests associated with the new rice varieties kept upward pressure on rural prices; therefore, maintaining the floor price was relatively easy at the prices actually set, which merely kept pace with inflation. As world rice markets returned to normal in the late 1970s and Indonesia's foreign exchange reserves remained ample, BULOG turned increasingly to imports to meet rising demand in urban markets. Imports from 1977 to 1980 averaged nearly two million metric tons per year, or about one-fifth of the total amount of rice traded internationally.

The combination of disease and pest problems, which led to the widening import gap, and deteriorating rural-urban terms of trade as a by-product of Dutch Disease, which caused severe problems of rural poverty, forced a reevaluation in 1978 of development strategy and the role of rice in it. Once again, BULOG was ill equipped to take the lead in rethinking its mission in the context of broader objectives and constraints. It was not a key player in either of the two basic policy changes in 1978 that set the rural economy in a new direction: the surprise devaluation of the rupiah in November 1978, which was partially intended to provide "exchange rate protection" to the rural economy; and the decision to keep fertilizer prices constant while continuing to increase the floor price for rice at about the rate of inflation, which was to result in a sharply enhanced degree of food security.[20] *Nominal* urea prices were unchanged from 1976 to 1983, and they were increased only slightly in 1983. When IR-36, an IRRI rice variety resistant to the most troublesome pests and diseases, was introduced on a nationwide basis in 1978, the stage was set for a surge in rice production that would transform BULOG's role. By 1984 the country was self-sufficient in rice, domestic procurement replaced imports as BULOG's sources of supply shifted, and the agency's success in defending the floor price was widely cited as a key factor in the unprecedented increase in rice production.

The switch in primary source of supply had a radical effect on the management of BULOG. Far more logistical capacity was required; local warehouses, mills, and transportation facilities were needed as domestically produced rice had to be stored and transported to points of distribution—a more complicated task than ordering imports for delivery at the time and location desired. Financial operations became much more complex when the variance in domestic procurement increased and the average time rice stayed in storage (and storage losses) rose. BULOG's outstanding credits from the central bank became a significant proportion of total bank credit for the whole economy. The agency became a significant macroeconomic actor.

Comparative experience would suggest that this was a dangerous time for the agency. It needed huge sums of money on a flexible basis for fixed investments, seasonal inventory, and operational expenses. None of this financing was provided in the Routine Budget of the Ministry of Finance. Finding funding mechanisms was a major challenge. They had to be sufficiently stable to permit long-range planning, sufficiently flexible to accommodate large variations in procurement financing on short notice (before rural market prices fell below the floor), and yet not too distorting to the rest of the economy. Senior leaders in the agency and their advisers worked closely with senior members of the economic team (the Ministry for Economic Coordination [EKUIN] and the "Economic Cabinet") and their advisers to find pragmatic solutions. Several measures contributed to keeping BULOG's finances off the front burner of political concerns.[21] Although some individual components of the agency's finances were public knowledge and officials in the Ministry of Finance reviewed BULOG's costs each year in order to calculate the "book price" for sales to the Budget Groups, no one outside BULOG understood all the components of the financing mechanisms. It is probably true that no one inside BULOG knew how the individual components related to each other or how dependent they were on the external dynamics of Indonesia's rice economy.

Those dynamics changed radically as Indonesia approached and then surpassed self-sufficiency in rice. Substantial surpluses emerged in 1985, BULOG's warehouses were still full from the record 1984 procurement, and support of the floor price was unsuccessful. Rice prices fell 20 to 30 percent below the floor price in many areas. Once again, BULOG was unprepared for an unexpected new mission, managing surplus stocks. A major external review undertaken in August 1985 revealed several fundamental problems with the design of rice policy and BULOG's structure for implementing it. The structural problems related mostly to financing mechanisms; the report concluded that without significant changes, BULOG would be bankrupt before the end of the decade. The government acted quickly; by January 1986, a special line item had been inserted in the Routine Budget in response to that concern. Although the budget allocation was never funded because of the collapse of oil prices later in 1986, it focused the attention of senior economic policymakers on problems with BULOG financing mechanisms and increased their understanding of the large costs of implementing a price-stabilization policy.

Price policy was reconsidered and a new pricing model was proposed that would treat the floor price and fertilizer price policy as short-run tools to manage production trends, subject to constraints imposed by world price levels for both rice and fertilizer, and the availability of budget resources to finance wide price divergences.[22] This call to use price policy to fine-tune BULOG's stock position relative to trends in domestic production and consumption required yet another ratcheting upward in the agency's capacities to analyze and implement policies that affected the rice economy. The new pricing model was used to reduce incentives gradually to rice farmers. Rice production slowed its rapid expansion and rested at a plateau from 1986 to 1988 which left procurement sharply below the levels of the previous five years. BULOG's surplus stocks were exported and used for distributions to the Budget Groups; by late 1987 the agency was unable to inject enough rice into retail markets to maintain price stability.

This experience raised several crucial questions for policymakers with respect to the rice economy. Will Indonesia retain self-sufficiency in rice regardless of the consequences for domestic rice prices, or will imports (and exports) be used as a balance wheel to lower the costs of price stabilization? How large do buffer stocks have to be to manage self-sufficiency within an acceptable band of price movements? What impact do substantial price movements, up or down, have on the rural economy? Several of these questions had been addressed since the mid-1960s as Indonesia's rice economy evolved and policies adapted to the change. Several were new or recast under the rapid succession of rice surpluses and deficits. The technical analysis used to address these questions has put Indonesia on economists' maps because the modeling has produced surprising and controversial results and fueled an exciting policy debate in Indonesia.

The Technical Debates

It might seem surprising that technical economic analysis played a significant role in the institutional development of BULOG. Although it might not seem very relevant to the organizational and institutional dimensions of building the agency, the argument here is precisely the opposite. The technical economic analysis conducted for BULOG, incorporated by it and other policymakers in defining its mission, and ultimately endogenized as an internal capability, provided two key elements in BULOG's success. From the time Mears and Afiff laid out its original mission of price stabilization, careful economic analysis of the Indonesian rice economy provided the foundation for the agency's role and the feasible measures it could implement.[23] Although much of this analysis was conducted by foreign advisers in the first decade of the agency's development, its internal capacity to analyze its own problems and mission rose significantly in the 1980s. Staff members who were sent abroad returned with sophisticated analytical skills, and the agency invested heavily in upgrading its middle management through intensive courses on food policy analysis and applied problem solving. Consequently, technical economic analysis enabled the agency to structure its mission in line with realities in the rice economy. Its sharply enhanced capacity in policy analysis in the 1980s allowed it to be at the forefront of the policy agenda in the Economic Cabinet on issues of direct relevance to the agency, and this technical expertise assured representation in a broad set of policy debates that had indirect impact on BULOG.

Three areas in which technical analysis reinforced institutional development are discussed below, in roughly chronological order. Each has engendered professional debate, application of methodologies to other countries, subsequent methodological developments applicable to a wider range of issues and settings, and, often, renewal of the policy debate in Indonesia. This iterative process has enriched the field of policy analysis as well as Indonesian policy itself.

Marketing Margins—An underlying goal of early efforts at price stabilization was to integrate Indonesia's far-flung rice markets as well as to defend floor and ceiling prices in individual locales. Because BULOG was always intended to serve as a buyer and seller of last resort rather than as a monopolist in rice markets, margins over space, time, and form were important parameters in the design and implementation of price policy. Mears (1961) had researched his classic study on rice marketing in 1956, and many of its findings on marketing structure remained valid in the late 1960s. But as BULOG became more successful in implementing floor and ceiling prices and transportation networks were reestablished, the structure and size of margins changed substantially.

The most important margin for policy purposes was between the floor and ceiling price. This margin contained all three components of marketing functions: transformations in space (farm price to urban price), time (harvest price to preharvest price), and form (paddy to milled rice). Each component required analytical attention. The spatial margin was addressed first.[24] Integration of Indonesia's rice markets was tested roughly by comparing the relative price spread across provinces between high and low prices during the same month. By 1971 this spread had narrowed dramatically from levels in the mid- to late-1960s, thus confirming that BULOG was succeeding in integrating regional rice markets.

Within regions, the spread between the floor price and the urban retail price during the same month was an important indicator for policy monitoring and for the role of the private sector. If the two locations were well connected by either private traders or BULOG activities, the urban price, when the size of the margin was known, could be used as an indicator of the agency's success in defending the floor price. Measuring the degree of market connection and the size of the margin turned out to be quite complex analytically. Early attempts in Indonesia stimulated substantial literature on techniques and applications in other settings.[25] The results showed that the actual marketing margin was substantially larger than would have been indicated by differences between average annual prices; when the urban ceiling price was successfully defended, the flow of rice sometimes reversed between rural and urban sources. Consequently, urban prices had to be correspondingly higher during the harvest to be commensurate with a given floor price. Because rural paddy prices were difficult to collect on an unbiased basis, reliance was placed on urban prices as a quick indicator of rural prices. The model clarified the means of calculating these prices, thus giving BULOG improved short-run monitoring capacity.

The milling conversion ratio for rice was a key parameter of the model, but relatively little was known about the Indonesian rice milling sector in the early 1970s. An analysis of technology choice in rice milling revealed the rapid development of a small-scale milling industry on Java and illuminated two important factors of concern to policymakers. Rice milling carried out by thousands of small entrepreneurs was the appropriate choice of technique; these small mills were neither the most labor intensive nor the most capital intensive.[26] An intermediate technology was economically efficient, a lesson first shown empirically in this setting. In addition, the Indonesian planning process was shown to have a substantial bias in favor of capital-intensive projects. This finding legitimized long-standing concerns in the planning agency (BAPPENAS) for creating employment and reducing poverty in addition to maximizing the rate of growth. Demonstration of the economic efficiency of greater employment creation meant the concerns could be integrated into the mainstream activities of the planning agency.[27]

The temporal dimensions of rice-marketing margins became a serious policy concern only when BULOG began to hold substantial buffer stocks from one crop year to the next. BULOG considered storage costs in the private sector in setting the width of the margin between the floor and ceiling price, but no significant analytical issues arose in determining the rough dimensions of these costs. Monthly interest rates to rice traders gave a first-order approximation. But by 1984 Indonesia was self-sufficient in rice, and the pressing question was how large the agency's buffer stocks should be to ensure price stability. The prevailing political judgment was the more, the better (at least up to five million tons, or about double what the agency held at the time), but BULOG's storage costs were escalating rapidly. Some analytically defensible level was sought. BULOG sponsored several studies of the problem, both within the agency and with outside consultants. The results were surprisingly similar: buffer stocks on the order of one million tons were adequate to ensure a low probability of imports (5 percent); and additional working stocks of 1.5 million tons were needed in storage immediately after the domestic procurement season. When stocks exceeded this level, as they did in 1985, BULOG was plunged into a major crisis. It failed to support the floor price and faced imminent bankruptcy.[28] The million-ton buffer stock was then accepted as an appropriate size, and the government budget was used to finance the costs of storing it.[29]

Each of these three components of the marketing margin between the floor price and the ceiling price—space, time, and form—influences private traders and the rice economy in separate and analytically distinct ways, and yet all are affected by the policy decision that determines the size of the margin itself.[30] On several occasions the government has consciously narrowed the margin in order to ease the food price dilemma—the opposite effects of any change in food prices on the welfare of producers and consumers. Because the private sector handles such a large share of rice marketed in Indonesia, a decision to squeeze the margin is also a decision to squeeze the private sector.[31] This squeeze thus alters the tasks for BULOG; a simple model of BULOG operations shows that its procurement and distribution role tends to be directly proportional to the extent it squeezes the private marketing sector, but the financial burden rises with the square of the squeeze.[32]

The dependence of BULOG's role on the relative size of the marketing margin took on renewed importance in 1988. BULOG's reduced stock position and a political ban on imports allowed margins to widen. The drought-reduced crop and wide margins meant the agency could procure very little rice at its announced floor price. Suddenly, the monthly distribution requirements for the Budget Groups loomed large relative to BULOG's reduced stock position, and history seemed ready to repeat itself despite all the lessons learned in the previous twenty years. Perhaps the sharpest lesson is that technical analysis and a thorough understanding of the functioning of rice markets remain subordinate to political objectives. In this case, they were subordinate to the desire of the president to maintain self-sufficiency in rice in Indonesia, an achievement for which he received a gold medal from FAO in November 1985. There is, of course, a price at which Indonesia is self-sufficient in rice. Recognition of how high this price might be led to authorization to secure "external supplies" for arrival in the first half of 1989. No government official called them imports. Substantial efforts have been under way since early 1988 to find a means to define self-sufficiency on a trend basis as a way of softening the political constraint that prevents BULOG from rationalizing its price-stabilization activities and lowering the costs of its operations.

The Fertilizer Subsidy—A contentious debate has been waged since the early 1980s over the social profitability of Indonesia's fertilizer subsidy. Modest fertilizer subsidies had been used since the earliest days of the BIMAS Rice Intensification Program to stimulate adoption of the technological package that included high-yielding varieties along with fertilizer and pesticides. But the subsidy became a substantial budgetary factor only in the late 1970s and early 1980s after the nominal price of fertilizer had been held constant for over half a decade at the same time that the nominal floor price for rice nearly doubled, about in line with the general price level. By 1983 as budgetary pressures began to be felt after the first drop in petroleum prices, officials in the Ministry of Finance as well as World Bank analysts pointed to the fertilizer subsidy as an obvious place to cut expenditures and improve the efficiency of resource allocation.

At the same time, the Ministry of Finance was sponsoring a major review of the BIMAS program under the auspices of the Development Policy and Implementation Study, with technical assistance from the Harvard Institute for International Development (HIID). The BIMAS Evaluation Study took a careful look at program design, management, and implementation and carried out valuable village-level surveys, which highlighted the extreme regional diversity with which the rather monolithic BIMAS approach had difficulty coping. The study team noted the rapid rise in fertilizer use on rice during the fifteen years of the program, but because fertilizer and rice price policy were not controlled by the BIMAS secretariat, the role of prices was not discussed in the initial draft of the evaluation report. In the summer of 1983, the BIMAS analysts and the price policy analysts intersected; the result was a quick and rough study of the role of price policy in the rice production success. Using aggregate time series from 1968 to 1982, the study estimated a fertilizer demand function, a rice production function, and the social profitability of the fertilizer subsidy in total and at the margin.[33]

The analysis and conclusions raised very troubling issues for most development economists, including the author, who was as surprised as anyone. The trend of experience and thought in the late 1970s and 1980s had reinforced the emphasis by economists on the superior performance of economic growth under market prices rather than prices altered by government taxes or subsidies. The high and robust social profitability of Indonesia's fertilizer subsidy seemed to challenge these hard-won gains for the role of free markets. At the very least, the results confirmed what economists knew in principle but hoped to neglect in fact—that such pricing interventions could only be evaluated empirically. There were perfectly sound theoretical reasons why market failures might justify a fertilizer subsidy on *efficiency* grounds—the subsidy corrected a dynamic disequilibrium. No a priori arguments based on static models could settle the issue.

Throughout the vigorous policy debate, Indonesian price policy for fertilizer followed a consistent goal: to reduce the size of the budget subsidy commensurate with maintaining food security, i.e., a balance between domestic production and consumption of rice. This balance is monitored by the level of BULOG's stocks.

242

When stocks were large and surplus rice was being exported at subsidized prices, increases in the nominal floor price for rice were kept below the inflation rate, whereas the prices of fertilizer rose by more than the inflation rate. In short, the fertilizer price was used in tandem with other prices and programs to fine-tune the Indonesian rice economy around a trend of self-sufficiency. Given Indonesia's substantial impact on the world rice market, this approach seemed to be the only way to guarantee food security for the country.

Rice Price Policy—The floor price of rice relative to the price of fertilizer and relative to the ceiling price are only two of several important price relationships for rice. Two others with substantial medium- and long-term significance are the real price of rice to the economy—that is, relative to the costs of other goods and services—and the cost of domestic rice relative to the cost of imports or exports. As with all the price relationships discussed so far, these two are closely related, although the foreign exchange rate enters as a key factor as well.

The impact of rice prices on production was included in the above discussion, but only with respect to fertilizer prices. The issues to be treated here are broader: what are the consequences of rice price policy for consumption and the distribution of nutrient intake, the dynamics of the rural economy, and the stability of the macroeconomy and the political environment?

Indonesia has served for more than a decade as a testing ground for empirical and methodological inquiries into the impact of changes in staple food prices on the distribution of nutrient intake by income class. When a single commodity such as rice forms a large share of a consumer's budget, the Slutsky Equation requires that real income effects will cause substantial changes in consumption of rice as its price changes, even if the pure substitution term in the equation is zero. The income component of the equation varies systematically by income class because of Engel's and Bennett's Laws.[34] Economists and nutrition planners knew roughly that higher food prices hurt the poor in the short run. When the world food crisis hit in 1973-74, however, the lack of specific empirical knowledge hindered efforts to determine the impact of the higher prices on the poor and to target food aid with precision.

Using data from the three rounds of sampling a total of 50,000 households in the 1976 National Socio-Economic Survey (SUSENAS), commodity demand functions disaggregated by income class were estimated. For the first time, separate price terms for each class were included in the analysis. The results were robust and analytically satisfying: the pure substitution coefficient in the Slutsky Equation varied systematically by income class; and, after compensation for the income effect of the price change, the poor were shown to be substantially more responsive to price changes than the wealthy. These results have been confirmed with further work in Indonesia and other countries. They allow planners to determine with far more confidence than a decade ago the extent to which demand for food changes by income class when prices change.[35] The methodological problems involved in estimating these parameters have also stimulated a new area of work in econometrics.[36]

High prices of rice during the world food crisis in the mid-1970s stimulated a concern for the impact of prices on poor consumers. By the mid-1980s rice prices in the world market had collapsed, and attention turned to the impact on farmer welfare and the health of rural economies. Understanding this impact has turned out to be a far more difficult problem both analytically and empirically. Analytically, the issue cannot be treated in a partial-equilibrium framework because of the significant spillover of effects from rice markets to labor, land, and credit markets in rural areas. Because of the importance of rice as a wage good and of rural-urban migration in determining equilibrium wages in the nonagricultural economy, changes in rice prices raise significant issues for general equilibrium as well. But the computable general-equilibrium models constructed so far for the Indonesian economy have suffered from several serious problems: the structure of the models does not reflect the apparent complexity of market-clearing in rural Indonesia, investment functions from rural incomes are not included, and the parameters used are not based on reliable empirical evidence.

The lack of understanding of rural dynamics in Indonesia, especially as driven by changes in rice prices, is very troublesome. Although substantial research addressing these issues is underway, there is neither an agreed methodological framework for organizing the research (especially the dynamic dimensions that capture the response of rural investments to changes in rice prices) nor a valid sampling procedure to guarantee that results from individual local markets can be aggregated with confidence to achieve an economywide understanding. On the other hand, this is the frontier of research on rural economics. Substantial progress is likely to be reported in the 1990s, and Indonesia is likely to serve as a home for much of that research.

Indonesian experience can also be used to examine the hypothesis that society places a large premium on stability of food prices for reasons that are not apparent in economists' models of the impact of price-stabilization policies. If both producers and consumers demand price stability, there should be a way of including this desire in the specification of their welfare functions and testing empirically which models and specifications best explain actual behavior with respect to price changes. This approach involves macrodynamics and political economy, not just narrow microeconomics. But if no microeconomic foundations can be found in consumer theory for the strong public desires for price stability, price-stabilization policies will remain ad hoc, repeatedly subjected to attacks by economists, and defended by policymakers. Such a hostile relationship on a key element of national policy is not healthy for either side, especially when the economists implicitly carry with them the resources of outside donors and investors. Indonesia's record on rice price stabilization has been remarkably successful by historical and comparative standards. The technical analysis, both in amount and sophistication, that has supported implementation of the policy offers an excellent foundation for further research in three directions: the choice-theoretic basis in welfare economics of demand for price stabilization; the political economy of the supply of price stabilization that grows out of both popular support for price stability and an analytical understanding of the macrodynamic consequences of it; and the institutional responses that determine its equilibrium cost.

Concluding Observations

An early reviewer of this paper remarked that it was on a very slippery slope. The acknowledged relevance of political stability and consumer aversion to price changes offers too much scope for an analyst's own tastes to dominate policy recommendations. Such considerations simply overwhelm "the hard economics of observable quantities."

Even if the charge were accurate, it would serve to highlight the growing irrelevance of such narrowly focused economic methodologies when the prey refuses to sit quietly and be measured. In fact, precisely the opposite point is being made here. What look like nebulous consumer tastes and "soft" political concerns are actually grounded in a more realistic theory of consumer decision making and in the dynamic contributions of price stability to economic growth. Both of these are grist for the hard-nosed economist, but no simple mill can produce an appropriately textured and subtle output. Both empirical research, in the form of detailed country studies conducted within the framework outlined in this paper, and theoretical developments that widen substantially the scope for benefits from price stabilization for the basic food grain, will be needed to see our analyst safely off these slippery slopes. But always in policy analysis, and ideally in economics, the goal must be to model, measure, and interpret what is important, not necessarily what is easy or mathematically tractable.

Often the best policy is the enemy of good policy, and bad policy wins by default. A persuasive argument can be made that endogenous rent-seeking activities nearly always overwhelm desirable but limited government interventions into food prices, and the resulting policies harm poor people, drain the budget, and significantly impair prospects for economic growth.[37] For governments that are always captured by either consumer or producer interests, it might be argued that a "good" policy is free trade, even though some management of domestic prices might offer additional benefits in the absence of such capture. But this judgment is empirical. A country that can manage to stabilize its food prices long enough to provide support for economic growth to become firmly entrenched and for the political process to reach a workable maturity—and a significant number of countries in Asia have managed precisely that—should not have its options limited by the failure of others.

There are broader lessons as well. No neoclassical growth model has demonstrated any relevance to the actual process of economic development. This process is inherently historical, and it is subject to precisely the same complex and subtle forces that determine whether price stabilization makes a positive net contribution to a society in the long run. By studying the narrower and more quantifiable topic of price stabilization, perhaps some analytical light can also be shed on the larger topic of the factors influencing economic development. No narrow economic model of trade liberalization or monetary reform can provide such illumination. ௸

Notes

1 The author would like to thank Carol F. Timmer for her considerable assistance in helping to assemble this chapter, and Wally Falcon, Frank Ellis, Mark Mitchell, Michael Roemer, and Dwight H. Perkins for suggestions on how to make the chapter more comprehensible.

2 This school of price policy is usually associated most closely with T. W. Schultz and his colleagues and students from the University of Chicago. See Schultz (1978) for a review of this philosophy and chapter 2 of Timmer (1986a) for an introduction to the border price paradigm that serves as its intellectual foundation.

3 See the work of Taylor (1980), Streeten (1987), de Janvry (1978), Lipton (1977), and Rao (1989).

4 An excellent review of this debate from a neoclassical perspective is in Little (1982); the structuralist perspective is best presented in Taylor and Arida (1988).

5 As a simple example of the problems, there is no reliable technique for estimating trends in prices. See Schwartz (1987).

6 See especially work by Newbery and Stiglitz (1981), Runge and Myers (1985), Stiglitz (1987), Just (1988), Pradhan (1988), Myers (1988), and Timmer (forthcoming).

7 See especially Stiglitz (1987), Srinivasan (1985), Braverman and Guasch (1986), and Bates (1981).

8 This is the key conclusion in Newbery and Stiglitz (1981), Stiglitz (1987), and Bigman, Newbery, and Zilberman (1988). The latter authors, for example, in their discussion of Just's arguments for price-stabilization policies, make the following comment: "Attempts to quantify the net (efficiency) benefits of institutional attempts to reduce risk, like commodity price stabilization or quota policies, suggest that they are usually small and often negative" (p. 461). Working from a different analytical framework, Ravallion (1987) comes to a related conclusion: "...although the results of this study [of the Bangladesh famine in 1974] suggest a case in favor of food-grain price stabilization, the most appropriate form of policy intervention remains unclear. The case for public storage [the most common mechanism used to stabilize prices in developing countries] rests on the nature of the distortions to markets; buffer stocks will not be able to stabilize a competitive market with rational expectations" (p. 172). Both approaches conclude there is little empirical rationale for governments to attempt to stabilize food-grain prices, a result so sharply at variance with actual experience that different approaches should be investigated.

9 The macroeconomic dimensions of price stability are stressed in Kanbur's (1984) review of Newbery and Stiglitz (1981). The extreme difficulty of building dynamic investment factors into general-equilibrium models of agricultural pricing can be seen in de Janvry and Sadoulet (1987).

10 These dimensions of the benefits to food-price stability are discussed in considerably more detail in Timmer (1989a).

11 For more extensive discussion of the operational issues in food price stabilization and market intervention, see Timmer (1986a); the "principles" section of Timmer (1988a); the Indonesian experience summarized in Timmer (1986c); and in Timmer (1989b).

12 See Timmer (1988b) for a discussion of the relationship between agricultural diversification and price policy.

13 Pinckney's analysis of the Kenyan experience with these issues presents several operational guidelines for coping with the deviation between planned and actual intervention levels. See Pinckney (1988).

14 See Timmer, Falcon, and Pearson (1983); and Timmer (1986a).

15 See Salant (1983) for an analysis of the conditions leading to successful speculative attacks on public food agencies, and their impact on price stability.

16 The free-market approach has been in vogue for much of the 1980s, but community development, central planning, rural development, basic needs, and redistribution with growth were enthusiastically pursued in earlier periods. Sustainable development seems likely to become the next enthusiasm.

17 See, in particular, Badan Urusan Logistik (BULOG) (1971), Timmer (1975b), and Mears (1981).

18 The original policy memorandum was published in 1969. See Mears and Afiff.

19 Although there were no policy analysts present at the creation, the basic rationale and institutional design are reasonably well understood. See Badan Urusan Logistik (BULOG) (1971); Mears and Afiff (1969); and Timmer (1975b).

20 See Timmer (1984) and Warr (1984).

21 These measures included interest rate subsidies on an open line of credit at the central bank, annual increases in book profits from revalued rice inventories as nominal rice prices rose each year, "cost-based" pricing for rice delivered to the Budget Groups, and profits from importing additional commodities put under BULOG's responsibility.

22 The proposal was contained in the Falcon Team Report issued in September 1985.

23 See Mears and Afiff (1969). The publication of this article, which was originally a memorandum to the chairmen of the Planning Agency and of BULOG, also foreshadowed another important dimension of Indonesia's approach to economic analysis in the food policy arena: a willingness to let the analysis be published after the policy debate was resolved. Such publication kept the analysis subject to professional scrutiny and attracted scholarly interest from analysts not immediately connected with the policy dimensions of the issues. *The Bulletin of Indonesian Economic Studies*, published in Canberra by the Australian National University, played a major role in this dissemination process in the early years of the New Order government. By the mid-1970s

articles on Indonesian food and agricultural policy issues were appearing in *Review of Economics and Statistics, American Journal of Agricultural Economics, Economic Development and Cultural Change, Food Research Institute Studies,* and other leading journals.

24 See Afiff and Timmer (1971) and Timmer (1974).

25 See Harriss (1979) and Ravallion (1986).

26 In particular, neither hand-pounding or large-scale integrated rice mills using mechanical drying and bulk handling were economically optimal.

27 Both topics are reviewed in Timmer (1975a).

28 See the Falcon Team Report (1985).

29 As noted above, the budget allocation was made, but funds were never paid to BULOG because of the general budget crisis in 1986 caused by the collapse of petroleum prices.

30 In recent years the ceiling price has not been formally announced, but traders have a reasonable estimate of what prices BULOG will defend in different cities by observing market operations and by having regular discussions with DOLOG officials.

31 BULOG has never bought more than 12 percent of the total harvest or perhaps 25 percent of total marketings.

32 The model is developed in Timmer (1986a, 63-66).

33 An early draft of this analysis was widely circulated in Indonesia and to analysts in the donor community, especially the World Bank. After widespread criticism of the conclusion—the fertilizer subsidy had been highly profitable in private and public terms in total, and remained profitable at the margin as long as Indonesia remained an importer of rice—a much more carefully documented and developed version was produced and published, with the same conclusions. See Timmer (1986c).

34 See Timmer, Falcon, and Pearson (1983), especially chapter 2, for a fuller explanation of these relationships.

35 The evolution of this analysis is reported in Timmer (1978), Timmer (1981), and Waterfield (1985).

36 For a review, see Deaton (1986). An application of the most recent econometric techniques to Indonesian data is in Monteverde (1987). SUSENAS data have also been used recently in a sophisticated application of optimal taxation theory to the welfare impact of changes in rice prices. See Van de Walle (1989).

37 In particular, Bates (1981) makes this argument for Africa.

9

Smallholder Rubber Development in Indonesia[1]

Thomas P. Tomich

Thomas P. Tomich, who joined HIID in 1984, served as HIID's resident adviser at the Center for Policy and Implementation Studies in Jakarta, Indonesia, from 1987-1990, where he led research on smallholder tree crop development strategy and other aspects of agricultural policy. An Institute associate at HIID, he teaches and conducts research on agricultural policy.

Introduction

Tree Crop Development Policy and Problems

Indonesia has pursued the largest smallholder tree crop development program in the world. Targets for government-sponsored projects involved planting hundreds of thousands of hectares of rubber, oil palm, coconut, and other trees; expenditures of trillions of rupiah; and foreign borrowing of hundreds of millions of dollars during REncana PEmbangunan LIma TAhun (REPELITA) III and REPELITA IV.[2]

For almost a decade, this ambitious tree crop investment strategy has relied exclusively on block planting projects as a means of aiding smallholders in raising productivity. These management-intensive project designs strained the implementation capacity of public agencies. Too often, projects failed to produce yields that would justify their high costs. As a result, many participants will not be able to repay their loans. Furthermore, realization fell short of targets. (See Appendix, Table 1.) With the exception of oil palm, average yields remained low for most smallholder tree crops, and over 85 percent of smallholders were untouched by projects after nearly ten years of massive government effort.

Historical, social, economic, technical, and institutional factors all contributed to the smallholder tree crop development strategy that emerged and its ultimate failure to raise smallholder productivity. Tree crops present special challenges, but these disappointing results were not inevitable. Pressure is mounting for change, either toward reform of the development programs or *de facto* abandonment of smallholder development. These pressures resulting from the fall in oil revenues are accompanied by an increased need to expand output of traditional export commodities and concerns about income and employment in the Outer Islands, where tree crops and petroleum both are important in local economies.

This paper examines Indonesia's experience with smallholder rubber development as a case study of general problems of tree crop development in Indonesia. The objective is to understand not only why the smallholder rubber development strategy evolved as it did, but also why it has persisted, and why crucial questions regarding the success of block planting projects and prospects for potential alternatives were not addressed.

Overview of a Decade of Smallholder Rubber Projects

Rubber projects are the biggest problem in Indonesia's tree crop investment portfolio. Over 290,000 ha of rubber were planted in block schemes between 1978 and 1987.[3] The cost of this effort was huge: about Rp. 1 trillion at 1987 prices.

All block planting schemes in Indonesia are variations on two basic project models: Nucleus Estate-Smallholder (NES) schemes and Project Management Units (PMUs).[4] Although they differ in scale—PMUs generally cover 100-200 ha/block while NES schemes cover 500 ha up to 10,000 ha—they involve similar objectives and financing arrangements and share an integrated approach to raising productivity.

NES schemes have been financed either solely with government funds or jointly with soft loans from international organizations such as the World Bank. Similarly, rubber PMUs include the Smallholder Rubber Development Project

250

(SRDP), financed jointly by the World Bank and the Indonesian Government, and *Peremajaan Rehabilitasi dan Perluasan Tanaman Ekspor* (PRPTE), financed solely with Indonesian government funds.

Projects headquartered on these administered blocks are designed to provide 2 ha of high-yielding rubber clones per farmer along with fertilizer, pesticides, herbicides, and cover crops—all financed largely by credit extension and marketing assistance, processing facilities, and other services in an integrated package. Typically, farmers were "paid" for a portion of their time during the seven years or so before rubber should be tapped, with these wages being added to the loan outstanding.

Project benefits are limited to farmers who agree to be full participants. Farmers can get neither more nor less than 2 ha planted with rubber clones, nor can they select among the various elements of the input package. Due to administrative problems and delays in disbursement of project funds, few projects have been implemented as designed.

Rubber block planting schemes get low marks for technical achievement. About 22 percent of SRDP, over 40 percent of NES, and 74 percent of PRPTE area fell below a "satisfactory" technical standard, according to a recent sample survey of smallholder rubber projects (World Bank 1987).[5] "Satisfactory" means a reasonable prospect of attaining 70 to 80 percent or more of the level of yields assumed in *ex ante* appraisals. For rubber, this corresponds to yields of 900-1,200 kg/ha at maturity.[6]

Project yields from continuing to try to plant large areas for smallholders often are not much higher than levels that appear attainable through a market-oriented strategy at a fraction of the cost of block planting. Perhaps more important than the apparent waste of funds were the missed opportunities for development of the sector as a whole. As discussed below, the focus on projects meant that virtually no development assistance was going to the majority of rubber smallholders.

Some changes in smallholder development programs have already been dictated by the budget crisis triggered by the fall in oil prices in 1983. Disbursement of funds for the PRPTE program has halted; the international development banks no longer seem willing to lend for rubber NES schemes, and the Indonesian government no longer can fund many of its own rubber NES schemes.

Changes made so far, however, only represent reductions in the level of funding and areas targeted for government-sponsored block planting. As yet, there has not been any fundamental shift in the tree crop development strategy.

Evolution of the Project-based, Block Planting Strategy

By the late 1970s—well before the oil price collapse in 1983—policymakers became convinced that channeling public funds into traditional exports was necessary to diversify sources of foreign exchange and desirable as a means of exploiting Indonesia's comparative advantage in production of tropical agricultural commodities. Among these, rubber exports had been the traditional leader.

Although ideas for a major initiative in smallholder rubber development appear to have originated within the Indonesian government, foreign agencies—especially the World Bank—played an important role in identifying specific project models and were entrusted with a substantial share of the responsibility for initial design and monitoring of implementation. Both the NES schemes and PMUs were imported concepts.

As the story is told now, many officials felt at the time that Indonesia's comparative advantage in production of rubber, as well as coconut, palm oil, and other tree crops, was so strong that virtually any development strategy was bound to be profitable. This view seems to have been shared by Indonesians and foreign personnel.

The issue, as interpreted by some foreign advisers, was not the identification of the most profitable strategy for development of the smallholder sector, but, due to the long gestation periods involved, the need to get on with any sort of strategy that was available. In other words, it appeared to many at that time that almost any technically feasible strategy would be economically satisfactory.

Then, as today, large-scale plantations in Indonesia and elsewhere in Southeast Asia provided the main reservoir of organizational experience and technical information on rubber production, as well as a ready supply of expatriate advisers. Thus, it is not surprising that this stock of experience was tapped to meet demands for smallholder rubber development.

Combined with faith in Indonesia's comparative advantage in rubber production was the strong conviction that smallholder rubber development would not occur without government planting projects. Specifically, the most widely held opinion then, and now, was that smallholders would do no planting without substantial government assistance. Whether or not it was shared by World Bank personnel from the outset, this notion eventually became the basic premise of World Bank lending for smallholder development.

Prior to the emergence of block planting schemes as the dominant strategy in the late 1970s, Indonesia experimented with a market-oriented strategy for smallholder rubber development. From the 1950s through 1973, a cess scheme was operated to finance small nurseries to supply higher-yielding selected seedlings to rubber smallholders (Barlow and Muharminto 1982b; Barlow and Jayasuria 1984b; Barlow, Shearing, and Dereinda 1991).

The cess scheme in Indonesia was a failure. Few nurseries were set up and the effort never received adequate financing (Barlow, Shearing, and Dereinda 1991). A substantial share of the money collected by provincial-level, quasi-governmental organizations ended up in civil servants' pockets and never was used for replanting grants for smallholders.

Paradoxically, the problems of bureaucratic corruption that emerged in the cess scheme in the early 1970s contributed to a shift toward greater bureaucratic control of smallholder rubber development by 1978. Specifically, the rubber cess experience convinced certain senior economic policymakers that the bureaucracy could not be trusted to administer planting grants. This distrust, sources report, was the origin of the "credit component" and "conversion process" that characterized the past decade of smallholder development schemes. Tree crop planting and credit became inseparable in many policymakers' minds. It also was the beginning of a long period in which project documents promised high economic returns if only management and implementation problems could be overcome.

Distrust of Market Mechanisms

The apparent contradiction of this shift toward greater bureaucratic control despite the dismal performance of bureaucrats responsible for the cess scheme reflects the widely held belief that markets could not be relied on as institutions for smallholder tree crop development. This suspicion of markets ranges throughout the bureaucracy and was abetted by the oil boom, which made it possible to fund massive public projects. Of course, it also provided a rationale for the bureaucratic, project-based approach to smallholder development that served organizational interests in the line agencies.

The premise of the extra export tax—the nationwide successor to the provincially administered cess schemes—was that markets for smallholder rubber were dominated by powerful traders who manipulated prices and gouged farmers.[7] In particular, one version of the argument underlying the extra export tax was that price increases in world markets were *not* passed back to smallholders. Following this logic, the extra export tax was to be invoked when prices in world markets increased; the incidence of the tax would fall solely on traders; and the funds gathered by the tax and passed back to smallholders through planting projects would come as a net addition to smallholders' resources. Thus, one attraction of a project-based strategy is that it seems to provide an opportunity for direct intervention in marketing of smallholder output. By concentrating production, it was hoped that marketing channels could be organized to circumvent the private trade.

At least three other aspects of distrust of market mechanisms have had even more profound effects on smallholder rubber development strategy than the familiar concerns regarding middlemen gouging farmers. The first concern is that reliance on markets will lead to a less equitable outcome than can be accomplished through administrative efforts to target benefits. This concern that, in the absence of bureaucratic control, a few producers will get rich while the majority remain poor, is legitimate, but the presumption that projects will result in greater participation and a more equitable outcome does not necessarily follow.

The second concern—closely related to the premise that there is no unassisted planting—is that a market-oriented strategy would be allocatively inefficient. In other words, if smallholders do not plant on their own, planting projects are needed to capture the benefits of Indonesia's comparative advantage in rubber production.

The third concern is that a market-oriented strategy would be technically inefficient. More precisely, the technical deficiencies resulting from either allegedly irrational smallholder behavior or from constraints and economic imperfections characteristic of a smallholder setting would reduce yields sufficiently to eliminate any economic gains from distribution of improved rubber varieties through market channels. The gestation period and long potential productive life of rubber trees lend special cause for concern about the prospect of locking-in an inferior technical outcome.

Each of these three notions of market failure and the belief that bureaucratic control can lead to better outcomes will be examined below. Each notion contains plausible elements, particularly for the case of smallholder rubber. In practice, however, these ideas biased the choice of smallholder development strategy toward a bureaucratic, control-oriented strategy and, ultimately, failed to increase productivity.

Conceptual Basis of the Block Planting Strategy

Equity

The main fear seems to have been that under a market-oriented strategy, benefits would be restricted to richer farmers while the majority of smallholders would be left behind. However, it was believed that benefits could be targeted to compensate for limited access to credit, lower levels of education, and other real disadvantages facing lower-income groups, and that this could be accomplished most effectively through an administrative, project-based approach.

In this context, NES schemes were seen as having particular advantages as a way to assist the poorest segments of rural society. Because landlessness is a serious problem on Java, but much less common on the Outer Islands, and because of the disappointing results with transmigration projects based on food crops, the NES model for tree crops came to be seen as an answer to the transmigration imbroglio and a means of addressing poverty problems on Java. Indeed, "tree crops for transmigrants" continued to develop into a major program even as most smallholder tree crop investment plans were cut back during REPELITA IV.

NES schemes, however, are the most expensive project model, with development costs of over Rp. 4 million per ha when infrastructure is included. Although this model may play a positive social role in transmigration schemes—a topic of substantial controversy—these costs ruled it out as a mass approach to smallholder development even before the onset of severe budget problems in 1983 (Baharsyah and Soetatwo 1982, 174).

PRPTE was intended to replicate the World Bank's SRDP model for many more traditional rubber producers. In many ways, PRPTE was the only option in the block planting strategy with a prospect of significant effects on productivity. The clear failure of the PRPTE is particularly significant as an indicator that a block planting strategy cannot hope to assist a significant share of smallholders. PRPTE did not fail simply because of lack of funds. Indeed, funding was cut because of overwhelming evidence of failure. PRPTE proved fundamentally unimplementable in Indonesia because of the complexity of its approach and because it did not fit smallholders' needs.

Two more approaches also were intended, but in practice received little or no attention from Indonesian officials or foreign agencies. The so-called partial approach of providing planting material and sometimes fertilizer, as well as extension services, was envisioned as a way to raise productivity among the upper strata of smallholders. The second approach was to form a "self-reliant" (*swadaya*) group of farmers, who needed only information supplied by the provincial tree crops advisory services (*Dinas Perkebunan Daerah*).

Project design problems, limited administrative capacity in implementing agencies, and difficulties in establishing financial control proved to be much more serious than shortage of funds as constraints to implementation of block planting through NES schemes and PMUs. These problems generated two responses, each of which further limited the percentage of smallholders assisted.

254

First, the block planting targets were scaled back, most dramatically in the case of PRPTE, thereby reducing opportunities for smallholders to join block planting schemes. Second, concern about implementation and management of block planting increasingly focused resources and attention on efforts to improve NES and PMU performance to the exclusion of any efforts toward farmers not included in projects.

Thus, the more market-oriented "partial" and "self-reliant" models that might have picked up some of the slack left by the contraction of block planting never really were tried.[8] During the peak of the block planting strategy through the early and middle 1980s, these two groups tended to be grouped together as "spontaneous" planters. Because the majority of Indonesian officials and their foreign advisers operated under the assumption that "spontaneous" planting was negligible, and because area targets reflected only NES and PMU activities, these notions reinforced the neglect of market-oriented alternatives.

From a narrow project perspective, it is something of an accomplishment to have operated the biggest tree crop planting program in the world and to have established about 294,000 ha of higher-yielding trees—albeit, often of disappointing quality—in nine years. In comparison, the Kenya Tea Development Authority (KTDA) earned a reputation as the most successful smallholder tree crop scheme in the world by organizing the planting of 54,000 ha of tea in a comparable period (Lamb and Muller 1982).

And yet, to the surprise of many Indonesians and foreigners alike, the biggest rubber planting scheme in the world had no effect on the vast majority of rubber smallholders. The size of the smallholder sector—covering almost 2.5 million ha scattered across Sumatra and Kalimantan (Biro Pusat Statistik 1987)—is a formidable challenge for any bureaucratic program. After more than a decade of effort, less than 15 percent of the smallholder area had been reached by block planting projects.

This means that there are still about 2.2 million ha of low-yielding rubber, with peak yield potential of about 500 kg/ha/year. At an average rate of 38,000 ha per year, which was sustained at high cost and with mixed results during REPELITA III, it would take fifty-eight years to replant this area under block projects. Now that NES schemes are curtailed and PRPTE is cancelled, smallholder rubber development relies solely on SRDP-type block planting. Even if funds are available in coming years, it seems unlikely that SRDP projects can be extended faster than 15,000 ha/yr. At that rate, it would take over 140 years to replant the entire area still occupied with unselected, low-yielding rubber. Past experience suggests that 7,500 is closer to the sustainable rate for SRDP expansion.

Ironically, the block planting strategy seems to have achieved exactly the opposite of what was intended, as a result of concern about participation and equity. Benefits were restricted to a few farmers while the majority of smallholders were left behind. It is difficult to argue that a development strategy that only benefits 15 percent of the target population is equitable.

Project Bias

The premise that there was no unassisted rubber planting, combined with the knowledge that without planting of higher-yielding rubber there would be no increase in productivity, appears to have provided the driving force behind a large-scale project bias in smallholder development strategy.[9] In other words, to raise yields, planting was necessary; to induce planting, it was believed projects were necessary; and to make significant progress in the enormous task, big projects were necessary.

Thus, the main points of controversy about equity, effectiveness, and feasibility of market-oriented alternatives to the block planting strategy concern prospects for the spread of higher-yielding rubber varieties beyond project boundaries or in the absence of projects. Under the current strategy, projects are the sole source of higher-yielding planting material; there is virtually no higher-yielding material available to nonparticipants. If there is no demand for planting material outside projects, no one is excluded, and no opportunities are missed by this strategy. Furthermore, absence of demand for planting material outside projects would mean that a market-oriented development strategy cannot work.

These beliefs are completely compatible with economic theory and the nature of tree crops. In its neoclassical formulation, the general "tree crop problem" is a standard application of dynamic programming: maximize the present discounted value of net profits over the planning horizon. In practice, this problem involves decisions about allocations of labor, capital, and land to the tree crop, intercrops, and alternative activities, as well as determination of optimal tree density, maintenance, harvesting, uprooting, and replanting patterns.

Relative to most other crops, the greatest difficulty in finding an optimal solution for the tree crop problem stems from the time that separates various decisions and their outcomes. This is complicated further by the high cost of reversing decisions, uncertainty about future prices of inputs and outputs, and risks from natural hazards. Decisions in one period affect options in the future, but they must be made without a clear picture of the options the future holds. Even if perfect information about the technical nature of the process were available to the producer, if risks were ignored, and if there were perfect markets for commodities and factors of production plus secure property rights, the calculations required to identify an optimal solution to the tree crop problem would be daunting (Bellman and Hartley 1985).

Given the nature of the tree crop problem, it is perfectly plausible that smallholder rubber producers may not be following an optimal economic program. Indeed, if there ever were a commodity in which significant market failures were likely to occur, it is smallholder rubber. The gestation period of six to ten years is among the longest for commercial tree crops and the productive life can extend to thirty years. This compounds the effects of risk and uncertainty on planting decisions, which are perfectly rational worries for a smallholder household attempting to meet its needs from a meager income. Furthermore, rubber smallholders must make investment decisions in an environment that includes high investment costs relative to cash income; capital market imperfections; limited access to information about markets and technology; output price variation around a declining trend; breakdown of traditional land tenure practices in the absence of formal tenure institutions; and uncertainty about future rubber export policies.

Under these circumstances, smallholder planting rates are likely to be below the economic optimum. Furthermore, given the fluctuations in rubber prices and the expansion of off-farm employment opportunities, unassisted planting by smallholders could be insignificant, despite a strong comparative advantage over the long run. If true, these plausible assertions provide a rationale for bureaucratic intervention through projects designed to ameliorate market imperfections. They are also consistent with the emphasis on credit, land title certification, and extension in the design of block planting schemes.

However, nothing ensures that bureaucracies can realize a better solution to the tree crop problem than individual smallholders. Furthermore, even though projects can be designed to address these market imperfections, there is no guarantee that they can be implemented through imperfect bureaucratic institutions. As with the equity issues discussed above, the practical question reduces to one of relative imperfections between bureaucratic techniques and market forces. This set of potential imperfections is an agenda for research. However, much can be deduced from the answer to two simple questions: (1) Are smallholders planting rubber on their own? and (2) If so, how much?

Despite the importance of the answer and the amount of resources put into smallholder rubber development, a good estimate of how much unassisted rubber planting takes place in Indonesia each year is surprisingly difficult to obtain because virtually no attention is paid to "spontaneous" planting. Local government office charts indicate precise areas of rubber projects, often down to the last tenth of a hectare. Yet, statistics on unassisted planting are incomplete, if they are kept at all. Thus, most official statistics support the official line. In this way the project bias works to confirm the major premise of the block planting strategy.

The history of rubber in Southeast Asia suggests that, despite economic imperfections, smallholders planted massive areas of rubber without assistance or, more often, in the face of policies designed to discourage them (Bauer 1948, Thee Kian Wee 1977, Barlow 1978, Pelzer 1978a, Dillon 1985). Indeed, the first rubber seedlings planted by Indonesian smallholders probably were stolen from plantations. However, world prices have fallen substantially since the introduction of rubber. The rubber price records set around 1910 have not been approached since in real terms.

Evidence from field visits supports the view that unassisted planting and the demand for higher-yielding planting material are substantial. In fact, smallholders are still stealing rubber seedlings from projects. Some farmers gather seed from abandoned colonial plantations, believing forty-five-year-old technology will be superior to what they usually can get.

Other data support the view that planting outside block projects has been substantial during REPELITA III and REPELITA IV. The Directorate General of Estates (DGE) compiles data from district offices of the tree crops advisory service regarding the age distribution of rubber trees. The areas of immature rubber reported by DGE must have come from somewhere, and only a portion can be accounted for as the result of block planting projects. For 1987, two different DGE sources provide estimates of 601,224 ha and 984,315 ha of immature rubber. Assuming that trees planted in projects have the same ten-year gestation period as unassisted planting, approximately 293,760 ha of this area of immature trees is due to block planting.[10] Thus, for the lower of the two estimates of immature area, 307,464 ha of replanting cannot be accounted for by block projects. Dividing by nine years of immaturity gives a minimum estimate of

34,000 ha/year of unassisted planting. Doing the same calculation with the more realistic assumption that the gestation period for project rubber is seven years yields an estimate of 43,000 ha/year of unassisted planting. Given the likelihood that these figures understate total immature rubber area, the rate of unassisted planting by smallholders is probably much closer to 50,000 ha/year than it is to zero.

Even the most conservative of these estimates, 34,000 ha/year, demolishes the key premise that unassisted planting by smallholders is negligible. Furthermore, this estimate suggests that unassisted planting, and not block planting schemes, accounts for more than half of the rubber planting in Indonesia.

Because smallholders are planting substantial amounts of rubber even though they are excluded from supplies of higher-yielding trees, an important opportunity is missed by restricting improved planting material to projects. Furthermore, increased availability of higher-yielding rubber varieties is likely to accelerate replanting. In the longer term, these missed opportunities will threaten Indonesia's comparative advantage if wages rise without an offsetting rise in productivity.

Plantation Bias

Even if the premise can be refuted that little or no unassisted rubber planting occurs in Indonesia, one additional argument against a market-oriented strategy for smallholder development must be considered: smallholders may not be able to realize higher yields on their own even if they could obtain higher-yielding planting material.

If this is true, then markets cannot be relied on as a means of distributing technology or raising productivity, even if there is demand among smallholders for improved rubber varieties. The corollary, of course, is another rationale for block planting: projects are deemed necessary to establish a controlled, plantation-like environment in order to realize the productive potential of the trees.

The most extreme version of this perspective holds that smallholders are irrational, that they ignore economic incentives, and that their behavior is contrary to their self-interest. A weaker version is the feeling that agents of the government know smallholders' interests better than smallholders themselves, and that these agents can guide smallholders to realizing a better outcome despite themselves.

Thus, a project setting designed to replicate plantation conditions is seen by some as an opportunity to control smallholder decision making and ensure that it conforms to the requirements of modern technology. With smallholder-to-agent ratios as low as 25:1 in NES oil palm schemes, the agents' role seems to be as much "guidance" and "discipline" as "extension" and "advice." These views are expressed most frequently in conversation but have been recorded for a variety of circumstances and especially in colonial settings (Green and Hymer 1966).

What will happen if smallholders get their hands on improved varieties? This issue is especially difficult to resolve since there has been so little experience with high-yielding rubber varieties under actual smallholder conditions in Indonesia. Empirical studies of smallholder behavior in low-income countries suggest that the perceived need for tight supervision of smallholders on NES schemes and PMUs indicates deficiencies in project design rather than problems in the smallholders' sense of their economic interests. Furthermore, behavior of Indonesian tree crop smallholders not involved in projects demonstrates that they can perceive and profit from investment opportunities. For example, a recent case study of the diffusion of a farmer-selected coffee variety in Indonesia illustrates smallholders' ability not only to seek out profitable investment opportunities but also to realize their potential (Messi 1988).

Although exaggerated notions about irrational behavior do influence attitudes regarding the feasibility of various approaches to smallholder development strategy in Indonesia, the debate about smallholder rubber technology tends to focus on the resource constraints typical of the smallholder setting and the characteristics of the available technology rather than on shortcomings in smallholder decision making.

Resource constraints present a more formidable challenge to the feasibility of a market-oriented strategy for smallholder rubber development. The basic idea behind this perspective is that a minimum—and relatively high—threshold of capital investment is required to realize any of the potential increase in yields from improved rubber varieties. As a result, it is argued, the high-yielding technology does not provide a smooth set of intermediate options across a range of factor intensities. The implications flowing from that argument are that (a) introducing high-yielding planting material to the capital-scarce smallholder setting can only lead to failure; (b) there can be no step-by-step transition from low-yielding traditional rubber to higher-yielding varieties; and (c) significant productivity gains can only come by placing smallholders in a plantation-like project setting.

The history of rubber development in Southeast Asia provides ample reasons to suspect that research programs would generate technology suited to relatively capital-intensive rubber production (Barlow and Jayasuriya 1984a). In a pattern similar to other cases of induced innovation biased toward the factor endowments of a few producers, the plantation bias in rubber development during the colonial era in Southeast Asia reflected the political economy of those societies (de Janvry 1978; Sanders and Ruttan 1978; Chambers 1983; Hayami and Ruttan 1985, 362).

Once institutionalized through patterns of research funding and accumulation of human capital regarding specific research topics, this institutional bias has persisted. Its cumulative effect could, in principle, require much time and work to reverse. Despite this, the appropriateness of the plantation-biased technology "on the shelf" to smallholder producers with different factor endowments depends on the degree of factor substitution possible within the technology (Barlow and Jayasuriya 1984a and 1984b; Yee and Longworth 1985).

Thus, the key issue regarding feasibility of a market-oriented smallholder development strategy is not the history of bias in research that favored plantations, but the scope for capital-labor substitution in the existing technology of high-yielding rubber. If biased research and development makes "modern" technology inappropriate to the constraints faced in traditional farming systems, a plantation setting could be necessary to realize yield increases because adapting technology to a smallholder setting would take too long. One may not like it, but the legacy of plantation bias in rubber research still must be faced.

Capital-Labor Substitution and Existence of a Market-oriented Alternative

Technology embodied in rubber trees at planting depends on the variety planted, the propagation method and planting techniques used, the variety's responsiveness to fertilizer and yield stimulants, and its maintenance requirements and susceptibility to disease. Once the tree is in the ground, these attributes are fixed. Disembodied technology includes the tapping systems used, application of fertilizer and yield stimulants, actual disease and weed control provided, and other practices that can have a varied effect on yield over the life of the tree (Sepien and Etherington 1980).

Studies of rubber production in Malaysia indicate that although disembodied technology may have a strong, capital-using, management-intensive bias, technology embodied in rubber planting material displays substantial scope for capital-labor substitution (Barlow and Jayasuriya 1984a, Yee and Longworth 1980, also Sepien and Etherington 1980).

Thus, there is an element of truth in each of the competing arguments about the appropriateness of existing high-yielding rubber varieties to smallholder production. On one hand, higher-yielding planting material may be easily adaptable to smallholder conditions. On the other hand, yield increases dependent on application of substantial amounts of other purchased inputs are unlikely because they are particularly dependent on sustained outlays of scarce capital.

The apparent opportunity to exploit higher yield potential embodied in planting material is the basis for the dispersal strategy for smallholder development advocated by Barlow and others (Barlow and Muharminto 1982a and 1982b; Barlow and Jayasuriya 1984b; Barlow, Shearing, and Dereinda 1991; also see Dillon 1985). This market-oriented strategy establishes small nurseries from which improved planting materials are sold to surrounding farmers who want to plant rubber. The concept of dispersing high-yielding rubber varieties widely among smallholders has a long history of advocates (Bauer 1948, 321; Thomas 1975). It also makes sense to farmers and is endorsed by a number of officials responsible for managing smallholder projects.[11]

Although the dispersal strategy relies on market mechanisms to distribute higher-yielding planting material to smallholders and for most other aspects of rubber production and distribution, it is not a laissez-faire strategy. In particular, the strategy includes bureaucratic intervention to establish nurseries and to assist in dissemination of information about the response of higher-yielding varieties to various inputs. Drastic reduction in the cost of participation is the primary approach to alleviating smallholders' cash constraints. However, if direct intervention is deemed necessary to alleviate financial barriers to smallholders' access to improved planting material, input price policy is the suggested instrument rather than the government-administered credit programs that characterize block planting.

An important, but unfortunate, result of the block planting strategy that restricted supply of high-yielding planting material to project participants is that there is very little evidence on performance of improved rubber varieties under typical smallholder conditions in Indonesia.[12] Furthermore, one outcome of the plantation bias in rubber research is that important questions regarding the application of technology in smallholder settings have not received serious attention. This bias in applied research has often been noted in the literature on agricultural development (Green and Hymer 1966, Chambers 1983, Richards 1985).

Nevertheless, project appraisal exercises performed with the available evidence provide estimates of economic and financial rates of return for a market-oriented dispersal strategy that are comparable with block planting. Under extremely conservative assumptions regarding costs, yields, and output prices, Barlow, Shearing and Dereinda (1991) estimate real financial rates of return of 17 to 19 percent and real economic returns of 11 to 14 percent for the dispersal strategy for rubber. Conservative assumptions were used in their analysis to provide reasonable certainty that productivity would rise even if farmers retained most traditional management practices. *Ex ante* appraisals of block planting schemes by the World Bank projected economic rates of return ranging between 11 and 17 percent, but these returns presumed significant changes in farmers' practices. It is unlikely economic rates of return for block planting schemes will reach 11 percent (Barlow, Shearing, and Dereinda 1991). Indeed, in the case of PRPTE, returns probably have been negative. Furthermore, even if projected rates of return for block planting can be reached for a few farmers, these results suggest the dispersal strategy deserves much more attention, even if only as a supplement to block planting, because of its potential to benefit many more smallholders at much lower cost to the government.

Even if planting in a dispersal strategy grew to cover 40,000 hectares per year and if substantial incentives were provided to field workers, the administrative costs of the full-scale program would be under Rp. 5 billion per year. A large unit subsidy on planting materials would double costs to the Indonesian government. Even under these generous assumptions, the total cost of a five-year, full-scale effort would total Rp. 50 billion (less than U.S. $30 million). The complete program just reaches the threshold of previous foreign loans for tree crop development and is about one-tenth of the comparable costs under the block planting strategy of REPELITA III and REPELITA IV. The next section considers how this might be viewed as a drawback.

Political Economy of Project Finance

Debates about tree crop development strategy are confused by an abundance of plausible arguments and a shortage of hard evidence. Yet, the conceptual basis for block planting discussed above should have been suspect, based on casual empiricism, even if formal analyses were not feasible. In practice, however, one or more of these notions seem to be accepted uncritically by a surprising number of foreigners and Indonesians. Many key people continue to accept the premises that block planting schemes were affecting a significant share of the smallholder rubber subsector and that unassisted planting by smallholders is negligible. They believe this despite the apparent contradiction between these premises and information that is available to almost anyone concerned with smallholder rubber development.

Although the issues regarding choice of technology are more complex than other basic premises favoring a project-based strategy, evidence available at least ten years ago indicated that a dispersal strategy could be an attractive alternative and suggested the need to take a closer look. Yet key foreign experts did not appreciate this information, or rejected it because it conflicted with their notions about an appropriate approach to smallholder development.

Although substantial amounts of money were involved, economic analysis seems to have played little or no role in steering the choice of smallholder development strategy. Of course, many of the warning signals about the chosen development strategy and the hints about possible alternatives emerged only after the commitment was made to large investments in block planting. As stressed in the *Introduction*, there seems to have been an initial consensus among Indonesians and foreigners that given the faith in Indonesia's comparative advantage in rubber production and the abundance of funds available at the time, almost any technically feasible strategy could yield a satisfactory development outcome. In this context, it made sense to seize the most readily available strategy and, once the commitment was made, to try to see it through. As long as results were satisfactory, there would be no particular pressure to devote substantial time and attention to experiments and the search for an optimal strategy among uncertain alternatives (Simon 1985).

As long as funds were abundant, uniform technical success could be allowed to mask underlying economic losses. Yet, years of denying the implications of the disappointing technical and economic record, and the efforts to preserve a consensus on block planting after 1983 raise the question of what interests really were being satisfied by the persistence of block planting projects. In principle, a variety of personal and organizational considerations could contribute to the lack of incentives—indeed, apparent disincentives—to analyze critically the chosen strategy and to search for alternatives.

Rent Seeking

Expensive, complex projects provide opportunities for personal gain through diversion of funds or material to private uses. In terms of opportunities for rent seeking, administrative control of projects is far superior to a market-oriented strategy. Furthermore, the opportunity to extract rents is usually proportional to the flow of funds through a project and is abetted by ambiguous project performance. Thus, the "management" and "implementation" problems associated with tree crop block planting could be seen, at least in part, as symptoms of opportunities for bureaucrats to divert funds.

The scandals associated with the PRPTE, and, most recently, reports of widespread mismanagement by top officials of some state plantation companies suggest certain individuals could benefit from perpetuation of a project-based, block planting strategy rather than a shift to a lower-cost, market-oriented strategy. However, attributing the entire history of tree crop development strategy to rent seeking alone would be misleading as well as unfair to the large number of conscientious staff members in implementing agencies.

Indeed, although rent seeking may have thrived at times as a result of the project bias in smallholder development, neither rent seeking nor any response to it is the force that has perpetuated the block planting strategy. First of all, scandal-ridden programs have been among the first to be cut. Concern about the massive corruption evident in the cess planting scheme was a driving force in the move toward centralized bureaucratic control in the late 1970s. Second, the block planting strategy continued not with the mere acquiescence of the World Bank and other international agencies but with their active support.

Although policymakers naturally turn to centrally administered projects in an effort to impose financial control, this is not the only possible solution nor has it been effective in combating rent seeking. Financial control mechanisms could have been applied to management of nurseries, planting material distribution, and other administrative aspects of a market-oriented dispersal strategy and probably with greater success. The shift from planting grants to a credit-based scheme appears to have provided only a temporary challenge to officials intent on extracting money from their association with smallholder tree crop development. Inventing fake participants in block planting schemes could be done without risk of much outside oversight because of the isolation of many projects. This was hardly an original approach (see Snodgrass and Patten, chapter 13). Furthermore, it is easier to escape detection in the case of tree crops than with rice projects because the fraud generally would not be discovered until many years later when repayments from nonexistent rubber trees became due. Frequent transfers of civil servants helped obscure evidence by the time problems were uncovered.

Organizational Interests

Indonesian implementing agencies and international lenders share organizational interests in large expenditures for tree crop development. These mutual organizational interests are the primary explanation for continuation of the block planting strategy.

Large-scale, expensive block planting projects are a way of "moving" money that government agencies and foreign lenders find particularly satisfactory. In this sense, the project bias and the plantation bias work together to reinforce arguments for large expenditures: total budgets increase with rising unit costs as well as with expansion of area targets.

Initially, the strategy may have been adopted based on sincere expectations of technical success and satisfactory economic returns that went beyond organizational benefits. However, once the strategy was in place, an elaborate rationale developed to sustain it despite mounting evidence of problems. This parallels the Egyptian experience with land reclamation, which evolved from idealistic objectives and faith in superior technology into a maze of vested interests based on bureaucratic control and large budgets (Springborg 1979).

In the late 1970s, the Department of Agriculture lost the bureaucratic battle for control of the extra export tax, which was to be introduced to replace the discredited cess scheme as a source of funds earmarked for smallholder development. The extra export tax revenue ended up in the general budget instead. Large projects with budgets of their own must have been an attractive alternative for expanding the Department of Agriculture's budget.[13] This effort was successful; funding for block planting increased dramatically in REPELITA III.

Implementation of the block planting strategy in REPELITA III and REPELITA IV affected the structure and orientation of the DGE and the provincial tree crop advisory services. The development funds allocated for block planting investments became an important source of supplements to routine operating budgets. Thousands of temporary employees were added, and their salaries were paid out of development funds. Permanent staff involved with projects received incentive payments to supplement their inadequate civil service salaries. It is not surprising that most bureaucratic attention shifted to block planting projects. Abandonment of block planting would be a financial disaster for the DGE and the provincial *Dinas*, particularly if nothing else replaced it.

The project and plantation biases of the block planting strategy are quite compatible with organizational incentives in international organizations to design and manage substantial lending programs. The U.S. $30 million cost of a generous—some would say, extravagant—five-year dispersal strategy for small-holder rubber development barely attains the threshold of interest for agricultural sector lending in Indonesia.

Neither the staff of the international agencies involved, nor the DGE, nor the provincial *Dinas* is monolithic in its support of the block planting strategy. Each organization has dissenters who question the results of block planting, whether privately or publicly. However, because of overriding organizational interests in big projects, plentiful institutional incentives abound for doing a satisfactory job of the difficult task of running an expensive smallholder development project.[14] Active criticism of existing projects is considered antisocial: it can mean the end of a person's career.

It is not possible to isolate a single personal or organizational factor as the major cause of persistence in the block planting strategy. However, these factors all seem to support continuation of the project-based, bureaucratic approach. Furthermore, technical information is most readily accessible to people directly involved in implementing projects—the very people who typically have the least interest in questioning those projects (Grindle 1980). The arcane nature of the controversy about choice of technology makes it difficult for people with general interests in smallholder development and without vested interests in large-scale projects to enter the debate in a meaningful way.

Pressure for Retrenchment and Prospects for Reform

Budget Constraints

In broad terms, tree crop investment in Indonesia has followed Allison's (1971) observation that policy changes are likely to coincide with periods of "budgetary feast" or "budgetary famine." Yet recognition of the full budgetary implications of failure of block planting was complicated by the special arrangements for smallholder project financing and the long gestation period of these crops.

In the beginning, optimistic plans for block planting in REPELITA III seemed to be an appropriate response to the abundance of development funds during the oil boom years. Tree crop investments were viewed as one element of a strategy to ensure against future "famines" in foreign exchange and public finance when the oil boom eventually ended. Massive investment programs for traditional export commodities like rubber were one plausible way of converting the flow of oil revenue into a renewable base for exports in the future.

The oil price decline in 1983 coincided with the expected start of production of the first oil palms, coffee, and other trees planted at the beginning of major investments in block planting in REPELITA III. If the block planting strategy had been successful, the timing of the expansion of tree crop production could not have been better. However, this was only the beginning of what eventually became a stream of evidence about serious technical problems with block planting. The first undeniable evidence of problems with rubber block planting, however, would not appear until trees reached productive ages of approximately seven to ten years. This did not occur until well into the REPELITA IV period.

The "credit component" that was an essential part of the high-cost block planting strategy was based on the notion that liability for debt would be "converted" from Indonesian government loan guarantees to smallholder repayment obligations. This "conversion" would occur after plots were certified to have met the technical standards specified in project designs and land ownership certificates had been issued to serve as collateral for state bank loans to smallholders. The "conversion" process was scheduled to be completed by the time trees started producing.

The success of block planting, in general, and the conversion process, in particular, would eventually have created a revolving fund to finance ongoing tree crop projects in which repayments by earlier smallholder participants financed planting by later groups. If things had gone according to plan, block planting could have become self-financing as more and more trees came into production.

Due to external shocks and internal problems, the plan did not succeed as expected. Optimistic planting targets had to adjust to accommodate lower oil prices, which reduced the flow of funds into the tree crop development program during REPELITA IV. The long gestation period for tree crops and concentration of some of the major technical problems in crops with longer gestation periods meant that the full financial implications of the "conversion" problem resulting from internal technical failures in investments made during REPELITA III emerged only gradually over the REPELITA IV period. In this second stage of financial problems it became apparent that a substantial share of the stock of funds intended to sustain the scheme would never be recovered. In the case of rubber, it took almost a decade for the internal technical problems to emerge fully—which brings the story up-to-date.

Retrenchment and "Privatization"

Policy decisions regarding what steps to take next will have an important long-term effect on the subsector. Ultimately, the balance-of-payments problems and crisis in government finance resulting from the fall in oil prices may be viewed as the beginning of a move away from the block planting strategy that provided lower-than-expected benefits at high cost. Unfortunately, it is not clear that the lessons of block planting experience have been appreciated. Indeed, there is a real risk that these expensive lessons of failure are being ignored.

Some policy changes have already been dictated by economic circumstances. On top of cuts in government-sponsored block planting that occurred during the REPELITA IV period, the scale of government-sponsored NES schemes and PMUs will inevitably have to be curtailed further due to the anticipated shortage of development funds for REPELITA V. However, the tendency has been to continue retrenchment rather than to explore opportunities for reform.

Efforts to promote private investment in tree crops have been the main policy response to the necessary reduction in public investment.[15] So far, this strategy has taken a narrow view of the private sector by focusing on large-scale investors and providing incentives to induce investment in tree crops.

Private investment in tree crops by smallholders has been neglected in this shift toward the private sector. The mistaken premise that there is little unassisted planting still exerts a strong influence over perceptions of policy options. If the block planting strategy simply continues on a reduced scale and the bulk of smallholder planting goes on without assistance in obtaining higher-yielding varieties, an opportunity to raise productivity and to enhance Indonesia's long-run comparative advantage in rubber production will be missed.

Prospects for Reform

The financial problems of rubber and other tree crop block planting schemes are much more apparent than they were even two years ago. The stakes for the Department of Agriculture must appear very different than they did at the beginning of the last planning cycle. Instead of a situation where organizational interests could be optimized by seeking the largest possible package of development projects, a real possibility exists that no major new projects will be planned for the next five years. Although a market-oriented dispersal strategy might not have served organizational interests as well as block planting in 1978, it must look better than a zero option today.

In the field, meanwhile, the situation of PRPTE PMUs is similar to that of the BRI Unit Desas when Proyek Bimbingan Massal (BIMAS) collapsed in 1983 (see Snodgrass and Patten, chapter 13). Approximately 10,000 project staff members are still assigned to PRPTE, despite the fact that they apparently have little or nothing to do. A pilot project for the dispersal strategy could be initiated in a few of these PMUs, which are already established in the main rubber producing regions.

Something bearing a rough resemblance to the dispersal strategy has sprung up spontaneously in a few areas where smallholders have arranged to obtain planting material from the nurseries established for defunct projects. It remains to be seen, however, whether the suggested reforms can evolve into the tree crop analog of Kredit Umum Pedesaan (KUPEDES)—or even whether it will have an adequate trial. ✑

Notes

1   The author acknowledges the assistance of a number of individuals in the preparation of this paper. Conversations with Marzuki Usman, Alirahman, Soetardjo Soewarno, C.P.A. Bennett, Colin Barlow, Colin Shearing, Ridwan Dereinda, S. Budiman, David Dapice, and many others provided inspiration for ideas in this paper. This paper would also not have been possible without the contributions and hard work of Nawir Messi, Sulton Mawardi, Dradjad Hari Wibowo, Listyowati Kusumo, Suyanto, and other members of HIID's Center for Policy Implementation Studies (CPIS) research staff. Cooperation from the DGE, Dinas Perkebunan Daerah, and SRDP staff members was

essential in arranging field research, especially in South Sumatra, West Kalimantan, Jambi, and North Sumatra. Finally, but not least, Sri Darmastuti deserves acknowledgment for her dedicated and efficient secretarial assistance.

2 REPELITA means "five year development plan." REPELITA III covers the period 1979/80 to 1983/84; REPELITA IV covers 1984/85 to 1988/89; REPELITA V was scheduled to begin implementation in April 1989. For example, at the beginning of REPELITA IV, over 1.5 million ha of planting was planned for rubber, oil palm, and coconut alone. Of this, over 1.1 million ha involved smallholders (DGE 1984).

3 Counting from the beginning of smallholder rubber block planting projects in 1974, the total is about 306,000 ha.

4 In Bahasa Indonesia, NES schemes are called "PIR" (*Perusahan Inti Rakyat*) and PMUs are called UPP (*Unit Pelaksanaan Proyek*).

5 These percentages correspond to sample areas in Class C and D according to the classification scheme used, with Class A being best and D worst.

6 All rubber yields in this paper are expressed as dry rubber content (DRC).

7 For example, former Minister of Agriculture Achmad Affandi, speaking on February 23, 1987, to a forum sponsored by the Chamber of Commerce and Industry, was reported to have said: "... high agricultural trade margins [are] due to the strong position of the intermediary institutions compared with the position of the producers. The collecting traders who directly buy the commodities, products of the farmers, are generally in a stronger bargaining position toward the great number of small farmers. It has become public knowledge that the greatest profit in this business chain is not enjoyed by the farmers, but by the collectors, the processors, and the wholesalers." (Reported by *NERACA*; translated by *Business News* [1987].)

8 Over the past ten years, the "partial approach" has been tried on a total of only 23 ha, according to DGE figures. Although it may have serious problems in its current design, this same drawback has not been a barrier to massive efforts in block planting. In this sense, the skepticism about the potential effect of market-oriented strategies has been self-fulfilling.

9 Economies of scale—either in planting, production, or processing—are a standard argument for the economic advantages of a large-scale organization of tree crop plantations (Graham and Floering 1984, Pryor 1982). Large-scale projects are seen as a means of organizing smallholders' activities to capture the technical economies of scale attributed to plantations. However, there do not seem to be important economies of scale in rubber production or marketing. Even though there are technical economies of scale in land clearing, it is hard to argue that the high costs and mediocre results of land clearing and planting contracted by NES schemes and PMUs are superior to smallholders' efforts on their own. Certainly in maintenance and harvesting there are few scale economies. Indeed, plantations have sought protection from the competition of smallholders throughout the history of rubber production in Southeast Asia (Bauer 1948, Thee Kian Wee 1977, Barlow 1978, Pelzer 1978a, Dillon 1985).

10 This estimate corresponds to the total of five years of planting in REPELITA III and four years so far of planting in REPELITA IV (Appendix, Table 2).

11 The dispersal strategy is analyzed in detail in Barlow, Shearing, and Dereinda (1991).

12 This also means that few Indonesian smallholders have had an opportunity to learn by using higher-yielding varieties.

13 The Department of Agriculture did not have complete control over these funds, however. Under this funding scheme, the National Planning Board (BAPPENAS) had to approve project proposals and the Department of Finance monitored disbursement of funds.

14 John Thomas's 1975 study of tubewell irrigation in East Pakistan is an early example of the organizational cultures that lead donors to support large-scale, capital-intensive projects.

15 A comparable pattern appeared in the evolution of the land reclamation program in Egypt. A joint venture period ensued after the demise of the state farm reclamation strategy. The difference is that in Egyptian land reclamation there was little or nothing that the public sector should have been doing other than regulating access to land and, perhaps, funding applied research. In Indonesia, the risk is that the opportunity for a promising market-oriented approach to smallholder development will be lost while effort and funds go to encourage large-scale private investments that perpetuate questionable development models.

Appendix

Table 1 **Planned Actual Government-Sponsored Planting Projects for Major Smallholder Tree Crops** (Ha)

	Repelita III (1979/80 to 1983/84)			Repelita IV (1984/85 to 1988/89)		
	Planned	Actual	%	Planned	Actual[a]	%
Rubber	269,000	190,193	71%	416,000	103,567	25%
Palm Oil	96,500	35,116	36%	694,000	77,836*	11%
Coconut	227,400	186,858	82%	471,500	56,202	12%
Coffee	94,100	58,849	63%	40,500	58,169	144%
Pepper	48,000	16,138	34%	35,000	14,428	41%
Cocoa	27,500	4,671	17%	22,500	n.a.	
Cloves	20,450	2,189	11%	47,500	0	0%
Tea	5,000	2,346	47%	15,311	8,626	56%
Other[b]	n.a.	n.a.		36,500	n.a.	

a. Through 1987/88, the fourth year of the five-year plan.
b. Other = nutmeg, kapok, cassiavera, vanilla
n.a. not available
 * preliminary

Source: DGE

| Table 2 | Ha Planted Smallholder Rubber Block Planting and Preplanting, 1979/80 to 1987/88 |
Block Planting	1979/80	1980/81	1981/82	1982/83	1983/84	1984/85	1985/86	1986/87	1987/88	Total
NES/PIR	4,858	13,723	18,545	27,317	30,236	33,235	15,108	11,687	2,978	157,687
SRDP Type		4,066	5,698	8,866	7,808	4,771	2,992	8,150	20,000	62,351
PSRSB (West Sumatra)	330.5	963.5	1,183	1,361	1,099	816	1,374	569		7,696
PRPTE :										
Replanting	4,530	9,965	18,272.1	27,199	3,539	0	0	1,886.6		65,392
Rehabilitation	0	634	0	0	0	0	0	0		634
Total Area										
Project (SH)	9,718.5	29,351.5	43,698.1	64,743	42,682	38,922	19,474	22,292.6	22,978	293,760

Source: DGE

Table 3 Planted Areas and Production of Rubber, 1973-1987

| | Smallholdings | | | | | Grand Totals | |
| | Area ('000 ha) | | | | Smallholdings | | |
Year	Immature	Mature & Tapped	Old and Productive	Total ('000 t)	Total Prodn. ('000 ha)[a]	Area ('000 t)	Prodn.
1973	331.7	1,226.1	298.2	1,856.0	497.0 (487)	2,347.4	844.2
1979	331.7	1,295.9	298.6	1,926.2	673.0 (519)	2,384.0	971.9
1983	473.9	1,329.1	314.9	2,117.9	673.6 (507)	2,529.0	907.0
1985	499.0	1,339.7	325.3	2,164.1	686.9 (514)	2,657.5	1,044.0
1987	984.315	1,497.8	b	2,482.1	801.1 (535)	3,006.8	1,131.7

a.   Figures in ( ) brackets are yields in kg. per ha. of mature tapped area.
b.   Included in "mature and tapped"

Source: Barlow, Shearing, and Dereinda (1991) and DGE data.

Trade Policy Reform in Indonesia

Richard R. Barichello and Frank R. Flatters[1]

Richard R. Barichello is head of the Department of Agricultural Economics, University of British Columbia, Vancouver, Canada. From 1986 to 1988, he served as senior resident adviser to HIID's Indonesia Fiscal Reform Project and the Customs and Economic Management Project. He continues to work on the analysis of agricultural, industrial, and trade policies in Southeast Asian countries and Canada.

Frank R. Flatters served as senior resident adviser to the HIID Fiscal Reform Project in Indonesia from 1983 to 1986 and is now professor of economics at Queen's University, Kingston, Canada. He has continued to consult on trade policy for HIID Indonesia projects and is also coordinating economic policy research projects at the Malaysian Institute of Economic Research and the Thailand Development Research Institute.

Introduction

For an oil-exporting country like Indonesia, the decade of the 1980s has tested the limits of resiliency of economic policies and of the economy itself. The massive swings in oil prices, the inflationary world conditions in the early 1980s, followed by the recession before the end of the first half of the decade, the significant fluctuations in nominal and real interest rates, and the dramatic realignments of the world's major currencies have all contributed to what might be an economist's dream, but a policymaker's nightmare. Partly by design, and partly by good fortune, Indonesia's response to these shocks included a significant reform of trade policies. This reform is a major cause of the remarkably good shape in which Indonesia has emerged from this turbulent decade. This paper reviews this reform process, focusing on the interplay of different currents of thought and interests concerning the design of trade and industrial policies over the period, and tries to trace the roles of the external economic environment and the economic views and political influence of and strategies followed by various significant actors in the policy process. We conclude with some observations on the lessons arising from the reform efforts.

Background[2]

Indonesia is a large country whose geography and history dictate an important role for international trade. Natural resource products have traditionally made up the major share of her exports—timber products, rubber, and coffee dominating until the early 1970s, and oil becoming the most important following the first OPEC oil boom in 1973. By the early 1980s oil accounted for about two-thirds of total exports and of government revenues.

Following the inward-looking, excessively regulated, and often corrupt policies of the late Sukarno years, the "New Order" government of President Suharto launched a long-term economic recovery program. This was based on improving the overall investment environment, achieving balance between the urban and rural sectors, and, most importantly, providing sound macroeconomic management. Responsibility for the New Order economic policies has been delegated in large part to a small group of foreign-trained "technocrats." These technocrats, who have occupied many of the important economic ministries over this period, have had little, if any, independent political base and have relied for their authority on their ability to provide the economic underpinnings for the president's continued political support.

While the New Order government has provided sound macroeconomic management, the success of its microeconomic policies has been more mixed. At this level, the government has often yielded to the temptation to interfere with and distort the signals given by market prices. Complex sales tax structures, widespread use of ad hoc investment incentives and tax exemptions, hidden subsidies to large numbers of state enterprises, and discriminatory credit subsidy programs are but a few examples of the policies in force by the beginning of the 1980s. In the microeconomic sphere, the New Order regime showed greater continuity with respect to the Sukarno policies. This reflected in part the difficulties in eliminating the rent-generating possibilities created by these sorts of policies (of which more below), but also a genuine paternalistic sense of the

272

need, for equity and efficiency reasons, to "guide" the "unsophisticated" local populace. This view is also a strong legacy of the Dutch colonial regime.

Early 1980s: Problems on the Horizon

Retrospect and Prospect

In many respects the Indonesian economy in the early 1980s appeared to be a great success story. Following a period of low and even negative economic growth in the mid-1960s, and a difficult period of recovery in the late 1960s and early 1970s, Indonesia showed remarkable growth afterwards. Overall GDP growth from 1965 to 1980 averaged 7.9 percent per year. Growth of manufactured goods production over the same period was 12 percent per year, one of the highest rates in the world, exceeded significantly only by South Korea.

These healthy signs notwithstanding, some gloomier prospects and symptoms were appearing on the horizon. A significant part of economic growth over this period had been due to increases in the volume and value of oil exports. Even without the (not yet foreseen) collapse of oil prices in the second half of the decade, it was becoming apparent that growing domestic consumption and leveling-off of production growth would reduce the future contribution of oil to exports and government revenues. And yet the rapidly growing manufacturing sector had not yet made any significant contribution to exports. Furthermore, the manufacturing sector so far had made less contribution to badly needed employment growth than might have been expected. Even more worrisome was that by the early 1980s overall growth, and, especially manufacturing growth, was beginning to slow down.

By the early 1980s these symptoms were not yet viewed as major problems. And even those who had recognized the symptoms were later surprised by the speed with which the oil price collapse of the second half of the 1980s brought it all to a crisis. In the meanwhile, the early 1980s saw the beginning of a clearer definition among policymakers of several different points of view about the appropriate policy stance at this stage of the country's development. This might best be discussed in conjunction with an outline of the interdepartmental distribution of powers over trade and industrial policies in the Indonesian government.

Policy Instruments and Players

The principal line departments and agencies concerned with these policies are the Departments of Finance, Industry, and Trade, and the Investment Licensing Board (BKPM). Other important players include the Ministry of Economic Planning (BAPPENAS), the Junior Minister of Administrative Reform, the Junior Minister for the Promotion of Domestic Products, and, performing a general guiding and coordinating role, the Economic Coordinating Minister f- Finance, Industry, and Trade (EKUIN). As in many other countries *¹ tend to be segregated into different groups according to th~' appropriate role and functions of government in econom, strongly dirigiste camp in Indonesia have been the Mir Industry, BKPM, and the Junior Minister for the Pron Products. Closer to the other end of the spectrum have beer Finance, BAPPENAS and EKUIN, and the Junior Minister

Reform. These differences in views tend to coincide with the policy instruments which these players control.

The Department of Trade sets regulations and issues licenses for a wide variety of business activities related to the conduct of domestic and international trade. It exercises formal control over all nontariff import and export policies. The basis for much of their regulatory activity through most of the 1980s, at least over imports, was a set of decrees issued in 1982, and revised in 1983, concerning the regulation of imports of major groups of industrial commodities. These set out a variety of categories of import licenses, from the fairly general category of "general importer" (IU) to that of "state trading company." In between were the categories of producer-importers and sole agents. Under these decrees the department was authorized to determine, for each of the covered commodities, the type of import license that would be required to import it, the companies that would be granted these licenses, and, if desired, the quantities and types of imports permitted of each good by each licensed importer. The exercise of these powers became a large part of the story of trade policies and reforms therein for the remainder of the 1980s.

BKPM is responsible for granting investment licenses to all foreign or joint venture firms and to domestic firms wishing to use investment incentives administered by this board. These incentives in the early 1980s included income tax holidays together with sales tax and import duty exemptions on capital equipment and on imported raw materials. In addition to approving individual investment applications and incentives, BKPM developed, maintained, and revised lists of sectors and types of projects that were open or closed to new investments, according to type of investor. This List of Investment Priorities (DSP) is prepared in consultation with the Department of Industry.

The Department of Industry is charged with encouraging and monitoring industrial development according to its views of the appropriate patterns and timing of this development. Aside from granting certain industrial licenses, the Department of Industry has little formal power over important policy instruments. However, through its general influence and its active participation on an interdepartmental (finance, industry, and trade) import policy team, it obtained significant indirect control over most of the important instruments of trade and industrial policy.

The Department of Finance assists in determining overall government spending levels and priorities, and has primary responsibility for raising taxes. Nonoil revenues in the early 1980s came primarily from domestic sales and excise taxes, import duties and sales taxes, and income taxes. Much of the authority to change individual tariff rates in response to special needs and to grant full or partial import tax exemptions was vested in Customs. The import policy team played a major advisory role on these questions.

Preparing for the Future

The successes of the first decade-and-a-half of the New Order government were cause for well-deserved self-congratulation among policymakers. But the early 1980s also brought the first indications of problems to come. Control over trade and industrial policies was dispersed, as were the views of the appropriate form of such policies. The need for major reforms was not at the top of anyone's agenda. There was a general wariness of excessive reliance on oil income. But this concern was expressed primarily through a cautious approach to the fiscal position of the government—tight control over public expenditures and the search for ways of improving nonoil revenue collections.

The decision to explore the need for reform of trade and industrial polices was a byproduct of the reform of the tax system.[3] In 1982, while planning this tax reform, it was realized that attempts to increase the simplicity and neutrality of the tax system would make more sense if some of the major distortions in the structure of import duties and other elements of trade policy could also be removed. Therefore, the government decided to broaden the work on reform of the tax system to include an examination of trade policies. This work got under way in 1983, soon after the appointment of the new cabinet, and became a principal source of information to the government on the structure and major economic effects of the trade policy regime. In the following section we present an overview of the methods and major conclusions of this work.

The Structure and (Unintended) Effects of Trade Policy

The examination of the structure and effects of trade and industrial policies followed several paths. Some of it was a byproduct of assistance in dealing with special petitions to the government for changes in protection. This involved investigating and making recommendations on requests, developing systematic procedures that could be used to handle such cases in the future, and training government officials to do this themselves. Longer-term, more "research-oriented" work included: a) cataloging and monitoring the development and application of all trade and industrial policy instruments; b) an economywide effective protection study encompassing the effects of a large number of trade policy instruments; and c) a number of case studies of particular sectors of the economy.

By the end of two years, considerable information had been accumulated. Although much of it had been passed on to the government as it had been completed, the government requested at this time (early 1985), and was given, a consolidated and detailed review of the principal conclusions, together with recommendations for future policy directions. The conclusions would have been familiar to analysts who had worked in a large number of other countries over the previous decade or two. What might have distinguished this work was the amount of detailed documentation, especially in the form of case materials, that had been accumulated. These detailed case materials, with their well-documented "horror stories," were an important source of the value of this work in persuading policymakers of the need for change.

Previous work had classified Indonesia's trade policy regime as of the "moderate import substitution" type. The work commissioned by the government confirmed the strong import substitution bias of trade policies in the early 1980s. The bias was achieved through the use of a wide variety instruments. Ad valorem import duty rates ranged from 0 a large number of specific rates as well. Import and don varied considerably across products, but much less so than i sales tax rates were generally greater than domestic rates or yielding a further degree of protection for domestic good: restrictions had also become very important; by the mid-1980 of the line items in the Tariff Book, or 35 percent of total imports by (1982) value, were covered by some form of such restrictions. These ranged from a few outright bans and zero quotas, to nonzero quotas and a wide variety of restrictive import licensing arrangements that provided varying degrees of protection against imports. Increased local content of manufacturing was encouraged by "deletion programs" that forced producers of finished products to source certain components locally. Investment and industrial licensing regulations also were used to protect existing producers against further domestic competition. This protection was usually in the form of tight investment restrictions in industries in which domestic capacity was judged to be sufficient to meet local market demand.

Exports of a variety of goods were restricted to ensure that local supplies would be adequate to "meet domestic needs." And exports of some commodities, most importantly logs, were being increasingly restricted, both to encourage domestic downstream processing and to attempt to exercise monopoly power in world markets. Quality control requirements were having similar restrictive effects on the export of some commodities. On the other hand, certain measures, most notably the "export certificates program," were being used as a form of export subsidy. Although designed to provide relief from import duties on imported raw materials used by exporters, its implementation had turned it into a direct subsidy program for selected exporters.

The resulting trade policy regime was characterized by levels of protection that were on average high and at the same time highly varied across sectors. The effective protection study based on the 1980 input-output table and trade policies in effect in early 1984 (but excluding the effects of investment licensing arrangements and industrial deletion programs) provided confirmation and some quantification of these effects. Figure 1 shows the wide distribution of

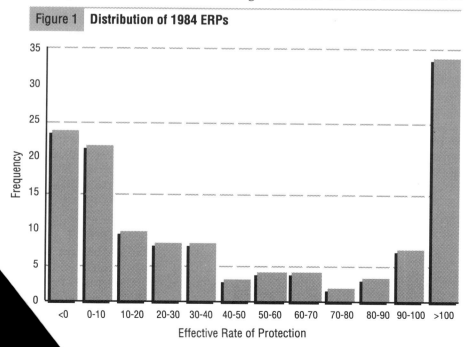

Figure 1   Distribution of 1984 ERPs

effective protection rates across sectors. Table 1 aggregates these rates in several different ways and shows some of the patterns or biases of the protection structure. Most of these patterns are familiar to those who have done similar work in other developing countries. Imports are very heavily protected relative to exports. Manufacturing is strongly favored relative to agriculture and resource-based sectors. Under some weighting schemes the usual pattern of escalating protection from primary to intermediate to final goods sectors appears. Under other weights, intermediate goods seem to get more protection than final goods. This less typical result reflects the growing tendency at that time to promote certain basic industrial raw materials sectors, especially steel and plastics.

Given the inefficiency and relatively low labor intensities of highly protected sectors compared to the less protected ones, it was possible to give some indication of the perverse employment and foreign exchange earning effects of these policies. The usual argument of advocates of protection was that it generated employment and saved foreign exchange. Using numbers from this and other studies, it was possible to show that investments induced by high protection of import substitutes generated only one-quarter of the jobs as would the same investments in export production. Similarly, a switch of investment from import sectors to exports would result in four U.S. dollars' worth of new foreign exchange earnings in the growing sector for every dollar lost in the shrinking sector. Similar, but smaller, results followed simply from switching investments from heavily protected import-competing sectors to less heavily protected ones.

Table 1	Average Effective Rate of Protection (ERP)		
Sector	Unwtd. Avg.	Wtd. Avg.	Median
1. Imports	349	319	70
2. Nonoil exports	86	29	1
3. Mfg. imports	431	500	92
4. Mfg. exports	222	123	9
5. All nonoil	271	203	30
6. All mfg.	395	410	70
7. All nonoil, nonmfg.	19	27	4
8. Capital goods	24	17	9
9. Inputs (nonoil)	216	252	30
10. Final goods	401	149	38

As dramatic as were these results from the effective protection work, the conclusions and evidence from the case studies were more persuasive and more useful to the policymakers who wanted to understand the effects of the poli regime and to begin to reform it. Particularly helpful was a pro approach to measuring the effects of protection that was for this work. This method was designed both to analyze trade policies and to assist in appraising requests for chang financial analysis of trade policies was a generalization of the method to measure the protective effects of different policies value of a firm or investment over its entire lifetime. Capital expenditures were specifically included in the calculation of cash flows. The economic analysis replicated the financial analysis except that it used shadow prices rather than market prices in evaluating cash flows. This method is most analogous to the traditional domestic resource-cost literature. In addition to the quantitative results derived from the use of this method, the information about the methods of implementation of trade policies gathered during the process of interviewing and data gathering at the firm level was also very useful.

The results of these case studies reinforced and amplified those of the effective protection exercise. Protection was shown to provide strong incentives to import substitution activities, even for firms and sectors that could have been export competitive. Protection raised costs of Indonesian producers and caused many types of inefficiencies. The combination of capacity-licensing and import protection policies often resulted in premature and excess investment. Trade and industrial policies reduced the demand for labor, decreased competition, increased the concentration of industry and wealth, and caused major distortions in investment allocation. The growing use of import restrictions on basic industrial raw materials discouraged the development of assembly activities into full manufacturing industries. This problem was compounded by the use of deletion programs to force assemblers into high-cost domestic components production. All of this precluded the development of a low-cost, labor-based, manufacturing export sector.

At least as important as the direct economic effects of these policies were the results of their method of implementation. Most pertinent in this respect were: a) the growing use of nontariff import restrictions, and b) the increasingly ad hoc way in which changes in policy were occurring. These two phenomena were quite closely related. By the mid-1980s, a clearly understood pattern for the granting of protection had developed. Firms that were willing to invest in "priority" sectors, as identified in discussions with the government (primarily the Department of Industry), felt assured that as soon as the capacity of that sector was "sufficient to meet domestic demand" and as long as there were at least two domestic producers, they would be rewarded with a ban on the import of competing products and often the closing of the industry to further investment. This was not felt to be an ironclad guarantee, but the feeling was that meeting the additional requirement of having the "right" local partners would increase the certainty of such favorable treatment. These understandings were based not only on promises and assurance given by government officials, but also by continued and increasing observation of the system in action. As might have been expected, this sort of regime encouraged the allocation of a major portion of entrepreneurial energies to the game of securing a clear or near monopoly in the domestic market.

This system of protection provided arbitrary and sizable subsidies to particular firms and individuals. Their value to protected firms (and their costs to users of protected goods) depended very much on the implementation of nontariff import restrictions. The powers authorized in the Department of Trade's 1982 and 1983 general decrees on import regulation were used in many different and creative ways. In some instances import licenses were granted only to the sole domestic producer(s) of the restricted goods. In others they were granted to a few state trading companies. And in yet others they were provided to "importer-producers," or industrial users of imported goods. In almost all cases, the amounts and allocations of imports of restricted goods were subject to intense and costly negotiations with the Departments of Trade and Industry. The sizes of the subsidies (negative or positive) provided by these restrictions could be very large—often as much as one-and-one-half to two times (in present value terms) the total amounts invested by the affected firms. In these circumstances it was not surprising to hear many stories about the importance of rent-seeking activities in the conduct of business in Indonesia. The returns from these activities, when successful, clearly exceeded those from any conceivable investments in productivity improvement and market promotion.

To the economist, the general need for and direction of trade and industrial policy reforms was clear. Most important, the ad hoc and arbitrary nature of these policies had to be changed. The use of nontariff trade restrictions had to cease. Existing nontariff restrictions had to be rolled back and, if necessary, replaced by tariff protection. The general level of import protection had to be reduced, as did the variance in protection across activities. This would require a general reduction in the level and variance of nominal tariffs. The use of industrial licensing restrictions, especially capacity licensing, industry closures, and deletion programs, had to cease.

To some policymakers these conclusions were not surprising. In these cases, the background documentation was viewed as useful material for persuading others. For them, the main questions concerned the appropriate timing of reforms and the strategy for persuading others. The general view with respect to timing was that eliminating the use of nontariff restrictions should be the first order of business. There were others who, when briefed on the research findings, were initially surprised, but eventually convinced of their validity. And there were others who were firmly wedded to the existing policy regime. It was the latter who would have to be either persuaded or overruled in the ensuing discussions. The strong emphasis on consensus in decision making in Indonesia made the former the much preferred route.

External Events, Internal Pressures, and the Beginning of the Reforms

Antecedents: Tax and Customs Reform

Several steps in the direction of trade policy reform had been attempted and/ or taken even before these debates had begun. In 1981 the Department of Finance had prepared a new tariff schedule which involved a moderate reduction in the average level and variance of nominal rates. Unfortunately, a variety of factors, including fear of being perceived to be responding too directly to pressures from international organizations, prevented this from being implemented.

The tax reform of 1984-85 had several direct and indirect impacts on trade and industrial policy. The replacement of the complex system of domestic and import sales taxes by a uniform value-added tax (VAT) on domestically marketed manufactured goods reduced the levels and variance of nominal protection to domestic goods and reduced the bias of the fiscal system against exports. The elimination of tax holidays and other forms of tax-based investment incentives reduced some of the distortions of investment policies and significantly lessened the leverage of the Investment Licensing Board over investors. Finally, in 1985, the Department of Industry argued that increases in input costs caused by the VAT required offsetting adjustments in tariff rates to compensate producers for decreases in protection. Despite the obvious fallacy of the basic argument, the proposals, which turned out to be quite similar to those which had been withdrawn by the Department of Finance in 1981, were accepted and incorporated in a new tariff. The result was a tariff structure with a mildly reduced average level and variance of effective rates of protection across sectors.

The most important trade policy reform in the first half of the 1980s occurred in April 1985 with a set of decrees issued under Presidential Instruction No. 4 (Inpres 4). Inpres 4 introduced an unprecedented reform of importing and exporting procedures aimed at reducing the costs of clearing goods through Indonesian ports. The most important single change was the replacement of Indonesian Customs as the agent for customs processing of all Indonesian imports (except for shipments of less than U.S. $5,000 in value) and exports (where necessary). Their responsibilities were assigned, on a contract basis, to a Swiss surveying company, SGS, who would inspect, classify, and value shipments to (and from) Indonesia in the foreign port of export (or import). In addition, these decrees abolished a large number of other costly and unnecessary port and shipping regulations. These sweeping reforms had an immediate and direct impact on port costs. The Indonesian Importers' Association reported that within months of the introduction of these reforms importing costs had fallen, on average, by more than 20 percent. Exporters had similar stories. A food processing company, for instance, found that its shipping costs had fallen by U.S. $500 per container, or about 25 percent of their previous levels, as a direct result of these reforms.

Inpres 4 represented a major contribution to the reform of trade policies in Indonesia. Its design and implementation, however, were not viewed at the time as part of such reforms. Rather, its design was coordinated by the Minister of Administrative Reform, and it was thought of as that—a major reform of administrative machinery. Its genesis was unrelated to the ongoing work on trade and industrial policies. It arose instead out of frustration with the high costs and corruption of port clearance procedures and undoubtedly had the support of important businessmen who were able to persuade authorities of the necessity for radical change. And radical changes these were. The Customs Department had long been a secure and lucrative source of unofficial income. Inpres 4 put an immediate end to this. In addition to its direct effects on the costs of foreign-trade-related activities, Inpres 4 provided a clear signal of the government's intent to make other major reforms where necessary, and it also opened up a very fruitful public debate on the reasons for and possible solutions to the problems of Indonesia's "high-cost economy." These discussions soon came to focus on the unintended effects of trade and industrial policies.

Internal Discussions, External Events, and the May 6th Reform Package

The growing public debate and cabinet-level discussions covered many issues. But two of the recurring themes were the cost-raising effects of policy-induced private and public monopolies in many key sectors of the economy and the poor performance of nonoil exports, which also came to be recognized as being due in large part to the inward-looking trade and industrial policies. There was by the mid-1980s a growing consensus among policymakers and increasing numbers of private entrepreneurs that the import substitution regime was no longer delivering on many of its promised benefits and was not contributing to the growth of the economy. Investment in protected sectors had fallen badly as a result of the excess capacity that had been induced by the nature of the "protection game." And now that the "easy" import substitution and growth possibilities in consumer goods sectors had been exhausted, further development along these lines required protection of upstream industries. These sectors were more capital intensive and, hence, often were less competitive than many basic consumer goods sectors and generated far less employment and very little export growth. Equally important, in terms of the changing political pressures facing the government, was the fact that protection of upstream industries imposed immediate costs on other sectors that used these products in their own production. This was especially true in the case of nontariff import restrictions, whose arbitrary effects were not borne equally by different producers. While this was true of almost all nontariff barriers (NTBs), it was most important, and most obvious, in cases where some vertically integrated producers had access under the import licensing arrangements to imported inputs, while others were forced to rely on these licensed importers *cum* sole domestic producers for the same inputs. This general phenomenon had implications for all domestic producers, not just exporters.

The concern over nonoil export performance was given greater focus by the threat, beginning in late 1984, of countervailing action against Indonesian textile exports to the United States market. The basis of the United States complaint was primarily the export certificates program. As mentioned before, this program was drawn up originally as a method to compensate exporters for tariff-induced high costs of imported inputs. But the method of implementation, with import content ratios and cost increase factors determined (on a narrowly defined commodity-by-commodity and firm-by-firm basis) by separate interdepartmental teams several times per year, and implemented separately by the Departments of Trade and Finance, had turned it into a specific subsidy program for particular exporters. The relationship between the size of the subsidy and the appropriate duty drawback equivalent had become increasingly tenuous. In the case of textiles, there clearly was very great abuse of the system, with most of the benefits accruing to a small number of exporters.

By early 1985 it was clear that a ruling unfavorable to Indonesia was inevitable and that it would be necessary for Indonesia to take some action to avoid considerable damage to its growing textile exporting sector. The agreement that emerged was for Indonesia: a) to sign the GATT Export Subsidy Accord, and b) to undertake to phase out the export certificates program by mid-1986. The latter was a condition for the former. In addition to removing the immediate danger of the United States countervailing action against Indonesian textiles, this had several other longer-term implications. The first was the necessity to replace the export certificates program with a duty drawback program that was consistent with the newly signed GATT Accord. Without some such program, most Indonesian producers, burdened by protection-induced high raw material costs, would be unable to become export competitive. Unfortunately, the GATT rules do not permit any form of subsidy to compensate exporters for high costs due to nontariff import restrictions; only drawbacks on import duties actually paid are permitted. Since a large and growing segment of Indonesian production was protected by nontariff barriers, this meant that the GATT rules would be a serious constraint on Indonesia's ability to relieve exporters of the burdens of import protection. The alternative, of course, was to begin to attack the problems of import protection head-on by beginning to dismantle the entire system of import regulation.

The textile episode, therefore, and its result in the signing of the GATT Accord, placed an important weapon in the hands of those wishing to draw attention to the need for major trade policy reforms. By focusing attention on the need to expand nonoil exports and showing the harmful effects of import protection in this regard, they were able to make a persuasive case for reform. For the first time, the interrelated and cumulative harmful effects of the trade and industrial policy regime became evident to a wide audience. Furthermore, a logical sequencing of reforms became evident. Aside from the urgent need to replace the export certificates program, the inability to compensate exporters for the harmful effects of nontariff restrictions under any such program made it clear that the first order of business in trade policy reform would have to be this form of protection. The reform of tariff rates and of investment licensing rules could come later.

By far the other most important external event at this time was the collapse of world oil prices that began at the end of 1985. Oil prices had been declining steadily since 1981. But the precipitous fall of over 60 percent in only a few months, provoked by the disintegration of the OPEC production arrangements, was a major shock to Indonesia's balance of payments. This provided the most urgent argument imaginable for the elimination of policy-induced barriers to the development of nonoil exports and for major deregulatory reforms to eliminate the policy-induced causes of Indonesia's high-cost economy.

These external events helped to provoke major discussions of the trade policy regime. The two initial results of these discussions were: a) some convergence of opinion on the role of nontariff import restrictions, and b) the development of a replacement for the export certificates program. We discuss these in turn.

By the end of 1985 there was general agreement among the major economic ministries to discontinue the use of nontariff import restrictions. This meant, in the first instance, that any new import restrictions would be in the form of tariffs; no new nontariff barriers would be imposed. The import policy team, in effect, was restricted to recommending only changes in tariff rates. In the longer run, the agreement meant that existing nontariff barriers eventually would be dismantled. No schedule or procedures for this longer-run process were agreed to at that time. The shorter-run decision changed the momentum that had developed with respect to the use of nontariff import restrictions.

For several months no new nontariff restrictions were imposed. Although domestic firms continued to press for import bans, there was now at least some doubt as to whether they would be granted almost automatically as in the past. A transitional problem arose, however, from the fact that some firms had already invested under the assumptions of the "old system." As might have been expected under these circumstances, several firms managed to have the "EKUIN agreement" overruled in their cases. When this happened, in early 1986, a cloud of doubt was placed over the government's real intentions and its power to act in a consistent manner in the realm of trade policy reform. The momentum of trade policies certainly had shifted in the direction of less regulation, but how much and for how long were still uncertain.

In the meanwhile, the planning for the replacement of the export certificates program was also well under way by late 1985. With external assistance provided by an international organization, a duty drawback system modeled after the highly successful Korean program was being developed. This system was based on representative input coefficients calculated and continually updated by technical experts in the Department of Industry. What was overlooked in the design of this system was the question of Indonesia's administrative capacity to operate it. While this system might have been successful in Korea, the likely outcome in Indonesia would be a replication of the old export certificates program. Only in very late 1985 were these proposals brought to the EKUIN level and these dangers recognized. The problems were viewed as sufficiently serious to begin to explore, even at this late date, the possibility of a completely different system. For this purpose, the Department of Finance began a parallel, independent planning exercise to develop a simple drawback system based on the model of Indonesia's new value-added tax. In less than a month the Finance Department had prepared a complete set of draft laws for such a system, and the general principles of this alternative were agreed to by the drafting team working under the supervision of the minister of Administrative Reform.

A problem common to any type of duty drawback program, as mentioned before, is that it could not compensate exporters for high input costs resulting from nontariff import barriers on these products. And direct subsidies for this purpose were ruled out under the terms of the GATT subsidy accord. Yet, it was now recognized that failure to deal with this problem, until the longer-term plan to eliminate nontariff import barriers was implemented, would leave the new system seriously flawed. The innovative solution devised in Indonesia was to extend import privileges for exporters to include the right to import required inputs *free of any import licensing or quota restrictions on these products*. Thus, the set of decrees issued on May 6, 1986, (the May 6th package) included provisions not only for duty drawbacks and duty exemptions for exporters, but also for the relaxation of all import licensing regulations on inputs required for export production.

All of this still would be insufficient to unburden exporters from the effects of import restrictions if the program were not administered smoothly and efficiently. For this reason a new administrative unit (the Pusat Pengelolaan Pembebasan dan Pengambilian Bea Masuk, or P4BM) in the Department of Finance was charged with this task. The P4BM was provided very strict time guidelines for processing applications and issuing payment authorizations for duty drawbacks, and its own internal operating procedures were developed so as to minimize the opportunities for and possibilities of administrative corruption.

In addition to the relaxed import restrictions for exporters, the May 6th package also included provision for the setting-up of bonded warehousing facilities for exporters and for the simplification of investment licensing rules administered by BKPM.

The May 6th package represented a fundamental change in the direction of Indonesian trade and industrial policies. It signaled a shift from exclusive attention to import substitution to a recognition of the importance of export-oriented development. It resulted from a new understanding of the contradictions between these two modes of development. It indicated some resolve to move away from nontariff barriers as a method of protection against imports. And it marked the beginning of a more general drive to deregulate trade and industrial policies in Indonesia.

Continuation of the Reform Process

The problem now, especially in light of the continuing stagnation of the world oil market, was to keep up the momentum of this reform process. The May 6th package was an important first step, but no more than that. While there was a growing constituency in favor of continuing the reform process, there was at the same time strong resistance to further fundamental deregulation. Despite the general recognition of the need to promote nonoil exports, the cabinet was not allowed to ignore the "need" to continue to protect domestic industries.

The next major policy move, the devaluation of September 12, 1986, was in the realm of macroeconomic management rather than regulatory reform. But it was an important measure, both in light of the overall macroeconomic situation and as an accompaniment to continued import deregulation. As other countries had learned, import deregulation without realistic exchange rate management could have disastrous consequences.

The continuation of the trade reforms proceeded as four further policy packages, on October 25, 1986; January 15, 1987; December 24, 1987; and November 21, 1988. The economic ministers made it clear that the reforms would be an ongoing process, with each new package introducing additional deregulatory measures. At the same time, the wide spectrum of views represented in the cabinet—changed very little since the beginning of the process—shaped the details of each package. The difference was that the discussions now seemed to concern primarily the speed rather than the direction of the policy reforms.

The first two of these packages were concerned almost exclusively with the import restrictions. Deregulation took the form of changes in import licensing arrangements ("simplification of import procedures") and changes in tariff rates. One slight complication pertaining to import licensing procedures was the addition of one further category ("producer-importers") to the list of importer types. But beyond that, the reform of nontariff restrictions consisted of simplifying and codifying the bewildering number and types of import licensing arrangements and shuffling commodities between licensing categories in a general pattern intended to reduce their restrictiveness. There were relatively few instances of complete deregulation of previously restricted goods; that is, permitting such goods to be imported by anyone with a general importing license. The October 25th and January 15th packages together completely deregulated about 17 to 21 percent, by 1982 import values, of previously restricted imports. Most of these were sectors that were becoming export competitive and had not previously been subject to significant import restrictions. The main thrust of the deregulatory reforms was to attempt to increase the range of importers and reduce the number of restrictions for designated commodities. For instance, under the October 25th decrees, the import of forty-eight commodities was simplified by permitting them to be imported by designated sole agents for particular brand names, and another fifty-seven items could now be imported by importer-producers. And in the January 15th package, 142 categories of goods became importable by producer-importers and/or state trading companies. When all these changes were added up, a significant number of import restrictions had been modified by the two reform packages. Aside from the instances of complete deregulation, up to another 25 percent of imports had been, in some sense, partially deregulated.

At the same time, a considerable number of tariff rates were changed. In some cases they were adjusted (usually raised) to compensate for the removal of nontariff protection; i.e., NTBs were replaced by tariffs. But in most cases the story was more complex, with both tariff and nontariff restrictions remaining as sources of protection. In the October 25th package, for instance, there were 154 tariff rate increases and 198 decreases. The stated rationale varied across products. In some cases tariff rates on outputs were increased to compensate for losses in nontariff import protection. In other cases input tariff rates were decreased to compensate for cost increases on these products arising from the September devaluation. And for another group of products, input tariffs were decreased to "improve the competitiveness of Indonesian exporters." In almost all of these instances, the net effect of the tariff changes was to increase protection given to domestic producers. In some of these cases, just as with VAT compensating tariff changes of 1985, the stated rationale did not always stand up to close scrutiny. The 1986 devaluation, for instance, tended to *increase* rather than decrease protection for domestic producers. And the May 6th package had made input tariffs generally irrelevant in determining the competitive position of Indonesian exporters.

The final tariff measure in the October 25th package was the introduction of a provision for the levying of tariff surcharges on selected commodities. This was meant to accomplish several purposes that could be achieved through temporary tariff increases: a) to deal with legitimate claims of foreign dumping behavior; b) to provide short-term increases in protection for other legitimate purposes; and c) to provide temporary adjustment assistance to sectors facing decreased protection due to the removal of nontariff import restrictions. Use of this import surcharge was to be coordinated by a new interdepartmental tariff team, similar in many respects to the old import policy team. The formation of the new team was felt to be necessary partly because of the relative inactivity of the old one, but most importantly because of its inability to stem the growing tide of (successful) special protection requests. Although the general intent of this new tariff surcharge seemed generally clear, the methods and guidelines for its implementation were not clear.

The December 24th package was a compilation of fifty-eight decrees from at least a dozen departments. In addition to further changes in import licensing regulations and tariff rates, it covered export licensing, immigration rules, customs procedures, ownership and capacity licensing requirements for foreign investors, and export credit facilities, and provided a host of licensing and regulatory simplifications for particular sectors, especially tourism. The changes in import licensing were of the same type as those in the previous two packages: a relaxation of restrictions by changing the licensing requirements for particular goods. The main change on the export side was to permit all goods that were not specifically regulated by government decree to be exported by anyone with a general business license. The changes in customs regulations were also designed to assist exporters and investors, as were most of the changes in immigration and investment rules. Major changes in this regard included provisions to permit foreign investors to export products of other Indonesian firms and to increase export production capacity without the need to obtain a new investment license.

The November 21st package included, in addition to a large number of further relaxations of import regulations and associated adjustments in import duties, a considerable deregulation of sea transport. The latter involved reductions in the number of necessary licenses for shipping companies, relaxation of many restrictions on the activities of foreign shippers, and removal of many regulations on route setting and choice of cargoes. These have gone a long way towards reducing costs of international and especially interisland sea transport. The NTB relaxations involved over 300 import categories, over 95 percent of which had all import restrictions removed; i.e., they can now be imported by anyone licensed to be a general importer. The most exciting of the changes were the removal of all NTBs on the import of plastic raw materials and the relaxation of a number of import restrictions on steel products.

These packages do not by any means mark the end of the trade policy reform process. The economic ministers were preoccupied through most of 1989 with the introduction of comprehensive deregulatory reforms in the Indonesian financial sector. Despite this, a significant deregulation of foreign and domestic investment procedures was completed in May of that year. Further deregulation packages are under preparation, and undoubtedly more will follow.

But it is not inappropriate at this time to offer some preliminary evaluation of the success of the reforms. The first measure of success is the performance of the economy in relation to the goals of the reforms. The primary goal of the initial measures, including Inpres 4, the May 6th package, and the September devaluation, was to ease the direct and indirect regulatory burdens faced by Indonesian exporters and investors in the nonoil sectors of the economy. The export figures for 1987 until 1989 provide a strong indication of at least the short-run success of these measures. While oil exports grew by less than 1 percent per year over the period, nonoil exports grew at an annual rate of 26 percent. And manufacturing exports grew by 37 percent per year (40 percent if wood products are excluded). In 1987, for the first time in many years, nonoil exports exceeded oil exports, and by 1989 they exceeded them by more than 50 percent. Manufactured exports alone were 80 percent of the value of oil and gas exports in 1989, compared with only 3 percent in 1980. Similarly, actual and approved investment, after a brief decline following the pretax reform boom in 1984, have shown steady and accelerating growth in recent years. There can be little doubt that much of this growth is attributable to the recent deregulatory measures.

A more indirect indication of the success of the reform process would be a measure of the amount of economic activity that has been deregulated in some form or other. Inpres 4 significantly reduced importing and shipping costs across a very wide range of economic activities. The May 6th package reduced or eliminated the direct cost-raising effects of import regulation on inputs used by many export producers. And the subsequent packages reduced the number of import categories that were subject to nontariff restrictions. By the end of 1989, less than 550 of the approximately 1,250 previously (pre-1986) NTB-regulated Tariff Book categories remained subject to some form of nontariff import restrictions, and many of these had had their import licensing restrictions somehow modified. In addition, many previous restrictions on foreign and domestic investment had been eliminated or relaxed.

According to these general indicators, the reform process appears to be moving rapidly, smoothly, and successfully toward its goal of deregulating trade and industrial policies. But, as we shall see, a closer look at the implementation of the reforms, the process of generating new reforms, and the emergence of new types of regulatory activities suggests that there remains some deepseated resistance to the reforms.

Resistance to the Reforms

In evaluating the significance of the trade reforms to date, it is useful as well to look a little more closely at their implementation. First, if we look beyond a mere "head count" of deregulated import categories, we find that the extent of reform is less than it first appears. While the proportion of regulated items has fallen from just over 30 percent of all those in the Tariff Book to just over 10 percent since 1986, the proportion of domestic production that is covered by these restrictions has fallen by less—from 43 percent to 29 percent. In other words, the goods whose imports have been freed of nontariff restrictions so far have tended to be those that do not compete with domestic production. This reflects, at least in part, a strategy to establish the momentum of the deregulation process by first tackling the "easy" cases, those that will not generate too much resistance from vested producers' interests. But it also indicates that these interests are resisting and using their influence to thwart the reforms.

To get a better appreciation of the nature (and at least partial success) of this resistance, it is instructive to look at the commodities that, in the first stages of the reforms, have been "partially deregulated." Here the gap between appearances and reality is often even greater. The usual claim in these cases has been that certain categories of imports have gone from prereform regulation by a set of restrictions, X, to postreform regulation by another set of restrictions, Y, where Y is allegedly less restrictive than X. Upon closer inspection of some cases, either or both of the following have been discovered to be true: a) The actual prereform restrictions were not X, but another set of rules, Z, which were less restrictive than either X or Y. In some cases goods have gone from being completely unregulated to being quite heavily regulated. b) The postreform restrictions, Y, either in law or in implementation, turn out to be more, or at least no less, restrictive than X, the prereform rules. For instance, in one of the early packages, a large number of goods went from being importable by only one or two state trading companies to being importable by either authorized sole domestic agents for these goods or by producers importing for their own use. Later investigation showed that, many months after the reform, *no* import licenses had been granted for these goods; their import, in effect, had been banned.

Besides the slippage in the implementation of nontariff deregulation, the other major difficulty with the process has been the way in which the tariff system has been used as NTBs have assumed reduced importance. A deliberate part of the initial strategy, of course, had been to replace nontariff protection with tariffs. The tactical issue was whether to try to apply a simple rule for replacing NTBs with tariffs, or to negotiate on a case-by-case basis the size of the tariff surcharge that would be necessary to compensate for reduced NTB protection. Largely out of necessity, it was decided to follow the latter approach. The result was considerable aggravation of the old problem of ad hoc procedures for granting protection. The tariff structure has become even more arbitrary and complex than it had been, with large variations in rates within similar categories of goods, considerable uncertainty about the evolution of protection for particular activities, and the granting of many prohibitive tariffs.

How did these difficulties arise? There is no simple answer, but a number of contributing factors can be identified. First, there was, and continues to be, strong resistance to the reforms on the part of investors in sectors which are heavily protected by the regulatory regime and who have learned how to use the regulatory system to produce commercial success. Such investors had been able to use their often very strong political influence to turn the regulatory regime to their own interests, and they continue to use this power to thwart the intent of the reforms. This, together with a strong and sincere belief at the highest levels of the political leadership in the necessity of paternalistic control and guidance of the economy, has contributed to resistance to deregulation.

Second, at the bureaucratic level, those responsible for issuing import and investment licenses and for creating and administering incentives through the regulatory regime not only remain firm believers in the necessity of these regulations, but also face the prospect of considerable losses of administrative power and privilege in the event of successful implementation of the suggested reforms. This creates another important source of resistance.

Third, the administrative machinery for the design and implementation of the detailed reform packages has been in many respects quite similar to the old import policy team and the new tariff team. While cabinet-level discussions produced consensus and general guidelines concerning the nature and direction of the reforms, the details of the changes were left to be worked out at lower levels. At these levels there was not a strong constituency with an understanding of the reasons or the needs for reform. And those who did represent the reformist view were not sufficiently well versed in the intricacies of the operation of the regulatory regime. In effect, then, the reforms were being designed and then implemented by the officials from the regulatory agencies who had considerable interest in maintaining the status quo. It is not surprising in these circumstances to find various forms of reregulation being slipped by in the form of deregulation.

On the import side, therefore, the reforms are not proceeding as quickly and as smoothly as might have been desired; there is some evidence that the process on occasion has been put in reverse. On the export side, however, some of the arguments that had been used so successfully in promoting the need for deregulation have been employed to launch a direct offensive against the reformers. Recall that one of the primary arguments in favor of deregulating imports and investment was the need to expand nonoil exports. On the basis of some twisting or misunderstanding of the underlying argument, and a favorable interpretation of recent log export policies, a new set of programs has been directed at the control of a variety of primary product exports. Their goal is to encourage increased value added and/or employment in nonoil exports. The basic argument is that Indonesia's dominant position in world markets for these primary products makes it possible to gain from increased prices and/or increased downstream processing that would result from export restrictions and other regulations on these exports. The result of acceptance of these claims has been the implementation of export restrictions, almost always of a quantitative nature, and a variety of other investment and marketing regulations on a wide variety of raw materials, including logs, rattan, latex, and several spice products.

What this represents is a transplant of the familiar import regulation mindset to the field of exports. The headlong rush into export regulation is reminiscent of, but even more precipitous than, what had happened with imports in the late 1970s and early 1980s. And also as in the case of imports, but even more so, the design and implementation of the new policies has been put largely in the hands of a small number of private industrial interests who stand to reap considerable financial returns from them. The principal economic ministers, especially those behind the import policy reforms, have not played a major role in the design of these policies and have not been well positioned to counter them. At the moment, therefore, the reformers are faced with both the difficult struggle to maintain the momentum of the import deregulation process, and the longer-run task of building up evidence, arguments, and support to counter the new trend in export regulation.

While the sources of resistance to the reforms are relatively easily identified, it is important not to forget the dynamics of the proderegulation lobby. The strongest part of this lobby has consisted of exporters whose competitiveness is reduced by trade restrictions of all types and by downstream producers of goods for the domestic market whose costs are increased by reduced competition in the supply of important inputs. The strength of their concerns has been diluted somewhat by several factors. The direct cost-raising effects of import policies on exporters were removed at a stroke with the May 6th, 1986, package. Furthermore, Indonesia's largest nonoil export industry, plywood, is further protected behind the comfortable effects of the log export ban. While the development of other integrated export-oriented manufacturing industries will continue to be hindered by the import regime, *potential* industries have seldom been an effective lobby on behalf of any cause. And while producers for the domestic market continue to be injured by the high costs of protection on their inputs, the regularization of importing procedures and the continued high protection of their own products in the domestic market has blunted somewhat their interest in major new reforms. However, the gradual freeing up of the economy has brought with it more and more competitively oriented investors whose interests are directly tied to continued deregulation. A slowing down, or even worse, a reversal of this process would impose unacceptably higher costs on their activities and destroy their competitive position. Thus, the momentum of the reform process also has some tendency to build its own political support in opposition to those who would resist it.

Some Lessons from the Indonesian Experience

A major reform of trade policies is unlikely to go smoothly even in the best of circumstances. Vested interests in political, administrative, and business circles are bound to resist change, and reputable economists, even when they agree on the broad direction, will disagree on the appropriate speed, ordering, and details of reforms. Especially in light of these observations, it is fair to say that the Indonesian trade policy reform, at least so far, has been a major success. Despite massive external shocks, most importantly the precipitous fall in oil prices and the major currency realignments of the 1980s, and their consequent effects on exports and the debt service burden, Indonesia has continued to prosper and to enjoy the confidence of the international investment and lending communities. We conclude with a discussion of some of the lessons that emerge from or are confirmed by the Indonesian trade policy reform process.

1. Trade policy reforms are more likely to be successful if they are generated from within the country. There are really two points here that can be illustrated from the Indonesian case. First, solutions that are perceived to have been imposed by outsiders might be doomed to political failure. The aborted tariff reform of 1981 is an example. Second, outsiders are prone to suggest solutions that might work in other environments but not in the country being advised. The duty drawback scheme proposed by an outside agency's consultant in late 1985 is an example. This does not mean that external assistance cannot be helpful. It just means that it must work closely with and be sensitive to the economic circumstances, administrative capabilities, and political needs of the client.

2. Careful analysis of the nature and effects of current policies is essential. It is not sufficient just to make the case that "free trade is good." Evidence, both macro and very micro, of exactly how current policies detract from achieving the country's economic goals is important in making this case even to those who are predisposed to agree with the position, but much more so in assisting them to persuade the ultimate decision makers. The gathering and synthesizing of this evidence, unfortunately, is not something that most officials have the time or resources to do.

3. Close and continuous monitoring of the implementation of reforms is necessary. This is just an extension of the previous point. Once they learn the rhetoric of the reforms, those who are opposed to the reforms will be able to clothe their reregulation in the garb of deregulation. Much of this sort of activity in Indonesia would have gone undetected without such monitoring.

4. Regulators often make poor deregulators. In large part this simply represents a perception of policy making ingrained by the habits of many years of regulating economic activity, but self-interest also plays a role. Without a doubt, the two most successful components of the Indonesian reforms so far have been Inpres 4 and the May 6th package. Both of these measures were coordinated largely by a minister without line responsibilities in the affected areas. And, in both cases, the administration of the postreform system was turned over to entirely new agencies. The four reform packages since May 1986, on the other hand, have been developed, and more importantly, implemented, to a much greater extent by the old line departments and agencies. The pace here has been somewhat slower.

5. Adverse exogenous shocks are of great importance in generating a perception of the need for major reforms. The United States countervailing action against Indonesian textiles forced the replacement of the "export certificates" program and resulted in the May 6th package. But most important, the oil price collapse, by slashing Indonesia's major source of government revenues and foreign exchange earnings, made the need for fundamental policy changes urgent and irresistible. At a stroke, this made immediately obvious the reformers' case for the removal of trade policy biases against the development of nonoil exports. And it enabled attention to be focused on the role of the regulatory regime in distorting and raising the costs of economic activity in Indonesia. These were the arguments that legitimized the deregulation not only of trade policies, but also of transport, capital markets, and many other sectors of the economy.

6. The greater the need for reform, the less attainable it will be. Restrictive foreign trade regimes are usually characterized by large opportunities for rent-seeking behavior and coalitions of interests among important subsets of the business, administrative, and political power structures, to take advantage of these opportunities. The tighter these relationships and the higher the rents, the greater will be the strength of the vested interests resisting reform. The proreform interests are generally much more dispersed, and hence less effective. Although many would agree that a deregulated economy runs more smoothly than a heavily regulated one, the actual process of deregulating it can turn out to be much more complex and difficult than that of regulating it.

7. The reforms, once begun, create a constituency for their own continuation. As investors, especially those directed at competitive export markets, are induced by the deregulation to acquire a stake in these activities, they become a lobby in favor of further reforms and opposed to those who would resist and reverse them. The growth of this support might be slow and irregular, but it provides a source of self-perpetuating and increasing momentum for the reform process. ∾

Notes

1   The authors served as the senior resident advisers to HIID's Indonesia Trade Policy Reform Project, Flatters from 1983 until 1986, and Barichello from 1986 until 1988. The advisory team, on whose work much of this paper is based, also consisted of a number of other resident and short-term consultants. Overall, HIID supervision of the project was undertaken initially by Malcolm Gillis, followed by Glenn Jenkins, Michael Roemer, and Joseph Stern. The authors are grateful for comments directly pertinent to this paper from Glenn Jenkins, Sean Nolan, and Michael Roemer.

2   A more complete summary and discussion of Indonesia's postindependence economic performance can be found in Malcolm Gillis (1984).

3   For useful discussions of the Indonesian tax reform, see Malcolm Gillis (1985 and 1989).

Tax Reform: Lessons Learned

Glenn P. Jenkins

Glenn P. Jenkins has been an adviser on tax reform projects in Bolivia, Indonesia, Kenya, Malawi, Sri Lanka, and the Dominican Republic. He was the assistant deputy minister of tax policy and legislation in Canada's Department of Finance from 1981 to 1985. Currently, he is an Institute fellow at HIID and director of the International Tax Program at Harvard University.

Introduction

ince 1984 the world has witnessed a virtual revolution in the field of applied public finance. During the past six years there have been at least twenty-five major tax reforms that have taken an approach to the design of tax systems that is radically different from the norm of the previous three decades.[1] While these tax reforms differ in degree, the common objective of the reforms has been to simplify the structure of the tax systems and to remove incentives for tax avoidance or evasion.

The implementation of reforms to achieve these objectives for income tax systems has led to a dramatic lowering of the top marginal tax rates on personal and corporate taxable income, and the elimination of many specific tax incentives in order to broaden the tax base. In many cases these tax reforms have included the implementation of a simple system of value-added taxation. These value-added taxes (VATs) have been levied at 1-to-3 rates, on a consumption base, while using the tax credit method of administration.

These tax reforms have produced larger changes in tax policies than experienced during the past three decades. Not only have the recommendations of the technical experts changed, but the recommendations are being implemented. As compared to the situation a decade ago, the present design of tax systems and their implementation is far better suited to the realities of the state of development and resources of the country's tax administration.

The Royal Commission on Taxation in Canada (1966) (known as the Carter Commission), and the Musgrave Commission in Colombia (1969), represented the finest work done up to that time in applied public finance. They were comprehensive in nature and set out the analysis, rationale, and recommendations for what was believed to be the best tax system for a developed (Canada) and developing (Colombia) country. Both the Carter Commission's report[2] and the Musgrave Commission's report[3] became the classic references in the area of tax reform and set the standards by which other tax reform studies have been judged.

In terms of implementation, the results were not so dramatic. The recommendations of the Carter Commission became the subject of a heated political debate. The government of the day quickly distanced itself from the commission and gave the impression that the Carter Commission was more or less an academic exercise, certainly not something totally practical.

The resulting Canadian tax reform in 1972 was a pale shadow of what was recommended. One might say that the Carter Commission aimed for the moon, but the tax system landed in the United States. Although the Carter Tax Commission did not accomplish what it set out to do, it did train a number of civil servants and academics in the area of applied public finance. The tax system in Canada is probably better off today because of the commission's work, but the evidence is not overwhelming.

The impact of the Musgrave Commission on Colombia's tax system was less in the short run, but probably more significant in the longer run. The government at that time did virtually nothing to implement the recommendations of the report. It was not until another government took power some four years later (it contained a number of the individuals that had worked with the Musgrave Commission) that many of the recommendations were implemented.[4]

Immediately following the tax reform in Canada in 1972 and the reform in Colombia in 1974, there has been an almost continuous tinkering with the tax systems in both countries. In large part the tinkering in Colombia made things worse, as was the case in Canada until 1981.[5] Most of the tax changes came as a response to the pleading of special interest groups and were aimed at relieving some of the "fine tuning" imposed by the tax reforms.[6]

These two highly public tax reform studies by domestic and foreign tax professionals and academics represented the best of a tradition that began with the Tax Mission to Japan, 1949-50, by Professor Carl S. Shoup.[7] This was followed by the tax reform proposals by Professor Nicholas Kaldor for India (1956)[8] and Sri Lanka (1959),[9] the Musgrave Tax Reform Study for Bolivia (1976),[10] and others. The most recent tax reform study that has followed this tradition is the Tax Reform Commission Report for Israel (1987).[11]

All of these tax reform studies were either only partially implemented or pronounced dead upon publication. Those that were partially implemented, with the exception of the Japanese tax reform, quickly disintegrated.

In contrast to these high profile tax reform studies that have yielded little institutional reform, the tax reforms of Chile (1974),[12] Indonesia (1984-85),[13] New Zealand (1986),[14] and Bolivia (1986)[15] were preceded with little fanfare, but all have had a great impact on their tax systems.

In a similar fashion, Singapore has made a series of tax changes in its annual budgets since the late 1970s. As a result it has transformed and modernized its structure of income taxes. The structure and administration of the income tax system in Singapore is now a model for the developing world to strive toward.[16]

During the past four budget cycles the government of Kenya and the government of Malawi have made major improvements in the structure of their tax systems. The cumulative impact of the changes made is of much greater significance than the advances made by many more dramatic tax reforms of other countries.

Let us consider a number of issues that might have contributed to the success of the tax reform process in these countries.

The Political Economy of Tax Reform

Tax reforms are proposed by ministers, legislated by congresses or parliaments, and implemented by bureaucrats. Unless all three of these governmental bodies support the reform proposals, there is little hope that the ultimate outcome will be favorable. If the tax reform has been a "commissioned" study, as was the case of Bolivia in 1976 or Israel in 1987, the tax reform proposals can easily be branded as an academic publication and be simply ignored.

Alternatively, the recommendations can be distorted in the political process by special interest groups, resulting in retrogression rather than reform. This appears to be what happened in Sri Lanka between 1978 and 1986.[17] If the reform measures have been successfully legislated but are resisted by the tax administration, it is possible that the new system will be so poorly administered that it will eventually collapse, and the old ways of taxation with their familiar irregularities will become the fallback position.

This outcome was the fate of the tax reforms designed by Nicholas Kaldor for India (1956) and Sri Lanka (1959).[18] Even the reform of the income tax system in Indonesia is displaying worrisome signs in that regard. A byproduct of the confusion and embarrassment of an aborted tax reform is that systematic reform of taxes usually becomes politically taboo for some decades.

Successful tax reforms are best illustrated by the comprehensive tax reforms implemented in Indonesia (1984-85), Bolivia (1986), New Zealand (1986), and Jamaica (1986-88).[19] In each of these cases there are a number of common elements, although there are significant differences in the approaches taken.

In all of these tax reforms a key minister, usually the minister of finance, and a number of senior officials in the government were heavily involved in the analysis and preparation of the proposals and legislation. They became committed to the reform as they worked through, or around, the institutional and political constraints. They did not become committed to tax reform as a result of a set of pristine recommendations delivered by a set of outside experts.

In the cases of the Indonesian and the Jamaican tax reforms, much of the analysis and technical advice was undertaken by a large number of foreign advisers. Although academics, these advisers were experienced in the field of taxation and in each case worked closely with their national counterparts for a period of four to five years in the preparation of the reforms.

Particularly in the case of Indonesia, great care was taken at each point in the analysis to present the results to the key ministers and officials.[20] Decisions were made continuously on issues by the authorities throughout the process of preparing the tax reform. Over a hundred policy memos were written and discussed with the ministers and officials of the Ministry of Finance. In the case of Jamaica, thirty-seven formal staff working papers were prepared along with many other policy memoranda.

Continuous political and bureaucratic input is critical in the study stage of a tax reform. In designing a tax system there is usually more than one "right" way to tax a particular type of income to treat a certain type of expense. On most taxation issues the technical analysis requires one to look at the economic efficiency considerations, the administrative and compliance issues, and the magnitude and nature of the adjustment costs that will be incurred.

Political considerations of how a proposal might be "sold" to the other members of the government, the bureaucracy, and the public should always be an essential input when deciding how to treat contentious aspects of the design of a tax system. The economic and administrative solution to a taxation issue that takes into consideration all of these various aspects of the operating environment of the tax system is likely to be more efficient both economically and politically than a solution which ignores any of these aspects.

In the design of tax reform proposals, it is critical to recognize that the tax system affects the largest number of people of any governmental institution in a country. The administrative arm of the tax system is also likely to be the government body with the most regular and frequent contact with the population.

Businesses are in contact with the sales tax authorities perhaps monthly. The ordinary citizen will have some contact with the revenue authorities to pay income taxes or property taxes. Most people are aware almost daily of the sales taxes they pay when they purchase goods and services. As a result, the tax system often becomes the most political of all the economic functions of government.

Because of this reality, tax systems that are unduly complicated, perceived to be unfair, or are implemented in an uneven manner will likely generate political pressures. If the grievances with the tax system continue, one can expect to have changes imposed on the tax system that will relieve this political irritation. If tax relief does not come quickly enough, as was the case with the introduction of the VAT in Guatemala in 1984 and the Stamp Act in the American colonies in 1765, the result is often a revolution.

The end result of a hastily designed or unduly complicated tax reform is generally more tax changes. The United States is a prime example of a process where systematic analysis and tax reform is very difficult to formulate and implement. As a result, for the past ten years the tax system has tended to be in a constant state of flux with massive changes made in almost every budget cycle. Unfortunately, the U.S. tax reform of 1986 is no exception, although the low marginal tax rates will reduce the pressures for special exemptions and incentives. Colombia after the 1974 tax reform, Canada after 1972, and Sri Lanka after its so-called tax reform of 1979 are all prime examples of institutionally destabilizing tax reforms.

In summary, the process of tax reform seems to be carried out best when the analysis of the current situation and what should be done is conducted over a fairly long period of time. At each stage, there should be continuous interaction with the political leadership to determine what is feasible and what will not be possible to implement. When a particular approach to a problem is either administratively or politically impossible, there are likely to be other ways of getting close to the same result but with fewer bureaucratic or political obstacles. Compromises will have to be made. On important issues it is better to design the measures with the compromises already imbedded in them before they are submitted for public examination. If this is not done, there is a high risk that pressures for changes will arise and the managers of the tax reform will have little control over the outcome.

The Evolution of Tax Policies

Direct Taxation

For most of the period since the Second World War, the income tax has been synonymous with modern tax policy. Although the concept of a value-added tax was put forward by Professor Carl Shoup as part of the tax reform proposals for Japan in 1948, it was not implemented until some forty years later.

The income tax has had a great deal of appeal to economists and policymakers alike. It seemed to be the fair way to distribute the burden of financing the expanding demand for public services. People thought it would be possible to design an income tax system that shifted the burden of government finance to high income earners, hence bringing about a redistribution of income. Perhaps more important, from the political point of view, the statutory marginal tax rates could be announced with great fanfare ahead of the actual collection of the taxes. Great claims could be made by the politicians and bureaucrats of their intent to tax the rich to help the poor. At the same time, plenty of tax incentives can be distributed to the politically influential groups in ways that are incomprehensible to those other than direct beneficiaries of tax preferences.

Two aspects of the income tax have been of concern to economists. First, income earned from work is taxed while benefits enjoyed from leisure are not. As a consequence, an income tax tends to discourage work relative to leisure. Unless a tax system were broadened to include in the base of the income tax an imputed amount of "potential income" derived from leisure, this distortion is not eliminated. Thus, there appears to be no viable way to deal with this problem.

Second, an income tax tends to overtax savings relative to consumption (the so-called problem of the double taxation of savings). Under an income tax, savings are cumulated from after-tax income. Furthermore, income from savings is taxed, while enjoyment received from consumption is not. As a consequence, consumers are given an incentive to consume when the gross of tax returns from consumption is less than the gross return from savings.

A solution to this problem is to tax on the basis of the amount of income consumed instead of the amount earned. This idea was developed and eloquently promoted by Nicholas Kaldor.[21] Under this system of taxation, it was the value of the consumption expenditures incurred, not income earned, that would be taxed. It could be administered in the same way as an income tax, with some additional complexity with respect to the accounting of the amounts of income saved. Proposals for the implementation of such a tax system usually called for a progressive rate structure based on the amount of consumption expenditures incurred. There was a concern that the consumption tax would not satisfy the objective of taxation according to the ability to pay. It was feared that those with wealth would cumulate more wealth through untaxed savings and enjoy unwarranted power from the ownership of such wealth. As a result, Kaldor's proposals for implementing a consumption tax system were accompanied by a proposal for a wealth tax.[22]

Whether through taxation of income or through taxation of annual consumption, it was thought by most public finance specialists in taxation, and certainly by policymakers, that a highly progressive statutory rate structure was desirable. The result of such a process caused most tax structures in the 1970s to have statutory rates of tax ranging all the way from 10 to 15 percent at the lowest brackets of taxable income to top marginal tax rates of 70 percent and beyond.

The Carter Tax Commission recommended in 1968 that the top marginal tax rate on individual income be lowered to 50 percent,[23] but when the tax reform came in 1972 the top statutory rate was set at 60 percent. By 1981, the top tax rate in Canada was in excess of 65 percent. As late as 1975, the top marginal tax rate in the United States was in excess of 70 percent. At that time, the United Kingdom had marginal tax rates above 90 percent. New Zealand had a top marginal tax rate of 66 percent until 1986.

Developing countries followed the pattern with high marginal rates of income taxation. For example, as late as 1980, India had marginal statutory rates of taxation on personal income of above 90 percent. Sri Lanka had marginal tax rates in excess of 75 percent. In Colombia the Taylor Mission in the early 1960s[24] recommended a top tax rate of 62 percent, and the Musgrave Commission (1969) proposed the top rate be raised to 55 percent. In 1986, the top marginal tax rate in Jamaica was 57.5 percent, and in Kenya it was 65 percent.

298

Table 1 **Reductions of Top Marginal Rates since 1984**[25]

Top Marginal Income Tax Rates for

	Individuals		Corporations	
	Before Changes	After Changes	Before Changes	After Changes
Country	(no. of tax brackets)			
Australia[26]	57%	47%	46%	39%
Austria[27]	62%(11)	50%(5)	55%	30%
Bangladesh	60%	55%	60%	55%
Barbados[28]	60%	50%	45%	35%
Belgium	72%	55%	45%	43%
Bolivia[29]	40%	10%	30%	2%
Botswana[30]	75%	50%	35%	40%
Canada[31]	34%(10)	29%(3)	36%	28%
Colombia[32]	49%	31%	40%	30%
Denmark[33]	45%	40%	50%	40%
El Salvador[34]	60%	35%	30%	35%
Finland[35]	51%	43%	33%	25%
France	65%	57%	45%	37%
Gambia[36]	75%(12)	35%(6)	47%	47%
Germany (F.R.)[37]	56%	53%	56%	50%
Ghana	65%	55%	60%	45%
Greece	63%	50%	49%	46%
Grenada[38]		0%		0%
Guatemala[39]	42%	34%	48%	34%
Hong Kong	17%	15%	18.5%	16.5%
Iceland	38%	33%	51%	50%
India[40]	62%	50%	55/60%	50/55%
Indonesia[41]	45%	35%	45%	35%
Ireland	58%	53%	50%	40%
Italy	62%	50%	36%	36%
Jamaica[42]	58%	33%	45%	33%
Japan	70%	50%	43%	37%
Kenya[43]	65%	45%	45%	42.5%
Kiribati	50%	40%	35%	35%
Luxembourg	57%	56%	40%	34%
Malawi[44]	50%	45%	50%	45%
Malaysia	55%	40%	40%	35%
Mauritius[45]	70%	35%	66%	35%
Netherlands	72%	60%	42%	40%
New Zealand[46]	57%(5)	33%(3)	45%	33%
Nigeria[47]	70%	55%	45%	40%
Norway	40%	20%	28%	28%
Papua New Guinea[48]	50%	45%	36.5%	30%
Portugal[49]	41/48%	37%	47%	36%
Saint Lucia	60%	30%	45%	33.3%
Singapore[50]	45%	33%	40%	33%
Spain	66%	56%	35%	35%
Sri Lanka[51]	55%	40%	50%	50%
Sweden	50%	20%	52%	52%
Tanzania[52]	75%	55%	50%	50%
Trinidad & Tobago	70%	45%	49.5%	45%
United Kingdom[53]	60%	40%	52%	35%
United States[54]	50%(15)	28%(2)	46%	34%
Western Samoa[55]	60%	50%	42%	39%
Zambia[56]	80%	35%	50%	35/45%

Over time the public finance profession, tax professionals, and politicians came to realize that these very high marginal tax rates were not assisting them in achieving their objective of a more equitable distribution of income. Neither were they taxing according to the principle of the "ability to pay." Conversely, these high marginal tax rates were providing a powerful incentive for the high-income individuals to either evade taxes or to purchase tax advice on how to avoid paying taxes.

In countries with weak tax administrations, the expected cost of tax evasion was often significantly lower than the cost of either paying taxes or buying tax avoidance schemes. The result has been a massive amount of tax evasion and a general breakdown in the ability of the direct tax system to make a substantial contribution to the financial requirements of the public sector.

By the late 1970s, there was some recognition of the destructive effects of higher marginal tax rates on income. A number of studies were carried out showing that although the marginal *statutory* rates increased, the marginal *effective* tax rates stayed almost constant as incomes rose. Such work was also done for Indonesia and Jamaica as part of the studies leading to their respective tax reforms.

The ineffectiveness of high marginal tax rates to bring about income redistribution was not, however, the most serious defect of this type of tax structure. While these high rates determine the taxes due on the highest levels of income, they also are the rates of subsidy given for tax avoidance schemes or compensation towards the penalties of getting caught evading taxes. High marginal tax rates are subsidies for the destabilization of the income tax system. Most tax shelters are not worth creating when the marginal rate of tax is less than 35 percent.[57]

Many of the other stubborn tax policy issues one faces when designing an income tax system disappear or are greatly reduced when the top marginal tax rates are reduced. For example, capital gains are heavily concentrated in the top income brackets. Such gains tend to be periodic; hence, if the income tax is highly progressive some sort of system for income averaging is usually demanded. With a single rate of tax this problem is completely eliminated, or it is greatly reduced if there are only two or three fairly low rates.

Problems created by companies paying for a wide variety of employee benefits (instead of paying additional wages and salaries) also are easily eliminated when the top rates of individual taxation are equal to or lower than the corporate income tax rates. The most difficult problem of income taxation, control over the deductibility of interest expense, is largely solved once capital gains are fully taxed and the lower rates of income tax reduce the value of interest deductions.

Responding to this awareness, in the late 1970s and early 1980s a number of developed countries began to lower their top marginal tax rates on individual income from above 50 percent to approximately 50 percent. In the early 1980s the United Kingdom and the United States both brought their rates down to approximately 50 percent. In 1982, Canada lowered its statutory marginal rate of personal income tax to 50 percent. Singapore made similar moves to lower its top bracket income tax rates to 40 percent. But with only a few exceptions, most developing countries still maintained income tax systems with high top marginal tax rates and masses of special tax preferences until well into the 1980s.

With the implementation of the tax reform in Indonesia, a new mold was struck with respect to the definition of the tax base and rate structure of income taxes. They decided to have only three tax brackets—15 percent, 25 percent, and 35 percent—and apply the same rate structure to both individuals and corporations.[58] At the same time, all special tax incentives were eliminated, and none have been introduced since.[59] Interest expense is not deductible by individual taxpayers, and all capital gains are taxable.[60]

Since 1984 a wave of developing and developed countries have followed these tax policies (see Table 1). New Zealand reduced its top rate of individual income tax from 57 percent to 33 percent and the rate on corporate taxable income from 45 percent to 33 percent. The Philippines lowered its top rate to 35 percent, the United States to about 30 percent, Jamaica to a flat rate of 33.33 percent, the United Kingdom to 40 percent, Colombia to 31 percent, Singapore to 33 percent, and India to 50 percent. While both individual and corporate income tax rates generally have been lowered, there has also been a tendency for the top rates of the two taxes to converge.

Accompanying this lowering of the tax rates has been a dramatic broadening of the base. From the evaluation done to date it would appear that this policy has generally resulted in an increase in income tax revenues. One of the few exceptions has been Indonesia, where the weak administration of the new income tax system has hampered revenue collections. In most countries, the stated policy of the income tax reform was to keep revenues neutral. For increasing tax revenues governments have turned to the indirect tax system, and particularly the value-added tax.

Indirect Taxation

Accompanying the changes in income tax policy has been a movement for a significant improvement in the indirect tax system. Few fiscal innovations have spread as rapidly across both developing and developed countries as has the value-added tax. In 1950 no country used this form of taxation. In contrast, in 1988 over sixty nations used one or another form of the VAT.[61] Over forty are classified as developing countries. Since 1984 at least seventeen countries have implemented value-added taxes. Malawi and Jamaica are now preparing to implement such a tax. Most countries that have adopted the value-added tax have chosen a consumption type of VAT imposed on the destination principle and utilizing the tax credit method of collection. Japan is an exception to that generalization. They are going to calculate the base for the VAT by the subtraction method.

Uruguay and Brazil in the 1960s were the first countries to adopt a comprehensive form of VAT. The adoption of this system of taxation as a requirement for countries entering the European Community (EC) has been a powerful force to recommend this form of taxation to both developed and developing countries. As is the case for the EC countries, most developing countries are very open to international trade. The value-added tax has the great advantage of being a tax system where the indirect tax content of the cost of producing items can be eliminated at the time of export. No other single-stage sales tax has in practice been administered in a way that will allow exported goods to be sold abroad completely free of indirect tax.

Table 2 **Introduction of VAT since 1984**

Country	Year Introduced	Rates Normal	Reduced	Increased	Other
Bolivia[62]	1985	10%	—	—	0%
Greece[63]	1987	18%	6%	36%	0%
Grenada[64]	1987	20%	—	0%	—
Hungary[65]	1988	15%	—	22%	0%
Indonesia[66]	1985	10%	—	—	0%
Japan[67]	1988	3%	—	—	0%
Kenya	1990	17%	multiple rates		0%
Malawi	1988	35%	10%	55%	85%/0%
Morocco[68]	1986	19%	7%	30%	14/12%/0%
New Zealand[69]	1986	10%	—	—	0%
Niger[70]	1986	25%	15%	35%	0%
Philippines[71]	1988	10%	—	—	0%
Portugal[72]	1986	16%	8%	30%	0%
Spain[73]	1986	12%	6%	33%	0%
Taiwan[74]	1986	5%	—	—	0%
Tunisia[75]	1988	17%	6%	29%	0%
Turkey[76]	1985	12%	5%	—	1/0%

Except Japan, all countries that have introduced the VAT (see Table 2) have employed the tax credit method of computation. This type of value-added tax is more easily audited than many other types of indirect tax. To those countries that want to improve the administration of their indirect taxes, this feature has been an added attraction.

On revenue grounds, the value-added tax has had a very credible record. In all cases the revenue from the value-added tax has been significantly higher than the indirect tax system that it replaced.[77] It is also clear that the administrative cost of operating such a taxation system can be substantial. This is the particular case when there are multiple rates and a number of exemptions.

An important attraction of introducing a value-added tax system in a developing country is that it requires the design of a completely new adminis-trative system. At the same time, it is close enough in structure to a sales tax that much of the knowledge that the current tax administration will have is useful when operating a new value-added tax. The clean break from the previous administrative system provides an opportunity to eliminate many of the previous inefficient and perhaps corrupt procedures. While the amount of training required to operate a value-added tax system efficiently may be substantial, it is not likely to require more than twelve months of preparation.

The introduction of a new value-added tax administrative system also provides the government with the opportunity to introduce computerization.

Microcomputers, combined with the audit trail that the tax credit type of value-added tax provides, are very complementary features for improving the detection of tax evasion. Because the tax credit method requires the issuing of receipts, taxpayers are automatically made very aware of the existence of an audit trail. When this feature is combined with a well-publicized program of computerization, taxpayers will generally improve their degree of compliance substantially.

The administration of a value-added tax system becomes highly complex and expensive if there are multiple rates and many exemptions from the tax. Because the tax that is paid at one level of manufacturing or processing is carried forward to a next level, the tax authorities are more or less forced to evaluate what is or is not being taxed at various stages. If there are multiple rates and diverse exemptions, the administrative cost of a value-added tax becomes enormous. If this is the case, then the administrative arm of the government will likely try to resist special interest groups that campaign for tax preferences. Ministers quickly become acutely aware that any tax preference will continue to create a continued and expensive irritation. In the political economy of tax administration and tax policy, this is a good thing.

Recently the history of value-added taxes around the world has been one of increased simplicity rather than increased complexity. While the initial value-added tax introduced in Europe and Latin America often had multiple rates and numerous exemptions, we find that these systems are becoming more stream-lined,[78] and the new ones being introduced are models of simplicity. In the case of Bolivia, Indonesia, New Zealand, Grenada, Taiwan, the Philippines, and the proposed value-added taxes in Jamaica, all have only one rate of tax on almost all items, with very few exemptions. In the field of indirect taxation such simplicity, heretofore, has been unheard of. In the past there has been considerable discussion of the income distribution effects arising from a value-added tax. It has often been alleged that the poor would bear more than their share of tax burden. This has proven not to be true. The main reason this tax is not regressive in developing countries is that it is virtually impossible to tax unprocessed food and items manufactured and sold directly to consumers by small enterprises. These items tend to make up a large proportion of the expenditures of the poor in any developing country. As a result, the bulk of the expenditures by the very poor are exempted from the value-added tax.

In developed countries where more of the basic food items go through the formal economy and are of a processed nature, the income distribution impact of a value-added tax can be less progressive than desired. Because countries tend to have income tax systems, progressivity at the bottom end of the income distribution can be easily added through an increase in the basic personal deduction or tax credit.[79]

This method of redressing the income distribution impacts of increased indirect tax revenues has been implemented in a number of European countries and was part of the proposals put forward by the Canadian tax authorities in their efforts to introduce the value-added tax.

Administration of Tax Systems in Developing Countries

A tax system is no better than its administration. Conversely, bad tax policies can never be transferred into good taxes by superb tax administration. The relationship between tax policy and tax administration is very close. Good tax policies can be made either easy or very difficult to administer depending on how they are structured or the degree of perfection desired.

The practical limits of administration of something as complex as a tax system are very real. As a result, finely tuned tax policies that are designed to deliver near perfection in economic efficiency and justice often end up generating gross inefficiency and unjust outcomes.

The potential for modernization of tax administration in less-developed countries has been revolutionized by the advent of the microcomputer. Because these tax systems deal with fewer taxpayers and are somewhat simpler, the desired information systems are ideally provided by the microcomputer. Often the support personnel in less developed countries are well suited for the operation of microcomputers as they have had considerable experience in manual data processing and typing. Because of the absence of the massive education opportunities available in developed countries, those people who have to settle for a career as a clerical staff member in the public sector of developing countries often have relatively strong native abilities. This potential can often be much better utilized when they have access to microcomputers in their work.

Accurate, up-to-date information is the most powerful tool for tax administration. If the tax administration has the ability to notify the taxpayer immediately after he is in arrears, the chances of improving taxpayer compliance are very high. Computerized systems that would have taken tens of millions of dollars only a decade ago can now be put in place for a fraction of the cost. As a result, in a matter of one or two years a country such as Malawi or Indonesia can have a computerized tax information system which would rival those of developing countries that built their systems over several decades.

It is clear that the biggest obstacle to the use of microcomputers and the information they can help produce is not the inability to understand or use computers, but the unwillingness of the tax authorities to use them. Because computerization often brings about a complete break in the previous patterns and relations between taxpayers and the tax authorities, the stream of irregular payments received by the tax administrators is usually greatly disrupted. When this happens the tax administrators are usually in a psychological frame of mind to try to see if the new system will quietly go back to its previous form.

It is generally only when it becomes clear that the system will not collapse that bureaucrats or tax administrators or authorities will have an incentive to mobilize and improve the tax administration. This pattern seems to fit the case of the value-added tax and the income tax systems in Indonesia.

After the introduction of the tax reforms, both tax administrations operated at a very slow pace to implement their new tax systems. Because over 70 percent of the value-added tax revenues came from imports, public enterprises, and oil products, tax revenues kept flowing in after the reform, even though the tax authorities did almost nothing to implement the system. The chance of the value-added tax collapsing was very small. As a result, the value-added tax administrators shifted their attitude relatively quickly to promote and improve the implementation of the system in order to capture credit for the new system's success. In the case of the income tax, the authorities moved very slowly to implement the new system. Revenues fell, and the emerging tendency is to go back to the previous methods of income tax administration.

In the case of the income tax, although the tax laws have been dramatically changed, the actual effect on the taxpayers has been much less. The income tax reform has given the government a much simpler tax law to implement, but the challenge will be to see if it is possible to mobilize the tax administration to move back to what the law states and away from old practices.

In considering how one might introduce new administrative practices with a tax reform, there have been a number of lessons learned. First, it is critical that the computerization effort be seen as part of the existing tax administration and not something that is going to be controlled outside of the administration. At the same time, it is critical that the new computerization unit report to the top of the tax administration and not to directors and subdirectors in the administrative system. In this way the people running the computer system are able to get access to the top administrators, who tend to be committed to the reforms, and who will reinforce the position of the computerization unit.

It is clear that in some cases there are substantial financial disincentives to work in the new computer information sections of the tax administration. Individuals in the computer sections may be intellectually rewarded but at the same time become financial paupers. In a system where much of the income of a staff member is obtained in extra payments, the computer unit employees often will not receive their share of these extra payments. In this way, further pressure is put on the reform process because those involved in the computerization will have greater financial incentives to spend only short periods of time in the unit. There tends to be a high degree of turnover between the computer units of the tax administration and the private sector. Alternatively, people will simply want to leave the computerization unit and go back to their old responsibilities in the tax administration.

While we have learned a great deal about how to design a modern tax structure, our knowledge of how to reform tax administrations is, at best, in its infancy. In the 1960s and 1970s the motto of many tax reform efforts could be summarized as "Dead upon Publication." At the current time, I am afraid that in a number of cases the motto is being changed to "Death through Administration." ఐ

Notes

1 The following sources and papers, published since 1984, have been reviewed for tax reforms as reported in Tables 1 and 2 below.

Bulletin for International Fiscal Documentation (BIFD), International Bureau of Fiscal Documentation, Amsterdam, 1984/1 to 1988/8-9.

CATA Newsletter, Commonwealth Association of Tax Administrators, London, 1984 to September 1988.

Editor's Note. "Tax Reform Around the World" in *The International Tax Journal*, vol. 13, no. 4, 1987.

Foreign and U.S. Corporate Income and Withholding Tax Rates, Ernst & Whinney, 1984 to 1988.

Price Waterhouse, *Individual Taxes (PWIT), A Worldwide Summary*, 1984 to 1988.

Price Waterhouse, *Corporate Taxes (PWCT), A Worldwide Summary*, 1984 to 1988.

Vito Tanzi, "Tax Reform in Industrial Countries and the impact of the U.S. Tax Reform Act 1986," in *BIFD*, vol. 42, 1988/2, 51-64.

Tax News Service (TNS), International Bureau of Fiscal Documentation, Amsterdam, 1984 to September 1988.

Tax Reform in the Asian Pacific Countries, papers presented at the Asian Pacific Tax Conference of the Asian Pacific Tax and Investment Research Centre, Singapore, November 1986.

2 Canada, Royal Commission on Taxation, *Report of the Royal Commission on Taxation* (Ottawa: Queens Printer, 1966).

3 Richard Musgrave and Malcolm Gillis, *Fiscal Reform for Colombia: Final Report and Staff Papers of the Colombian Commission on Tax Reform* (Cambridge: Harvard University, International Tax Program, 1971).

4 Guillermo Perry, who had played a key role in the work of the Musgrave Commission and later became director general of Internal Taxes, was intimately involved in the formulation of the 1974 reforms.

5 Colombia has had a history of tax reforms dating from the 1960s. In 1986 it had another major tax reform. This time simplicity and low marginal tax rates have made this reform very similar to the tax reform in countries such as Indonesia and New Zealand. Canada since 1981 has made several changes in its tax system that have tended to lower the marginal rates of tax while eliminating tax exemptions and shelters. In 1987 it removed many of the personal deductions and substituted a system of tax credits. This was accompanied by a lowering of the personal and corporate rates of taxation.

6 Charles E. McLure Jr.,"Analysis and Reform of the Colombian Tax System," in *Lessons from Fundamental Tax Reform in Developing Countries*, ed. Malcolm Gillis (Durham: Duke University Press, Spring 1989).

7 Carl S. Shoup, "The Tax Mission To Japan, 1949-1950," in *Lessons from Fundamental Tax Reform in Developing Countries.*

8 Nicholas Kaldor, *Indian Tax Reform, Report of a Survey,* New Delhi, 1957, reprinted in Nicholas Kaldor, *Reports on Taxation,* vol. 2, New York, 1980, 31-189.

9 Nicholas Kaldor, *Suggestions for a Comprehensive Reform of Direct Taxation in Ceylon,* Colombo, Government Press, 1960, reprinted in Nicholas Kaldor, *Reports on Taxation,* vol. 2, New York, 1980, 189-213.

10 Richard Musgrave, *Fiscal Reform in Bolivia: Final Report of the Bolivian Mission on Tax Reform* (Cambridge: Harvard University, International Tax Program, 1981).

11 For a summary of the study and recommendations, see Dan Galai, Dov Sapir, Ephraim Sadka, Amnon Raphael, and Eytan Sheshinski, *Personal Income Tax Reform: Report of the Committee of Experts,* presented to the Minister of Finance, Jerusalem, February 1988.

12 Arnold C. Harberger, "Lessons of Tax Reform, From the Experiences of Uruguay, Indonesia and Chile," in *Lessons from Fundamental Tax Reform in Developing Countries.*

13 Malcolm Gillis, "Comprehensive Tax Reform: The Indonesian Experience, 1981-1988," in *Lessons from Fundamental Tax Reform in Developing Countries.*

14 John Prebble, "Tax Reform in New Zealand," in *Tax Reform in the Asian Pacific Countries.* See also footnote on New Zealand in Table 1, below.

15 Arthur J. Mann, "The Role of Tax Reform in Bolivia Under Economic Liberalization and Stabilization," presented at the Harvard Institute for International Development (HIID) Conference on Systems Reform in Developing Countries, Morocco, October 1988.

16 Mukul G. Asher, "Tax Reform in Singapore," in *Tax Reform in the Asian Pacific Countries.*

17 For a more complete discussion of the tax reform process in Sri Lanka see Glenn P. Jenkins, "Tax Changes before Tax Policies: Sri Lanka 1975-1988," chapter 7 in Malcolm Gillis ed. *Tax Reform in Developing Countries* (Durham: Duke University Press, 1989, 233-51).

18 See Introduction to Nicholas Kaldor, *Reports on Taxation,* vol. 2 (1980), ix.

19 For Indonesia, New Zealand, and Bolivia, see notes 13, 14, and 15 above. For Jamaica, see Roy Bahl, "The Political Economy of the Jamaican Tax Reform," in *Lessons from Fundamental Tax Reform in Developing Countries.*

20 It is my impression that a similar process was carried out in Jamaica. In Jamaica the tax reform effort had the additional advantage of having the prime minister, who was also the minister of finance, involved in the reform process from the beginning.

21 Nicholas Kaldor, *The Expenditure Tax,* London, 1955.

22 See Nicholas Kaldor (1955 and 1980).

23 Canada, Royal Commission on Taxation (1966).

24 *Fiscal Survey of Colombia* (1965), a report by Professor Milton Taylor, head of a joint program of the Organization of American States and the Interamerican Development Bank.

25 Y.D. Chimombo, (commissioner of Taxes, Malawi), president of CATA 1990, "Recent Tax Reform Initiatives in CATA Countries: An Overview," paper presented at the Symposium on Taxation Relationships and International Investment Flows organized by the OECD's Committee on Fiscal Affairs and held at the OECD Headquarters in Paris on June 26 and 27, 1990.

J. Owens, "Taxation Relationships and International Investment Flows," Committee on Fiscal Affairs, Development Centre, International Monetary Fund, June 26 and 27, 1990.

26 In 1985 individual income taxes were reduced from 60 percent to 49 percent, and corporate taxes increased from 46 percent to 49 percent. See D. C. Orrochi: "Australia: Tax Reform," in *BIFD*, vol. 39, 1985/11. In 1988 another reform was introduced as announced in the Economic Statement for the Fiscal Year 1988/89, reducing the corporate tax rate from 9 percent to 39 percent. TNS-162 (1988).

27 Reform should become effective as of January 1, 1989. TNS-66 (1988).

28 Reported in *CATA Newsletter*, March 1987. Previous individual income tax rate from PWIT, 1985.

29 By Supreme Decree 21,060 of August 29, 1985, TNS-147-85. Previous individual income tax rate from PWIT, 1985.

30 The following changes are reported in *CATA Newsletter*, December of 1988, appendix II, 21. The previous rates are prior to 1984, but the exact year and scope of the reform are not reported.

31 The tax rates reported are for the federal government only. Additional income taxes of about 50 percent of the federal rate are levied by the provinces. *Tax Reform White Paper*, TNS-155 (1987). Tax reform motion introduced on June 13, 1988, to the House of Commons. The rates for corporate income apply for manufacturing. The reduction will be graduated between 1987 and 1990. For general business it is 36 percent to 28 percent and for small business 15 percent to 12 percent.

32 Law 75/86 from December 23, 1986, TNS-22 (1987). The previous income tax rate for individuals is from *PWIT 1985*.

33 Tax amendment law 1986, published July 12, 1986. *TNS*-106 (1986).

34 Published in the *Official Gazette* of December 22, 1986. *TNS*-99 (1987).

35 Corporate income was taxed at 33 percent and a Municipal Tax of 14 to 18.5 percent was added. The new rate is unified. *TNS*-80 (1988).

36 In March 1988 an Income Tax Reform was passed by Parliament. See McPherson, M. and Radelet, S. C., "Economic Reform in the Gambia...," chapter 4, this volume.

37 The government approved in March of 1988 a tax reform bill that will apply in 1990. *TNS*-89 (1988).

38 Income tax for both individuals and companies abolished with effect from March 1987, and replaced with a VAT applicable to all sales of goods and services. See Wendell A. Samuel, "Tax Reform in Grenada," in *BIFD*, vol. 42, 1988/3; and *TNS*-75 (1987).

39 Reform effective October 1987. *TNS*-227 (1987)

40 The rates for corporate income are for public/private enterprises. See Nishite Desai: "Tax Reform in India" in *Tax Reform in the Asian Pacific Countries*. Papers presented at the Asian Pacific Tax Conference of the Asian Pacific Tax and Investment Research Centre, Singapore, November 1986.

41 See Jap Kim Siong: "Indonesia: The Tax Reform Laws" in *BIFD*, Vol. 38, 1984/3; and *TNS*-140 (1983). Previous corporate income tax rate from Ernst & Whinney: Foreign and United States Corporate Income and Withholding Tax Rates, 1983, 11.

42 Effective January 1, 1987. See *TNS*-97 (1986), *TNS*-109 (1987), and *CATA Newsletter,* vol. 1, 1988, March.

43 Individual income tax rates as reported by *TNS*-139 (1987) for the budget 1987/88. It has already been announced that the tax rate for corporations will be reduced to 40 percent in 1991.

44 For resident companies.

45 The following changes are reported in the *CATA Newsletter*, December of 1988, appendix 2, 21. The previous rates are prior to 1984, but the exact year and scope of the reform are not reported.

46 *TNS*-239 (1987), *PWIT*, 1987 edition, and *CATA Newsletter*, vol. 1, 1988 (March), 15.

47 Similar to the case of France, the reduction in rates reported for Nigeria in the table below is also based on changes on the rates trough the budget law. Finance decree as part of the budget, *TNS*-115 (1987), and *CATA Newsletter*, vol. 1, 1987, March.

48 For resident companies.

49 See Cunningham, William T.: "Portuguese Tax Reform," in *BIFD*, vol. 42, 1988/2; and *TNS*-122 (1988).

50 Corporate income rates as reported in *CATA Newsletter*, March 1987. Individual income tax rates have declined from 45 percent in 1984 to 40 percent in 1985, and to 33 percent in 1987; see *PWIT*, corresponding years.

51 The following changes are reported in *CATA Newsletter*, December of 1988, appendix 2, 21. The previous rates are prior to 1984, but the exact year and scope of the reform are not reported.

52 The following changes are reported in *CATA Newsletter,* December of 1988, appendix 2, 21. The previous rates are prior to 1984, but the exact year and scope of the reform are not reported.

53 The following changes are reported in *CATA Newsletter,* December of 1988, appendix 2, 21. The previous rates are prior to 1984, but the exact year and scope of the reform are not reported.

54 *TNS*-153 (1986).

55 For resident companies.

56 Corporate income rates as reported in *CATA Newsletter*, March 1987. Individual income rates as report by *PWIT*, 1986 and 1987.

57 Glenn P. Jenkins, "Tax Shelter Finance: How Efficient Is It?", *Canadian Tax Journal*, vol. 38, no. 2, 270-285, March 1988.

58 It was initially proposed that there would be only one rate of tax, 30 percent. See Gillis (1989).

59 This may be a record for any country.

60 It is not expected that much of the normal capital gains will actually get taxed. This measure will, however, prevent other income such as salaries from being converted into capital gains and escape taxation.

61 Malcolm Gillis, Carl Shoup, and Gerardo Sicat, *Lessons From Value-Added Taxation For Developing Countries,* World Bank, February 9, 1987.

62 Tax reform law #843. *TNS*-147 (1985). This tax does not come into force until detailed regulations have been published.

63 VAT system introduced on January 1, 1987. *TNS*-181 (1986).

64 Income tax for both individuals and companies abolished with effect from March 1987, and replaced with a VAT applicable to all sales of goods and services. See Wendell A. Samuel,"Tax Reform in Grenada," in *BIFD*, vol. 42, 1988/3; and *TNS*-75 (1987).

65 *TNS*-168 (1987).

66 Government Regulation 1 of 1985 from January 1985; VAT introduced as of April 1, 1985. *TNS*-22 (1985).

67 "A 3 percent consumption tax, with the value-added computation based on companies books rather than on invoices. Small Businesses with annual turnover of less than Y30m are exempt, as are financial transactions, medical services under the national health insurance plan and school tuition fees." *Financial Times*, no. 30, 696, Thursday, November 17, 1988. p. 1.

68 VAT system effective on April 1, 1986. *TNS*-111 (1986).

69 Goods and Service Tax (GST) in force since October 1986. International Bureau of Fiscal Documentation: *Taxes and Investment in Asia and the Pacific, New Zealand Country Survey.*

70 Finance Law 1986 (Ord. No. 85-29). VAT applied as of January 1, 1986. *TNS*-25 (1986).

71 Contemplating introduction as of January 1988. *TNS*-171 (1987).

72 Decree Law 504.M, from December 30, 1985. In force since January 1, 1986, coinciding with Portugal's membership to the EC. International Bureau for Fiscal Documentation: *Guides to European Taxation IV: Value-Added Taxation in Europe, Portugal Survey.*

73 Law 30 of 2 August 1985. In force since January 1, 1986, coinciding with Spain's membership to the E.C. International Bureau for Fiscal Documentation: *Guides to European Taxation IV: Value Added Taxation in Europe, Spain Survey.*

74 Effective on March 1, 1986. See Jap Kim Siong: "Taiwan: An Outline of the Proposed Value Added Tax System" in *BIFD*, vol. 40, 1986/1, and "Taiwan: The VAT Law in Force" in *BIFD*, vol. 40, 1986/7; and *TNS*-18 (1986).

75 Introduction as of July 1, 1988. *TNS*-123 (1988).

76 Effective January 1, 1985. *TNS*-95 (1984). Rates from *PWCT*, 1987 edition.

77 In Indonesia the value-added tax has increased the indirect tax revenues about 600 percent above the revenues from the sales taxes it replaced.

78 For example, both the United Kingdom and France have greatly simplified their VAT through time.

79 Canada, Department of Finance, Tax Reform 1987; Sales Tax Reform, June 18, 1987, 29.

12

Reform of Financial Systems

David C. Cole and Betty F. Slade

David C. Cole has served as adviser on financial and economic policy to the governments of Korea and Indonesia since the mid-1960s and has written extensively about the two countries. He has, for many years, taught a course at Harvard on financial policy in developing countries, and, from 1984 to 1989, he directed HIID's Summer Workshop on Banking and Monetary Policy in Developing Countries.

Betty F. Slade wrote her doctoral thesis on the Turkish financial system, taught economics, and was a policy consultant for USAID in Turkey for many years. She also taught a course on monetary and fiscal policy in developing countries at Vanderbilt University for five years. She has served as an adviser to the Indonesian government for three years.

Both authors are HIID project associates and co-coordinators of the Program for Financial Policy Studies and Training Project in Indonesia. They are also involved in the direction and writing of a major study on money markets in seven East Asian countries, conducted jointly by HIID and Harvard Law School.

Introduction

he attempts at reform of financial systems in developing countries that have proven most successful have consisted of a fundamental reordering of the regulatory structure rather than some simple process of deregulation. The objectives of financial reforms have generally been to reduce bureaucratic controls over prices and allocation of financial transfers and to permit market forces to exert a greater influence over such transfers, thereby contributing to improved efficiency and equity of the whole economy. But financial systems, as Minsky (1982) has argued, are prone to generate instability and—as many practitioners, from Ponzi to Boesky and beyond, have demonstrated—are extremely susceptible to fraud. Competition does not necessarily protect the innocent or prevent panics in financial markets, so there is continuing need for some form of regulation to try to limit such abuses.

In developing countries, especially, financial systems have been used by government bureaucracies to try to guide the allocation of investment and to influence the distribution of income. Common examples are to give preferential financing to industrial investment and to grant low-cost loans to farmers. Such bureaucratic interference has frequently led not only to inefficient allocation of resources and a worsening of income distribution, but also to increasingly segmented and ineffective financial systems. As some countries have come to recognize the harmful effects of their financial policies, they have attempted to undertake financial reforms for the purpose of reducing these allocational and distributional distortions and promoting a healthier, more vigorous financial system without, at the same time, opening up that system and the economy to fraud and instability.

The guidelines, or models, for carrying out financial reforms are neither clear nor well established. As Perkins suggests in the first chapter of this volume, simple maxims like "get the prices right" or "eliminate bureaucratic interference" are not helpful. Among the many factors that bear upon the process are historical experience, the current structure of the political and economic systems, and susceptibility to external pressures or shocks. The challenge to which this paper is addressed is to determine whether there are any useful generalizations that can be offered as to the appropriate objectives of or approaches to financial reform.

In attempting to meet this challenge, we first take up the question of defining the characteristics of a healthy financial system. In the process, we suggest why it is so difficult to measure both the size and quality of a financial system, or even its contribution to the overall growth of the economy. Next, we present a stylized historical sketch of how the financial systems of many developing countries evolved in the years following their independence, to show how they were often used by governments for narrow, short-sighted purposes and, as a consequence, became deformed and inefficient. Then we turn to the reform process itself: classifying various conditions and external forces precipitating the reforms, delineating different approaches to reform, and describing outcomes. In this context, we present three case studies from countries that represent quite different circumstances, approaches, and outcomes. These are not meant to be a representative sample of countries but simply ones with which the authors have extensive personal experience. Finally, we offer some tentative guidelines for successful reform processes.

Four themes emerge from this paper. The first is that financial systems are multifunctional. Therefore, it is misleading to try to measure their development on a unidimensional scale, and misguided to try to emphasize any one function, for example, to promote real growth, while neglecting the other functions. The multifunctional aspect of the financial system suggests that we need a multidimensional measure of financial development with appropriate weights for the different functions based upon their relative contribution to real development—a kind of financial decathlon where what matters is the overall performance in a number of different events, rather than excelling in just one. We can identify the different functions and even suggest some measures of performance for each function, but we do not yet have a useful set of weights that relates functional performance to overall development. This should be an important objective for future research.

The second theme is that most financial systems can best be viewed for analytical purposes as consisting of two parts: a formal, registered, regulated, and recorded part; and an informal, unregistered, unregulated, and unrecorded part.[1] Furthermore, if the formal part of the system is failing to perform one or several of the financial functions effectively, then it is almost inevitable that the informal part will move in and try to fill the void. As a financial system develops, there tends to be a substitution of formal for informal finance. This process can be frustrated, most frequently by governmental policies that attempt to use the formal institutions in a distorted, unifunctional way. The informal part is generally a market-based system but has many imperfections due to limited information, lack of access to the legal system, and absence of governmental protection. The two parts are clearly not perfect substitutes in all functions and, consequently, the relative roles of formal and informal finance have a bearing on the overall performance of the system.

The third theme is that the financial sector does not stand alone, but is just one part of the overall economic system. The effectiveness of financial policies is greatly influenced by the configuration of other policies. The most important of these are likely to be the fiscal and balance-of-payments or trade policies. If these other policy areas are being managed in ways that deter economic development, then there is little that can be done through financial policies to rectify the problems. On the other hand, if the other policy areas are supporting economic development, then bad financial policies may do some harm, but the more likely effect will be to shift the weight of financial activity to the informal part of the system.

The fourth theme is that, for most countries, the optimal mix of financial policies lies in some middle ground between bureaucratically regulated and free-market approaches, more likely closer to the free-market end of the range, but supported by regulations that limit monopoly, fraud, and instability. Many developing countries worked their way over to the bureaucratic end of the spectrum in their early years of independence. Some are contemplating or are in the process of moving toward the market-based end, but wondering how far to go and how to get there.

The Theory of Finance and Development

The theory of how competitive financial markets contribute to efficient mobilization of savings and allocation of investment was laid out clearly by Irving Fisher over half a century ago (Fisher 1930). He demonstrated that, in well-functioning competitive financial markets, savers would receive the highest possible return on their savings and would thus be able to make optimal choices between saving and current consumption. Producer-investors, on the other hand, would be able to obtain financing at the lowest possible cost consistent with savers' preferences, and would be guided to invest optimal amounts in the most profitable activities. This optimal situation could be disturbed by failure of markets to operate under competitive conditions or by governmental interference in the functioning of the markets.

Subsequently, Gurley and Shaw (1960) presented a theoretical model of how financial systems evolve as countries develop. They were among the first to elaborate the several functions of a financial system and to indicate the kinds of institutional changes that normally accompany financial development. Modern financial theory, building upon their insights, now postulates that a financial system can promote or impede economic development in many different ways.[2]

Economic development theorists, as distinct from financial theorists, have tended to emphasize a single function for the financial system. The policies deriving from these theories have failed to take account of the complex nature of finance and its multidimensional role in the economy. Instead, they have led to distortion and misuse of finance.

Initially, the development specialists saw the role of finance primarily as a means of paying for, or carrying out, investment which, for them, was the essential requirement for growth. But as many countries became overzealous in pushing investment without sufficient concern about the growth of money and credit unmatched by real savings, the focus of both the theorists and the dominant aid donors shifted to inflation and balance-of-payments problems. There was a realization that excessive growth of nominal finance could undermine real financial and economic growth. Subsequent attempts to control monetary expansion while still carrying out government-determined essential investment activities led to distortion and repression of the financial system, usually through a combination of interest-rate and credit ceilings and credit allocation to priority sectors, which resulted in low financial savings and continuing inflation. The "financial repression" school of Shaw and McKinnon was largely responding to this set of problems when they recommended restrictions on growth of money supply and setting nominal interest rates above the inflation rate as the way to achieve a more healthy and effective financial system.

The Functions of the Financial System

We see seven functions which, if performed well by the financial system, would increase savings and investment, reduce the cost of financial resources to investors, improve the allocation of resources, enhance stability of the economy, and reduce risk. All of these changes are likely to contribute to development.

A first function of the financial system is to provide a safe, convenient, and beneficial form in which to hold savings. The monetary return on financial savings is only one of the important characteristics, which can be offset to some extent by safety and convenience.[3]

A second function of the financial system is to transfer control over resources from savers to investors at low transaction costs compared with such alternatives as direct transfers, inflation, government intermediation through taxation or foreign savings.

Third, a financial system channels purchasing power to a wide variety of investors with varying needs, degrees of risk, and probable rates of return that permit more diversified and generally more efficient investment.

Fourth, financial institutions can exert pressure on investors to use resources in an efficient and productive manner in order to repay existing obligations and to qualify for new financing.

Fifth, a well-functioning financial system rewards efficient and capable financial managers who make wise, or lucky, choices or develop attractive new financial instruments.

A sixth function of a financial system is to maintain a stable *numeraire* or unit of account for comparing values within the country, across countries, and over time.[4]

Seventh, a financial system provides a safe, efficient payments system that makes possible quick settlement of all types of obligations. This reduces the risk and cost of financial transactions.

Very few financial systems perform every function effectively, but the deficiencies have tended to be especially severe in those developing countries which have attempted to control and direct finance through excessively bureaucratic means.

How Financial Systems Become Deformed

The financial history of today's developing countries differs from that of industrialized countries in that the former were often colonies of or dominated by the latter. This meant that at the time of *de jure* or *de facto* independence the developing countries inherited financial systems created by the colonial power to serve its own interests. Generally, the modern part of the system consisted of a few foreign-owned commercial banks that dealt mainly with foreign trade transactions, plus a currency board or primary note-issuing bank that supplied the currency. A traditional set of informal financial institutions often existed to serve the needs of indigenous farmers and small businesses because only a few of the wealthier businesses or individuals had access to the modern institutions. Some modern institutions took deposits and made short-term commercial loans; there were few, if any, markets for negotiable instruments, precluding either open-market operations by the monetary authorities or the issuance of long-term capital instruments to the public by business.

In the early decades after independence, most governments either set up new central banks or took over the management of currency boards which, in turn, assumed responsibility for note issue and for assuring the liquidity of the banking system.

The newly independent governments also tended to become frustrated with the independent actions of privately owned, especially foreign-owned, banks, and increasingly intervened in the operations of domestic commercial banks or nationalized the foreign-owned banks. Others established government-owned

317

banks not only to do regular commercial banking business but also to meet the special financing needs of selected sectors of the economy.

To assure the parastatal banks a market share that would keep them viable, the government often directed state-owned enterprises to carry out their banking business exclusively with the government-owned banks, and channeled both central bank and foreign aid funds to them. Dependence on captive markets, the obligation to open branches in unprofitable areas, and requirements to lend to favored sectors of the economy progressively weakened the competitive capacity of these banks.

Foreign banks that continued to exist were often relegated to niches that, though they decreased in relative size, were still profitable because they were protected from entry by new foreign banks. Many of the remaining private banks became linked to industrial groups that drew heavily on their financial resources. Commercial banking activities became increasingly segmented and noncompetitive.

Most governments quickly discovered that their new central banks were convenient sources of funds to meet fiscal deficits at low interest rates. Central bank credit could be used to support the directed credit programs at low interest rates. This led to excessive credit expansion by many of the central banks. Inflation rose and foreign exchange reserves fell. Directed credit programs encouraged commercial banks and new special purpose banks (like industrial, agricultural, or housing banks) to become increasingly dependent on the central bank for funds. With such a source, the banks needed only to make limited efforts to mobilize deposits from the domestic economy. Businesses that had access to these banks or received direct credit programs came to depend on these sources. When some of their investments turned out to be unprofitable, the businesses resisted or at least delayed repayment of their loans. Thus, the central bank and its major banking customers became locked into portfolios of uncollectible, low-interest loans to the government, government-sponsored businesses, and small farmers.

Continuing pressures for central bank credit expansion and few opportunities to contract credit ultimately led to balance-of-payments crises. In many cases, governments turned to the International Monetary Fund (IMF) for both financial and technical assistance to design and implement financial stabilization programs. The IMF approach to stabilization policy in the 1960s and 1970s focused on controlling the growth of bank credit and money supply. Initially this was attempted by controlling the growth of the net domestic assets of the central bank, but as many central banks experienced difficulty in limiting the subsequent expansion of bank lending, there was a shift to greater reliance on loan ceilings for both commercial and special banks. Rationing of bank loans that carried low nominal interest rates resulted in large excess demand for bank credit. The high economic rents implicit in such loans became major sources of corruption of the bank and government officials who controlled their allocation. Those borrowers who obtained the loans often used them for other than the intended purposes, and in some of the worst cases the funds were used to finance political campaigns and payoffs.

Both potential borrowers, who were unable to obtain bank loans, and potential savers, who found banks uninterested in their deposits or limited to paying low nominal interest rates on such deposits, tended to turn to other channels to meet their needs. This distortion led to the growth of two sorts of financial institution. One was an extension of long-standing, traditional, informal financial institutions that were largely unregulated, often illegal, and about which very little was known.[5]

Another channel for financial intermediation, which evolved in response to the distortions in the banking system, was the nonbank financial institution (NBFI). These institutions either took regular deposits or issued notes that were deposit substitutes and loaned the funds to many of the regular bank customers who could not get adequate accommodation from their banks.[6]

Market forces neither died nor faded away even in those countries with the most repressed financial systems; they just shifted to other venues. Funds obtained from the banks were often re-lent in the unregulated markets at much higher rates of interest. Many businesses, even the larger ones, became dependent upon the unregulated markets for at least part of their funds and made their investment decisions on the basis of the interest rates prevailing in those markets rather than the controlled bank interest rates. The disparity between nominal interest rates of banks and those in the unregulated markets became a measure of the segmentation and distortion of financial markets as well as a bargaining zone between borrowers and dispensers of bank funds. It also explained why those who succeeded in obtaining bank loans were so reluctant to ever repay them.

While the commercial banking part of the financial system grew ever more convoluted, some of the NBFIs, which were able to circumvent interest rate and credit controls, became quite significant in a number of countries. On the other hand, the development finance institutions supported by foreign donors, investing domestic and foreign funds at medium- and long-term, found their books choked with troubled loans because governments had used them to support investments and companies that were politically important, but often economically nonviable.

A number of developing countries accumulated large foreign debts, but this was due in the first instance more to fiscal deficits arising from excessive spending and weak tax systems than to the deficiencies of the financial system. On the other hand, the inflow of foreign capital in the heyday of foreign borrowing often led to postponement of financial reforms because the foreign capital substituted for domestic savings mobilization.

The overall result of this pattern of policies and approaches to the financial system was remarkably common across developing countries. The central banks became heavily involved in administering an elaborate system of direct controls over interest rates, credit allocation, loan approval, and continuing support for nonperforming bank loans and nonmarketable government debt. They had little room for discretionary monetary policy other than to try to restrict the growth of their credit. They also had little control over, or interest in, evaluating the quality of bank assets.

The commercial and specialized banks were not good mobilizers of deposits, preferring to rely on the central bank for low-cost funds. Their loans were often of questionable quality, hard to collect and not very profitable. The banks functioned more like bureaucracies than profit-motivated institutions and sought to maintain the appearance of soundness rather than to face up to the realities of their loan portfolio. They survived only with the help of the central bank.

Governments came to depend on the central banks and foreign loans as major sources of supplementary low-cost finance for the budget and also as underwriters of cheap credit to agriculture, industry and government-owned enterprises engaged in everything from grain purchasing to producing steel and other products of heavy industry.

Nonbank financial institutions and the informal, unregulated money brokers grew into increasingly important channels for mobilizing savings from many sources and lending them to all types of borrowers, from small consumers to large enterprises. The interest rates were often well above the nominal, but not necessarily the effective bank rates, and were differentiated according to risk and administrative cost. To the extent that there was market guidance for investment decisions, it emanated from the unregulated financial markets, which governments sometimes tried to suppress, rather than from the official money and capital markets that the government was ostensibly trying to promote.

The Process of Financial Reform

In recent years a number of countries have attempted to reform their deformed financial systems. Although most such reforms have had the underlying theme of opening up the financial systems to market forces, there has been great variation in the approaches and the outcomes.

To assess better the relative efficacy of alternative approaches to financial reform, it is important to understand both the underlying forces that precipitated the reforms and the different approaches followed in carrying them out. Among the many forces that have been influential in generating the impetus for financial reforms, four seem most significant. They are:

a. popular dissatisfaction with the inefficiencies and inequities of the existing system;

b. new governments or cabinets that have entered office partly in response to popular dissatisfaction or that are otherwise committed to carrying out various economic reforms;

c. external shocks from changes in world markets;

d. pressures from international institutions.

Sometimes all four of these forces converged in a particular country at one time, creating a very strong impetus for the reforms.

The following distinctions among alternative approaches to financial reform seem most significant:

a. all-out market-oriented financial reforms versus more limited or partial reform efforts;

b. financial reforms which were part of a broad reorientation of economic policies versus financial reforms which were relatively unique events, unsupported by other major policy changes;

c. countries which either already had, or adopted as part of the reform, a relatively free foreign exchange system, versus those which maintained relatively strong controls over foreign exchange flows even while freeing up internal financial markets.

When financial reforms are carried out as part of a broad economic policy reform package there is less likelihood that some internal distortion, such as a fiscal deficit, or external pressure from a growing balance-of-payments surplus or deficit, will undercut the development of the financial system. On the other hand, a multifaceted change in economic policies can cause uncertainty and instability that often is manifested in speculative attacks in the newly liberalized financial markets. If the financial system can weather these early assaults, it then has a better chance of continuing improvement. Often new governments which enter office with a mandate for drastic change in economic policies can carry out a broad set of reforms, but later encounter increasing resistance to even minor changes in policy because of shifts in the popular mood or because new vested interests do not want to be disadvantaged. This inability to respond flexibly to changing conditions can turn a successful reform into a failure.

Some countries, such as Chile and Argentina, adopted all-out market-oriented reforms, of which the financial reforms were a part, in the late 1970s and early 1980s. These reforms also included a shift to very open foreign exchange regimes. Both Chile and Argentina experienced serious difficulties with large capital movements and extreme fluctuations in their foreign exchange rates, causing them to retreat from the reforms, and leading to the cautionary propositions, from McKinnon (1982) and Edwards (1984), that some continuing regulation of the international payments system should be retained until the domestic financial reforms had been thoroughly implemented.

Other countries have carried out all-out market liberalizations of their domestic financial systems, but have retained fairly tight controls over their international payments systems. Turkey provides an example and will be described in detail below.

Most often, countries have carried out partial domestic financial reforms while retaining foreign exchange controls. The partial domestic financial decontrol has consisted of raising deposit and loan rates above the inflation rate or allowing banks to set their own interest rates within ranges specified by the monetary authorities; or removing loan ceilings and giving the banks more discretion over the allocation of their loans.[7]

Some countries which carried out partial financial reforms also freed up their foreign exchange controls to some extent, but were reluctant to go all the way to unrestricted capital flows or totally free exchange rates.[8]

Finally, some countries have open foreign exchange regimes, but have only partially freed up their domestic financial markets. In such countries the effects of domestic financial changes on international capital flows or the exchange rate have been a central concern of policymakers and have tended to curtail their willingness to reform and deregulate the domestic financial system.

Measuring the overall effectiveness of a particular reform effort is fraught with problems. There is no good universal standard for measuring financial performance that combines all the financial functions in a composite index. Some improvement in the performance of each function would be a clear indicator of success, but even that is not likely to occur in many cases. More frequently, there will be noticeable improvement in some areas, no progress in others, and possibly even some deterioration in others.

Time poses another complication. During some periods, it will appear that a particular reform measure has been very successful. But then subsequent developments, emanating from either internal or external sources, or rigidity or change in key officials, can lead to loss of momentum or loss of confidence in the continuity of basic policies, which turns the whole reform sour. Therefore, in evaluating a particular reform effort it is usually necessary to specify a time period, such as three to five years, within which the effects of the reform measures might normally be expected to work themselves out.

In what follows we will review financial reform efforts in three countries, characterizing them in terms of the various motivating forces and types of approaches suggested above as well as evaluating their effectiveness.

Financial Reform in Indonesia

The financial reform process in Indonesia occurred in several phases: the first, from 1966 to 1971, followed by a period of retrogression; then a second round in 1983, followed by a third effort in late 1988. The first reform was part of a massive push by a new government to stop hyperinflation. The second, also as part of a broad stabilization program introduced by a new cabinet, involved a removal of credit ceilings and interest rate controls on the existing commercial banks and a shift to indirect instruments of monetary control. The third, which is just getting under way, is mainly a freeing-up of entry for new banks and other financial institutions to engage in a wide range of financial activities subject to strengthened prudential regulation. This latest financial reform is being initiated by a new cabinet as part of a broader effort to deregulate markets and increase competition.

In 1966, the full effects of President Sukarno's profligate economic policies, exacerbated by attempted coups and countercoups, came home to roost. National production had been declining absolutely and inflation accelerating for several years. Faced with price increases of 40 to 50 percent per month and negative foreign exchange reserves, the new Suharto government, with assistance from the IMF and encouragement from the World Bank, embarked upon a broad-gauged financial stabilization program in October 1966.

The main elements of the program were:

a. balancing the government's budget;

b. adoption of a dual exchange rate system, with one rate fixed and the other floating, the latter to give a bonus to exporters and provide a free-market source of foreign exchange for nonpriority imports;

c. restriction on the extension of central bank credit, but no other major changes in banking or financial policy;

d. financial support from the IMF and other aid donors to meet urgent import needs and generate local currency for budgetary support.

This program was pursued with great diligence and probably would have succeeded in bringing the inflation rate down from over 1,000 percent per annum in 1966 to one-tenth that rate in 1967, except for poor rainfall and a reduced rice crop in 1967 that pushed rice prices up sharply so that the consumer price index rose by 170 percent. In 1968 and 1969, better crops and larger grain imports helped to stabilize food prices and bring the overall rate of inflation down to 126 percent in 1968 and 16 percent in 1969.

In late 1968, with prices stabilizing and the economy gradually recovering, the first major move was made to revive and reform the financial system. This consisted of a large increase in bank time deposit interest rates from 30 to 72 percent per annum on one-year time deposits and a rise in maximum bank lending rates to 60 percent. The difference between the deposit and lending rates was covered in part by central bank subsidy payments. This measure led not only to a rapid increase in bank time deposits, but also to a large inflow of foreign exchange and a 25 percent appreciation of the floating exchange rate in a six-month period. It also permitted more rapid expansion of central bank credit which, together with the growing deposit resources of the commercial banks, led to a substantial real increase in the availability of bank financing. As both domestic credit and foreign exchange became more available and less expensive, in real terms, businesses were able to rehabilitate and, in some cases, expand their productive capabilities.

Over the next few years, economic conditions improved steadily so that by 1971 the government was able to move to a free foreign exchange system with a unified rate pegged to the U.S. dollar. Nominal and real deposit interest rates had been brought down to 24 percent and 20 percent respectively and the direct subsidy on time deposit interest reduced. Financial institutions continued to grow and provide a mixture of commercial and term financing, which was augmented by a large inflow of foreign financing for major development projects as well as for business investment.

At that point, it was reasonable to conclude that the partial financial reform process, in the context of a broad macroeconomic policy reorientation and, after 1971, an open foreign exchange regime, was moving ahead very successfully. There was still much room for improvement in the management and operation of financial institutions and a deepening of financial markets, but progress on all these fronts was readily apparent.

The rise in oil prices in 1973 had immediate impact on Indonesia, generating balance-of-payments surpluses and budgetary revenues that soon boosted domestic spending and inflation. The central bank was unable to control the growth of reserve money and, therefore, shifted to credit ceilings on the commercial banks in an attempt to control growth of the money supply. Interest rate ceilings, which had been carried over from earlier years, were kept well below the inflation rate, and bank deposits stopped increasing as a share of GNP.

Much of the investment and working capital of business for the next decade was financed by the government budget or by loans from abroad. The government budget was funded through a combination of oil export revenues and continuing inflows of foreign assistance. The foreign borrowings of the business sectors consisted of direct foreign loans and equity investments, and also sizable borrowings from banks in nearby financial centers such as Singapore and Hong Kong.

Because of the ceilings on domestic bank lending and the low interest rates on bank deposits, many Indonesian businesses found it expedient to hold substantial deposit balances abroad and then to use those balances as collateral for loans from foreign banks. At the same time, any domestic banks that had surplus funds beyond their loan ceilings tended to place those funds abroad in order to obtain the best possible rates of return. The free foreign exchange payments system and the stability of the foreign exchange rate made these relatively risk-free operations. Thus, the ceilings on domestic credit did not become a significant constraint on the availability of financial services for most Indonesian businesses of medium to large scale. They simply shifted their financial activities offshore. Smaller businesses and households, especially in the rural areas, were not well served by the formal financial institutions, but there was ample liquidity within the country as a whole, and the informal institutions saw to it that financial services were available wherever they were profitable. The abundance of financing and domestic spending raised the inflation rate to an annual average of 21 percent from 1973 through 1977. The ratio of commercial bank assets to GDP declined from 22.7 percent to 21.2 percent during the same period.

The tranquility of this combination of domestic and foreign financing was shaken in 1978 when the government carried out a surprise 50 percent devaluation of the rupiah relative to the U.S. dollar. The primary purpose of the devaluation was to correct relative prices between Indonesia and the rest of the world, to avoid serious disincentives to domestic producers of traded goods. But the financial effect was to give those domestic banks and businesses which had large credit balances abroad a sudden windfall profit on their net foreign exchange holdings, and to impose a corresponding cost on all those with net foreign indebtedness. The positive effects seemed to outweigh the negative ones, and were then reinforced by the second increase in oil prices in 1979. Indonesia continued to have ample sources of financing despite repression of the domestic banking institutions.

The decline in oil prices beginning in 1982 signaled a sharp reversal in Indonesia's circumstances and brought on a second round of retrenchment and reform of macroeconomic policies in 1983, again coinciding with the installation of a new cabinet following reelection of President Suharto. The first move was in the fiscal area, as the government scaled back sharply on budgetary commitments for large investment projects. This was followed by another large devaluation of the rupiah by 38 percent at the end of March 1983. This devaluation was intended not only to encourage exports and restrain imports, but also to help make up for the loss in budgetary revenues from oil exports.

The third major move was in financial policy, when the central bank announced removal of all bank credit ceilings and also of interest ceilings on the government-owned banks. (Previously, private banks had not been subject to interest rate ceilings, but they were subject to credit ceilings, and this had limited their interest in mobilizing deposits.)

The fourth measure, announced in September 1983, was a broad tax reform, introducing a value-added tax and shifting from a schedular to a global income tax. Implementation of the tax reform was a gradual process over the next several years and proved crucial in sustaining government revenues in the face of further declines in oil prices. The financial reform, on the other hand, was quicker to take effect and produced a substantial increase in bank deposits and loans within the first seven months of its enactment.

One of the great unknowns in Indonesia, with its totally open capital account system, is how much of any financial change is simply a shifting of activity from offshore to onshore or vice versa. The growth of total bank assets between June

1983 and December 1987 was equal to 74 percent of the growth of nominal GNP. This caused a rise in the ratio of total bank assets to GNP from 26 to 42 percent. Such a high rate of growth of bank assets, occurring during a period when GNP per capita was growing at only about 3 percent per annum in real terms and the terms of trade were moving strongly against Indonesia, did not reflect a comparable real increase in national saving. It also did not reflect accurately the increase in financial saving. Instead, the high rate of growth resulted from some combination of increased real saving, increased saving in the form of financial assets, and repatriation of past financial savings from overseas.

At the time of the financial reform in June 1983, one of the major concerns was that there might be a rapid inflow of past foreign asset accumulations, which could cause a sudden increase in domestic reserve money, credit, and money supply, with possible inflationary consequences that could undermine the positive effects of the devaluation. Similar inflows of foreign capital in 1973/74 had led to imposition of credit ceilings in the first place, and removal of those ceilings in 1983 left the monetary authorities with no real instruments for controlling the growth of the money supply, except possibly through increases in reserve requirements. As it turned out, there was some return flow of foreign exchange in response to both the devaluation and the rise in domestic interest rates, but there was no large increase in bank credit, domestic spending, or inflation.

A major reason for this was the sluggish response of the government-owned commercial banks to the removal of loan ceilings. The "state" banks, still operating in the bureaucratic control mode, were accustomed to making prospective borrowers wait for months for loan approvals, and they did not change their style quickly, despite the rapid build-up of their deposits in response to higher interest rates. Instead, the state banks found it expedient to increase their foreign exchange holdings abroad or to lend excess funds through the newly active Jakarta interbank market to the private banks, which were much more aggressive in expanding lending. Over the next several years, the private banks increased their share of total bank assets from 20 to 25 percent, reflecting their strong response to removal of credit ceilings.

This pattern of deposit mobilization by the state banks, which was then intermediated through the private banks to the ultimate borrowers, worked quite well without causing any serious pressures on interest or exchange rates until September 1984, when the Indonesian financial system experienced not an excess of liquidity from foreign capital inflow, but a liquidity squeeze. This was due to the absence of any effective instrument for supplying liquidity and adjusting the available liquidity to changes in other factors affecting the supply of reserve money in the financial system. A sudden transfer of government deposits to the central bank reduced the supply of reserve money and, without any offsetting adjustment from the central bank, caused the liquidity squeeze.

Normally such a squeeze would have been met by a short-term inflow of funds from abroad under Indonesia's open foreign exchange system, but this liquidity squeeze was exacerbated by a concurrent steady depreciation in the exchange rate set by the central bank, which made the commercial banks very reluctant to sell foreign exchange, even for a few days to cover their reserve requirements. As a consequence, the domestic interbank interest rate shot up to 90 percent per annum, which was the annualized rate of daily depreciation of the exchange rate. The central bank overreacted and dumped large amounts of liquidity credits into the banking system, bringing the interbank interest rate down below 15 percent in a few days.

This experience demonstrated the many problems of indirect monetary controls and the necessity of building up the institutional base for such management. Specifically, it highlighted the need for the central bank to keep better track of the available supply of reserve money in the financial system, to develop further its instruments for controlling the supply of reserve money and to avoid too steady a depreciation of the currency. All of these measures are more or less taken for granted in an established, market-oriented financial system, but they do not exist in a bureaucratically managed system. When trying to make the transition from one to the other, it is important to make sure that these information flows and reactive instruments are available when needed.

The central bank had introduced one new instrument for reserve money control in February 1984, the Bank Indonesia Certificate or SBI. The SBI was a short-term liability of the central bank, comparable to a treasury bill, that was sold periodically by the central bank to commercial banks and other financial institutions to reduce the supply of reserve money. It was intended as a means of offsetting the expected inflow of foreign funds for conversion into reserve money, and it proved ineffective when there was a need, as in September 1984, to supply additional reserves. This led to the introduction in early 1985 of a second instrument in the form of a standardized commercial bill (SBPU), either issued or endorsed by the commercial banks, which could be discounted at the central bank. These two instruments, the SBI and the SBPU, provided readily available means to either withdraw reserves from, or add reserves to, the banking system.

Although the original plan had been for the prices of these two instruments to fluctuate according to changing market conditions, and for secondary markets to develop, the central bank in effect stood ready to supply or buy whatever amounts the banks wished to buy or sell at cut-off interest rates set by Bank Indonesia. While this practice did succeed in stabilizing the interest rates on these instruments and accustomed the banks to buying and selling them, it precluded the development of a real secondary market and reduced the central bank's control over reserve money.

In addition to setting the short-term interest rate, the central bank also set the foreign exchange rate and the premium on foreign exchange swaps that it offered to those financial institutions and businesses with future foreign exchange commitments. (Initially, the swap facility was offered in limited quantities, but the limits were removed in October 1986, following another large devaluation of 45 percent.) Thus, the central bank controlled three key prices: the SBI and SBPU money market interest rates, the foreign exchange rate and the swap rate on forward foreign exchange. It also stood ready to be the residual supplier of any excess demand or buyer of excess supply, within broad limits, in all three markets.

This pattern of price setting and willingness to meet excess demand by the central bank was particularly vulnerable to speculation about changes in the foreign exchange rate. And such speculation had been fostered by the three

326

sudden and large devaluations in 1978, 1983, and 1986. Whenever rumors spread in the financial markets that there might be another devaluation, most financial institutions and businesses took advantage of the free capital markets and bought foreign exchange or sold it to the central bank under a currency swap agreement. Very large moves in short-term interest rates would have been required to counteract such speculation, and the central bank was reluctant to permit such moves in the short-term rates that it controlled. As a consequence, the interbank borrowing rate, which the central bank did not control, became very volatile.

In June 1987, there was a speculative run on the rupiah and the interbank rate rose to 37 percent. The authorities, having concluded that there was no underlying justification for a devaluation, took drastic measures to reduce the supply of reserve money and force a return flow of foreign exchange to cover bank reserve requirements. The forced reduction in reserve money was accomplished through two measures. First, all commercial banks were required to repurchase their commercial bills (SBPUs) from the central bank; the ceilings on such rediscounts for each bank were suddenly reduced to zero. The second measure was an instruction to four state enterprises with large time deposit balances at the commercial banks to use those deposits to buy central bank bills (SBIs). Both measures shifted large amounts of reserves from the commercial banks to the central bank. The forced repurchase of commercial bank bills (SBPUs) eliminated that instrument of monetary policy for the time being, and the forced purchase by the state enterprises of SBIs with six-month maturity at a set interest rate did much to undermine the SBI as a flexible tool of monetary policy.

The effect of these strong measures was positive in one sense: it made clear that the government was prepared to defend the exchange rate and perhaps avoid any further large devaluations. This was very important for the psychological factors influencing domestic interest rates. The cost of these measures, however, was at least a temporary loss to the central bank of the market-based instruments for short-term liquidity management.

In late 1988, the Indonesian authorities announced a new set of reform measures. This time the focus was primarily financial and the main themes were to open up entry to new participants in the financial markets, to broaden the range of financial services, to shift from fixed to flexible interest and exchange rates, and to encourage the development of both domestic money and capital markets.

Licensing of new banks, opening of new branches, and entry of foreign banks in the form of joint ventures, all of which had been prohibited or highly restricted previously, were to be permitted. Similarly, new financial services such as factoring, consumer credit, venture capital, and securities dealing and underwriting were opened up to commercial banks either directly or through subsidiaries.

Bank reserve requirements were lowered to a uniform 2 percent on all deposits and the banks were initially required to hold increased quantities of SBIs as secondary reserves. The monetary authorities supported the development of a secondary market for SBIs and SBPUs to enhance their liquidity and encouraged a number of financial institutions to act as market-makers in these money market instruments.

Both exchange rate and money market interest rate management became more flexible. Gradual depreciation of the rupiah against the U.S. dollar, through a kind of crawling peg, was designed to further discourage speculation over a major devaluation, and at the same time give an indication of a steady spread between rupiah and dollar interest rates. Regular weekly auctions by the central bank of four-week SBIs were more accepting of and consistent with the prevailing rates in the secondary market.

All of these new measures are too recently implemented for one to predict how they are going to work out. But the direction of government policy at this time is clearly to free up the domestic financial markets to easier entry and flexible price movements. It is another step in the process of repatriating financial services from neighboring financial centers. At the same time, it opens up the Indonesian financial markets even more to the potential pressures and instabilities that may intrude from abroad.

Indonesia has, for twenty years, offered the interesting example of a country which has carried out financial reforms within the context, or constraint, of an open international capital system. This has necessitated a fairly gradual approach to freeing up domestic markets while always keeping an eye on movements in foreign exchange reserves. When faced with actual or anticipated runs on the currency, the authorities did not hesitate to carry out large devaluations, but this, in turn, caused expectations of further large devaluations, which meant that extreme fluctuations in short-term interest rates or other drastic measures were required to defend the exchange rate when that seemed to be an appropriate objective. A major challenge now and for the future is to convince participants in the Indonesian financial markets that large devaluations are no longer likely to occur so that more moderate adjustments in the exchange rate and domestic interest rates can exert a sufficient influence over short-term liquidity movements.

For over twenty years, Indonesia has managed to maintain a basic continuity of policy and direction of its economy that is rare in the developing world, and in sharp contrast to the experience of Turkey, discussed below. While some specifics of financial policy changed significantly during the era of high oil prices, the basic principles of a balanced fiscal budget and open capital account were maintained. Then, as financial resources again became scarce after 1982, the approach to financial reform was to free up prices and allocative controls rather than to tighten them. Further reform measures have recently been implemented despite, or perhaps because of, new external pressures from uncertain oil prices and a rising burden of foreign debt. The pattern in Indonesia since 1966 has been that when economic conditions become difficult and financial resources are scarce, there is a shift in policies toward greater reliance on market forces. When resources become more abundant, there is a shift to more bureaucratic, nonmarket-oriented allocation of those resources. The recent reforms are consistent with this pattern.

Financial Reform in Turkey

Turkey began in earnest the process of financial and other reform after the 1980 military takeover. Conditions in Turkey at that time were similar to those in Indonesia in 1966, the culmination of years of political strife, near civil war, economic disruption, and inflation. Economic and political changes were initiated during the 1980-83 military regime; they were continued and intensified by the elected government of Prime Minister Ozal. The reforms have expanded the role of market forces in the financial and real sectors by purposefully restricting the role of the central government in the enterprise decision-making process.

At the macroeconomic level, the government has been unsuccessful in its efforts to maintain stability during the attempted transformation from a controlled, state-dominated economy to a more market-oriented economy. Rapid depreciation, high rates of inflation, and erratic year-to-year changes in the financial and real variables characterize the entire period from 1980 to 1988. This instability seems to stem mainly from the inability to curb government spending.

Since 1980, Turkey has taken important measures to develop its financial system. These measures can broadly be classified as development of a sound financial infrastructure, more market-oriented interest rate and foreign exchange policies, and improvement in indirect tools of monetary control. Financial reform efforts in Turkey can be characterized in the context of the scheme developed in this paper as (1) all-out market-oriented domestic financial reforms; (2) with relatively strong controls over foreign exchange movements; and (3) part of a broad reorientation of economic policies.

The motivation and ability to move towards a more market-oriented economy grew out of a combination of factors. First, by 1980 the economy was in dire straits, with a negative GNP growth rate, rampant inflation, negative real interest rates, and a high public sector debt. Second, there was a personal commitment to a market-oriented economy by the head of the State Planning Organization, a strong and influential leader who in 1983 became prime minister. Third, the military, which was in power from 1980 to 1983, tended to support the reform process. Fourth, there was a need to increase foreign exchange earnings in the face of a large current account deficit. Fifth, the IMF and the World Bank, as a prerequisite to financial aid and debt restructuring, prodded the Turkish government to implement stabilization and structural adjustment programs that included more market orientation. Sixth, Turkish economists and businessmen living abroad were willing to return and take up key management positions in the public and private sectors. Last, the government wished to join and needed to be able to compete in the European Economic Community.

The reform measures in the period following 1980 covered both the financial and the real sectors of the economy. The domestic financial markets, long repressed, were opened up by a series of measures designed to maintain positive real rates of interest in order to encourage financial savings, to stimulate competition in lending and mobilizing funds both in liras and foreign exchange, and to provide for more diverse but sound financial instruments and institutions. Three main themes underlay the financial liberalization: to allow a greater reliance on the operation of the price mechanism (free up interest rates and maintain more flexible exchange rates); to build the necessary legal and institutional infrastructure to support money and capital markets (new laws, better accounting, new market arrangements, new institutions); and to improve monetary control through development and better use of instruments of monetary policy (reserve requirements, interbank markets, and open market operations). At the same time, the government began to promote change in the real sectors. Some of the more important reforms focused on government price controls, taxes, the foreign trade regime, state economic enterprises, and wages.

Interest rates and foreign exchange rates were key prices which the Turkish government set out to free up in 1980, but they have encountered many difficulties, especially in the area of interest rates. In fact, interest rate policy has been very erratic since 1980, with the authorities seemingly being forced to act on an ad hoc basis, experimenting with various alternatives whenever a crisis arose. They have vacillated between freeing up interest rates entirely, setting both deposit and loan rates, and setting only deposit rates. Their goal was maintenance of positive real deposit rates to encourage funds mobilization. Reaching this goal was stymied by several factors, including the oligopolistic behavior of the big banks in setting nominal rates below inflation rates, the response of the unregulated financial sector to disequilibrium rates, the erratic behavior of inflation itself, of exports, imports, and the government deficit and the lags in adjusting interest rates.

In July 1980, the monetary authorities lifted all controls on both deposit and loan rates. Upward pressure on these rates began to be exerted by smaller banks and a new group of unregulated, but not illegal, financial institutions called "brokers." These brokers were poorly capitalized and engaged in very risky investments, but they promised a better return than the banks. Many millions of people invested their savings with these brokers. In mid-1982, liquidity problems beset the brokers because even reliable brokerage houses had overextended themselves. The market collapsed, taking some small banks with it. The potential damage to the financial liberalization effort was great. The government acted quickly, salvaging many of the losses and attempting to dampen the panic that swept through the financial markets. By early 1983, under different circumstances, the central bank used moral suasion to get banks to lower nominal deposit rates. To offset inflationary pressures, the central bank again set deposit rates in late 1983. The deposit rate continued to be adjusted up and down by the central bank until the summer of 1987, when it was freed but again set by gentlemen's agreement among the banks at 38 percent. In February 1988, the inflation rate was running at nearly 70 percent, while the deposit rate was still 38 percent. The central bank intervened again, raising the nominal deposit rate to 52 percent, in response to a serious foreign exchange crisis.

Exchange rate policy has been more consistent than interest rate policy since 1980, when Turkey abandoned its fixed exchange rate system. Throughout the 1980-88 period, the government adhered to a managed but flexible exchange rate policy. The formula-driven adjustments in rates have resulted in significant depreciation of the lira. This inflation-related depreciation has undermined confidence in the Turkish lira and made it impossible for the government to make the lira fully convertible, despite the prime minister's full intention and actual announcement of his plan to do so. As a consequence, foreign exchange operations of the banks have had to be restricted.

One of the positive consequences of the 1982 "broker's crisis" was that the government came to realize the urgent need for a more secure underpinning of the financial system. It was seen that market-oriented policy measures needed to be supported by a strong financial infrastructure, including a sufficient level of regulation and supervision. Many elements of the regulatory infrastructure were

330

put into place from 1982 to 1987. They included a Capital Markets Law, a new Banking Law, reorganization of the stock exchange, rules on disclosure, capitalization, and issue of financial instruments. Accounting standards and external auditing were required for financial institutions. Banks were given the right to establish unit trusts, but under strict supervision.

In the pre-1980 period, monetary policy goals were pursued through direct controls. Interest rates and exchange rates were fixed by the monetary authorities, and there were strict foreign exchange controls. Reserve requirements were kept at high levels, but were subject to loose management. There were no flexible indirect monetary control instruments available to the central bank. Rediscount rates were used to allocate credit to priority sectors. There was no viable interbank market from which the central bank could get signals, and no open market operations.

In the post-1980 period, the monetary authorities began to set up the instruments and institutions that would allow them to operate through indirect monetary control measures. Several reform measures have been initiated, but with varying success. These include an improvement in the effectiveness of reserve requirements, the establishment of an interbank market, and initiation of open market operations.

In April 1986, the central bank opened an interbank money market in which it acted as a blind broker between lender and borrower. The purposes of this new market were to improve the efficiency of interbank borrowing and to give early indications to the central bank of the state of liquidity in the market. Previous to this, banks transacted on a bilateral basis. The central bank began open market operations in February 1987 by initially injecting TL 500 billion into the banking sector's reserves. In May 1987, the central bank expanded active open market operations by selling government bonds.

In the introduction to this paper, we identified recurring themes in the relationships between financial development and economic development. One theme is that the formal financial system should substitute for informal finance as the financial system develops. Two aspects of the Turkish story clearly reflect the influence of informal finance. The first, the 1982 "brokers crisis," resulted from the disequilibrium interest rate set by the bankers' oligopoly. The imperfections in this "informal market" (lack of governmental prudential regulation and lack of information) led to a crisis, which, in turn, had a positive influence in that it gave impetus to the development of a regulatory infrastructure, the establishment of unit trusts, and better supervised capital market operations. A second informal market is that of the *tahtakale* or parallel foreign exchange market. Though illegal, this market is tolerated because movements in the exchange rates away from the official rates give indications to the monetary authorities of speculative pressures against the lira. This market's negative reaction to the January 1988 announcement of the impending opening-up of foreign exchange markets forced the prime minister to retrench. The signal was that Turkey's macroeconomic instability made it impossible to free up foreign exchange markets. Since that time, the government has found it necessary to impose an "austerity program" to try to get its macro variables in order.

Another recurring theme, that "finance does not stand alone," is supported by the Turkish case. Inappropriate macroeconomic policies have undermined the financial progress. Although the government has made important advances in improving the financial structure, the failure, in particular, to contain the public deficit has resulted in inflation, which has led to many distortions, especially of the key financial policy variables that the government wanted to free up. There has had to be continuous and large-scale depreciation to keep exports competitive, increasing the costs of imports and leading to speculative behavior, particularly the desire to hold foreign exchange rather than Turkish lira. The attempt, and often failure, to keep real interest rates positive resulted in uncertainty, fluctuations in the demand for money, and shifts between demand and time deposits. At times very high real interest rates attracted funds to the banks but discouraged productive investment; at other times negative rates caused funds to flow from the banks to real estate speculation and gold. In general, smaller firms were starved of credit or forced to pay very high interest rates. Nonperforming loans of banks as well as business failures grew.

A third recurring theme is that complete deregulation of prices and markets is undesirable. The Turkish case supports the suggestion that there is some optimal middle ground during the liberalization process for government price-setting policies. The Turkish government has attempted to disengage from the role of setting financial prices—the interest rate and the exchange rate. We have briefly traced the chronology of the various attempts at freeing up these variables. The evidence is quite clear that the complete hands-off policy towards interest rates, adopted initially, was undermined by the collusion of the large banks to set deposit rates at too low levels. The Turkish government then opened up entry to both foreign and domestic banks, and many new banks started operations. However, a new problem arose when large holding companies established their own banks, thus segmenting and "protecting" their markets to some extent.

In the process of implementing financial reforms in Turkey, some important issues have arisen concerning the functions of a financial system. The first function of banks that we identify is that they can provide for an efficient form of savings, but must provide an adequate return to attract them. In Turkey, first, in order to provide for an efficient form of savings, banks had to be transformed from inefficient to efficient enterprises. The authorities hoped to promote competition and lower bank costs and lending rates, but they have not been very successful. The government has sought to bring about the reorganization and rationalization of the highly inefficient, but politically powerful and dominating, state-owned banks, to battle with the collusive practices of the large banks, and to deal with small banks that failed because of risky practices. Bank entry was opened up, but new types of market-segmenting behavior emerged. On the whole, concentration of bank assets did not change significantly in the period 1980-85; state-owned banks retained their 52 percent share, and the three largest private domestic banks slightly increased their share (43 percent), as did foreign banks (4 percent). There is evidence that bank interest margins have increased over the period rather than narrowed.

Second, the government desired that banks provide a reasonable, positive real rate of return in order to mobilize funds. The interest rate policy results were excellent in the initial years, but disappointing in the latter years. Inflation rates fluctuated considerably over the period; nominal interest rates were often less than inflation rates. Third, a function of a financial system should be to maintain a stable unit of account. This has clearly not been the case since 1980, resulting in the unfavorable side effects of instability and inflation.

National income statistics (subject to some doubt) indicate high average, but erratic, real GDP growth since 1981. Domestic investment by both the public and private sectors has grown significantly, financed by private savings. On the whole, there has been strong real economic performance, but it has been based on poor macroeconomic foundations: inflation, continuous depreciation, and public sector deficits causing instability.

Turkey's instability may simply reflect the severe strains that the transition from a controlled to a market-oriented economy in a relatively short time can put on an economic and political system. These strains can occur despite a country's effort to take significant measures to bolster its financial system. Fiscal and balance-of-payments deficits, partly due to domestic political pressures and partly due to external events, can overwhelm the authorities' efforts to contain inflation. The failure is reflected in the erratic behavior of the financial variables. Political factors are particularly important. During the reform process, the government may find it necessary to diverge from its all-out, market-oriented path, to use government expenditure to achieve political ends. This may have seemed necessary to the prime minister to stay in power in a democratic country with a strong statist history and vested interests.

In February 1988, the prime minister announced that the lira would be "floated" in March; the value of the lira on the parallel market plunged. The government had to retreat from many of its market-oriented policies to contain the speculation. The prime minister took this opportunity to announce an austerity program to deal with inflation. Monetary control was tightened and taxes raised. It is conceivable that Prime Minister Ozal, who attacked the banks as the culprits in the foreign exchange speculation, may have hoped to use this episode to wring out inflation, and then continue on with his reform process. One step back; two steps forward.

Financial Reform in Korea

The story of Korea is quite different from that of either Indonesia or Turkey. In 1965, Korea carried out one of the early partial financial reforms involving an increase in the bureaucratically determined bank deposit and loan rates. This partial reform was just one aspect of a major reorientation of economic policy from import substitution to export-oriented development. Korea managed to achieve very high rates of investment and economic growth after 1965 despite a relatively undersized banking system and highly controlled bank interest rates. Admittedly, the banking system did grow rapidly from 1965 to 1972 in response to positive real interest rates on deposits, but as these rates turned negative after 1972, growth of the banking system practically stopped while the economy continued to grow at nearly 10 percent each year.

Then in the early 1980s, following the assassination of President Park, a new government initiated a second round of financial reform that was supposed to turn over the banking system from public to private ownership and remove governmental controls over banking operations. What happened in fact was that the banks were so insolvent, after many years of bureaucratic abuse, that they had to continue to depend heavily on the central bank for funds and inevitably for direction. Despite this there occurred a very substantial financial reform and liberalization "through the back door." A combination of changes in macro policies and fortuitous events contributed to rapid growth of various types of nonbank financial institutions and capital markets, which took over much of the responsibility for financial accumulation and intermediation.

The shift in Korean economic policies from import substitution to export-led growth, in the mid-1960s, was accompanied by three significant changes in financial policy (Cole and Park 1983). The first was a rise in government-controlled interest rates on time deposits offered by banks: the maximum rate of 30 percent per annum was well above the average inflation rate. This led to a rapid build-up of time deposits in the banks and a rise in the ratio of M2 to GNP from 12 percent in 1965 to 36 percent in 1972.

The second policy change was to instruct the banks to give immediate and automatic financing to their customers upon presentation of export letters of credit (LC). The terms of this financing were 80 percent of the value of the LC, 90 to 120 days to repay, and interest rates of 6 percent. The volume of these loans grew very rapidly, and because the approval was automatic, it was not possible for banks to extract any rents above the stated interest rate. The banks would obviously have incurred a big loss by paying 30 percent on deposits and lending at 6 percent, but the central bank rediscounted the export loans at 3 percent and paid a partial subsidy on the time deposit interest to more than offset the negative spread. The commercial banks at the time were all owned by the government, which was less interested in profit and efficiency of the banks than in using them to support the savings and export campaign.

Korea's third policy change was to instruct both the commercial and the development banks, all government-owned, to guarantee repayment of all foreign loans approved by the government. This led to a large inflow of foreign loans that financed most of the capital investment of the new export industries as well as some of the infrastructure needed to support those industries. The growing exports helped to pay for both rising imports of intermediate goods and, eventually, the repayment of the foreign credits.

Thus, Korea's banking system was used to mobilize domestic savings by paying high interest rates and to attract foreign savings by guaranteeing foreign loans. It was also used to channel working capital and guarantee investment capital for the new export industries, both at very low rates of interest. Central bank subsidies and takeover of nonperforming loans helped the government-owned banks to minimize their losses. The question arises, why were the investments so efficient in the face of low interest rates and abundant financing?

Two forces made investment efficient. The first was the drive for exports in intensely competitive world markets. Government prodded and rewarded both the firms and the responsible government agencies that contributed to high export growth. The incentives for export growth were very great. Export markets were very competitive because not only Korea, but also Taiwan, Hong Kong, and Singapore were all trying to take existing markets away from Japan. To succeed in these markets, Korean producers had to be efficient in order to make good quality products at low cost. Their investment decisions were not guided by the cost of their capital, but by what would sell in the export market. Low-cost capital helped them compete.

Korean businesses, like their Japanese counterparts, could also accurately estimate the opportunity cost of the capital they were investing. In the large informal curb market where nonexporting businesses had to obtain their capital, interest rates were consistently high in real terms, about 20 percent per annum. These rates reflected the prevailing marginal return on capital in Korea at the time and served as a reference rate for investment decisions. If a business could not earn more than a 20 percent real rate of return on a new investment, it would do better to lend out any surplus funds on the informal market. But in the surging Korean economy, there were many investment opportunities that could earn those rates.

In the 1970s, the Korean government not only let bank deposit rates become negative, thereby stopping the growth of deposits at the banks; it also sought to extend the system of subsidized credit to finance large investments in the capital-intensive heavy and chemical industries. Typical of the development bank financing activities described above, these loans carried low interest rates and long repayment periods for investments that could never hope to earn the rates of return prevailing elsewhere in the economy. The loans absorbed much of the financing available from the banking system and forced other, more profitable businesses to seek financing elsewhere. Initially, they turned to the domestic informal market and to foreign lenders, but these sources began to dry up in the early 1980s as the Korean economy was hit by a recession, world-market interest rates shot up, and the Latin American debt crisis curtailed lending by foreign banks.

In 1980, following the death of President Park, the Korean economy experienced a crisis of confidence. Real output declined for the first time in over twenty years. The rice crop failed due to bad weather. There was political unrest as various groups vied for power. After a new government took power late in the year, it repudiated the heavy industry strategy and set out to reduce bureaucratic interference in the management of the economy. One aspect of the new program was to turn the banking institutions over to private ownership, and, at the same time, try to prevent them from being taken over by the large conglomerates which were heavily dependent on the banks for both loans and guarantees of foreign credits.

The government did manage to sell its interests in the commercial banks to private owners without fully disclosing that nonperforming loans made them technically insolvent. But since the banks were still so heavily dependent on central bank subsidies, the government continued to control them even though they were technically privately owned. The banks were in no position to move out and seek new funds or take on new activities. Instead, they have continued to play a limited role under the watchful eye of the central bank.

A second aspect of the new government's policy was to bring inflation under control by cutting back on government spending, raising taxes, and restricting growth of the money supply. The decline in world oil and other raw material prices in 1982 helped to reinforce the domestic policies so that inflation dropped to very low levels (2 to 3 percent) for the next several years. The restraints on the banking system, plus a crisis in the unregulated money-broker markets that made them temporarily very risky, forced a search for new channels of financial savings and intermediation.

Fortunately, the nonbank financial institutions, such as insurance, finance, trust, commercial paper companies, and the securities markets, which had been growing moderately for some time, were able to move into the breach. Between 1981 and 1985, the NBFIs increased their share of both deposits and loans from roughly one-third to one-half, with the shares of the banking sector declining correspondingly. Capital markets also became more active so that the share of banks in total corporate financing had dropped below 25 percent by 1985 (Cho and Cole 1986).

Thus, rather than becoming submerged by the troubled loans of commercial and development banks, the Korean financial system has continued to grow since 1980 by isolating the problems in the banks and permitting the NBFIs and the capital markets to increase the supply of funds at market interest rates to Korean firms for productive investment.

Foreign financing, which had been so important from 1965 to 1980, declined in importance during the 1980s both because of reduced world supply and reduced domestic demand. The Korean government had controlled foreign capital movements throughout this period, but even those controls relaxed in the latter part of the 1980s as the trade balance became highly positive and Korea moved from a net borrower to a net lender. Appreciation of the exchange rate made Korean financial assets increasingly attractive to domestic savers and helped to hold down nominal interest rates.

By early 1989 the Korean government, under political pressure for greater democracy and freedom from bureaucratic controls, announced plans to carry out a "real" financial reform. The main problem continued to be what to do with the insolvent commercial banks. Officials had hoped that the banks would grow out of their problem loans, but this has not happened because bank growth has been slow and the bad loans have increased. The rest of the financial system is functioning well on a largely market-determined basis, and the economy continues to grow at a high rate.

Some Generalizations about Financial System Reforms

The experience of a few countries does not provide an adequate basis for generalizing about the importance of, or the best approaches to, financial system reform. Nevertheless, the combined experiences of the relatively successful reform cases of Indonesia and Turkey, the many examples of deformed systems and even those cases of successful economic development with distorted financial systems, as in Korea, suggest some propositions that might be subjected to further testing.

The transition from a highly controlled to a market-oriented financial system is a very complicated process that can easily be derailed by political changes, external shocks, or lack of other complementary basic policies. Disequilibria in either the fiscal or balance-of-payments spheres put severe strains on the financial system and can easily overwhelm newly emerging instruments of monetary policy, thereby forcing a return to direct controls or acceptance of high rates of inflation and foreign capital surpluses or deficits, which further undermine financial reform. Many of these problems existed in the Turkish case and, although they did not stop the financial reforms, they made their continuation more difficult.

A market-oriented financial system requires a considerable infrastructure of institutions, information, and regulation, but these are all fundamentally different from those which prevail under a bureaucratically controlled financial system. The financial institutions have to be product and price conscious, offering services that are demanded in the market and pricing them to meet the competition. New types of information flows on bids and offers, transactions and prices, and, most of all, accurate financial accounting statements are needed for financial markets to work well. A supervisory and regulatory system oriented to asset quality and measures of liquidity and solvency must replace a system primarily concerned with following bureaucratic directives as to prices and credit allocation. All these changes not only take time, but also often require a change in leadership or, at least, in attitude of those directing key institutions. Failure to allow for and even support such changes slowed down the financial reform efforts in Indonesia.

Governmental bureaucracies seem to find it very difficult to give up their controls over operations of the banking system, especially those banks which are owned by the government and have been used for many years to favor special interests or support bureaucratic programs. In Indonesia the privately owned banks have been the ones that capitalized on deregulation, whereas the state-owned banks have been slow to respond, and the government has continued to use them to support special programs. In Turkey the banking sector has continued to be an oligopolistic group that has resisted market-determined prices or modernization of operations. Foreign banks and various channels of foreign financing have been the major new suppliers of funds for economic expansion. In Korea the banking system is still caught up in the problem of old nonperforming, government-directed loans, but the nonbank financial institutions and the money and capital markets have taken on much of the responsibility for mobilizing savings and financing development. Thus financial reform, at least in these three countries, has encountered great difficulty in bringing change to the banking system, which has continued to operate in the "old style" and to serve narrow bureaucratic purposes. Rather than leading the financial reform process, the older banking institutions have had to be dragged along or bypassed by the process.

The appropriate depth, breadth, and diversity of a market-oriented financial system depends upon the degree of complexity and decentralization of decision-making of the underlying economy. A simple agricultural, foreign trade-oriented economy does not need a sophisticated set of financial institutions. But as an economy becomes more specialized, interdependent, and decentralized, the financial needs become more diverse and complex. This transition of the real economy often highlights the weaknesses of an overly controlled financial system and generates pressure for reform such as has been taking place in Japan over the past decade, and now seems to be getting serious consideration in Korea.

The degree of openness of a country's financial system to international financial markets has a crucial influence on the process of financial reform. Clearly, there is more risk of large capital flows in and out of the country under an open system and, if the monetary policy instruments are not available to counteract such flows, domestic markets will be very unstable. On the other hand, unrestricted capital movements need not preclude domestic financial reforms, but they do require a more careful approach, such as that followed in Indonesia, to avoid excessive instability.

Restrictions on foreign capital movements are probably a necessary concomitant of domestic financial reform in those cases where the fiscal system is not well controlled or where instability of external trade receipts or payments subject the economy to severe shocks. Turkey has been able to carry out significant financial reforms in the face of erratic fiscal and trade deficits because it retained foreign exchange controls and steadily devalued the lira. Even the suggestion of full foreign exchange deregulation recently precipitated a crisis and forced some retrenchment on the reforms.

A well-functioning, market-driven financial system is not essential for economic development, but if it exists, it will tend to facilitate economic development, and, if it does not, its absence may eventually retard development. An over-controlled and distorted financial system is not likely to affect resource allocation seriously if the other aspects of basic economic policy (i.e., fiscal and trade-exchange rate policy) are not distorted, and if unregulated domestic or foreign financial markets can mobilize and reallocate the available financing. Perhaps the most severe limitation of an over-controlled financial system is that it either undersupplies or misprices longer-term financing, as was the case in both Korea and Indonesia in the 1970s. Some enterprises get very cheap long-term funds while others have to use short-term funds to finance long-term investment, thus taking on the risk of term transformation. In economies that are growing steadily and rapidly, such as postwar Japan, South Korea, and Taiwan, this risk is not very great, but in less dynamic or more unstable economies the distortions of the capital structure can retard longer-term growth. Also, in time a high-growth economy will become more diversified and may experience difficulty in allocating resources efficiently without improved financial markets. ๛

Notes

1 The boundary line between formal and informal parts of a financial system varies across countries. In some countries the division can be approximated by banks versus moneylenders. In other cases smaller banks and finance companies, although they are registered and supposedly regulated, nevertheless function as largely unregulated institutions. In still other cases, such as that of Korea, a three-way distinction among regulated, semi-regulated, and unregulated may be more appropriate. Banks tend to be the heart of the regulated and bureaucratically controlled part of the system; finance companies, money, and capital markets may be semi-regulated; and a wide range of borrowing and lending institutions, from large corporations to small village stores, make up the informal, unregulated part. For analytical purposes, the three-way division is not much different from the two-dimensional one. The main question is whether the semi-regulated middle part functions more like the highly controlled banking sector, or like the uncontrolled informal sector.

2 McKinnon (1973) and Shaw (1973), while recognizing the multiple functions of a financial system, believed that financial systems became "repressed" because of interest rate controls and inflationary credit expansion. They advocated "liberalization" of the financial system by removing interest rate controls, or raising controlled interest rates, and also by controlling the growth of the money supply. Their ideas have had an important influence on the approaches to financial reform in a number of countries. In our view, they overlooked the broader needs for regulatory change, institutional reform, and the influence of other policy actions on the development of the financial system.

3 Whether a positive real interest rate on savings deposits has an impact on the overall rate of savings, in national income accounting terms, is still subject to debate. Nevertheless, positive real interest rates are likely to increase the share of total savings held in the form of financial assets, thereby causing such assets to rise as a share of GNP even if real savings do not grow, and permitting financial institutions to play a larger role in meeting the needs of savers.

4 The benefits to development of an inflation tax, supported by some in the past, seem much less apparent after the recent hyperinflations in Latin America. With low or moderate inflation, savers are less inclined to hold their assets in gold, other property, or abroad, thus making more of their savings available to domestic investment.

5 Some of the informal financial institutions were private savings associations that would take periodic deposits and lend them sequentially to members. Others were regular moneylenders, or even large money brokers, who amassed large pools of funds for big business borrowers. Also, many large industrial or trading corporations that were able to gain access to subsidized commercial bank credit or foreign loans extended credit to their suppliers or distributors in lieu of direct bank financing. Interest rates on these credits were generally positive in real terms and sometimes very high. Since the informal, unregulated institutions are not included in the national financial statistics, the migration of financial activity from the banking system to the informal sector showed up only as a relative decline in financial services.

6   Some NBFIs were described as merchant banks even though their true function was a variation of commercial banking. Other forms were finance companies, commercial paper dealers, leasing companies, and even insurance companies. The assets and liabilities of NBFIs are at least partially recorded in national financial statistics, but they are generally omitted in the more common comparative measures of financial services, such as the ratio of "broad money" (M2) to GNP.

7   Usually the removal of loan ceilings has been accompanied by greater reliance on indirect monetary controls over the reserve base to maintain some control over credit expansion. In the past, some countries used adjustments in reserve ratios to control the growth of credit and money supply, but reserve requirements are increasingly recognized as a type of tax on the banking system which discourages its growth, so that in recent years there has been a trend toward general lowering of reserve ratios in both developed and developing countries.

8   Taiwan is a rather amazing example of a country that has retained moderate foreign exchange controls even though its foreign exchange reserves are among the highest in the world in absolute dollar terms. Taiwan still maintains a controlled exchange rate and retains many controls over the lending activity of its financial institutions. Hong Kong, on the other hand, as befits an international financial center, has no restraints on international capital movements, but is committed to a fixed exchange rate between the Hong Kong and the U.S. dollar.

Reform of Rural Credit in Indonesia:

Inducing Bureaucracies to Behave Competitively

Donald R. Snodgrass and Richard H. Patten

Donald R. Snodgrass is a development economist who has spent much of the past decade working with the Center for Policy and Implementation Studies in Indonesia on rural banking and other development programs and policies. He is an Institute fellow at HIID and lecturer on economics at Harvard University.

Richard H. Patten has worked for HIID since 1961 as an adviser on rural development and credit in Bangladesh (East Pakistan), Ghana, and Indonesia. He is a project associate with HIID's Bank Rakyat Indonesia Project.

Introduction: The Problem of Rural Credit Reform[1]

The Need for Reform

The volume of rural credit extended in developing countries has risen enormously over the past three decades, spurred by the desire to finance input purchases required by new agricultural technologies.[2] This expansion of rural lending has been accompanied by widespread difficulties. Default rates have been high in most programs (Donald 1976, Sanderatne 1978, Adams 1980, Sanderatne 1986, Meyer and Nagarajan 1988). Critics have charged that more money went to rich than to poor farmers (Adams 1981, Adams and Graham 1981, Gonzales-Vega 1983, Vogel 1984) and did little to raise agricultural production (Vogel and Larsen 1980). Some lending agencies were not permitted to accept deposits that could have provided funds for lending, while others put little effort into deposit mobilization because subsidized loan interest rates made it unprofitable. Most loan finance came either from the national government concerned or from international assistance. When the funding source tired of continual appeals for additional contributions, the integrity of the primary lending agency, usually a specialized rural lending institution, was often jeopardized.

As these problems became evident, a "new view" of rural credit emerged from the United States Agency for International Development's *Spring Review of Agricultural Credit* in 1972-73. Vigorously propounded by Dale Adams and his colleagues at Ohio State University, the "new view" became orthodoxy among economists but was slower to influence practitioners. Its fundamental tenet was that "commercial" rather than subsidized interest rates should be charged in small-scale and rural lending programs. This, "new view" advocates argued, would ensure a positive real rate of interest and promote the development of rural financial markets, rather than impeding their development as traditional credit programs had done. Funds for relending could be generated through the savings that now became profitable and through reinvested earnings. Although higher interest rates for poor borrowers might seem unfair, "new view" proponents argued that equity would actually improve because access to credit would be open to anyone willing and able to pay the going interest rate. This would be both more equitable and more efficient than the rationing of credit on nonmarket criteria (cf. Claudio Gonzales-Vega's "iron law" of credit allocation [1984]) that allocates funds in subsidized lending programs, which inevitably face excess demand.

The Path to Reform

Although the "new view" critique clearly stated that interest rates should be decontrolled and government regulation generally should be reduced, it provided little more specific guidance on how to carry out a credit reform.

Traditional credit programs were undertaken in the belief that farmers and other small-scale rural entrepreneurs had credit needs that went unmet because commercial banks would not serve such customers and the moneylenders who were their primary source of credit charged very high interest rates. It is now recognized that the "informal financial sector" has major advantages as a source of small enterprise finance—that, contrary to popular belief, its high interest rates are more a reflection of risk and lender transaction costs than of monopoly power (Long 1968, Bottomley 1975), and even that its interest rates may not be so much higher than those of institutional lenders (Fernando 1988). Nevertheless, the potential contribution that developing financial markets and financial institutions can make to economic development by stimulating savings and facilitating intermediation between savers and investors provides support for public intervention to build up the formal financial sector and extend its services to classes of business that it has not yet served (Shaw 1973, McKinnon 1973).

Nor does the "new view" tell us what form the primary lending institution should take (Bottrall and Howell 1980). While a few students of rural finance have favored cooperatives (Schaefer-Kehnert 1986) or specialized lending institutions, most agree that a bank or other institution that takes deposits as well as makes loans is to be preferred (Von Pischke 1981, Vogel and Burkett 1986). As a rule, private banks are regarded as better agents of the commercial approach favored by the "new view" than public sector institutions (Graham and Cuevas 1984).

This paper discusses a case of rural credit reform in which the initiating and implementing body was a government-owned commercial bank. If private banks had been expected to do the lending under the reformed system, the fundamental policy problem would have been to devise a policy framework consisting of incentives and disincentives that would induce them to make small loans effectively. In our case, with a public financial enterprise implementing the reform, the critical need was to restructure incentives for managers at several different levels of the organization in ways that would make the bank as a whole operate less like a bureaucracy and more like a business responding to market signals.

The Indonesian Case

Commercial banking in Indonesia is dominated by five large government-owned banks. There are also about seventy domestically owned private banks, mostly small, and ten foreign and joint-venture banks. The system is urban-oriented. Foreign banks have been restricted to Jakarta and private domestically owned banks have also concentrated on the capital (Nasution 1983). Even government-owned banks other than the one with which we are concerned here have rarely operated below the level of the district (*kabupaten*) capital. General banking reforms adopted in October 1988, December 1988, and March 1989 are intended to widen the coverage of the banking system.

A number of secondary (market and rural) banks operating on a local or regional basis make small loans to traders and petty producers. Various nonbank institutions, including the perennially illiquid cooperatives, also make loans. A successful and well-known example of a small regional lending operation is the *Badan Kredit Kecamatan* (Subdistrict Loan Board) of Central Java (Goldmark and Rosengard 1983). Another type of lending institution that is long-established and well patronized by low-income borrowers, especially in rural Java, is the government-owned pawnshops.

Rural Indonesians also borrow extensively from noninstitutional sources such as friends, neighbors, relatives, professional moneylenders (officially scorned), and retailers and wholesalers who give trade credit. The rotating savings and credit association (ROSCA), known in Indonesia as the *arisan*, is popular at all levels of society. There are also self-styled community groups, sometimes called cooperative saving and loan societies (KOSIPA), which lend at high interest rates and may be little more than camouflage for moneylenders. A rural borrower who is unable to obtain an interest-free or preferential loan from a friend, relative, or patron (and even this is likely to involve reciprocal obligations in some form) must usually borrow short-term at an interest rate of 10 percent a month or more.

People borrow for both consumption and production purposes. Before 1970 farmers used few purchased inputs but suffered from seasonal fluctuations in the price of rice, so they borrowed primarily to fill consumption needs in times of low cash inflow (Mears 1981, 311-13). Financing rice intensification became the main objective of government-sponsored credit programs in the 1970s, but close observation of the rural economy indicates that rice intensification is only one of many sources of demand for production credit, especially small working capital loans. Most rural households have several sources of income, and many on Java obtain more income from nonagricultural activities than from agriculture. The scarcity of working capital makes the marginal return on capital high, and innumerable rural producers have shown that they can successfully amortize loans at high rates of interest. Credit targeted for a particular purpose tends to be added to a family's pool of working capital and used wherever the expected return is highest.

Kredit Umum Pedesaan (KUPEDES) or General Rural Credit, the form of rural lending introduced in 1984, is provided through the village units of the Indonesian People's Bank, Bank Rakyat Indonesia (BRI). BRI is a state-owned commercial bank which has been assigned responsibility for rural and small-scale lending. One of five state-owned commercial banks, BRI is the latest in a line of officially promoted people's banks stretching back to 1895. At the end of 1985, BRI had a central office in Jakarta, fifteen regional offices, and 294 branches, located in all of Indonesia's twenty-seven provinces (Nasation 1983). Below the branch level are the *BRI Unit Desa*, which numbered 3,626 at the end of 1985 according to BRI statistics. *Unit Desa* means village unit, but the average Unit Desa actually serves fifteen to twenty villages.[3] Its village units were established in the early 1970s to provide credit to rice farmers (Robinson and Snodgrass 1987). The introduction of KUPEDES in 1984 marked the start of an effort to develop a network of village offices and service posts providing simple but reasonably comprehensive banking services at locations convenient to people in the rural areas throughout Indonesia.

KUPEDES differs from the typical government-sponsored credit program, which focuses on a narrow "target group" defined by a government department, not by a bank. Indonesia has more than one hundred such programs, in which interest rates are set at levels intended to persuade members of a target group to undertake particular activities which the department concerned thinks would be beneficial (fish pond construction, livestock purchase, rural electrification, hand tractor use, purchase of four-wheeled vehicles by teachers, etc.). These interest rates are too low to permit the handling bank to perform the normal intermediation function of mobilizing savings and lending these savings for viable economic activities with a spread that covers operating costs and loan losses.

Sponsored credit programs in Indonesia, as elsewhere, are funded either from the government budget or from foreign aid. Savings generation is not emphasized. Loan interest fails to cover operating costs and loan losses, both of which are high. The result is a crippled banking institution, dependent on the government both for resources to lend and for continuing subsidization to cover operating costs. By contrast, KUPEDES aims at development of a financially viable, unsubsidized rural banking system offering a wide range of banking services to the majority of the Indonesian population, which has no effective access to banks other than the BRI village unit.

An earlier paper (Patten and Snodgrass 1987) described the background and content of KUPEDES. Here we briefly recapitulate that description, updating it to the end of 1988. We then consider why the reform was undertaken, why it took the shape it did, what the outcome has been, and what lessons would-be credit reformers elsewhere can learn from its experience.

Background of Rural Banking Reform

BIMAS Rice Credit and the Establishment of the BRI Village Units

From 1970 to 1984 the largest rural lending program of the Indonesian government was a component of the Improved National *Bimbingan Massal* (BIMAS) or Mass Guidance program. BIMAS encompassed a set of activities— agricultural extension, improved and subsidized input supply, and rice price support, in addition to credit—intended to induce farmers to intensify rice production by using new seeds, fertilizer, insecticides, and improved cultivation methods. BIMAS credit was provided partly in kind (participating farmers received chits redeemable for fertilizer and other inputs) and partly in cash (a small "cost of living" component and sometimes other elements). It was repayable in cash at a 12 percent annual interest rate. While earlier forms of rice credit had been extended through farmers' groups, the design adopted in 1970 called for loans to be made directly to millions of individual farmers through the village units of BRI, a new type of institutional network that would make loans and collect repayments.

Early experience with BIMAS was favorable. Until 1975 farmer participation rose and loan losses stayed below 5 percent. Then farmers began leaving the program as they encountered difficulties with pests, flooding, and drought. Many found easier ways to acquire the fertilizer and other inputs required for high rice yields. BIMAS borrowers whose rice crops were disappointing either repaid with difficulty from other sources of income (and often dropped out of the program thereafter) or defaulted and were barred from further borrowing.

With participation and repayment both falling in the late 1970s and early 1980s, the government vacillated between policies (such as selective debt forgiveness) that encouraged enrollment but weakened repayment and those (such as heavy-handed debt collection campaigns) which had the opposite effects. The number of farmers enrolled in BIMAS fell by 60 percent from 1975 to 1983, while the share of credit ever repaid dropped from 95 percent or more to 80 percent or less, and the percentage repaid on time fell even more sharply. By the early 1980s, surviving BIMAS participants tended to be either the richest farmers, who used their eligibility to obtain cheap credit which they put to various uses, or the poorest ones, who were driven to borrow by their poverty. In October 1983, responding to charges that BIMAS was only for the rich, the government banned loans to farmers cultivating one hectare or more of rice land. This virtually ended the BIMAS credit program.

This is a highly condensed version of a story that has been told in greater detail elsewhere. (See DPIS 1983 and Robinson and Snodgrass 1987.)

BIMAS credit probably did promote the growth of rice production in the early 1970s. After 1975 most farmers no longer needed BIMAS credit to induce or permit them to increase yields, and production continued to rise, despite the decline of BIMAS.[4] Regardless of its effect on rice production, BIMAS left Indonesia an important legacy in the form of the BRI village units.

BRI had little autonomy in BIMAS lending. Farmers certified by the Ministry of Agriculture's extension workers as participants in the BIMAS program as a whole in effect were preapproved as borrowers. In principle, the village units could reject loan applicants, but they were often pressed to accept all comers by local officials who were themselves under pressure to achieve the area targets that were used to motivate the bureaucracy to expand the program and which served as a major criterion for evaluating local officials. Some officials conspired to make loans to fictitious borrowers and pocket the money, which eventually became a bad debt. This was a common form of corruption under BIMAS.[5]

Except during sporadic loan collection campaigns, neither the extension workers nor the local officials had much interest in collecting BIMAS debt. Even BRI's incentive to obtain loan repayments was limited, since the central bank and Ministry of Finance absorbed 75 percent of the bad debt (although they were often slow to pay) and an administrative subsidy from the government covered much of the cost of operating the village units.

With BIMAS collapsing in the early 1980s and BRI faced with possible losses of Rp. 30 billion a year, there was every possibility that the village unit system would be dismantled.[6] Closing the village units would have eliminated formal banking services in about 90 percent of all locations in the country that had such services at the end of 1982, destroying a socially useful and potentially profitable institution.

Other Forms of BRI Village Unit Credit

During the 1970s the BRI village units were asked to manage several smaller credit programs similar to BIMAS, with similar results. Collection problems eventually caused most of these programs to be transferred to the BRI branches for closer administration. Two credit programs, however, did much better than the others. Kredit Mini, initiated in 1974, made loans of up to Rp. 200,000 (then $482) to individuals involved in any form of rural enterprise. The loans were made at a 12 percent annual interest rate and the staff of the BRI village unit was permitted to judge the borrower's repayment capacity. Grant funds for Kredit Mini were provided to BRI by the Ministry of Finance. Kredit Midi, begun in 1980, was intended for "graduates" of Kredit Mini. It made loans of up to Rp. 500,000 (equivalent to $797 in 1980), also at 12 percent, and was funded by 3 percent liquidity credits from Bank Indonesia.

Although Kredit Mini and Kredit Midi worked better than BIMAS and other targeted loan programs, they used the same artificially low interest rate. Lending at 12 percent, BRI would have had to increase the value of Mini and Midi loans outstanding from Rp. 110 billion ($120 million in 1983) to at least Rp. 600 billion ($660 million) to break even.

Savings

Tabungan Nasional (TABANAS), the National Savings Scheme, was devised by Bank Indonesia for use throughout the banking system and introduced into the village units in 1977. To attract small depositors, a 15 percent interest rate on the first Rp. 1 million (then $2,410) deposited in an account was introduced in June 1983. TABANAS balances held in the village units grew slowly over the years, reaching Rp. 38 billion ($37 million) at the end of 1984, but BRI had a disincentive to raise savings because it lent at 12 percent and the spread was thus negative. If pressed, BRI officials would explain that the provision of TABANAS accounts, like BIMAS lending, was something the bank did in its role as an "agent of development," not in its role as a bank.

Institutional Development

The network of village units grew rapidly in the early 1970s. By the end of 1975 there were 2,981 BRI village units in operation. Later growth was steady but much slower. The maximum number of units, 3,626, was reached in 1984.

A standard village unit has a staff of four. In the late 1970s the volume of business in many units no longer justified a staff of four and the actual number of staff was permitted to fall to three. A unit head (*Kepala Unit Desa*) is its general manager, responsible for all its activities and for supervision of the other staff. A field agent (*mantri*) works mainly outside the office, investigating loan applications and collecting loan repayments. A cashier handles all cash transactions in the village unit office. Finally, a bookkeeper maintains the individual loan and savings accounts, makes normal bookkeeping entries, balances the books, and prepares reports to be sent to the branch. These employees are members of a special cadre (unlike other BRI employees, they do not have civil servant status) and are given special training in the jobs they will hold. All village unit staff members are male (as far as we know), most are of rural origin, and the great majority are high school graduates, often from the commercial stream. By rural standards, these are attractive and well-paid jobs. BRI was able to hire from a large pool of applicants until late 1988, when it tried to upgrade its educational standard and ran into a shortage of qualified candidates.

On average, in 1983, twelve village units were supervised by a single BRI branch office through a special officer or division within the branch office and a network of field inspectors (*penilik*) selected from among the best village unit heads. The village unit operated less like a separate branch office than as a remote window of the supervising branch. It had no independent authority to make loan decisions, even for Kredit Mini and Kredit Midi, but only put together a file of loan application documents, which was then examined and approved or disapproved in the branch office. The village unit was permitted to hold only tiny amounts of cash overnight—in some cases, none at all. Although separate books were kept for each village unit, the bookkeeping format did not permit a clear cut appraisal of the unit's performance to be made.

Initiation of the Reform

The 1984 rural credit reform was not undertaken in response to a crisis, but it does not exactly fit the "politics-as-usual" framework either (Grindle and

Thomas; see chapter 3). Rather, it was a response to problems and opportunities that had arisen, informed by the lessons of experience both in Indonesia and in other countries. By 1982 the shortcomings of the existing rural credit system had become obvious and desirable features of a better system had already been listed: financially viable lending institutions; an ability to respond to all kinds of credit requests from rural family enterprises; loans made on the basis of character references without a collateral requirement; flat, previously announced weekly or monthly amortization schedules; similar interest rates on all types of loans; and, most important, transactions conducted at the village level (Patten 1982).

Although the general lines of reform were clear, actual or potential objections to the proposed changes blocked a decision to go ahead until late 1983. There were four important obstacles.

(1) **The regulatory stance of the Central Bank**. The Central Bank had a long history of intervention in banking matters and had installed a number of direct controls aimed at influencing both the volume and composition of credit. However, increasing recognition that this type of regulation was ineffective and self-defeating led to a general banking deregulation in June 1983. This freed the banks from quantitative restrictions on lending and permitted them to set the interest rates they charged on loans and those they paid on deposits other than TABANAS. The new regulatory framework permitted BRI to set higher interest rates on its rural loans, but, as discussed below, political objections to exercising this freedom remained in force.

(2) **Preferences of the Ministry of Agriculture**. The ministry preferred a credit system that directed loans to clients selected by its own representatives. This preference outlived BIMAS and is still evident in a number of directed agricultural credit programs sponsored by the Ministries of Agriculture and Cooperatives. These programs require government subsidization.

(3) **Commitment to cooperatives**. Indonesia is ideologically committed to the development of cooperatives as an important form of economic enterprise. Many government officials continue to believe that cooperatives should be subsidized and given monopolies over various rural economic activities, including the provision of credit.

(4) **Sensitivity about commercial interest rates**. As the government bank charged with lending to rural and small-scale producers, BRI was in a good position to initiate and carry out a rural credit reform, despite these objections. But it faced a final barrier to action: uncertainty that the government would permit higher interest rates to be charged. Higher rates, it was feared, would draw public and parliamentary charges of discrimination against poor rural borrowers vis-à-vis richer urban borrowers. The fact that higher interest rates could increase the availability of institutional credit in rural areas by permitting the bank to generate loanable funds was not widely recognized. Nor did urban critics realize that most rural borrowers would happily pay more in return for improved access to bank credit because their alternative was to borrow from the informal market at 10 percent per month or more.

That it proved possible to overcome these objections and opt for reform in late 1983 is attributable to three factors.

(1) **The choice forced by the collapse of BIMAS**. As we have seen, the fall of BIMAS left the BRI village units without a function and at risk of being shut

down. Problems had also arisen with Kredit Mini and Kredit Midi. Although repayment rates in these programs had generally been good, some branches and village units had accumulated large arrears by 1982. BRI responded by forbidding these units to extend additional credit, even to good borrowers. This caused the repayment rate to fall as borrowers became uncertain about their ability to refinance after repaying an existing loan and thus increasingly opted to hold on to the credit that they already had. The BRI village units were clearly at a fork in the road: they had to be either given a new function or closed down.

(2) **The declining acceptability of subsidized programs**. The 1983 bank deregulation and other policy reforms undertaken in the early 1980s were motivated largely by a basic change in Indonesia's macroeconomic prospects. During the 1970s the country had enjoyed historically unprecedented rates of economic growth, resulting mainly from its ability to export petroleum and natural gas at high prices. Even if oil prices had not fallen in the early 1980s, changes would eventually have been mandated by exhaustion of Indonesia's oil and gas reserves, which were not large in relation to rapidly growing domestic demand for petroleum products. High oil and gas receipts during the 1970s fueled rapid expansion of the public sector, which in 1981 received as much as 70 percent of its revenue directly from the oil and gas industry (Gillis 1984, 3). The desire to reduce dependence on oil and the government budget which it fed prompted a number of policy measures, ranging from tax reform to privatization. In rural banking it meant that the government could no longer afford to pass large amounts of budget funds through the banking system into rural credit. A credit program carried out by a bank on a largely self-financing basis became more attractive.

(3) **Key personnel changes**. Two offices critical to the reform decision changed hands in 1983 when a new minister of finance and a new president-director of BRI were appointed. Although the new incumbents of both offices were no more sympathetic to rural credit reform than their predecessors had been, their appointments accelerated the decision to proceed. Each of the new men seemed to seize on the reform plans that were being formulated when he took over as something that could be done quickly to get his term of office off to a productive start. Both therefore became actively involved in the final stages of defining the reform and issuing the administrative decrees needed to begin its implementation.

These factors tipped the balance in favor of reform, but only barely. Lingering concern about potential opposition was indicated by the lack of a public announcement when KUPEDES lending began in early 1984, and by the fact that the rate of interest charged was not stated explicitly but was left implicit in the repayment schedules shown to potential borrowers.

Within the Ministry of Finance, the Center for Policy and Implementation Studies (CPIS) had formed a Rural Credit Working Group (RCWG) in late 1982. This group produced a series of discussion papers on rural credit reform. In September 1983 the minister of finance decided to go ahead with the reform. KUPEDES was initiated in January 1984.

Aims of the Reform

The rural credit reform was intended to improve access to bank credit for all types of rural producers. The means of improving access was to be the profit motive. Rather than exhorting BRI to be an "agent of development" against its own business interests, the reform tried to create a Smithian situation in which profit opportunities would induce BRI to work for the good of society.

The starting point was the loan interest rate. Rather than setting this rate low to attract borrowers, the main concern was to set it high enough to make the program viable and attractive to BRI. With little or no government subsidy in prospect and savings likely to be the main source of loanable funds, this meant that the spread between the lending and saving interest rates should offer BRI the prospect of a profit, given its administrative costs and expected loan losses.

Savings interest rates in Indonesia must meet two criteria: they must be positive in real terms and provide a sufficient premium over Singapore rates to deter capital flight by people who estimate the risk of devaluation to be high. The second criterion is important because Indonesia has maintained an open foreign exchange market for many years. It is less significant for rural than for urban savers, but it controls the general level of savings interest rates in the country.

Up to 1986 the main savings instrument provided by the BRI village units was TABANAS. The 15 percent rate paid on TABANAS deposits of Rp. 1 million or less exceeded the prevailing rate of inflation and thus satisfied the basic requirement for the village units to mobilize savings. Using this 15 percent savings interest rate as the potential cost of funds and assuming that the operating costs of the village units (mainly the cost of staff) would increase by no more than 15 percent a year, the RCWG projected that the system would begin to break even at Rp. 200 billion of loans outstanding if the interest rate provided a 15 percent spread over the cost of funds and the loss ratio was no more than twice that experienced in Kredit Mini. The calculation thus indicated that the effective loan rate should be approximately 30 percent. Although this was much more than the 12 percent charged in earlier subsidized official programs, it was far less than rural borrowers had to pay on loans from alternative sources available to them. Because of the excess capacity then existing in the village unit system, the RCWG believed that the projected break-even point of Rp. 200 billion in loans outstanding could be reached in eighteen months without adding staff.

Rp. 200 billion was twice the amount of Kredit Mini and Kredit Midi outstanding at that time. Doubling credit in eighteen months would require additional capital injections. Further growth in the volume of credit beyond the break-even point would generate increasing profits, provided that the repayment rate held up and costs did not escalate unduly. These profits could then be used to retire debt or to pay "dividends" to the government, BRI's sole "stockholder." In theory, profits could also be used to increase loanable funds. However, as we shall see, Indonesian public enterprise regulations do not permit this.

The projections indicated that a socially beneficial improvement in access to rural credit and a profitable expansion of BRI's business could be realized simultaneously. Making the projections a reality, however, would require an appropriate behavioral response from BRI, a large organization with staff spread around the country in its central, regional, and branch offices as well as the village

350

units. While the opportunity for BRI to make a profit is undoubtedly stronger institutional motivation than simply being acclaimed as an "agent of development," it would have been naive to assume that this profit opportunity alone would motivate all of BRI's employees to carry out their duties enthusiastically and effectively and thereby make the program a success. For the goal to be reached, it would be necessary to devise a set of incentives and sanctions that would induce BRI employees at all levels to work hard to achieve the overall objective.

Content of the Reform

Loan Terms and Arrangements

A KUPEDES loan of up to Rp. 3 million[7] can be obtained for any kind of productive enterprise operated by a rural resident. Since most families have more than one source of income, loans are often repaid from income generated by activities other than the one for which the loan was obtained. Consumption loans are not permitted, but there is no effective way to prevent the increase in available funds from being used to increase consumption if that is what the borrower wants.

A loan applicant lists a particular enterprise as the one for which the loan is taken. The BRI village unit staff looks at the cash flow of that enterprise and recommends an appropriate repayment schedule from a list of alternatives prescribed by the central office and posted in the village unit office. Repayment schedules are available for working capital loans of three, six, nine, twelve, eighteen, twenty-four, and thirty-six weeks with no grace period or with grace periods of three, six, or nine months. Single payment tables for loan periods from three to twelve months are also available for working capital loans. Investment loan schedules call for a similar range of repayments and grace periods up to thirty-six months. When the borrower has several enterprises, the one chosen is usually the enterprise with the most regular cash flow. As a result, the majority of KUPEDES loans are listed as being for trade and most loans are for twelve months with monthly installments.

The interest rate for a KUPEDES working capital loan is 1.5 percent per month, calculated as a flat rate on the full amount of the loan. The effective interest rate is the same for all repayment schedules.

There is a penalty of 0.5 percent a month for failure to pay on time. Since the penalty is unlikely to be collectible after the borrower has already defaulted, all borrowers are charged a 2 percent flat rate and the extra 0.5 percent is returned to those who paid all installments in full and on time. This Prompt Payment Incentive (IPTW) is paid into the savings account of the borrower and may be withdrawn whenever the customer wishes. This is a control measure which allows easier audit.

The interest rate for KUPEDES investment loans is 1 percent per month, again calculated as a flat rate. The 0.5 percent penalty and IPTW provision are the same as for working capital loans. Bank Indonesia provides liquidity credit at 3 percent per annum for KUPEDES investment loans. Thus, the spread is approximately the same for working capital and investment loans. The liquidity credit constitutes a continuing subsidy, but it is not important since investment credit outstanding at the end of April 1987 was only Rp. 13.6 billion out of a total of Rp. 389 billion for all forms of KUPEDES. The subsidy for investment loans was retained at the insistence of Bank Indonesia. It is surprising that the volume of lending in a subsidized category of lending is so small, since borrowers have an incentive to apply for investment credit whenever possible. The reason may be that the individual loan ceiling for KUPEDES is so low that few forms of fixed equipment qualify. The extensive paperwork (bids, receipts, etc.) required on investment loans may also inhibit some potential borrowers.

Although the RCWG had proposed that KUPEDES loan decisions be based solely on the borrower's character and previous repayment experience, Indonesian banking law and practice have mandated the continuation of a collateral requirement. A borrower must provide collateral sufficient to cover the value of the loan. While in principle any type of property may serve as collateral, in practice it usually takes the form of land. For an initial loan of Rp. 400,000 or less, any document that indicates ownership of land, such as a signed statement of local officials or evidence of having paid land tax, may be used to satisfy the collateral requirement. Above Rp. 400,000, a land certificate to prove ownership is required.

Classification of borrowers on the basis of their repayment records sets personal loan limits for subsequent loans. For example, a borrower who pays all installments on time is put in Class A; his personal loan limit will be twice the value of the previous loan. The borrower may use the same proof of ownership of collateral for a subsequent loan as he used for the first, provided the value of the collateral is sufficient for the new amount.

Legal procedures for taking possession of collateral in a case of loan default are relatively complicated and expensive, and are rarely used. For loans as small as those made in KUPEDES, the documentation of collateral is more an expression of the borrower's ability and intent to repay than a basis for possible legal action.

Incentives and Controls

BRI is a state-owned enterprise which has operated much like a government department in the past. In an effort to strengthen staff incentives at various levels and permit performance to be monitored, administrative changes intended to bolster both incentives and controls were made as part of the reform.

■ *For the Village Unit*

The effort to develop the village unit into a full-service rural bank began by giving it authority over KUPEDES loans. Loan decisions were now to be made by the *Kepala Unit Desa*, subject to general supervision by the branch. A number of measures were taken to support this change.

□ *Accounting.* The books of the village unit had to reflect its business performance. This required four major accounting changes: (1) reconstruction of each unit's balance sheet to show its true position at the start of the KUPEDES program; (2) supply of additional liquidity from the branch as a loan on which the village unit would pay interest; (3) provision for the village unit to deposit excess funds in an interest-bearing account in the branch; and (4) payment by the village unit of the branch's cost of supervising the village unit.

☐ *Service network.* When KUPEDES replaced BIMAS as the main type of loan handled by the village units, BRI branch heads in Java, Bali, South Sulawesi, and West Sumatra were asked to reassess the potential of each village unit. These plans were reviewed by the respective regional offices, and units judged to have poor potential were consolidated with units regarded as more promising, which now acquired larger staffs. The former village unit sites were then designated as village service posts (*Pos Pelayanan Desa*), to be visited one to three times a week by two-person mobile teams working out of the remaining village units. As a result of this consolidation, the number of active units declined from 3,617 at the end of 1983 (and 3,626 at the end of 1984) to 2,469 by the end of 1985. Total staff employed in the village units was allowed to fall from 14,334 to 12,954 over the same period. This was the result of natural attrition and the firing of some staff for misappropriation of funds. The reallocation itself did not reduce staff.

☐ *Cash management.* As autonomous units, the village units needed greater freedom to manage their own cash holdings. In March 1986, after two years of experience with KUPEDES, cash management rules were liberalized, so that each village unit could keep enough cash on hand to cover its transactions and did not have to turn all its cash in periodically to the branch, as had been required by some branches. Since the village unit pays interest on funds borrowed from the branch and earns interest on idle cash deposited with the branch, its profit is affected by its ability to manage cash effectively.

☐ *Staff incentive.* Village unit staff members were given the opportunity to earn a cash incentive payment if they increased efficiency and were energetic in looking for additional credit and savings customers. The payment was geared to the profitability of the unit and its success in attracting savings. Branch staff received no such incentive and the payment offered to the village unit staff was capped so that their pay could not exceed that of the branch staff. As a result, most units reached their cap within the first two years of the program and then had no further incentive to increase profits or savings. Recently BRI management decided to reinstate the incentive to renew the inducement for village units to perform.

☐ *Staff training.* In a large organization with nationwide operations like BRI, communication of new goals and procedures to staff at all levels is a massive job, not to be taken lightly. The formal means of conveying such information is a circular letter (*Surat Edaran*) issued by the central office. An initial circular letter on KUPEDES issued in early 1984 was followed by a number of subsequent letters providing clarifications and changes. Supplementary instructions were issued by the regional and branch offices. Experience shows, however, that these instructions may fail to arrive at their destinations, may be countermanded at intermediate levels, or may be misunderstood by their ultimate recipients. Accordingly, instructions to implement the reform have been supplemented by extensive training programs for staff of the regional offices, branches, and village units.

■ *For the Branch*

The branch office head is no longer supposed to make individual loan decisions but it remains responsible for supervising and auditing the work of the village units. Supervision involves a wide range of activities, including follow-up to ensure that all regulations issued by the central office are understood and implemented, staff training, appointment of new staff (with the formal concurrence of the BRI regional office), merger of village units, and creation of village service posts. Field supervision is carried out by the *penilik*, who generally covers six village units, visiting each of them at least once a week.

The willingness of branch heads to grant the prescribed autonomy to the village units has varied widely. Some have taken an entrepreneurial approach, encouraging units under their supervision to build up their KUPEDES loans and Simpanan Pedesaan (SIMPEDES) or General Rural Savings accounts, while others are more control-minded and emphasize the avoidance of arrears.

■ *For BRI as a Whole*

The incentive for BRI as a whole is that there is a large potential for profit in the development of KUPEDES and SIMPEDES, given the wide spread between the loan interest rate and the cost of funds.

Funds for KUPEDES came from several sources. At the start, BRI had about Rp. 100 billion to put into the program. This consisted of the capital of the Kredit Mini program (Rp. 66.7 billion at the end of 1983, originally from government grants), which became available for KUPEDES lending as Kredit Mini loans were repaid, plus Rp. 43 billion in Bank Indonesia liquidity credits for Kredit Midi, which the central bank converted to KUPEDES liquidity credits as they fell due for repayment. Since the break-even point for the BRI village unit system was projected as Rp. 200 billion, an additional Rp. 100 billion was needed. This amount was provided by Bank Indonesia as a line of credit. The original interest rates on this credit were 15 percent for funds on-lent as working capital loans and 3 percent for funds on-lent as investment loans.

By 1986, liquidity credits drawn from Bank Indonesia by BRI to support KUPEDES had risen to Rp. 243 billion, including the rolled-over liquidity credits originally provided for Kredit Midi. This sum was then consolidated into a single liquidity credit, repayable over a fifteen-year period at 12 percent interest. This rate approximated the average rate of interest on all BRI interest-bearing accounts at that time.

In May 1987 the government signed an agreement with the World Bank for a U.S. $100 million loan to provide additional resources for KUPEDES lending. The interest rate on these funds is the average rate on all of BRI's interest-bearing accounts. Each quarter, funds from this loan become available to BRI at the rate of 10 percent of the amount loaned or 50 percent of the increase in the amount outstanding during the quarter, with an upper limit of 65 percent of the increase in the amount outstanding. The upper limit drops to 60 percent in the second year of the loan agreement. These limitations were intended to encourage BRI to increase savings mobilization in the village units.

The other important source of funds for the BRI village units is deposits. As expected, BRI became more interested in promoting TABANAS accounts once KUPEDES provided a profitable outlet for these relatively expensive funds. TABANAS funds in the village units rose strongly during 1986, reaching Rp. 78 billion ($61 million) by year's end.

SIMPEDES was introduced by BRI through the village unit system as a pilot project in November 1984 and "went national" in April 1986. SIMPEDES pays no interest on accounts with minimum monthly balances of less than Rp. 25,000 ($19 in 1986), 9 percent on minimum balances from Rp. 25,000 to Rp. 200,000

($156 in 1986), and 12 percent on balances which remain above Rp. 200,000. Savers are permitted unlimited withdrawals (unlike in TABANAS), a feature which has proven important for the success of the program, even though few customers actually make two withdrawals in a single month. There is a prize drawing every six months, using account numbers and the amount in the SIMPEDES account as the basis for issuing coupons. The eighteen-month test period proved SIMPEDES to be the savings instrument of choice among village unit customers.

A potential source of funds that BRI is precluded from using to finance KUPEDES lending is reinvested profits. BRI pays a 35 percent tax on its profits and may devote up to 55 percent of its after-tax profit to dedicated uses agreed to by the Ministry of Finance. These uses include staff bonuses and reserves for pensions and bad debts. Remaining profits revert to the government.

BRI's top management values KUPEDES as a source of profit for the bank. Countering this attraction, however, is fear that the decentralization of authority involved in KUPEDES could lead to a loss of control and unwise or dishonest loan decisions that would discredit bank management. While the desire to attain and improve profitability was dominant in the first two or three years of the reform, by 1987 the rapid expansion of both lending and saving activities, plus some increase in arrears, had caused management to adopt a more cautious approach.

Results of the Reform

Growth of Activity

■ *KUPEDES*

The volume of KUPEDES credit rose rapidly during the first three and a half years of the program (Table 1). There was Rp. 111 billion outstanding by the end of 1984, Rp. 229 billion by the end of 1985, Rp. 334 billion by the end of 1986, and Rp. 403 billion by June 1987. Thereafter, growth in the volume outstanding slowed considerably. The total for December 1988 was Rp. 540 billion (about $310 million), divided among 1.4 million borrowers.

■ *SIMPEDES*

In November 1986, seven months after SIMPEDES "went national," SIM-PEDES balances passed the total for TABANAS funds held in the village units (Table 2). Rapid growth of SIMPEDES continued, and by the end of 1988 the village units had Rp. 334 billion ($190 million) in SIMPEDES, compared to Rp. 88 billion ($50 million) in TABANAS. In the first two years after SIMPEDES became available nationally, total savings in the village units increased by 145 percent; SIMPEDES accounted for 92 percent of the increase. Besides SIMPEDES and TABANAS, some village units also offer liquid accounts (*giro*) and time deposits (*deposito berjangka*). The amounts involved are small (Table 2).

By the end of 1988, village unit savings represented 89 percent of the amount outstanding in KUPEDES lending, while SIMPEDES alone had reached 62 percent of the total lent out. If recent trends continue, SIMPEDES deposits will soon exceed the amount of credit outstanding. As noted by some of the "new view" advocates, savings activities reach far more people than lending activities. By January 1989, BRI had opened more than 5.1 million accounts in its village units, including 1.7 million SIMPEDES accounts.[8]

Table 1   Volume of KUPEDES Credit Outstanding, 1984-88

	Month	Amount (Rp. billion)
1984:	March	30
	June	72
	September	89
	December	111
1985:	March	143
	June	180
	September	200
	December	229
1986:	March	260
	June	285
	September	297
	December	334
1987:	March	374
	June	403
	September	416
	December	429
1988:	March	461
	June	494
	September	503
	December	540

Source: BRI

Table 2   Savings in BRI Village Units, 1983-88 (Rp. billion)

	Month	TABANAS	SIMPEDES	Giro	Deposito	Total
1983 :	December	25	-	2	-	27
1984 :	December	39	0	2	1	42
1985 :	December	64	5	14	2	85
1986 :	December	78	83	11	4	176
1987 :	March	73	107	7	4	192
	June	67	122	17	5	210
	September	68	144	19	8	240
	December	80	183	13	13	287
1988 :	March	75	206	7	17	305
	June	70	215	10	22	317
	September	74	265	22	31	392
	December	88	334	16	42	479

Note: Discrepancies attributable to rounding.

Source: BRI

Table 3 **Profit and Loss of the Village Unit System, 1984-88**

Year	Profit/Loss (Rp. billion)
1984	-25.1
1985	-0.9
1986	+9.8
1987	+22.5
1988	+30.7

Source: BRI

System Profitability

The RCWG's forecast that the village unit system could achieve profitability at a KUPEDES lending volume of Rp. 200 billion within eighteen months proved accurate when that level of lending was attained in September 1985. The village units lost Rp. 0.9 billion in 1985 as a whole, a minuscule sum by past standards. From 1986 on, a growing profit was realized (Table 3). In September 1988, 82 percent of the individual village units operated at a profit.

A dramatic indication of the difference between the old and new systems came in 1987, when BRI as a whole drew profit from just three activities: the operations of the village units; special banking services provided to the National Logistics Agency (BULOG); and interest earned by lending on the interbank market. Earnings from these three sources exceeded the total profit of the bank. Thus, in contrast to the earlier period when BIMAS losses were cross-subsidized from profits made in other BRI operations, the village units not only paid for themselves but helped to cover losses incurred in BRI's regular commercial banking business. In 1988 the village units provided about 30 percent of BRI's total profit.

Problems Encountered and Corrective Measures Taken

Contraction of Village Unit Network

The initial impetus of many branch and regional managers was to reduce the number of village units. By the end of 1986 the number of active units had fallen further to 2,273, supplemented by 1,266 village service posts. However, early estimates of potential proved too pessimistic in many cases. By June 1988 the number of village units had risen again to 2,543, largely through the reconversion of village service posts, which now numbered 915. The number of village unit staff also fell, reaching 11,967 at the end of 1987. By 1988 staffing had become a constraint on KUPEDES lending and a major hiring exercise was initiated.

Concern with Arrears

Although loss ratios under KUPEDES have generally been low, they have risen steadily over time (Table 4). The long-term loss ratio (cumulative payments missed as a percentage of payments due) is our preferred indicator of the long-term status of the program. It has increased gradually over the years but remained relatively low at 3.3 percent in December 1988. The short-term loss ratio (payments missed as a percentage of payments due in a particular month) was under 1 percent. The more familiar portfolio status measure (cumulative arrears as a percentage of current outstanding) was 7.5 percent in December 1988. This ratio almost inevitably rises as a program grows older, especially if the lending institution is slow to write off bad debts. The tendency of all loss measures to rise slowly but steadily has caused concern among bank management. Unfortunately, it has sometimes reinforced the widespread perception that small loans are inherently risky. In fact, the arrears problem is largely concentrated in a relatively small number of branches and village units, where heightened management attention is needed.

Table 4 KUPEDES Loss Ratios, 1984-88 (%)

Month		Long-Term Loss Ratio	Short-Term Loss Ratio	Portfolio Status
1984 :	December	0.98	1.36	0.54
1985 :	December	1.70	3.02	2.12
1986 :	December	2.23	2.71	4.49
1987:	March	2.29	1.98	4.81
	June	2.44	1.67	5.49
	September	2.50	2.31	6.15
	December	2.55	4.40	5.74
1988 :	March	2.80	4.21	6.64
	June	3.12	3.71	7.68
	September	3.25	3.44	8.36
	December	3.28	0.90	7.46

Source: BRI

Table 5 KUPEDES Credit Outstanding by Type and Sector, April 1986

	Number of Loans (thousand)	Value Outstanding (Rp. billion)
Investment loans		
Agriculture	15.7	4.9
Industry	1.3	0.4
Trade	10.2	2.9
Other	8.4	2.4
Total	35.6	10.6
Working capital loans		
Agriculture	306.2	69.5
Industry	18.2	3.9
Trade	760.0	184.4
Other	9.1	2.1
Total	1,093.5	259.9
Grand Total	1,129.1	270.5

Source: BRI

Lending for Agriculture; Seasonal Loans

In April 1986, there were 1.1 million current KUPEDES borrowers (Table 5). The average loan balance outstanding, which had been rising steadily since the start of the program, was Rp. 240,000. Sixty-nine percent of the amount lent was listed as credit for trading purposes. A disturbingly low 28 percent was officially for agriculture, although field investigations did reveal that two-thirds of those who borrowed for trade also had agricultural enterprises which benefited indirectly from the loans, since they tapped their cash flow to buy agricultural inputs. More than 96 percent of the credit outstanding was listed as working capital.

Collateral Requirements

As discussed earlier, collateral continues to be required of all borrowers and, in most cases, must consist of evidence of land ownership. Since most KUPEDES loans are for trading activities (at least nominally) and land ownership has little to do with the success or failure of a trading enterprise, this requirement seems arbitrary. Yet Indonesian policymakers and bankers apparently remain persuaded that a pledge of collateral improves the bank's chance of being repaid, even though foreclosure is virtually unknown.

Very Small Loans and New Borrowers

The RCWG had hoped that BRI would make loans as small as Rp. 25,000. BRI has steadfastly avoided very small loans, in part because there is a significant fixed element in loan processing costs which makes small loans more expensive in percentage terms. While refusing to deal in very small loans, BRI has shown a strong preference for larger repeat loans to borrowers who have repaid in the past over smaller loans to first-time borrowers. As concern about arrears mounted in 1987, growth in the number of borrowers came to a virtual halt.

Efficiency of BRI Village Units

To help overcome initial resistance within BRI, the spread between KUPEDES lending rates and the cost of funds was deliberately made very large. Since loan repayment rates and BRI's own operating costs were somewhat unpredictable at the start, this wide spread bolstered the bank's confidence to go ahead with the program. As it turned out, the average lending rate, taking into account IPTW collections and the mix of working capital and investment loans, has been around

Table 6 **KUPEDES Interest and Intermediation Costs, 1984-88**
(as a % of credit outstanding)

	Month	Cost of Funds	Labor Cost	Total Intermediation Cost
1984 :	December	12.1	50.9	58.6
1985 :	December	11.0	19.2	21.6
1986 :	December	9.3	13.5	15.5
1987 :	March	9.3	11.2	12.5
	June	9.4	12.3	13.5
	September	9.4	11.8	13.0
	December	9.0	11.8	13.2
1988 :	March	9.1	12.4	13.7

Source: BRI

30 percent per annum, while the average cost of funds, allowing for the existence of small savings account balances that earn less than 12 percent and for the fact that interest is paid on the minimum monthly balance, has been 9.0 to 9.5 percent since 1986 (Table 6). Since the resulting spread is 20 percent or so, the observer with 20-20 hindsight might have been more surprised if BRI had failed to make a profit on KUPEDES than if it had succeeded.

The intermediation cost of the village unit system declined sharply over the first three years of the program, reaching 13.7 percent of the volume of credit outstanding in March 1988. Labor was the dominant cost element.

Economic Impact

Assessing the economic impact of a credit program is a methodologically intractable problem (Cole and Slade, see chapter 12), especially when borrowers have multiple economic activities. Since credit given for one nominal purpose frequently finances some totally different activity, it is hard to measure the economic impact of KUPEDES. There is, however, indirect and inferential evidence that KUPEDES credit is economically beneficial. The fact that the loans are popular and generally repaid successfully suggests that the ultimate uses of the additional capital, whatever they may be, are sufficiently productive in private terms to keep the loan fund turning over. Since KUPEDES is unsubsidized, the existence of high private rates of return may be taken to mean that social benefits are also substantial. There is anecdotal evidence that secondary banks and informal sector lenders who lend at higher rates of interest have lost business as a result of competition from KUPEDES. The average effective rate of interest paid by rural producers has been reduced by some unknown amount. This must have permitted them to undertake projects that would not have been feasible at the higher borrowing rates that they faced before 1984.

Conclusions

Effectiveness of the Reform

■ Successes

The KUPEDES story shows that commercial banks can operate relatively successful lending programs for small rural borrowers if appropriate economic incentives are provided for both borrowers and credit providers and there is vigorous managerial follow-through. Customer interviews in rural Indonesia reveal a widespread preference for dealing with a government bank. Although people associate BRI more with sponsored loan programs than with savings accounts, they feel safer putting their savings in BRI than elsewhere, provided they can withdraw the funds when they need them. In the past, loans available from BRI carried attractive interest rates but were tied to participation in official programs that were not always in people's individual interests, and the credit provided was not always available on a reliable basis. Uncertainty about refinancing prospects was probably the largest cause of arrears. With the flow of credit assured, BRI has now become a popular source of loans, even at a relatively high rate of interest.

The surest way to ensure a continuing flow of funds is to make it in the interest of the credit provider to generate the funds from within. Creating a large positive spread between the loan rate of interest and the cost of funds is thus likely to be the starting point for any successful credit reform, but it is far from the whole story. If a large and complex institution such as BRI is to implement the reform, specific actions must be taken to induce appropriate behavioral responses from the thousands of individuals involved.

The reform required the village units to transform themselves from subordinate bureaucratic units to profit-maximizing businesses. The instruments used to bring about this transformation were instruction, training, and a cash incentive. Meanwhile, the branch offices were to transfer the responsibility for making individual loan decisions to the village units while still supervising these units and retaining overall responsibility for their performance. Regional offices were supposed to continue supervising the branches, but were asked to be more promotional and less control-minded in their approach. The branches and regional offices shared responsibility for reshaping the service network—closing units located in areas of low potential for KUPEDES and SIMPEDES, opening new units and village service posts. The incentives used to induce these behaviors from the branches and regional offices were similar to those used with the village units, except that no cash incentive was offered.

An important issue at all levels of BRI is the bank's staff promotion policies. It has not yet been sufficiently emphasized that officials are more likely to be promoted when they act in ways that promote the success of KUPEDES and SIMPEDES than when they behave in ways that impede the development of these parts of BRI's business. Being in charge of a village unit, branch, or region that experiences unusually high arrears or misuse of funds will definitely harm one's promotion prospects, but the message that aggressive expansion of KUPEDES and SIMPEDES can put one on the fast track to promotion still needs to be promoted. It is hard to fire anyone from a government institution, and even extreme misbehavior is sometimes punished lightly. We have met former village unit heads who were punished for misappropriating funds by being demoted to cashier!

This ambiguity may reflect weakness in the incentives offered to BRI as an institution. As noted earlier, government rules on the use of profits of public sector enterprises leave BRI little control over its own profits. While the bank had good reason to eliminate the losses it was incurring on the village units once the government subsidy was removed, its motivation to raise the profit that the system has been generating since 1986 may be weak. The directors of the bank will definitely be held responsible for massive arrears or fraud, but it is less clear that their status will rise along with the profits generated by the village units. It would be understandable if this asymmetry in incentives caused them to take a somewhat cautious approach.

A related danger posed by government rules on distribution of the profits of public sector enterprises is that these enterprises will be encouraged to raise their cost bases, thus retaining control over the funds by eliminating the profits which are not theirs to dispose of. Within BRI, there are pressures to provide village unit staff with the civil service benefits enjoyed by other BRI employees. Giving in to these pressures could raise intermediation costs for KUPEDES to a level that would make the program unworkable.

■ Limitations

It has not proven possible to persuade BRI to make very small loans, lend without collateral, make a large number of seasonal loans for agricultural activities, or expand its service network as aggressively as the potentials of KUPEDES and SIMPEDES appear to merit. Some of these limitations may result from accurate judgments on the part of BRI officials that particular classes of business are too costly or risky to undertake, while others may reflect undue caution resulting from persistent habits or an incentive structure that makes the cost of failure disproportionately high relative to the rewards of success.

Transferability of the Approach

Although no one should contemplate wholesale transfer of the KUPEDES model to another developing country, aspects of the KUPEDES experience do address four general points that have been widely discussed in the literature.

(1) KUPEDES validates, with two qualifications, the "new view" argument that the use of commercial terms will provide wider access to institutional credit. But the qualifications are also important. The first one has already been stated by Anderson and Khambata (1985): it takes time for lending institutions to learn which types of small borrowers they can safely lend to and on what kinds of information. Second, some types of loan will never be attractive to institutional lenders because of the high cost of obtaining the kind of information that would reduce the risk to the lender to an acceptable level. These issues are still to some extent being sorted out in the case of KUPEDES.

(2) KUPEDES shows that it is possible to persuade a bank to deal with small-scale borrowers. Indeed, providing credit to small producers through a commercial bank creates an opportunity to mobilize savings that could be missed if loans were made by specialized lending institutions that do not take deposits.

(3) Although the use of borrower groups to pool risk among small-scale borrowers has received favorable note in the literature (Adams and Ladman 1979, Schaefer-Kehnert 1983, Mosley and Dahal 1987), KUPEDES succeeded by lending to individual business men and women. Borrower groups have generally not been very successful in Indonesia.

(4) Politically, reforming rural credit in Indonesia proved less difficult than many expected. In retrospect, one can speculate that rural credit reform might be easier to achieve than urban banking reform because the vested interests involved have less power in national politics. The favored urban borrowers of the state banks are not threatened by KUPEDES and SIMPEDES—indeed, they may benefit from relending of rural savings—and the amount of money involved is a small share of total bank assets. As noted earlier, in 1987 BRI made money on rural banking and certain other operations but was still unable to turn a profit on its general commercial banking business. At the same time, those who prefer sponsored credit programs have never given up their efforts to downgrade KUPEDES and restore sponsored programs to their former prominence. In April 1989, for example, there was public criticism of KUPEDES by advocates of directed credit, centering on its collateral requirement.

We conclude by calling attention to the magnitude of KUPEDES relative to small loan programs elsewhere: with the equivalent of U.S. $310 million outstanding at the end of 1988, KUPEDES already dwarfs all other small loan programs in developing countries, except perhaps those in India. An article in the *New York Times* of February 21, 1988, listed "the principal providers of very small loans" in Latin America, Asia, and Africa. Although the amount of credit outstanding in two of the programs mentioned was listed as "not available," the totals given for the remaining programs add up to U.S. $48 million, less than one-fifth the total for KUPEDES! ∞

Notes

1 The authors are grateful to conference participants for their comments on an earlier draft and particularly grateful to Dwight Perkins, Michael Roemer, and C. Peter Timmer, who provided detailed commentaries. Their largest debt, however, is to the many people with whom they have worked on rural credit in Indonesia, especially Mr. Kamardy Arief, president-director of Bank Rakyat, Indonesia, and the many members of his staff in the central office, regional offices, branches, and village units who have provided innumerable courtesies and forms of assistance to us over the years.

2 Until recently, rural credit was usually referred to as agricultural credit. Recognition of the importance of nonfarm rural enterprise and its participation in rural financial markets came late (Kilby, Liedholm, and Meyer 1984).

3 When the number of village units reached its peak of 3,626 in 1984, there were about 63,000 officially recognized villages in Indonesia. The average BRI village unit thus served seventeen to eighteen villages at this time. Most village units did 90 percent or so of their loan and deposit business with residents of no more than five or six nearby villages. Effectively, therefore, the system covered about one-third of the villages in the country.

4 This odd juxtaposition of a collapsing agricultural credit program with growing production is not unique and may be common. See, for example, Graham and Bourne (1980).

5 Kane (1984) argues that in bureaucratically managed credit programs success is often equated with a growing volume of lending, and politically powerful groups tend to be favored. BIMAS experience bears out these generalizations.

6 Rp. 30 billion in 1983 was equivalent to U.S. $33 million. Since 1978 there have been three major rupiah devaluations and continual depreciation of the rupiah against the dollar. To assist the reader, some of the rupiah values cited in the text have been converted into dollars at the exchange rate prevailing in the year in question.

7 The individual loan limit was Rp. 1 million until April 1986, when it was raised to Rp. 2 million (then equivalent to nearly U.S. $1,800). The devaluation of September 1986 and further rupiah depreciation subsequently reduced the dollar equivalent of Rp. 2 million to less than $1,200. In 1988 the limit was raised again, this time to Rp. 3 million as a general rule and Rp. 5 million in exceptional cases. The new urban banking units, which are not discussed here, may lend up to Rp. 10 million to a single customer.

8 There were 3.3 million TABANAS accounts, many of them uneconomically small. Many of these accounts were opened during campaigns that urged masses of people to open nominal savings accounts.

Strategic Interventions and the Political Economy of Industrial Policy in Developing Countries

Tyler S. Biggs and Brian D. Levy

Tyler S. Biggs is a research associate at HIID. During 1986 to 1991, he managed the Employment and Enterprise Policy Analysis (EEPA) Project at HIID, which conducted research in Korea, Taiwan, the Philippines, Thailand, Bangladesh, and Indonesia, providing information for this paper.

Brian D. Levy is a staff economist at the World Bank. During 1986 and 1987, as an HIID research associate and consultant to the EEPA Project, he spent a year in Korea, Taiwan, and the Philippines, conducting research upon which this paper is based.

As the previous papers in this volume highlight, governments differ in their commitments to socially beneficial policies and in their capacities to sustain and administer such policies over the long haul. In "soft" states, vulnerable to socially costly rent-seeking behavior by powerful private interests and government officials, the costs of stifling bureaucracies and blocked, noncompetitive markets have been all too evident. The appropriate policy remedies—getting prices right and promoting market competition—are explored in other sections of this volume. However, in "hard" states where governments are able to devise, implement, and sustain socially beneficial industrial policies, the scope for activist government is more substantial, and the menu of desirable reform options more varied, than is implied by unqualified laissez faire policy nostrums.

Industrialization in particular can be promoted via a variety of strategies, each involving a different role for government, and each with the potential to achieve sustained, efficient development. It follows that a crucial component of successful reform of industrial policy is the goodness of fit between the chosen strategy of industrialization and the institutional environment in which the strategy is to be implemented.

This paper delineates some alternative strategies for industrialization and draws some general lessons for industrial strategy from the authors' field research and related work in Korea, Taiwan, Bangladesh, and the Philippines. Field experience has strengthened our conviction that dynamically efficient industrialization is not possible in the long run in the face of egregious misallocations of resources. But it has also persuaded us that the promotion of industrialization, as earlier theorists recognized, involves additional considerations to those of pricing policy. For one thing, as has increasingly been recognized, the successful efforts of East Asian governments to promote industrialization went beyond a commitment to relatively efficient pricing policies. More fundamentally, policy prescriptions that focus exclusively on prices implicitly assume that markets are frictionless, that economic agents are omniscient, and that externalities are limited in magnitude, with the costs and benefits of actions largely internalized in the calculations of private decision makers. Contrary to the first assumption, transactions-cost economists have explored the determinants of the costs of market transactions, and the character of mechanisms to conserve on these costs.[1] Contrary to the second assumption, economists who study organizations have taken as their starting point the proposition of bounded rationality and have explored mechanisms of organizational learning.[2] And, contrary to the third assumption, students of industrialization and industrial policy highlight increasingly the centrality of externalities in the industrialization process.[3]

Taken together, organizational learning, externalities, and transactions costs point to a conception of industrialization that extends beyond efficient allocation. In this broader conception, industrialization involves a transition from a low-level equilibrium characterized by transactionally costly markets, limited organizational capabilities, and pervasive, uncaptured positive externalities, to a dynamic disequilibrium in which markets operate with increasing efficiency over time, participants in industry reciprocally take advantage of, and in turn create, positive externalities, and organizations progressively improve their capabilities. We will argue that a variety of interventionist industrial strategies can set in motion and accelerate the achievement of dynamically efficient industrialization, with the choice of strategy dependent upon a nation's economic and political environment.

The paper is divided into two sections. The first focuses on industrial strategy in "hard" states, and also delineates some relations between initial economic conditions, the character of the interventions, and the nature of the subsequent transitions. The second section explores what might be the consequences of adopting industrial strategies suited for "hard" states in "soft" states and suggests some alternative policies that might be better suited for these "soft" states.

Figure 1 **A Typology of Development Strategies**

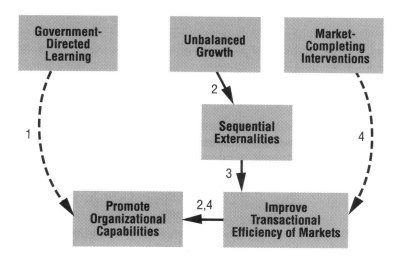

Industrial Policies in "Hard" States

A Typology of Industrial Strategies

As a prelude to delineating the industrial strategies of Korea and Taiwan, it is helpful heuristically to distinguish among some analytically divergent classes of industrial strategy. Our conception of industrialization focuses attention on the ways in which industrial strategies help promote the performance of the institutions responsible for production and allocation. Given this institutional orientation, the fundamental distinction is between market-oriented and hierarchy-oriented strategies. We discuss the class of strategies that work to promote the capabilities of hierarchical organizations under the rubric of government-directed learning, and the class of strategies that work to improve the transactional efficiency of markets under the rubrics of strategies of unbalanced growth and of market-completing interventions.[4] Figure 1 summarizes the channels through which each strategy is hypothesized to promote industrialization.

Government-directed learning refers in this paper to specific efforts on the part of government to improve the capabilities of individual firms by inducing them to move down their learning curves. The learning curve, illustrated in

Figure 2, depicts the dynamic internal economies enjoyed by firms as they increase productivity and reduce unit costs with cumulative increases in production.[5] Governments have two central tasks in industrial strategies of government-directed learning. The first task is to "pick winners," to select individual firms and industries where the potential magnitude of dynamic internal economies is substantial. The second task is to refine instruments of "partial mutuality,"[6] instruments that simultaneously induce firms to enter and oblige them continually to expand and secure improvements in productivity. As Figure 1 summarizes, a successful strategy of government-directed learning enables individual firms progressively to expand and enhance productivity and technical proficiency.[7] But, insofar as the strategic focus is on enhancing administrative coordination and enterprise capability, a learning strategy may do little, even in the long run, to promote the transactional efficiency of markets. As will be evident below, government-directed learning promoted by the vigorous use of instruments of partial mutuality appears to have been unusually important in Korea.

Figure 2   The Learning Curve

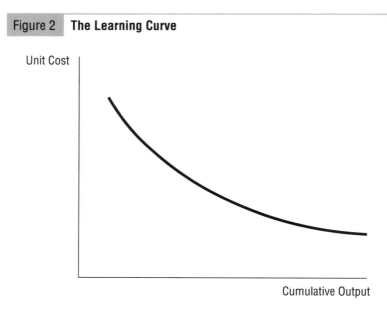

Positive externalities are taken to be central to industrialization in the strategy of "unbalanced growth." New firms enter to take advantage of externalities created by earlier entrants; by the act of entry they, in turn, create externalities that induce yet more firms to enter. Industrialization via this strategy thus involves an ongoing proliferation of small and medium enterprises.[8] As Figure 1 summarizes, the sequential externalities set in motion via this strategy induce ongoing entry, expanded competition and transactional efficiency in markets, and, as a result of the press of competition, progressive gains in organizational capabilities.

Hirschman summarized succinctly the role of government in an unbalanced growth strategy:

...the two principal roles of government economic policies in the cause of the development process are...to initiate growth through forward thrusts that are meant to create incentives and pressures for further action; and then to stand ready to react to, and to alleviate, these pressures in a variety of areas.[9]

In short, Hirschman proposes an *inducing* and an *induced* role for government. Government's inducing role revolves around strategic interventions to promote a continuing outcropping of profitable opportunities. The task of government, in Hirschman's words, is to set in motion a "compulsive sequence" sustained by sequential externalities and associated with ongoing entry of firms. Such a role requires a certain amount of active leadership in industrialization. An associated role for government results in active involvement in promoting what Hirschman calls "purely permissive sequences." The task here is to lay down the prerequisites for further growth and development by such things as construction of physical infrastructure and maintenance of law and order. As prerequisites, "they permit and invite, rather than compel, other activities to follow suit."[10] We would add to Hirschman's list the development of institutional infrastructure (our market-completing interventions) in the areas of marketing, finance, technical information, subcontracting, and quality control.[11] The magnitude of the endogenous response to any exogenous government intervention (or policy reform) will vary depending on such infrastructure.

Government's induced role, according to Hirschman, emanates from the endogenous growth process touched off by government's exogenous strategic interventions to get things going. As the endogenous expansion makes rapid strides through market forces, shortages and bottlenecks will be revealed in education, health, public utilities, and pollution. Government's function is to remedy these revealed deficiencies.

As will be evident below, endogenous expansion sustained by sequential externalities and associated ongoing entry of small and medium enterprises subsequent to initial, externality-creating investments promoted (and sometimes undertaken directly) by government appear to have been unusually important in Taiwan's successful industrialization.

The final strategy explored here, the one that conforms most closely to laissez faire prescriptions, amounts to a set of programs—interventions in financial markets, in product markets, and in input markets—to improve transactional efficiency. Programmatic market-completing strategies are ubiquitous; however, our field research suggests that they played at best a marginal role in securing dynamically efficient industrialization in either Korea or Taiwan (or in any other country of which we are aware). The virtue of this third strategy is that it points to tasks for government that are at the same time activist and unlikely to be seriously distortionary, even if poorly implemented. We shall have more to say on the potential role of this strategy in our discussion of industrial policies that might be suitable in soft states.

Figure 3 summarizes some hypotheses as to how, in the context of a "hard" state, the incremental benefits relative to laissez faire of adopting either a government-directed learning or an unbalanced growth strategy might vary with the level of a nation's organizational capability or market efficiency. At very low levels, a strategy of unbalanced growth is hypothesized to have little impact insofar as markets will be too incomplete to signal new opportunities, and agents will be too lacking in skill and experience to interpret and respond to any signals of opportunity they indeed receive. By contrast, insofar as a strategy of government-directed learning bypasses markets and takes as its starting point pre-existing limitations in organizational capability, it is hypothesized to be capable of yielding substantial cumulative gains, even in the face of severe initial institutional shortfalls. As the initial level of capabilities rises, the unbalanced growth strategy becomes better able to generate sustained positive dynamic externalities and thereby to promote cumulative advances in market efficiency, organizational capability, and the capture of sequential externalities. At the same time, however, as Figure 3 illustrates, a higher level of initial capabilities means smaller net gains over laissez faire from either strategy. At high enough levels of market efficiency and organizational capability, explicit industrial strategy is hypothesized to add little to a nation's ability to pursue dynamically efficient industrialization.[12]

Figure 3   The Benefits of Industrial Strategy in a "Hard" State

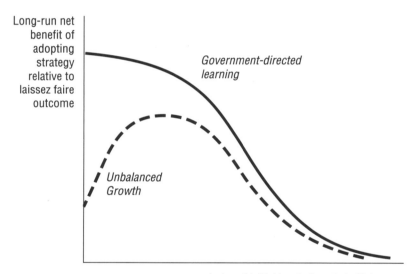

Long-run net benefit of adopting strategy relative to laissez faire outcome

Government-directed learning

Unbalanced Growth

Index of initial level of market efficiency and organizational capability

Industrial Strategies in Korea and Taiwan

Industrial policy in any given country is shaped at least in part by incremental, ad hoc responses to specific, complex circumstances, not simply by a consistent application of some coherent strategic view. Even so, as we shall attempt to demonstrate in this section, the heuristic strategies of government-directed learning and unbalanced growth highlight some important differences between Korea and Taiwan in their paths of industrial expansion. In turn, the disparate experiences of the two nations highlight the relations between industry strategy and industry structure: the ways in which initial conditions shape the choice of industrial strategy, and the ways in which the choice of strategy shapes, in turn, the subsequent evolution of industry structure.

Since the early 1960s, both Korea and Taiwan have enjoyed unusually rapid, and unusually equitable, economic growth.[13] Between 1965 and 1983, GNP per capita grew at an average annual rate of 6.5 percent in Taiwan, and 6.7 percent in Korea, as compared with an average rate of 3.8 percent for a larger sample of upper-middle-income less developed nations. Gini coefficients for after-tax household income amounted to .285 (in 1978) and .389 (in 1980) for Korea and Taiwan respectively, placing both nations in the low-inequality group of countries. Interestingly (and consistent with our analysis of differences between the two countries), between the late 1960s and late 1970s inequality widened in Korea but narrowed in Taiwan.

Although our primary interest is in differences, we note briefly some important similarities in historical legacies, political conditions, and subsequent economic policies lying behind these economic successes. To begin with similarities in historical legacy and political conditions,[14] a first similarity is the common experience of colonization by the Japanese in the first half of the twentieth century.[15] A second similarity is the absence of politically influential rural elites at the outset of the period of rapid industrial expansion: in both nations, rural elites were first weakened by the Japanese and then destroyed by land reform subsequent to decolonization. A third similarity is the absence of competitive politics at the height of industrial expansion in the 1960s and 1970s: authoritarian rule was imposed on Taiwan by the Kuomintang after their withdrawal from China in 1949, and was imposed on Korea by the military in the early 1960s, after a decade of political turmoil. A fourth similarity was in the common suppression of activist labor movements by governments in the two countries and associated commitments to competitive labor markets and market-determined wages.[16]

As for economic policies, governments in both countries took on the productive economic tasks assigned to the public domain by conventional economic analysis: both countries invested heavily in infrastructure and education and both countries pursued coherent macroeconomic policies that avoided imbalances of a kind which could choke off economic expansion, although Korea's policies were rather more inflationary than those of Taiwan.[17] Additionally, after a decade or so of import-substituting industrialization; and both countries shifted in the early 1960s to outward-oriented policies that, at the very least, did not on average discriminate against exports in favor of production for their domestic markets.[18]

Given these similarities as background, we turn now to analysis of the distinctive features of industrial expansion in each of the two countries.

The Korean Pattern. What distinctive policies account for Korea's extraordinarily rapid expansion of manufactured exports and national income since the mid-1960s? Although the standard neoclassical explanation highlights the shift from socially inefficient incentives for private firms associated with import substitution to socially efficient incentives associated with the subsequent shift to outward-oriented policies,[19] following Amsden (1989) we emphasize here the role of government-directed learning.[20]

Consistent with the emphasis of the neoclassicals, evidence suggests that the move from multiple rates to a uniform exchange rate, and the associated cessation of zero-sum opportunities for rent-seeking by importing at an overvalued exchange rate, was important in sustaining the initial burst of export activity.[21] Moreover, again consistent with the neoclassical explanation, since the mid-1960s Korea has offered a wide range of nondiscretionary incentives for exports. As of 1968, gross export incentives amounted to 29.8 percent of the value of total merchandise exports; over 80 percent of this total was provided automatically to all firms that met the relevant performance criteria.[22] But along with nondiscretionary export incentives, the Korean policy arsenal included a series of instruments that, from a neoclassical perspective, have a more dubious impact.

First, long-term credit was 100 percent government-controlled and provided selectively to individual firms at interest rates well below market equilibrium, often according to criteria so general that they left virtually complete discretion as to who would benefit in the hands of the relevant government officials.[23] Second, direct tax breaks also were proferred on a discretionary basis. Some tax incentives were linked explicitly to exports in ways that limited the scope for discretion, but others involved such vague criteria that firms had little basis for predicting whether they might qualify in advance of negotiations with the bureaucracy.[24] Additionally, in the absence of prespecified criteria, firms were continually vulnerable to tax audits at the more or less arbitrary discretion of government bureaucrats.[25] Third, dating back to 1962, the Korean Ministry of Commerce and Industry set and monitored export targets for individual firms, sometimes in collaboration with the firms, sometimes not.[26] Fourth, even after the shift to export-oriented policies, the Korean government continued to use extensively tariffs and quantitative restrictions to limit imports. Viewed from the perspective of their impact on efficient allocation, discretionary tax and credit subsidies and import protection appear thoroughly undesirable, and export targets an unimportant curiosity. But viewed from the perspective of an industrial strategy of government-directed learning, export targets, import protection, and discretionary tax and credit subsidies emerge as a coherent package of non-neoclassical policy instruments to force the pace of organizational learning.

Table 1 reveals that although barriers to import in Korea were low on average in 1968,[27] their magnitudes varied substantially across sectors. On average, the magnitudes of protection and subsidy were low for export sectors (for sales to both domestic and export markets), but high for export-and-import-competing and import-competing sectors; most of the subsidy for the latter groups of sectors took the form of protection for domestic sales. The data imply that the Korean government did not use subsidies in the latter sectors simply to enable manufacturers to earn rents from domestic sales; the substantial difference between levels of effective protection and effective subsidy for export sales points to very high tax and credit subsidies for exports by firms in import-competing sectors in particular. Indeed, almost 40 percent of Korea's major export sectors enjoyed above average levels of subsidy for domestic sales, largely in the form of protection.[28] Thus Westphal and Kim (1977) conclude that "the government has subsidized exports that were inefficiently produced.... through high nominal protection on the domestic market."[29] Pack and Westphal (1986) go further, suggesting that "inefficiently produced" exports often were exports from infant industries. As they put it, "the Korean government discriminated in its treatment between established, internationally competitive industries and new, infant industries that were deemed worthy of promotion.... Something closely approximating neutrality has characterized the government's policies affecting the established industries.... but there has been substantial bias in favor of the promoted infant industries."[30]

Table 1	Effective Protection and Effective Subsidies in Korean Manufacturing (1968) by Trade-orientation of Products (%)					
	Effective Protection [1]			Effective Subsidies		
	Export Sales	Domestic Sales	Average	Export Sales	Domestic Sales	Average
Export[2]	5	-18	-11	13	-26	-13
Export-and-Import-Competing[3]	-2	73	45	9	55	38
Import-Competing[4]	-9	93	92	35	91	91
Non-Import-Competing[5]	-1	-16	-16	6	-24	-24
All Manufacturing	3	-1	-1	12	-9	-7

Source:
Westphal and Kim (1977), 231.

Notes:
1. Effective protection is measured using the Balassa method.
2. Export sectors are defined to be those sectors where exports exceed 10% of production and imports amount to under 10% of consumption.
3. Export-and-import-competing sectors are defined to be those sectors where exports exceed 10% of production, and imports exceed 10% of consumption.
4. Import-competing sectors are defined to be those sectors where exports amount to under 10 percent of production and imports exceed 10% of consumption.
5. Non-import-competing sectors are defined to be those sectors where exports amount to under 10% of production and imports amount to under 10% of consumption.

A strategy of government-directed learning involves more than protection for infant industries. The goal of the strategy is to promote dynamic internal economies within individual firms by inducing them to enter and obliging them continually to expand and secure improvements in productivity via ongoing increases in export volumes.[31] Thus, along with import protection the government needs, in addition, instruments of partial mutuality, mechanisms to target individual firms and oblige them to expand progressively their export volumes rather than settle for the quiet life of inefficient, yet profitable, production for the protected domestic markets. Export targets and selective credit and tax instruments can in principle provide the requisite tools. Targets can be used to challenge individual firms and to evaluate the extent to which they meet these challenges. Credit and tax instruments also can be used to reward success and punish failure, showering successful firms with selective subsidies and tax breaks, and threatening unsuccessful firms with tax audits, the loss of subsidies, and even the calling-in of outstanding loans. In the context of their high levels of indebtedness,[32] the last would be tantamount to a threat to shut down unresponsive firms.

Survey results reported by Rhee (1984) provide some evidence that the Korean government indeed employed its export targets and controls over taxation and credit as instruments of partial mutuality. Sixty-two percent of 106 firms surveyed in 1976 felt that their export targets had led to increases in exports, while only 14 percent claimed the targets had made no difference in the growth of production.[33] Additionally, over 60 percent of the firms agreed that monthly export promotion meetings attended by both businessmen and government officials, and often chaired by the nation's president, significantly affected their export performance. Underlying these positive responses appears to be the implicit threat of government sanction. Almost three-fourths of the respondents viewed the most important advantage of good export performance to be its implied assurance of continued government support for the firms' efforts. Fifty-five percent of firms felt that the rigor of tax collection depended on their export performance. And 36 percent felt that export performance influenced the facility and speed of their dealings with government.[34] Hong (1979) provides a particularly evocative depiction of the centrality of partial mutuality in Korean business-government relations. "After the sixties," he suggests, "Korean entrepreneurs soon learned that generous subsidies and other promotional schemes would be provided for production activities that the government wished to support, while various disincentives would be applied to nonfavored activities.... As the emphasis of the government shifts...the successful entrepreneur begins to adapt to this shift...if this does not happen, the chances are good that he will soon no longer be a successful entrepreneur in the Korean economy."[35]

Pursuit of a strategy of government-directed learning appears to have influenced both the rate and direction of Korea's industrial expansion, and the pattern of industrial organization within Korean manufacturing. The relation between industry strategy and industry structure is explored later for both Korea and Taiwan. An aggregate empirical analysis of the relation between government-directed learning, industrial growth, and economic welfare is beyond the scope of the present paper. What must suffice here are four illustrative, industry, and firm-specific summary examples of Korean successes that highlight policy interventions of the sort associated with the strategy of government-directed learning.

■ **Shipbuilding.**[36] Hyundai Shipbuilding and Heavy Industries was established in 1973. The project almost was abandoned in 1972 after Hyundai's chairman had come up empty handed in efforts to raise international finance. Hyundai persevered only after a "thinly veiled threat" from the Korean president "that 'if you only want to do what's easy, you'll get no more help from us.'" In April 1972, Hyundai won orders to supply two 250,000 ton vessels (this from a country that had never produced a vessel larger than 10,000 tons). The dry-dock was built, workers trained, supplementary facilities completed, and the ships completed for delivery by November 1974. By 1976, almost 30,000 people were employed in the construction of steel cargo ships; a decade later annual production capacity had tripled.[37] But the industry remained dependent on government largesse. Thus, when a 1975 world shipbuilding slump led to the cancellation of orders for three virtually completed tankers, the Korean government arranged for Korean oil refineries to lease the vessels to transport crude from the Middle East to Korea. And both the 1976 Planned Shipbuilding Program and the 1981 Shipping Promotion Fund subsidized the purchase of domestically built ships by Korean shipping companies.[38]

■ **Automobiles.**[39] Domestic assembly of automobiles got underway in 1962 when the Korean government enacted a ban on the imports of fully assembled cars into Korea (the ban continued into the 1980s). Between 1962 and 1974 the Korean government made no effort to use the protected local market as a springboard for high volume exports; rather, the focus was on increasing domestic content, which rose from 21 percent in 1966 to over 60 percent in 1972.

Government policy shifted in 1974 with the promotion of Korean designed and engineered vehicles with 100 percent domestic content. Then in 1979, after sharp declines in demand, the government intervened to restructure the industry, arranging the closure of two of Korea's four producers of passenger cars. That same year "exports came on the agenda (of Hyundai Motor Company, which since 1976 had produced more than half of Korea's passenger cars) partly in response to the government's machinery export promotion policy." By 1982, the share of exports in total automobile output had reached 15 percent, with Hyundai accounting for 99.9 percent of the export total.

■ **Diesel engines.**[40] The foundations for diesel engine production in Korea were laid with the establishment in 1963 of the autonomous public enterprise Han'gi. Subsequent to operating difficulties, Han'gi was sold in 1968 to the private auto company, Shinjin. In 1972, after continuing difficulties, Shinjin was provided with extensive long-term credit subsidies, conditional upon its providing equity finance for a planned Han'gi plant to manufacture diesel engines under license from a German firm. Financial difficulties continued, and in 1975 the government consummated a deal in which Han'gi was sold off to the Daewoo group. Daewoo immediately requested a ban on the importation of diesel engines from foreign countries; the ban was granted, on the condition that the price of diesel engines would fall. With the subsequent expansion of automobile production in Korea (and after overcoming technical problems of design compatibility between the engines and Korean cars), Daewoo was able to realize economies of scale and transform diesel engine manufacture into a profitable operation.

■ **Television.**[41] In 1966 Goldstar began to assemble black and white TVs for sale in a domestic market from which imports were entirely barred (the ban on TV imports continued into the 1980s). Three years later the government began its effort to promote television exports, with the promulgation of the Electronics Industry Promotion Law of 1969. The law provided for a series of tax concessions and credit subsidies for TV exporters (as well as for exporters of other electronics products). By 1975, production of black and white TVs (now by Samsung as well as Goldstar) exceeded one million sets; exports accounted for over 50 percent of shipments. By the late 1970s, production capacity exceeded five million sets; Korea had become the largest monochrome television supplier in the world.[42]

Initially the production of color television (under way since the mid-1970s) was entirely for export. But in 1980 the government reversed its longstanding ban on color TV broadcasts. Color TV manufacture took off, spurred by high prices on the protected domestic market. Local sales went from zero in 1979 to over U.S. $399 million in 1982 and $465 million in 1983. Export sales rose almost as rapidly—from about $50 million in 1979, to $185 million in 1982, and $353 million in 1983. Cost and pricing data for color TVs that emerged in the course of a United States antidumping suit provide indirect evidence of cross-subsidization of export sales with domestic rents. According to one calculation, in 1983 the average cost of production of a color TV was $222, average f.o.b. export price was $159, and average sales price on the Korean market was $307. Some fraction of the gap between production cost and retail sales price was, however, captured by the Korean government in the form of indirect taxes.[43] Along with protecting the domestic market from import competition, the Korean government also sought to limit competition (and associated declines in rents earned domestically) among local manufacturers. Thus, Hyundai appears to have been dissuaded in 1983 from including manufacture of color TVs in its new venture into the electronics industry;[44] and in 1984 the threat of administrative litigation for "disturbing orderly marketing" restrained domestic price cutting by one of Korea's three color TV makers.[45]

The Taiwanese Pattern. Pricing policies in Taiwan have followed a similar pattern to those of Korea; however, the nonprice mechanisms of governmental intervention—and the associated mechanisms of industrial expansion—were quite different.

Table 2 Incentives in Taiwan's Trade Regime, Compared to Five Other Countries *(about 1969,[1] in %)*

		Taiwan	Korea	Singapore	Israel	Colombia	Argentina
1	Manufacturing[2]	14	13	4	76	35	112
2	Agriculture[2]	-4	18	—	48	-14	-13
3	Effective Subsidy to Manufactured Exports[3]	9	-14	-7	-17	7	-46
4	Intersectoral Dispersion[4]	8	36	2	25	71	38
5	Effective Subsidy to Manufactures for Domestic Market Sale[3]	10	14	1	16	28	45
6	Intersectoral Dispersion[4]	23	47	7	32	56	35

Source:

R. Wade (1998b), which uses Balassa 1982; rows 1 and 2, Table 2.3; rest derived from Balassa Table 2.6.

Notes:

1. The data are for 1969 except for Korea (1968), Singapore (1967), and Israel (1968).

2. Effective protection measures the extent to which tariffs and quantitative trade restrictions increase the domestic value-added price over the world market value-added price. The figure of 14 percent for Taiwan manufacturing means that the combined effect of Taiwan's tariffs and quantitative restrictions in 1969 was to increase the domestic value-added price of manufactures by 14 percent, on average, above the world market value-added prices of the same items.

3. Effective subsidy is a more comprehensive measure than effective protection. It attempts to factor into the calculation of the domestic value-added price not only the effects of tariffs and quantitative restrictions but also the effects of as many tax and subsidy schemes as can be measured, such as export credit.

4. The dispersion index refers to the standard deviation from the unweighted manufacturing mean of the seven manufacturing sectors (construction materials, intermediate products I [lower levels of fabrication], intermediaries II [higher levels of fabrication], consumer nondurables, consumer durables, machinery, and transport equipment. The averages given in rows 1 and 2 are weighted, and come straight from the source; those in rows 3 and 5 are unweighted and differ from those in the source. The problem of bias resulting from high effective subsidy rates for quantitatively insignificant sectors is reduced by the relatively large size of each subsector.

To begin with the pricing regime, barriers to import into Taiwan have been characterized as historically low on average, but their magnitudes varied substantially across sectors. The low average manufacturing effective rate of protection in Taiwan at the end of the 1960s has generally been interpreted as low government intervention in trade. Similarly, the relatively low manufacturing difference in effective subsidy for export sale versus domestic sale is interpreted as a low "trade bias." But if one looks at the disaggregated data the picture changes somewhat. Taiwan has an intersectoral dispersion of effective subsidy rates to seven manufacturing sectors around the manufacturing average of twenty-three (Table 2). This is lower than in the other countries shown but not far from the rates in Argentina and Israel. A standard deviation of 23 percent still leaves plenty of room for big intersectoral differences in effective subsidy rates. Indeed, in two important sectors, consumer durables and intermediate products II (higher levels of fabrication), Taiwan had the second highest subsidy levels in the six-country study, after Argentina.

Two effects of the dispersion of rates are important. First, the resource pull effect (or industry bias) of a given standard deviation will probably be greater the lower the average. Second, when dispersion is at a low average, it is more likely to result from *intended* differences between sectors; whereas when it is at a high average, it is more likely to result from unintended, even quite accidental, causes, because all numbers are large and the dispersion is calculated as the difference between large numbers.[46] If these effects are true, then Taiwan's standard deviation may have as much or more resource-pulling effects as that of Israel or Argentina, and these effects are more likely to be the intended result of industrial policies.

Table 3 shows the relative strength of resource pulls towards export versus domestic sale for each subsector. The figures indicate that, for Taiwan, resource pulls created by government policies have the net effect of *favoring export sale* in the so-called "export industries," while they have the net effect of *favoring domestic market sale* in the import-competing industries. In other words, as in

Table 3 **Difference Between Effective Subsidy for Export Sale and that for Domestic Market Sale (E – D): Taiwan Compared to Five Other Countries** *(about 1969, in %)*

		Taiwan	Korea	Singapore	Israel	Colombia	Argentina
1	All Manufacturing	4	7	-5	-44	-22	-145
	Industries by Trade Orientation:						
2	Export	12	31	0	-130	10	-91
3	Import-Competing	-46	-61	-3	-88	-76	-190
4	Export-and-Import-Competing	-4	-46	-7	-65	-15	-164
5	Non-Import-Competing	21	16	3	-5	-4	-153

Source:
Balassa and Associates, Table 2.5, pp. 34-35 (1971).

Notes:
1. See notes for Table 1.
2. See notes for Table 2 for a definition of effective subsidy.

Korea, the trade regime has been dualistic. Government policies created different incentives for different industries.

A final point on Taiwan's trade regime: the Kuomintang (KMT) government has been anxious not to be seen as doing anything which might provide a pretext for other countries to put up export barriers, and thus has taken care to keep the instruments of quantitative import control out of sight. We would support Wade's contention that these hidden controls cause Balassa's measures of effective protection to be understated. Government in the late 1960s, 1970s, and 1980s classified imports as "prohibited," "controlled," and "permissible." But this categorization did not capture the real scope of the system of quantitative restrictions, because many items on the "permissible" list were in fact not allowed to be freely imported. All imports are required to have a license. This requirement is used by government to restrict certain products on the "permissible" imports list by requesting a would-be importer to establish that the domestic supplier cannot meet his terms (cost, quality, delivery date) as a precondition to obtaining the license.[47]

There are also restrictions based on who can import (agency restrictions) and on where the imports can come from (origin restrictions). For example, some items can only be imported directly by end users (many capital goods items are restricted in this way) or by government agencies. Traders can get import licenses only if they meet certain minimum asset and export requirements. Most garments are "permissible," but only from Europe or America, thus excluding the most competitive sources of supply. According to Scott, yarns, artificial fibers, fabrics, some manufactured food stuffs, chemicals, machinery, and electrical apparatus are all subject to origin restrictions.[48] Some big items on the import bill, such as crude oil, have agency restrictions.

Exporters in Taiwan generally pay no duty on most intermediates used for export production. However, some important intermediates are not freely importable, because they are subject to evidence that domestic substitutes are not cost effective. As for capital goods, exporters *do* have to pay duty unless they are concerned with products which appear on a list of specific items to be encouraged, and unless a domestic substitute is not available. A variety of capital goods are subject to quantitative import controls, even if they are to be used for export production.

Fiscal incentives run the usual gamut in Taiwan from tax holidays to accelerated depreciation allowances. What is unusual about Taiwan's system, however, is its degree of selection between products specified in the eligibility requirements. In heavy electrical machinery, for example, six types of product are identified as eligible for reduction of business income taxes from 25 to 22 percent, one of which is transformers—but not all transformers, only 154 KV class or above. In electronics not just any semiconductor devices are eligible, but only those equipped with "diffusion facilities" or "ion implantation facilities." Reading the lists of items eligible for various fiscal incentives, one has the distinct impression that the Taiwanese planners know exactly where they want the economy to go. The compilation of the lists involves them in a considerable exercise of judgment about which products should be promoted.

Taiwan also had preferential selective credit controls, as did Korea (concessionary export financing and strategic industry loans), but the volume of these loans in Taiwan and the preference margins on interest rates were not anywhere near Korea's (just on export loans alone the rents accruing to Korean borrowers were six to seven times larger than in Taiwan). Hence, the artificial financial economies for large-scale enterprise were largely absent in Taiwan. Furthermore, because of heavy financial regulation in Taiwan, a large portion of business credit (particularly for new firms and for smaller businesses) came from curb markets and from internal finance. Such heavy reliance on curb markets (friends and relatives, lending between enterprises, postdated checks and the like) and accumulated profits for business finance cut in the opposite direction from Korea's subsidies for large-scale operations. In Taiwan, firms had artificial financial diseconomies for large-scale enterprise.

For all the similarities in pricing regimes, there are striking differences between Korea and Taiwan in their industrial structures. Taiwanese firms tend to be smaller than their Korean counterparts and to depend more heavily on market transactions. Manufacturing establishments tend to be larger, individual product markets more highly concentrated, and the extent of conglomerate control greater in Korea than in Taiwan. The five largest Korean conglomerates accounted in 1982 for 22.6 percent of that nation's manufacturing shipments; the corresponding figure for Taiwan was only 4.7 percent.[49] As Table 5 reveals, the fifty largest firms (not conglomerates) accounted in the most recent estimate for 37.5 percent of Korean, but only 16.4 percent of Taiwanese, manufacturing sales. Table 4 shows that establishments with 500 or more workers accounted in 1981 for 41 percent of Korean but only 28 percent of Taiwanese manufacturing employment. Table 4 highlights a further difference between Korea and Taiwan: between 1966 and 1976 the share of employment in the largest establishments progressively increased in Korea but declined in Taiwan. Indeed over that decade the number of manufacturing firms in Taiwan increased by 150 percent, while the average enterprise size, measured by number of employees, increased by only 29 percent. By contrast, in Korea the number of manufacturing firms increased by only 10 percent, and the number of employees per enterprise by 176 percent.[50]

Turning to differences in dependence on market mechanisms, associated with small and medium firms is a proliferation in Taiwan of subcontracting between final assemblers and independent suppliers of intermediate inputs, and of ongoing entry by export traders who function as conduits to the international

Table 4	**Percentage of Total Manufacturing Employment in Establishments with 500 or More Workers, 1966-81**	
	Korea	*Taiwan*
1966	25.7%	34.7%
1971	35.6	36.1
1976	45.1	26.0
1981	40.5	27.5

Sources:
Republic of Korea Economic Planning Board, Mining and Manufacturing Surveys, *selected years; Republic of China, Directorate-General of Budget, Accounting and Statistics, Executive Yuan,* The Reports on the Industrial and Commercial Census, Taiwan-Fukien Area, *selected years.*

Table 5   Share of Manufacturing Sales by Largest Fifty Firms (percent)

	Korea	Taiwan
1970	30.3%	—
1972	32.9	—
1974	—	16.9%
1975	—	15.8
1977	35.0	15.2
1980	—	16.4
1982	37.5	—

Source:
World Bank (1987), 31.

market. In contrast to the Taiwanese pattern, Korean firms engaged in subcontracting only to a limited degree, relying instead on vertically integrated, in-house manufacture of their local inputs.[51] As for export trading, Table 6 reveals that the number of export traders expanded apace with the growth of industrial exports in Taiwan, but lagged behind export growth in Korea.

What are the mechanisms by which small- and medium-sized Taiwanese firms compete with large enterprises from other countries? What was the role of the Taiwanese government in facilitating growth via the proliferation of small firms?

We suggested earlier that government interventions in Taiwan can best be viewed as efforts to promote industrial expansion via unbalanced growth. But before we summarize the details of the relevant interventions, it is helpful to make that strategy more concrete by outlining in some detail the competitive advantages of small and medium enterprises.

The competitive strategy adopted by most Taiwanese firms followed the highly flexible, niche-producer pattern. Such a strategy concentrates on short product cycles, quick product delivery schedules, short production runs, and mixes of products aimed at particular market niches. So while the cost leaders compete by extending the length of production runs, and by increasing product standardization, flexible-niche producers compete by increasing production flexibility and focusing on market segments.

Taiwan was compelled to develop capacity in increasing production flexibility and progressive development of marketing capability, two areas key to competitive success with the flexible-niche strategy. Competitive pressures, together with sequential externalities generated by Taiwan's particular endogenous expansion process, provided most of the stimulus. In particular, sequential externalities that increased the transactional efficiency of markets in production and marketing activities, as well as technical learning by doing that progressively built up technological capability, facilitated Taiwan's competitive strategy and, in doing so, became a driving force in the expansion process.

Let us take the transactional efficiency of markets first.[52] As small firms entered and expanded, as subcontractors, suppliers, and traders, they continuously created external effects which tended to improve the transactional efficiency of markets. Two factors were responsible for improved transaction efficiency. First, increases in the number of "participants" created positive agglomeration

Table 6 **Export Traders in Korea and Taiwan**, 1973-84 (selected years)

	Korea		Taiwan	
	Number of Export Traders[1]	Average Value of Industrial Exports per Trader (U.S.$000s)	Number of Export Traders	Average Value of Industrial Exports per Trader (U.S.$000s)
1973	1,200	$2,400	2,777	$1,400
1975	1,900	2,500	4,430	1,000
1978	—	—	8,899	1,300
1980	2,300	7,000	13,320	1,300
1982	3,500	5,800	14,117	1,500
1984	5,300	5,200	20,597	1,400

Sources

Republic of China, Council for Economic Planning and Development, Taiwan Statistical Data Book, *1986 (Taipei) p. 207; Republic of China, Executive Yuan, Directorate-General of Budget, Accounting and Statistics,* The Report on 1981 Industrial and Commercial Census (see Table 4) Taiwan-Fukien Area *Vol. 6, pp. 156-7; Republic of China, Ministry of Finance,* Monthly Bulletin of Financial Statistics, *1987, p. 94; Republic of Korea, Economic Planning Board,* Major Statistics of Korean Economy, *1986 (Seoul) p. 225; and data supplied by Korea Traders Association.*

Notes

1. The Korean Traders Association represents the best available proxy. Membership of the trade association includes those manufacturers who choose to join as well as import and export trades. Only enterprises that are members of the Korean Traders Association are permitted to operate as export traders.

externalities, as a consequence of the increased social and physical proximity among larger factories and subcontractors and among traders and sellers, stemming from reduced search costs. Second, as the number and history of market transactions expanded with ongoing entry, norms and standards, coupled with greater general understanding about how market transactions worked in various industries, built up progressively, reducing the costs of contract negotiations and monitoring and the probability of postcontract opportunism. Declining transaction costs drove Taiwanese businessmen continuously in the direction of greater use of the market rather than the firm (hierarchies) for production. Production thus became more disintegrated and flexible as producers succeeded with the flexible-niche competitive strategy.

In essence, declining transaction costs facilitated the flexible-niche competitive strategy by reducing the trade-off between production flexibility and scale economies. Normally, smaller rivals have a difficult time competing with larger firms because of economies of scale and scope, especially in standardized products where price competition is important. But, by adopting a more flexible production technology, one that enables a small enterprise to absorb more demand fluctuations, and by targeting market niches, small firms can offset the competitive disadvantage of higher average production costs. In highly developed countries, small firms take up competitive positions in many industries by adopting flexible manufacturing systems (e.g., by using flexible, computer-controlled machine tools, which allow a high variance in production runs and mixes) for production of specialized products. In Taiwan, such flexibility was achieved through continuously declining transaction costs.

As small and medium Taiwanese firms entered into domestic and foreign markets and transaction costs declined, extreme forms of subcontracting and specialization in production became the accepted way to do business. This enabled many firms to differentiate their products on the basis of production flexibility (short production runs, tight delivery schedules, and diversified product mixes), which in turn allowed a slightly higher product price and facilitated competitive positions in certain high-end, niche products. As an American buyer for a large department store chain put it, "When we need five thousand pairs of shoes, we go to a Korean firm for its long production runs and lower cost; when we need five hundred pairs at the end of the season, with pink laces, in two weeks, we go to Taiwan."[53] Most important, government interventions in the areas of finance (e.g. laws to facilitate informal financial transactions, back-to-back letters of credit at banks, etc.), marketing (support for trading companies), technical information, and subcontracting laws, to name a few, supported this transactions-based business environment.[54]

In addition to the transactional efficiency of markets, the second force driving industrial expansion in Taiwan is technical change. One only has to look at statistical evidence from the capital goods sector, where Taiwan was transformed in a matter of five to ten years "from an amateurish supplier of machine tools to Southeast Asia into the fourth largest exporter of machine tools to the United States,"[55] and from the high-tech consumer electronics sector, where Taiwan has become a significant player on world markets in a few short years. Details of the process whereby Taiwan accumulated technological capability have been examined elsewhere and will not be recapitulated here.[56]

How did government facilitate industrial expansion via the mechanism just outlined? We highlight here three different sets of policies: interventions by government to set in motion the "compulsive sequence" that underlies un-balanced growth, induced interventions to help sustain the endogenous expansion, and interventions to promote the acquisition of technological capability on the part of progressive small and medium enterprises.

To begin with the inducing interventions, industrialization in Taiwan has moved through several phases, from primary import substitution in the 1950s to export-led growth in the 1960s, and turning to a mix of secondary import substitution and higher-value export commodities in the mid-1970s and 1980s. Throughout, government has been directly involved in leading the economic transitions and in shaping the successful expansion within each development phase. The KMT's top government managers already had experience trying to develop modern industry on the mainland. They had a fairly clear idea of what industries ought to exist in Taiwan and—with some disagreement—in what sequence to establish them. Japan also provided them with a source of ideas, a justification for their conception of the role of government and the main external reference economy for emulation.[57]

Since the early 1950s, government's inducing role has been defined by the KMT as taking the lead in establishing new industries—often single factories. It then either found selected private investors to run the factories or, when nobody would invest, ran them as public enterprises. Throughout the 1950s more than half of industrial production came from public enterprises (a much higher percentage in the upstream basic industries). As the projects got bigger and more technologically advanced, government entered into joint ventures with foreign multinationals. In this way, the basis was laid for production of petrochemicals, plastics, artificial fiber, glass, cement, fertilizers, plywood, textiles, and many other products. A variation on this theme has come through government policy to encourage multinational companies to enter into upstream basic industries and into selected new industrial areas (for example, electronics) to induce the growth of local suppliers and to build the foundation for a high-tech change in comparative advantage.

Downstream production was left as a preserve for local private enterprise. Government promulgated various policies and programs to promote entry and investment into the new industries it had initiated with such instruments as restrictions on imports, sectoral allocation of foreign exchange, and concessional credit. As firms and new activities sprang up downstream, the proportion of state ownership of industrial production declined; nevertheless, key upstream sectors tended to be put under control of public enterprises. Even today, Taiwan's upstream industries tend to be highly concentrated and dominated by public enterprises (see Table 7 and Figure 4).

Thus, by direct government investment and joint ventures, by encouraging entry of multinationals in selected areas, and by changes in various incentives, government has tried to influence the direction of the choice of consecutive leading industrial sectors and has attempted to spark an endogenous downstream expansion of private firms as a result of its initiatives. The aim has been somewhat different in each development phase. But, in general, it has been to change Taiwan's comparative advantage in *anticipation* of changing market conditions and to respond to exogenous shocks unforeseen.

As for interventions to promote the induced, endogenous process of expansion, one key set of policies here has to do with efforts by government to promote ongoing entry by small and medium firms rather than expansion in the size of large firms.[58] Private investors, because of capital constraints, government restrictions, and the uncertain international political situation of Taiwan, were constrained from investing in upstream industries, which tended to be relatively capital-intensive, but relegated to the more labor-intensive downstream activities. Moreover, the government-controlled, formal financial intermediaries (dominated by the banks) were inclined to be very conservative. As in Korea, there were also preferential selective credit controls, discussed earlier.

Investment incentives, tax laws, labor laws, and a host of other policies (business licensing procedures, antitrust laws, bankruptcy laws, export quota management) presented strong incentives (though often unintended by the authorities) to limit company size. For example, a five-year tax holiday provision in the government's investment incentives for new startups in strategic industries created an incentive to start new companies rather than expand existing companies. The corporate income tax was graduated by size categories in terms of net income (NT 50,000 to 10,000, 15 percent of net income; NT 100,000 to 500,000, 25 percent; above NT 500,000, 35 percent), and there was a large gap between *maximum rates* on corporate taxes (25 percent before 1974 and 35 percent after) and personal income (maximum 50 percent before 1969 and 60

Table 7 The Role of State-Owned Enterprises in Taiwan's Raw Materials Industries, 1966-86

Industry Core Company[a]	Share of State-Owned Enterprises in Revenues of the Industry [f]					Industry Size (Revenues in US$)		SOE Share of Value Added	
	1966	1970	1976	1981[b]	1986	1966	1981	1966	1982
Oil & gas extraction	n.a.	n.a.	n.a.	n.a.	90%[c]	n.a.	n.a.	n.a.	n.a.
Petroleum & coal products	86.3%	69.3%	90.8%	96%	98%[c]	108	5384	92.2%	79.8%
thereof Petroleum refining (China Petroleum Group)[d]	95.8%	97%	100%	100%	n.a.	100	5327	97.3%	94.3%
Chemical Materials	44.4%	18.2%	17.9%	17.3%	n.a.	144	3283	40.3%	15.4%
Chemical fertilizers (Taiwan Fertilizer Co.)	77.4%	81.3%	90.4%	91.3%	n.a.	77	217	62.5%	n.a.
Chem. mats. excl. fertilizer	6.7%	1.5%	7.7%	3%	n.a.	67	3053	6%	n.a.
but: Larges private group (Formosa Plastics Group)[c,e]	n.a.	n.a.	n.a.	23%	26%				
Mining (except oil & gas)	n.a.	n.a.	n.a.	n.a.	75%[c]	n.a.	n.a.	n.a.	n.a.
Basic metals	35%	19%	13.3%	13.9%	n.a.	82	3429	39.7%	32.6%
Ferrous metals thereof (China Steel Co.)	22.7% —	11.1% —	9% —	14.8% 31.9%	n.a. 21.2%	67	2857	21.4%	34.9%
Nonferrous metals thereof	97.1%	91.3%	n.a.	n.a.	n.a.	15	571	94.3%	n.a.
Aluminum refining (Taiwan Aluminum Co.)	n.a.	n.a.	73.6%	43.2%	n.a.	n.a.	217	n.a.	n.a.
Nonmetal mineral products	0%	0.1%	0.2%	0.2%	n.a.	10	2273	0%	0.3%
but: Largest private company (Taiwan Cement)[g]	n.a.	22%	n.a.	14%	n.a.				
Electricity (Taiwan Power Co.)	n.a.	n.a.	n.a.	98%[a]	97.3%	n.a.	3016	n.a.	n.a.

a The listed enterprises account generally for more than 90% of the revenues of all state-owned enterprises in the industry.
b For some industries revenues were not available, hence production value was used there instead. Moreover, for some industries 1981 data was not available, hence 1982 data was employed there.
c Estimated.
d Including China Petrochemical Development Co., which is held by China Petroleum Co.
e In 1980, the Formosa Plastics Group accounted for about 48% of man-made fiber sales and 30% of plastics sales. The group's market share was much larger in individual segments of these industries (e.g., 66% of domestic PVC production, and 63% of HDPE, in 1986). The group member Nan Ya Plastics is the world's largest PVC processor. In 1985, the group had about NT$ 26 billion sales in man-made fiber, NT$ 20 billion in plastics, and NT$ 26 billion in plastics processing.
f The underlying data is potentially unreliable. Both private and public enterprises have reason to under-report output to save tax or because of national security. The share of SOEs does not change substantially.

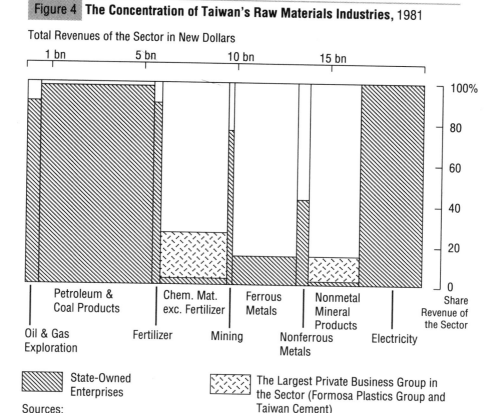

Figure 4 The Concentration of Taiwan's Raw Materials Industries, 1981

Total Revenues of the Sector in New Dollars

State-Owned Enterprises

The Largest Private Business Group in the Sector (Formosa Plastics Group and Taiwan Cement)

Sources:
See Table 7

percent after). Finally, labor laws and their weak enforcement reinforced the already strong incentive to become one's own boss by starting a small company rather than working for someone else.

Finally, there were interventions to promote the acquisition of technological capabilities. Interventions ranging from trade policies, to the pricing policies of state-owned enterprises, to control of labor unions, all helped indirectly to promote technological acquisition. But three more direct interventions stand predominant.

First has been the government's policies towards multinational companies. Multinationals were invited to Taiwan directly by individual government officials in some cases, and by a system of profitable incentives—in particular, "strategic" product arrears, where the government wanted to develop technological capability. In the early 1960s, technological improvements were sought in product areas like textiles and sewing machines; later on, capacity was developed in secondary import-substitution industries and electronics. Once foreign companies began setting up operations in Taiwan, their production methods and capital equipment were imitated by local producers very rapidly, facilitated by both word of mouth and by the mobility of labor from multinational company factories to independent or company-connected supplier operations. It was facilitated as well by government-imposed conditions on multinational direct investments.

Second, search, adoption, and diffusion of technology by private firms was also facilitated more directly by the government. Examples of government-negotiated (and sometimes subsidized) foreign technology licensing agreements[59] abound in textiles, basic industries, electronics, and machine tools. Moreover, government set up technology research centers, which imported foreign technology and adapted it to local requirements (for example, the Machine Institute Research Laboratory (MIRL) developed machine tool prototypes for local producers, and the Industrial Technology Research Institute (ITRI—the Electronics Research and Service Organization [ERSO] division, to be exact) introduced redesigns of imported technologies and prototypes in electronics and other areas). But more than the technology prototypes, these government institutes made influential contributions to training and practical experience for a host of engineers and a large number of skilled technicians. It has also been government policy to provide incentives to these research institutes to spur the development of *marketable* technologies, whether they be the product of reverse engineering, local adaptations, or new innovations. Local researchers, or those overseas Chinese lured to Taiwan by high pay and prominent positions, can expect government financial subsidies in the form of concessional loans and government investments to establish companies for the purpose of producing the (proven) marketable technologies they have developed. This allows engineers and research scientists to capture some of the financial gains generated by their efforts. Additionally, extensive technical libraries are operated for business; the government heavily subsidizes trips abroad for businessmen to attend equipment shows and to visit foreign factories; government agencies, such as the China Productivity Center, have been influential in various "strategic" industries in giving direct assistance in upgrading production technology and management; and teams of experts (subsidized by government) are sent to factories to give technical assistance.

Third, government has paid a lot of attention to the kind of education that benefits the economy. Government expenditures on education have been second only to defense, averaging about 21 percent of the budget (15-20 percent above the world average). And government education planning has fostered a formal education system that is heavily biased towards churning out scientists and engineers, rather than lawyers and liberal arts majors. It has also developed an extensive technical training network in close cooperation with the business community, as well as lent its support to private technical training institutions.

Industrial strategy and industry structure in Korea and Taiwan. The analyses of Korea and Taiwan have revealed that the two countries differ both in industry strategy and in the organization of their industrial sectors. What are the relationships between these divergent industrial structures and the divergent industrial strategies adopted in the two countries?

First, strategy appears to influence structure. The Korean strategy of government-directed learning appears to have fostered that nation's concentrated economic structure by encouraging individual firms progressively to increase their export volumes. The strategy, however, appears also to have saddled Korea with an organization-heavy institutional structure, with administrative negotiation and hierarchical command substituting to an unusual degree in a mixed economy for market mechanisms of coordination. By contrast, the Taiwanese unbalanced growth strategy appears to have supported that island's diffusion of economic power through its emphasis on investments that induce entry, and thereby expand market competition and transactional efficiency.

Second, structure appears to influence the efficiency with which strategy can be implemented. Korea's concentrated structure enhanced the efficiency of the strategy of government-directed learning insofar as government officials could target their firm-specific efforts at a small number of large firms, each capable of a substantial absolute response, rather than at a large number of small and medium enterprises. And Taiwan's transactionally relatively efficient market environment was crucial to the success of the unbalanced growth strategy insofar as it enabled a ready supply of agents to enter and take advantage of the government's externality-creating stimuli.

Third, strategy and structure appear to reinforce one another at the micro as well as the aggregate level. Students of corporate strategy identify two alternative strategies that firms might adopt in competitive international market environments: a strategy of securing market leadership, and a strategy of identifying and occupying market niches. The former strategy typically is most appropriate for large firms, the latter for their smaller counterparts.[60] Policies to promote government-directed learning both promote large firms and cost reduction through volume increases, and thus broadly reinforce cost leadership corporate strategies. And policies to promote unbalanced growth are consistent with a proliferation of smaller firms, each pursuing potentially profitable market niches.[61]

Two opposite implications for industrial policy might be drawn from the mutually reinforcing character of strategy and structure. One possible implication is that structure is entirely endogenous, and thus that a nation is free to choose whichever strategy promotes in the long run the preferred structure of industry. From this perspective, the observed differences between Korea and Taiwan in industry structure can be interpreted as the result of more or less arbitrary (or politically determined[62]) strategic choices. An alternative implication, one that underlies much of the analysis in this paper, is that initial economic conditions matter a great deal in determining which industrial strategy will yield more substantial benefits.

Initial conditions were quite different in Korea and Taiwan. As Table 8 reveals, per capita income and levels of education were substantially higher in Taiwan than in Korea at the outset of outward-oriented industrialization. More fundamental, if less readily measurable, the nineteenth-century population of Taiwan—migrants from Fukien located between the major trading ports of Hong Kong and Shanghai—appears to have enjoyed more substantial experience in business than did Koreans, who at that time were emerging only gradually from their status as citizens of a "Hermit Kingdom" and, in the absence of a fully monetary economy, were dependent in part on barter as a vehicle for domestic trade.[63] Perhaps most fundamental of all are differences in culture. In Korea a combination of social homogeneity and a deep rooted centralist Confucian tradition has long encouraged both hierarchy and loyalty on the part of subordinates to their hierarchical superiors. In Taiwan a migrant frontier ethos, combined with the tensions between Kuomintang officials who came to Taiwan in 1949 and the predominantly Taiwanese business class, the Kuomintang adherence to the economic philosophy of Sun Yat Sen, and a strong sense of political precariousness on the part of businessmen, all tended to discourage large-scale organization and the accumulation of economic power in private hands.

Table 8 Levels of Development in Korea and Taiwan

	Korea	Taiwan
1. GNP per capita (in constant 1965 US$)		
1955	$81	$140
1960	95	157
1965	103	216
1970	150	312
2. Total population (millions)		
1955	21.5	9.1
1960	25.0	10.8
1970	31.5	14.7
3. Population over six years of age with twelve or more years of education ('000s and percentage)		
1952	—	650 (10.2%)
1960	1,038 (5.3%)	1,207 (14.2)
1965	—	1,788 (17.4)
1970	2,729 (10.4)	3,740 (30.2)

Sources:
Republic of China, Council for Economic Planning and Development, Taiwan Statistical Data Book 1986 *(Taipei); Republic of Korea, Economic Planning Board,* Korea Statistical Yearbook *(various years); Republic of Korea, Economic Planning Board,* Handbook of Korean Economy; *Republic of Korea, Economic Planning Board, National Bureau of Statistics,* Population and Housing Census Report *(1960, 1970, 1975).*

Evidence of substantial initial differences between the two nations suggests that there was nothing arbitrary about their choices of industrial strategy. With the cost of market transactions relatively high at the outset of export-led industrialization, a strategy of unbalanced growth is not likely to have afforded Korea the success it enjoyed through its strategy of government-directed learning. Nor is a government-directed learning strategy likely to have had much prospect of success in Taiwan, as is evident from the failure of recent efforts to pursue Korea-style policies. On the contrary, a significant fraction of the development successes of Korea and Taiwan can be attributed to the ability of their governments to identify industry strategies that fitted well with their respective economic environments, and to implement them effectively, willing to experiment, to plunge in, learn from error, and adjust as the results of initial efforts became apparent.[64]

Industrial Policies in "Soft" States

The focus thus far has been on industry strategies for countries with governments capable of devising, implementing, and sustaining socially beneficial

388

policies. However, a sobering lesson of post-World War II development efforts has been recognition that in many less developed nations the extent and character of intervention often is shaped by forces that have little to do with the promotion of dynamically efficient industrialization. What industrial policies are appropriate for these soft states? We analyze first what might be the consequences of adopting government-directed learning or unbalanced growth strategies in soft states. Second, we examine ways in which industrial policies in soft states might usefully extend beyond an exclusive focus on prices and free markets. Third, we discuss briefly some industrial policies that might help overcome initial price distortions.

Hard Strategies in "Soft" States

In the face of the analysis and evidence thus far, it might be tempting to advocate interventionist industrial strategies for a wide range of less developed countries with initially low levels of organizational capability and market efficiency. However, as Figure 5 summarizes, many of our earlier propositions as to the efficiency of various industrial strategies look quite different for "soft" states.

First, government-directed learning now emerges as the least, rather than the most, desirable strategy. The combination of highly selective instruments of intervention and concentrated economic power associated with government-directed learning affords enormous opportunities for socially unproductive rent-seeking behavior on the part of business elites and government officials, opportunities that are likely to prove irresistible in soft states. Second, across a wide range of levels of market development the net benefit relative to laissez faire of promoting endogenous expansion via the initial stimulus of lumpy, publicly supported investments is shown to be positive, although the magnitude of the benefits is less than in "hard" states. The implied hypothesis here is that, even in a relatively weak state, the interventions associated with unbalanced growth could help promote sequential externalities, while being less likely to undermine spontaneous, laissez faire industrialization than are interventions associated with purported learning strategies. To be sure, the weaker the state, the less efficient will be the targeting of investments, the greater will be the risks of undermining industrialization via distortionary intervention, and thus the narrower the range in which efforts to promote unbalanced growth are likely to be desirable. Third, as with the analysis of "hard" states, the case for intervention-ist industrial strategy weakens in countries with substantial initial capabilities. In "hard" states, the case weakens because net benefits relative to laissez faire decline but remain positive. In "soft" states, however, the net benefits of strategies of government-directed learning in particular turn sharply negative with increases in initial levels of market development, reflecting increases in the potential for spontaneous laissez faire industrialization with higher initial capabilities, and thus a rising opportunity cost of blocking the spontaneous process.

Figure 6 brings together the various propositions as to the relationship between the desirability of alternative industrial strategies and levels of political and market development. The broken lines divide the figure into three areas. Area I represents the range of political and market development for which government-directed learning represents the preferred strategy; area II the range

Figure 5
The Benefits of Industrial Strategy in a "Soft" State

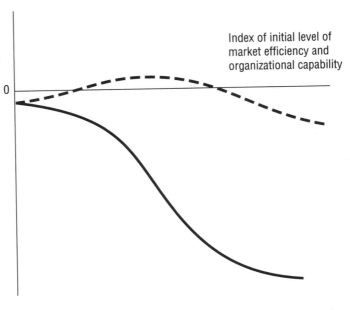

Long-run net benefit of adopting strategy relative to laissez faire outcome

Index of initial level of market efficiency and organizational capability

0

Figure 6
Initial Conditions and the Choice of Strategy

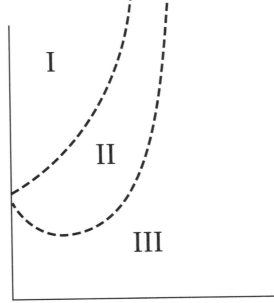

Index of political development

I

II

III

Index of market development

for which an unbalanced growth strategy is preferred; and area III the range for which a nation is likely to do best if its government adopts a laissez faire industrial policy. The figure thus illustrates our central hypothesis: there is no single industrial strategy appropriate for all less developed nations at all times. What matters rather is the goodness of fit between, on the one hand, the chosen strategy of industrialization, and on the other, a nation's economic environment and the kind of policies that nation's government has the capability of administering effectively over time, given the character of the political mechanisms of decision making.

Promotional Interventions in "Soft" States

A wide range of countries is likely to be in area III of Figure 6. Given their initial levels of market and political development, they would do better with laissez faire industrial policies than with either unbalanced growth or government-directed learning strategies. This section explores ways in which laissez faire might be usefully supplemented in "soft" states by market-completing programs and other market-completing interventions (strategy 4 in Figure 1). We make no claims to comprehensive coverage. Rather, our goals are to delineate a framework for thinking about potentially desirable interventions and to lay out a few, very preliminary, ideas for intervention.

Interventions to promote dynamically efficient industrialization in soft states need to be structured in ways that limit the risk of redirection into socially unproductive rent-seeking. Three principles can help guide their formulation.

First, interventions should be designed with careful attention to their impact on industry structure. They should support the "dynamic middle" of progressive small and medium enterprises, rather than either the largest firms or micro-enterprises. The dismal experience of "crony capitalism" in the Philippines subsequent to President Marcos's efforts in the 1970s to push industrialization via Korea-style policies suggests that in "soft" states interventions targeted to large firms are very likely to be hijacked to promote the enrichment of favored public and private elite groups. Interventions targeted to microenterprises are both less vulnerable to hijack and, in the event of hijack, are likely to result in less extreme distortions. However, our experience suggests that while microenter-prises can offer a welfare safety net on the margins of society, they have little potential to spark and sustain industrial expansion.[65] By contrast, the experience of Taiwan confirms that progressive small and medium enterprises can be the mainstay of prolonged dynamically efficient industrialization, particularly in the early and middle stages of industrial growth, when labor-intensive products are important. Small and medium enterprises require transactionally efficient markets to thrive. So policy commitments to promote competition, to remove all bureaucratic obstacles to entry and exit, and to pursue market-completing programs, can be important in promoting the dynamic middle of the industrial structure and thereby navigating successfully between the pitfalls of socially unproductive rent seeking and dead-end welfare-oriented policies.

Second, interventions in "soft" states should minimize discretion by govern-ment officials as to who will enjoy access to the available benefits. Nondiscre-tionary interventions minimize the opportunities for allocating benefits according to criteria unrelated to potential performance. And guaranteed access is a reliable signal to firms lacking connections in government (more likely progressive small firms than large enterprises) that they might also benefit from the relevant program.

Third, interventions should be performance-based. Observing this principle means that interventions in "soft" states should be linked to export performance wherever possible. As the earlier analysis of Korean industrial policy suggested, tying interventions to export performance has benefits additional to those highlighted by standard considerations of efficient resource allocation. The extent of a firm's success in export markets is a uniquely unambiguous "practical yardstick for measuring progress towards international competitiveness;"[66] firms engaged in exports enjoy opportunities for learning about technology, product design, and market preferences not open to firms that produce only for domestic markets; and continual change in the international marketplace ensures that learning and productivity gains are ongoing and not one-time efforts.

The close link between export success and productivity suggests that, contrary to our second principle, interventions linked to export performance can sometimes be discretionary even in "soft" states. For one thing, the Korean experience suggests that, even if they are granted discretionary advantages which might under some circumstances be construed as socially unproductive, successful exporters have little incentive to backslide on their efforts to improve productivity: once they had successfully penetrated export markets, protection at home and associated rents added to the incentive of Korean exporters to increase their export volumes, thereby moving further down the learning curve, reducing costs, and increasing productivity and—with no downward pressure on domestic prices—profits.[67] For another thing, export-oriented interventions afford fewer opportunities for government officials to stray, for whatever reason, from dynamically efficient actions. As Anne Kreuger put it, "Since even the most unrealistic policy-maker recognizes that foreigners cannot be forced to accept domestically produced goods, any decision to encourage a line of exports that happens to be uneconomic will be accompanied by large losses, either to the exporter, who will then contract production, or to the government, if it is inducing exports by subsidies. Either way the costs are highly visible and provide feedback that policy is inappropriate, feedback that is far stronger than an implicit or explicit tariff of comparable magnitude under import-substitution regimes, where firms have captive markets."[68]

Five examples of potential interventions that we think hold substantial promise illustrate how the three principles might be applied.

■ **Promote informal financial markets.** Our field research in Taiwan revealed that a combination of formal and informal sources of credit, rather than specific, "supply-leading" government lending programs, were the mainstay of finance for that island's progressive small firms.[69] Indeed, long experience of failure in a wide range of countries confirms that formal credit institutions lack the information and incentives to lend to promising, newly established progressive small and medium enterprises.[70] Governments cannot directly promote lending in curb markets. But the Taiwanese experience points to a range of possible mechanisms for strengthening the complementarity between formal and informal lenders and the efficiency of the curb market. All of these interventions are nondiscretionary and increase the transactional efficiency of a market that can raise the allocative efficiency of credit by meeting the financial needs of small borrowers rationed out of the formal market and by reallocating financial resources that are misallocated because of official credit programs.

■ **Guarantee working capital for exports.** A shortfall of working, rather than investment, capital has emerged as a major constraint on expansion by progressive small and medium firms.[71] Both Korea and Taiwan have programs that offer central bank rediscount facilities to banks who provide working capital to exporters against the assurance of letters of credit from buyers.[72] A program of guaranteed working capital for exports (on indirect exports) can serve as one certain channel of access to finance for progressive firms seeking to grow. The nondiscretionary character of guaranteed access to working capital for exports limits the opportunities for arbitrary refusal or grants by government officials,[73] and its link to exports ensures that the financing will go to relatively productive activities.

■ **Provide incentives to promote the entry of export traders and other export marketing mechanisms.** Both theory and evidence from Taiwan suggest that the proliferation of medium-sized export traders, and associated reductions in the costs of international transactions, were important in sustaining the participation of the dynamic middle in Taiwan's export expansion.[74] Without traders, the relatively high cost of learning about unfamiliar foreign environments would have been a major obstacle to international trade by small manufacturers and by the buyers in small volumes on whom small manufacturers depend for orders. Although the proliferation of medium-sized traders proceeded spontaneously in Taiwan, we are persuaded that government programs could provide an important initial spur to promoting trader entry. Once entry and exports are under way, we expect that an ongoing proliferation of traders and small manufacturers would continue spontaneously. A program to promote export traders might be implemented by such interventions as working capital loans based on foreign letters of credit and tax credits to trading companies. The risks associated with even discretionary incentives are likely to be low, as long as the incentives are targeted to small and medium traders, and nonparticipants in any trader-promotion program remain free to enter and engage in export trading.[75]

■ **Provide selective incentives for entry by multinational exporters of final products**, with the magnitude of incentives calibrated to the extent of local content procurement from independent component suppliers. As with the promotion of traders, the objective here—again influenced by field research in Taiwan, where backward linkages from multinational exporters represented an important channel of entry and technological learning for small manufacturers, who often subsequently became direct exporters themselves[76]—is to promote the demand for production by progressive small and medium manufacturers. We interpret the Taiwanese experience to imply that once markets for efficient subcontractors include a threshold number of participants, expansion and entry by additional final manufacturers and subcontractors can be self-sustaining;[77] thus, the objective of the proposed intervention is to get the process started.[78] The linkage between subcontracting and final-good exports is consistent both with our principle that selectivity should be considered only in the context of export activities, and with evidence from the Philippines and elsewhere that local content programs tied to final suppliers of protected domestic markets tend to promote intermediate activities in which domestic producers have no prospects for achieving dynamic efficiency in the long run.[79]

■ **Provide selective, firm-specific incentives to national exporters of manufactures.** Of the five examples, we have least confidence in the desirability of this proposal; it highlights, one final time, the opportunities and pitfalls of selective export promotion in "soft" states. The opportunities are substantial; as with multinational firms, national exporters can generate important backward linkages to independent subcontractors. Additionally, when national firms grow to become significant players in oligopolistic world markets, they are more likely than multinational firms with already established market positions to act as national champions, willing to challenge for increased world market share from national factories, even if their challenge entails significant disruption of global markets.[80] The dilemma is that (unlike multinational firms already endowed with expertise) national firms cannot be full blown exporters right from the startup of production; so a sustained program of selective support for potential national exporters cannot be linked exclusively to actual export performance. Selective incentives in Korea appear to have been contingent on initially modest but progressively rising shares of exports in a firm's total production. But for a soft state, the risk is that initially modest export performance requirements will progressively be debased. Thus, as a crude rule of thumb, we would suggest that selective firm-specific support of potential exporters should be considered in "soft" states only if firms can from the outset export at least 50 percent of their production.[81]

Strategies for Overcoming Price Distortions

Our discussion of promotional interventions in soft states presupposed a laissez faire environment, with more or less undistorted prices. This presupposition is naive: a central dilemma "soft" states pose for economic policymakers is precisely their willingness to create and tolerate price distortions as a way of channelling rents to favored clients. Would the net benefits of our proposed promotional interventions be positive even in "soft" states with distorted price environments? And would the proposed interventions help move policy away from the pre-existing distortions? Happily, as a few final comments suggest, the answer to both questions appears to be yes.

Powerful special interests that gain from price distortions—inefficient industrialists who can profit only behind high tariff walls and government officials who can extract rents by virtue of the rationing power afforded by disequilibrium prices—typically oppose efforts to move from a more to a less distorted price environment. In the face of these interests and their influence, proposals to eliminate distortions directly are extremely difficult to enact and to implement. By contrast, our proposed interventions help promote the move towards nondistorted prices via a more roundabout route;[82] rather than confront directly the interests blocking reform, the proposals work to strengthen interests that stand to gain from subsequent changes in policy.

The promotion of exporters can be a central ingredient of roundabout strategies for effecting policy change. Exporters rarely are the beneficiaries of the most egregious distortions associated with import-substituting regimes. Rather, import restrictions make their lives more difficult, denying them access to imported inputs of requisite price and quality, or affording access via cumbersome, time consuming, and unpredictable bureaucratic procedures that effectively foreclose the possibility of participating in those international markets where rapid response is crucial for success. Our proposals to guarantee working capital to exporters, to promote export traders, to promote multinational exporters with backward linkages to domestic subcontractors, and to selectively subsidize exporting national firms all would help strengthen factions of society that, as they gain in influence, are likely to become increasingly vocal advocates of policy reform.

One last point: our proposals have been presented as desirable on their own merits in "soft" states with undistorted price environments. Export processing zones, tariff drawback schemes for direct and indirect exporters, bonded warehousing programs and the like are additional mechanisms for promoting exporters by affording tariff-free access to otherwise protected inputs,[83] mechanisms that have no attraction in already undistorted price environments. But they are exceedingly attractive options in "soft" states riddled with distortions, where the objective is the roundabout one of working to strengthen the hand of interests favoring reform.[84] Our work in the Philippines and in Bangladesh provided evidence that, for all of the shortfalls in implementation, export processing zones, tariff drawback schemes, and bonded warehouses were crucial in enabling export manufacturers to take root; and these exporters were among the most vociferous advocates of continuing policy reform. Indeed, it was Korea and Taiwan that pioneered the use of zones, drawbacks, and the like in the early 1960s, a time when both countries were themselves working to navigate the shift from inward- to outward-oriented industrial strategies.

Bangladesh unquestionably provides the most dramatic example. It was generally assumed that Bangladesh was largely incapable of breaking into world markets in manufactured goods and of implementing an outward-oriented development strategy. But in spite of a distorted policy environment and a rigidly bureaucratic system of business regulations, garment exports jumped from almost nothing to U.S. $300 million in just six years.[85] Growing at an average annual rate of 106 percent, the share of garment exports in Bangladesh's total exports rose from .5 percent 1980/81 to 28.3 percent in 1986. Even by comparison with the explosive growth achieved by East Asian manufactured exports in the 1960s, Bangladesh's extraordinary performance is impressive.

Three factors were responsible for this success with garments exports. By far the most important element was the involvement of a large Korean multinational exporter, Daewoo, in Bangladesh industry. Daewoo, after selling the government some rolling stock in the late 1970s, proposed an ambitious joint venture involving the development and operation of tire, leather goods, cement, and garments factories. The government put the garments business first, and a local company, Desh, entered into a joint venture with Daewoo for technical assistance and international marketing of the product. More than 100 workers were recruited by Desh and sent to Korea for intensive training in management, maintenance, and production techniques in Daewoo's garments factory. Subsequently, Daewoo engineers helped Desh set up its factory in Bangladesh and stayed on for several years to offer technical assistance. The final product was marketed through Daewoo's extensive international marketing network. Raw materials and machinery were also purchased through Daewoo subsidiaries. For its part, Daewoo received 5 percent of Desh sales. In roughly five years after this initial startup, 120 new Bengali garments exporters had entered the business, largely as a result of the original Desh workers going out on their own.

Second, on the urging of Desh and Daewoo, the government initiated a system of duty drawbacks and bonded warehouses, allowing garments exporters to import machinery and raw materials duty-free. Preshipment export financing was also provided on a limited basis through a rediscount facility at the central bank. And tax exemptions were extended to firms devoted exclusively to export.

Third, in the early 1970s, the taka exchange rate was revised to offset its substantial overvaluation. Between 1973 and 1976, the real trade-weighted exchange rate was devalued by more than 70 percent. From 1976 onward, however, the real trade-weighted exchange rate appreciated about 10 percentage points, somewhat offsetting the earlier realignment. This exchange rate incentive to nontraditional exports provided a modest boost to the garments boom on top of the other factors outlined above. ✍

Notes

1 For important contributions, see Coase (1937), Williamson (1985), and Cheung (1983).

2 For key contributions, see Nelson and Winter (1982), Rosenberg and Birdzell (1986) and, again, Williamson (1985). For applications of a learning perspective to development economics, see Amsden (1989).

3 See, for example, Pack and Westphal (1986); also, in the context of debates over industrial policy in developed countries, Krugman (1986). Externalities were, of course, central to the earlier analyses of Hirschman (1958) and Scitovsky (1954).

4 One strategy, which we do not consider, is that of balanced growth. In a balanced growth strategy, the task of government is to select and coordinate investment decisions in industries that simultaneously create positive externalities for one another. In our judgment, and that of Amsden (1989), coordination per se was not central to the successful industrial strategies of Korea and Taiwan.

5 Corden (1974, 250-255) highlights dynamic economies as a plausible rationale for infant industry protection. Learning by doing has been analyzed by Arrow (1962) and Nelson and Winter (1982). For applications to Korea and Taiwan, see Westphal (1982), Kim (1985), and Amsden (1989).

6 The phrase is from Jones and Sakong (1980).

7 Note that insofar as a learning strategy tends to promote an industrial structure characterized by a small number of giant enterprises, it promotes the capture of simultaneous externalities, in part by enabling large individual enterprises by virtue of their size and associated diversification to internalize

externalities; and in part by facilitating coordination among a small number of large enterprises, coordination that would be exceedingly difficult to achieve in a more diffuse industrial structure.

8 See Levy (1989) for a formal model of interactions among traders and small manufacturers that highlights how an initial endogenous stimulus can set in motion dynamic expansion driven by ongoing gains in the efficiency of market transactions.

9 Hirschman (1958, 202).

10 *Ibid.*, 203.

11 For a discussion of the importance of institutional infrastructure in conditioning the response to policy reform, see Myint (1982).

12 But, as Krugman (1986), Brander and Spencer (1985), and Yamamura (1986) illustrate, even industrialized nations can reap benefits from strategic trade policies where world markets are oligopolistic, and high-profit firms from different countries engage in complex games of strategy with one another.

13 The summary data presented here are from Kuznets (1988, 14-17).

14 For further analysis of the points raised in the text, and more broadly of the political roots of industrial policy in Korea and Taiwan, see Cheng (1987).

15 See the articles in Myers and Peattie (1984) for analysis of Japanese colonial rule in Korea and Taiwan.

16 For further discussion of the implications of these labor market policies, see Kuznets (1988, 27-29).

17 For overviews of macroeconomic policies, see Kim and Roemer (1979) and Galenson (1979).

18 See Balassa and Associates (1981) for analyses of the trade policies followed by the two countries.

19 For important examples of the neoclassical explanation, see Frank, Westphal, and Kim (1975), Kim and Roemer (1979), and Balassa and Associates (1981).

20 Pack and Westphal (1986), Jones and Sakong (1980), and Westphal and Kim (1977) develop related explanations of Korea's industrial successes that endeavor to go beyond an exclusive focus on efficient pricing.

21 But note that the earlier multiple exchange rates included incentives for exporters; so, as Jones and Sakong (1980, 86-97) demonstrate, the policy reforms did not increase the absolute returns to exports.

22 As Westphal and Kim (1977, 217) note, these incentives included both compensation for domestic price distortions and net incentives on top of returns in a free trade regime. The nondiscretionary incentives included rebates of indirect sales taxes and of import duties on inputs for items produced for export (both compensating rather than net incentives; together these accounted for 72 percent of the total value of the incentive package); subsidized short-term credit to cover shipment costs, carrying costs, and raw material procurement costs of exports; and wastage allowances that enabled exporters to resell some fraction of their inputs ostensibly procured for export production on the protected domestic market at inflated prices.

23 For detailed analyses of the operation of controlled credit markets, see Cole and Park (1983) and Jones and Sakong (1980, 101-110).

24 For details of the various direct tax incentives on offer, see Hong (1979, 79-95).

25 Jones and Sakong (1980, 114-115) illustrate how government officials used the threat of audit as a way of securing compliance from firms.

26 Thus Rhee (1984, 89) report that fifty of ninety-seven firms that responded to a 1976 survey claimed to have a say in setting their export targets, with the remainder claiming to have no say.

27 The year 1968 is the most recent for which disaggregated, analytically useful estimates of effective protection based on price comparison data are available. Data summarized in World Bank (1987, 57-60) reveal that effective protection rose subsequent to 1968, and the nature of the protected sectors shifted as Korea embarked on its push (curtailed after 1979) to develop heavy and chemical industries.

28 These were sectors whose exports accounted for more than one percent of total merchandise exports; Westphal and Kim (1977, 242-43).

29 Westphal and Kim (1977, 243).

30 Pack and Westphal (1986, 94).

31 The standard neoclassical objection to infant industry intervention to promote dynamic internal economies is that firms have private incentives to invest to capture internal economies, and that if capital market imperfections limit the opportunities to make the relevant investments, then the appropriate policy response is to intervene to improve the efficiency of capital markets. But Corden (1974, 255), notwithstanding his impeccable neoclassical credentials, concludes that "one has to face the fact that capital markets are imperfect, especially in less-developed countries, and it is often easier or cheaper to impose tariffs than to create an effective capital market. There seems little doubt that, in spite of many qualifications, a valid, practically relevant infant argument for subsidization of new manufacturing industries resting on capital market imperfections can be made for many less-developed countries."

32 The average debt/equity ratio peaked at 390 percent in 1971 and remained in the 300-400 percent range throughout the 1970s; Jones (1980, 105-112); also Jones and Sakong (1980, 101-102).

33 Rhee (1984, 91).

34 *Ibid.*, 92.

35 Hong (1979, 71).

36 This example is adapted slightly from Jones and Sakong (1980, 119, 357-58).

37 Data are from Economic Planning Board, *Report on Mining and Manufacturing Survey, 1976*, and Economic Planning Board, *Major Statistics of Korean Economy, 1986*, 110.

38 World Bank (1987), vol. 2, 138-39.

39 This example is adapted slightly from Amsden and Kim (1985).

40 This example summarizes material from Jones and Sakong (1980, 128-131) and Amsden and Kim (1985, 11-12).

41 This example summarizes material compiled from Kim (1985): World Bank (1987), vol. 2, chap. 8; Goldstar Co. Ltd. (1985); and business periodicals cited below.

42 *Business Korea* (October 1983, 14-20).

43 Data in the text are from *Business Korea* (September 1984a, 80-82). According to data provided by an anonymous spokesman of one of Korea's TV manufacturers, as of early 1984 indirect taxes accounted for two-thirds of the gap between factory gate price and domestic retail sales price; see *Business Korea* (April 1984, 63).

44 *Business Korea* (September 1983, 16-20).

45 *Business Korea* (September 1984b, 85-86) and (September 1984a, 81).

46 Wade (1988a).

47 *Ibid.*, 41. Exporters could import these or "controlled" items (raw materials and intermediates) with a license obtainable if the price of domestic substitutes was more than 110 percent of the c.i.f. price. Domestic producers had a more stringent requirement of 125 percent plus many additional charges.

48 Scott (1979).

49 Lee (1983, 239); the Taiwanese estimate is calculated from China Credit Information Service and Republic of China, 1986.

50 Data are from Scitovsky (1954, 146).

51 See Levy and Kuo (1991) and Levy (1991) for evidence of a Korean tendency towards vertical integration and a Taiwanese tendency to procure inputs from independent subcontractors in computer keyboard and footwear production.

52 See Biggs and Lorch (forthcoming) for a discussion of how increasing transactional efficiency of markets in production facilitated Taiwan's flexible-niche competitive strategy and its industrial expansion. See Levy (1989) for a discussion of how increasing transactional efficiency of markets in marketing had similar effects.

53 Interview with the authors in Taiwan, September 1987.

54 See Biggs and Lorch (forthcoming) for a detailed description of the government interventions.

55 Amsden (1982).

56 Biggs (forthcoming).

57 Wade (1988a, 39).

58 See Levy (1989) for analysis of the reasons why the endogenous expansion will be larger with small rather than with large firms.

59 Gold (1981).

60 For a detailed analysis of these and related strategies, see Porter (1980).

61 For evidence and analysis of divergent strategic orientations along these lines by Korean and Taiwanese firms, see Levy (1988).

62 For an analysis that highlights political determinants of differences between Korean and Taiwanese industrial strategies, see Cheng (1987). As Jones (1980) discusses, the hypothesis that industry structure is entirely a consequence of government policy enjoys substantial support in Korea.

63 For a discussion of the evolution of Taiwan's business elite, see Gold (1981). For evidence of the incomplete development of a monetary economy in the nineteenth century in Korea, see Amsden (1989).

64 See Jones and Sakong (1980, 290-295) for a vivid depiction of the flexible, learning orientation of Korean policymakers.

65 Supply-side interventions to promote the growth of microenterprises can also have unintended, perverse effects. For example, preferential credit and programs to subsidize the cost structures of firms with less than ten employees, because they are undiscriminating, can widen the "survival space" for relatively inefficient small firms that would otherwise be forced by competitive market mechanisms to upgrade production technology or go out of business. Subsidies aimed at the bottom of the size distribution of enterprises can also result in a "growth trap." If firms receiving subsidies lose them by growing up, "marginal tax rates" on firm growth, which are already substantial in most countries, will be increased. The increment in costs due to reduced tax breaks, soft loans, and other cost advantages may be enough to tip the balance against the decision to expand.

66 Pack and Westphal (1986, 100). Neoclassical arguments against trade protection generally dwell on the notion of x-inefficiency due to reduced competition. The real cost of protection from international competition may be more involved with the dynamics of the opportunity to learn, which exposure to world markets permits.

67 For a persuasive theoretical explanation of these relationships between import protection and export promotion, see Krugman (1986). For compelling evidence of a parallel relationship between import protection and export promotion in Japan, see Yamamura (1986).

68 Kreuger (1980, 151).

69 For a detailed analysis of Taiwanese financial markets, see Biggs (forthcoming).

70 See Little (1979, 218-221, 233) for a useful overview; also Anderson (1982).

71 See, for example, Anderson (1982); Biggs, Levy, Oppenheim, and Schmitz (1986); Biggs (forthcoming).

72 A letter of credit is a commitment from a bank designated by the buyer to pay for an order upon the buyer's receipt of merchandise in satisfactory condition. See Rhee (1984) for details of how export credit guarantee schemes might be implemented. In practice, coverage in Taiwan proved less than universal in the face of the extreme conservatism of that country's formal banking system, but well-established informal financial markets were able to take in the slack. See Biggs (forthcoming) for further details.

73 But, as in the Philippines, especially conniving businessmen and government officials might be able to extract (and abscond with) very substantial loans with letters of credit for orders they had no intention of fulfilling. Thus, care must still be taken to screen and monitor export loans.

74 For a theoretical analysis, see Levy (1989); for detailed evidence from Taiwan, see Biggs and Lorch (forthcoming).

75 It is worth making note of a related program to promote trade: subsidizing trade shows in the exporting country, and subsidizing exporters to attend and exhibit in trade shows abroad. Our field experience suggested strongly that trade shows were important channels for learning and marketing for exporters from the Philippines, Taiwan, and Korea.

76 For evidence of this pattern in Taiwan, see the case study of Singer Sewing Machines by Schive (1978), reported in Amsden and Kim (1985).

77 Levy (1989) delineates the relevant mechanism.

78 One possible extension of the proposal in the text in countries that are shifting from import-substituting to outward-oriented regimes is to mandate the breakup of inefficient vertically integrated enterprises. This gets subcontracting markets started for activities where experience elsewhere with independent subcontracting has demonstrated that vertical integration has no overwhelming transactional or technological advantages. See Lall (1980) for evidence that although final producers (in his case for the domestic Indian market) might initially be reluctant to shift from vertical integration to subcontracting, the arrangement often proved efficient subsequent to their being forced by government to establish ties with independent subcontractors.

79 See Biggs, Levy, Oppenheim, and Schmitz (1986) for evidence of this pattern in the Philippines electronics and automobile components industry.

80 For vivid examples of the aggressive Japanese challenge in the television and semiconductor industries, see Yamamura (1986) and Borrus, Tyson, and Zysman (1986).

81 It is perhaps worth noting explicitly that this condition says nothing about potential advantages of programs that provide firms, with fewer than 50 percent exports, either guaranteed working capital for their export sales or any other incentives linked directly to actual export performance.

82 For two important contributions to the analysis of roundabout routes to policy reform, see Hirschman (1963) and Tendler (1982).

83 Described in detail in Rhee (1984).

84 Given their bureaucratic character, however, they are likely to discriminate against small and medium enterprises for whom the opportunity costs of the requisite paperwork may exceed the benefits.

85 Bangladesh's boom in nontraditional garments exports is described in detail in Rhee (1988).

Antitrust as a Component of Policy Reform:

What Relevance for Economic Development?

Clive S. Gray

Clive S. Gray, an Institute fellow at HIID, has led overseas advisory and research projects of the Institute in Colombia, Ethiopia, Indonesia, Morocco, and the West African Sahel. He has served as adviser on competition policy, the subject of this paper, to the governments of Kenya and Morocco.

People of the same trade seldom meet together, even for merriment and diversion, but the conversation ends in a conspiracy against the public, or in some contrivance to raise prices. It is impossible indeed to prevent such meetings, by any law which either could be executed, or would be consistent with liberty and justice. But though the law cannot hinder people of the same trade from sometimes assembling together, it ought to do nothing to facilitate such assemblies; much less to render them necessary.

—Adam Smith, *The Wealth of Nations,* 1776

Section I. Background

Most years see a meeting in Geneva, under the auspices of the United Nations Conference on Trade and Development (UNCTAD), of a body called the "Intergovernmental Group of Experts on Restrictive Business Practices" (IGE). The writer observed the opening of its sixth session, where the scale and setting were reminiscent of a miniature United Nations General Assembly. Over fifty countries were represented, and the usual caucuses of the Group of 77 (non-aligned countries), Group B (member countries of the Organization for Economic Cooperation and Development [OECD], and Group D (the Soviet bloc) convened between plenary sessions.

The vast majority of Group-77 delegations, i.e. developing countries, were represented by members of their permanent diplomatic missions in Geneva, whose sole "expertise" on restrictive business practices (RBP) derived from whatever they had absorbed from attending previous one- to two-week sessions of the group. Even so, it appears that these delegates were more knowledgeable than the governments to which they would subsequently report. Most of the delegates were presumably aware that the IGE's main object is to help developing countries establish mechanisms to combat RBP in their national economies. Conversely, anecdotal evidence suggests that many developing country national authorities still understand the IGE, some thirteen years after its founding, to be an extension of UNCTAD's mission of rectifying North-South imbalances in international trade, notably by way of combatting collusive tendering by transnational corporations (TNCs) on development projects.[1]

The UNCTAD secretariat office that services the IGE (the Restrictive Business Practices Unit of the Protectionism and Market Access cluster) lists only a dozen developing countries (out of some 125 identified as such in the World Bank's 1988 *World Development Report* [WDR-1988]) as having adopted RBP control legislation by late 1987.[2] According to UNCTAD and the IGE this is far too few; in other words, RBP control would be a good thing for many more developing countries.

To encourage and assist member states in this direction, apart from regularly convening the IGE, the UN and/or UNCTAD have issued major policy statements and other documents and convened two regional seminars (in Nairobi and Bangkok). The principal policy statements/documents are:

1. *The Set of Multilaterally Agreed Equitable Principles and Rules for the Control of Restrictive Business Practices* (known as *The Set* to IGE veterans);[3]

2. A *First Draft of a Model Law or Laws on Restrictive Business Practices to Assisting Developing Countries in Devising Appropriate Legislation;*[4]

3. A series entitled *Annual Report on Legislation and Other Developments in Developed and Developing Countries in the Control of Restrictive Business Practices,* published from 1978 to 1985; and, most recently,

4. At least four components of a *Handbook of Restrictive Business Practices Legislation.*[5]

At the regional seminars UNCTAD and cooperating bilateral sponsors distribute agenda papers entitled *The Need for Restrictive Business Practices Legislation,* quoting the following exhortation from *The Set*:

> States should, at the national level or through regional groupings, adopt, improve and effectively enforce appropriate legislation and implementing judicial and administrative procedures for the control of restrictive business practices, including those of transnational corporations.[6]

An UNCTAD secretariat working paper prepared for the 1987 IGE session cites a need to "redouble efforts to sensitize Third World countries to the pernicious effects of restrictive business practices on their trade and development."[7]

A search through the UNCTAD/IGE literature reveals that it comprises primarily a description of (i) different categories of RBP, illustrated with many more examples from industrial than from developing countries, and (ii) alternative techniques for controlling the practices in question, likewise supported by more illustrations from industrial than developing economies. Little is said on the balance of costs and benefits of alternative approaches to RBP control in different categories of low-income countries at successive stages in their evolution, or on how RBP control dovetails with other measures for policy reform as means of combatting economic decline or stagnation and accelerating growth. Clearly, the literature on these issues is very limited.[8]

The present paper is conceived as an attempt to stimulate debate on the political economy of RBP control as a component of policy reform in developing countries. Following a note on terminology in Section II, Section III reviews some indicators of the prevalence or otherwise of competition in low-income economies. Section IV reviews briefly the current status of RBP control in industrial market economies, whose experience underlies the doctrine promulgated by UNCTAD. Section V then seeks to do the same with respect to most of the dozen or so developing countries that have adopted legislation in the RBP field.

Next, Section VI examines RBP control as part of a spectrum of reform measures, addressing in particular concerns which have inspired many developing countries to adopt the *dirigiste* approach of price controls. Its interaction with more widely discussed measures for trade policy reform is analyzed. Section VII raises the issue of implementation of RBP control, examining political constraints to which it is particularly subject in a developing country environment, as well as merits and demerits of alternative modes of enforcement. Particular attention is paid to the role of judicial review, and the issues posed by the relative backwardness that afflicts some developing countries in this sector.

Section VIII concludes by asking what objectives an enlightened government of a small developing country might strive to attain through RBP control, and under what conditions it might conclude that such measures would be premature.

Section II. Terminology

The subject of this paper is the set of measures designed to control practices by which producers of goods and services[9] exploit market position to secure economic advantages, including, but not limited to, profit enhancement, over and above those that would accrue to them in an imaginary base-line situation with markets ranging from perfectly competitive to Chamberlinian large-group oligopolistic, and economic agents being free to maximize utility in the light of near-perfect information about present, though not necessarily future, conditions.

Two authoritative international agencies concur in applying the term "restrictive business practices" to the manifestations which are the object of these control efforts: the United Nations, as we have already seen, and the OECD, which has maintained a standing Committee of Experts on Restrictive Business Practices since at least the early 1960s. The OECD (but not UNCTAD) now uses the term "competition policy" to apply to the set of measures designed to control RBP.

Although the legal form of the United States "trusts" against whom the first modern legislation was enacted via the Sherman Act of 1890 has long since vanished, the term "antitrust" is still the official title of United States policy in this field. The word is used, without quotation marks, in official references to United States policy published in other languages.[10] Even though it has not been incorporated in the legal or bureaucratic lexicon of any other country, anglophone or otherwise, some non-United States authorities prefer it over their own legal jargon in unofficial discussion of the relevant body of law and practice.[11]

Table 1, summarizing the apparatus of RBP control in ten industrial and ten developing countries, gives a picture of the legal terminology used in the respective jurisdictions. One sees at a glance that anglophone countries other than the United States use the word "trade" where UNCTAD and OECD, following American usage, say "business."

In French and Spanish both terms are represented by "com[m]ercial." However, the current laws of France and Spain give priority to a different terminology: the French ordinance, in a subheading not shown in Table 1, refers to "anticompetitive practices," while the Spanish law prohibits "practices in restraint of competition."

The concept of "fairness" figures in the titles of laws in Britain, Sri Lanka, Japan, and Korea, which indicate an intent to promote "fair trade" or "fair trading."

The laws of most of the anglophone developing countries declare their intent to address both "monopolies" and "restrictive trade practices." Law and precedent in India, which has arguably the most sophisticated RBP case law of any developing country, distinguish between monopolistic, restrictive, and unfair trade practices (documents of the administering authority occasionally use the shorthand "MTPs/RTPs/UTPs"[12]). In brief, these are defined as follows:

(i) **Monopolistic trade practices**. Practices engaged in by single enterprises or combinations of enterprises having a dominant position in a market, the effect of which is to reap advantages from such position;

Table 1 Apparatus for Control of Restrictive Business Practices in Selected Countries

Country	Principal Authorizing Legislation (as amended)	Year Enacted (Note A)	Quasijudicial Commission/ Tribunal and Other Deliberating Body(ies)	Responsible Executive Branch Agency(ies)	Issues of Substance Appealable to Courts of Law? (Note B); Locus of Appeal
1. ANGLOPHONE INDUSTRIAL COUNTRIES (Note C)					
Australia	Restrictive Trade Practices Act (1906)	1971–73	Trade Practices Commission	Attorney-Gen.'s Dept. (Competition Policy Branch)	Yes; Trade Practs. Tribunal/Federal Ct.
Canada	Combines Investigation Act	1889	Restrictive Trade Practices Commission	Min. of Consumer and Corporate Affairs (Directorate of Investigations and Research)	Yes
New Zealand	Commerce Act	1975	Commerce Commission	Dept. of Trade and Industry (Examiner of Commercial Practices)	Yes; High Court Admin. Division
United Kingdom	Fair Trading Act Restrictive Trade Practices Act	1973 1976 (1949)	Monopolies and Mergers Commission; Consumer Protection Advis. Commission	Min. of Trade and Industry (Office of Fair Trading)	Yes; Restrictive Practices Court
United States	Sherman Antitrust Act Clayton Antitrust Act Federal Trade Comm. Act	1890 1914 1914	Federal Trade Commission	Justice Dept. (Antitrust Division)	Yes; Federal Judiciary
2. OTHER INDUSTRIAL COUNTRIES					
France	Ordinance on Freedom of Prices and Competition	1986 (1945)	Competition Council	Min. of Finance (Dir. Gen. of Competition, Consumption, and Suppression of Fraud)	Yes; Paris Court of Appeal
Germany	Unfair Competition Act Restraint of Competition Act	1957	None	Federal Cartel Office	Yes; Berlin Court of Appeal/Federal Supreme Court

407

Country	Principal Authorizing Legislation (as amended)	Year Enacted (Note A)	Quasijudicial Commission/Tribunal and Other Deliberating Body(ies)	Responsible Executive Branch Agency(ies)	Issues of Substance Appealable to Courts of Law? (Note B); Locus of Appeal
Japan	Act for Prohibition of Private Monopolies and Maintenance of Fair Trade	1947	Fair Trade Commission	Attorney General (acting on request of FTC)	Yes; Tokyo High Court
Spain	Act against Restraints to Competition	1963	Tribunal for the Defence of Competition; Council for the Defence of Competition	Min. of the Economy and Fin. (Directorate Gen. for Defence of Competition – Note D)	Leave to appeal must be sought from full Tribunal (except as regards enforcement of fines)
Sweden	Competition Act	1983 (1953)	Market Court	Competition Ombudsman; National Price and Cartel Office	No
3. ANGLOPHONE DEVELOPING COUNTRIES (Note C):					
India	Monopolies and Restrictive Trade Practices Act	1969	Monopolies and Restrictive Trade Practices Commission	Ministry of Industry (Dept. of Company Affairs, Dir. Gen. Investigations and Research)	Yes; Supreme Court
Kenya	Restrictive Trade Practices, Monopolies and Price Control Act	1987	Restrictive Trade Practices Tribunal	Ministry of Finance (Monopolies and Prices Commissioner)	No
Pakistan	Monopolies and Restrictive Trade Practices (Control and Prevention) Act	1970	Monopoly Control Authority (functions simultaneously as Corporate Law Authority)	None	Yes; High Court
Sri Lanka	Fair Trading Comm. Act	1987	Fair Trading Commission	Ministry of Trade and Shipping (Secretary-General of FTC)	Yes; Court of Appeal

Country	Principal Authorizing Legislation (as amended)	Enacted (Note A)	Tribunal and Other Deliberating Body(ies)	Responsible Executive Branch Agency(ies)	of Law? (Note B); Locus of Appeal
4. LATIN AMERICA					
Argentina	Act for the Defence of Competition	1980 (1946)	National Commission for Defence of Competition	Secretary of Domestic Trade	
Brazil	Restrictive Business Practices Act	1962	Administrative Council for Economic Defence (CADE)	Ministry of Justice	No
Chile	Anti-Monopolies Act	1973 (1959)	Adjudicatory Com. (Note E) Central Preventive Com. (+ provincial counterparts)	National Economic Prosecutor (independent but reports to presidency through Min. of Econ., Development and Reconstruction)	Yes
Colombia		1959	None (as of 1978)	Superintendency of Industries (Division of Price Control)	
5. OTHER DEVELOPING COUNTRIES					
Greece	Competition Law	1977	Competition Commission	Service for the Protection of Competition, Ministry of Trade	
Korea	Monopoly Regulation and Fair Trade Law	1980	Fair Trade Commission	Economic Planning Board (Office of Fair Trade)	
Portugal	Law for the Defence of Competition	1983	National Competition Council	Directorate General of Competition and Prices	
Thailand		1979	None	Dept. of Internal Trade (Merchandise Division)	Yes

Note A: Year of enactment of law currently in force. Earlier year in parentheses (if any) refers to enactment of country's first major law in RBP area.

Note B: Answer of "Yes" indicates that law or precedent hitherto allows judiciary scope for reviewing substantive aspects of commission/tribunal/executive agency ruling. Negative answer indicates law/precedent limits judiciary to enforcement of sanctions and review of narrow matters of law.

Note C: Anglophone in the sense that English is the language (or one of the languages) in which the country's laws are promulgated.

Note D: Was initially established as a Service in Ministry of Commerce.

Note E: Comisión Resolutiva.

(ii) **Restrictive trade practices**. Practices engaged in by enterprises lacking a dominant position, which "have or may have the effect of preventing, distorting, or restricting competition";

(iii) **Unfair trade practices**. Acts by sellers causing "loss or injury" to consumers.[13]

Clearly there is a difference in usage as between the concept of "fair" or "unfair" in the laws of the four countries cited above (Britain, etc.), and that of India. Nearly all legal systems, including those in which competition policy figures little or not at all, punish consumer fraud. Most countries pursuing RBP control regard protection of the consumer as a distinct issue and cover it in separate legislation, even if, as in the United States, a single agency (the Federal Trade Commission) handles enforcement at the national level in both areas.

Following the lead of OECD, the present paper will refer principally to restrictive business practices (RBP) and competition policy, and treat consumer protection as a separate though closely related field.

Section III. Assessing the Extent of Competition in Developing Economies

Activity in all economies other than those categorized by the United Nations as "centrally planned," including the most market-oriented industrialized nations, ranges along a spectrum of competitive modes between the two extremes of (i) monopoly and (ii) at least one major sector, small-farm agriculture, for example, that approaches the model of perfect competition.[14] No society's entrepreneurs are exempt from the law of human nature expressed by Adam Smith in the celebrated quotation opening this article, the implication of which is that few will resist the temptation to collude with supposed competitors if it is profitable to do so.

On the other hand, countries certainly differ in the degree of competition characterizing their markets, even if construction of an overall index to measure this would be a highly complex and subjective exercise. To assess the prevalence or otherwise of competition in low-income countries, one begins by looking for certain features distinguishing these economies as a class from their industrialized counterparts.

At the competitive end of the spectrum, low-income countries feature a large informal sector sufficiently competitive to limit the bulk of its participants to real incomes comparable to those of agricultural laborers. Moreover, at the margin between the modern and informal sectors, one can identify a small-enterprise sector, accounting for an appreciable share of commerce, transport, and manufacturing in low-income countries, which operates in more competitive conditions than its counterpart in the industrialized world.

This difference is explained in large part by the fact that the sector in question supplies goods and services that absorb a significantly larger share of consumer purchasing power in low-income than in industrialized economies. Hence the higher marginal utility which Third World consumers gain by negotiating down sellers' margins, compounded by the lower opportunity cost of time spent in bargaining and seeking low-cost outlets.

Third World shopkeepers conduct the bulk of their trade in relatively homogeneous goods at margins of 5 to 10 percent. By contrast, their counterparts in industrial countries exploit greater product differentiation—i.e. they face more steeply sloping demand curves within the framework of Chamberlinian "large groups"—to mark up analogous products by 30, 50, even 100 percent.

At the other end of the spectrum, the recent dissection of Third World economies that has identified their need for "structural adjustment" has shown that the share of output in medium- and large-scale industry accounted for by enterprises operating behind high walls of protection, against not only foreign but also domestic competition, is greater in those countries than in industrialized market economies. One explanatory factor is the contrast between (i) the postwar movement towards industrialization with minimal attention to efficiency, conducted by newly independent states, and (ii) the growing acceptance by their industrialized counterparts of the net advantages of enhanced international competition.

Another factor is the relatively greater role of the state as entrepreneur in developing nations. Whatever the underlying factors, e.g. genuine socialist ideology *versus* material gain by decision makers (notably through bribes accompanying government purchase of turn-key factories), Third World states play a larger role in industry.[15] These ventures are concentrated at the capital-intensive end of the spectrum, and typically labor under a chronic overhang of unutilized capacity. Hence the use by sponsoring governments of the numerous regulatory devices at their disposal to limit competing investments, whether by foreign or domestic firms.

Reports of activity by RBP control agencies in the dozen or so developing countries that have instituted measures in this area provide anecdotal evidence of the occurrence of relevant practices in the Third World. Section V summarizes recent reports from Argentina, Chile, India, Korea, Pakistan, and Portugal.

Conversely, the quantification of phenomena that are or would be subject to RBP control measures in developing countries has been largely confined to measurement of concentration in industry. Countries/regions for which such studies have been carried out include Egypt (Forsyth 1985), India (Gupta 1968, Chaudhuri 1975, and Ghosh 1975), Kenya (House 1973), Korea (Jones and Sakong 1980), Latin America (Meller 1978), Malaysia (Gan and Tham 1977), Morocco (Sagou 1984), and Pakistan (L. White 1974 and Amjad 1977). These studies typically measure concentration and correlate it with industry profitability, but attempts to measure the welfare loss from monopolistic/oligopolistic market structures are rare or nonexistent. The Kenya study and an ongoing research effort in Morocco will be reviewed here.

Drawing on Kenya's 1963, 1967, and 1972 Censuses of Industrial Production, House used a mix of three criteria to classify Kenyan industry according to a market structure taxonomy comprising three groups: I. "monopoly and concentrated oligopoly"; II. "unconcentrated oligopoly"; and III. "competitive." The criteria used were:

1.   A "hybrid concentration index" derived by computing a•b, where "a" is the proportion of an industry's total employment situated in its three largest plants, and "b" is the ratio of the industry's output (excluding exports) to its total domestic sales plus imports regarded as competitive with the domestic output;

2.   The "size-ratio" of plants, equal to employment in the three largest plants divided by employment in the industry's remaining plants; and

3. The number of firms in the industry.

Out of 1,057 firms allocated by the 1972 census to specific industries, 51 percent of value added was by industries falling into Group I and 30 percent by those in Group II, with the remaining 19 percent of value added by sectors qualifying as competitive. In other words, House found about half of Kenyan industry fitting the characterization "monopoly and concentrated oligopoly," and only one-fifth to be "competitive."

Lacking usable data on firms' net worth, House computed the ratios of gross and net cash flow—gross and net of depreciation—to sales, and correlated these with his indices of concentration. Excluding industries dominated by loss-producing state enterprises, he concluded from 1963 and 1967 census data (corresponding 1972 data was not yet available) that both gross and net profit margins were positively and significantly correlated with his "hybrid" concentration index.

No less relevant is House's finding that the size of the minimum capital required to enter an industry, comprising a classical barrier to entry, was not independently significant in explaining net profit margins. This implies that other barriers, particularly government regulatory policies, were more important in explaining both profitability and concentration. A decade after House wrote, it was clear to staff engaged in designing RBP control machinery for Kenya (including the present writer) that government intervention by way of (i) licensing of industrial investment, (ii) contracting with foreign machinery salesmen to establish large state enterprises, and (iii) discrimination in allocating foreign exchange for imported inputs, bore a hefty share of the responsibility for concentration in many sectors.

A subsequent review of market structure in Kenya by the present writer (Gray 1977) dwelt on the place of imports in definition of domestic concentration. It was suggested that replacing House's "b" term with 1.0 plus an industry's effective rate of protection (ERP) would be a superior way of introducing the notion of international competitiveness into measurement of industrial concentration. Application of this procedure shifted some of House's sectors—cement, soft drinks, chemicals, bakery products, tanning and leather, motor vehicle bodies, and confectionery—into more competitive subcategories, while others—cordage, rope and twine, paints, dairy products, paper products, and textiles—emerged from the analysis looking more concentrated. Correlation of the new index with profitability rates was suggested as a field for further investigation.

House's blend of concentration indices, leaving him with eight permutations and combinations to fit within his three market categories, testifies to the uncertainties involved in measuring monopoly power. It will be instructive to digress for a moment and look at the evolving approach to measurement in the United States.

Traditionally, studies of industrial organization in the United States focused on the share of a market held by the four largest sellers (concentration ratio = CR4). This approach was given quasilegal status by inclusion in the 1968 Department of Justice Horizontal Merger Guidelines, which defined a CR4 of 75 percent as a threshold for "high concentration."

Increased access to computerized data bases on United States industrial structure facilitated adoption, in the rewritten guidelines of 1982, of the more precise Herfindahl-Hirshman Index (HHI), which is the sum of squares of individual market shares of all firms in an industry, the shares being treated as whole numbers (e.g. if a firm has a 25 percent share, it contributes $25^2 = 625$ to its industry's HHI). Values of the HHI range from 0 (perfect competition) to 10,000 (100^2 = pure monopoly). The latest (1984) revised guidelines treat an HHI of 1,800+ as signaling "high concentration," while mergers that leave the industry's HHI below 1,000 are unlikely to be challenged. White (1987) cites econometric evidence from United States industry indicating that HHIs of 1,000 and 1,800 translate empirically into four-firm concentration ratios (CR4s) of 50 percent and 70 percent, respectively.[16]

As to the implications of foreign competition for measuring concentration, some writers—see Landes and Posner (1981), quoted in Schmalensee (1987)—have gone so far as to say that, provided (i) any part of the relevant market's domestic sales currently comprises imports, and (ii) quotas that would prevent additional imports are not in effect, total worldwide capacity should be taken into account in defining the market and domestic sellers' shares in it. Clearly, such an approach would reduce HHIs in a number of United States industries by a significant amount.

Schmalensee accepts the relevance of foreign capacity but calls for assigning it a weight well below 1.0, to take account of market segmentation and special entry barriers such as exchange risk and the high cost of marketing in the United States.[17] He does not suggest how the weight should be calculated.

Moroccan government economists are currently analyzing concentration in that country's manufacturing sector, based on a more detailed classification (ninety-eight subsectors) and 1986 data on four times as many firms as were available to House for Kenya. They have so far found that 54 percent of the ninety-eight industries exhibit HHIs in excess of 1,800, and only 28 percent fall below the United States threshold of 1,000. Although the indices used differ, these results parallel House's description of half of Kenyan industry as "monopoly and concentrated oligopoly."

Table 2 and the accompanying Figure 1 compare four-firm concentration ratios (CR4s) between Morocco (1986) and the United States (1972). About 34 percent of manufacturing sales in Morocco were accounted for by industries with CR4s of between 80 and 100 percent, as against 9 percent of value added in United States manufacturing. CR4s of 60 percent and above characterized industries accounting for 59 percent of sales in Morocco, as compared with 23 percent in the United States.

At the normative level the current Moroccan study will have to face the question of what HHI or CR4 values should trigger close surveillance by any RBP control apparatus that may eventually be established in Morocco (none exists at present, excluding the provincial administration's intervention in local markets—see Section VI below). Given the scale of the Moroccan market—1986 GNP equivalent to $13.3 billion, according to WDR-1988, or only 6 percent of India's, for example—there will be pressure to set threshold values higher than those that would draw the attention of the authorities in India, let alone the United States.

Table 2 **Distribution of Four-Firm Concentration Ratios in Moroccan and U.S. Manufacturing**

Range of Four-Firm Concentration Ratios	Number of Industries Morocco	U.S.	% of All Industries Morocco	U.S.	% of Total Output* Morocco	U.S.
80-100%	45	22	46%	4.9%	33.7%	8.9%
60-79%	21	55	21%	12.2%	24.9%	13.9%
40-59%	19	118	19%	26.2%	18.3%	20.5%
20-39%	11	169	11%	37.5%	16.2%	33.9%
0-19%	2	87	2%	19.3%	6.9%	22.8%
Total	98	451	100%	100%	100%	100%

* Measure of output is sales in Morocco, value added in United States.

Sources: U.S. – L. G. Reynolds, *Microeconomics* - Third Edition, Irwin, 1979, 212, based on U.S. Bureau of the Census, Census of Manufactures, 1972, Special Report Series: Concentration Ratios in Manufacturing.
Morocco – analysis of 1986 Industrial Survey, T. Mounsif and C. Gray (in progress).

Figure 1 **Distribution of Four-Firm Concentration Ratios in Moroccan and U.S. Manufacturing**

Share of manufacturing output in each CR4 range

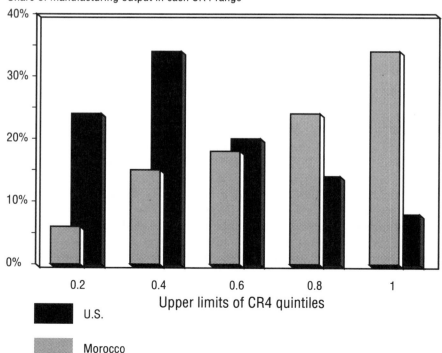

Upper limits of CR4 quintiles

■ U.S.

▨ Morocco

Section IV. Status of Competition Policy in Industrial Market Economies

To set the backdrop for a review of RBP control initiatives in the Third World, a brief update on the status of competition policy in OECD-member countries is in order.

The OECD's annual reports on the status of competition policy in its member countries reflect the fact that RBP control has long since attained maturity in the large majority of those economies. In particular, there is no longer any doubt concerning the state's obligation to combat two major categories of RBP, viz. (i) horizontal collusion in oligopolistic markets, i.e. agreements through which independent suppliers fix prices and/or divide up markets, and (ii) practices by which firms in dominant positions, acting singly or in concert, abuse their market power to suppress current or potential competitors in a weaker position (e.g. predatory pricing and tied sales).

In a third area of competition policy, control of vertical restraints, notably exclusive dealing and resale price maintenance between successive stages of the distribution chain, maturation of policy has meant in some countries a retreat from earlier blanket prohibition. For example, recent case law in the United States permits resale price maintenance with regard to sophisticated consumer products where the manufacturer can claim a legitimate commercial interest in requiring retailers to provide buyer instruction and after-sales service.[18] Regulators in other industrial countries are paying close attention to this evolution of United States policy, and some show signs of following suit.

A fourth policy area, control of market concentration, not unexpectedly features a relatively wide range of philosophies and degrees of state intervention. Britain, France, and Germany define thresholds of market control—most commonly, 25 percent—beyond which a merger is either in principle forbidden, or cannot be consummated without government approval. Most smaller countries, considering that firms in some industries cannot exploit economies of scale and compete internationally without larger shares of the domestic market, eschew quantitative criteria.

Apart from intervening directly to combat RBPs affecting trade among member states—cf. 58 million European currency units (ECUs) worth of fines imposed on fifteen petrochemical producers in 1985—the European Economic Community has played a major role in harmonizing national competition policy among its members. In practice, this has meant that members starting out with less comprehensive legal and administrative machinery for RBP control, and/or less vigorous enforcement of existing legislation, have upgraded their apparatus and its enforcement to standards set by the leaders in the field. The EEC Commission admits, however, that its lack of merger control legislation has prevented it from serving as a guide to its members in this field.[19]

Spain. The experience of the community's two newest members, Spain and Portugal, testifies to the EEC's role in stimulating laggard European states to strengthen their RBP control systems. Spain's first RBP legislation, adopted in 1963, was inspired directly by Articles 85, 86, and 90 of the Treaty of Rome (1957). However, according to the Spanish authorities themselves, enforcement of this legislation during the next generation was "mediocre," absent a political will as well as an awareness on the part of the citizenry.[20]

Interest in the subject quickened as Spain was on the verge of entering the EEC. The authorities perceived RBP control as a means of imposing "internal discipline" on Spanish enterprises to prepare them for European competition.[21] In 1985 the Court for the Defence of Competition was reorganized and a new directorate-general established in the Ministry of Commerce. A subsequent move to the Ministry of Economy and Finance gave this office increased status. Major amendments to the law were adopted in 1988.

Portugal. This country adopted its first RBP control law in 1983, having relied up to that time on price controls to accomplish related objectives. In this respect Portugal may be viewed as a current role model for many developing countries. Indeed, since *WDR-1988* classifies it as a developing country, with 1986 per capita GNP below that of twenty-two similarly classified states, its experience will be examined more closely in the following section.

Greece. The only other EEC member appearing in *WDR-1988* as a developing country is Greece, with a 1986 per capita GNP 64 percent above Portugal's. Its first RBP control legislation came on the books in 1977.

France. Although well in advance of Spain and Portugal, France lagged behind other founding members of the EEC in RBP control. Its immediate postwar legislation, heavily accenting price controls, remained in effect from 1945 until late 1986. Although some RBP prohibitions were included at the outset (additional measures were gradually added) and an advisory commission on restrictive agreements and abuse of dominant positions had been established in 1953, Finance Minister Édouard Balladur could say in December 1986 that France's economic regulatory system was still "essentially that of a postwar economy, closed to the outside, marked by scarcity and the imperative for reconstruction."[22]

The new ordinance enacted at that time revoked the 1945 law and established the "general and irreversible principle of freedom of prices." It created an independent Competition Council, revoked the power of the executive branch to impose sanctions for RBP violations, and entrenched the principle of judicial review in this area. Attributing the prosperity of the 1960s to the establishment of the Common Market, Minister Balladur described the overriding object of the reform as that of preparing French firms for the 1992 advent of the unified European market—"a constraint we have freely imposed on ourselves"—by giving an impetus to "imagination, dynamism and productivity."

It will be argued below that the main economic rationale for RBP control in developing countries is no different from that adduced by the French finance minister for his own economy.

Section V. Evolution of Competition Policy in Developing Countries

Table 1 shows that RBP control in the Third World was pioneered by the three largest Latin American countries. The status of control measures in Argentina, Brazil, Colombia, and subsequently Chile, was documented twice during the 1970s by Eduardo White, then with the Institute of Latin American Integration (INTAL), via consultant reports to UNCTAD.[23] UNCTAD has subsequently paid more attention to RBP control efforts in Asia. The writer's access to current data in regard to Latin America has been limited to materials from Argentina and Chile.

According to White, the RBP of primary concern to most Latin American countries have historically been those conducted by subsidiaries of transnational corporations (TNCs). The countries' responses, formulated in a more or less *dirigiste* ideological framework, have been measures such as price controls, establishment of state enterprises to place countervailing market power in local hands, and regulation of foreign investment and technology transfer, in lieu of adopting or actively enforcing the antitrust measures that are familiar to Latin governments through their exposure to United States law and practice.[24]

Those responses notwithstanding, in the latter part of the 1970s White noted a trend in the four above-mentioned countries away from direct intervention (notably price control and state enterprise) as a means of controlling market power, in favor of market-oriented competition policy.[25] Highlights of his findings are:

(i) A pragmatic, flexible approach was favored against, for example, a quantitative threshold for defining unacceptable market dominance. The authorities argued that the national interest, notably domestic control of production in "basic" sectors, might be served by bending classical RBP control formulae in selected cases.

(ii) The general approach was to control *abuses* of market power, not growth and mergers *per se*. Indeed the authorities felt that modernization required larger domestic enterprises.

(iii) The enterprises most frequently accused of abusing market power, especially in Brazil, were subsidiaries of TNCs. Similarly, in the concentration field, control measures were generally directed at foreign attempts to take over local enterprises.

(iv) The Brazilian and Chilean approaches diverged, in that Brazil was particularly concerned about the negative impact of oligopolistic behavior on small-scale enterprises, while Chile sought to promote greater market transparence throughout the economy.

(v) The Argentinean, Chilean, and Colombian authorities argued that monopoly/oligopoly behavior could be effectively countered by price controls. The Brazilians seemed to be less convinced of this.

(vi) Most of the countries were having difficulty institutionalizing the administrative machinery needed to enforce RBP control.

A recent UNCTAD report includes the Latin American countries among the majority of those developing countries having RBP control systems where "the bulk of the control activity of the authorities involves practices employed in the distribution of products."[26]

Argentina. A 1987 report from Argentina's Comisión Nacional de Defensa de la Competencia (CNDC) indicates that RBP control in that country began to move as recently as 1981, with the enactment in 1980 of a new Law for the Defence of Competition that replaced 1946 antimonopoly legislation treating every anticompetitive act as a criminal offense subject to sanction only through prosecution in the courts. Out of 105 actions during the thirty-four years of the former law, only one led to a firm conviction.

Conversely, seven years of the new law have seen the CNDC conclude 144 cases, applying sanctions in 27 percent of them. Out of twenty-four court appeals concluded, CNDC action was confirmed in fourteen cases and reversed in ten. The offense most frequently sanctioned by the CNDC is price fixing, followed by abuse of dominant position, predatory pricing, and refusal to sell. Other infractions relate to specialization agreements, collusive bidding, and exclusive distribution. State-owned enterprises are among those sanctioned by the CNDC.[27]

Chile. For its part, Chile reports the following actions in 1987:

(i) The Comisión Resolutiva decided twenty-four cases in the areas of price fixing, seller discrimination, exclusive dealing, refusal to sell, resale price maintenance, transparency of pricing, anticompetitive government regulations (minimum spacing of commercial establishments), economic concentration, abuse of monopoly power by public utilities (telecommunications and electric power), regulation of entry to stock exchange concessions, and collusion to forestall entry in transport.

(ii) In related fields the Central Preventive Commission issued forty-eight advisory judgments, complemented by sixty-nine investigations conducted by its regional counterparts.

(iii) Apart from regular submission of dossiers and advice to the central and regional commissions, the office of the National Economic Prosecutor (Fiscalía Nacional Económica) appeared in six cases of appeals before the Supreme Court, and conducted several studies of market structure.[28]

India. The roots of India's intervention in the RBP control field go back to the recommendations of a Monopolies Inquiry Commission in the early 1960s. The Monopolies and Restrictive Trade Practices Act (MRTP), adopted in 1969, followed closely Britain's then Restrictive Trade Practices Act (1956) and Resale Prices Act (1964). The administering agencies (MRTP Commission and Department of Company Affairs in the Ministry of Industry) pay close attention to British and American antitrust/RBP case law. Thus, out of 280 cases cited in a recent treatise on Indian law and practice published by the responsible government of India (GOI) officer, 48 percent are British or American and 52 percent domestic.[29]

Table 3 summarizes the principal actions of India's RBP control apparatus during 1985. An initial impression on viewing the table is that of an entrenched bureaucratic apparatus operating actively in a large economy. During 1985 the MRTP Commission employed twenty-three staff at or above the level of assistant director/director-general, an additional eight vacant posts being gazetted at year-end. Its 1985/86 budget was Rs. 43 million, then equivalent to U.S. $3.5 million.

The more than 1,600 enterprises registered as "large" (assets equivalent to U.S. $81 million or more) operated in the context of an economy with a GNP of around U.S. $227 billion.[30] WDR-1988 shows only two other developing countries, China (U.S. $316 billion) and Brazil (U.S. $250 billion), as exceeding that figure, and only one additional country, Mexico (U.S. $149 billion), as coming within range of it. (The next largest economy on the list is South Korea, with a GNP of U.S. $98 billion).

Table 3 India's MRTP Act - Principal Transactions During 1985

Part A - Actions of Dept. of Company Affairs, Ministry of Industry

I. Registration of MRTP Undertakings (Note A)

Transactions during 1985:	"Large" [assets = Rs.1 b.+, but not "Dominant"]	"Dominant" [assets = Rs.10m. to 1b.]	Both "Dominant" and "Large"	Total
1. Default notices issued to unregistered firms considered by department to be potentially subject to the law				88
2. Gross new registrations	244	1		245
3. Net cancellations of registration (arising mainly from five-fold increase of asset threshold in 1985)				256
Number of undertakings registered as of 12.31.85	1,563	60	59	1,682
Applications for registration pending as of 12.31.85				44

II. Registration of Agreements Relating to Restrictive Trade Practices

Registered during 1985	Registered at End of 1985 (cumulative)	Pending
7,129	34,670	613

III. Actions in Regard to Economic Concentration

Section of MRTP Act:	No. of Proposals Disposed of during 1985	...of which: (percentages) Approved	Rejected	Withdrawn	Ruled Exempt
21 - substantial expansion of existing undertakings	144	58%	19%	9%	14%
22 - establishment of new undertakings	332	55%	23%	12%	10%
21 - modification of previous orders under Sec. 21	5	100%			
22 - modification of previous orders under Sec. 22	14	93%		7%	
23(2) - mergers/amalgamations of existing undertakings	11	91%		9%	
23(4) - takeovers	7	72%		28%	
References to MRTP Commission under Secs. 21-23	0				
25 - authorization for single person to hold more than ten company directorships	0				
27 - references to MRTP Com. to consider divestiture orders (Note B)	(5 applications received during 1985)				
30 - share capital transactions involving MRTP undertakings	187	51%	26%	23%	

For row 30, the 23% value spans both the Withdrawn and Ruled Exempt columns (indicated by a brace).

Part B - Actions of MRTP Commission – Transactions during 1985

Section of MRTP Act:	References Received/ Enquiries Instituted	Reports Submitted/Enquiries Disposed of:				Cases pending at end of 1985
		Cease and Desist Order	Consent Order or "Undertaking Accepted"	Enquiry Closed	Total	
31 - monopolistic trade practices	1					3
Other provisions regarding monopolistic trade practices	1					2
10(a) – restrictive trade practices, case originating from:						
(i) complaint by trade or consumers' assoc. or 25+ consumers	4					13
(ii) reference from central or state gov't.	0					0
(iii) applications filed by Dept. of Company Affairs	16	5	9	5	19	28
(iv) "Commission's own knowledge or information"	113	4	5	48	57	138
36(B) – unfair trade practices, case originating from:						
(a) complaint by trade or consumers' assoc. or 25+ consumers	13		1	2	3	15
(b) reference from central or state gov't.	0					0
(c) applications filed by Dept. of Company Affairs	0					0
(d) "Commission's own knowledge or information"	83		29	28 (Note C)	57	74

Notes to Table 3:
India's MRTP Act - Principal Transactions During 1985

Note A - An "MRTP undertaking" is any firm or interconnected group of firms with total assets of not less than Rs.1 billion (equivalent to U.S. $81 million at the average official exchange rate in 1985), or any "dominant" firm or interconnected group of firms with assets of not less than Rs. 10 million (= U.S. $0.8 million).

Note B - Few transactions take place under this section. No references were made in 1985 and no cases were pending as of year-end. A single case of a textile mill, on GOI appeal to the courts since 1974, was finally dismissed during 1985.

Note C - One of the twenty-eight cases was referred to the police and another is described as having been "rejected."

Source: Min. of Industry, Dept. of Company Affairs, 15th Annual Report on Execution of MRTP Act (New Delhi, 1987).

The extent of business practices regarded as potentially subject to scrutiny under the act is illustrated by the more than 34,000 agreements registered by the end of 1985. The 1985 MRTP report provides capsule summaries of hundreds of current RBP cases, categorized by the report itself as follows:

1. Area restriction (producers or distributors limiting the area of operation of their dealers/stockists);

2. Tied sales (most frequent example: gas connection or supply of cylinders made conditional on purchase of a gas stove);

3. Refusal to supply (considered an RBP only where a supplier cannot prove a legitimate interest in restricting the number of its outlets); also boycott of a supplier by dealers;

4. Differential pricing or discounting (resulting in unequal treatment of dealers/distributors/stockists despite similar circumstances);

5. Exclusive dealing (restricting a client's freedom to purchase and deal in products of other suppliers);

6. Resale price maintenance (RPM; the act provides for exempting classes of goods where the MRTP Commission judges that, absent RPM, the public interest would be harmed by a reduction in the quality or variety of goods for sale, eventual increase in prices, or reduction of after-sales service);

7. Collusive tendering (all the cases cited involve response to tenders issued by state agencies or corporations);

8. Concertation in pricing; and

9. Manipulation of prices/imposition of unjustified costs on consumers by a single supplier (this practice clearly involves overlap between restrictive and monopolistic trade practices).

GOI policy statements in the RBP field point towards a trade-off between the competing objectives of "economic and industrial growth" *versus* "social and economic justice," indicating that control of economic concentration and RBP serves the latter and implying that it may do so at some sacrifice in growth.[31] The MRTP Commission's stress on social and ethical factors in its own evaluation of its role is instructive:

> While it is difficult to measure the impact of the role of the Commission in tangible terms it is felt that the Commission has been able to create a sense of awareness in the business community about the provisions of the Act and resultant social obligations...The Commission hopes that its efforts will create conditions for a free play of competition in production and a fair and ethical pricing and distribution system of goods and services to the consumers.[32]

The place of RBP control in Indian industrial development policy is most clearly illuminated by examining the Ministry of Industry's actions in the concentration field. We see from Table 3 that during 1985, in disposing of nearly 500 proposals for establishment of new enterprises or substantial expansion of existing ones, the ministry rejected over 20 percent, another 10 percent being withdrawn (some of these doubtless anticipating a negative reception by the authorities).

According to the ministry, rejection occurs most often on one or more of nine grounds:[33]

1. A "fair possibility" that non-MRTP companies—i.e. other than "large" and/or "dominant" undertakings—might "take up manufacture of the proposed item";

2. Adverse impact on existing manufacturers, especially small- and medium-scale enterprises (SME);

3. Applicant is "dominant" with respect to production of the item proposed for expanded capacity;

4. Applicant refuses to locate new capacity in accordance with GOI regional development policy;

5. Applicant is unable or unwilling to assume a GOI-specified export commitment;

6. "Existence of adequate capacity in the country and lack of scope for creation of additional capacity";

7. Applicant is a foreign-controlled company unable or unwilling to reduce foreign equity share;

8. Proposal falls short of establishing what the GOI considers to be "minimum economic capacity"; and/or

9. "Nonavailability of the feed-stock or the raw material to sustain the proposed project."

Significantly, although it is the MRTP Act that provides authority for the ministry's review of investment proposals, only the first three grounds involve concentration of economic power. Another three relate to GOI policy on regional development, export promotion, and domestic control. The final three grounds (nos. 6, 8, and 9) are tantamount to government saying one of the following: either (i) we (government) are better qualified than the applicant to assess commercial aspects of the project, or (ii) (particularly with respect to nos. 6 and 9) the project will, if successful, undercut existing producers, and that would be a bad thing.

Seen in this light, the government of India's competition policy stops well short of the philosophy expounded by French Finance Minister Balladur in introducing his country's new RBP control legislation in 1986 (see Section V). Balladur was saying, in effect, that competition has dynamic effects which no one, least of all government, can foresee, and if a new enterprise comes along or an existing one expands in such a way as to undercut an existing producer's market or access to inputs, then one of three outcomes will ensue and any of the three is more likely than not to have a positive impact on economic growth:

(i) Existing producers will react by becoming more efficient, increasing domestic absorption at lower prices and economizing on inputs;

(ii) The industry concerned will be driven to more aggressively seek foreign outlets for its goods, eventually expanding exports irrespective of bureaucratically determined export targets; or,

(iii) Some existing producers will be driven to the wall, leading to creative destruction of capital in a Schumpeterian sense and freeing resources for commitment to more efficient endeavors.

Pakistan. Pakistan's Monopolies and Restrictive Trade Practices (Control and Prevention) Ordinance came into effect two months after India's (February 1970 versus December 1969), and, like it, drew on British precedent. Also as in India, the government views its RBP control policy in the context of a trade-off between "the policy objectives of rapid capital formation and economic development on the one hand, and of social justice and consumer protection on the other."[34] Pakistan's practice diverges from that of both India and Britain in that administration of the ordinance is exclusively the responsibility of a quasi-judicial body, the Monopoly Control Authority (MCA), whose annual reports make no reference to collaboration with any executive branch agency.

The MCA's "monopoly" extends even to handling of concentration, in contrast to India, where all initiative in this area is reserved to the administration, which has referred only a handful of cases to the MRTP Commission. According to the Indian Ministry of Industry, an investment proposal raising concentration issues "is referred to the Commission only if it is felt that the facts and circumstances of the case are such that a proper decision cannot be taken on it by the Government without further enquiry."[35] Any decision by the commission in the concentration area is in the nature of a recommendation to the central government.

Conversely, Pakistan's MCA can go so far as to order divestiture, and indeed it had a number of cases pending in this area at the end of 1986 (see below). However, a 1986 review by the government of major actions since enactment of the ordinance does not cite any decisions with respect to concentration, confining itself to RBP of a classical nature in the area of distribution.[36]

In 1981, a Corporate Law Authority was established to administer all of Pakistan's major company legislation including the MRTP ordinance. Its membership subsumed that of the MCA. The authorities' relative preoccupation with company law issues is indicated by the fact that, out of 124 cases decided by the MCA in 1986, all but five concerned protection of shareholders against siphoning of resources by management—hardly an RBP issue. Of 243 cases pending at the end of 1986, the breakdown was: shareholder protection—47 percent; conversion into public limited companies of enterprises with assets above a threshold level—16 percent; disinvestment by individuals—18 percent; unreasonable monopoly power—16 percent; restrictive trade agreements—3 percent.[37]

Thailand. The next developing country to adopt RBP legislation appears to have been Thailand in 1979. The Thais' approach has been low-key. In lieu of an independent regulatory commission, the Department of Internal Trade's Merchandise Division administers the law, seeking to settle complaints through consultation with businessmen accused of RBP. Enforcement action, if any has in fact taken place, is the responsibility of the Justice Department. The law does not cover concentration. The responsible agency does not produce annual reports.[38] UNCTAD's annual reviews of developments in RBP control law and practice throughout the world contain no references to Thailand.

Korea. The Korean Monopoly Regulation and Fair Trade (MRFT) Act entered into effect in April 1981. The Korean government's pronouncements on

RBP control contrast markedly with those of India and Pakistan by stressing a direct link with economic growth. According to a policy statement supplied to and published by UNCTAD:[39]

> By early 1980, the following adverse effects of the government-directed economic policy had become obvious:
> - Distortion of resource allocation, particularly in the area of capital;
> - Weakening of initiative and entrepreneurship in the private sector;
> - Overconcentration of economic power among the nation's large conglomerates;
> - Unfair trade practices by monopolistic enterprises;
> - Deteriorating international competitiveness of domestic industries due to relatively high import restrictions and other protection...
>
> By encouraging competition, the [MRFT] Act protects consumers, stimulates business creativity and innovation and promotes a balanced development of the national economy.

The Office of Fair Trade in Korea's Economic Planning Board (EPB) reports nearly 3,000 "corrective actions" during its first six-and-a-half years of activity, of which 47 percent related to agreements between Korean and foreign firms, 42 percent to unfair trade practices, 7 percent to mergers, and the remaining 5 percent to collusion and abuse of dominant position. In addition it has tabulated close to 11,000 reports, registrations, and consultations during the same period.

Although the EPB did not furnish any analytical materials in response to the Moroccan government's explicit request, it seems not unlikely that EPB economists may have at least attempted some quantitative evaluation of the impact of RBP control since 1981.

The Third World RBP control scene now shifts to three countries in as many continents—Portugal, Sri Lanka and Kenya—in whose experience one finds the common thread of a price control apparatus coming under increasing criticism as antidevelopment, and incorporating functions of an RBP control authority.

Portugal. The Law for the Defence of Competition came into effect in December 1983, transforming Portugal's long-standing price control office into a Directorate General of Competition and Prices (DGCP) and establishing a National Competition Council (NCC). Significant actions in the RBP control field date from 1985, a year which also saw significant reduction of price controls, these being replaced, according to the authorities, by a strategy of "monitoring the evolution of prices" in a large number of sectors.[40] The DGCP remains responsible for control of "administrative prices," i.e. ratemaking for public services. The same government source claims that coordinated and simultaneous adjustment of rates to reflect previous cost increases, an approach adopted for the first time in 1985, led to a significant reduction in the overall inflation rate.[41]

RBP cases handled by the DGCP and NCC in 1985 were classified under eleven headings: (1) exclusive distribution agreements, (2) boycott of supplier by dealers, (3) discriminatory selling practices, (4) concerted practices by suppliers, (5) abuse of market dominance, (6) refusal to sell, (7) issue of price lists by trade associations, (8) collusive selling, (9) specialization agreements, (10) resale price maintenance, and (11) tied sales.

Sri Lanka. This country's Fair Trading Commission Act became effective in January 1987, taking as models the British and Australian laws and repealing a National Prices Commission Law adopted in 1975 near the end of the last Bandaranaike administration. Arguing that controls had driven significant sectors of trade in wage goods underground and stimulated corruption, the United National Party (UNP) government, which took power in 1977, eased out of directly setting prices for any goods except rice (the price of which is still fixed by the cabinet), flour, and bread. Still, any increase in prices of some 30 "prescribed" items remained subject to government authorization.

The 1987 act vests power to authorize such increases, as well as to establish price ceilings for any item at the request of the Controller of Prices, in the Fair Trading Commission, which has also been given typical responsibilities for control of RBP and concentration. The commission has commenced dealing with RBP complaints, but as of early 1989 no case had arisen in the field of concentration. The policy for the time being is to maintain a low profile and try to settle complaints via informal consultation with the parties concerned. The commission hopes to avoid recourse to sanctions provided in the law (imprisonment, fines, and/or suspension of trading), relying instead on publicizing commission decisions. An obstacle reported to have surfaced here is reluctance on the part of the press to offend its advertisers.[42]

Kenya. So far as is known to UNCTAD or to the writer, Kenya is currently (early 1989) the only African country with RBP control legislation. Its Restrictive Trade Practices, Monopolies and Price Control Act was adopted in late 1988, eleven years after the institution of RBP control machinery was first proposed in a consultant's report linked to the preparation of Kenya's 1979/80 to 1983/84 Five-Year Development Plan. The proposal attracted the interest of a government economist, who, from a subsequent vantage point as senior civil servant in the finance ministry, observed first hand the drawbacks of Kenya's price control system and argued that encouraging competition was a better way of protecting the consumer.

Since long before independence in 1963, the government of Kenya, like many of its peers, had intervened regularly in the determination of prices for basic foodstuffs, starting at producer level and building up, through a chain of authorized margins, to consumer prices of the processed commodities. In 1956 the colonial administration adopted a Price Control Act giving the minister of finance broad powers to establish price ceilings for any good or service. However, application of the act to nonfood items remained dormant until the early 1970s.

At that time two things happened to arouse the government's interest in such application. First, price inflation of nonfood consumer goods, construction materials, and agricultural inputs began to accelerate under the impetus of such factors as (i) the government's industrialization policy under which imposition of high tariffs and nontariff barriers against imports competing with domestic manufactures enhanced local industries' market power, (ii) modest devaluation of the currency, and (iii) the first oil crisis in 1973. Second, politicians began to perceive rising prices of these items as an issue on which they could contend either for direct electoral support or for influence within the government.

The control system that evolved was similar to that described above in regard to Sri Lanka. Under a so-called Price Control (General) Order, prices of a gazetted list of items, mainly manufactured goods but also including some services, were frozen as of a specific date, and could not be increased thereafter without the approval of the Price Controller, who in turn required authorization from the finance minister. A 1983 gazette notice lists some forty-eight line items or categories of items (cf. the figure of thirty in Sri Lanka).[43]

Predictably, no Kenya finance minister felt comfortable about authorizing price increases, even in the face of inflation, which averaged 13 percent annually from 1975 through 1985. The practice was to, in effect, dodge each new application as long as possible by first imposing formidable requirements for supporting documentation on the applicant, then delaying face-to-face negotiations, and finally, in many cases, waiting for the applicant to mobilize support from the Office of the President. The law permitted such tactics because it imposed no deadline for responding to an application.

In a number of cases an official preference was revealed—a perverse one, considering the duties of a finance minister—to let an enterprise become a burden on the credit system, or compensate an ex-factory price increase with an excise tax reduction, rather than let the consumer price rise. In 1982 a new minister took office who instructed his staff that no price increases for items subject to the General Order would be approved on any grounds during the fiscal year 1982/83. This was in the face of a measured overall inflation rate of 12 percent during 1981, rising to 20 percent in 1982.

Government economists became concerned that this policy, pursued for the sake of short-term political advantages, was beginning to act as a drag on Kenya's industrial development. Firms were being forced to decapitalize, with a predictable effect on incentives for expansion and new investment, and thus employment creation. There were cases of industries that had once invested ahead of domestic demand and exported a surplus that was subsequently absorbed by expansion of the local market; now the policy of the price control authorities, arguing among other things that a 5 percent nominal return on equity was adequate considering the Kenya consumer's struggle to make ends meet, was discouraging expansion and foreclosing the creation of a new exportable surplus.[44]

The technocrats hoped that Kenya's political leadership would recognize the long-run cost of continuing a strict price control policy, and would accept the argument that introduction of RBP control would give the government adequate, even if less direct, means of forestalling excessive price rises. RBP control was not, to be sure, envisaged as government's sole instrument in this respect; an ongoing effort (under IBRD and IMF pressure, needless to say) to relax exchange controls and open up the economy to import competition was expected to be no less important a factor in restraining inflation.

In seeking political acceptance for RBP control it was felt that the politicians would respond to a proposal for combatting trade practices by which the powerful Asian business community was arguably restraining competition from emerging African entrepreneurs.

Accordingly, in late 1983, the price control department was ordered to draft an RBP control law and accompanying policy statement. The statement called for reforms in the price control system as well as establishment of a new apparatus for RBP control, including a Restrictive Practices Court. The proposal failed to interest the then finance minister, remaining dormant for two years. At that point pressures for price control reform from an exasperated business community became irresistible, and the minister was requested to submit an immediate policy statement on the issue. His only recourse was to submit the 1983 document, which he did after complaining to his staff about the irrelevant material on RBP control in it.

However, the dual approach had a better reception elsewhere in government, and the cabinet instructed the legal department to prepare an integrated law, which finally passed Parliament in November 1988. The law provided a comprehensive set of criteria for government control of RBP, and established the Monopolies and Prices Department in the finance ministry with a monopolies and prices commissioner at its head, in addition to an independent Restrictive Trade Practices (RTP) Tribunal to be appointed by the finance minister.

The law incorporated the existing Price Control Act with only minor changes. In particular it refrained from imposing any of the restrictions on the minister's or commissioner's conduct of price control that had been called for in the policy statement, such as deadlines for action on price increase applications and a proviso that an application could take effect in the absence of written disapproval up to a deadline. The law also excluded the RTP Tribunal from any intervention in price control matters. Thus, as a measure for price control reform the Kenya act stops short of Sri Lanka's, which as noted above provides an active role in price regulation for the Sri Lankan counterpart agency (the Fair Trading Commission).

Section VI. RBP Control within the Spectrum of Development Policy Reform Measures

There is a certain uniformity about World Bank and IMF prescriptions for structural adjustment in the Third World, arising from the fact that strategies followed by political elites in different countries, whether to consolidate their power and acquire material assets or out of genuine ideological conviction, have engendered similar weaknesses in the economic fabric.

The standard manifestation of an economic crisis leading to a structural adjustment prescription is default on service of foreign debt, as a result of which a country experiences or is threatened with interruption of commercial financing of imports, with the disruption that implies for consumption, production, investment, and thence growth.

Most prescriptions contain the following elements, subject to varying degrees of emphasis and packaged in a variety of ways:

1. *Harmonization of incentives to export and import substitute.* Comprises steps pointing towards an effective foreign exchange rate that is the same for all actors and ensures balance in the country's international payments without quantitative controls. Subsumed here are measures such as nominal devaluation of the currency, uniformization of import taxes at a modest level, removal of export taxes except those capturing resource rents, and removal of nontariff trade barriers.

2. *Pricing of other factors and public services at opportunity cost.* Relaxation of controls that depress interest rates and raise the cost of labor; revision of public utility and transport rates to cover long-run marginal cost.

427

3. *Other measures designed to mobilize initiative and skills of private economic actors.* Minimization of bureaucratic intervention in market determination of producer decisions on investment, product mix, and pricing; transfer, to private operators, of state enterprises in sectors other than public services.

4. *Reduction of burden of public sector on productive activity.* Compression of the government bureaucracy, freeze or reduction of new hiring, and liquidation of unproductive state enterprises that cannot be sold.

5. *Anti-inflationary monetary policy.* Maintenance of classical controls over credit creation by banking system.

6. *Tax reform.* Design and administration of a tax system ensuring sufficient revenues to bring public sector deficit within desired limits, even generate surplus on recurrent account, with neutral impact on producer incentives across sectors.

Control of RBP and economic concentration does not figure in this list. Moreover, in an admittedly nonrandom sample of documents pertaining to IMF "programs" and, since late 1986 in Africa, structural adjustment facilities, as well as IBRD/IDA global and sectoral structural adjustment loans and credits in perhaps a dozen developing countries, the writer has found no suggestion that introducing control of concentration and RBP would be a desirable reform. The closest that several World Bank-proposed reform programs reviewed in this connection have come to RBP control is a call for machinery to combat "dumping" by foreign sellers. The object of such a step is to soften the opposition of domestic producers to relaxation of trade controls out of fear that it would open them up to predatory pricing by TNCs.

The only relevant World Bank initiative known to the writer occurred in early 1987 when a four-person project identification mission was sent to Morocco to look at internal trade and market structure. The mission did a case study of the leather industry, where, notwithstanding the presence of an enterprise controlling 25 percent of tanning capacity, it concluded barriers to entry were minimal and found no evidence that the large enterprise was abusing its position of dominance. Back in Washington the mission personnel were assigned to other duties before they could write their report, and World Bank intervention in Morocco's internal trade sector has remained moribund.

Current lack of IMF and World Bank interest in RBP control does not necessarily imply that the two institutions would oppose it as counterproductive to structural adjustment. Proponents of structural adjustment programs do not claim that the policy packages they recommend encompass everything a government should be doing to promote its citizens' welfare. Urging a government to adopt measures such as those listed above is not tantamount to saying that it should not bother simultaneously to improve its legislative and enforcement machinery to fight common crime, for example.

What would, however, seem to be implied by IMF and World Bank silence on RBP control is that, for the countries in which they are currently promoting structural adjustment, they side with the attitude we have previously attributed to the Indian and Pakistani authorities, to the effect that RBP control is more an instrument of social justice than a means of dynamizing the economy by unleashing the energies of private entrepreneurs otherwise shackled by oligopolistic combines. In effect, the IMF and World Bank are overlooking, or at the very least according only minor importance to, the opposing view expressed by the Koreans, that RBP control "stimulates business creativity and innovation and promotes a balanced development of the national economy."

It is not intended to imply here that, in the absence of national legislation on RBP control and concentration, a country necessarily lacks instruments to combat any of the nine categories of practices identified by the Indian RBP control authority in the preceding section. In the first place, legislation against collusive tendering on contracts with public sector agencies is already common in developing countries.[45] Second, examination of local government administration in Morocco shows that provincial governors and their staffs intervene actively, both with the help of the police and through mediation, to implement wide powers held by the governors to regulate the local economy. This includes (i) enforcing controls on prices and/or trade markups, which may be set by the central government or by the provincial administration itself; (ii) taking other measures of consumer protection—e.g. ensuring display of prices, checking weights and measures, or punishing refusal to sell; and (iii) protecting local—virtually by definition, small—businessmen from predatory practices by one another.

On the other hand, in the absence of effective RBP control at the national level, given universal human instincts,[46] one can predict with a high degree of certainty that in any country, industrialized or developing, manufacturers and distributors operating outside the reach of provincial governors will engage actively in RBP. The key questions for development policy are then (i) how much of an obstacle such practices pose with respect to the adoption of other policy reforms and to economic growth in general and (ii) how likely it is that measures introduced to control them may have side effects more detrimental than the practices themselves.

Assessing the economic cost of RBP in any economy is, needless to say, a highly subjective exercise. The debate over an imaginative effort by Harberger (1954) to measure the deadweight welfare loss attributable to monopolistic organization in United States manufacturing during 1924 to 1928 continues to the present. Harberger estimated the loss at about 0.1 percent of GDP, suggesting that economists should not lose much sleep over it. Conversely over the next twenty-five years some writers arrived at ranges as high as 4 to 7 percent of GDP. In his authoritative recent text Scherer (1980) derives a figure close to 1 percent.[47]

Recently the most active debate about gains attainable through opening up monopolistic and oligopolistic markets has focused on the impact of heightened international competition on industry operating behind protective walls following national and regional boundaries. This discussion can be viewed as a vindication of Leibenstein's X-efficiency thesis. It was not until they observed the impact on British industry of United Kingdom membership in the Common Market, or the reaction of both European and North American industry to invasion of their markets by Japan and, more recently, the East Asian Gang of Four, that many observers realized how far away from its production possibility frontiers manufacturing industry in the once leading economies was operating.

Comments of the French and Spanish authorities quoted in Section III, although they refrain from describing their national industries as monopolistic or oligopolistic, testify to their anticipation of efficiency and, thence, welfare gains as a result of increased competition arising from, in the French case,

Europe-1992, and in the Spanish case, entry into the EEC. Similarly, it is certainly first and foremost the dynamic effect of international competition that the IMF and World Bank have in mind when they pressure developing countries to reduce trade barriers and propel their industries into export markets.

There are at least two good reasons for the World Bank and IMF to argue that intensification of foreign competition through reduction of trade barriers will bring more efficiency gains than establishing an RBP control apparatus, *at least with respect to tradable goods and services*. First, given the growing pains likely to be experienced by any new bureaucratic intervention in a developing economy (see Section VII below), there is a risk that the remedy may cause more harm than the ills it is designed to counter. Second, the relatively small size of most developing country markets, coupled with technological factors creating economies of scale in modern industry, means that the number of producers that is consistent with efficiency in many branches will be much smaller than in either developed economies or large developing ones. The relatively high concentration indices observed for Kenya and Morocco in Section III—cf. in particular the comparison between Morocco and the United States—are basically a reflection of this phenomenon.

In effect, just as certain public utilities may be classified as "natural monopolies," some branches of manufacturing certainly constitute "natural oligopolies" in small developing countries. The price control route taken by many governments, however perverse its impact, reflects in part an appreciation of this fact. Members of a Chamberlinian small-group oligopoly can charge high prices and rig markets through implicit collusion—"mutual interdependence recognized"—without leaving tangible evidence for an RBP control authority to act on.

Today most economists agree with the IMF and World Bank that, for tradable goods and services, liberalization of trade policy—provided it is coupled with a realistic exchange rate policy that inspires confidence in the business community—is the most efficient option. However, this precept still leaves open two areas where RBP control could be useful under appropriate conditions: (i) production of nontradable goods and services, and (ii) countries where a political will to liberalize trade and exchange policy, thereby exposing domestic industry to the shock of international competition, is not forthcoming in spite of continued IMF and World Bank pressure.

Some nontradables are produced by natural monopolies, notably public utilities, and the railroad and transport terminal authorities; a number of others, e.g. urban public transport, air transport, and shipping, are in the hands of state monopolies that are not so natural but persist under the control of politically influential groups. Regulation of these mainly service sectors is handled by ministries or commissions that will stay in business even with the advent of an RBP control apparatus.

Such an apparatus would, however, have plenty of business to transact with respect to activities such as those financial services whose regulation is not preempted by the ministry of finance or central bank; road transport; construction contracts; and the various facets of goods distribution above petty shopkeeper level that seem prone to market rigging (cf. the Indian authorities' inventory of RBP categories cited in Section V above). The apparatus would also receive calls to intervene at the producer level in regard to nontradable commodities with high weight/value ratios permitting monopoly rents at prices below import parity—notably cement and other bulk construction materials.

As for countries where trade and/or exchange reform is sluggish—and that includes many where other facets of structural adjustment are making solid advances—RBP control should be weighed as an approach to strengthening domestic competition in potential tradables and thereby enhancing efficiency. *Ceteris paribus*, assuming RBP control is managed at the same level of efficiency and honesty as price control, it is a superior regulatory instrument. Among other things RBP control does not lend itself to the political inertia that Section IV indicated may have distorted Kenya's price control system into an obstacle to development.

Moreover, experience suggests that political forces will deter many governments from relaxing price controls until they are confident that they have an alternative mechanism for limiting monopoly rents in the distribution of sensitive goods and services. As shown in Section V, several of the developing countries entering the RBP control area most recently have associated it administratively with an existing price control function without necessarily relaxing the latter at the outset. Clearly these authorities want to see RBP regulation yield results before they relinquish the instrument that ensures them direct control.

Section VII. Issues of Implementing RBP Control in a Developing Country

It is useful to approach the problem of implementing any reform program from two different points of view. The first is that of the political scientist who examines the political context determining the constraints to which implementation of the program will be subject. The second is that of the technician, normally an administrator, an economist or other social scientist. Most frequently, the two points of view will be blended by an adviser or official whose job is to consider what regulations, procedures and institutions will accomplish the objectives of the reform most efficiently.

The writer's current role being that of a technician much more than that of a political analyst, not much space will be devoted here to the first viewpoint. It would, however, be ingenuous to recommend adoption of RBP control measures with no regard for the confluence of political forces that will determine whether or not the measures will be adopted, and if adopted, to what effect.

Obviously, groups whose economic and political power would be reduced by a program of RBP control, administered with the objectivity that is now fairly characteristic of industrial countries, will oppose the reform and, if they cannot deflect it, seek to distort its implementation. A question on which we may seek enlightenment from our political science colleagues: are such groups currently more influential in developing than in industrial countries, and how is their role likely to evolve in the future?

A provisional answer, based on the writer's own experience: in the majority of developing countries there is now greater confluence of economic and political power than in the industrial democracies. This has resulted from a blend of processes whereby interests that have established themselves in commerce have bought into political power, while political powers, for example military officers without initial ties to commerce staging coups d'état, have used their status to elbow their way into citadels of commerce. Such confluence is, of course, easier to manage in small economies featuring the "natural oligopolies" cited above, than in economies the size of Brazil, India, Mexico, etc.

In consequence, the modern industrial and commercial sectors of most developing countries feature concentrations of power that can summon political influence to resist not only divestiture, but also other restraints on their exercise of market power. This is certainly one reason why so little has happened in fifteen years of UNCTAD promotion of RBP control for the Third World.

Abstracting from this political reality, we now resume the role of technician to consider options for design of an RBP control system in a hypothetical country whose government has a few degrees of freedom to seek ways of dynamizing the economy even at the risk of dislodging some vested commercial interests. Options may be classified under two headings: (1) regulatory substance and (2) enforcement machinery.

Numerous options regarding substance are presented in the UNCTAD secretariat's two major contributions towards preparation of a "model law" (UNCTAD 1979 and 1984). One of the most important is the choice between designating specified practices as *prima facie* illegal, as opposed to outlining criteria by which the responsible authority will be asked to judge whether a given practice has a harmful effect in a particular context. The latter alternative gives wide discretion to the authority, which may exacerbate uncertainty about application of the system (see below); on the other hand it also gives the authority latitude not to interfere in the commercial strategy of sellers in essentially competitive markets, an attribute that most of the recent literature reviewed for this paper treats as desirable.

If the law refrains from treating all listed practices as illegal *per se*, it can ask that restrictive agreements be registered, in other words brought out into the open where the authority can take a look at them and order offending provisions to be modified or removed. This is a practice which Britain pioneered and has been followed by a number of industrial as well as developing countries.

Another legislative option concerns applicability of the RBP control system to state-owned enterprises (SOEs). The general practice is to exempt SOEs from the provisions regarding concentration, and (where applicable) from the requirement to register if assets exceed a threshold value. On the other hand it is a truism that SOEs are no less apt than private firms to engage in restrictive practices. The literature reviewed here suggests that developing country RBP control authorities treat their SOEs with considerable deference, but some decisions critical of SOE behavior are cited (cf. especially 1987 reports of the Argentinean and Chilean authorities).

Institutional options may be summarized as follows:

(i) Whether to make RBP control exclusively a bureaucratic function, or alternatively to establish a commission or other deliberative body enjoying some autonomy from the administration;

(ii) Which ministry or department should host the apparatus or refer cases to the commission;

(iii) Who should appoint the commissioners and what kind of tenure they should enjoy;

(iv) Whether the commission should have quasijudicial powers, or merely make recommendations to a minister;

(v) Whether the ministerial unit or the commission should be empowered to determine sanctions for violations; and

(vi) What the parties' rights of appeal to the judiciary should be, and how far the judiciary should delve into questions of substance.

Before reviewing each option in a developing country context it is useful to define a set of constraints that the control system should satisfy in order to meet its policy objectives:

(a) Financial and political corruption should be held sufficiently in check to limit the bureaucratic burden which RBP control imposes on the productive sectors;

(b) The system should evolve a transparent set of rules which the business community can understand, such that uncertainty about what is and is not permitted will not unduly deter productive activity; and

(c) The system's decision makers should be persons in whose objectivity and fairness in applying the rules the business community is likely to acquire confidence.

(i) *Autonomous commission versus bureaucratic line agency.* Out of twenty-one developed and developing countries listed in Table 1, only two, Germany and Thailand, appear not to have established an autonomous or semiautonomous commission. The drafters of UNCTAD's 1979 "model law" on RBP assumed such a body; five years later when the secretariat, while on the whole backing away from the 1979 draft, circulated a document subtitled "Elements for provisions of a model law on restrictive business practices," it felt sufficiently confident of the superiority of the commission formula to write:[48]

> Probably the most efficient type of administrative authority is one which is a quasi-autonomous body of the government, with both strong judicial and administrative powers for conducting investigations, taking decisions, applying sanctions, etc., while at the same time providing for the possibility of recourse to a higher judicial body.

It may well be argued that the business community in most countries would have more confidence in the rationality and objectivity of a semi-autonomous deliberative body deciding which trade practices are fair and which are not, than in such attributes on the part of a bureaucratic line agency. In not many countries, industrial or developing, does the bureaucracy enjoy the reputation for objectivity and professionalism that it does in Britain, for example.

With respect to control of concentration, the United States doctrine that policy in this area can be based on objective standards of economics and law, subject to application by quasijudicial or judicial bodies, appears not to be widely shared. Authorities of EEC-member countries are more inclined to treat concentration as raising broad political issues, bringing it within the purview of officials qualified to implement the current government's perception of the national interest.[49]

(ii) *Host ministry/department.* Table 1 indicates a wide variety of practice in this regard. The formula occurring with the greatest frequency has an agency within the ministry of commerce and/or industry intervening in alleged RBP situations on a consultative and advisory basis, referring to the autonomous commission those dossiers which the agency cannot close by itself. However the spectrum also includes the following formulae: all activity short of judicial deliberation is handled by (i) an independent commission, (ii) an autonomous executive agency, or (iii) the ministry of trade; ministries/departments other than commerce/industry which perform the executive branch's support role in RBP control are finance, economic planning, or justice. To governments seeking his advice in the matter the writer has suggested that a ministry of commerce and industry's likely susceptibility to influence by major actors in the business community makes it a less than ideal locus for the RBP control apparatus.

(iii) *Appointment and tenure of commissioners.* Appointment may be exercised by the national president or by the department head most directly involved; tenure is usually for a fixed term, but it may be as short as two years. Systems vary in the ease with which the administration of the day can dislodge an uncooperative commissioner other than for cause. *Ceteris paribus*, one would suppose that the higher the appointing authority, and the longer the commissioners' tenure, the greater the commission's independence from vested interests.

(iv) *Quasijudicial powers vs. advisory role.* Issues raised by this option overlap with those discussed above. In most countries playing a mere advisory role to a minister dilutes a commission's power and prestige.

(v) *Power to impose sanctions.* A number of RBP control agencies have the authority to impose sanctions for infractions under the law; in other countries legal procedure limits this power to the mainstream judiciary. (This is apart from the fact that only the judiciary can summon the police power to enforce sanctions if an offender refuses to pay a fine or otherwise disobeys orders.)

In introducing the new French ordinance of December 1986 Finance Minister Balladur gave an eloquent justification for withdrawing his ministry's long-standing power to fine RBP offenders and restricting it instead to the courts. Noting that this power, "inherited from the days of rationing and the black market," put the administration in the simultaneous role of judge and interested party, the minister asserted that the system did not provide "the minimal guarantees to be expected in a society of laws."[50]

(vi) *Role of the judiciary.* Table 1 points to a variety of practices regarding the role of the judiciary in the implementation of RBP control. The prevailing pattern is that offenders are entitled to lodge appeals with the courts against decisions by the responsible executive branch agency or autonomous deliberative body. Some systems feature a special commercial court from whose decisions there is no appeal on substance, although presumably almost anywhere one can appeal to the supreme court on grounds of deprivation of rights through procedural error.

In some systems, including that of the United States, the judiciary delves deeply into issues of substance, receiving volumes of expert testimony from economists and accountants, among others, and ruling on such issues as how a market for a particular good or service should be delineated, and what percentage of sales in the market confers a dominant position such that an enterprise created by merger would be able to hold the price at least 5 percent over the competitive level for not less than one year. Conversely, in other systems the courts stay aloof from such issues, confining their attention to questions of procedure.

In some developing countries currently considering introduction of RBP control, allocation of a role to the judiciary is questioned on the ground that traditional judges have no preparation in modern commercial law and are not well enough educated to absorb it. Reference is also made to severe congestion in the courts, and the concern is expressed that RBP cases arriving there could not be resolved quickly enough to make RBP control a credible form of regulation.

It is indeed true that litigation over some branches of RBP law, particularly concentration, has become a veritable tangle even in jurisdictions with a good deal of experience in modern commercial law. For example, the Indian Ministry of Industry has so far referred only three cases of alleged monopolistic trade practices to the MRTP Commission. The references, involving the multinationals Coca-Cola, Cadbury Fry, and Colgate-Palmolive, were made in 1973 and 1974. The companies submitted appeals, which the Delhi High Court took until the end of 1979 to dismiss. As of the end of 1985, eleven to twelve years after the references, appeals of the dismissals were still pending in the Supreme Court, and the enquiries had not gotten underway.

If one wants to reassure businessmen about the rule of law, as suggested by French Finance Minister Balladur, there is surely no alternative to having the judiciary play a role in implementation of RBP control. It may have to start modestly by accepting the facts as decided by quasijudicial authorities or even executive branch agencies, and merely fixing or confirming the sanctions. Meanwhile it will gradually become more familiar with the ground. If a judiciary is so corrupt that businessmen fear it will only add to the arbitrary nature of enforcement measures taken by the executive, then that is the obvious place to begin one's reform efforts.

There is no question that a commercially, even economically, literate judiciary is one of the components of a modern industrial state. If a developing country aspires to such a state, then creation of a qualified judiciary is as much a development imperative as is building dams or expanding literacy. Of interest in this connection is a communique issued by the Moroccan employers' federation (CGEM) and association of civil engineers (AIPC) at the conclusion of an April 1988 colloquium on "The Public and Private Sectors: Towards a Better Balance," which called for instituting

> ...clear rules of competition, in particular via reforms of the stock exchange, accounting standards and the commercial code, as well as by modernization of judicial administration and training of the judiciary to understand the problems posed by the workings of competition.[51]

Section VIII. Conclusion

It is useful to abstract momentarily from political reality and imagine how a benevolent dictator in a small developing country engaged in a "typical" IMF/ World Bank-supported structural adjustment program could put RBP control to good use. (We also abstract here from pure social justice considerations, while expressing the belief that the dictator could probably strengthen his political base by taking steps to control exploitation of weak market participants by strong ones.)

From the viewpoint of promoting economic growth, the dictator's overriding objective vis-à-vis tradable sectors should be to complement trade policy reform by intensifying domestic competition, thereby forcing producers to cut costs to the point where they can compete externally. If this leads to creation of excess capacity, so much more likely will producers be to turn their attention to foreign markets.

The question of what concentration policy to pursue in this situation is a complex issue. Classical policy objectives do not lose all their validity in a small market—thus, one wants to prevent expansion and mergers that confer market power unaccompanied by cost reduction and stimuli to export. On the other hand there will be "natural oligopoly" sectors where development of an export capability will depend on consolidation of some existing enterprises and, sadly but unavoidably, closure of others, among them units falling into the politically sensitive small- and medium-scale category.

As for nontradable goods and services, considering that their prices affect indirectly the competitiveness of tradables, the object will be not only to forestall seller collusion, making for prices above competitive levels, but once again to reduce costs of inputs and wage goods by stimulating price competition.

To ensure effective pursuit of these policies, the dictator should strive to establish an RBP control apparatus that respects the constraints outlined in the preceding section. That is, the apparatus should shun corruption, operate under transparent rules and be staffed by persons deserving of the business community's respect. To promote these ends a quasijudicial machinery should complement the bureaucratic line agency charged with RBP control, and decisions of either should be subject to review by a qualified judiciary.

Insofar as the level of institutional development in the country denies the dictator access to regulators and judges meeting these conditions, it may well be that passage of an RBP control law would be premature, such that creation of new openings for corrupt officials to bleed the business community would offset any concrete achievements of the system. In that case the dictator should rather confine his immediate attention to making a success of trade policy reform, while initiating a program of training and institution-building, looking towards introduction of RBP control at a later date. ∾

Notes

1 For example, in May 1986 Kenya's commerce and industry minister strummed this theme in keynoting an African regional seminar sponsored by UNCTAD and two Scandinavian governments to sensitize participants on the desirability of instituting national antitrust programs. Cf. Ng'eno (1986).

2 UNCTAD (May 1986, 2), updated orally in November 1987. The figure of twelve excludes six Latin American countries identified as having anti-RBP clauses in their written constitutions (but apparently lacking administrative machinery to enforce these).

3 United Nations (1981). Adopted by the United Nations Conference on Restrictive Business Practices (Geneva, November-December 1979 and April 1980) and subsequently by the 35th United Nations General Assembly (December 1980).

4 United Nations (1979). Carries subtitle "Prepared by the UNCTAD Secretariat."

5 TD/B/RBP/33 and 42 of July 1986 and August 1987.

6 UNCTAD (May 1986, 1).

7 UNCTAD (November 1987), cover page.

8 Rabat is not the easiest vantage point from which to mount a literature search. The principal component in the search has been a series of letters directed by the Moroccan government to known RBP control authorities in developing countries, asking them inter alia for citations (and, if possible, copies) of analytical writings on the local RBP situation. Up to the present, nothing that merits the title of economic analysis has turned up.

9 Not including labor services. Practices of trade unions, while potentially no less restrictive than those of price-discriminating monopolists, are traditionally excluded from the antitrust field.

10 Cf. OECD (1987, 137).

11 Cf. Indian Law Minister Kaushal's foreword to Dugar (1984), which begins: "Anti-trust legislation is now an integral part of the economic life all the world over."

12 Government of India (GOI) (1987, 153).

13 Definitions based on Dugar (1984, 66-67, 69-70, 298-300). Dugar cites the Monopolies Inquiry (Sachar) Commission of 1977-78 as observing that every monopolistic trade practice is on its face also restrictive.

14 State subsidies administered via nondiscriminating farm price supports, while widespread in industrialized countries, do not vitiate the competitive character of small-farm agriculture.

15 On the basis of admittedly incomplete data and differing classifications of industry, Peter Short (1984) finds state-owned enterprises accounting for larger shares of manufacturing output and investment in developing than in industrialized countries.

16 White (1987, 17). These relationships have been found to hold in Morocco, based on analysis of 1986 survey data in that country.

17 Schmalensee (1987, 50-51).

18 The latest move in this direction is the Supreme Court's May 1988 ruling in a Sharp Electronics case. Cf. *International Herald Tribune*, May 9, 1988.

19 Cf. M. Caspari, director general of competition, Commission of the European Communities, statement in government of France (GOF) (May-June 1988, 7).

20 M. Comenge, director general of the Defence of Competition, Government of Spain (GOS) in *ibid* (May-June 1988, 10).

21 OECD (1987, 87).

22 GOF (December 1986, 5-6).

23 E. White (1974 and 1978).

24 E. White (1978, 1).

25 White also refers to the introduction of RBP control legislation in Venezuela's Congress in 1975, although an UNCTAD document issued twelve years later describes this bill or its successor as being still under consideration. Cf. UNCTAD (November 1987, 11).

26 UNCTAD (1985, 23).

27 Rovira, (1986 and 1987).

28 Government of Chile (GOC) (1988).

29 Dugar (1984, xxi-xxxi). At the time of publication, Mr. Dugar was joint secretary in the Ministry of Industry's Department of Company Affairs.

30 Cf. WDR-1988, appendix Table 1, population of 765 million times per capita GDP of $270.

31 Cf. GOI (1987, 1).

32 Ibid., 158.

33 Ibid, 9.

34 UNCTAD (1986), section entitled "Commentary by the Government of Pakistan on the Monopolies and Restrictive Trade Practices (Control and Prevention) Ordinance," p. 22. Notwithstanding the reference to consumer protection, the ordinance does not intervene in this field.

35 GOI, Ministry of Industry (1987, 10).

36 Government of Pakistan (GOP) explanatory memorandum, UNCTAD (1986).

37 GOP (1987).

38 Information obtained in November 1987 interview with Thai officials.

39 UNCTAD (August 1987, 18).

40 OECD (1987, 234).

41 According to the IMF's International Financial Statistics, inflation of Portugal's consumer price index dropped from 25.1 percent in 1983 and 28.9 percent in 1984 to 19.6 percent in 1985.

42 Information on Sri Lanka taken from government of Sri Lanka (GOSL) (1987) and interviews with Sri Lankan authorities.

43 Government of Kenya (GOK) (1983). The schedule of items remained essentially unchanged from the late 1970s at least until mid-1986.

44 A study conducted by the writer in 1983 pointed to this state of affairs in the dry-cell battery industry.

45 UNCTAD (1984, 21).

46 Cf. quote from Adam Smith at the beginning of this paper.

47 0.86 percent. Scherer, 465.

48 UNCTAD (1984, 51).

49 For an analysis of United States doctrine see the symposium on merger policy in AEA Fall 1987; regarding European positions see the symposium on competition policy and Europe-1992 in French Ministry of the Economy, etc., May-June 1988.

50 GOF, French Ministry of the Economy (1986, 10).

51 Morocco, AIPC-CGEM (1988, 402).

Bibliography

■ *Chapter 1: Economic Systems Reform in Developing Countries.*
D. H. Perkins

See notes on page 48 for references.

■ *Chapter 2: Macroeconomic Reform in Developing Countries.*
M. Roemer, S. C. Radelet.

Adelman, Irma, and Sherman Robinson. 1978. *Income Distribution Policy in Developing Countries: A Case Study of Korea.* Stanford, Calif.: Stanford Univ. Press.

Ahluwalia, Montek. 1976. "Inequality, Poverty, and Development." *Journal of Development Economics* 3 (December): 307-42.

Amsden, Alice. 1989. *Asia's Next Giant: South Korea and Late Industrialization.* New York: Oxford Univ. Press.

Balassa, Bela. 1971. *The Structure of Protection in Developing Countries.* Baltimore, Md.: Johns Hopkins Univ. Press.

_____. 1978. "Exports and Economic Growth: Further Evidence." *Journal of Development Economics* 5 (June): 181-89.

_____. 1982. "Structural Adjustment Policies in Developing Economies." *World Development* 10:23-38.

_____. 1986. "Policy Responses to Exogenous Shocks in Developing Countries." *American Economic Review* 76 (May): 75-78.

Balassa, Bela, and John Williamson. 1987. *Adjusting to Success: Balance of Payments Policies in the East Asian NICs.* Washington, D.C.: Institute for International Economics.

Bates, Robert H. 1981. *Markets and States in Tropical Africa: The Political Basis of Agriculture Policies.* Berkeley: Univ. of California Press.

Berg, Elliot. 1981. *Accelerated Development in Sub-Saharan Africa.* Prepared by Elliot Berg for the World Bank. Washington, D.C.: World Bank.

Bergsman, J. 1974. "Commercial Policy, Allocative, and 'X-Efficiency.'" *Quarterly Journal of Economics* 58 (August): 409-33.

Bhagwati, Jagdish. 1978. *Foreign Exchange Regimes and Economic Development: Anatomy and Consequences of Exchange Control Regimes*. Cambridge, Mass: Ballinger.

———. 1988. "Export-Promoting Trade Strategy: Issues and Evidence." *Research Observer* 3 (January): 27-57.

Brunner, Karl, and Alan Meltzer, eds. *Economic Policy in a World of Change*. Carnegie-Rochester Conference Series on Public Policy. Vol. 17. Amsterdam: North-Holland.

Bruno, Michael. 1985. "The Reforms and Macroeconomic Adjustments: Introduction." *World Development* 13:867-69.

Bruton, Henry J. 1970. "The Import Substitution Strategy of Economic Development." *Pakistan Development Review* 10:123-46.

———. 1989. "Import Substitution as a Development Strategy." In *Handbook of Development Economics*, edited by Hollis Chenery and T. N. Srinivasan. Vol. 2. Amsterdam: Elsevier Science Publishers B. V.

Chenery, Hollis, Jeffery Lewis, Jaime de Melo, and Sherman Robinson. 1986. "Alternative Routes to Development." In *Industrialization and Growth: A Comparative Study*, edited by Hollis Chenery, Sherman Robinson, and Moshe Syrquin. Washington, D.C.: World Bank.

Chenery, Hollis, Montek S. Ahluwalia, C. L. G. Bell, John H. Duloy, and Richard Jolly. 1974. *Redistribution with Growth*. London: Oxford Univ. Press.

Cheng, Tun-Jen. 1986. "Sequencing and Implementing Development Strategies: Korea and Taiwan." San Diego: Univ. of California.

Corbo, Vittorio, and Jaime de Melo. 1985. "Overview and Summary." *World Development* 13:863-66.

Corbo, Vittorio, Jaime de Melo, and James Tybout. 1986. "What Went Wrong with the Recent Reforms in the Southern Cone?" *Economic Development and Cultural Change* 34:607-40.

Corden, W. Max. 1989. "Macroeconomic Adjustment in Developing Countries." *Research Observer* 4 (January): 51-64.

Crockett, Andrew. 1981. "Stabilization Policies in Developing Countries: Some Policy Considerations." International Monetary Fund Staff Papers no. 28 (March): 54-79.

Darrant, A. F. 1986. "Trade and Development: The Asian Experience." *CATO Journal* 6:695-700.

de Melo, Jaime, and Sherman Robinson. 1982. "Trade Adjustment Policies and Income Distribution in Three Archetype Developing Economies." *Journal of Development Economics* 10 (February): 67-92.

Demery, Lionel, and Paul Addison. 1987. "Stabilization and Income Distribution in Developing Countries." *World Development* 15:1483-98.

Dethier, Jean-Jaques. 1986. "Nutritional Implications for the Poor of Macroeconomic Stabilization Policies in Developing Countries." Paper presented at the annual meeting of the United Nations Subcommittee for Nutrition (Administrative Coordination Committee), April 7-11, in Tokyo, Japan.

Devarajan, Shantayanan, and Dani Rodrick. 1989. "Trade Liberalization in Developing Countries: Do Imperfect Competition and Scale Economies Matter?" *American Economic Review* 79 (May): 283-87.

Devarajan, Shantayanan, Christine Jones, and Michael Roemer. 1989. "Markets under Price Controls in Partial and General Equilibrium." *World Development* 17 (December): 1881-93.

Diaz-Alejandro, Carlos F. 1981. "Southern Cone Stabilization Plans." In *Economic Stabilization in Developing Countries*, edited by William R. Cline and Sidney Weintraub. Washington, D.C.: Brookings Institution.

Donges, J. 1976. "A Comparative Study of Industrialization Policies in Fifteen Semi-industrial Countries." *Weltwirtschaftliches Archiv* 112:626-59.

Edwards, Sebastian. 1987. "Sequencing Economic Liberalization in Developing Countries." *Finance and Development* 24 (March): 26-29.

Edwards, Sebastian, and Sweder Van Wijnbergen. 1989. "Disequilibrium and Structural Adjustment." In *Handbook of Development Economics*, edited by Hollis Chenery and T. N. Srinivasan. Vol. 2. Amsterdam: Elsevier Science Publishers B. V.

Eicher, Carl K., and John M. Staatz. 1984. *Agricultural Development in the Third World*. Baltimore, Md.: Johns Hopkins Univ. Press.

Feder, Gershon. 1983. "On Exports and Economic Growth." *Journal of Development Economics* 12 (February-April): 59-74.

_____. 1986. "Growth in Semi-industrial Countries: A Statistical Analysis." In *Industrialization and Growth: A Comparative Study*, edited by Hollis Chenery, Sherman Robinson, and Moshe Syrquin. Washington, D.C.: World Bank.

Fei, John C. H., and Gustav Ranis. 1964. *Development of the Labor Surplus Economy*. Homewood, Ill.: Richard D. Irwin.

Fei, John C. H., Gustav Ranis, and Shirley W. Y. Kuo. 1979. *Growth with Equity: The Taiwan Case*. London: Oxford Univ. Press.

Fischer, Stanley. 1986. "Issues in Medium-Term Macroeconomic Adjustment." *Research Observer* 1 (July): 163-82.

Foxley, Alejandro. 1981. "Stabilization Policies and Their Effects on Employment and Income Distribution: A Latin American Perspective." In *Economic Stabilization in Developing Countries*, edited by William R. Cline and Sidney R. Weintraub. Washington, D.C.: Brookings Institution.

_____. 1983. *Latin American Experiments in Neo-conservative Economics*. Berkeley: Univ. of California Press.

Foxley, Alejandro, and Laurence Whitehead. 1980. "Economic Stabilization in Latin America: Political Dimensions." *World Development* 8:823-32.

Frank, Charles R., Kwang Suk Kim, and Larry E. Westphal. 1975. *Foreign Trade Regimes and Economic Development: South Korea*. New York: Colombia Univ. Press.

Gillis, Malcolm, Dwight H. Perkins, Michael Roemer, and Donald R. Snodgrass. 1983. *Economics of Development*. New York: W. W. Norton.

Grais, W., et al. 1986. "A General Equilibrium Estimation of the Reduction of Tariffs and Quantitative Restrictions in Turkey in 1978." In *General Equilibrium Trade Policy Modelling*, edited by T. N. Srinivasan and J. Whalley. Cambridge: M.I.T. Press.

Grindle, Merilee S. 1989. "The New Political Economy: Positive Economics and Negative Politics." HIID Development Discussion Paper no. 311 (August). Cambridge: Harvard Institute for International Development.

Haggard, Stephan. 1985. "The Politics of Adjustment." *International Organization* 39:505-34.

Haggard, Stephan, and Cung-In Moon. 1983. "The South Korean State in the International Economy: Liberal, Dependent, or Mercantile?" In *The Antinomies of Independence*, edited by John Ruggie. New York: Columbia Univ. Press.

Harberger, Arnold C. 1959. "The Fundamental of Economic Progress in Underdeveloped Countries: Using the Resources at Hand More Effectively." *American Economic Review* 49 (May): 134-46.

———. 1982. "The Chilean Economy in the 1970s: Crisis, Stabilization, Liberalization, Reform." In *Economic Policy in a World of Change*, edited by Karl Brunner and Alan Meltzer. Carnegie-Rochester Conference Series on Public Policy. Vol. 17. Amsterdam: North-Holland.

Harris, Richard. 1984. "Applied General Equilibrium Analysis of Small Open Economies with Scale Economies and Imperfect Competition." *American Economic Review* 74:1016-32.

Helleiner, G. K. 1986. "Outward Orientation, Import Instability, and African Economic Growth: An Empirical Investigation." In *Theory and Reality in Development*, edited by S. Lall and F. Stewart. London: Macmillan.

———. 1987. "Stabilization, Adjustment, and the Poor." *World Development* 15 (December): 1499-1514.

Heller, Peter. 1988. "Fund-Supported Adjustment Programs and the Poor." *Finance and Development* 25 (December).

Hirschman, Albert O. 1958. *The Strategy of Economic Development*. New Haven, Conn.: Yale Univ. Press.

Huang, Yukon, and Peter Nicholas. 1987. "The Social Costs of Adjustment." CPD Discussion Paper no. 1987-6. Washington, D.C.: World Bank.

Hyden, Goran. 1983. *No Shortcuts to Progress: African Development Management in Perspective*. Berkeley: Univ. of California Press.

Johnson, H. G. 1958. "The Gain for Free Trade for Europe: An Estimate." *Manchester School* 26:241-55.

Jones, Hywel. 1976. *An Introduction to Modern Theories of Economic Growth.* New York: McGraw-Hill.

Jones, Leroy P., and Il Sakong. 1980. "Government, Business, and Entrepreneurship in Economic Development: The Korean Case." *Studies in the Modernization of the Republic of Korea: 1945-75.* Cambridge: Council on East Asian Studies, Harvard University.

Jung, W. S. and P. J. Marshall. 1985. "Exports, Growth, and Causality in Developing Countries." *Journal of Development Economics* 18:1-12.

Kahkonen, Juka. 1987. "Liberalization Policies and Welfare in a Financially Repressed Economy." International Monetary Fund Staff Papers no. 34:531-47.

Khan, Mohsin. 1986. "Macroeconomic Adjustment in Developing Countries: A Policy Perspective." World Bank Development Policy Issues Series, Report no. VPERS 6. Washington, D.C.: World Bank.

Khan, Mohsin and M. D. Knight. 1985. "Fund-Supported Adjustment Programs and Economic Growth." IMF Occasional Paper no. 41. Washington, D.C.: International Monetary Fund.

Killick, Tony. 1984. *The Quest for Economic Stabilization: The IMF and the Third World.* London: Heinemann Educational Books.

Kim, Kwang Suk, and Michael Roemer. 1979. *Growth and Structural Transformation.* Studies in the Modernization of the Republic of Korea: 1945-75. Cambridge: Council on East Asian Studies, Harvard University.

Kovoussi, Rostam M. 1985. "International Trade and Economic Development: The Recent Experience of Developing Countries." *Journal of Developing Areas* 19 (April): 379-92.

Krueger, Anne O. 1974. "The Political Economy of the Rent-Seeking Society." *American Economic Review* 64:291-303.

———. 1978. *Foreign Trade Regimes and Economic Development: Liberalization Attempts and Consequences.* Cambridge, Mass: Ballinger.

———. 1984. "Problems of Liberalization." In *World Economic Growth*, edited by Arnold C. Harberger. San Francisco: Institute for Contemporary Studies.

Krueger, Anne O., and B. Tuncer. 1982. "Growth of Productivity in Turkish Manufacturing." *Journal of Development Economics* 11 (December): 307-26.

Kuo, Shirley W. Y. 1983. *The Taiwan Economy in Transition.* Boulder, Colo.: Westview Press.

Lal, Deepak, and Sarath Rajaptirana. 1987. "Foreign Trade Regimes and Economic Growth in Developing Countries." *Research Observer* 2 (July): 189-219.

Lancaster, Carol. 1986. "Political Economists and Policy Reformers in Africa: Dialogue of the Deaf? Tower of Babel? Or Ships Passing in the Night?" World Bank Workshop on the Political Economy of Policy Reform in Africa, December 3-5, in Washington, D.C.

Lange, Oskar. 1938. "On the Economic Theory of Socialism." In *On the Economic Theory of Socialism*, edited by B. Lippincott. Minneapolis: Univ. of Minnesota Press.

Lewis, W. Arthur. 1954. "Economic Development with Unlimited Supplies of Labor." *Manchester School* 22:139-91.

Lipton, Michael. 1977. *Why Poor People Stay Poor: A Study of Urban Bias in World Development*. London: Maurice Temple Smith.

Little, Ian M.D. 1982. *Economic Development, Theory, Policy, and International Relations*. New York: Basic Books.

Little, Ian M.D., Tibor Scitovsky, and Maurice Scott. 1970. *Industry and Trade in Some Developing Countries: A Comparative Study*. London: Oxford Univ. Press.

Lueder-Neurath, Richard. 1986. *Import Controls and Export Oriented Development: A Reassessment of the South Korean Case*. Boulder, Colo.: Westview Press.

Mason, Edward S., Mahn Je Kim, Dwight H. Perkins, Kwang Suk Kim, and David C. Cole. 1980. *The Economic and Social Modernization of the Republic of Korea*. Cambridge: Council on East Asian Studies, Harvard University.

Michaely, Michael. 1977. "Exports and Growth an Empirical Investigation." *Journal of Development Economics* 4:149-53.

———. 1986. "The Timing and Sequencing of a Trade Liberalization Policy." In *Economic Liberalization in Developing Countries*, edited by Armeane M. Choksi and Demetrius Papageorgiou. New York: Basil Blackwell.

Michalopoulos, Constantine. 1987. "World Bank Programs for Adjustment and Growth." World Bank Development Policy Issue Series, Report no. VPERS 11. Washington, D.C.: World Bank.

Michalopoulos, Constantine, and K. Jay. 1973. "Growth of Exports and Income in the Developing World: A Neoclassical View." Discussion Paper no. 28. Washington D.C.: United States Agency for International Development.

Myers, Ramon H. 1986. "The Economic Development of the Republic of China on Taiwan, 1965-81." In *Models of Development*, edited by Lawrence J. Lau. San Francisco: ICS Press.

Nelson, Joan M. 1984. "The Political Economy of Stabilization: Commitment, Capacity, and Public Response." *World Development* 12:983-1006.

———. 1988. *Comparative Perspectives: The Politics of Economic Adjustment in Developing Nations*. Washington, D.C.: Overseas Development Council.

Nishimizu, Meiko, and Sherman Robinson. 1986. "Productivity Growth in Manufacturing." In *Industrialization and Growth: A Comparative Study*, edited by Hollis Chenery, Sherman Robinson, and Moshe Syrquin. Washington, D.C.: World Bank.

Nurkse, Ragnar. 1961. *Equilibrium Growth in the World Economy*. Cambridge: Harvard Univ. Press.

Olson, Mancur. 1982. *The Rise and Decline of Nations*. New Haven, Conn.: Yale Univ. Press.

Pack, Howard. 1989. "Industrialization and Trade." In *Handbook of Development Economics*, edited by Hollis Chenery and T. N. Srinivasan. Vol. 1. Amsterdam: Elsevier Science Publishers B. V.

Pastor, Manuel. 1987. "The Effects of IMF Programs in the Third World: Debate and Evidence from Latin America." *World Development* 15:249-62.

Power, John H. 1966. "Import Substitution as an Industrialization Strategy." *Philippines Economic Journal* 5:167-204.

Prebisch, Raul. 1950. *The Economic Development of Latin America and Its Principal Problems*. Lake Success, N.Y.: United Nations.

_____. 1959. "Commercial Policy in the Underdeveloped Countries." *American Economic Review* 49 (May): 251-73.

Rodrick, Dani. 1988. "Imperfect Competition, Scale Economies, and Trade Policy in Developing Countries." In *Trade Policy Issues and Empirical Analysis*, edited by Robert E. Baldwin. Chicago, Ill.: National Bureau of Economic Research; distributed by Univ. of Chicago Press.

Roemer, Michael. 1982. "Economic Development in Africa: Performance since Independence and a Strategy for the Future." *Daedalus* 111 (Spring): 125-48.

_____. 1986. "Simple Analytics of Segmented Markets: What Case for Liberalization?" *World Development* 14:429-39.

Rosenstein-Rodan, Paul N. 1943. "Problems of Industrialization in Eastern and Southeastern Europe." *Economic Journal* 53:202-11.

Sachs, Jeffrey. 1986. "The Bolivian Hyperinflation and Stabilization." National Bureau of Economic Research Working Paper no. 2073. Chicago, Ill.

Schultz, Theodore W. 1964. *Transforming Traditional Agriculture*. New Haven, Conn.: Yale Univ. Press.

Scitovsky, Tibor. 1958. *Economic Theory and Western European Integration*. London: Allen and Irwin.

_____. 1985. "Economic Development in Taiwan and South Korea: 1965-81." *Food Research Institute Studies* 19:215-64.

Sheahan, John. 1980. "Market-oriented Economic Policies and Political Repression in Latin America." *Economic Development and Cultural Change* 28:267-92.

Singer, Hans W. 1950. "The Distribution of Trade between Investing and Borrowing Countries." *American Economic Review* 40:470-85.

Singer, Hans W., and P. Gray. 1988. "Trade Policy and Growth of Developing Countries: Some New Data." *World Development* 16 (March): 395-404.

Solow, Robert M. 1956. "A Contribution to the Theory of Economic Growth." *Quarterly Journal of Economics* 70:65-94.

Stolper, Wolfgang, and Paul Samuelson. 1941. "Protection and Real Wages." *Review of Economics and Statistics* 9:58-73.

Streeten, Paul. 1987. "Structural Adjustment: A Survey of the Issues and Options." *World Development* 15:1469-82.

Syrquin, Moshe. 1986. "Productivity Growth and Factor Reallocation." In *Industrialization and Growth: A Comparative Study*, edited by Hollis Chenery, Sherman Robinson, and Moshe Syrquin. Washington, D.C.: World Bank.

Taylor, Lance. 1983. *Structuralist Macroeconomics*. New York: Basic Books.

———. 1988. *Varieties of Stabilization Experience: Toward Sensible Macroeconomics in the Third World*. Oxford: Clarendon Press.

Timmer, C. Peter. 1986. *Getting Prices Right: The Scope and Limits of Agricultural Price Policy*. Ithaca, N.Y.: Cornell Univ. Press.

Turnham, David, assisted by Ingelies Jaeger. 1971. *The Employment Problem in Less Developed Countries: A Review of Evidence*. Paris: OECD.

Tyler, William G. 1976. *Manufactured Export Expansion and Industrialization in Brazil*. Tübingen, West Germany: J. C. B. Mohr.

Williamson, John, ed. 1983. *IMF Conditionality*. Washington, D.C.: Institute for International Education.

World Bank. 1981. *Accelerated Development in Sub-Saharan Africa*. Prepared by Elliot Berg for the World Bank. Washington, D.C.: World Bank.

———. 1984. *Toward Sustained Development in Sub-Saharan Africa*. Washington, D.C.: World Bank.

———. 1987. *World Development Report 1987*. New York: Oxford Univ. Press.

———. 1988. "Adjustment Lending: An Evaluation of Ten Years of Experience." Washington, D.C.: Country Economics Department, World Bank.

■ *Chapter 3: Policymakers, Policy Choices, and Policy Outcomes: Political Economy of Reform in Developing Countries*. M. S. Grindle, J. W. Thomas.

Adler, Emanuel. 1987. *The Power of Ideology: The Quest for Technological Autonomy in Argentina and Brazil*. Berkeley: Univ. of California Press.

Allison, Graham. 1971. *Essence of Decision: Explaining the Cuban Missile Crisis*. Boston, Mass.: Little, Brown & Company.

Almond, Gabriel, and James Coleman, eds. 1960. *The Politics of the Developing Areas*. Princeton, N.J.: Princeton Univ. Press.

Alt, James A., and K. Alec Chrystal. 1983. *Political Economics*. Berkeley: Univ. of California Press.

Ames, Barry. 1987. *Political Survival: Politicians and Public Policy in Latin America*. Berkeley: Univ. of California Press.

Amin, Samir. 1976. *Imperialism and Unequal Development*. New York: Monthly Review Press.

Anderson, Kym, and Yujiro Hayami. 1986. *The Political Economy of Agricultural Protection*. Sydney, Australia: Allen and Unwin.

Apter, David E. 1965. *The Politics of Modernization*. Chicago, Ill.: Univ. of Chicago Press.

Balassa, Bela, Gerardo M. Bueno, Pedro-Pablo Kuczynski, and Mario Enrique Simonsen. 1986. *Toward Renewed Economic Growth in Latin America.* Washington D.C.: Institute for International Economics.

Bardhan, Pranab. 1984. *The Political Economy of India.* New York: Basil Blackwell.

Bates, Robert. 1981. *Markets and States in Tropical Africa.* Berkeley: Univ. of California Press.

Bennett, Douglas C., and Kenneth E. Sharpe. 1985. *Transnational Corporations Versus the State: The Political Economy of the Mexican Auto Industry.* Princeton, N.J.: Princeton Univ. Press.

Bennett, James T., and Thomas DiLorenzo. 1984. "Political Entrepreneurship and Reform of the Rent-Seeking Society." In *Neoclassical Political Economy*, edited by David C. Colander. Cambridge, Mass.: Ballinger.

Braybrooke, David, and Charles Lindblom. 1963. *A Strategy of Decision: Policy Evaluation as a Social Process.* New York: Free Press.

Brock, William A., and Stephen M. Magee. 1984. "The Invisible Foot and the Waste of Nations." In *Neoclassical Political Economy*, edited by David C. Colander. Cambridge, Mass.: Ballinger.

Buchanan, James M. 1980. "Rent Seeking and Profit Seeking." In *Toward a Theory of Rent-Seeking Society*, edited by J. M. Buchanan, R. D. Tollison, and G. Tullock. College Station, Tex.: Texas A & M Univ. Press.

Cardoso, Fernando E., and Enzo Faletto. 1979. *Dependency and Development in Latin America.* Berkeley: Univ. of California Press.

Carnoy, Martin. 1984. *The State and Political Theory.* Princeton, N.J.: Princeton Univ. Press.

Cohen, John, Merilee S. Grindle, and S. Tjip Walker. 1985. "Foreign Aid and Conditions Precedent: Political and Bureaucratic Dimensions." *World Development* 13 (December): 1211-30.

Colander, David C. 1984. "Introduction." In *Neoclassical Political Economy*, edited by David C. Colander. Cambridge, Mass.: Ballinger.

Dahl, Robert. 1961. *Who Governs?: Democracy and Power in an American City.* New Haven, Conn.: Yale Univ. Press.

———. 1971. *Polygarchy, Participation, and Opposition.* New Haven, Conn.: Yale Univ. Press.

Dos Santos, Teotonio. 1970. "The Structure of Dependence." *American Economic Review* 60:235-46.

Engels, Friedrich. 1968. "The Origin of the Family, Private Property, and the State." In *Selected Works*, Karl Marx and Friedrich Engels. New York: International Publishers.

Frohock, Fred M. 1979. *Public Policy: Scope and Logic.* Englewood Cliffs, N.J.: Prentice Hall.

Grindle, Merilee S. 1977. *Bureaucrats, Politicians, and Peasants in Mexico: A Case Study in Public Policy*. Berkeley: Univ. of California Press.

————. 1986a. *State and Countryside: Development Policy and Agrarian Politics in Latin America*. Baltimore, Md.: Johns Hopkins Univ. Press.

————. 1986b. "The Question of Political Feasibility: Approaches to the Study of Policy Space." Employment and Enterprise Policy Analysis Discussion Paper no. 3 (March). Cambridge: Harvard Institute for International Development.

Haggard, Stephan. 1985. "The Politics of Adjustment: Lessons from the IMF's Extended Fund Facility." *International Organization* 39 (Summer): 505-34.

Haggard, Stephan, and Chung-In Moon. 1983. "The South Korean State in the International Economy: Liberal, Dependent, or Mercantile?" In *The Antinomies of Interdependence*, edited by John Ruggie. New York: Columbia Univ. Press.

Halperin, Morton. 1971. *Bureaucratic Politics and Foreign Policy*. Washington, D.C.: Brookings Institution.

Hampsen, Fen. 1986. *Forming Economic Policy: The Case of Energy in Canada and Mexico*. New York: St. Martin's Press.

Hirschman, Albert O. 1981. "Policymaking and Policy Analysis in Latin America—A Return Journey." In *Essays in Trespassing: Economics to Politics and Beyond*, edited by Albert O. Hirschman. Cambridge: Cambridge Univ. Press.

Killick, Tony. 1976. "The Possibilities of Development Planning." *Oxford Economic Papers* 28 (July): 161-84.

Kinder, Donald R., and Janet A. Weiss. 1978. "In Lieu of Rationality: Psychological Perspectives on Foreign Policy Decision Making." *Journal of Conflict Resolution* 22 (December): 707-35.

Krasner, Stephen. 1978. *Defending the National Interest: Raw Materials Investments and U.S. Foreign Policy*. Princeton, N.J.: Princeton Univ. Press.

Krueger, Anne O. 1974. "The Political Economy of the Rent-Seeking Society." *American Economic Review* 64:291-303.

Lane, Robert E. 1959. *Political Life*. Glencoe, Ill.: Free Press.

March, James A. 1978. "Bounded Rationality, Ambiguity, and the Engineering of Choice." *Bell Journal of Economics* 9:587-608.

March, James A., and Herbert Simon. 1958. *Organizations*. New York: John Wiley and Sons.

Nordlinger, Eric. 1977. "Taking the State Seriously." In *Understanding Political Development*, edited by Myron Weiner and Samuel Huntington. Boston, Mass.: Little, Brown & Company.

Olson, Mancur Jr. 1965. *The Logic of Collective Action: Public Goods and the Theory of Groups*. New York: Schocken Books.

————. 1982. *The Rise and Decline of Nations*. New Haven, Conn.: Yale Univ. Press.

Orren, Gary R. 1988. "Beyond Self-Interest." In *The Power of Public Ideas.* Cambridge, Mass.: Ballinger.

Poulantzas, Nicos. 1973. *Political Power and Social Classes.* London: New Left Books; Sheed and Ward.

Robinson, James A., and R. Roger Majak. 1967. "The Theory of Decision-Making." In *Contemporary Political Analysis,* edited by James C. Charlesworth. New York: Free Press.

Skocpol, Theda. 1985. "Bringing the State Back In: Strategies of Analysis in Current Research." In *Bringing the State Back In,* edited by Peter B. Evans, Dietrich Rueschemeyer, and Theda Skocpol. Cambridge: Cambridge Univ. Press.

Srinivasan, T. N. 1985. "Neoclassical Political Economy, the State, and Economic Development." *Asian Development Review* 3:38-58.

Stallings, Barbara. 1978. *Class Conflict and Economic Development in Chile, 1958-73.* Stanford, Calif.: Stanford Univ. Press.

Stepan, Alfred. 1981. *The State and Society: Peru in Comparative Perspective.* Princeton, N.J.: Princeton Univ. Press.

Thomas, John. 1975. "The Choice of Technology for Irrigation Tubewells in Eastern Pakistan: An Analysis of a Development Policy Decision." In *The Choice of Technology in Developing Countries: Some Cautionary Tales,* edited by C. Peter Timmer, et al. Harvard Studies in International Affairs no. 32. Cambridge: Center for International Affairs, Harvard University.

Trimberger, Ellen. 1978. *Revolution from Above: Military Bureaucrats and Development in Japan, Turkey, Egypt, and Peru.* New Brunswick, N.J.: Transaction Books.

Truman, David. 1951. *The Governmental Process.* New York: Knopf.

United States Agency for International Development. 1982. *Approaches to the Policy Dialogue.* Washington, D.C.: USAID (December).

Wellisz, Stanislaw, and Ronald Findlay. 1984. "Protection and Rent Seeking in Developing Countries." In *Neoclassical Political Economy,* edited by David C. Colander. Cambridge, Mass.: Ballinger.

World Bank. 1984. *Toward Sustainable Development in Sub-Saharan Africa.* Washington, D.C.: World Bank.

_____. 1986. *Financing Adjustment with Growth in Sub-Saharan Africa, 1986-90.* Washington, D.C.: World Bank.

■ *Chapter 4: Economic Reform in The Gambia: Policies, Politics, Foreign Aid, and Luck.* M. M. McPherson, S. C. Radelet.

Duesenberry J. S. 1986. "Fiscal and Monetary Policy in The Gambia." Banjul: Ministry of Finance and Trade, Government of The Gambia (February).

Galbraith, J. K. 1979. *The Nature of Mass Poverty.* Cambridge: Harvard Univ. Press.

Gray, Clive S. 1983. "Terms of Reference for the Committee on Income Tax Reform." Banjul: Ministry of Finance and Trade, Government of The Gambia (March).

———. 1985. "Ministry of Finance and Trade Tax Reform Committee Final Report on Personal Income Tax." Banjul: Ministry of Finance and Trade, Government of The Gambia (November).

The Government of The Gambia. 1984. *Country Economic Memorandum for the Donor's Conference on The Gambia*. 3 vols. Banjul: Ministry of Economic Planning and Industrial Development.

———. 1985. "The Economic Recovery Programme." Banjul, August.

———. 1981. *Five Year Plan for Economic and Social Development, 1981/82-85/86*. Banjul.

———. 1987. "Memorandum by the Honourable Minister of Finance and Trade on the Economic Recovery Programme." Banjul, November.

———. 1988. "Policy Framework Paper 1988/89 to 1990/91." Banjul, November.

Grindle, Merilee S., and John W. Thomas. 1991. "Policymakers, Policy Choices, and Policy Outcomes: Political Economy of Reform in Developing Countries." In *Reforming Economic Systems in Developing Countries*, edited by Dwight H. Perkins and Michael Roemer. Cambridge: Harvard Institute for International Development.

International Monetary Fund. 1982. "The Gambia—Request for Stand-By Arrangement and Approval of Multiple Current Practice." Washington, D.C.: IMF EBS/12/17 (January 26).

———. 1989. "Structural Adjustment in Fund Supported Programs." Washington, D.C.: IMF (March).

Lewis, John P. 1989. "Government and National Economic Development." *Daedalus* 118 (Winter): 69-88.

McPherson, Malcolm F. 1979. "An Analysis of the Recurrent Cost Problem in The Gambia." Sahel Recurrent Cost Study. Cambridge: Harvard Institute for International Development (September).

———. 1983. "Monetary Policy in The Gambia." Harvard Institute for International Development, Cambridge, December. Mimeo.

Nelson, Joan M. 1984. "The Political Economy of Stabilization: Commitment, Capacity, and Public Response." *World Development* 12:983-1006.

Radelet, Steven C. 1987. "The Potential Inflationary Impact of the 1986/87 Groundnut Crop." *Economic Note* no. 2/87. Banjul: Statistics and Special Studies Unit, Ministry of Finance and Trade, Government of The Gambia.

———. 1988. "Rescheduling of The Gambia's Official Debts." *Economic Note* no. 1/88. Banjul: Statistics and Special Studies Unit, Ministry of Finance and Trade, Government of The Gambia.

Shipton, Parker M. 1987. "Borrowers and Lenders in The Gambia: Preliminary Report on a Study of 'Informal' Financial Systems in Some Sahelian Farming

Communities." Economic and Financial Policy Analyses Project Working Paper (June 21), Banjul.

United States Agency for International Development. 1985. "An Economic and Operations Analysis of The Gambia Produce Marketing Board." Banjul: USAID (May).

World Bank. 1981. *Accelerating Development in Sub-Saharan Africa: An Agenda for ACTION.* Washington, D.C.: World Bank.

———. 1984. *Towards Sustained Development in Sub-Saharan Africa.* Washington, D.C.: World Bank.

———. 1985. "The Gambia: Development Issues and Prospects." Report no. 5693-GM. Washington, D.C.: World Bank.

———. 1986. *Financing Adjustment with Growth in Sub-Saharan Africa, 1986-90.* Washington, D.C.: World Bank.

■ *Chapter 5: The Politics of Health Reform in Chad.* A. M. Foltz, W. J. Foltz.

See notes on page 156 for references.

■ *Chapter 6: Structural Adjustment and Economic Reform in Indonesia: Model-Based Policies vs. Rules of Thumb.* S. Devarajan, J. D. Lewis.

Barichello, Richard R., and Frank R. Flatters. 1991. "Trade Policy Reform in Indonesia." In *Reforming Economic Systems in Development Countries*, edited by Dwight H. Perkins and Michael Roemer. Cambridge: Harvard Institute for International Development.

Behrman, Jere, Jeffrey D. Lewis, and Sherif Lotfi. 1989. "The Impact of Commodity Price Instability: Experiments with a General Equilibrium Model for Indonesia." In *Economics in Theory and Practice: An Eclectic Approach*, edited by L. R. Klein and J. Marquez. Advanced Studies in Theoretical and Applied Econometrics. Vol. 17. Dordrecht, The Netherlands: Kluwer Academic Publishers.

Biro Pusat Statistik. 1986. *Social Accounting Matrix: Indonesia 1980.* Jakarta: Bureau of National Accounts, Central Bureau of Statistics, Government of Indonesia (October).

———. 1988. *National Income of Indonesia: 1983-86 (Main Tables).* Jakarta: Government of Indonesia (April 27).

Corden, W. Max. 1971. *The Theory of Protection.* Oxford: Oxford Univ. Press.

Dahl, Hendrik, Shantayanan Devarajan, and Sweder van Wijnbergen. 1986. "Revenue-Neutral Tariff Reform: Theory and an Application to Cameroon." World Bank, Washington, D.C. Mimeo.

de Melo, Jaime, and Sherman Robinson. 1988. "On the Treatment of Foreign Trade in Computable General Equilibrium Models." *Journal of International Economics* 27 (August): 47-67.

Dervis, Kemal, Jaime de Melo, and Sherman Robinson. 1982. *General Equilibrium Models for Development Policy*. Cambridge: Cambridge Univ. Press.

Devarajan, Shantayanan. 1987. "Models of Adjustment and Growth in Developing Countries." Paper presented at the symposium commemorating the twenty-fifth anniversary of the West African Monetary Union, Dakar, Senegal, October.

Devarajan, Shantayanan, and Chalongphob Sussangkarn. 1987. "Effective Rates of Protection When Domestic and Foreign Goods Are Imperfect Substitutes: The Case of Thailand." Thailand Development Research Institute, Bangkok. Mimeo.

Devarajan, Shantayanan, and Jaime de Melo. 1987. "Adjustment with a Fixed Exchange Rate: Cameroon, Cote d'Ivoire, and Senegal." *World Bank Economic Review* 1:447-87.

Harberger, Arnold C. 1988. "Trade Policy and the Real Exchange Rate." Economic Development Institute, World Bank, Washington, D.C., March. Mimeo.

International Monetary Fund. 1988. "Indonesia: Recent Economic Developments." Report SM/88/89. Washington, D.C.: IMF (April 27).

Lewis, Jeffrey D., and Shujiro Urata. 1984. "Anatomy of a Balance of Payments Crisis: Application of a Computable General Equilibrium Model to Turkey, 1978-80." *Economic Modeling* 1 (July): 281-303.

Mallon, Richard D., and Joseph J. Stern. 1991. "The Political Economy of Trade and Industrial Policy Reform in Bangladesh." In *Reforming Economic Systems in Developing Countries*, edited by Dwight H. Perkins and Michael Roemer. Cambridge: Harvard Institute for International Development.

Newbery, David M. G., and Nicholas Stern. 1987. *The Theory of Taxation for Developing Countries*. Oxford: Oxford Univ. Press.

Robinson, Sherman. 1988. "Multisectoral Models of Developing Countries: A Survey." In *Handbook of Development Economics*, edited by Hollis Chenery and T. N. Srinivasan. Amsterdam: North-Holland.

World Bank. 1988. "Indonesia: Adjustment, Growth, and Sustainable Development." Report no. 7222-IND. Washington, D.C.: World Bank (May 2).

_____. 1989. "Adjustment Lending: An Evaluation of Ten Years Experience." Policy and Research Series no. 1. Washington, D.C.: Country Economics Department, World Bank.

■ *Chapter 7: The Political Economy of Trade and Industrial Policy Reform in Bangladesh.* R. D. Mallon, J. J. Stern.

Ahmad, Junaid Kamal. 1986. "A Note on the Implications of the World Bank Suggested Tariff Reform on the Operation of the Bangladesh Steel and Engineering Corporation." TIP Document, TIP-MU-H.5. Dhaka, Bangladesh.

Bruton, Henry J., and Swadesh R. Bose. 1963. *The Pakistan Export Bonus Scheme*. Research Monograph no. 11. Karachi: Pakistan Institute of Development Economics.

Devarajan, Shantayanan, and Jeffrey D. Lewis. 1991. "Structural Adjustment and Economic Reform in Indonesia: Model-Based Policies vs. Rules of Thumb." In *Reforming Economic Systems in Developing Countries*, edited by Dwight H. Perkins and Michael Roemer. Cambridge: Harvard Institute for International Development.

Faaland, Just, and J. R. Parkinson. 1976. *Bangladesh: The Test Case for Development*. London: C. Hurst and Company.

Floyd, Robert H., Clive S. Gray, and R. P. Short. 1984. *Public Enterprise in Mixed Economies: Some Macroeconomic Aspects*. Washington, D.C.: International Monetary Fund.

Griffin, Keith, and A. R. Khan, eds. 1972. *Growth and Inequity*. New York: Macmillan.

Grindle, Merilee S., and John W. Thomas 1989. "Policymakers, Policy Choices, and Policy Outcomes: Political Economy of Reform in Developing Countries." In *Reforming Economic Systems in Developing Countries*, edited by Dwight H. Perkins and Michael Roemer. Cambridge: Harvard Institute for International Development.

Hirschman, Albert O. 1958. *The Strategy of Economic Development*. New Haven, Conn.: Yale University Press.

Hutcheson, Thomas L., and Joseph J. Stern. 1986. "Methodology of Assistance Policy Analysis." HIID Development Discussion Paper no. 226 (April). Cambridge: Harvard Institute for International Development.

Muhith, A. M. A. 1978. *Bangladesh: Emergence of a Nation*. Dhaka, Bangladesh: Bangladesh Books International.

Rab, Abdur. 1984. "Assistance to Export Development in Bangladesh: An Evaluation." TIP Document, TIP-PPIU-G.3. Dhaka, Bangladesh.

Rhee Yung Whee. 1988. "The Catalyst Model of Development: Lessons from Bangladesh's Success with Garment Exports." Washington, D.C.: World Bank.

Stern, Joseph J. 1971. "Growth, Development, and Regional Equity." In *Development Policy II: The Pakistan Experience*, edited by Walter P. Falcon and Gustav F. Papanek. Cambridge: Harvard Univ. Press.

Stern, Joseph J., and Walter P. Falcon. 1970. *Growth and Development Pakistan: 1955-69*. Occasional Paper no. 23. Cambridge: Center for International Affairs, Harvard University.

TIP Management Unit. 1985. "Overview of Assistance Policies for the Steel and Engineering Industries." TIP Document, TIP-MU-A. Dhaka, Bangladesh.

————. 1986. "Overview of Industrial Investment Incentives." TIP Document, TIP-MU-F. Dhaka, Bangladesh.

World Bank. 1983. *Bangladesh: Recent Economic Trends and Medium Term Development Issues*. World Bank Draft Report, Washington, D.C.

————. 1988. *Bangladesh: Adjustment in the Eighties and Short-term Prospects*. Vol. 2, Table 6.3: 40. Washington, D.C.: World Bank.

■ *Chapter 8: Food Price Stabilization: Rationale, Design, and Implementation.* C. P. Timmer.

Afiff, Saleh, and C. Peter Timmer. 1971. "Rice Policy in Indonesia." *Food Research Institute Studies* 10.

Badan Urusan Logistik (BULOG). 1971. *Seperempat Abad Bergulat dengan Butir-butir Beras (A Quarter Century's Struggle with Rice)*. Jakarta: BULOG.

Bates, Robert H. 1981. *Markets and States in Tropical Africa: The Political Basis of Agricultural Policies*. Berkeley: Univ. of California Press.

Bigman, David, David M. G. Newbery, and David Zilberman. 1988. "New Approaches in Agricultural Policy Research: Discussion." *American Journal of Agricultural Economics* 70 (May): 460-61.

Braverman, Avishay, and Luis Guasch. 1986. "Rural Credit Markets and Institutions in Developing Countries: Lessons for Policy Analysis from Practice and Modern Theory." *World Development* 14:1253-67.

Deaton, Angus S. 1986. "Demand Analysis." In *Handbook of Econometrics*, edited by Zvi Griliches and Michael Intriligator. Amsterdam: North-Holland.

de Janvry, Alain. 1978. "Social Structure and Biased Technical Change in Argentine Agriculture." In *Induced Innovation*, edited by Hans P. Binswanger and Vernon W. Ruttan. Baltimore, Md.: Johns Hopkins Univ. Press.

de Janvry, Alain, and Elisabeth Sadoulet. 1987. "Agricultural Price Policy in General Equilibrium Models: Results and Comparisons." *American Journal of Agricultural Economics* 69 (May): 230-46.

The Falcon Team Report. 1985. "Rice Policy in Indonesia, 1985-90: The Problems of Success." BULOG, Jakarta, September. Typescript.

Harriss, Barbara. 1979. "There is a Method in My Madness, or is It Vice Versa? Measuring Agricultural Market Performance." *Food Research Institute Studies* 17:197-218.

Just, Richard. 1988. "Making Economic Welfare Analysis Useful in the Policy Process: Implications of the Public Choice Literature." *American Journal of Agricultural Economics* 70 (May): 448-53.

Kanbur, S. M. Ravi. 1984. "How to Analyse Commodity Price Stabilization? A Review Article." *Oxford Economic Papers* 36:336-58.

Little, Ian M.D. 1982. *Economic Development: Theory, Policy, and International Relations*. New York: Basic Books.

Lipton, Michael. 1977. *Why Poor People Stay Poor: A Study of Urban Bias in World Development*. London: Temple-Smith.

Mears, Leon A. 1961. *Rice Marketing in the Republic of Indonesia*. Jakarta: P. T. Pembangunan.

————. 1981. *The New Rice Economy of Indonesia*. Yogyakarta: Gadjah Mada Univ. Press.

Mears, Leon A., and Saleh Afiff. 1969. "An Operational Rice Price Policy for Indonesia." *Ekonomi dan Keuangan Indonesia*. Jakarta.

456

Monteverde, Richard T. 1987. *Food Consumption in Indonesia*. Ph.D. diss., Economics Department, Harvard University.

Myers, Robert J. 1988. "The Value of Ideal Contingency Markets in Agriculture." *American Journal of Agricultural Economics* 70 (May): 255-67.

Newbery, David. M. G., and Joseph E. Stiglitz. 1981. *The Theory of Commodity Price Stabilization: A Study in the Economics of Risk*. Oxford: Clarendon Press.

Pinckney, Thomas C. 1988. *Storage, Trade, and Price Policy under Production Instability: Maize in Kenya*. IFPRI Research Report no. 71. Washington, D.C.: International Food Policy Research Institute.

Pradhan, Sanjay. 1988. *Market Failures and Government Failures: Industrial Restructuring and Pricing Policy Analysis for the Indian Fertilizer Industry*. Ph.D. diss., Economics Department, Harvard University, and Harvard Business School.

Rao, Mohan. 1989. "Getting Agricultural Prices Right." *Food Policy* 14 (February): 28-42.

Ravallion, Martin. 1986. "Testing Market Integration." *American Journal of Agricultural Economics* 68 (February): 102-09.

_____. 1987. *Markets and Famines*. New York: Clarendon Press for Oxford Univ. Press.

Runge, Carlisle Ford, and Robert J. Myers. 1985. "Shifting Foundations of Agricultural Policy Analysis: Welfare Economics When Risk Markets are Incomplete." *American Journal of Agricultural Economics* 67 (December): 1010-16.

Salant, Stephen. 1983. "The Vulnerability of Price Stabilization Programs to Speculative Attack." *Journal of Political Economy* 91 (February): 1-38.

Schultz, Theodore W., ed. 1978. *Distortions of Agricultural Incentives*. Bloomington: Indiana Univ. Press.

Schwartz, Robert J. 1987. *Optimal Trends for Forecasting Prices: An Empirical Assessment of Three Grains*. Ph.D. diss., Economics Department, Harvard University, and Harvard Business School.

Srinivasan, T. N. 1985. "Neoclassical Political Economy, the State, and Economic Development." *Asian Development Review* 3:38-58.

Stiglitz, Joseph E. 1987. "Some Theoretical Aspects of Agricultural Policies." *World Bank Research Observer* (January): 43-60.

Streeten, Paul. 1987. *What Price Food? Agricultural Price Policies in Developing Countries*. London: Macmillan.

Taylor, Lance. 1980. *Macro Models for Developing Countries*. New York: McGraw-Hill.

Taylor, Lance, and Persido Arida. 1988. "Long-run Income Distribution and Growth." In *Handbook of Development Economics*, edited by Hollis Chenery and T. N. Srinivasan. Amsterdam: North-Holland.

Timmer, C. Peter. 1974. "A Model of Rice Marketing Margins in Indonesia." *Food Research Institute Studies* 13:145-67.

_____. 1975a. "The Choice of Technique in Indonesia." In *The Choice of Technology in Developing Countries: Some Cautionary Tales*, edited by C. Peter Timmer, et al. Harvard Studies in International Affairs no. 32. Cambridge: Center for International Affairs, Harvard University.

_____. 1975b. "The Political Economy of Rice in Asia: Indonesia." *Food Research Institute Studies* 14:197-231.

_____. 1978. "The Impact of Indonesian Price Policy on the Distribution of Protein-Calorie Intake by Income Class and Commodity." Ford Foundation, Jakarta, February. Typescript.

_____. 1981. "Is There 'Curvature' in the Slutsky Matrix?" *Review of Economics and Statistics* 62 (August): 395-402.

_____. 1984. "Energy and Structural Change in the Asia-Pacific Region: The Agricultural Sector." In *Energy and Structural Change in the Asia-Pacific Region: Papers and Proceedings of the Thirteenth Pacific Trade and Development Conference,* edited by Romeo M. Bautista and Seija Naya. Manila: Philippines Institute for Development Studies and the Asian Development Bank.

_____. 1986a. "Implementing Price Policy: The Impact of Markets and Marketing." In *Getting Prices Right: The Scope and Limits of Agricultural Price Policy*, edited by C. Peter Timmer. Ithaca, N.Y.: Cornell Univ. Press.

_____. 1986b. "Private Decisions and Public Policy: The Price Dilemma in Food Systems of Developing Countries." MSU International Development Paper no. 7. Lansing, Mich.: Department of Agricultural Economics, Michigan State University.

_____. 1986c. "The Role of Price Policy in Increasing Rice Production in Indonesia, 1968-82." In *Research in Domestic and International Agribusiness Management,* edited by Ray A. Goldberg. Vol. 6. Greenwich, Conn.: JAI Press.

_____. 1988a. "Analyzing Rice Market Interventions in Asia: Principles, Issues, Themes, and Lessons." In *Evaluating Rice Market Intervention Policies: Some Asian Examples.* Manila, Philippines: Asian Development Bank.

_____. 1988b. "Crop Diversification in Rice-Based Agricultural Economies: Conceptual and Policy Issues." In *Research in Domestic and International Agribusiness Management,* edited by Ray A. Goldberg. Vol. 3. Greenwich, Conn.: JAI Press.

_____. 1989a. "Food Price Policy: The Rationale for Government Intervention." *Food Policy* 14 (February): 17-27.

_____. 1989b. "Food Price Policy in Indonesia." In *Food Price Policy in Asia,* edited by Terry Sicular. Ithaca, N.Y.: Cornell Univ. Press.

_____. Forthcoming. "Free Markets and Food Security: Indonesian Experience with Rice Price Stabilization." Manuscript.

Timmer, C. Peter, Walter P. Falcon, and Scott R. Pearson. 1983. *Food Policy Analysis.* Baltimore, Md.: Johns Hopkins Univ. Press for the World Bank.

Van de Walle, Dominique. 1989. *The Welfare Analysis of Rice Pricing Policies Using Household Data for Indonesia*. Ph.D. diss., Department of Economics, Australian National University, Canberra, Australia.

Warr, Peter G. 1984. "Exchange Rate Protection in Indonesia." *Bulletin of Indonesian Economic Studies* 20 (August): 53-89.

Waterfield, Charles. 1985. "Disaggregating Food Consumption Parameters." *Food Policy* 10 (November): 337-51.

■ *Chapter 9: Smallholder Rubber Development in Indonesia*. T. P. Tomich.

Allison, Graham T. 1971. *Essence of Decision: Explaining the Cuban Missile Crisis*. Boston, Mass.: Little, Brown & Company.

Baharsyah, S., and Soetatwo S. Hadiwigeno. 1982. "The Development of Commercial Crop Farming." In *Growth and Equity in Indonesian Agricultural Development*, edited by Mubyarto. Jakarta: Yayasan Agro Ekonomika.

Barlow, Colin. 1972. "Smallholder Rubber: A Comment." *Bulletin of Indonesian Economic Studies* 8 (November): 142-45.

_____. 1978. *The Natural Rubber Industry: Its Development, Technology, and Economy in Malaysia*. Kuala Lumpur: Oxford Univ. Press.

_____. 1984. "Institutional and Policy Implications of Economic Change: Malaysian Rubber, 1950-83." Canberra: Australian National University.

_____. 1985. "Indonesian and Malaysian Agricultural Development, 1870-1940." *Bulletin of Indonesian Economic Studies* 21 (April): 81-111.

Barlow, Colin, and J. Drabble. 1983. "Government and the Emerging Rubber Industries in The Netherlands' East Indies and Malaya, 1900-40." Canberra: Australian National University.

Barlow, Colin, and Muharminto. 1982a. "The Rubber Smallholder Economy." *Bulletin of Indonesian Economic Studies* 18 (July): 86-119.

_____. 1982b. "Smallholder Rubber in South Sumatra: Towards Economic Improvement." Balai Penelitian Perkebunan Bogor and Australian National University.

Barlow, Colin, and S. K. Jayasuriya. 1984a. "Bias Towards the Large Farm Subsector in Agricultural Research: The Case of Malaysian Rubber." Canberra: Australian National University.

_____. 1984b. "Problems of Investment for Technological Advance: The Case of Indonesian Rubber Smallholders." *Journal of Agricultural Economics* 35:85-95.

_____. 1987. "Structural Change and Its Impact on Traditional Agricultural Sectors in Rapidly Developing Countries: The Case of Natural Rubber." *Journal of Agricultural Economics* 1:159-74.

Barlow, Colin, C. Shearing, and R. Dereinda. 1991. "Alternative Approaches to Smallholder Rubber Development." HIID Development Discussion Paper no. 368 (January). Cambridge: Harvard Institute for International Development.

Bauer, P. T. 1948. *The Rubber Industry: A Study in Competition and Monopoly*. Cambridge: Harvard Univ. Press.

Bellman, Richard E., and Michael J. Hartley. 1985. "The Tree-Crop Problem." Washington, D.C.: World Bank.

Binswanger, Hans P., and Mark R. Rosenzweig. 1982. *Behavioral and Material Determinants of Production Relations in Agriculture*. World Bank Discussion Paper ARU 5. Washington, D.C.: World Bank.

Biro Pusat Statistik. 1987. *Sensus Pertanian 1983*. Seri F4 and F5.

Business News. 1985. "Expansion of Rubber Planting Not Followed by Proper Increase in Rubber Production." Vol. 4250 (August 30): 3-4.

Chambers, R. 1983. *Rural Development: Putting the Last First*. London: Longman.

Coates, Austin. 1987. *The Commerce in Rubber: The First 250 Years*. New York: Oxford Univ. Press.

Collier, W., and Suhud T. Werdja. 1972a. "Smallholder Rubber: A Reply." *Bulletin of Indonesian Economic Studies* no. 3:146-48.

————. 1972b. "Smallholder Rubber Production and Marketing." *Bulletin of Indonesian Economic Studies* 8:67-92.

de Janvry, Alain. 1978. "Social Structure and Biased Technical Change in Argentine Agriculture." In *Induced Innovation: Technology, Institutions, and Development*, edited by Hans P. Binswanger, Vernon W. Ruttan, et al. Baltimore, Md., and London: Johns Hopkins Univ. Press.

Departemen Pertanian Direktorat Jenderal Perkebunan (DGE). 1984. *Rencana Pembangunan Lima Tahun Keempat: Sub Sektor Perkebunan 1984/85-88/89*. 4 vols. Jakarta.

Dillon, H. S. 1985. "Development of Rubber Smallholders in North Sumatra." ACIAR, *Smallholder Rubber Production and Policies*. Proceedings of an international workshop held, February 18-20, 1985, at the University of Adelaide, South Australia.

Gotsch, C., and W. Dyer. 1982. "Rhetoric and Reason in the Egyptian New Lands Debate." *Food Research Institute Studies* 18:129-47.

Graham, E., and I. Floering. 1984. *The Modern Plantation in the Third World*. New York: St. Martin's Press.

Green, R. H., and S. H. Hymer. 1966. "Cocoa in the Gold Coast: A Study in the Relations between African Farmers and Agricultural Experts." *Journal of Economic History* 26:299-319.

Grindle, Merilee S., ed. 1980. *Politics and Policy Implementation in the Third World*. Princeton, N.J.: Princeton Univ. Press.

Hayami, Yujiro, and Vernon W. Ruttan. 1985. *Agricultural Development: An International Perspective*. Baltimore, Md., and London: Johns Hopkins Univ. Press; first edition, 1971.

The Jakarta Post. 1987. "Debt Laden Farmers Over-Exploit Jambi Rubber Plantations." 17 (November): 3.

Lamb, G., and L. Muller. 1982. *Control, Accountability, and Incentives in a Successful Development Institution: The Kenya Tea Development Authority.* Washington, D.C.: World Bank.

Mansvelt, W. M. F., and P. Creutzberg. 1975. *Changing Economy in Indonesia: Indonesia's Export Crops 1816-1940.* Amsterdam: Royal Tropical Institute.

Messi, Nawir. 1988. "Pola Penyebaran Varietas Baru: Kasus Kopi 'Marzuki' di Sumatera Selatan." Jakarta: Center for Policy and Implementation Studies.

NERACA. 1987. "Business in Agricultural Products is Marked with High Margin." Translated by *Business News* (March 4): 7.

Pelzer, Karl J. 1978a. *Planter and Peasant: Colonial Policy and the Agrarian Struggle in East Sumatra, 1863-1947.* 'S-Gravenhage: Martinus Nijhoff.

————. 1978b. *Planters Against Peasants: The Agrarian Struggle in East Sumatra, 1947-58.* 'S-Gravenhage: Martinus Nijhoff.

Pryor, F. L. 1982. "The Plantation Economy as an Economic System." *Journal of Comparative Economics* 6:288-317.

Purseglove, J. W. 1968. *Tropical Crops: Dicotyledons.* London: Longman.

Richards, Paul. 1985. *Indigenous Agricultural Revolution: Ecology and Food Production in West Africa.* London: Hutchinson.

Sanders, John H., and Vernon W. Ruttan. 1978. "Biased Choice of Technology in Brazilian Agriculture." In *Induced Innovation: Technology, Institutions, and Development*, edited by Hans P. Binswanger, Vernon W. Ruttan, et al. Baltimore, Md., and London: Johns Hopkins Univ. Press.

Schultz, Theodore W. 1983. *Transforming Traditional Agriculture.* Chicago, Ill., and London: Univ. of Chicago Press.

Sepien, Abdullah bin, and Dan M. Etherington. 1980. "Economic Efficiency with Traditional and New Inputs on Smallholder Rubber Holdings in Malaysia." *Oxford Agrarian Studies* 9:63-88.

Simon, H. 1985. *The Sciences of the Artificial.* Cambridge, Mass., and London: M.I.T. Press.

Snodgrass, Donald R., and Richard H. Patten. 1991. "The Reform of Rural Credit in Indonesia: Inducing Bureaucracies to Behave Competitively." In *Reforming Economic Systems in Developing Countries*, edited by Dwight H. Perkins and Michael Roemer. Cambridge: Harvard Institute for International Development.

Springborg, R. 1979. "Patrimonialism and Policy Making in Egypt: Nasser and Sadat and the Tenure Policy for Reclaimed Lands." *Middle Eastern Studies* 15:49-69.

Thee Kian-Wie. 1977. *Plantation Agriculture and Export Growth: An Economic History of East Sumatra, 1863-1942.* Jakarta: National Institute of Economic and Social Research.

Thomas, John W. 1975. "The Choice of Technology for Irrigation Tubewells in East Pakistan: An Analysis of a Development Policy Decision." In *The Choice of Technology in Developing Countries: Some Cautionary Tales*, edited by C. Peter Timmer, et al. Harvard Studies in International Affairs no. 32. Cambridge: Center for International Affairs, Harvard University

Tomich, Thomas P., and C. Gotsch. 1987. "Private Land Reclamation in Egypt: Development Policy and Project Design." *Food Research Institute Studies* 20:107-39.

Voon, Phin Keong. 1976. *Western Rubber Planting Enterprise in South East Asia, 1876-1921*. Kuala Lumpur: Universiti Malaya.

Warta Cafi. 1983. "Elasticity of Demand: Indonesia's Rubber Industry Hopes to Capitalise on Improving World Market Conditions–but First It Must Boost Productivity." NL/21/11:3-6.

_____. 1985. "World Bank Lends U.S. $131 Million to Indonesia for Rubber Production." WT/19/03.

World Bank. 1984. *Nurseries and Field Development*. Staff Appraisal Report, Working Paper C. Jakarta: Projects Department, East Asia and Pacific Regional Office, World Bank.

_____. 1985. *Indonesia—the Major Tree Crops: A Sector Review. A Study of the Prospects for Rubber, Oil, Palm, and Coconuts, during Repelita IV (1984-88)*. World Bank Report no. 5318-IND. Washington, D.C.: World Bank.

_____. 1986. *World Development Report*. "Rubber Replanting Programs in Thailand." Washington, D.C.: World Bank.

_____. 1987. *Upgrading of Substandard Smallholder Plantings on Indonesian Tree Crop Projects: Technical, Economic, and Social Aspects—A Review and Recommendations for Action*. Main Report and Annexes. Washington, D.C.: World Bank.

_____. 1988. *Indonesia: Cost Recovery Issues under Ongoing Estate Crop Projects*. Main Report and Annexes. Washington, D.C.: World Bank.

Yee, Yuen L., and John W. Longworth. 1985. "Biases in Research: The Case of Rubber Growing in Malaysia." *Journal of Agricultural Economics* 36 (January): 15-29.

■ *Chapter 10: Trade Policy Reform in Indonesia.* R. R. Barichello, F. R. Flatters.

Gillis, Malcolm. 1984. "Episodes in Indonesian Economic Growth." In *World Economic Growth*, edited by Arnold C. Harberger. San Francisco: Institute for Contemporary Studies.

Gillis, Malcolm. 1985. "Micro and Macro Economics of Tax Reform: Indonesia." *Journal of Development Economics* 19.

Gillis, Malcolm. 1989. "The Indonesian Tax Reform after Five Years." Mimeo.

■ Chapter 11: Tax Reform: Lessons Learned. G. P. Jenkins.

Asher, Mukul G. 1987. "Tax Reform in Singapore." *Bulletin of the APTIRC* 5:111-21.

Bahl, Roy. 1989. "The Political Economy of the Jamaican Tax Reform." In *Lessons from Fundamental Tax Reform in Developing Countries*, edited by Malcolm Gillis. Durham, N.C.: Duke Univ. Press.

Canada, Department of Finance, Tax Reform. 1987. *Sales Tax Reform.*

Canada, Royal Commission on Taxation. 1966. *Report of the Royal Commission on Taxation.* Ottawa: Queens Printer.

Chimombo, Y. D. 1990. "Recent Tax Reform Initiatives in CATA Countries: An Overview." Paper presented at the symposium on Taxation Relationships and International Investment Flows, June 26-27, at OECD Headquarters, Paris.

Commonwealth Association of Tax Administrators. 1984-88 (September). *CATA Newsletter.* London.

Cunningham, William T. 1988. "Portuguese Tax Reform." *Bulletin for International Fiscal Documentation* 42 (February): 78-80.

Desai, Nishite. 1986. "Tax Reform in India." In *Tax Reform in the Asia Pacific Countries*. Singapore: Asian-Pacific Tax Conference of the Asian-Pacific Tax and Investment Research Center (November).

Ernst & Whinney. 1984-88. *Foreign and U.S. Corporate Income and Withholding Tax Rates.*

Financial Times. 1988. No. 30 (Thursday, November 17): 696.

Galai, Dan, Dov Sapir, Ephraim Sadka, Amnon Raphael, and Eytan Sheshinski. 1988. *Personal Income Tax Reform: Report of the Committee of Experts.* Presented to the Minister of Finance, February, in Jerusalem.

Gillis, Malcolm. 1989. "Comprehensive Tax Reform: The Indonesian Experience, 1981-88." In *Lessons from Fundamental Tax Reform in Developing Countries*, edited by Malcolm Gillis. Durham, N.C.: Duke Univ. Press.

Gillis, Malcolm, Carl Shoup, and Gerardo Sicat. 1987. *Lessons from Value-Added Taxation For Developing Countries.* Washington, D.C.: World Bank.

Harberger, Arnold C. 1989. "Lessons of Tax Reform: From the Experiences of Uruguay, Indonesia, and Chile." In *Lessons from Fundamental Tax Reform in Developing Countries*, edited by Malcolm Gillis. Durham, N.C.: Duke Univ. Press.

International Bureau of Fiscal Documentation. 1984-88 (September). *Tax News Service (TNS).* Amsterdam.

_____. 1984 (January)-1988 (September). *Bulletin for International Fiscal Documentation (BIFD).* Amsterdam.

_____. 1984. *Taxes and Investment in Asia and the Pacific.* New Zealand Country Survey.

_____. 1985. *Guides to European Taxation IV.* Value-Added Taxation in Europe, Portugal Survey.

_____. 1986. *Guides to European Taxation IV.* Value-Added Taxation in Europe, Spain Survey.

The International Tax Journal. 1987. "Tax Reform Around the World." Editor's Note. Vol. 13.

Jenkins, Glenn P. 1988a. "Tax Shelter Finance: How Efficient is It? *Canadian Tax Journal* 38 (March): 270-85.

_____. 1988b. *The Cost Effectiveness of After-Tax Financing.* March. Mimeo.

_____. 1989. "Tax Changes Before Tax Policies: Sri Lanka 1977-88." In *Tax Reform in Developing Countries*, edited by Malcolm Gillis. Durham, N.C.: Duke Univ. Press.

Kaldor, Nicholas. 1955. *The Expenditure Tax.* London: George Allen and Unwin Ltd.

_____. [1957] 1980. *Indian Tax Reform: Report of a Survey.* New Delhi. Reprinted in Nicholas Kaldor, *Reports on Taxation* (New York) 2:31-189.

_____. [1960] 1980. *Suggestions for a Comprehensive Reform of Direct Taxation in Ceylon.* Colombo: Government Press. Reprinted in Nicholas Kaldor, *Reports on Taxation* (New York) 2:189-213.

Mann, Arthur J. 1988. "The Role of Tax Reform in Bolivia under Economic Liberalization and Stabilization." Paper presented at the Harvard Institute for International Development Conference on "Systems Reform in Developing Countries," October, in Marrakech, Morocco.

McLure, Charles E., Jr. 1987. *The Value-Added Tax.* Washington, D.C.: American Enterprise Institute Studies in Fiscal Policy.

_____. 1989. "Analysis and Reform of the Colombian Tax System." In *Lessons from Fundamental Tax Reform in Developing Countries*, edited by Malcolm Gillis. Durham, N.C.: Duke Univ. Press.

McPherson, Malcolm F., and Steven C. Radelet. 1991. "Economic Reform in The Gambia: Policies, Politics, Foreign Aid, and Luck." In *Reforming Economic Systems in Developing Countries*, edited by Dwight H. Perkins and Michael Roemer. Cambridge: Harvard Institute for International Development.

Musgrave, Richard. 1981. *Fiscal Reform in Bolivia: Final Report of the Bolivian Mission on Tax Reform.* Cambridge: International Tax Program, Harvard University.

Musgrave, Richard, and Malcolm Gillis. 1971. *Fiscal Reform for Colombia: Final Report and Staff Papers of the Colombian Commission on Tax Reform.* Cambridge: International Tax Program, Harvard University.

Orrock, D. C. 1985. "Australia: Tax Reform." *Bulletin for International Fiscal Documentation* 39 (November): 490-93.

Owens, J. 1990. "Taxation Relationships and International Investment Flows." From the Committee on Fiscal Affairs, Development Centre, International Monetary Fund. Paper presented at the symposium on Taxation Relationships and International Investment Flows, June 26-27, at OECD Headquarters, Paris.

Prebble, John. 1987. "Tax Reform in New Zealand." *Bulletin of the APTIRC* 5:3-21.

Price Waterhouse. 1984-88. *Individual Taxes (PWIT)*. A Worldwide Summary.

Price Waterhouse. 1984-88. *Corporate Taxes (PWCT)*. A Worldwide Summary.

Samuel, Wendell A. 1988. "Tax Reform in Grenada." *Bulletin for International Fiscal Documentation* 42 (March): 123-30.

Shoup, Carl S. 1989. "The Tax Mission to Japan, 1949-50." In *Lessons from Fundamental Tax Reform in Developing Countries*, edited by Malcolm Gillis. Durham, N.C.: Duke Univ. Press.

Siong, Jap Kim. 1984. "Indonesia: The Three Tax Reform Laws: Overhaul of an Inherited Tax System." *Bulletin for International Fiscal Documentation* 38 (March): 130-34.

————. 1986a. "Taiwan: An Outline of the Proposed Value-Added Tax System." *Bulletin for International Fiscal Documentation* 40 (January): 18-19.

————. 1986b. "Taiwan: The VAT Law in Force." *Bulletin for International Fiscal Documentation* 40 (July): 315-18.

Tait, Alan A. 1988. *Value-Added Tax, International Practice, and Problems*. Washington, D.C.: International Monetary Fund.

Tanzi, Vito. 1988. "Tax Reform in Industrial Countries and the Impact of the U.S. Tax Reform Act 1986." *Bulletin for International Fiscal Documentation* 42 (February).

Taylor, Milton. 1965. *Fiscal Survey of Colombia*. Report by Professor Taylor, mission chief of the Joint Tax Program of the Organization of American States and the Interamerican Development Bank. Baltimore, Md.: Johns Hopkins Univ. Press.

Tax Reform in the Asian-Pacific Countries. 1986. Papers presented at the Asian-Pacific Tax Conference of the Asian-Pacific Tax and Investment Research Center, November, in Singapore.

■ Chapter 12: *Reform of Financial Systems*. D. C. Cole, B. F. Slade.

Central Bank of Turkey. 1988. *Turkey Economic Developments: Policies and Prospects*.

Cho, Y. J., and David C. Cole. 1986. "The Role of the Financial Sector in Korea's Structural Adjustment." HIID Development Discussion Paper no. 230 (May). Cambridge: Harvard Institute for International Development.

Cole, David C., and Y. C. Park. 1983. *Financial Development in Korea, 1945-78*. Cambridge: Harvard Univ. Press.

Edwards, Sebastian. 1984. "The Order of Liberalization of the External Sector in Developing Countries." *Princeton Essays in International Finance* 156 (December).

Fisher, Irving. 1930. *The Theory of Interest*. New York: Macmillan.

_____. 1987. *Structural Reform, Stabilization, and Growth in Turkey*. IMF Occasional Paper no. 52. Washington, D.C.: International Monetary Fund (May).

Gurley, John G., and Edward S. Shaw. 1960. *Money in a Theory of Finance*. Washington, D.C.: Brookings Institution.

Kopits, George. 1987. "Turkey's Adjustment Experience 1980-85." *Finance and Development* (September): 8-11.

McKinnon, Ronald I. 1973. *Money and Capital in Economic Development*. Washington, D.C.: Brookings Institution.

_____. 1982. "The Order of Economic Liberalization: Lesson from Chile and Argentina." Carnegie-Rochester Conference Series on Public Policy 17 (Autumn): 159-86.

Minsky, Hyman P. 1982. "The Financial-Instability Hypothesis: Capitalist Processes and the Behavior of the Economy." In *Financial Crises: Theory, History, and Policy*, edited by Charles Poor Kindleberger and Jean-Piere Laffargue. Cambridge: Cambridge Univ. Press.

Saracoglu, Rusdu. 1987. "Economic Stabilization and Structural Adjustment: The Case of Turkey." February. Manuscript.

Shaw, E. S. 1973. *Financial Deepening in Economic Development*. London: Oxford Univ. Press.

■ *Chapter 13: Reform of Rural Credit in Indonesia: Inducing Bureaucracies to Behave Competitively.* D. R. Snodgrass, R. H. Patten.

Adams, Dale W. 1980. "Recent Performance of Rural Financial Markets." In *Borrowers and Lenders*, edited by John Howell. London: Overseas Development Institute.

_____. 1981. "Rural Financial Markets and Income Distribution in Low Income Countries." *Savings and Development* 5:105-12.

Adams, Dale W., and Douglas H. Graham. 1981. "A Critique of Traditional Agricultural Credit Projects and Policies." *Journal of Development Economics* 8:347-66.

Adams, Dale W., and Jerry R. Ladman. 1979. "Lending to the Poor through Informal Groups: A Promising Financial Market Innovation?" *Savings and Development* 3:85-92.

Adams, Dale W., Douglas H. Graham, and J. D. Von Pischke, eds. 1984. *Undermining Rural Development with Cheap Credit*. Boulder, Colo.: Westview Press.

Anderson, Dennis, and Farida Khambata. 1985. "Financing Small-Scale Industry and Agriculture in Developing Countries: The Merits and Limitations of 'Commercial' Policies." *Economic Development and Cultural Change* 33 (January): 349-71.

Bottomley, Anthony. 1975. "Interest Rate Determination in Underdeveloped Rural Areas." *American Journal of Agricultural Economics* 57 (May): 279-91.

Bottrall, Anthony, and John Howell. 1980. "Small Farmer Credit Delivery and Institutional Choice." In *Borrowers and Lenders*, edited by John Howell. London: Overseas Development Institute.

Cole, David C., and Betty F. Slade. 1991. "Reform of Financial Systems." In *Reforming Economic Systems in Developing Countries*, edited by Dwight H. Perkins and Michael Roemer. Cambridge: Harvard Institute for International Development.

Donald, Gordon. 1976. *Credit for Small Farmers in Developing Countries*. Boulder, Colo.: Westview Press.

Development Program Implementation Studies (DPIS). 1983. *Rice Intensification*. Report no. 2 (December).

Fernando, Nimal S. 1988. "The Interest Rate Structure and Factors Affecting Interest Rate Determination in the Informal Rural Credit Market in Sri Lanka." *Savings and Development* 12:249-67.

Gillis, Malcolm. 1984. "Micro and Macroeconomics of Tax Reform: Indonesia." HIID Development Discussion Paper no. 174 (July). Cambridge: Harvard Institute for International Development.

Goldmark, Susan, and Jay Rosengard. 1983. *Credit to Indonesian Entrepreneurs: An Assessment of the Badan Kredit Kecamatan Program*. Report prepared for the United States Agency for International Development. Washington, D.C.: Development Alternatives, Inc.

Gonzales-Vega, Claudio. 1983. "Arguments for Interest Rate Reform." *Savings and Development* 6:221-29.

——. 1984. "Credit-Rationing Behavior of Agricultural Lenders: The Iron Law of Interest-Rate Restrictions." In *Undermining Rural Development with Cheap Credit*, edited by Dale W. Adams, Douglas H. Graham, and J. D. Von Pischke. Boulder, Colo.: Westview Press.

Graham, Douglas H., and Carlos F. Cuevas. 1984. "Agricultural Lending Costs in Honduras." In *Undermining Rural Development with Cheap Credit*, edited by Dale W. Adams, Douglas H. Graham, and J. D. Von Pischke. Boulder, Colo.: Westview Press.

Graham, Douglas H., and Compton Bourne. 1980. "Agricultural Credit and Rural Progress in Jamaica." In *Borrowers and Lenders*, edited by John Howell. London: Overseas Development Institute.

Grindle, Merilee S., and John W. Thomas. 1991. "Policymakers, Policy Choices, and Policy Outcomes: Political Economy of Reform in Developing Countries." In *Reforming Economic Systems in Developing Countries*, edited by Dwight H. Perkins and Michael Roemer. Cambridge: Harvard Institute for International Development.

Howell, John, ed. 1980. *Borrowers and Lenders*. London: Overseas Development Institute.

Kane, Edward J. 1984. "Political Economy of Subsidizing Agricultural Credit in Developing Countries." In *Undermining Rural Development with Cheap Credit*, edited by Dale W. Adams, Douglas H. Graham, and J. D. Von Pischke. Boulder, Colo.: Westview Press.

Kilby, Peter, Carl E. Liedholm, and Richard L. Meyer. 1984. "Working Capital and Nonfarm Rural Enterprises." In *Undermining Rural Development with Cheap Credit*, edited by Dale W. Adams, Douglas H. Graham, and J. D. Von Pischke. Boulder, Colo.: Westview Press.

Long, Millard. 1968. "Interest Rates and the Structure of Agricultural Credit Markets." *Oxford Economic Papers* 20:275-88.

McKinnon, Ronald I. 1973. *Money and Credit in Economic Development.* Washington, D.C.: Brookings Institution.

Mears, Leon A. 1981. *The New Rice Economy of Indonesia.* Yogyakarta: Gadjah Mada Univ. Press.

Meyer, Richard L., and Geetha Nagarajan. 1988. "Financial Surveys for Small and Micro Enterprises: A Need for Policy Changes and Innovation." *Savings and Development* 12:363-71.

Mosley, Paul, and Rudra Prasad Dahal. 1987. "Credit for the Rural Poor: A Comparison of Policy Experiments in Nepal and Bangladesh." *Manchester Papers on Development* 3 (July): 45-59.

Nasution, Anwar. 1983. *Financial Institutions and Policies in Indonesia.* Singapore: Institute of Southeast Asian Studies.

Patten, Richard H. 1982. "Kredit Pedesaan" (Rural Credit). Memorandum to Drs. Atar Sibero and Drs. Hotman Sitanggung, December 2, 1982.

Patten, Richard H., and Donald R. Snodgrass. 1987. "Monitoring and Evaluating KUPEDES (General Rural Credit) in Indonesia." HIID Development Discussion Paper no. 249 (November). Cambridge: Harvard Institute for International Development.

Robinson, Marguerite S., and Donald R. Snodgrass. 1987. "The Role of Institutional Credit in Indonesia's Rice Intensification Program." HIID Development Discussion Paper no. 248 (November). Cambridge: Harvard Institute for International Development.

Sanderatne, Nimal. 1978. "An Analytical Approach to Small Farmer Loan Defaults." *Savings and Development* 2:290-303.

———. 1986. "The Political Economy of Small Farmer Loan Delinquency." *Savings and Development* 10:343-53.

Schaefer-Kehnert, Walter. 1983. "Success with Group Lending in Malawi." In *Rural Financial Markets in Developing Countries*, edited by J. D. Von Pischke, Dale W. Adams, and Gordon Donald. Baltimore, Md.: Johns Hopkins Univ. Press for the Economic Development Institute, World Bank.

———. 1986. "Agricultural Credit Policy in Developing Countries." *Savings and Development* 10:5-29.

Shaw, Edward S. 1973. *Financial Deepening in Economic Development.* New York: Oxford Univ. Press.

Vogel, Robert C. 1984. "The Effect of Subsidized Agricultural Credit on Income Distribution in Costa Rica." In *Undermining Rural Development with Cheap Credit,* edited by Dale W. Adams, Douglas H. Graham, and J. D. Von Pischke. Boulder, Colo.: Westview Press.

Vogel, Robert C., and Donald W. Larsen. 1980. "Limitations of Agricultural Credit Planning: The Case of Colombia." *Savings and Development* 4:52-61.

Vogel, Robert C., and Paul Burkett. 1986. "Deposit Mobilization in Developing Countries: The Importance of Reciprocity in Lending." *Journal of Developing Areas* 20 (July): 425-38.

Von Pischke, J. D. 1981. "The Political Economy of Specialized Farm Credit Institutions in Low-Income Countries." World Bank Staff Working Paper no. 446 (April). Washington, D.C.: World Bank.

Von Pischke, J. D., Dale W. Adams, and Gordon Donald, eds. 1983. *Rural Financial Markets in Developing Countries.* Baltimore, Md.: Johns Hopkins Univ. Press for the Economic Development Institute, World Bank.

■ Chapter 14: *Strategic Interventions and the Political Economy of Industrial Policy in Developing Countries.* T. S. Biggs, B. D. Levy.

Amsden, Alice. 1982. "The Division of Labor is Limited by the Rate of Growth of the Market: The Taiwan Machine Tool Industry in the 1970s." *World Development* 11.

———. 1983. "The Division of Labor is Limited by the Rate of Growth of the Market: The Taiwan Machine Tool Industry Revisited." Harvard University, Graduate School of Business Administration. Mimeo.

———. 1989. *Asia's Next Giant: South Korea and Late Industrialization.* New York: Oxford Univ. Press.

Amsden, Alice, and K. S. Kim. 1985. "The Acquisition of Technology Capability in South Korea." Report to the Research Department, Productivity Division, World Bank, Washington, D.C.

Anderson, Dennis. 1982. "Small Industry in Developing Countries: A Discussion of Issues." *World Development* 10-11.

Arrow, K. J. 1962. "The Economic Implication of Learning by Doing." *Review of Economic Studies* 29.

Balassa, Bela A., and Associates. 1971. *The Structure of Protection in Developing Countries.* Baltimore, Md.: Johns Hopkins Univ. Press.

———. 1982. *Development Strategies in Semi-industrial Economies.* Baltimore, Md.: Johns Hopkins Univ. Press for the World Bank.

Biggs, Tyler S. Forthcoming. "Structure, Dynamics, and Performance of Taiwan's Industrial Sector." Employment and Enterprise Policy Analysis Project Discussion Paper. Cambridge: Harvard Institute for International Development.

Biggs, Tyler S., and Klaus Lorch. Forthcoming. "The Boundary between Firm and Market in Taiwan." Employment and Enterprise Policy Analysis Project Discussion Paper. Cambridge: Harvard Institute for International Development.

Biggs, Tyler S., Brian D. Levy, Jeremy Oppenheim, and Hubert Schmitz. 1986. "The Small Business Policy Directions Study." Prepared for the Ministry of Trade and Industry, Republic of the Philippines, December.

Borrus, M., L. Tyson, and J. Zysman. 1986. "Creating Advantage: How Government Policies Shape International Trade in the Semi-conductor Industry." In *Strategic Trade Policy and the New Industrial Economics*, edited by Paul R. Krugman. Cambridge: M.I.T. Press.

Brander, J. A., and B. J. Spencer. 1985. "Export Subsidies and International Market Share Rivalry." *Journal of International Economics* 18 (February): 83-100.

Business Korea. 1983 (September). "An Electronics War? Hyundai Plans to Storm the Market."

Business Korea. 1983 (October). "Consumer Electronics: Seeking the Right Switch."

Business Korea. 1984 (April). "Korea Considers Dumping Charge Dubious."

Business Korea. 1984a (September). "High Domestic TV Prices Buoying Export Effort."

Business Korea. 1984b (September). "Samsung-Goldstar Rivalry: The Two Companies that Put Korean Electronics on the Map."

Cheng, H. S. 1986. "Financial Policy and Reform in Taiwan." In *Financial Reform in Pacific Basin Countries*, edited by H. S. Cheng. San Francisco: Federal Reserve Bank of San Francisco.

Cheng, Tun-Jen. 1987. "Sequencing and Implementing Development Strategies: Korea and Taiwan." San Diego: Univ. of California.

Cheung, Steven. 1983. "The Contractual Nature of the Firm." *Journal of Law and Economics* 26 (April): 1-21.

China Credit Information Service (CCIS). 1977. *Top 500.* Taipei, Taiwan.

———. 1986. *Top 500.* Taipei, Taiwan.

Coase, R. H. 1937. "The Nature of the Firm." *Economics* 4.

Cole, David C., and Y. C. Park. 1983. *Financial Development in Korea, 1945-78.* Studies in the Modernization of the Republic of Korea: 1945-75. Cambridge: Council on East Asian Studies, Harvard University.

Corden, W. M. 1974. "Effective Protection Rates in the General Equilibrium Model: A Geometric Note." *Oxford Economic Papers* 21 (July).

Dosi, G. 1988. "Sources, Procedures, and Microeconomic Effects of Innovation," *Journal of Economic Literature* 26 (September).

Economic Planning Board, Republic of Korea. 1976. *Report on Mining and Manufacturing Survey.*

Economic Planning Board, Republic of Korea. 1986. *Major Statistics of Korean Economy*.

Frank, C. R., K. S. Kim, and L. E. Westphal. 1975. *Foreign Trade Regimes and Economic Development: South Korea*. New York: National Bureau of Economic Research.

Galenson, W., ed. 1979. *Economic Growth and Structural Change in Taiwan: The Postwar Experience of the Republic of China*. Ithaca, N.Y.: Cornell Univ. Press.

Gold, Thomas. 1981. *Dependent Development in Taiwan*. Ph.D. diss., Sociology Department, Harvard University.

Goldstar Company Ltd. 1985. Harvard Business School Case no. 9-385-264.

Hirschman, Albert O. 1958. *The Strategy of Economic Development*. New Haven, Conn.: Yale Univ. Press.

_____. 1963. *Journeys toward Progress: Studies of Economic Policy Making in Latin America*. New York: Twentieth-Century Fund. Reprint, New York: Greenwood Press, 1968.

_____. 1970. *Exit, Voice, and Loyalty*. Cambridge: Harvard Univ. Press

Hong, W. T. 1979. *Trade, Distortions, and Employment Growth in Korea*. Seoul: Korea Development Institute.

Jones, Leroy P. 1980. "Jae-Bul and the Concentration of Economic Power in Korean Development: Issues, Evidence, and Alternatives." Boston University. Mimeo.

Jones, Leroy P., and Il Sakong. 1980. *Government, Business, and Entrepreneurship in Economic Development: The Korean Case*. Studies in the Modernization of the Republic of Korea: 1945-75. Cambridge: Council on East Asian Studies, Harvard University.

Kim, K. S. 1985. *The Timing and Sequencing of a Trade Liberalization Policy: The Korean Case*. Washington, D.C.: World Bank.

Kim, K. S., and Michael Roemer. 1979. *Growth and Structural Transformation*. Studies in the Modernization of the Republic of Korea: 1945-75. Cambridge: Council on East Asian Studies, Harvard University.

Kreuger, A. 1980. "Export-Led Industrial Growth Reconsidered." Paper prepared for the Eleventh PAFTA Conference, Seoul, Korea.

Krugman, Paul R. 1986. "New Trade Theory and the Less-Developed Countries." Economics Department, M.I.T. Mimeo.

Kuznets, P. W. 1988. "An East Asian Model of Economic Development: Japan, Taiwan, and South Korea" *Economic Development and Cultural Change*.

Lee, J. M. 1983. "Problems of Late Industrialization: An Interpretation from Industrial Organization's Perspective." Ph.D. diss., Economics Department, Harvard University.

Levy, Brian D. 1988. "Korea and Taiwan as International Competitors: The Challenges Ahead." *Columbia Journal of World Business* (Summer).

471

_____. 1989. "Export Traders, Market Development, and Industrial Expansion." *Research Memorandum Series* no. 114. Williamson, Mass.: Williams College (March).

_____. 1991. "Transactions Costs, the Size of Firms, and Industrial Policy." *Journal of Development Economics* (Amsterdam: North-Holland) 34:151-78.

Levy, Brian D., and Wen-Jeng Kuo. 1991. "The Strategic Orientation of Firms and the Performance of Korea and Taiwan in Frontier Industries: Lessons from Comparative Case Studies of Keyboard and Personal Computer Assembly." *World Development* 19.

Little, Ian M.D. 1979. "The Experience and Cause of Rapid Labour-Intensive Development in Korea, Taiwan, Hong Kong, and Singapore, and the Possibilities of Emulation." *ARATEP, ILO-ARTEP APII-1*. Bangkok, Thailand (February).

Lorch, Klaus, and Tyler S. Biggs. 1988. "Traders and Transactors: The Role of Trading Companies in Taiwan's Market-Based Economy." Employment and Enterprise Policy Analysis Project Discussion Paper no. 19. Cambridge: Harvard Institute for International Development.

Myers, Ramon, and Mark R. Peattie, eds. 1984. *The Japanese Colonial Empire, 1895-45*. Princeton N.J.: Princeton Univ. Press.

Myint, H. 1982. "Comparative Analysis of Taiwan's Economic Development with Other Countries." In *Experience and Lessons of Economic Development in Taiwan*, edited by K. T. Li and T. S. Yu. Taipei, Taiwan: Academia Sinica.

Nelson, Richard R., and Sidney G. Winter. 1982. *An Evolutionary Theory of Economic Change*. New Haven, Conn.: Yale Univ. Press.

Pack, H., and L. Westphal. 1986. "Industrial Strategy and Technological Change: Theory vs. Reality." *Journal of Development Economics* 22 (June): 87-128.

Park, Y. C. 1985. "Economic Stabilization and Liberalization in Korea, 1980-84." Korea University. Mimeo.

Porter, M. 1980. *Competitive Strategy: Techniques for Analyzing Industries and Competitors*. New York: Free Press.

Republic of China, Ministry of Economic Affairs, Department of Statistics. 1986. *Report on Industrial and Commercial Survey*.

Rhee, Y. W. 1984. "Export Policy and Administration in Developing Economies." World Bank Staff Working Paper no. 725. Washington, D.C.: World Bank.

_____. 1988. "The Catalyst Model of Economic Development: The Boom in Nontraditional Exports in Bangladesh." World Bank. Mimeo.

_____. 1989. "The Role of Catalytic Agents in Entering International Markets." Industry and Energy Department Working Paper, Industry Series Paper no. 5. Washington, D.C.: World Bank.

Rosenberg, N., and L. E. Birdzell. 1986. *How the West Grew Rich: The Economic Transformation of the Industrial World*. New York: Basic Books.

Schive, C. 1978. "Direct Foreign Investment, Technology Transfer, and Linkage Effect: A Case Study of Taiwan." Ph.D. diss., Case Western Reserve University, Cleveland, Ohio.

Scitovsky, T. 1954. "Two Concepts of External Economies." In *The Economics of Underdevelopment*, edited by A. N. Agarwala and S. P. Singh. New York: Oxford Univ. Press (1986).

Scott, Maurice. 1979. "Foreign Trade." In *Economic Growth and Structural Trade in Taiwan: The Postwar Experience of the Republic of China*, edited by W. Galenson. Ithaca, N.Y.: Cornell Univ. Press.

Tendler, Judith. 1982. "Urban Project through Rural Eyes." World Bank Staff Working Papers. Washington, D.C.: World Bank.

Wade, R. 1988a. "Export Promotion and Import Controls in a Successful East Asian Trading Economy." Trade Policy Division, Country Economics Department, World Bank, Washington, D.C.

———. 1988b. "State Intervention in 'Outward-Looking' Development: Neoclassical Theory and Taiwanese Practice." In *Development in States in East Asia*, edited by Gordon White. New York: Macmillan.

Westphal, L. 1982. "Fostering Technological Mastery by Means of Selective Infant Industry Protection." In *Trade Stability, Technology, and Equity in Latin America*, edited by Moshe Syrquin and Simon Teitel. New York: Academic Press.

Westphal, L., and K. S. Kim. 1977. "Industrial Policy and Development in Korea." World Bank Staff Working Paper no. 263. Washington, D.C.: World Bank.

Williamson, O. E. 1985. *The Economic Institutions of Capitalism*. New York: The Free Press.

World Bank. 1987. "Korea: Managing the Industrial Transition." World Bank Country Study. Vol. 1. Washington, D.C.: World Bank.

Yamamura, Kozo. 1986. "Caveat Emptor: The Industrial Policy of Japan." In *Strategic Trade Policy and the New Industrial Economics*, edited by Paul R. Krugman. Cambridge: M.I.T. Press.

■ *Chapter 15: Antitrust as a Component of Policy Reform: What Relevance for Economic Development?* C. S. Gray.

American Economic Association. 1987. "Symposium on Mergers and Antitrust." *Journal of Economic Perspectives* 1 (Fall): 3-54.

Amjad, R. 1977. "Profitability and Industrial Concentration in Pakistan." *Journal of Development Studies* 1 (April): 181-98.

Chaudhuri, Asim. 1975. *Private Economic Power in India: A Study in Genesis and Concentration*. New Delhi: People's Publishing House.

Dugar, S. M. 1984. *MRTP Law and Practice*. New Delhi: Taxmann Publications.

Fisher, F. M. 1987. "Horizontal Mergers: Triage and Treatment." *Journal of Economic Perspectives* 1 (Fall): 23-40.

————. 1987. "On the Misuse of the Profits-Sales Ratio to Infer Monopoly Power." *Rand Journal of Economics* 18:384-96.

Fisher, F. M., and J. J. McGowan. 1983. "On the Misuse of Accounting Rates of Return to Infer Monopoly Profits." *American Economic Review* 73:82-97.

Forsyth, D. 1985. "Government Policy, Market Structure, and Choice of Technology in Egypt." In *Technology, Institutions, and Government Policies*, edited by J. James and S. Watanabe. New York: St. Martin's Press.

Gan, W. B., and S. Y. Tham. 1977. "Market Structure and Price-Cost Margins in Malaysian Manufacturing Industries." *Developing Economies*, pp. 280-92.

Ghosh, A. 1975. "Concentration and Growth of Indian Industries, 1948-68." *Journal of Industrial Economics* 23:203-22.

Government of Chile, Fiscalía Nacional Económica. 1988. *Memoria 1987.* Annual report. Santiago.

Government of France, Ministry of the Economy, Finance, and Privatization. 1986. *Liberté des Prix et Nouveau Droit de la Concurrence.* Supplement to *Les Notes Bleues* of December 15-21. Paris.

————, Directorate General of Competition, Consumption, and Suppression of Fraud. 1988. *Revue de la Concurrence et de la Consommation: Prix et Marchés* (Paris) 43 (May-June).

Government of India, Ministry of Industry, Department of Company Affairs. 1987. *The Fifteenth Annual Report Pertaining to the Execution of the Provisions of the Monopolies and Restrictive Trade Practices Act, 1969.* New Delhi.

Government of Kenya. 1983. *The Price Control (General) Order.* Legal Notice no. 249 (October 26).

————. 1987. *Restrictive Trade Practices, Monopolies, and Price Control Act.* Nairobi: Government Printer.

Government of Korea, Economic Planning Board, Office of Fair Trade. 1987 (November). *Monopoly Regulation and Fair Trade in Korea.*

Government of Pakistan, Monopoly Control Authority. 1987 (July). Annual report for the year ending December 31, 1986.

Government of Sri Lanka, Parliament. 1987. Fair Trading Commission Act no. 1.

Gray, Clive. S. 1977. "Costs, Prices, and Market Structure in Kenya." Consultant's report. Ministry of Economic Finance and Planning, Government of Kenya, Nairobi, December.

Gupta, V. 1968. "Cost Functions, Concentration, and Barriers to Entry in Twenty-nine Manufacturing Industries in India." *Journal of Industrial Economics* 17/18:57-72.

Harberger, Arnold C. 1954. "Monopoly and Resource Allocation." *American Economic Review* 44 (May): 77-87.

Horton, B. 1982. "The Structure of Incentives in the Industrial Sector." Moroccan Ministry of Commerce, Industry, and Tourism.

House, W. J. 1973. "Market Structure and Industry Performance: The Case of Kenya." *Oxford Economic Papers* 25 (November): 405-19.

International Herald Tribune 1988. Paris, May 9.

Jones, Leroy P., and Il Sakong. 1980. *Government, Business, and Entrepreneurship in Economic Development: The Korean Case.* Studies in the Modernization of the Republic of Korea: 1945-75. Cambridge: Council on East Asian Studies, Harvard University.

Meller, P. 1978. "The Pattern of Industrial Concentration in Latin America." *Journal of Industrial Economics* 27:41-47.

Morocco, Amicale des Ingénieurs des Ponts et Chaussées (AIPC) and Confédération Générale Economique Marocaine (CGEM). 1988. Actes du Colloque - Secteur Public Secteur Privé: Vers un Meilleur Équilibre. Casablanca, March 31-April 2.

Ng'eno, J. 1986. "Speech on Official Opening of African Regional Seminar on Restrictive Business Practices." UNCTAD, Nairobi, May 12.

OECD. 1987. *Politique de la Concurrence dans les Pays de l'OCDE—1985-86.* Paris: OECD.

Phelps, M. G., and B. Wasow. 1972. "Measuring Protection and Its Effects in Kenya." IDS Working Paper no. 37. Nairobi: Institute for Development Studies, University of Nairobi.

Reynolds, Lloyd George. 1979. *Microeconomics: Analysis and Policy.* 3rd edition. Homewood, Ill.: R. D. Irwin.

Rovira, R. L. 1986. "Observaciones al Proyecto de Ley de Defensa de la Competencia." *La Ley* (Buenos Aires) (May 9).

_____. 1987. "Funcionamiento y Experiencia en la Aplicación de Normas Sobre Prácticas Comerciales Restrictivas en la República Argentina–Año 1987." Summary of statement to sixth session of Intergovernmental Group of Experts on Restrictive Business Practices, November, at UNCTAD, Geneva.

Sagou, M. 1984. "La Structure de l'Industrie Marocaine." *Révue Marocaine de Droit et d'Economie du Développement* 8.

Scherer, F. M. 1980. *Industrial Market Structure and Economic Performance.* 2nd edition. Chicago, Ill.: Rand McNally.

Schmalensee, R. 1987. "Horizontal Merger Policy: Problems and Changes." *Journal of Economic Perspectives* 1 (Fall): 41-54.

Short, R. P. 1984. "The Role of Public Enterprises: An International Statistical Comparison." *Public Enterprise in Mixed Economies: Some Macroeconomic Aspects,* edited by Robert H. Floyd, Clive S. Gray, and R. P. Short. Washington, D.C.: International Monetary Fund.

Smith, Adam. 1776. *The Wealth of Nations.* New York: The Modern Library (1957).

UNCTAD. 1984. "Consideration of the Revised Draft of a Model Law or Laws on Restrictive Business Practices." TD/B/RBP/15/Rev.1, September.

————. 1985. "Annual Report on Legislation and Other Developments in Developed and Developing Countries in the Control of Restrictive Business Practices." Latest version, covering the two years 1983-84. United Nations publication no. TD/B/RBP/29.

————, Restrictive Business Practices Unit, Manufactures Division. 1986. "Reference Notes" for African Regional Seminar on RBP..Nairobi, May 12-16. Processed.

————. 1986 and 1987. Components of a "Handbook of Restrictive Business Practices Legislation." TD/B/RBP 13 and 42, July 1986 and August 1987, respectively.

————. 1987. "Information Note on Restrictive Business Practices." Bulletin No. 13. TD/B/RBP/INF.19. November 1987.

United Nations. 1979. "First Draft of a Model Law or Laws on Restrictive Business Practices to Assisting Developing Countries in Devising Appropriate Legislation." TD/B/C.2/AC.6/16/Rev.1.

————. 1981. "The Set of Multilaterally Agreed Equitable Principles and Rules for the Control of Restrictive Business Practices." TD/RBP/CONF/10/Rev.1.

White, E. 1974. "Control of Restrictive Business Practices in Latin America." UNCTAD/ST/MD/4. Processed.

————. 1978. "Recent Developments in the Control of Restrictive Business Practices in Latin America." UNCTAD/TD/B/C.2/AC.6/17. Processed.

White, Lawrence J. 1974. *Industrial Concentration and Economic Power in Pakistan*. Princeton, N.J.: Princeton Univ. Press.

————. 1987. "Antitrust and Merger Policy: Review and Critique." *Journal of Economic Perspectives* 1 (Fall): 13-22.

World Bank. 1988. *World Development Report—1988*. Washington, D.C.: World Bank. (Cited in text as WDR—1988).

————. 1984. *Morocco—Industrial Incentives and Export Promotion*. Washington, D.C.: World Bank.

Index

Abortion, 143
Adams, Dale W., 342, 362
Addison, Paul, 75, 76
Adelman, Irma, 76
Ad Valorem duties, 275
Afiff, Saleh, 235, 239
Africa, 12, 44, 70, 79, 220; banking system in, 17; clientelism in, 78; development in, 82; factionalism in, 139; productivity growth in, 30; profit maximization theory and, 38; raising food prices and, 77; sequencing reforms and, 72; trade policies and, 64
Africa, sub-Saharan, 15
African Development Bank, 126
Agarwala, Ramgopal, 20; price distortion study by, 20-21, 25
Aggregate production function, 28
Agricultural sector, 12, 60, 221; in Bangladesh, 192; farmer-investor analysis and, 224; food prices and, 77, 221-22; price distortions and, 35; seasonal loans and, 359; sequencing reforms and, 73
Ahluwalia, Montek, 61
Alliance for Progress, 93
Allison, Graham, 87
Alt, James, 86
Ames, Barry, 86
Amjad, R., 411
Amsden, Alice, 70, 371
Anderson, Dennis, 362
Anderson, Kym, 86
Antitrust legislation, 5, 404-39
Aquino, Corazon C., 98
Argentina, 71, 94, 97, 104; competition in, 411, 417-418; financial reform and, 321; planning reform in, 98-99
Arifin, Bustanil, 236
Asia, 15, 79, 221, 222; growth rates in, 82; profit maximization theory and, 38; raising food prices and, 77; rice price stabilization in, 225-26, 228; state intervention in, 17

Automobile firms, Korea's, 375
Average effective of protection, 20
Awami League Government, 192; exchange controls and, 202

Badan Kredit Kecamatan (Subdistrict Loan Board), 343
Badan Urasan Logistik (BULOG), 104-05, 357; fertilizer subsidy and, 242-43; institution building (1968-88) and, 235-39; marketing margins and, 239-42; price-stabilization policy and, 236; role in rice markets, 234-35; technical debates and, 239
Baharsyah, S, 254
Balanced growth, 59-60
Balance-of-payments, 117; Bangladesh's crisis and, 214; devaluation and, 35; developing countries and, 35, 160; disequilibrium of, 6; financial reform and, 315, 321, 336; governmental intervention and, 41; IMF stabilization package and, 66; Indonesia and, 323; market efficiency and, 35
Balassa, Bela, 61, 63, 64, 68, 69, 70, 378
Balassa-Corden (BC) formula, 172-74
Balladur, Edouard, 416, 435
BAMA (Foundation for Food), 235
Bangladesh, 4, 5, 8, 10, 80, 229, 395; banking system of, 17; centralized command economy in, 190, 210; context for reform (1969-80), 191-193; governmental regulation in, 18, 190; industrial protection reform, 206-10, 366; inventory calculations and, 27; manufacturing sector in, 192, 202; political economy reform in, 193-98; price reform in, 202-06; public sector in, 192, 197, 199; reform of controls in, 198-202. *See also* TIP program
Bangladesh Shipla Bank (BSB), 198, 201
Bangladesh Textile Mill Corporation (BTMC), 210, 212, 215

477

CGE models. *See* Computable general equilibrium (CGE) models

Chad, 9; context for reform in, 138-41; health care sector reform in, 141-46

Chadian administrative system, 144-45

Chamberlinian frameworks, 406, 411, 430

Chambers, R., 259, 261

Chaudhuri, Asim, 411

Chenery, Hollis, 64, 68

Cheng, Tun-Jen, 70

Chile, 61, 72, 76, 210; devaluation and, 73; evolution of competition in, 418; financial reform and, 321; RBP control and, 411, 417; sequencing programs in, 71-72; stabilization and, 76; tax reform in, 295; trade policy and, 64

China, 7, 220; bankruptcy laws in, 38; capital formation in, 30; discretionary bureaucratic commands and, 44; financial system of, 17; government regulation in, 18; growth in, 30, 70; inflation and, 41; market system in, 12, 33, 35; public enterprise and, 15; soft budget constraints and, 38; training health care workers in, 144

Chinese Communist Party, 44

Chittagong Steel Mill (CSM), 197, 207-08, 212

Cho, Y. J., 336

Chrystal, K. Alec, 86

Chun Doo-Hwan, 7

Clientelism, 78-79; factionalism in Chad and, 139, 151

Cobb-Douglas functions, 179

Colander, David C., 86

Cole, David C., 5, 10, 334, 336, 360

Collateral, loan, 352, 359

Colombia, 2, 61, 104; high marginal tax rates in, 298, 301; noncrisis reform in, 97; policy elites in, 88, 105; tax reform in, 294-95, 297, 298

Comisión Nacional de Defensa de la Competencia (CNDC), Argentina's, 417-18

Commission on the Health Information System (CSIS), 148

Competition, 3, 57; bureaucratic commands and, 37; devaluation and, 40; effective markets and, 5; industrialized economies and, 415-16; investment controls and, 18; perfect competition, 410; structural adjustment and, 34, 39, 62, 68; trade barriers and, 430

"Competition policy," 406

Computable general equilibrium (CGE) models, 162-64; Balassa-Corden ERPs

and, 172-74; income distribution and, 75-76; price stability and, 224-25

Computerized tax systems, 303-05

Concentration, market, 412-13, 415; Kenya and, 411-12; policy for, 436

Confederal Parliament, 128

Conglomerates, 12

Congo-Brazzaville, 139

Constant elasticity of transition (CET), 163

Constant elasticity substitution (CES), 163, 170

Cooperatives, 343-344; rural credit reform and, 348

Cooperative saving and loan societies (KOSIPA), 343

Corbo, Vittorio, 66, 71, 72, 73

Corden, W. Max, 67, 73

Corporate Law Authority, Pakistan's, 423

Costa Rica, 89, 95; elite consensus and, 103

Cotton textile industry, Bangladesh's, 209-10, 215

Court of the Defence of Competition, Spain's, 416

Credit rationing, 39, 59; Bangladesh and, 197

Crisis-ridden reforms, 94-95, 160; Bangladesh and, 194; decision makers status and, 95-96; Gambia's reform program and, 128-29; hypothetical reasons behind, 97-98; innovation versus incrementalism and, 96; international donor pressure and, 214; political stability and, 97; stakes involved and, 95; timing and, 96-97

Crockett, Andrew, 76

Cuba, 44

Cuevas, Carlos E., 343

Currency depreciation, 72

Current account: constant real exchange rate and, 165-66

Daewoo Group: Desh joint venture and, 395-96; diesel engine production and, 375

Dahal, Rudra Prasad, 362

Dahl, Hendrik, 171

Darrant, A. F., 63

Debt rescheduling, 66

Decision making, policy: decentralization of, 40, 82

Deficits, budget, 72, 321; central banks and, 318; foreign debt and, 319; Gambian disequilibria and, 117, 128; IMF stabilization package and, 66, 69; Turkey and, 332, 333

de Janvry, Alain, 259

Mason, Edward S., 78
Mass Guidance Program. *See Bimbingan Massal* (BIMAS)
May 6th reform package, 280-84, 286, 289, 290
Mears, Leon A., 235, 239, 240, 344
Médecins Chefs de Préfecture (MCP), 147, 150, 153
Médecins sans Frontières (MSF), 140; rebuilding Chadian health facilities and, 142
Meller, P., 411
Messi, Nawir, 259
Mexico, 24, 61, 432; stabilization sequencing in, 71
Meyer, Richard L., 342
Michaely, Michael, 63, 75
Michalopoulos, Constantine, 61, 63, 68, 72, 75
Military procurement, 38, 42
Milling conversion ratio, rice, 240
Ministry for Economic Coordination (EKUIN), 238
Ministry of Commerce and Industry, Korea's, 372
Ministry of Economic Planning (BAPPENAS), 240, 273
Ministry of Public Health, Chadian, 142; administrative system and, 144-45; health professionals and, 141; organizational reform and, 146-47
Minsky, Hyman P., 314
Money supply, 66, 160; Indonesia's financial reform and, 323, 325; nominal interest rates and, 316
Monopoly Control Authority (MCA), Pakistan's, 423
Monopolies, 57, 58, 223, 280, 410; competition and, 62; Kenya and, 411; "natural monopolies," 430; RBP control and, 406
Monopolies and Restrictive Trade Practice Ordinance, Pakistan's, 423
Monopolies and Restrictive Trade Practices Act (MRTP), India's, 418, 422
Monopolistic trade practices (MTP), 406
Moon, Cung-In, 70
Morocco, 2; concentration indices in, 430; manufacturing sector concentration and, 413; RBP control and, 411, 429; World Bank intervention and, 428
Mosley, Paul, 362
Muharminto, 252, 260
Muhith, 194
Muller, L., 255

Multinationals: Bangladesh's garment exports and, 395-396; India's RBP control and, 435; "soft states" industrialization and, 393-94; Taiwan's upstream industrialization and, 383; technology and, 385
Musgrave, Richard, 294; Bolivian tax reform and, 295; Colombian tax reform and, 295
Myers, Ramon H., 61
Nagarajan, Geetha, 342
Nasution, Anwer, 343
National Competition Council (NCC), Portugal's, 424
National Socio-Economic Survey (SUSENAS), 243
Nelson, Joan M., 73-74, 75
Neoclassical economics, 1, 71; free markets and, 67; intervention and, 58; Korean expansion and, 371-72; structuralists and, 12; structural problem solutions and, 61; system reform and, 57-59; trade-growth relationship and, 64; welfare-maximizing prices and, 3-4
Netherlands, 125; fuel grants and, 127; Gambian reform package and, 126; rice marketing and, 235
Newbery, David M. G., 170, 225
New Industrial Policy (NIP), 199; regional development incentives and, 200
New Order, Indonesia's, 272, 274
"New view" of rural credit, 342; KUPEDES and, 362
New York Times, 363
New Zealand: tax reform in, 295, 296; top marginal tax rates in, 298, 301; VAT implementation in, 303
Nicholas, Peter, 75
Nigeria, 139
Niushimizu, Meiko, 64
Nonbank financial institutions (NBFIs), 319, 320; Korean financial markets and, 336; rural Indonesians and, 343
Nontariff barriers (NTBs), 281, 286-87, 288
Nontraded commodities, 172, 436; RBP control and, 430-31
North Korea: financial system of, 17; government regulation in, 18; public enterprise in, 15
Nucleus Estate-Smallholder (NES), 250, 255, 258; international development banks and, 251; project-based approach and, 254; retrenchment and, 265
Nurkse, Ragnar, 60

Office of Fair Trade, Korea's, 424
Oil price, 56, 61, 117, 160, 323, 324, 335
Oligopolies, 57; competition and, 62; horizontal collusion in, 415; Kenya and, 411; "natural oligopolies", 430, 432, 436
Olson, Mancur, 78, 86, 101
OPEC, 272, 282
Optimal tariffs, 170-71, 176
Organization for Economic Cooperation and Development (OECD), 404, 410; RBP control and, 406
Outcomes, policy change, 99-100; administrative/technical content and, 102, 104; benefits dispersion and, 104; bureaucratic arena and, 103-06; cost dispersion and, 101-02, 104; government benefits from, 101-02; influential protagonists and, 195; international pressures and, 93; losers and gainers and, 78, 121-22, 123-24; public arena and, 101, 129-32; stabilization programs and, 76
Outward-looking strategy: definition of, 56-57; export-driven economies and, 77-78; import substitution and, 65, 371
Ozal, Turgut, 329, 333

Pack, Howard, 64, 372
Pakistan, 2, 8, 61; Bangladesh and, 191; evolution of competition in, 423; RBP control and, 411
Parastatals, 132; banking system and, 318; Gambian reform package and, 132; managers' political posi- tions and, 38; performance contracts and, 133; in The Gambia, 117-19
Pareto models: credit allocation and, 39; government intervention and, 224; markets and, 34, 40, 225
Paris Club, 121; Gambian reform package and, 126
Park, Y. C., 334
Park Chung Hee, 7, 333; economic goals of, 43-44
Pastor, John H., 76
Patten, Richard H., 7, 10, 263, 266, 348
Pelzer, Karl J., 257
People's Progressive Party (PPP), 116; reform package implementation and, 127
Peremajaan Rehabilitasi dan Perluasan Tanaman Ekspor (PRPTE), 251, 261, 266; block planting and, 255; rent seeking behavior and, 262; World Bank SRDP model and, 254
Perestroika, 12
Perkins, Dwight H., 4, 7, 9, 314

Peru, 71
Philippines, 5, 61, 394; agrarian reform in, 8, 92, 97-98, 103; bureaucratic corruption in, 43; crisis reforms and, 95; "crony capitalism" in, 391; governmental regulation in, 18; industrialization of, 366; marginal tax rates in, 301; VAT implementation in, 303
Piecemeal policy reforms, 213
Pigou, Arthur Cecil, 223
Planning, 1
Pluralism, 112
Policy change models, state-centered, 86-88
Policy decision making: analysis and communication in, 230-32; cost concentrations and, 104; crisis versus politics-as-usual in, 94-95, 128-29; decision makers status and, 96; duration time of implementation and, 102-03, 104-05; evaluation of policies and, 233; implementation and sustainability of, 99-100, 131-33, 153, 214-15, 230-34; innovation or incrementalism and, 96; role of circumstances and, 94-99; self-implementing changes, 102; stakes involved in, 95; timing of, 96-97; Walrasian economics and, 160
Policy elites, 8; bureaucratic interactions and, 91-92; definition of, 111-12; "first-best world" and, 160; hierarchical status and, 95-96; industrialization and, 391; international pressure and, 92-94; political stability-support and, 92; societal preferences and, 88-90; stakes involved and, 95; technical analysis and, 90-91
Policy reform packages, examining: exchange rate policy and, 164-68; Indonesian CGE model for, 162-64; politics of reform and, 176; tariff policy and, 168-74; two-sector analytic model for, 161-62
Political marketplace, 86
Political stability/support, significance of, 92
Politics-as-usual reforms, 94-95; bureaucratic interaction and, 97; decision makers status and, 95-96; hypothetical reasons behind, 98-99; innovation versus incrementalism and, 96; stakes involved and, 95; timing and, 96-97
Portugal, 411; evolution of competition in, 424; RBP control and, 416
Posner, Richard A. 413
Potential income, 298
Poverty, 75

PPP. *See* People's Progressive Party (PPP)

Prebisch, Raul, 60

Presidential Instruction No. 4 (Inpres 4), 280, 286, 290

Preventive Medicine Agency, Chadian, 150-51

Price Control Act, Kenya's, 425

Price Control (General) Order, Kenya's, 425-26

Price controls, 6

Price data, international, 21-23, 46-48

Price distortion index, 20-21, 23-24

Price distortions, 20, 36; interest and inflation effects on, 24-25; "soft states" industrialization and, 394-96

Prices: factors of production and, 57; IMF stabilization package and, 66; inflationary environment and, 65; market efficiency and, 34; reducing dispersion in tariffs and, 169-72; self-implementing change and, 102; state intervention and, 18; structural adjustment and, 67. *See also* Price stabilization

Price Stabilization: analytical case for, 221-23; budgetary costs and, 228-30; government intervention and, 223-25, 227; implementation of market interventions, 230-34; operational issues in, 226-28; policy evaluation and, 233; quantitative significance of, 225; single commodity price and, 226-27

Primary health care, 144, 146

Private sector investment: Bangladesh and, 193; state regulation of, 18

Privatization, 3, 19, 69, 160, 349; in Bangladesh, 193-95; definition of, 57; government's development role and, 15; Indonesian smallholder rubber projects and, 265-66; international agencies and, 39; market efficiency and, 39-40; structural adjustment and, 67

Production costs, external, 58

Productivity growth: competition and, 34; composition of, 29-30; developing countries and, 32; economic development and, 2-3; Gambian reform package and, 132; trade policies and, 64

Profit maximizing, 16; agriculture and, 60; BRI system and, 354-55, 357, 360, 361; bureaucratic state and, 37-38; marketing system success and, 34-35; "soft budget constraint" and, 38-39; state enterprises and, 40, 42

Project Management Units (PMUs), 250, 255, 258, 266; block planting and, 254; retrenchment and, 265

Prompt payment incentive (IPTW), 351; BRI village efficiency and, 359

Protectionism, 4, 60; effective rates of, 36; transition from, 65

Public debt, 74

Public enterprise, 15-16; profit distribution of, 361

Public Investment Program (PIP), Gambian, 120-21

Purchasing power, 317

Purchasing power parity, 22, 24, 37; price distortions and, 46-48

Pusat Pengelolaan Pembebasan dan Pengambilian Bea Masuk (P4BM), 283

Rab, Abdur, 204

Radelet, Steven C., 6, 8, 9

Rahman, Mujibur (Sheik Mujib), 191, 193

Rahman, Zia, 193, 211

Ranis, Gustav, 60

Rates of return, 317

Rational actor model, 87; technical analysis and, 90

Rational actor models, 87

RBP. *See* Restrictive business practices (RBP)

Real effective exchange rate, 20

Reform, characteristics of, 100-01

Reform triggering mechanisms, 211-13

Regulation, government, 6-7; market efficiency and, 41; market entry barriers and, 412; of private sector, 17-19; rent seeking incentives and, 58

REncana PEmbangunan Lima TAhun (REPELITA), 250, 267

Rent seeking behavior, 58, 68, 171, 245, 279, 371; bank loans and, 215, 318; BIMAS program and, 346; Indonesia's smallholder rubber projects and, 262-263; optimal tariffs and, 176; price stabilization and, 222; "soft" states and, 366, 389; trade policy and, 291

REPELITA. *See* Rencana Pembangunan Lima Tahun (REPELITA)

REPELITA III, 250; block projects during, 257, 261, 263, 264; technical failures during, 265

REPELITA IV, 250, 254; block projects during, 257, 261, 263; budget constraints and, 265

REPELITA V, 181, 265

Research and development, 29

Restrictive business practices (RBP) control, 404; definition of, 406; development reform policies and, 427-31; economic cost of, 429; implementing

Smallholder rubber development,
Indonesia's: block planting strategy, 251-52, 260; budget constraints and, 264-65; capital-labor substitution, 260-61; equity and, 254-55; financing projects for, 261-62; market mechanisms and, 253-54, 259-61; organizational interests and, 263-64; plantation biases in, 258-59; project-based approach in, 250-51, 254; project biases in, 255-58; prospects for reform and, 266; retrenchment and privatization in, 265-66; tree crop development and, 250
Smallholder Rubber Development Project (SRDP), 250-51
Smith, Adam, 223, 404, 410
Snodgrass, Donald R., 7, 10, 263, 266, 344, 346
Social accounting matrix (SAM), 181-83
Socialist countries, 35
Soetatwo, S., 254
"Soft budget constraint," 5; Bangladesh's reforms and, 196; banking reforms and, 39; profit maximization and, 38
Solow, Robert M., 57
South Asia, 70
Southern Cone, 72
South Korea. See Korea, Republic of
Soviet bloc, 404
Soviet Union, 7, 12; bureaucratic command system of, 13; capital to output ratio in, 31; industrialization in, 59; market system in, 33; structural growth in, 70
Spain, 406; EC entry and, 429-30; RBP control and, 415-16
Special Donors' Conference in London (GOTG 1985), 125
Speculation, 327
Sponsored credit programs, 344-45
Springborg, R., 263
Spring Review of Agricultural Credit, 342
Sri Lanka, 74, 210; evolution of competition in, 425; RBP control and, 406; tax reform in, 295, 296, 297; top marginal tax rates in, 298
Srinivasan, T. N., 86
Staatz, John M., 60, 61
Stabilization, definition of, 56
Stabilization programs, 65-67; central bank credit and, 318; credibility and, 73-74; outcomes of, 76; sequencing of programs in, 71-73; in The Gambia, 122; timing and magnitude in, 74-75
Stabilization school of pricing, 222
Stamp Act, U.S., 297
Standard Chartered Bank (London), 125

Standardized commercial bill (SBPU), 326; reserve money supply and, 327
State-interest approach models, 88; technical analysis and, 90
State-owned enterprises, 15, 69; banking and finance sector of, 17; good management principles and, 42-43; operating under market criteria, 40; profit maximizing and, 16, 37-38, 42; RBP control and, 432
Statistics and planning unit, Chad's, 148-51
Steel industry, Bangladesh's, 207-08
Stern, Joseph J., 2, 10, 202
Stern, Nicholas, 171
Stiglitz, Joseph E., 225
Stolper, Wolfgang, 75
Streeten, Paul, 68
Structural adjustment, 3, 19, 67-71; components of, 67; credibility and, 73-73; definition of, 56; income distribution and, 76; RBP control and, 427-28; sequencing reforms in, 71-73; Third World countries and, 411; timing and magnitude in, 74-75
Structural Adjustment Act (SAC), 126
Subcontracting, 379-80, 382, 393-94
Subsidies, 4, 19, 38; bank credit as, 40, 70, 195; high marginal tax rates and, 300; IMF programs and, 76; Indonesia's credit subsidies, 272, 342; Korean export promotion and, 372; Taiwan's industrialization and, 377-78; The Gambia and, 117, 123
Sudan, 139
Suharto, President, 221; BULOG and, 234; financial reform and, 322, 324
Sukarno, President, 272, 322
Summers, Robert, 21, 46
Sun Yat Sen, 388
Syrquin, Moshe, 61

TABANAS. *See Tabungan Nasional* (TABANAS)
Tabungan Nasional (TABANAS), 347, 348, 355; BRI village units and, 350, 354
Taiwan, 9, 12, 13, 61, 69, 338; acquiring technology in, 385-86; conglomerate control in, 379; effective rates of protection and, 377; egalitarian income distribution in, 77-78; exports and, 334, 377-78; flexible-niche strategy and, 380-81; governmental regulation in, 18; import substitution and, 371; industrialization of, 366, 367, 369-70, 376-86; investment incentives in, 378; pricing policies in, 376-77; private downstream

industrial inducement, 383; public upstream industrialization, 383; selective credit controls and, 378-79; structural reform and, 70; subcontracting in, 379-80; unbalanced growth strategy in, 380; VAT implementation, 303

Tanzania, 44, 61, 74

Target group, 344

Tariff Book, 276, 287

Tariffs, 19, 60, 72, 160; drawback schemes and, 395; Indonesia's trade policy and, 274, 285, 288; optimal tariffs, 170-71; promoting exports and, 372; rule of thumb policies for, 168-74; sequencing reforms and, 72-73

Taxes, 6-7, 9, 58; Bangladesh's industrial reform and, 206; computerized systems, 303-05; evasion and shelters, 300; export promotion and, 372-73; high marginal rates, 298-300; income taxes, 298, 305, 383; Indonesian taxes, 253, 272, 275, 279-80, 324; market efficiency and, 41; optimal tariffs and, 170-71; optimal tax, 172; state regulation and, 18; Taiwan's industrialization and, 383; wealth tax, 298. See also TAX reform

Tax Reform, 349; background for, 294-95; designing systems and proposals for, 296, 305; developing countries and, 303-05; direct taxation and, 297-01; indirect taxation, 301-03; institutionally destabilizing reform and, 297, 300; interest groups and, 295; political economy of, 295-97; special interest groups and, 295; successful examples of, 295, 296; systems administration and, 302-03; tax brackets and, 301

Taylor, Lance, 64, 66, 75, 76

Taylor Mission, 298

Technical analysis, 90; crisis-ridden reforms and, 97; noncrisis reform and, 98

Technocrats, 3, 426; Bangladesh's import policy and, 200-01; Bangladesh's TIP program and, 190-91, 196-97; Indonesia's New Order and, 272

Television firms, Korea's, 375-76

Terms-of-trade, 166-67; Bangladesh and, 194

TFP. See Total factor productivity (TFP)

Thailand: banking and finance in, 17; governmental control in, 19 ; interest rates in, 25; RBP control and, 423; rice pricing and, 228

Tham, S. Y., 411

Thee Kian-Wee, 257

Third World Countries, 138; competition in, 410; economic reform in, 143; health care reform in, 141-42; RBP control and, 405, 432. See also Develop- ing countries

Thomas, John W., 8, 9, 128, 130, 133, 153, 194, 260, 348

Timing, policy response, 96

Timmer, C. Peter, 4, 10, 77

TIP program. See Trade and Industrial Policy (TIP) Reform program

Tomich, Thomas P., 7, 10

Total factor productivity (TFP), 62; import substitution and, 64

Trade and Industry Policy (TIP) Reform program, 190, 199, 211; DFIs and, 201, 212; industrial protection reform and, 206-10, 213, 215; initiation of, 193; interest groups and, 200; Muhith and, 194; technocrats and, 190-91, 196-97; XPB program and, 205

Trade policies, 37; financial reform and, 315; income distribution and, 76; income growth and, 63-64; liberalization of, 62-63, 160; sequencing reforms and, 72-73; structural adjustment and, 69

Trade policy reform, Indonesia's: back-ground for, 272-73; devaluation and, 284, 286; GATT subsidy accord and, 281-83; Inpres 4 and, 280; lessons from, 290-91; May 6th package, 280-84; policies and players in, 273-74; policy packages for, 284-87; policy structure-effects and, 275-79; preparation for future and, 274-75; resistance to, 287-89; system of protection and, 276-78, 280; taxes and customs in, 279-80

Transaction costs, 366; improving market efficiency and, 380-82

Transitional Government of National Unity (GUNT), 139

Transnational corporations (TNC), 404; RBP control and, 417. See also Multina-tionals

Treaty of Rome (1957), 416

Tuncer, B., 64

Turkey, 34, 61; budget deficit and, 332, 333; devaluation and, 332; financial reform, 321, 328-33, 336, 338; import substitution in, 64; market-oriented transition and, 329; monetary policy in, 329-30; price deregulation, 329-30, 332

Turnham, David, 61

Tyler, William G., 61

Uganda, 74

Unbalanced-growth strategy, 368-70, 380,